An Introduction to Programming and Object-Oriented Design Using Java™

An Introduction to Programming and Object-Oriented Design Using Java™

Jaime Niño and Frederick A. Hosch
University of New Orleans

John Wiley & Sons, Inc.
New York   Chichester   Weinheim   Brisbane   Singapore   Toronto

ACQUISITIONS EDITOR	Paul Crockett
MARKETING MANAGER	Katherine Hepburn
PRODUCTION EDITOR	Ken Santor
DESIGNER	Harry Nolan
COVER DESIGNER	Norm Christiansen
ILLUSTRATION COORDINATOR	Sandra Rigby

This book was set in Adobe FrameMaker by the authors and Publication Services and printed and bound by R.R. Donnelley—Crawfordsville. The cover was printed by Lehigh press.

This book was printed on acid-free paper. ∞

The paper in this book was manufactured by a mill whose forest management programs include sustained yield harvesting of its timberlands. Sustained yield harvesting principles ensure that the numbers of trees cut each year does not exceed the amount of new growth.

Library of Congress Cataloging in Publication Data:

Nino, Jaime.
    An Introduction to programming and object oriented design using JAVA/Jaime Nino,
        Frederick A. Hosch. p. cm.
Includes bibliographical references and index.
ISBN 0-471-35489-9 (pbk. : alk. paper)
    1. Object-oriented programming (Computer Science) 2. Java (Computer program
        language) I. Hosch, Frederick A. II. Title.
QA76.64 .N57 2002
005.13'3--dc21

2001017636

Printed in the United States of America

10 9 8 7 6 5 4 3

In memory of my mother, Maria del C. Salcedo, a most unselfish being.

—J. N.

To Katherine and the rest, Andrew, Laura, Spike, Mary.

—F. A. H.

PREFACE

Purpose and approach

This book is an introductory text on programming using Java, intended for first-year computer science undergraduates. The approach is object-oriented, sometimes called "objects first." The text is intended to be supported by regular laboratories in which lecture concepts are reviewed and enforced.

We believe there is considerable benefit in beginning with the same fundamental methodology we expect students to be using when they complete the curriculum. We find this creates much less difficulty than starting with a procedural approach and asking students to "shift paradigms" (apologies, Thomas Kuhn) after they've experienced some initial success. With the conventional approach we've used in the past, students began by developing complete, self-contained solutions to simple, well-defined problems. This had the advantage of introducing fundamental algorithmic constructs and providing a grounding in the specifics of some programming language in a nicely confined context. The difficulty was that students found that these problems yield to an undisciplined, *ad hoc* approach. When later confronted with more substantial, less well-defined problems—problems for which design issues involving complex structural relations between components must be effectively addressed—they floundered, unwilling to abandon the "code now, think later" approach that had served them so well. We will go so far as to say that having students start by writing small, complete, self-contained programs is detrimental to their later development as competent programmers.[1,2]

---

1. See, for instance, Duane Buck and David J. Stucki, "Design Early Considered Harmful: Graduated Exposure to Complexity and Structure Based on Levels of Cognitive Development," *31st SIGCSE Technical Symposium*, Austin, March, 2000.
2. Another point of view is that this is complete hokum; the only useful programs are written by very clever people, and there's not much we can do to ruin them.

While traditional introductory programming texts approach the subject in a syntax- and example-driven format, we stress design and the discipline needed for developing complex software systems. The emphasis throughout the book is on problem modeling, using fundamental software engineering principles and concepts. Object orientation is presented using the specify-design-implement-test cycle. It takes considerable experience, of course, to acquire real proficiency in the design and construction of software systems. We hope to develop a set of fundamental skills in constructing system components and to introduce a point of view regarding system design that will be as useful in the construction of large systems as it is in the design of small components.

The programming language used in the text is Sun Microsystems' Java. We should be clear that this is not a text about Java. We are concerned with the design and construction of software systems, not language fluency. Nevertheless, since we assume our readers have no specific programming experience, we spend quite a bit of time covering Java syntax and semantics. We make no attempt, however, to cover the language completely or comprehensively. We chose Java because we felt it a good compromise between viability and semantic coherence. The language has become quite popular, and we expect adequate tools and libraries to be readily available. At the core, Java is a relatively clean and small language: one that supports the concepts we present without "getting in the way." We can spend a minimum amount of time explaining language peculiarities that have little to do with the fundamentals of software design. The UML is used (informally) for denoting objects, object relationships, and system dynamics.

Overview

There are several corollaries to the approach we have adopted. First, students must have at least an elementary appreciation of notions such as *object*, *object state*, and *object feature* before they attempt implementation exercises. Second, the distinction between an object's *specification* and its *implementation* is fundamental and must be emphasized throughout the presentation. Third, we must begin with small well-defined components, even though the payoff will be in the construction of large, evolving systems. This implies that the software elements students construct are carefully specified components of a conceptually large system.

The first three chapters are introductory. Chapter 1 provides some basic definitions and a simple operational model in which language semantics can be explained. Chapter 2 introduces the fundamental concepts of *object* and *class*, and relates them to the notions of *value* and *type*. Chapter 3 presents basic structural and lexical aspects of a Java program. These preliminary chapters can be covered quite quickly by moderately prepared students. Most of the items in

Chapter 3 and some details in Chapter 2 were included at this point to get them "on the record" and out of the way of subsequent presentations. These topics could have been placed in an appendix or distributed throughout the text, with some loss in coherence and some later disturbance in topic flow. The critical matters in these chapters are objects and classes, and the constitutive processes of abstraction and composition.

In Chapters 4–10 we progress through specifying simple, well-defined classes, implementing and testing these classes, and designing and building small collections of interacting classes. Chapter 4 deals with class specification, and provides the first substantive look at Java syntax and semantics. It is unfortunate that the language does not syntactically separate a class's specification from its implementation, and we must depend on some documentation tool to "extract" the specification. Nevertheless, the conceptual distinction is essential. It is not possible to provide a correct implementation for an incompletely or inconsistently specified class. Chapters 5 and 6 cover basic algorithmic matters, including assignments, conditions, and method invocations. Chapter 7 introduces the important notion of component correctness from the point of view of programming by contract. Chapter 8 deals with testing. The first "complete program" is developed in the form of a system to test a class implementation. Chapter 9 sketches some basic organizational possibilities for interacting objects. The section concludes in Chapter 10 with the design and implementation of a complete system of moderate complexity.

Much of this early material deals of necessity with elementary algorithmic concepts and rather low-level aspects of programming. Nevertheless, the context in which topics are presented is one of class development. Classes are specified and designed with the assumption that they are to be incorporated into a larger whole. Fundamental notions such as the distinction between specification and implementation, and the architectural distinction between model and user interface are emphasized. The basic structuring mechanisms of composition and extension are also introduced in this section.

Chapter 11, on software quality, presents a reflective pause in the material after the first substantial system has been seen. It is intended to hint at issues to be addressed, rather than detail a comprehensive inventory of software quality measures.

Chapters 12 and 13 introduce the sequential list as the paradigmatic container class. ("List" is simply a more fundamental notion than "array." Arrays are hardware architectural features—see the IBM 704—bubbling up into the language syntax.) Iteration is discussed in Chapter 12, and basic list-related sorting and searching algorithms are presented in Chapter 13.

Essential class structuring devices, specifically inheritance and composition, are examined and compared in Chapters 14 and 15. The discussion of inheritance and polymorphism necessitates a presentation of some of the more baroque aspects of Java's scoping and accessibility semantics. While it is tempting to skip much of the detail, enough must be covered to enable students to understand otherwise incomprehensible program behavior.

Chapter 16 applies some of the structuring concepts to the list container, and Chapter 17 introduces recursion, starting from the perspective of lists. Chapter 18 expands on the programming by contract methodology, addresses the complex problem of error handling, and introduces exceptions, an important notion in Java. Chapters 19 and 20 provide a brief survey of the Java Swing library and a presentation of the *model-view-controller* architecture. The discussions of MVC and Swing allow us to examine specific examples of additional fundamental design patterns such as *composite* and *observer*.

Chapters 21–25 cover optional material and provide an introduction to fundamental data structuring concepts. Computational complexity is informally introduced in Chapter 21, so that the complexity of algorithms can be compared in subsequent chapters. The remaining chapters provide a introduction to some fundamental data structuring concepts, and serve as a case study in which to present choices for class and library design. Arrays and linked structures are introduced, and examples of factory methods, *bridge* and *adapter* patterns are encountered. The final chapter introduces several common containers such as *stack* and *queue*.

Some key points of the presentation are as follows.

- Chapters 1–3 are introductory and can be presented relatively quickly, in a few classes.

- Object orientation is presented using the specify-design-implement-test cycle.

- Methods are categorized as commands that change state or queries that return some aspect of an object's state.

- System and class design are distinguished from algorithm design.

- Class specification is distinguished from class implementation.

- Design by contract, with preconditions and postconditions, is employed throughout.

- Assertions, in particular invariants, are used to design, document, and test classes.

- The MVC architecture is employed, regardless of system size.

A number of syntactic language topics have been omitted from the main body of the text. As we've said, language syntax is not the organizing feature of the text. Linguistic structures that we felt essential to support the conceptual material are presented in some detail. Other aspects of the language, important or interesting as they may be in their own right, are not included. Applets and file-based i/o are treated in appendices. A third appendix provides an overview of most fundamental core structures of the language. We have chosen not to include comprehensive specifications of standard library classes. These are readily available on the Web, and are much more complete and up-to-date than any we could provide in the text. We hope this approach is adequate for the needs of most instructors.

Implementation

As mentioned, the text is intended for beginning undergraduates in computer science. No previous programming experience is assumed, and the only mathematics required is elementary college algebra. We have taught the material several times as part of an introductory sequence in programming and software design. The material in the text is followed by traditional data structure topics, also presented in an object-oriented context. Our students are first- and second-year computer science majors with no previous computer science coursework. Though their backgrounds vary widely, a number have almost no prior computing experience. (In-class presentations can be a bit more formal than those given in the text if students have some knowledge of elementary topics from discrete mathematics.)

Laboratories

Although it may not be obvious from the text, the approach depends on students' regular participation in structured laboratories. In addition to laboratory work, of course, students should also complete homework assignments of a broader scope.

Initial laboratory exercises, associated with the first few chapters of the text, familiarize students with the concepts of *object*, *class*, *state*, and so on, and help them understand simple class specifications. In our labs, students begin by experimenting with simple software systems to identify objects, their properties, and their behavior. Next they work from class specifications to develop test plans for simple classes. Testing is done using implementations and test drivers provided by the instructor. Students then develop, code, and compile class specifications. Since Java does not separate a class's specification from its implementation in distinct compilation units, methods are coded with "dummy" bodies so that compilation can take place. Such exercises are fundamental, and inculcate students with an "object-oriented perspective."

Subsequent exercises involve implementing simple classes from instructor-provided specifications. Initially, testing is done with test harnesses provided by the instructor. It is not long, however, before students are able to mimic instructor-provided test code and create their own test drivers. The first "complete systems" students encounter are test harnesses exercising a few simple classes.

From the start, the distinction between model and user interface is emphasized. Initially, students design, specify, and implement model classes, and are supplied other classes needed to construct test systems. As they progress, they are able to write their own text-based user interface components, and begin developing small systems with a few interacting classes. Later laboratories provide reinforcement of algorithmic concepts, language constructs, and class structuring techniques such as extension and composition. Independent homework assignments involve designing and implementing well-defined systems of moderate complexity.

Since the approach depends on building well-specified components of a conceptually large system, exercises generally require a supporting environment provided by the instructor. We have developed an extensive set of laboratories that we use with the text. Material for these laboratories is continually being updated and expanded. Laboratory material, support code for laboratory and homework exercises, a class library that includes elementary i/o and fundamental classes used in the text, are available at our Web site. We invite suggestions and contributions, and anticipate serving as a clearinghouse for the exchange of ideas, exercises, and supporting code.

Lecture organization

Chapters 1–11 comprise the basic topics covered in the text. As mentioned, the first three chapters are introductory and can be covered rather quickly with well-prepared students. Chapters 4–8 present fundamental algorithmic constructs from an object-oriented perspective. While many students will be familiar with the elementary algorithmics, the object-oriented slant will be new. We have found, however, that students tend to find the approach natural and have far fewer problems with the object-oriented concepts than we originally anticipated.

Chapter 9 is intended to set the stage for more complex class relationships to come. It can be treated very lightly, almost as a reader.

Chapter 10 is a first opportunity to put together something substantial. We concentrate on the important class relationships and the few new constructs in the example, and generally let students read the obvious code segments on their own. (This chapter may go down too well. Designs in subsequent courses often inappropriately reflect the basic structure illustrated here.)

Chapter 11 offers an opportunity for making a few points regarding software quality. The topics in this chapter could be presented almost anywhere in the course. The chapter can also be treated lightly, mostly as a reader.

Chapter 12 presents containers, in the manifestation of a sequential list. As mentioned above, "list" is a more fundamental notion than "array," and we can do the same algorithmic development with an indexed list as with an array. Instructors who prefer to introduce arrays early can insert material from Section 22.1 at this point.

Chapters 13–20 form a second segment of the text. Much of this material can be considered optional in a first course. In particular, sections 13.4 (verifying correctness), 16.2 (ordered lists), 17.5 (indirect recursion), and 17.6 (object recursion) can be omitted on first reading. Chapter 15 (modeling with abstraction) and Chapters 19 and 20 (the graphical user interface) could also be omitted. (Though in our view, Chapter 15 is one of the most fundamental in the text.)

Chapters 14 and 15 on modeling with inheritance and composition are a bit more conceptually advanced than the previous chapters. These chapters are the first in which more general design issues are addressed in a substantial way.

Finally, Chapters 21–25 cover topics often considered to be part of a "data structures" course. These chapters are included to give students a idea of "where we go from here" and, by providing some concrete list implementation alternatives, to complete a picture begun in earlier chapters. We would not expect this material to be covered in a typical introductory course.

Supporting material

As mentioned above, considerable supporting material is available on the Web. This includes laboratories with supporting software, source and executables of library packages used in the text, source of examples used in the text, *etc.* Supporting material can be accessed through the Wiley server, at

```
http://www.wiley.com/college/nino/
```

or through our server, at

```
http://wakko.cs.uno.edu/
```

Additional complementary material made available by other contributors is also available through these sites.

Comments, suggestions, corrections, contributions, *etc.* can be forwarded through the above sites, or to the authors directly at `fred@cs.uno.edu` and `jaime@cs.uno.edu`.

Readers interested in learning Java *per se* should investigate the Sun Java tutorial at

```
http://java.sun.com/docs/books/tutorial/
```

For specifics on the language syntax and semantics, consult the *The Java language Specification*, available at `http://java.sun.com/docs/`.

The Java Software Development Kit can be downloaded, as of this writing, from

```
http://java.sun.com/j2se/
```

(You might also try

```
http://java.sun.com/products/
```

or

  `http://java.sun.com/.)`

Documentation for the standard Java libraries can be accessed at

  `http://java.sun.com/j2se/1.3/docs/api/`

Documentation for local libraries used in the text can be found at

  `http://wakko.cs.uno.edu/OOJ/docs/`

If you have difficulty accessing these sites, check the Wiley site at

  `http://www.wiley.com/college/nino/`

the Sun sites

  `http://java.sun.com/products/`, and
  `http://java.sun.com/`

or contact the authors directly.

Finally

We could not, of course, have completed this text without the help and support of many people. We are indebted to our colleagues for the confidence they showed in us by allowing us to overhaul the introductory programming curriculum and install an unproven approach. (Particularly noteworthy since most of them knew they'd end up trying to teach this stuff.) We are also indebted to the first few classes of students who endured our trials and errors—getting a first hand view of the design-implement-test cycle. They seem no worse for the experience, and didn't have much of a choice anyway.

We are grateful for the conscientious efforts of our reviewers, notably Fiona Gaston, Thaddeus F. Pawlicki, H.E. Dunsmore, Byron Weber Becker, and Alok Mehta. We'd like particularly to thank our colleague Bill Greene who labored through early versions of the notes on which this text was based and offered numerous helpful suggestions.

Special thanks to Robert Burton, for his many insightful and useful suggestions, and his careful reading of the text.

We are grateful for the help and guidance of the folks at Wiley, particularly Jenny Welter, Susannah Barr, and our editor, Paul Crockett; Ken Santor, who put up with us through production; Karen Tongish, our copy editor; Norm Christiansen, who did a great cover, even though we wanted a plain brown wrapper; and Bill Zobrist, who can recognize quality when he sees it but took our book anyway.

Finally, we are grateful for the support of our family and friends, and for Bill Joy, James Joyce, Thomas Kuhn, George Eliot, John Reynolds, Ray Witham, Stephen Kleene, Larry Landweber, Dana Scott, John Adams, Jacques Barzun, Arnold Schoenberg, Jacqueline Du Pré, Immanuel Kant, Karl Hoffman, and Bertrand Meyer.

I should without hesitation split the infinitive and write *to calmly consider.*

—Jacques Barzun

They lard their lean book with the fat of others' works.

—Robert Burton (1576-1640)[1]

---

1. Borrowed from the preface of [Joy 00].

CONTENTS

Chapter 5   Implementing a simple class   91

CHAPTER 1   Introduction

This book is about building software. Specifically, we examine fundamental tools and techniques essential for building large software systems. The first chapter sets the stage for our study of software development. After a brief general introduction to computer science, we analyze the important properties of large software systems, noting in particular that such systems are

- inherently complex, and
- constantly changing.

These observations lead us to a data-oriented software development strategy, based on composition and abstraction. This approach has proven to produce software systems of high quality, and is the one we follow throughout the text.

In the second part of the chapter, we present some fundamental hardware and software concepts that comprise part of the essential background for a software developer. In particular, we want to make sure that basic notions such as a processors, memories, file systems, programming languages, compilers, *etc.*, are familiar to the reader.

1.1   What is computer science?

> **computer science** *n.*   A study akin to numerology and astrology, but lacking the precision of the former and the success of the latter.
> — *Stan Kelly-Bootle*

> But fundamentally, computer science is a science of abstraction—creating the right model for a problem and devising the appropriate mechanizable techniques to solve it.
> — *A. Aho and J. Ullman*

Since this book is directed toward beginning students in computer science, it seems reasonable to start with the questions what is computer science, and where, in the scheme of things, does software development fall? As it is a relatively new discipline, there are, in fact, many different views of computer science. We'll briefly present our perspective, and outline one possible way to categorize the principal areas. Aho and Ullman's definition given above is particularly insightful, and succinctly describes the point of view we take in the text. Read it carefully.

First of all, we should note that computer science is not the "science of computers"—that is, it is not the study of electronic computing equipment *per se*. Rather it is the study of *computation*: mechanical or automated problem solving. As an interesting aside, some of the fundamental problems of computation were framed and studied many years before electronic computers existed. "Computability" issues were central to work in the foundations of mathematics in the 1920s and 1930s. Questions such as which problems can be solved by mechanical "program directed" computation and which cannot, were precisely formulated and answered by mathematicians before the first electronic computer was built. To mathematicians and logicians of this era, a "computer" was a person with pencil and paper.

Of course there is no doubt that the development of electronic computing devices made computer science a viable independent discipline. Even now much of what we do and how we do it is sometimes needlessly coupled to the structure of the hardware we use. In fact, despite several attempts at name changes, the two most prominent professional organizations in computer science are the Association for *Computing Machinery* and the IEEE *Computer* Society.

At any rate, the discipline of computer science, as we have said, is concerned with automated problem solving. Computer science revolves around the study of automated *systems* that actually produce the solutions, the study of *methods* used to develop solution strategies for these systems to follow, and the study of *application areas* in which automated problem solving is particularly useful. The fundamental mathematical and logical structures necessary for understanding the nature and limitations of computing, and for analyzing and verifying the correctness of both software and hardware, comprise the *foundations of computing*. Work in this area provides the mathematical underpinnings on which the rest of the discipline is based.

Foundations

The study of *computing foundations* is the study of the formal mathematical structures that provide the logical basis for computer science. Fundamental questions such as how to characterize the collection of problems that can be solved computationally, how to define mathematically the syntax and semantics of a programming language, how to measure the complexity of a software system, and how to verify the correctness of a system formally, are examined.

Systems

The "machine" that is our principle tool is constructed of both hardware and software components. The study of computing *systems* examines the hardware and supporting software that define the computing environment. It includes the areas of computer architecture, operating systems, and networking.

Computer architecture involves the organization and structure of the hardware. As we progress through lower and lower levels of detail, this investigation becomes computer engineering, electrical engineering, and ultimately physics. Where one discipline ends and another begins is neither precisely defined nor particularly relevant. The computer architect and the computer engineer are concerned with much the same problem: the design of computing hardware.

The area of *operating systems* deals with the design of fundamental resource management software. When we talk of a "computer," we usually imply both hardware and operating system. (Operating systems you may be familiar with include MS-DOS, UNIX, Windows NT.) Without an operating system, a user would be forced to handle details such as where a program should be put in memory, where a particular data item actually resides on a disk, whether a disk is spinning up to speed, and so on. The operating system manages system resources like disks, memory, and processors, and provides a user with a manageable environment in which to work. The areas of operating systems and computer architecture are closely related. The operating system is intimately concerned with the details of the hardware, and many management functions are accomplished cooperatively by the hardware and operating system software. In some systems, the *graphical user interface* or windowing facility is part of the operating system; in others it is an independent software component.

Networking and the study of *distributed systems* deal with methods for connecting computers together so that users can share resources and information. As you might guess, this area overlaps considerably with the study of operating systems. An operating system is responsible for managing a computer's resources. A network provides a means for several computers to share resources. A computer network may involve a few systems at the same location, or thousands of machines spread around the world. A user on a distributed network may be completely unaware that the resources he or she is using are located on remote systems.

Applications

Of course computers are used in numerous diverse *application areas*. In many instances an identifiable set of techniques has evolved that is uniquely applicable to a particular area. We give just a few examples:

- *artificial intelligence*, where the problems tackled—for instance, understanding English, proving mathematical theorems, playing games of strategy such as chess—are traditionally assumed to require "human intelligence";

- *database management*, where the essential issue is how to organize very large quantities of data so that particular items of information can be easily extracted;

- *computer graphics*, where the concern is rendering visual images by computer.

Methods

The study of computational *methods* encompasses the design and assessment of techniques and software tools for creating automated problem solutions.

The solution strategy for a problem must ultimately be expressed in some formal notation: this is a *programming language*. Programming languages and the software tools for using them are fundamental to computer science. A programming language provides a precise, formal notation in which it should be easy to express and analyze a natural, correct, efficient problem solution. Designing and implementing an effective programming language is not trivial. Much effort has been devoted to building hundreds of programming languages during the past forty years, only a few of which have proven particularly successful.

The general study of methods for producing and evaluating software is called *software engineering*. At an elementary level, this is primary topic of this text. We are interested in developing some very fundamental skills for designing software systems and for implementing these systems in a programming language. We'll elaborate on this in the following sections.

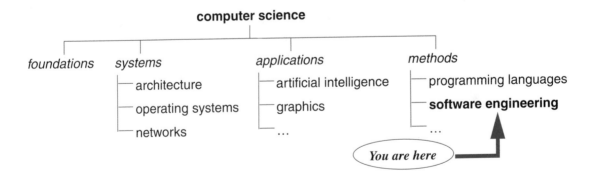

Figure 1.1 A simple taxonomy.

1.2 What is a software system?

You may ask why we say "software system" when we could get by with a smaller mouthful by simply saying "program." Basically, the term "program" has connotations we wish to avoid. A program is usually considered to be a self-contained piece of software that solves a particular, static, well-defined problem. In actuality, problems are seldom static and well-defined, and the software built to address them is rarely simple or self-contained. (Having said this, we'll proceed to use the terms "program" and "software system" more or less interchangeably throughout the text, much to the distress of one of the authors. We also use the term "application" as essentially synonymous with "software system.")

A key aspect of real systems is that the problems they solve are rarely clearly defined or stable over time. The environment in which a system is used, the needs of the users, and therefore what is required of the system, change constantly. A software system is at best a temporary solution to a changing problem. This is true even when the problem appears completely straightforward. For example, the basic text editor installed on the system being used to write this book is version 19.30. Without getting into version numbering details, it should be evident that there have been dozens of modifications to this piece of software, even though it is hard to imagine a more well-defined problem than editing text.

The dynamic nature of problems and the inherent complexity of software solutions unequivocally constrain the approaches we can take when developing a system. The approach we adopt in this text and the mind-set we hope to develop is largely driven by these two aspects of real-world systems: *i.e.*,

- they are *dynamic*: the demands made of a software system, and hence the software system itself, constantly change; and

- they are *complex*.

1.2.1 Dealing with complexity: composition and abstraction

The difference in size and complexity between a small program and a large application can be compared to the difference between a plank footbridge across a ditch and cantilever highway bridge across a river. It would be rash indeed to assume that techniques adequate for constructing one are also suitable for building the other. If we had nothing to do but build small programs, almost any approach would serve. We don't have to be structural engineers, after all, to build a footbridge. But real problems are another matter entirely. To manage the complexity of both problems and their solutions, we depend on *composition* and *abstraction*. These notions are introduced in the following sections.

Composition

The size of a typical software system implies that it must be broken down into manageable pieces—that it be dealt with as a *composite structure*. The smaller a component is, the easier it is to build and understand. On the other hand, the smaller the parts, the more parts one has to deal with. The more parts, the more possible interactions there are between parts and the more complex the resulting structure. Thus a critical balance must be achieved in a design: the parts must be simple enough to be understood and managed, but the interaction between them must be minimized to keep the complexity of the entire system under control. The quality of a design, and hence of the resulting system, is directly related to how successfully the problem has been decomposed into relatively independent parts.

To get an idea of what we mean, consider an audio system. The system is composed of a number of components—amplifier, tuner, speakers, and so forth—wired together. Each component has a carefully specified function that can be understood independently of the entire system. Their interaction is through connecting wires, each carrying a precisely specified signal with a clearly defined purpose. It is an easy matter to improve the system by replacing or adding components. A CD player can be added, for instance, or speakers replaced with ones of better quality. Furthermore, each component is itself constructed of smaller parts. But how these smaller pieces fit together inside a speaker or amplifier is not relevant to understanding how the speaker connects to the amplifier.

Figure 1.2 **A circuit board: clearly defined interacting components.**

At the other extreme, we might consider a "Rube Goldberg device" or a "house of cards." With a Rube Goldberg device, the parts are connected in intricate, clever, and unexpected ways. The functioning of the device is not obvious, and modification almost unthinkable. Understanding the parts independently is of little help in understanding the system as a whole, since the parts themselves are in no intrinsic way related to the problem the device solves. Though the number of parts might be relatively small, the complexity is considerable due to their intricate and unexpected interaction. With a house of cards, the components themselves are trivially simple. But the stability of each card is dependent on all the others: each component is related in a critical way to every other component. The slight movement of any card will cause the entire structure to collapse.

Pencil Sharpener   RUBE GOLDBERG (tm) RGI 038

Open window (A) and fly kite (B). String (C) lifts small door (D) allowing moths (E) to escape and eat red flannel shirt (F). As weight of shirt becomes less, shoe (G) steps on switch (H) which heats electric iron (I) and burns hole in pants (J). Smoke (K) enters hole in tree (L), smoking out opossum (M) which jumps into basket (N), pulling rope (O) and lifting cage (P), allowing woodpecker (Q) to chew wood from pencil (R), exposing lead. Emergency knife (S) is always handy in case opossum or the woodpecker gets sick and can't work.

Figure 1.3 **A "Rube Goldberg" device.**
Rube Goldberg is the ® and © of Rube Goldberg Inc.

Abstraction

The process of abstraction allows us to deal with system components and their interactions without worrying about the specific details that go in the building of each of the components. Suppose we are designing an automobile, certainly a complex system composed of many parts. In our initial design, we decompose the system into a few high-level components: engine, power train, frame, *etc*. We can describe, rather precisely, what each component does and how they interact without giving details of how the individual components are constructed. We are dealing with *abstractions* of the components. As we elaborate the design of one component, we view the others only as they relate to the one we're working on. For instance, when we design the power train, which connects the engine to the drive wheels, we probably need to know the torque and power specifications of the engine: but its size, weight, and shape are irrelevant. When we design the body panels, we need to know the size and shape of the engine, but are not concerned with power and torque. In neither case do we care about the engine's bore and stroke, combustion chamber shape, and so on. That is, in each case we have a distinct abstract view of the engine: a representation in which most details are not relevant to the task at hand and can be ignored. Note that "abstract" does not mean "vague" or "imprecise." It simply means that we limit our view of an object to a few of its properties. Imagine, for example, that two different engines—one a 16-valve twin cam fuel injected four cylinder, the other a single cam carburetted V-6—happen to have the same power and torque specifications. These two engines would be identical to the power train designer: at the level of abstraction from which the power train designer views the engine, they are equivalent. But whatever kind of engine we build, we must make sure that those properties used to specify its interaction with other components are maintained. If we use an engine with twice the torque assumed when designing the power train, we will not have a reliable vehicle. And of course, components like an engine or power train are complicated systems constructed of component subsystems.

Now in reality an automobile isn't designed in the simple manner implied above. The various components are designed simultaneously by teams composed of many individuals. Furthermore, the use of parts directly "off the shelf" with little or no modification greatly simplifies and speeds up the process. The same is true of large software systems, which are often more complex and have a less standardized "parts catalogue" than an automobile. But the notions of a *composite* system comprised of clearly identifiable interacting parts each of which can be dealt with independently, and of an *abstraction* in which only a few details need to be considered, are the two principal means the system designer has for coping with the complexity of large systems.

To summarize, abstraction can be defined as elimination of the irrelevant and amplification of the essential. To abstract is to eliminate details from consideration, and thus eliminate distinctions. Things considered different from one point of view become "equivalent" when viewed from a sufficiently abstract perspective. In this sense, we often consider abstraction as capturing the "commonality" between different things. And as Aho and Ullman have observed, computer science is fundamentally a science of abstraction.

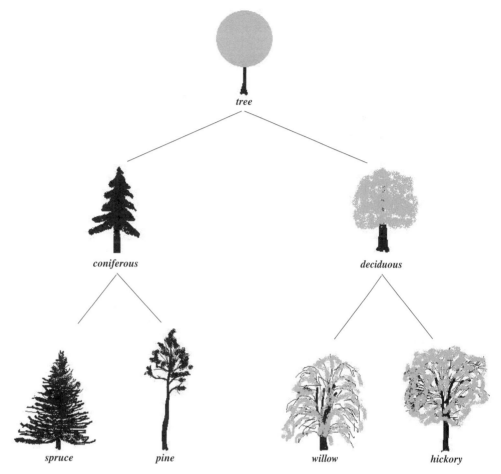

Figure 1.4 **Abstracting trees.**

1.2.2   Two aspects of a system: data and functionality

Two aspects of any program or software system are *data*—the information the program deals with—and *functionality*—what the program does with this data. ("Functionality" means the same thing as "function," but has more letters and so is preferred.) Data for an income tax program, for instance, are the pieces of information we write on our tax forms: number of dependents, gross wages, taxable income, gross tax, *etc.* The function of this program is to compute the amount of tax we owe. The data for a student record system relate to students and courses: names, addresses, social security numbers of students; courses taken, grades, credits earned, and so on. Functions of such a system might include producing transcripts and grade reports, determining if a student should be placed on probation, determining which students have completed degree requirements, *etc*. The data for the document processing software used to prepare this book are essentially text and graphics, and the functionality provided by the software includes facilities for displaying, printing, adding, deleting, modifying, rearranging text and graphics.

If we consider the data for a moment, it will be clear that the *data descriptions* for a program are fixed, while the individual *data values* change each time the program is run. Taking the tax program as an example, "number of dependents" is the *description* of a particular data item. The data *value* associated with this item is some integer number, like 3 or 12. We can imagine running the tax program many times to compute taxes for many different individuals. Each time we run the program, the number of dependents must be provided. But the *specific number* will be different for different individuals: 4 for me, 2 for you, and so on. The same is true for the other data items mentioned above. In the student record system, the same kind of information is kept for each student: name, address, credits earned, *etc*. But the particular values of these data items are, of course, different for different students. An important part of designing and constructing a software system is determining and describing the data items that the system will use.

Now let us briefly turn our attention to the system's functionality. The system must be able to perform some sequence of goal-directed actions with a set of data values. For instance, the tax system must perform the calculations required to compute a person's tax. We'll use the term *processor* to refer to whatever it is, person or electronic computer, that actually performs the actions. (If I fill out my tax return manually, I'm the processor.) The *sequence of actions* the processor performs to accomplish some end is a *computation*. (We imagine the harried taxpayer with pencil nubs and mechanical calculator slaving over a form 1040.) Clearly the particular actions the processor performs depend on the data values. If I do my tax return and then do yours, the same processor (me) performs two computations with the same goal—*i.e.,* to determine someone's income tax. But the particular actions I perform in each case—the numbers I manipulate, the sections of the form I fill in—differ because the data values I start with differ. Nevertheless there is an identifiable, common *pattern* to each of the two computations. This pattern is described by the *instructions* provided in the IRS booklet I follow in each case. That is, in each case I follow the same instructions but in fact perform different actions. The instructions define the *pattern* each computation will follow; the instructions plus specific data values determine the exact *actions* I perform. A precise set of instructions that describe a pattern of behavior guaranteed to achieve some goal is an *algorithm*. In addition to defining the data items, the software builder must also construct the algorithms that provide the functionality of the system.

---

computation: a sequence of goal-directed actions performed by a processor.

algorithm: a set of instructions describing a pattern of behavior guaranteed to achieve some goal.

1.3   Object-oriented systems

We now have the following general picture of a software system. The definition of the system includes a description of the data items that will be manipulated and a collection of algorithms that provide the system's functionality. Both are expressed in the formal notation of a programming language. A processor, given a particular set of initial data values, follows an algorithm and performs a sequence of actions, a computation, that produces a result. We also know that in the design of a system we must manage complexity (abstraction and composition are relevant tools here) and address the inevitability that the system will change.

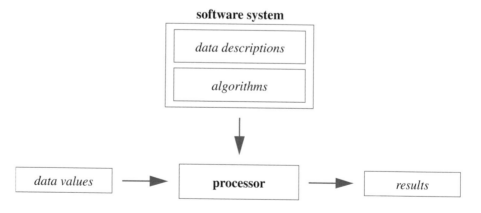

Figure 1.5 Components of a computation.

Several fundamentally different methods for structuring software systems have been developed during the past twenty-five or so years. The approach we take here is called *object oriented*. It is intended to produce systems that are composite, modular constructions, built using abstraction, and organized around the data. It is generally recognized that this approach provides the best-known solution to the design of large, evolving software systems. We sketch the approach next.

Before we can devise an automated solution to a problem, we need to design the right *model*—that is, create *abstractions* of the real-world problem that can be represented and manipulated with a computing system. A *software system* is a collection of such abstractions that work together to solve a problem or set of related problems. In the object-oriented approach, the abstractions used to describe the problem are called *objects*, and are often abstractions of the real-world entities in terms of which the problem is expressed. For instance, if we're building a student record system, we will have objects representing students, courses, and so on. For each student there will be a component of the student record system—a software *object*—that represents the student. The component will contain only information about the student that is relevant to the student record system: it will include the student's name, address, list of courses, *etc.*, but will likely not include the student's shoe size. In this sense, it is an "abstraction" of the student. The aspects of a student that we choose to represent with a student object are the *properties* of the object.

The functionality of the system is distributed to the objects: the tasks the system is required to perform are allocated to objects that perform them. A student record system, for instance, must be able to determine whether a student should be placed on probation. Some object will be assigned the responsibility for performing this job: for instance, it may be the responsibility of the object representing a particular student to determine if that student should be placed on probation. The algorithm for accomplishing this task is incorporated as part of the student object. In this sense, the system is structured on the *data objects* rather than on the *functions* that it will perform. This is not to say that the functions are unimportant: the objects themselves are created to support the basic functionality required of the system. But the fundamental organizational structure of the system is based on the data objects: objects provide the basic abstractions with which we model the problem, and are the elementary components from which we structure the solution.

One additional item to note. Software systems are modular constructions built from components—in our case, objects. Like the automobile designer, we want a stock of standard parts that we can put together to build a system. The availability of "reusable components" is key to the efficient production of reliable systems. We shall see that the design and use of modules that can be easily tailored to serve many needs is an important part of the object-oriented approach.

All this may seem a bit vague at the moment. That is to be expected. We have introduced a fair number of notions in a rather abstract setting. We will return to these ideas frequently in the ensuing chapters, though many of the points can be truly appreciated only after one has had some experience designing and building large software systems.

1.4   A model of a computer system

Before we start discussing software construction *per se*, we need to develop a model of the underlying computing system on which our software will run, and briefly describe some of the tools we use to build our systems. In this section, we sketch a simple operational model of a computing system; in the next section we describe some essential software tools.

We view a computer system as composed of four functional components: input/output, processor, memory, and file system.

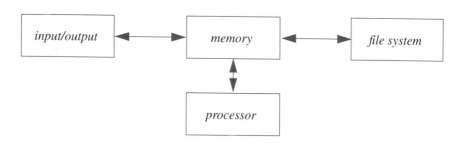

Figure 1.6 **Simple model of a computer system.**

Input/output

Input and *output devices* are the means by which the system communicates with the outside world. There are many possible ways for a system to interact with users and other devices. A system intended for use by a person typically has at least a keyboard and mouse for input and a monitor for output. A system used to control some other device, such as an anti-lock braking system controlling brakes on a vehicle, may have only simple environmental sensors for input and control signals to the other device for output. Other common input devices include cameras, microphones, digitizing pads, *etc.* Output devices include speakers, printers, plotters.

Processor

The *processor* is the component of the system that actually performs the actions of a computation. A processor has a set of actions that it can perform, a set of instructions it can carry out. This set of instructions is called the *instruction set* or the *machine language* of the processor. These instructions are generally very simple: "add two numbers," for example. The power of the processor comes from the fact that it can perform millions of these very simple instructions each second.

The instructions for a processor are encoded as sequences of *bits*: *i.e.,* sequences of *binary digits*, zeros and ones. For example, the instructions for Sun Microsystems' SPARC processor are sequences of 32 bits. Each action the processor can perform has its own unique representation as a string of 32 zeros and ones. These bit strings are what the processor actually understands.

Note that different kinds of processors have very different instruction sets. Instructions for Intel's Pentium processor, for instance, bear little resemblance to those for a SPARC processor. The SPARC instruction for, say, adding two numbers looks quite different from a Pentium instruction. It would be senseless to give a Pentium processor instructions coded for a SPARC processor, or *vice versa*.

Memory

The *memory*, sometimes called the store, main memory, or RAM, is where the data and algorithm the system is currently using reside. The algorithm is expressed in machine language, in terms of the instruction set of the processor. The processor can understand nothing else. The data must also be encoded as sequences of bits so that it can be stored in the system's memory.

Different kinds of data are encoded using different encoding schemes. But while there is considerable difference in the instruction sets of different machines, there is substantial uniformity in the manner in which data is encoded. Textual data—the letters, digits, punctuation marks that you key from a keyboard and are displayed on your monitor screen—are often represented as eight-bit sequences using the ASCII (American Standard Code for Information Interchange) code. That is, each character is assigned a unique eight-bit sequence: the letter A for example is represented by the sequence 01000001. When you key an upper-case letter A on the keyboard, this sequence of bits is sent to processor and stored in memory. It's also what gets sent as output to the monitor and displayed on the screen as the letter A. Numbers that are to be used in arithmetic operations are stored in a different way. Details are beyond the scope of the present discussion.

The memory is divided into a number of fixed size (typically eight bit) storage locations. Each location has a unique numeric *address* associated with it. The processor is able to access a data value or instruction stored in memory by knowing its address and its size. The processor repeatedly fetches instructions of the algorithm from memory, decodes and performs them. If we took a snapshot of the system, we would see the data values and algorithm stored in memory. Two successive snapshots might look something like what is shown in Figure 1.7. (Of course, everything would actually be encoded as bit sequences.) The figure shows a data value (the number 17) stored in the location with address 100. An instruction, which we assume to be 32 bits long, is stored in (four) locations 500 through 503. The processor knows the location and size of the next instruction it is to execute. The processor simply reads the 32-bit instruction from memory, and performs the action specified. Usually instructions are simply fetched one after the other from memory. So if one 32-bit instruction were located at address 500, the next one would be at location 504.

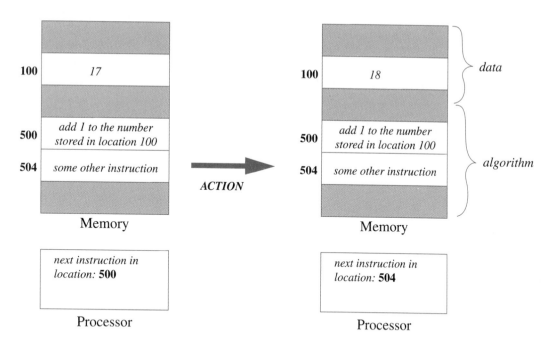

Figure 1.7 **Successive snapshots of a machine.**

As the processor successively executes the instructions of the algorithm, the data values stored in memory are changed. The algorithm, however, remains fixed during the computation.

File system

The *file system*, sometimes called secondary storage, is similar to the memory in that it stores data values and algorithms. However, while the contents of the memory are volatile and change constantly—the memory contains the data and algorithm the system is using *at the moment*—the contents of the file system are relatively stable. Algorithms and data remain in the file system whether the system is operational or not. To use the student record system as an example again, if the machine is in the process of producing a transcript for a particular student, data relevant to that student and the algorithm for producing a transcript are in memory. Data for other students, and algorithms for other functions, remain in the file system.

The file system is organized into a collection of *named files*, in which data and algorithms are stored. A file might contain a program expressed in the processor's machine language, data for a program, results from running a program, text such as this book chapter, *etc.* Exactly what a file name looks like depends on the particular computer system we are using. In general, though, one tries to give a file a name that is descriptive of its contents. For example, the file containing the text of this chapter is named "Chapter1.frame." (The software used to create and format the text is called FrameMaker. The suffix ".frame" gives a clue that the file is intended to be used with this software.) File systems are generally implemented on rotating magnetic disks.

Network

Finally, we conclude by hooking our computer to a *network*. We can view a network simply as a wire to which a number of computers and other devices are connected, permitting them to communicate with each other and share resources. (If we want to, we can view the network connection simply as a special input/output device.)

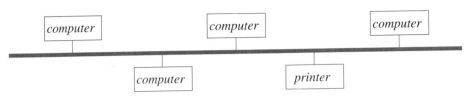

Figure 1.8 **A network.**

The description of a computer system we have given is, admittedly, rather abstract. While we have ignored many details in this sketch, it should provide an adequate model for understanding the subsequent material.

1.5   Software tools

Operating systems

The basic hardware computer, as described in the previous section, is a rather tedious beast. To make it usable, software called an *operating system* is almost always included as part of the system. Examples of operating systems include MS-DOS, Windows 98, Windows 2000, and various flavors of UNIX such as Solaris, Linux, and HP-UX. The operating system is the fundamental hardware-resource management software. Some portion of the operating system is always resident in the computer's memory. It performs functions such as verifying user name and password on a multi-user system, deciding exactly where in memory a program will be loaded, loading programs from disk into the machine's memory and starting their execution, managing the file system by allocating and freeing disk space for files. When a program needs to read data from or write data to an i/o device or the file system, the program actually makes a request of the operating system. The operating system handles all the low level details of moving the data between memory and the device or the disk. In some cases, the operating system is also responsible for managing the graphical user interface or windowing system through which the user interacts with the system. In other cases, the windowing system is a separate software component, independent of the operating system.

Programming languages

The data descriptions and algorithms that define a software system must at some point be expressed in a formal notation called a *programming language*. Unlike the machine languages discussed in the previous section, programming languages are intended to be written and read by people. They are designed to assist a programmer in structuring and building a problem solution in a natural way. That is, they are intended to be "problem oriented" rather than "machine oriented": the problem solution can be expressed in terms appropriate to the problem rather than in terms specific to some computing system. If we are developing a student record system, for instance, the programming language should allow us to write in terms of students and courses rather than in terms of bits and bytes. Programming languages are independent of the peculiarities of any particular processor or computing system.

Programming languages are defined in terms of a *syntax* and *semantics*. The syntax is the set of grammatical and punctuation rules for the language. The syntactic rules tell us how to write legal constructs. The semantics of the language is the set of rules that specify the meaning of syntactically legal constructs. A programming language is much more rigorous in both syntax and semantics than a natural language like English. Whether we punctuate an English sentence with a comma or semicolon isn't likely to affect its understandability. In a programming language, however, using a comma rather than a semicolon may make a construct invalid or completely change its meaning. Furthermore, most sentences in English have some degree of ambiguity: different readers construe slightly (or in some cases, seriously) different meanings from the same sentence. In a programming language, a construct has one unique meaning. This necessity for absolute precision is sometimes difficult for beginning programmers to grasp.

Many program languages have been designed and implemented during the past forty or so years. We use Sun Microsystems' Java™ language in this text.

Editors

Using the notation provided by the language, the programmer defines the data and algorithms appropriate for solving the problem. An essential tool for this activity is a *text editor*, a program which allows the user to create and modify text files in the computer's file system. If we're lucky, our editor is *language sensitive*. This means the editor has some understanding of the syntax of the language we're using, and can help by providing templates for common constructs, immediately identifying syntactic errors, and so on. Text files that contain data descriptions and algorithms expressed in a programming language are called *source files*. The text that makes up a program is often simply referred to as *code*.

Translators

It is all well and good to express our solution in a readable programming language. The difficulty is that the machine that is actually going to solve the problem doesn't understand our programming language: it only understands its own machine language. What to do? We need to *translate* our program from the *programming language* into something the machine we're going to run the program on can understand. A program that performs this translation is called a *compiler*. A compiler reads our source file as input and produces a version of the program translated into something more like machine language.

There are a number of different approaches that can be taken in this translation process. In the most straightforward approach, called compilation and linking, the program is translated into the actual machine language of the computer on which it's to be run. This is usually done in several steps, to make it easier to combine several modules, perhaps written at different times in different programming languages, into a single machine language program.

The language we use in this text is Java. The first implementations of this language were *interpreted*. In this approach, rather than producing a machine language version of the program, the compiler translates the program into a *machine independent* intermediate language, called "byte-code" in the case of Java. The Java byte-code "language" consists of low-level instructions, similar to machine language. However, the language is not tied to the architecture of any particular type of machine. Another program called an *interpreter* reads and executes the program after it has been translated into this intermediate language. Figure 1.9 shows a Java program being compiled on a SPARC workstation, and Figure 1.10 shows the program being interpreted on a Pentium PC.

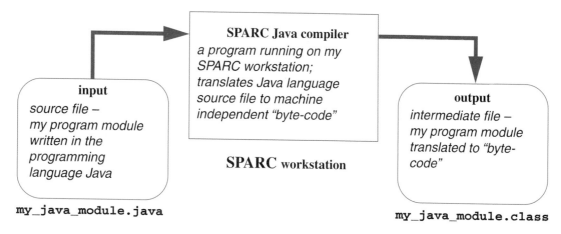

Figure 1.9 Translation to an intermediate language.

Note that with compilation and linking, a program is translated to the machine language of the computer on which it is to run. When the program is run, the machine language translation is loaded into the computer's memory and executed. With an interpreted implementation, as shown in Figure 1.10, when a program is run, the *interpreter* is loaded into the computer's memory and executed. The interpreter reads and executes the byte-code one step at a time. The principal disadvantage of an interpreter is efficiency. It is not surprising to find that an interpreted program runs 10 to 20 times slower than a similar compiled and linked program.

The reason that Java was initially implemented this way is that Java programs are intended to be executed across a network. That is, a program could be written, compiled, and reside on one machine and be executed on a completely different kind of machine. Since there is no way of telling when a program is compiled what kinds of machine will ultimately execute the program, it is not possible to translate the program into a specific machine language.

> **compiler:** a program that translates programs written in a specific programming language into a language more like machine language.

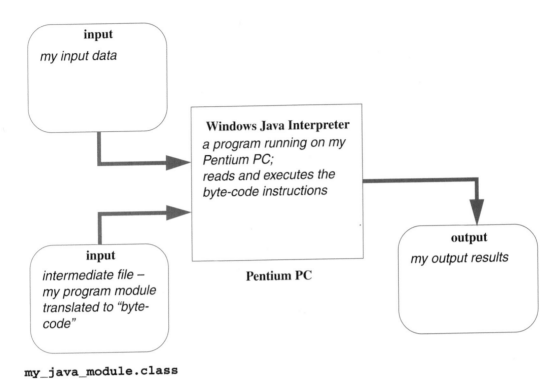

Figure 1.10   **Interpretation.**

There are other hybrid approaches, called "Just in Time (JIT) compilers," in which the "interpreter" translates the byte-code into machine language as it executes it. This provides the advantages of an interpreter, but with a less severe efficiency penalty. Details are well beyond our present discussion.

1.6   Errors in the programming process

Since we've just completed our brief initial discussion of programming languages and compilation, it seems appropriate to mention some of the kinds of errors that can arise in the programming process. On one hand, we tend to think of computers as extremely reliable systems. We even tend to attribute a degree of infallibility to computer produced output. (If your checkbook balance doesn't agree with your bank statement, where do you assume the error lies?) On the other hand, we've all heard stories of credit cards and million dollar water bills addressed to the family pet. The culprit in these cases is usually identified as "the computer."

This dichotomy is not entirely surprising. A computer can perform millions of additions in a second flawlessly. But the systems we build are so incredibly complex that it is almost inconceivable that they are completely correct.

We should, at this point, distinguish between *errors* and *failures*. An *error* is a mistake on the part of a system designer, programmer, or user that prevents a system from functioning properly. A *failure* is the inability of a system or system component to perform its intended function. If you forget to replace the oil pan drain plug when changing your car's oil, you have made an error. When the engine seizes because of a lack of oil pressure, the system has failed. Simply put, errors cause failures. Of course, a system failure may not be directly attributable to an error on the part of the user, designer, or builder. Your car's oil pump may break, for instance, even though it is well-designed, properly built, and you have meticulously and accurately followed the maintenance schedule.

Computer systems fail to function as expected because of *conceptual errors*, *data errors*, *hardware failures*, and *software errors*. A conceptual error is a misunderstanding on the part of the user of the function of the system or of how to use the system. The result can hardly be considered a system failure. Even a completely correct, flawlessly designed system can fail to meet a user's expectations if the user expects the wrong thing. (This is not quite as trivial as it may seem; probably more dissatisfaction with computing systems arises from conceptual errors than any other cause.)

Data errors are obvious: if the price for a can of beans is incorrectly entered into my grocer's data base, my bill won't be correct when I buy beans. We might expect the software to detect gross errors—if the price of beans were entered as $59 per can rather than $0.59. But if the correctness of the data could be completely determined by the software, there would be no need to enter the data at all.

Though there have been a few very well-publicized exceptions, hardware components are very carefully designed to insure their correct functioning. Hardware components are usually considerably simpler in design than large software systems, and the quantity in which they are produced justifies the expense of rigorously verifying design correctness. Hardware can, of course, fail during use. Fortunately such failures are usually easy to detect: rather than producing incorrect results, the system simply doesn't function at all.

We are concerned primarily with software errors. At this point, we introduce a few fundamental ideas; we'll treat the topic in some detail later. The simplest errors to deal with are *syntactic errors*, sometimes called *compilation errors*. A syntactic error occurs when what we write is not legal in the programming language we are using. We use a comma where a period is required for instance, or misspell the word "begin" as "beign." Though syntactic errors often cause us some aggravation when we're first learning a new programming language, they're easy to detect: the compiler (or even the editor) will point them out. Now we might need to be a bit ingenious to understand what the compiler tells us. The compiler will know what we've entered is not legal, but may not know exactly why. We can't expect the compiler to understand our intentions, after all. Nevertheless, there's never any danger of someone using a syntactically incorrect program: it won't compile much less run.

Since syntactic errors are easy to detect, programming languages are designed so that some key aspects of a program's correctness are built into the language syntax. For instance, a common programming error is attempting to perform an inappropriate operation on a data value. It's hard to explain fully this kind of error without a little more background, but the following example might give a bit of the flavor. Suppose you're mixing pastry dough, and I hand you a jar of powdered sugar. If you mistakenly use it as flour, the resulting product is not likely to be satisfactory. You've performed the "add three cups of flour" operation, an inappropriate operation to perform with the sugar jar. As we'll see, the *type structure* of the language allows this kind of error to be detected by the compiler.

Of course a software component can be syntactically correct—that is, legal in the programming language—and still not do what it's supposed to do. For example, a component generating an invoice might compute sales tax before applying a discount, when tax should be computed properly only on the discounted balance. Or a programmer may forget to take into account the possibility that a player can have zero at bats when writing a program to compute batting average. In these cases, the component is said to contain *logical errors*. Logical errors can be very difficult to detect. A logically incorrect program may produce results that appear reasonable but are in fact quite erroneous.

Logical errors can cause a program or component to experience *run-time failure*: that is, fail during execution. Exactly how a run-time failure appears to the user depends on many circumstances, but for the moment we can imagine a message popping up during program execution saying something like "General system failure." Run-time failure can also result from the inability of the operating system to provide some essential resource to the program. For instance, the program may attempt to access a file that has been locked by another user.

We'll further address the issues of logical errors and run-time failures in later chapters.

1.7   Summary

This chapter is intended to serve two distinct purposes. First, you should begin to have an appreciation for the challenges involved in building a large software system, and how the methodology adopted in this book applies. Specifically,

- large systems are complex; and
- large systems change over time.

To address these difficulties, we adopt a methodology that allows us to

- build systems that are modular, composite construction;
- make extensive use of abstraction;

To define a software system, we must include a description of the data items to be manipulated by the system and a collection of algorithms that provide the system's functionality. The object-based methodology we adopt structures the system around the data.

The second part of the chapter provides some fundamental concepts essential to building software systems. In particular, you should have

- a clear, conceptual model of the supporting hardware system;
- basic understanding of the purpose of fundamental software such as operating systems, compilers, and interpreters.

EXERCISES

1.1 Find the jargon file (a.k.a. *The New Hacker's Dictionary*) on the net. Find the definitions of all the terms you need to know that weren't defined in this chapter.

1.2 Read Thomas S. Kuhn's *The Structure of Scientific Revolutions*. Is it reasonable to call the object-oriented approach to software development a "paradigm"?

1.3 Find out some information about Alan Turing. How do his expectations regarding the development of computing compare to reality?

1.4 Assume that you are going to cook chicken stew. Determine the following:
   a. the algorithm;
   b. the data description;
   c. the data values;
   d. the computation.

1.5 Describe an algorithm to register for classes at your school. What is the data for this algorithm?

1.6 Discuss the differences between algorithms such as those of exercises 1.4 and 1.5 in which you are the processor, and algorithms carried out by a machine.

1.7 Illustrate composition and abstraction using a computer system as an example.

1.8 Suppose you want to write a program to play chess. What are some of the objects you might use to model the game? Suggest some properties and responsibilities these objects might have.

GLOSSARY

abstraction: elimination of the irrelevant and amplification of the essential. To abstract is to ignore certain differentiating details.

address: a number uniquely identifying a particular location in memory.

algorithm: a set of instructions describing a pattern of behavior guaranteed to achieve a specific goal.

application: a program or software system that is not part of the "system management" software. Specifically, a program not associated with the operating system.

compilation error: a syntactic error.

compiler: a program that translates programs written in a high level programming language into a language closer to machine language.

component: a well-defined part of a system.

composition: the process of building a system using simpler components.

computation: a sequence of goal-directed actions performed by a processor.

computer science: a science of abstraction—concerned with creating the right model for a problem and devising an appropriate mechanizable technique to solve it.

conceptual error: a misunderstanding on the part of the user of the function of the system or of how to use the system.

data: the information a program deals with.

data description: a description of the kind of data a program requires.

data error: an error caused by incorrect data being provided to a program.

distributed system: a collection of networked systems that share resources, and in some ways function as a single system.

editor: a program that allows the user to create and modify text files in a computer's file system.

error: a mistake by a system designer or user that prevents a system from functioning properly. Errors cause failures.

failure: the inability of a system to complete satisfactorily its intended purpose. Failures are caused by errors.

file: a named collection of information stored in a machine's file system.

file system: the collection of files, containing programs and data, that a machine has access to; usually stored on disk.

functionality: the actions a program is expected to perform, or the purpose it is expected to satisfy.

hardware failure: the failure of a system due to hardware malfunction.

input/output device: a mechanism by which a computer system communicates with the outside world.

interpreter: a program which reads and executes, step by step, another program that typically has been translated into an intermediate language.

instruction: a description of an action to be performed by a processor.

instruction set: the set of instructions that a particular processor can understand.

logical error: an error in program which causes it to produce incorrect results, even though the program is syntactically legal. A program containing logical errors is legal in the programming language, but does not produce the intended results.

machine language: the instruction set of a particular processor.

memory: a computer system component in which data and algorithm reside when the processor is using them.

network: a number of computers and other devices connected together so that they can communicate with each other and share resources.

object: a software abstraction representing some data component to be manipulated by the system.

object-oriented: a method of software development in which the system is organized around data objects.

operating system: the fundamental resource management software of a computer system.

processor: the component of the system that actually performs the actions of a computation.

program: a collection of data descriptions and algorithms, expressed in a programming language, designed to solve a problem. A program is usually considered to be a self-contained piece of software that solves a particular, static, well-defined problem.

programming language: a formal notation in which data descriptions and algorithms are expressed.

run-time failure: a failure that occurs while a program is executing (running).

semantic error: a logical error.

semantics: the set of rules that specify the meaning of a syntactically legal construct in a programming language.

software engineering: the study of methods for producing and evaluating software systems.

software error: a syntactic or logical error in a program.

software system: a collection of data descriptions and algorithms, expressed in a programming language, designed to solve a particular problem or set of related problems.

source file: a text file containing data descriptions and algorithms expressed in a programming language.

syntactic error: an error resulting from not adhering to the grammatical rules of a programming language. A program containing syntactic errors is not a legal program in the language in which it is written.

syntax: the set of grammatical and punctuation rules for a programming language.

CHAPTER 2

Data abstraction: introductory concepts

We now begin considering in detail how to build components of a software system. In this chapter, we introduce the foundational notions of value and type, and of object and class. *Values* are the basic items of data we manipulate with a program, and are grouped into *types*. *Objects* are the fundamental abstractions from which we build our systems, and are grouped into *classes*.

We also initiate our study of the programming language Java, looking at the primitive values and types provided by the language. Finally, we introduce *reference values*, an elementary mechanism by which objects can be related to each other. If objects are to function cooperatively in solving a problem, they must certainly know about each other. A reference value denotes a particular object, and so provides a "handle" that other objects can use to interact with it.

2.1 Values and types

We are now ready to begin learning how to build the components of a software system. But first we need to understand some fundamental concepts.

Values are the fundamental pieces of information manipulated by a program. The most obvious examples of values are numbers, both integers and reals. Other examples are characters (letters, digits, and punctuation marks), colors, points in a plane. A value can be *simple*, sometimes called *atomic*, in which case it cannot be broken down into simpler parts. Or it can be *composite*, in which case it is composed of other, simpler values. For example, an integer number is atomic: we don't think of the number 3 as having "simpler parts." On the other hand, a date, like 11/22/96, has month-day-year components: it is a composite value. Similarly, the word "Hello" is composed of five characters—*H, e, l, l, o*—each of which is atomic.

Values are abstractions used to represent, or *model*, various aspects of a problem. We use an integer, for instance, to denote the number of students in a class, or the number of words on a page. Integers represent or model aspects of a problem we want to count. We use real numbers to represent problem features we "measure": the width of a table, the voltage drop across a line. Representing problem characteristics with numeric values and then manipulating the values to solve the problem is exactly what we do when we solve an exercise in physics, or a "word problem" in mathematics.

Values are grouped together according to what we use them for and according to the *operations* we perform with them. A set of values along with the operations that can be performed with them is called a *type*. The idea is to collect in a type values that can be used in similar ways. We use integer numbers to model things we can count, for instance, and perform operations such as addition, subtraction, and multiplication with them. The operations we can perform with one integer (double it, subtract it from 10, *etc.*) we can also do with any other integer. Hence the set of integers along with the operations of arithmetic comprise a type. The integer values are all elements of the same type. A color, on the other hand, is a completely different kind of value. It wouldn't make much sense to use a color to denote the number of students in a class, or to multiply two colors. Operations we might want to perform with colors include combining, complementing, and so on. A set of colors along with a collection of appropriate operations can also form a type, but a color and an integer would not likely be in the same type.

> **value:** a fundamental piece of information that can be manipulated in a program.
>
> **type:** a set of related values along with the operations that can be performed with them.

A programming language provides some *primitive,* or *built-in,* types that are an integral part of the language. Many programming languages also include facilities that allow us to define our own types. That is, they provide a facility with which a programmer can group together a set of values, along with appropriate operations on them, as a type. We'll look at Java's built-in types next.

2.2   Primitive types in Java

Java's built-in types include `byte`, `short`, `int`, `long`, `float`, `double`, `char`, and `boolean`. We briefly describe each type here; we'll see them in more detail later. (Note that we use a recognizably distinct type font when we write something that has a specific meaning in the programming language.)

The types `byte`, `short`, `int`, and `long` all denote sets of integer values. The operations that can be performed with these values include the usual arithmetic operations of addition, subtraction, multiplication, and division. The only difference in these types is the size of the sets they denote. For instance, as shown in Figure 2.1, the type `int` contains the integers from –2,147,483,648 through 2,147,483,647, while the type `short` contains the integers from –32,768 through 32,767.

Type	Smallest value	Largest value
`byte`	–128	127
`short`	–32,768	32,767
`int`	–2,147,483,648	2,147,483,647
`long`	–9,223,372,036,854,775,808	9,223,372,036,854,775,807

Figure 2.1 Value ranges for integer types.

As is the case with most languages, Java distinguishes real numbers from integers. The types `float` and `double` contain sets of real (in fact, rational) numbers. These values are sometimes called "floating point" numbers because of the way in which they're encoded in the computer's memory. Computers represent integer numbers and floating point numbers by quite different encodings, and have different machine language instructions for manipulating them. An important distinction is that integer numbers are represented exactly while real numbers are approximated. Values of type `float` are stored to about seven places[1] of accuracy, and values of type `double` to about sixteen. If the `float` representation of the number 0.01 were summed 100 times, for instance, the sum would be very close to, but not exactly equal to, 1.0. The reason is that the computer's representation of 0.01 is not exact: it's an approximation, in much the same way that 0.33333 is an approximation of 1/3. For the same reason, the `float` representations of the numbers 17,000,000 and 17,000,001 are identical. The numbers differ in the eighth place, but are represented in the machine to only about seven places of accuracy. On the other hand, these numbers would be distinguishable if encoded as integers, since each would be represented exactly.

As mentioned above, we use integer values to represent things we count: the number of students in a class, the number of angels dancing on the head of a pin, the number of banking transactions this month, the number of pixels on a computer screen. We use real (floating point) values to represent things we measure: the width of a desk top, the voltage drop across a battery, the luminescence of a light bulb.

---

1 . We say "*about* seven places" because these numbers are stored using a *binary* representation which does not translate into an exact number of *decimal* places.

The type `char` consists of a set of characters called the *Unicode* character set. The Unicode character set extends the ASCII character set mentioned in the first chapter. Included are upper case and lower case letters, digits, punctuation marks, and many other special characters. Characters are principally used for input and output.

The type `boolean` contains only the two values *true* and *false*. We'll see operations on these values later.

Java neither provides for composite values, nor offers a mechanism for directly defining our own types. Situations modeled with composite values or user-defined types in some languages are handled with objects in Java. We consider objects and classes next.

2.3   Objects

As we mentioned in Chapter 1, *objects* are the fundamental abstractions from which we build software systems. Objects are often abstractions of real-world entities: students, employees, rooms, passageways, chess pieces, *etc.* Any system we design has a set of tasks that it must perform. We refer to this collection of tasks as the *functionality* of the system. Objects are designed to support the functionality of the system. That is, the tasks the system must perform are allocated to software objects that perform them. We say an object has the *responsibility* for performing certain specific tasks. Consider, for example, a university registration system. Among the functions this system must perform are enrolling students in courses and producing course rolls. (We say "course" rather than "class" to avoid confusion with the technical term "class" introduced later.) In designing such a system, we may well decide to model students and courses with objects. Each student and each course will be represented by a separate software object. The responsibility for enrolling a student in a course will be given to the object representing the student; the responsibility for producing a course roll will be given to the object denoting the course. In this way the functionality required of the system is distributed to the objects that comprise the system. Now to enroll a student in a course, the student object almost certainly needs to interact with the object representing the course. The software system is therefore composed of a collection of objects that *cooperate* to solve a problem.

2.3.1   Queries and properties

The importance of an object is the set of functions it is responsible for performing. But we have also said that objects model "real-world entities"—aspects of the problem that actually exist. The function of an object in modeling something is to furnish relevant information about whatever it is the object represents. Suppose we consider an object that denotes a student in the registration system. Characteristics of a student relevant to the registration system include things like the student's name and address, the number of credit hours the student is enrolled in, the student's course schedule, whether or not the student has paid fees, and so on. It is the responsibility of the object modeling a particular student to maintain this information about the student. There are of course many other characteristics of the student that are not relevant for the registration system and won't be represented: shoe size, eye color, the amount of change in the student's pocket, *etc.* (The object is an abstraction of the student.)

The characteristics the object will provide information about are called the *properties* of the object. Thus properties of a student object include *name*, *address*, and so on. At any given time, each property has an *associated value*. We can *query* the object to determine the current values of its properties: "What is your name?" "How many credit hours are you enrolled in?" "Have you paid your fees?" Thus one important aspect of an object's functionality is the set of properties the object has, and hence the set of queries it responds to.

Now we don't care how an object determines the value it returns in response to a query. For instance, if a student object is queried for the number of credit hours the student is enrolled in, it might simply remember (the value is stored in memory somewhere), it might add up the hours for each course on the student's schedule, it might even enlist the assistance of other objects. All that's important is that the object has a property (*credit hours*) whose value can be obtained by querying the object.

2.3.2   Commands and state

It should be clear that the particular values associated with an object's properties can change with time. A student might change her address, or drop a course when she learns who the instructor is. Thus the object denoting the student might, at different times, give different responses to the query "How many credit hours are you enrolled in?" The set of an objects's properties and associated values at a given time is called the state[1] of the object. We say an object's state changes over time.

> **state:** the set of an object's properties and associated values at any given time.

Note carefully the relationship between objects and values. At any given time, a particular *value* is associated with each *property* of an *object*. (The fact that objects can change is a key point of distinction between objects and values.)

---

1 . The term *state* properly refers to the object *as implemented* rather than as viewed by the user. We'll ignore this notational abuse for the present.

We represent an object graphically as shown in Figure 2.2. The state of the object, as a set of properties and their current values, is given below the horizontal line.

Student	
name	= R. Raskolnikov
address	= S. Place, Petersburg
social security number	= 000-00-0001
credit hours	= 9
fees paid	= no
course schedule	= Ethics 1001
	Law 6592
	Comp Sci 1583

Figure 2.2 **An object.**

The only way that an object's state changes is as a result of some action by the object itself. In addition to replying to queries, where an object simply reports some aspect of its current state, objects also respond to a specific set of *commands*. A command instructs the object to perform some action, which often results in the object changing state. For instance, we might instruct a student object to drop a course, changing the *credit hours* and *course schedule* properties of the object. Compare the illustration of an object performing a command and changing state (Figure 2.3) with that of the processor executing an instruction and changing data stored in memory (Figure 1.7). In performing a command and changing its state, an object is behaving much the same as a processor executing a command and changing the contents of memory.

The sets of queries and commands available for a particular object are collectively called the object's *features*[1]. Its features determine the view we have of the object: that is, we "know" an object only through its queries and commands. When we design an object, we choose queries (and hence properties) and commands relevant to the problem at hand. That is, we choose features supporting the functional responsibilities of the object. As we have previously mentioned, the functional behavior required of the system is distributed as responsibilities of the comprising objects.

---

1 . The terms *features* and *properties*, as we use them in the text, are not standard throughout the object-oriented community.

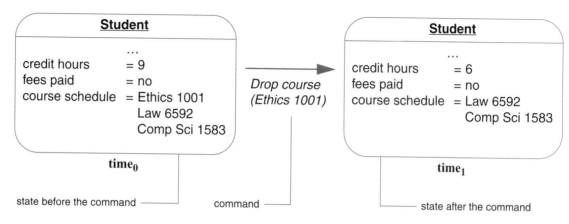

Figure 2.3 **Student object changes state in response to a command.**

> An object is characterized by its **features**, including:
>
> > **queries**, by which we determine the values currently associated with the object's properties; and
> > **commands**, which can change these values.

2.3.3 Designing with objects

Two questions must be addressed when designing a system with an object-based methodology:

- what are the objects? that is, what aspects of the problem should be represented as objects? and

- what features should these objects have?

Several techniques of varying degrees of sophistication have been proposed for identifying potential objects in a system design. In many cases, however, there are rather conspicuous candidates: certain aspects of the problem lend themselves to being modeled with objects in an obvious way. If we're designing a university registration system, for instance, it doesn't take a great leap of imagination to start by modeling students and courses as objects. Such objects are sometimes said to be "there for the picking."

In general, it takes a bit of experience to identify a suitable collection of objects for modeling a system. In a later chapter we'll offer some guidelines for deciding which system components should be abstracted as objects. Since our immediate goal is to learn how to design and implement simple objects, we assume for the present that the decomposition of the system into objects is rather obvious from the system specification. That is, we assume the objects are there for the picking.

Now assuming that we have identified a number of objects that can be used to build the system, we must determine what features each of these objects will have. As we've stated above, objects are designed to support the functionality of the system. That is, we determine a set of system requirements from the system specification: data the system must maintain and operations it must perform. These requirements are distributed as *responsibilities* to the objects. The functionality required of the system is *decomposed* or *partitioned* into responsibilities of the objects that will comprise the system.

In determining what responsibilities a particular object should have, it is useful to think in terms of what the object must *know* and what the object must *do*.

Knowing responsibilities include:

- knowing the properties of the entity the object is modeling;
- knowing about other objects with which it needs to cooperate.

Doing responsibilities include:

- computing particular values;
- performing actions that modify its state;
- creating and initializing other objects;
- controlling and coordinating the activities of other objects.

When we specify the object, "knowing responsibilities" generally translate into queries: if we want to find out some particular piece of information the object knows, we query the object. "Doing responsibilities" translate into queries and commands. If we want some particular piece of information that the object knows how to compute, we query the object. If we want the object to perform some action that will change its state, we give the object a command.

Consider, for example, the student object mentioned above. This object is to represent a student in a registration system. What must the object *know* about the student? It should know things like:

- student's name;
- student's address;
- student's social security number;
- number of credit hours the student is enrolled in;
- student's schedule;
- whether or not the student has paid fees.

These are some of the "knowing responsibilities" of the object. When we design the object, we will include *queries* for these values among the features of the object.

If we consider what the object must be able to *do*, we might come up with a list of responsibilities including:

- add a course to the student's schedule;
- drop a course from the student's schedule;
- change the student's address;
- determine the student's fees.

The first three of these responsibilities involve changing the state and will become *commands* when we design the object. The last involves computing a value, and will be a query.

When we define the object, the responsibilities enumerated above will translate into features:

- queries: name, address, social security number, credit hours, schedule, fees, fees paid;
- commands: add course, drop course, change name.

The student object will almost certainly have additional features. But a complete list of an object's responsibilities, and hence its features, can only be determined from a thorough analysis of system requirements. Suppose we are designing an object to model a simple wall switch. What information should the object know about the switch? Should it know the position of the switch, whether it's on or off? Should it know the color? If we're modeling electrical circuits, we would surely answer "yes" to the first and "no" to the second. On the other hand, if we're building an inventory system for a hardware store, the position of the switch is irrelevant, but color might well be important to know.

Determining an object's responsibilities is an important design activity, a process driven by the object's role in supporting the functionality of the system. However, in our initial examples, since we consider objects more or less in isolation, we will simply assume a set of responsibilities *a priori*. As our examples become more comprehensive, we will get a better idea of how an object's specification is driven by the demands of the system it is part of.

2.3.4 Some additional examples

As another example, suppose we want to model a ticket dispenser of the kind found at service counters. Upon entering the shop, a customer takes a numbered ticket from the dispenser. Customers are served in numeric order.

What are the responsibilities of such an object? As we've seen, we can't give a definitive answer without knowing more about the application. But let's assume that we want the object to know the number on the next ticket, and how many tickets remain in the dispenser. What should the object be able to do? Dispense a ticket, and refill the dispenser. Thus the object will have the following features:

- queries: next ticket number, number of tickets remaining.

- commands: dispense a ticket, refill the dispenser.

Figure 2.4 shows the object performing a "dispense ticket" command.

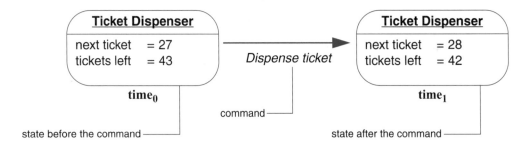

Figure 2.4 **Dispenser object changes state in response to a command.**

It might seem that "refilling the dispenser" should be some other object's responsibility. In reality, after all, ticket dispensers don't refill themselves. We must keep in mind that we're dealing with a *software object* that represents the ticket dispenser. The number of the current ticket and number of tickets left are part of the state of this object. "Refilling the dispenser" changes the state of the object, and we've seen that changing state is accomplished by the object itself, in response to a command. Thus any desired state changes are the responsibility of the object whose state is to be changed.

Next, consider a program that allows a person to play chess against "the computer." Such a program must be able to show the user the board configuration, get moves from the user, and evaluate and determine moves for the computer. In designing such a program, we might have objects representing the players (user and computer), objects representing each chess piece, an object representing the board. Each player object responds to a command "*make a move.*" One of the player objects (the computer) implements this command with an algorithm for determining which move to make next. The other player object (the user) gets its moves from the person playing the game. What are likely responsibilities for an object representing a playing piece? We want it to know the color and name of the piece (*e.g.*, black queen), whether it has been captured or is still in play, and its position on the board. We want it to move and get captured, both of which change its state. Thus the object will have queries like *color, name, position,* and commands like *"move,"* which changes its board position, and *"captured,"* which removes it from play.

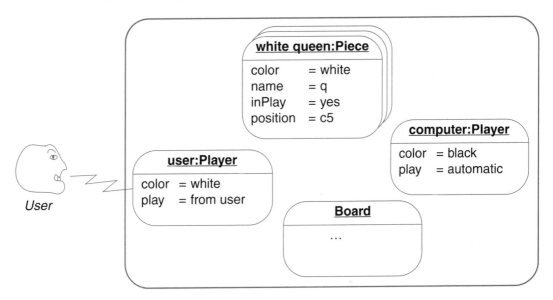

Figure 2.5 **Objects in a chess game.**

2.3.5   Objects denoting composite values: immutable objects

In Section 2.1 we noted that values could be simple, like integers, or composed of other, simpler, values. Java does not provide composite values directly. Rather, objects are used in Java to realize composite values. Suppose for instance we need to deal with dates, composite values having day, month, and year components. We can model such values with date *objects*, having day, month, and year features. That is, we expect a date object to know the day, month, and year of the date it represents, and we can query the object for these values. But these objects are inert: we don't expect them to *do* anything. They simply represent a particular *value*, and once they are created, they never change state. We refer to such objects as *immutable*.[1]

Strings of characters, such as the word "Hello", are handled in a similar way. We'll see later that string objects are provided for in the standard Java libraries. A string object represents a value whose components are the individual characters of

---

1 . The standard Java libraries provide for date objects that are not immutable, and are much more complex than the date objects illustrated here.

Date

day	= 29
month	= May
year	= 1999

Figure 2.6 **An immutable object representing a date: once created, it will never change state.**

the string. We can query the object to determine the number of characters it contains (its "length") and to determine the individual characters that comprise it. But once it is created, it cannot change. As with the date object, it is immutable.

2.3.6   Some cautions

We should be careful to note that software objects do not behave exactly like the real entities they are modeling. For instance, the real entities might change even though they are completely passive; software objects will not. People age, light bulbs burn out, switches are turned off and on, ticket dispensers are refilled. All this happens without any obvious active participation required of the people, light bulbs, switches, or ticket dispensers. If Sally is now 25 years old, she does not need to perform any specific action to turn 26. She will be 26 one year from now regardless of what she does or doesn't do. On the other hand, suppose a software object representing Sally (as part of the student registration system, for instance) stores the property *age* as part of its state. The only way this object will change state is in response to an explicit command. Thus if we want the software object Sally to age, it must be a responsibility of the object: for instance, a command "*update age*" might be included in the object's features.

As another example, suppose an object models a lamp. Two properties we might be interested in are whether the lamp is on and whether the lamp is burned out. To determine if an actual lamp is on, we simply look at it. But we can't just "look at" a software object. We must query the object to determine its state. To be specific, let's assume that boolean values are associated with the properties *lamp is on* and *lamp is burned out*. We query the lamp object to determine if it is on (we get a response of *true* if the lamp is on, *false* if it is off), and we query it to determine if it burned out. The only way the lamp object changes state is in response to a command. Thus we might have commands like "*turn on*" and "*turn off.*" How does the lamp burn out? Again, as with any state change, it must be the result of some specific action by the object itself. We might have a command "*burn out*" that explicitly changes the state of the lamp. Or the lamp might remember how many times it was turned on, and burn out when it is turned on for the 100th time.

How the lamp object works is a matter of design. The important thing to remember is that an object will only change state in response to an explicit command. It is the object's responsibility to change its state.

2.4 Classes

Just as we collect values and operations into types, we categorize objects according to their features. Objects representing students *me, you, him, her* are likely to have the same set of properties (though different values associated with these properties at any specific time) and respond to the same commands (though perhaps in different ways). A collection of similar objects, objects with the same set of features, is called a *class*. Every object is an element of some class: we say an object is an *instance* of the class. The student objects *me, you, him, her* all belong to the same class; the objects representing the pieces in the chess game are also instances of a common class. Again, a class specifies the features of a group of similar objects: if two objects (two instances) are of the same class, they will have the same set of queries and the same set of commands. They are the same kind of object, having the same functionality and properties, though of course they will likely have different values associated with their properties.

---

class: a set of objects having the same features: *i.e.*, supporting the same queries and commands.

Every object is an **instance** of some class, which determines the object's features.

A critical part of designing a software system is defining classes appropriate for modeling the various entities involved in the problem solution. When we define a class, we specify the features—queries and commands—for members of the class. The objects—the instances of the class—are created and destroyed dynamically as the system runs. For example, when we design a registration system, we decide what aspects of a student we want to model and what responsibilities an object representing a student should have. This is reflected in the design of the class *Student*. However, we have no idea who the actual students will be when we design the system. When the system is running, as each student is enrolled a new object of class *Student* is created to represent that student. (Note that we have a little different situation with the chess game. When we design the program, we already know all the objects that will be involved. Unlike students at a university, pieces don't come and go in a chess game.)

In our diagrams, we use a box to denote a class and a rounded box to denote an object. This is illustrated in Figure 2.7.

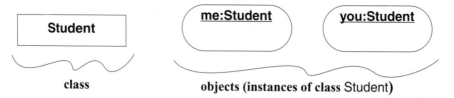

class   objects (instances of class Student)

Figure 2.7 **Class and instances.**

2.5   Objects as properties of objects

So now we have an object defined by a set of queries and commands. But what queries the object or gives it a command that causes it to change state? Well, simply some other object. Objects don't exist in isolation: as mentioned above, they cooperate to solve a problem. An important part of designing a software system is defining the *relations* between the objects: that is, defining exactly how the objects interact to solve the problem. A relation associates two or more objects in a specific, well-defined way. We explore relations between objects in a general setting in later chapters. For the moment, we concentrate our view on a single object.

One way in which a relation between one object and another can be expressed is by means of a property. Suppose we are modeling characters from literature. We might define a class *Person*, and determine that we want an object of that class to know the character's mother. Thus an object of class *Person* will have an attribute mother, as shown in Figure 2.8.

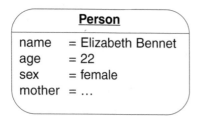

Figure 2.8 **An object of class *Person*.**

We expect the mother of one character to be another character, and so to be modeled by another *Person* object. This is an example of a simple relation between two objects: one *Person* object *has as mother* another *Person* object. From the perspective of the (first) object, *mother* is a property in much the same way that *age* is. We can query the object to determine its *age*, and we can query the object to determine its *mother*.

We've noted that at any given time each property of an object has a specific *value* associated with it. The object pictured in Figure 2.8, for instance, has the integer value 22 associated with the property *age*. What kind of value should be associated with the property *mother*? Quite simply, it should be a value that *denotes* or *refers to* another *Person* object. Such a value is called a *reference* value. Its type, in this case, is *reference-to-Person*, since the object it refers to is of class *Person*. (A value that refers to a *Student* object would be of type *reference-to-Student*, and so on.) We illustrate a reference value as arrow, as shown in Figure 2.9.

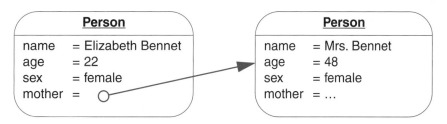

Figure 2.9 **A property of one object references another.**

Note that there can be many instances of a reference value, just as there can be many instances of an integer value. As shown in Figure 2.10, the objects denoting Elizabeth Bennet and her sister have the same value for the property *sex*, and the same value for the property *mother*.

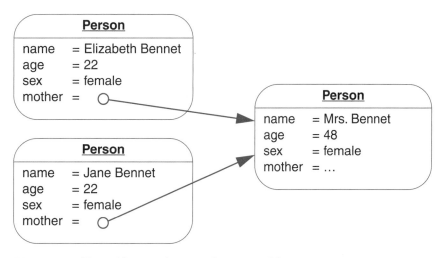

Figure 2.10 **Two objects reference the same object.**

We repeat for emphasis: *Person* is a *class*. A class specifies the features that objects of the class will have. One can think of a class definition as providing a pattern or template for creating objects. The entities representing Elizabeth Bennet and Mrs. Bennet are *objects*—instances—of class *Person*. Associated with an object is a reference *value* that identifies the object. The *type* of this value is *reference-to-x*, where *x* is the class of the object. The value that denotes the "Mrs. Bennet" object is of type *reference-to-Person*, since the object it denotes is an instance of class *Person*. In Figure 2.9 this value is associated with the property *mother* of the "Elizabeth Bennet" object.

---

reference value: a value that denotes an object.

Let's look at one more example. Assume the object representing the chess board mentioned above has a property for each square on the board. A value associated with one of these properties is a reference to the piece that occupies the squares. That is, the value associated with the square is of type *reference-to-Piece*, where *Piece* is the class of the chess pieces. Figure 2.11 shows square *a1* occupied by the white queen. Clearly this square will be occupied by different pieces at different points in the game. That is, the particular value associated with the property *a1* will change as the game progresses. But the value will always be a reference to some object of class *Piece*; that is, it will always be a value of type *reference-to-Piece*.

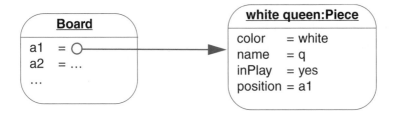

Figure 2.11   Board **object references a** *Piece* **object.**

One final observation before we end our first look at reference values. Suppose the square *a1* in the above example is not occupied by any piece. What would we expect in response to the query "Which piece is on square *a1*?" We'd expect a response that essentially says "None." There is a unique value in every reference type,[1] called the *null* reference, that doesn't denote any object. Getting this value in response to a query tells us "none." It will be pictured as shown in Figure 2.12.

---

1 . Technically, the *null* value is the unique value of the anonymous "reference-to-nothing" (null) type.

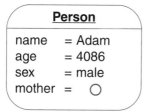

Figure 2.12 **The *null* reference.**

2.6   Summary

This chapter introduced the fundamental notions of values and objects. Values can be simple or composite, and are grouped along with their operations into types. Java provides as primitive:

- several integer types (`byte`, `short`, `int`, `long`);
- two real or floating types (`float` and `double`);
- the character type `char`, and
- the type `boolean` which contains two values, `true` and `false`.

Objects are the fundamental abstractions from which software systems are built. Objects are often abstractions of real-world entities, and are designed to support the functionality of the system. An object's role in the system is determined by the set of features the object is responsible for supporting. These features include

- queries, which provide the current values of the object's properties; and
- commands, which cause the object to preform some action.

The set of an object's properties and their current values is called the state of the object. Thus a query reports information concerning the state of the object, while a command usually causes the object to change state. The only way an object can change state is if the object itself performs some command.

In designing an object, we ask what should the object know and what should the object do. That is, we enumerate the "knowing responsibilities" and the "doing responsibilities" of the object. These responsibilities are determined by the object's role in supporting the functionality of the system. System functionality is distributed to the comprising objects by assigning a set of responsibilities to each object. "Knowing responsibilities" translate to queries when the object is defined. "Doing responsibilities" translate into queries or commands.

Objects are grouped into classes. A class defines the features of its members. All objects in a particular class have the same features. An object that is a member of a particular class is called an instance of the class.

For every object there is a value that denotes or refers to the object. Such a value is called a *reference value*; its type is *reference-to-x*, where *x* is the class of the object. We use reference values to establish relationships between objects.

EXERCISES

2.1   Assume that a type is defined to model each of the following. List some values of the types.

    a.   Months of the year.

    b.   Playing card suits.

    c.   Positions on a baseball team.

2.2   Consider a composite value that represents a playing card. What are the components of such a value? What are the types of the components?

2.3   Consider a composite value that represents a point in the Euclidean plane. What are the components of such a value? What are the types of the components?

2.4   For each of the following applications, suggest some objects that might be included in the system design. Give one or two responsibilities that might be assigned to each object.

    a.   Your favorite computer game.

    b.   A program modeling traffic flow on major thoroughfares in a city.

    c.   An inventory control system for a hardware store.

    d.   A program controlling a vending machine.

    e.   A university registration system.

    f.   A program that translates English into French.

    g.   A program for recording and manipulating genealogical data.

2.5   Suppose a simple object needs to be designed to model each of the following. Propose some responsibilities the object might have. Specify queries and commands (features) to support these responsibilities. Indicate the type of the value associated with each query.

    a.   A three-way lamp.

    b.   A traffic signal light.

    c.   A combination lock.

    d.   An inventory item in a hardware store.

    e.   An elevator.

2.6   In the University Registration System, objects must be designed to represent colleges, departments, and courses. Suggest some properties each of these might have.

2.7   Consider an object representing a student in the University Registration system. Specify the *type* of each of the following properties of this object.

   a.   Student's fees.

   b.   Student's name.

   c.   Department to which the student belongs.

   d.   Student's schedule.

   e.   Student's grade point average.

2.8   Consider a system to manage a library's holdings. What properties should an object representing a book include? Which of those properties have values that are references to other objects?

2.9   Could an object representing a student in the University Registration System be used to model a user of University Library? Are all properties of a student relevant for a library user? Are new properties needed?

2.10   When a student user of the library borrows a book, the system must have a record that, among other things, associates the book borrowed with the student borrowing it. How could such a record be represented? What information should it contain?

GLOSSARY

class: a collection of similar objects. Objects that are members of the same class have the same set of features.

command:[1] a constituent (feature) of an object used to instruct the object to perform some action which typically results in a change of the object's state.

doing responsibility:[1] a requirement that an object be able to accomplish some task.

feature:[1] a query or command to which an object responds.

immutable object: an object that does not change state after it is created.

instance: an object. An object that is a member of a class is called an "instance of the class."

---

1 . These definitions are with respect to an object.

knowing responsibility:[1] a requirement that an object know some piece of information.

null reference: a unique reference value that doesn't denote any object.

primitive type: a type provided as an integral part of the language. Java's built-in types include `byte`, `short`, `int`, `long`, `float`, `double`, `char`, and `boolean`.

property:[1] a characteristic of an object. A value is associated with each property of an object.

query:[1] a constituent (feature) of an object used to determine the current value of one of the object's properties. There is one query feature for each property of an object.
Also means use of the feature: "to query an object" means to obtain the current value of a property by using a query feature.

reference value: a value which denotes or refers to an object.

relation:[1] a specific, well-defined association between two or more objects.

responsibility:[1] something required of an object. Generally, a requirement that an object know some information ("knowing" responsibility) or be able to accomplish some task ("doing" responsibility).

state:[1] the set properties of an object and their current values.

system functionality: the set of tasks a system is required to be able to perform.

type: a set of similar values along with the operations that can be performed with them.

value: a fundamental piece of information manipulated in a program.

---

1 . These definitions are with respect to an object.

CHAPTER 3   Basic Java structural components

Java man *n.*   either of two small-brained prehistoric men known chiefly
from more or less fragmentary skulls found in Trinil, Java.
> — *Webster's New Collegiate Dictionary*

Before we see how to use the language for specifying and implementing our
designs, it will be helpful to begin with a few Java fundamentals. In this chapter,
we first consider the high-level structure of a system written in Java, introducing
packages and *compilation units*. Then, at the other extreme, we examine some
low-level lexical issues and see what the basic tokens that make up a Java program
look like. In neither case are we considering system design. We simply want to get
some basic notions on the record and behind us before moving ahead.

3.1   Syntactic structure of a system definition in Java

As we have explained, a software system consists of a collection of software
objects that cooperate to solve a problem. To create a system, we define the
classes to which the objects belong. A class definition determines the features and
behavior of the objects that are instances of the class. What we write—what the
"program source" consists of—is a *collection of class definitions*. Of course, we
also need some "spark" to create the first objects and get the whole thing going.
We'll worry about that later. At this point, all we want to do is see how the class
definitions are organized into a program. We'll learn exactly what class definitions
look like and why we organize them in a particular way in subsequent chapters.

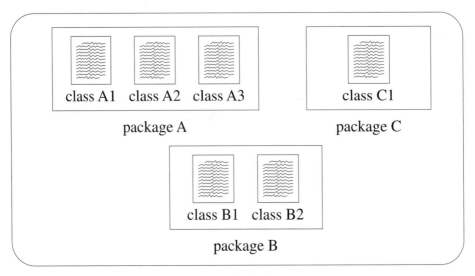

System Definition

Figure 3.1 **Class definitions are grouped into packages.**

Packages

A system definition is composed of a number of modules called *packages*. Each package contains the definition of one or more closely related classes. Suppose we have a class *Room* that models rooms in an architectural plan. We might well have a collection of classes closely related to *Room*—maybe *Door* and *Wall*—that would be conveniently grouped in the same package as *Room*.

A class defined in a particular package can make use of other classes defined in the package. In the above example, a *Room* object could reference a *Door* object. By default, classes defined in one package are not accessible (not visible) to classes defined in another package. We can change this situation by explicitly marking a class as accessible throughout the entire system. Such a class is called a *public* class.

Looking at Figure 3.1, an object of class *A1* for instance can access other objects of class *A1* as well as objects of classes *A2* and *A3*. Classes *A1*, *A2*, and *A3* are all defined in the same package. However, if we want an object of class *A1* to access an object of class *B1*, then we must mark *B1* as a public class. Otherwise, only instances of classes defined in package *B* will be able to access objects of class *B1*.

Don't worry why we might want to do this at the moment. In our initial examples, each class will be public and defined in its own package. We'll see examples later of why we might want to group classes together in a package, and why we might not want a class to be public.

Compilation units

The class definitions that make up a package are written in a set of source files called *compilation units*. A compilation unit can contain the definition of at most one public class. For instance, looking at Figure 3.1 again, if *A1* and *A2* are both public classes—that is, objects of these classes can be accessed from anywhere in the system—then the definition of class *A1* and the definition of class *A2* must be in different files. A package is made up of one or more files (compilation units), each containing the definition of one or more classes. At most one class in a compilation unit can be public. A possible organization of the packages of Figure 3.1 into compilation units is shown in Figure 3.2.

> **package:** a collection of closely related classes.
>
> **compilation unit:** a file containing the definition of one or more classes of a package.

```
package A;

public class A1 {
...
} // end of class A1

class A3 {
...
} // end of class A3
```
A1.java

```
package B;

public class B1 {
...
} // end of class B1

class B2 {
...
} // end of class B2
```
B1.java

```
package A;

public class A2 {
...
} // end of class A2
```
A2.java

```
package C;

public class C1 {
...
} // end of class C1
```
C1.java

Figure 3.2 **Four compilation units.**

3.2 Identifiers

Next we consider some low-level lexical details of the language. Two of the fundamental "tokens" that appear in Java programs are *identifiers* and *literals*. We see identifiers here, literals in the next section.

We use *identifiers* to name things in Java. Identifiers name packages, classes, objects, and features. A Java identifier is a sequence of characters consisting of letters, digits, dollar signs($), and/or underscores(_). An identifier can be of any length, and cannot begin with a digit. The following are examples of Java identifiers. (Recall we use a distinct type font when we write in the language.)

```
X      Abc    aVeryLongIdentifier      b29   a2b   A_a_x
b$2    $_     $$$    IXLR8
```

In practice, we follow a convention that doesn't use underscores and dollar signs in identifiers: we use only letters and digits. The following are not legal Java identifiers. (Why not?)

```
2BRnot2B      a.b    Hello!      A-a
```

Java identifiers are *case sensitive*. This means that upper and lower case characters are different. For example, the following are all different identifiers.

```
total         Total          TOTAL          tOtAl
```

Though it may be obvious, we also note that identifiers can't contain spaces, and that the digits 1 and 0 (one and zero) are different from the letters l and o (el and oh), though the difference is not always easy to see in print.

There are a number of *keywords* and *identifier literals* reserved for special purposes. These cannot be used as identifiers, and are given in Figure 3.3.[1]

---

identifier: a sequence of characters that can be used as a name in a Java program.

---

abstract	default	goto	null	synchronized
boolean	do	if	package	this
break	double	implements	private	throw
byte	else	import	protected	throws
case	extends	instanceof	public	transient
catch	false	int	return	true
char	final	interface	short	try
class	finally	long	static	void
const	float	native	super	volatile
continue	for	new	switch	while

Figure 3.3 **Identifier literals and keywords.**

---

1. `true`, `false`, and `null` are identifier literals; the rest are keywords. The distinction need not concern us.

Class, package, and compilation unit names

Packages and classes are named with identifiers. Our convention is to name a class with a capitalized identifier, and name a package with the lower case name of the principal class defined in the package, or its plural. (More about package names later.) Thus, if we are going to define a class `Student`, the package containing its definition will be named `student` or `students`.

Compilation units are text files, and so are named with *file names*. Exactly what a file name looks like depends on the operating system we are using. A file name is *not* a Java identifier. File names in some operating systems are not case sensitive, and many systems impose a limit on the length of file names. Furthermore, file names can generally contain characters (such as ".") that are not permitted in Java identifiers.

We'll assume that the name of a compilation unit is the same as the name of the public class defined in the file, with ".java" appended. Thus the compilation unit containing the definition of the class `Student` will be a file named `Student.java`.

Guidelines in choosing identifiers

The compiler insists only that we use legal identifiers when naming entities in a Java program; it does not matter to the compiler what specific identifiers we use. However, the intelligent choice of identifiers is one of the most crucial factors in producing a readable program. If we are defining a class to model a student, it is sensible to give the class a name like "`Student`" rather than "`S`" or "`X`" or "`Foo`." It is just as essential that your code be comprehensible to a human reader as to the compiler.

Here, we'll give a few general, common-sense guidelines in choosing identifiers. We'll be more specific as we examine syntactic constructs of the language in detail.

1. Choose identifiers that are descriptive of the named entity. Single-letter identifiers are seldom appropriate. Avoid unnecessary, cryptic, or unintelligible abbreviations, and cuteness.

    Use

        Student   KeyWord   ExpressionTree

    not

        X1   Vodka   XpsnTr

2. Avoid overly long identifiers. Generally, one or two words will suffice. In particular, don't use "noise words" in identifiers.

Use

    ExpressionTree

not

    TheParseTreeForAnExpression

3. Avoid abbreviations. If you abbreviate, be consistent. In particular, if a word is abbreviated as part of one identifier, its occurrence in any other identifier should be similarly abbreviated.

Use

    employeeRecord and masterRecord

or

    employeeRec and masterRec

not

    employeeRec and masterRecord

There are two common methods for choosing abbreviations: using the first few letters of a word or eliding vowels. Be consistent in your method of choosing abbreviations. If `msg` abbreviates "message" then `opr`, not `oper`, should abbreviate "operator."

4. Be as specific as possible. Identifiers like `ComputeResults`, `ProcessData`, *etc.* are virtually contentless.

5. Take particular care to distinguish closely related entities. Names should be as descriptive as you can make them, and differences in entities should be mirrored by differences in their names.

Use

    newMasterRecord and oldMasterRecord

not

    masterRecord1 and masterRecord2

or worse

    masterRec and masRec

6. Don't incorporate the name of its syntactic category in the name of an entity.

Use

    Student

not

    StudentClass

3.3 Literals

A *literal* is a representation of a particular value in a programming language. We write literals in our programs to denote specific values.

Integer literals look like ordinary decimal numbers, and denote values of the type `int`. The following all denote `int` values:

        25   0   1233456   289765   7

Integer literals can't contain commas and shouldn't have leading zeros. For instance,

        123,456

is not a legal literal, and

        0123

doesn't represent the value that it appears to.[1]

Numbers that include a decimal point denote values of type `double`. For instance,

        0.5   2.67   0.00123   12.0   2.   .6

all denote values of type `double`. Even though the last two numbers on the above line are legal, we prefer always to write digits before and after the decimal point. This makes the numbers a bit easier to read. Thus, we'll write

        2.0   0.6

to represent these values.

Exponential notation can also be used for `double` literals. The following are legal `double` literals:

        0.5e+3   0.5e-3   0.5E3   5e4   2.0E-27

They represent the values

$$0.5 \times 10^3 \ (=500.0), \ 0.5 \times 10^{-3} \ (=0.0005), \ 0.5 \times 10^3, \ 5.0 \times 10^4, \text{ and } 2.0 \times 10^{-27}$$

Note that the "e" can be upper or lower case, and that the mantissa (the number before the "e") need not contain a decimal point. The exponent (after the "e") is an optionally signed integer.

Character literals (denoting values of type `char`) consist of a single character between apostrophes. For instance:

        'A'   'a'   '2'   ';'   '.'   ' '

---

1. The leading zero means the number is given in *octal*, or *radix 8*, notation.

The last example on the previous line represents the "space" or "blank" character, the character that is generated by pressing the space bar on the keyboard. Note that uppercase letters are distinct from lower case letters. Thus the first two literals on the above line represent different characters. Also note that the following three literals

```
2      2.0     '2'
```

denote values of *different types*. The first denotes an `int`, the second a `double`, and the third a `char`. These three values are encoded quite differently in the computer's memory, and are manipulated with different instructions.

The apostrophe, quotation mark, and backslash must be preceded by a backslash in a character literal. Thus these characters are represented as

```
'\''    '\"'   '\\'
```

and not as

```
'''     '"'    '\'
```

Certain special characters are also represented by using a backslash. In particular, the "tab" character is represented `'\t'`, and the "end of line" character ("linefeed") is denoted `'\n'`.

Except for the space character, character literals shouldn't include spaces. Thus

```
' A '
```

is not legal, where there are spaces before and after the letter 'A'.

The two values of type `boolean` are written as follows:

```
true   false
```

Since Java is case sensitive, we must use lower case letters when writing these `boolean` values. We can't write `true` as `TRUE` or `True`.

A string literal is a possibly empty sequence of characters enclosed in quotations:

```
"ABC"        "123"        ""
```

String literals are a little different from those literals discussed above. *String* is a class defined in the standard package `java.lang`. A string literal denotes (a reference to) an instance of this class. Instances of the class *String* are immutable objects. (See Section 2.3.5) A string object represents a composite value whose components are the individual characters of the string.

A string literal cannot be split across more than one line. And the quotation mark and backslash must be preceded by a backslash in a string literal:

```
"He said, \"Let's go!\""
```

---

literal: a sequence of characters that denote a particular value in a Java program.

3.4 Lexical structure

A source file contains constructs (class definitions, for instance) made up of *tokens*—identifiers, keywords, literals, punctuation marks. How things are spaced and where a line ends are somewhat arbitrary. Spaces are required to separate words. For instance, the line

```
public class Student
```

contains two keywords followed by an identifier, but the line

```
publicclass Student
```

simply contains two identifiers.

Spaces are not required but are usually permitted around punctuation. For instance, the following two lines are equivalent:

```
class Student{
class Student {
```

(There are some cases where spaces are not allowed around punctuation marks; these will be obvious when we encounter them.)

Finally, several spaces can generally appear, and a line can end, wherever one space can appear. The following two lines are equivalent:

```
public class Student{
public        class        Student {
```

and are each equivalent to the following four lines:

```
public
            class
  Student
  {
```

However, we adhere to rather rigid rules for spacing in order to make our programs easier to read. We'll illustrate these conventions as specific syntactic constructs are introduced.

Comments

Comments are explanatory remarks included in a program strictly for the benefit of a human reader. They are completely ignored by the compiler. There are three kinds of comments in Java. We'll see them used throughout the text. The first begins with a pair of "slash" characters, and extends to the end of the line:

```
// This is a one-line comment.
```

The second form of comment begins with the character pair "/*" and extends to the character pair "*/". This form of comment may extend across several lines:

```
/* This is a comment that
extends across more than one line. */
```

The final form is called a "doc comment." It is similar to the second form above but starts with the three characters "/**". Doc comments are recognized by certain software tools that provide summaries of classes defined in a source file.

```
/** This is a doc comment. Like the above,
it can continue for more than one line. */
```

We use a convention of starting each line in a doc comment with an aligned "*", and putting the starting "/**" and ending "*/" on lines by themselves.

```
/**
 * This is a doc comment.
 * By convention, each line starts with a "*" and
 * the starting and terminating characters are put on
 * lines by themselves.
 */
```

Again, although comments are very important for programmers who need to use or understand our code, they have nothing to do with how the program behaves when it is run.

---

comment: explanatory remarks included in a program for the benefit of a human reader, and ignored by the compiler.

3.5   Summary

In this chapter, we saw some of the fundamental structure of a Java program. Looking at the overall organization, we saw that the class definitions that make up a program are grouped together into packages. Classes defined in the same package are closely related to each other. Instances of these classes can access each other automatically, simply because the classes are in the same package. On the other hand, if a class is to be visible throughout the entire system, it must be explicitly labeled as *public*.

Class definitions are written in source files called *compilation units*. A compilation can contain the definition of at most one public class. All the classes defined in a given compilation unit are part of the same package.

Looking at the lexical structure of a program, we saw that *identifiers* and *literals* are two forms of tokens that comprise a program. Identifiers are used to name classes, packages, objects, and object features. Literals denote specific values.

Finally, we saw that there are three kinds of comments in a Java program. Comments are ignored by the computer when the program is executed. Their purpose is to help a human reader understand the program.

EXERCISES

3.1 Suppose that a system is built from the classes shown in Figure 3.1, and that classes *A1*, *B1*, and *C1* are the only public classes. What is the minimum number of compilation units that can be used to define the system? What is the maximum number?

3.2 A class is being designed to model an item of inventory in a retail store. An instance of the class will have the following properties: item number, item description, price, and quantity on hand. It will have commands to modify or set each of its properties. Suggest reasonable identifiers for naming the class and its features. Give some examples of inappropriate identifiers, and indicate why they are inappropriate.

3.3 For each of the following, indicate whether or not it is a legal Java literal. If it is, give the type of the value denoted.

(a)	1000	*(b)*	10x5	*(c)*	2E2	*(d)*	2.e.2
(e)	'0'	*(f)*	'abc'	*(g)*	True		

GLOSSARY

case sensitive: a method of comparing identifiers in which identifiers that differ in the case (upper or lower) of the constituent letters are considered to be different identifiers. The identifiers ABC, Abc, and abc are all different in a case-sensitive language, all the same in a language that is not case sensitive.

comment: text included in a program purely for the benefit of a human reader. Comments are ignored by the compiler.

compilation unit: a text file ("source file") containing the definitions of one or more classes of a package.

doc comment: a specially-formatted comment that is recognized by system documentation-producing tools.

identifier: a sequence of characters that can be used to name entities in a program. A Java identifier can contain letters, digits, underscores, and dollar signs. It must not begin with a digit.

identifier literal: a sequence of characters that conforms to the rules for an identifier, but is in fact a literal. Identifier literals cannot be used as identifiers. `true`, `false`, and `null` are identifier literals in Java.

literal: a sequence of characters used in a program to denote a particular value.

keyword: a sequence of characters that conforms to the rules for an identifier, but is used for a special syntactic purpose, and cannot be used as an identifier.

package: a set of related class definitions. A package is the fundamental structural unit of a Java application.

public class: a class that is accessible from the entire software system. A class not identified as public is accessible only from within its package.

token: an identifier, literal, keyword, punctuation mark, or operator that is part of the program's text.

CHAPTER 4

Specification of a simple class

In this chapter, we begin the design of some simple classes. Our goal is to see how to write a *specification* for a class: that is, a precise description of the features common to all instances of the class.

We start by explaining what it means for one object to "use" another. This is the *client-server* relationship between two objects. The features of the server object as seen by the client comprise the *specification* of the server object. The object specification is distinct from the *implementation* of the object. The specification defines the object's behavior as seen by another object. The implementation, on the other hand, provides the internals that enable the object to behave according to its specifications.

We construct in Java the specification of several example classes: simple counters, players in a maze game, and students in a registration system. Our initial examples are, of necessity, oversimplified and incomplete. We settle for vague descriptions of the general problem, and assume our object design is "right" without a proper justification based on careful analysis of problem statement. This is adequate for our exposition, since we're concerned here more with illustrating various design and language constructs than with demonstrating a comprehensive design methodology. And while this degree of *nonchalance* about problem statement would hardly be suitable in "real life," the situation we present isn't too far from reality. We never create a "perfect" design on first try, and rarely, in fact, work from a complete and comprehensive problem statement.

4.1 Object specification: clients and servers

4.1.1 Client and server

Recall that an object has a set of *features*: queries and commands. We can query the object to ascertain the current value of one of its properties, and give it commands that change its state. We have also noted that objects are related to each other in various ways, and cooperate to produce a problem solution. An important structuring relation that can exist between two objects is that one object (call it object *A*) *uses* another object (object *B*) by query and command: *i.e.*, by using its features. In this relationship, object *A* is termed the *client*, and object *B* is the *server* or *supplier*. In the overall system design, any given object will sometimes play the role of client and sometimes the role of server.

A **client** queries and commands a **server**.

If we consider the chess playing program introduced in Section 2.3, a *Player* object might query a *Piece* object to determine its location, or command the *Piece* to move—*i.e.*, to change its location. The *Player* object is the client, the *Piece* is the server. This is illustrated in Figure 4.1.

As another example, suppose a *Student* object and a *Course* object are part of a registration system. We can imagine that the *Course* object might have a list of enrolled students as part of its state. To enroll in the course, the *Student* object instructs the *Course* object to add it (the *Student*) to the list of enrollees. The *Student* object gives the *Course* object a command that changes its (the *Course*'s) state. The *Student* object is the client, the *Course* object the server. At some later time, the *Student* object might be queried for the name and address of the student it represents, or instructed to change the student's address. In this case, the *Student* object is acting as server.

The relation of client to server is described as the *"uses"* relation. The client object (for instance, the *Player*) *uses* the server object (the *Piece*).

4.1.2   Specification and implementation

The collection of an object's features as seen by its clients is called the object's *interface* or *specification*. (We'll say "specification" to avoid confusion with the Java construct called an "interface.") The *implementation* provides the "internals" that actually make up the features. As a simple example, consider a standard 110 volt wall receptacle. The *specification* guarantees that if you plug an appliance into the receptacle, you will get alternating current with certain well-defined characteristics. How the current is produced and how it gets to the receptacle—the *implementation*—you have no information about. Nor do you care about these details: the specification *isolates* you from the details of the implementation. If the nuclear power plant that is suppling current to the receptacle blows up and the power company switches the feed to a coal-burning station, it makes no difference to the

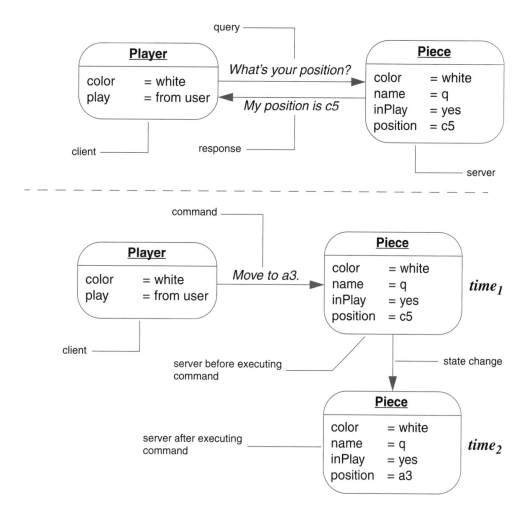

Figure 4.1 *Player* object is client; *Piece* object is server.

toaster plugged into the receptacle. Your toaster is content as long as it gets the expected kind of current: that is, as long as the receptacle's *specifications* are met. The toaster's operation is independent of *how* the current is created or delivered.

The situation with software objects is analogous. A client object knows only the queries and commands a server object will respond to: the server object's features are well-defined and completely specified. This is the *specification* of the server object. How the features are actually implemented is of no concern to the client. For instance, suppose a *Course* object in the registration system can be queried for a list of enrolled students either in alphabetical order or in the order in which they enrolled. These queries are part of the specification of the *Course* object, and are relevant to a client. *How* the ordering is actually accomplished is part of the object's implementation; it is not information available to the client.

> **specification (interface):** definition of an object's features, as seen by its clients.

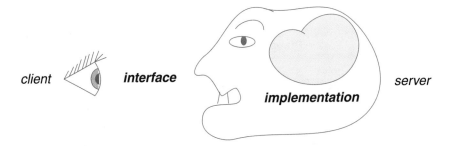

client   *interface*   *implementation*   *server*

Figure 4.2 **Interface (specification) and implementation.**

The importance of this simple distinction cannot be overemphasized. Understanding and preserving the distinction between specification and implementation is absolutely essential to good system design.

4.2   Specifying a class

We next give a few more examples of defining an object specification. A warning, though. In describing an object, we first enumerate the object's responsibilities, and then give the properties—the aspects of the object we can query—and the commands. In reality, the responsibilities of an object are determined by the *system's functionality*, and by the object's *relationships* with other objects in the system. That is, we first need a good idea of what we want an object to do in support of system requirements before we can enumerate its responsibilities and specify its features. Indeed, even the fact that a particular aspect of a system is to be modeled as an object requires some analysis of the system's required behavior.

4.2.1   A simple counter

To start with, consider an object modeling a very simple counter. What we have in mind is a hand counter such as a ticket-taker might use, or a device that counts cars as they pass a particular spot on a road. The function of a counter is very straightforward. The only property we are interested in is the count. Its responsibilities are simply to know the count, and to increment and reset the count.

Counter responsibilities:

Know:
    the value of the count

Do:
    set the count to 0
    increment the count by 1

Thus our object responds to only one query and two commands that change its state. We can query the object for the current count, and command the object to step the count or reset the count to 0. We summarize:

Class: *Counter*

Queries (Properties):
    count   the value of the count, a nonnegative integer

Commands:
    reset   set the value of *count* to 0
    step count   increment the value of *count* by 1

Note that we're actually defining a *class*. An object that represents a counter will be an instance of this class. The class definition determines the features of its instances. To define the class completely, we must provide both a *specification* and an *implementation* of each feature. As explained above, the specification describes the features that every object of the class will have; that is, the features seen by other (client) objects. We limit our attention here to the specification; we implement the class in the next chapter.

Let's start writing the class definition in Java. We name the class with the identifier Counter. (Recall that by convention we capitalize class names.) We have seen in the previous chapter that the class definition will be in a package. We name the package counters, following the convention that the name of a package is the lower case name of the principal class contained in the package, or its plural. We assume that there will be no other classes in the package.

The class definition will be in a source file named Counter.java. The file begins with a *package statement*, which identifies the package that the source file is part of. That is, the classes defined in the file are part of the package named in the package statement. The format for a package statement is the keyword **package**, followed by the name of the package (an identifier), followed by a semicolon.

    package *PackageName*;

For instance,

    package counters;

(We show keywords in boldface to distinguish them from identifiers.)

    Unfortunately, the Java syntax does not permit us to separate the class specification from its implementation. The class is defined with a *class declaration* or *definition*, which contains both the specification and implementation of the features of the class. A class declaration looks like this:

```
/**
 * A simple integer counter.
 */
public class Counter {
    ...                                            definitions of
}                                                  features go here
```

(Note: the ellipses (…) are not part of the class definition. They are used to indicate that something is missing and remains to be filled in.) The keyword **public** indicates that this is a public class: objects of this class will be accessible throughout the system. The specification and implementation of the features will be contained between the braces. (Note that braces—{ and }—*must* be used; parentheses or brackets are not equivalent.) The class definition is preceded by a doc comment that precisely describes what the class provides. Every class you define should be preceded by such a comment. Doc comments are used to create specification documentation, as described below. It is important that these comments be precise and concise. Someone who needs to use what you have written should be able to locate the class definition easily and quickly by scanning these doc comments.

Specifying a method for a query

We have determined that *Counter* objects have only one property: the *count*. The value associated with this property is a integer. That is, when a client queries a *Counter* for the value of the property *count*, it will get an integer in response. (We can be more precise in specifying the result of the query. The integer result is non-negative, and there is probably an upper limit on this value as well. We'll return to this issue later.) As we saw in Section 2.2, Java has four built-in integer types: **byte**, **short**, **int**, and **long**. With no compelling reason to do otherwise, we'll choose the built-in type **int**. The value associated with the property *count* will be of type **int**.

To enable a client to query a *Counter* object for this value, we provide a *method* or *function*. (We use the two terms interchangeably; they are not equivalent in all programming languages.) We specify a method or function to query the property like this:

```
/**
 * Current count; the number of items counted.
 */
public int count () {
    ...
}
```

type of value returned by query

name of method

the implementation of the method goes here

The keyword **public** stipulates that this method is part of the class specification: that is, it is a feature available to clients of *Counter* objects. The keyword **int** indicates the type of value the method will provide to the client. (The method implements a query, so it must provide a value when invoked.)

The name of the method, count, is simply an identifier.[1] We could have chosen any identifier at all, but it makes sense to name the method with the name of the property we are asking about. By convention we use lower case letters for methods, except for "embedded" words, which are capitalized. (For instance, we use creditHours rather than credithours.)

---

method (function): a language construct that defines and implements a query or command.

---

1. It is a Java convention that an identifier naming a query that accesses an object property begins "get." (A command changing the property is prefixed "set.") Thus the method that queries for the value of *count* would be named getCount. In this text, we prefer to name queries with nouns and reserve imperative verbs for commands.

Specifying methods for commands

Next, let's specify the commands for a *Counter* object. Recall that there were two: *step count* and *reset*. Here's the specification for these features:

```
/**
 * Increment the count by 1.
 */
public void stepCount () {
    ...
}

/**
 * Reset the count to 0.
 */
public void reset () {
    ...
}
```

the implementations of the methods go here

Both of these methods have the keyword **void** in place of the type name used in the query. This is because these methods are *commands*: they change the state of the object but do not provide the client with a value.

By convention we name commands with an imperative verbs (*e.g.*, step-Count, reset), while we name queries with nouns (or adjectives) descriptive of the value returned (*e.g.*, count).

Constructors

We've specified the methods for the class, but we haven't yet said how to create an instance of the class. A mechanism for creating a new object is called a *constructor*. Invoking a constructor creates a new instance of the class and gives initial values to the properties of the instance.[1]

The name of the constructor is the same as the name of the class. The specification for a *Counter* constructor is as follows:

```
/**
 * Create a new Counter object.
 */
public Counter () {
    ...
}
```

---

1. Technically, instance creation and constructor invocation are both part of evaluation of a class instance creation expression. We ignore the distinction.

Note that the constructor is part of the class definition but is clearly not a feature of an object. An object does not create itself.

Since we have a very simple class, we have a very simple constructor. All the constructor needs to do is create a new instance of the class and initialize the value of *count* to 0.

We now have a complete specification for the class *Counter*. Listing 4.1 shows the specification as a class declaration with the method implementations omitted. Of course, this is not yet a syntactically complete class definition. We must include implementations of the methods before we have a legal Java class definition.

Listing 4.1 **Specification for the class *Counter***

```
package counters;

/**
 * A simple integer counter.
 */
public class Counter {

    // Constructors:

    /**
     * Create a new Counter object.
     */
    public Counter () {
        ...
    }

    // Queries:

    /**
     * Current count; the number of items counted.
     */
    public int count () {
        ...
    }

    // Commands:

    /**
     * Increment the count by 1.
     */
```

continued

Listing 4.1   **Specification for the class *Counter (continued)***

```
public void stepCount () {

    ...

}

/**
 * Reset the count to 0.
 */
public void reset () {

    ...

}

} // end of class Counter
```

4.2.2 Specification documentation

As we've said, even though they are logically distinct, the Java syntax does not allow us to separate a class specification from its implementation. There are, however, software tools such as Sun's *javadoc* tool, that generate documents containing class specifications. *javadoc* generates a set of HTML[1] documents containing specifications extracted from program source files. For instance, the documentation produced for the methods of the class *Counter* is shown in Figure 4.3. We'll use a similar format when we want to specify a class or method in the text.

We should assume that a programmer who needs to use a class will have access only to the generated specification documentation. Since these documents include doc comment text, it is critically important to make doc comments complete and comprehensible. A programmer should be able to use a class correctly by reading nothing more than the specification documentation. Correspondingly, we should avoid verboseness and "noise" in doc comments. In particular, doc comments should never refer to implementation details. We'll see more detail about what goes into good documentation in later chapters.

4.2.3 Invoking a method

Before we move on to another example, let's take a quick look at how one object (a client) invokes another object's (a server's) methods.

---

1. HTML is *Hypertext Markup Language*, a standard notation for Web documents.

public class **Counter**
extends java.lang.Object

A simple integer counter.

Constructor Summary

Counter()
    Create a new Counter object

Method Summary

int	**count**() Current count; the number of items counted
void	**reset**() Reset the count to 0
void	**stepCount**() Increment the count by 1

Constructor Detail

Counter

public **Counter**()

    Create a new Counter object

Method Detail

count

public int **count**()

    Current count; the number of items counted

---

stepCount

public void **stepCount**()

    Increment the count by 1

---

reset

public void **reset**()

    Reset the count to 0

Figure 4.3 **Specification documentation, generated from the class *Counter*.**

Before a client can use a server, the client must somehow know about the server object. As we've seen in Section 2.5, reference values denote objects. A reference value provides a "handle" by which one object can know about another. We'll see how an object can get a reference to another object in the next chapter, when we implement some of the classes specified here. For the moment, we assume that c is a reference to a *Counter* object.

To query the object c for the current value of its property *count*, we write

```
c.count()
```

This construct is called a *function call* or *method invocation*. A function call causes the object (c in this case) to perform actions prescribed by the method implementation: actions determined by what we write between the braces in the definition of the method. In this case, the call results in the server object c delivering the current value of its property count to the client.

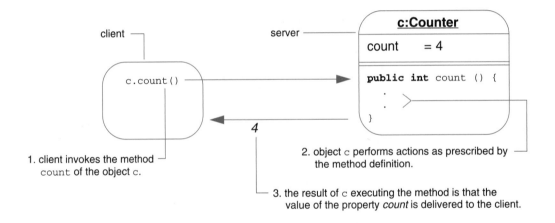

Figure 4.4   Steps in a query and response.

The method invocation for a command is similar. For instance, to invoke the command reset for the object c, we write

```
c.reset();
```

Note the semicolon is part of the syntax. Again, the object c performs actions as specified by the implementation of the method. The difference here is that the actions result in the state of the object c being changed, rather than a value being delivered to the client. This is illustrated in Figure 4.5.

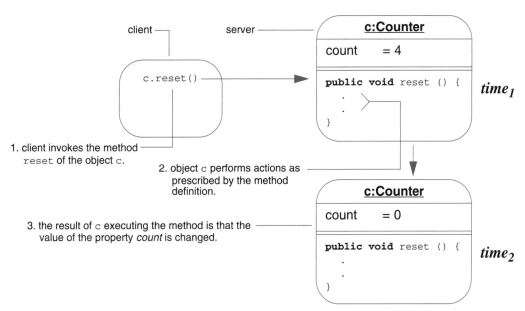

Figure 4.5 **Steps in a command execution.**

4.2.4   Interaction diagrams

A common technique for illustrating the order in which objects interact is to use an *interaction diagram*, as shown in Figure 4.6. Time advances from top to bottom in the diagram. Each vertical line or bar represents an object. A vertical rectangle signifies that the object is active; that is, it is executing one of its methods. A labeled horizontal arrow indicates that one object is invoking one of the features of another object. The object at the arrow point is acting as server; the object at the arrow tail is client. Sometimes we show the value being returned from a query as a horizontal arrow with a flag.

Figure 4.6, for instance, shows some client object interacting with a *Counter*. The object first queries the *Counter* for its current count, and then gives the *Counter* the command reset.

4.3   A maze game example

4.3.1   The class *Explorer*

As a second example, we consider a maze game: a game in which a player must find his way through a set of connected rooms to reach some goal. We can

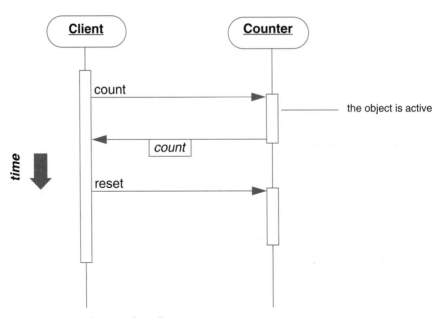

Figure 4.6 **An *interaction diagram*.**

imagine that there will be tricks the player must figure out and monsters of various kinds ("maze denizens") to be defeated along the way. Even from this minimal description, it seems clear that among the things we should model are the player, monsters, and rooms. We'll model the player first.

While there will be a number of rooms and monsters in our maze, we'll assume there is only one player. The player, each room, and each monster will be modeled by a distinct object. Monster objects will have a set of common features, which will be different from those of the room objects and from those of the player object. Thus monsters will all be entities of the same class, which we'll call *Denizen*. Similarly, room objects will be members of the class *Room*. Every object must be an instance of some class. So even though there will be only one player, that object will be an element of the class *Explorer*. (Sounds a little better than "Player.")

Queries for class Explorer

Let's consider some responsibilities we might expect an *Explorer* object to have. First of all, we give the player a name and want to know where he is in the maze. For location, we'll simply note the room in which the player is located. We might decide later that we want to be more specific about location—exactly where the player is in the room. But for now, we'll be satisfied with just the room. Since we expect the player to fight monsters, we need to model fighting ability. In our initial view, a player (modeled by the *Explorer* object) can relate to a monster (*Denizen* object) in two ways: the player can hit the monster, and the player can be hit by the monster. As a first cut, we'll include two properties, one describing how much damage the player does when he hits a monster, and a second measuring how much damage he can endure before he is defeated. Thus we expect the *Explorer* object to know the following:

Explorer responsibilities:

Know:

the explorer's name

location in the maze

how much damage he does when striking an opponent

how much damage he can endure when struck by an opponent

These responsibilities translate into properties in a rather straightforward manner:

name	the name of the *Explorer*
location	the room in which the *Explorer* is currently located
strength	a measure of the *Explorer*'s offensive ability: how much damage the *Explorer* inflicts when striking a monster
stamina	a measure of what it takes to defeat the *Explorer*

Before we go further, we might ask what type of value will be associated with each of these properties. For *name*, we'll be content with a string of characters like "Marjorie." For *location*, we could use a description or some identifying room number. But as suggested above, we also want to model rooms as objects. That is, we will have a class *Room* whose objects will be the rooms of the maze. The *Explorer* object is related to a *Room* object by a relation we might call *is-in*: the *Explorer is in* the *Room*. So we associate a reference to a *Room* object—a reference to the room containing the player—with the *Explorer*'s property *location*. The *type* of the value associated with the property *location* is *reference-to-Room*.

Finally, we'll simply model *strength* and *stamina* with integers. The general idea is that it will take ten blows of *strength* 10 or five blows of *strength* 20 to defeat a player (or monster) with *stamina* 100. An *Explorer* object is pictured in Figure 4.7.

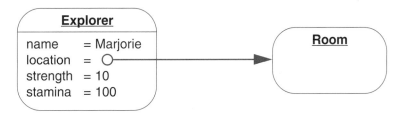

Figure 4.7 An *Explorer* object.

Commands for class Explorer

What should an *Explorer* be able to do? We need a general idea of how the object behaves in the system before we can even make a reasonable guess. The *Explorer* will move from room to room in response to input from the user, changing *location*, and sometimes encountering monsters. So the *Explorer* must be able to move, fight monsters, and we'll let him change his name as well.

Explorer responsibilities *(continued)*:

Do:

    change name
    change location in the maze (move from room to room)
    fight a maze *Denizen*

We need commands to tell the *Explorer* to perform these actions. We include a command *move* that changes the *Explorer*'s *location* and a command to change the *name* property:

    change name   change the *Explorer*'s name
    move   change *Explorer*'s *location*

When we give an object a command, we generally need to provide the object with some additional information. For instance, if we give an *Explorer* object a command to change its name, we must provide the new name. If we give it a command to change location, we must provide a new location, or some other information like direction of movement from which the new location can be determined. The elements of information that must be provided with a command are referred to as *parameters* (or sometimes *formal parameters*) of the command. We'll include parameters in parentheses when describing the command; *e.g.*,

    change name   change the *Explorer*'s name (new *name*)
    move   change *Explorer*'s *location* (new *location*)

The actual values provided by the client when invoking a command are called *arguments* (or sometimes *actual parameters*). Thus if a client commands an *Explorer* to change its name to "George," then "George" is the *argument* associated with the new name *parameter* of the command.

Now as we explained above, the *Explorer* must battle various monsters encountered in the maze. We need a command to instruct the *Explorer* to strike a *Denizen*. The additional information that must be provided with this command is the *Denizen* object to be hit:

    strike   strike a blow (*Denizen* to hit)

Note that performing this command doesn't change the state of the *Explorer*. (Unless we decide that striking a blow reduces the *Explorer*'s *strength*.)

Finally let's consider the case of a monster (a *Denizen* object) hitting the *Explorer*. We expect the *stamina* of the *Explorer* to be reduced as a result of the blow: that is, we expect the *Explorer* to change its state. If the *Explorer* has a *stamina* of 100 for instance and receives a blow of strength 5, the *Explorer*'s *stamina* is reduced to 95.

It is the *Explorer's responsibility* to change its state. In order to change its state, the *Explorer must execute a command*. So we have the *Denizen* acting as client in hitting the *Explorer*, and the *Explorer* acting as server. The *Denizen* gives the *Explorer* a command that causes the *Explorer* to change state; that is, to reduce its *stamina*. *The only way an object's state can change is by means of an action of the object itself in response to a command.*

What information must the client—the *Denizen*—provide with this command? It must provide the strength of the blow. This is illustrated in Figure 4.8, where the integer value 5 is provided as argument. (The situation is symmetric when the *Explorer* strikes a monster: the *Explorer* is the client in this case, and the monster is the server.)

To summarize, we have defined the following features for the class *Explorer*:

Class: *Explorer*

Queries (Properties):
     name   the name of the *Explorer*

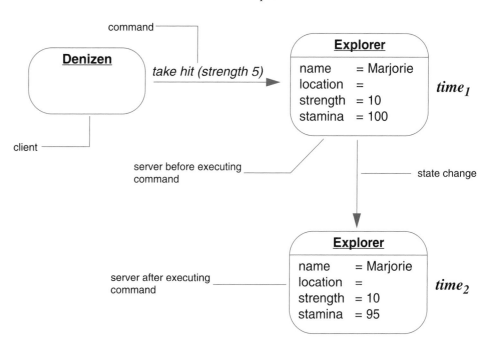

Figure 4.8   *Denizen* commands *Explorer*, causing it to change state.

Queries, continued:

location	the room in which the *Explorer* is currently located
strength	a measure of the *Explorer*'s offensive ability: how much damage the *Explorer* inflicts when striking a monster
stamina	a measure of what it takes to defeat the *Explorer*

Commands:

change name	change the *Explorer*'s *name* (new *name*)
move	change *Explorer*'s *location* (new *location*)
strike	strike a blow (*Denizen* to hit)
take hit	receive a blow—reduce *stamina* (strength of blow)

Three of these commands change the state of the object. The command *change name* changes the object's *name*. The command *move* changes the object's *location*. The client must provide the new location—in the form of (a reference to) a *Room* object. The command *take hit* reduces the *stamina* of the object. The client must provide the strength of the blow that the *Explorer* object takes. If an *Explorer* object with *stamina* of 100 takes a blow of strength 5, we expect the *stamina* to be reduced to 95. The command *strike* instructs the *Explorer* object to strike a monster. It requires the client to provide (a reference to) the *Denizen* object to be hit. This command probably doesn't change the state of the *Explorer*.

A few questions may have occurred to you at this point. There is no command to increase or restore *stamina*—perhaps we should add *heal*. There is no obvious way to change *strength*. There are in fact many additional properties and commands that could be part of the specification of an *Explorer* object. What we have is adequate for our exposition, and we'll be content without these for now.

It may also seem that the *strength* property should in some way be dependent on *stamina*. As *stamina* decreases, so might *strength*. This is a detail of implementation that should not concern us at this point. And if the relationship between *strength* and *stamina* can be dismissed as part of the implementation, an astute reader might ask if *strength* and *stamina* should be part of the specification at all. That is, should a client be able to query for specific *strength* and *stamina* values, or should these simply be implementation details of no concern to the client? We'll leave them as part of the specification, since we can imagine, at least, that we might want to display these values to the user.

A constructor for the class Explorer

As with the *Counter* class discussed above, we need a constructor for creating objects of the *Explorer* class. Our constructor has a little more work to do this time. When we create a new *Explorer*, we need to supply initial values for the object's properties. That is, we need to provide the *name*, *location*, *strength*, and *stamina* values that the *Explorer* will have when it is created. Thus the constructor for an *Explorer* will have four parameters:

create new Explorer   (*name, location, strength, stamina*)

A *Counter* object, on the other hand, has only one property, the *count*. The starting value of this property will always be 0 for a newly created *Counter*, so we don't need to provide an initial value when creating one.

4.3.2   Specifying the class *Explorer* in Java

Let's write the specification for the *Explorer* class in Java. Again, we write the class specification and omit the implementation parts. Since we don't know how the application is to be structured, we can't make any convincing argument about package organization. For the moment, we just put each class definition in its own package. We could just as well have put all the classes in a single package named something like mazeGame. As we'll see, to reference a class defined in another package we use a fully-qualified class name. That is, we prefix the package name to the class name, as

```
PackageName.ClassName
```

For instance, to refer to the class Counter specified above from outside the package counters, we write

```
counters.Counter
```

The definition of the *Explorer* class will be in a source file named Explorer.java, with the same basic structure we've seen with the class Counter:

```
package explorer;

/**
 * A maze game player.
 */
public class Explorer {
    ...                              definitions of
                                     features go here
}
```

Query specifications are not substantially different from the previous example.

```
/**
 * Name of this Explorer.
 */
```

```
public String name () {
    ...
}

/**
 * Room in which this Explorer is currently located.
 */
public rooms.Room location () {
    ...
}

/**
 * Damage (hit points) this Explorer does when
 * striking.
 */
public int strength () {
    ...
}

/**
 * Damage (hit points) required to defeat this
 * Explorer.
 */
public int stamina () {
    ...
}
```

The methods strength and stamina return values of type **int**. As we have explained, we use integer values to model these properties. And as with the *count* property of *Counter* objects, we could be more precise in specifying the results of these queries: the integer results are non-negative, and there are surely upper limits for *strength* and *stamina*. For now, though, we'll simply specify that these queries return **int** values.

The query name returns a *String*. As we've mentioned in Chapter 3, *String* is a class defined in the standard package java.lang. A *String* instance is immutable, and contains a string of characters, like "Marjorie" or "Helen."

The type of value returned by the query location is rooms.Room. From our previous discussion, we know that this query should return a reference to an object of class *Room*. This class will be defined in a different package from explorer. Specifically, it will be defined in the package rooms. This is what the notation indicates. Since the class *Room* is not defined in the package explorer—it is not "local"—we must prefix the class with the name of the package containing its definition. As we've seen, the syntax is

PackageName.ClassName

Thus the query `location` will return a reference to an object of class *Room*, which is defined in the package `rooms`. (Of course, if we had decided to put the classes *Room* and *Explorer* in the same package, we could omit the package name when referencing the class *Room* from the class *Explorer*.)

Note also that the class *Room* must be a public class; otherwise, we could not access it in the package `explorer`.

Next, let's specify the commands. Recall there are four: *change name*, *move*, *take hit*, and *strike*. Here's the specification for these features:

```
/**
 * Change the name of this Explorer to the
 * specified String.
 */
public void changeName (String newName) {
    ...
}
```
— parameter name
— parameter type

```
/**
 * Move to the specified Room.
 */
public void move (rooms.Room newRoom) {
    ...
}
```

```
/**
 * Receive a blow of the specified number of
 * hit points.
 */
public void takeHit (int hitStrength) {
    ...
}
```

```
/**
 * Strike the specified Denizen.
 */
public void strike (denizens.Denizen monster) {
    ...
}
```

As explained above, all four of these methods have the keyword **void** in place of the type name we find in queries because they are *commands*. They change the state of the object, but do not provide a value to the client. Also note that the parentheses after the method name are not empty. This is because each of these commands has a parameter. The client must provide information to the object when invoking the command. The parameter specification consists of a type followed by an identifier. The type is the type of value the client must provide; the identifier is an arbitrary identifier used to name the parameter. For instance, if the client calls the command `takeHit`, the client must provide an argument, an **int** value, to specify the strength of the hit. We can use any identifier as a parameter name, but as usual we try to choose something meaningful. In summary, the specification for the method `takeHit` indicates that this feature is a command (**void**) and requires that the client provide an **int** value as argument when invoking the command.

The method `move` requires an argument that is a reference to an object of class *Room*, and the method `strike` requires a reference to an object of class *Denizen*. (Since it will usually be clear from context when we are talking about an object and when we are taking about a reference to an object, we'll simply say "*Room*" rather than "reference to an object of class *Room*" from now on.) The class *Denizen* is defined in a package with the name `denizens`, just as the class *Room* is defined in the package `rooms`. Thus "`denizens.Denizen`" is the "full name" of the class *Denizen*, and "`rooms.Room`" is the full name of the class *Room*.

Finally, we need to specify a constructor. The specification is as follows:

```
/**
 * Create a new Explorer.
 */
public Explorer (String name, rooms.Room location,
                 int hitStrength, int stamina) {
    ...
}
```

Note that the name of the constructor is the same as the class. The client must provide four argument values when invoking the constructor: a *String*, a *Room*, and two **int**'s, in that order. Invoking the constructor creates a new object of the class, initializes the object's properties with the argument values, and returns a reference to the newly created object. We'll see how to do this later.

We now have a complete specification for the class *Explorer*. We show the specification in Listing 4.2, using a format similar to that produced by the documentation tools.

4.3.3   Invoking methods with parameters

We've seen the basic syntax for invoking a method in the previous example. In the present case, several methods have parameters. When a client invokes a method, the client must provide a value of the appropriate type for each parameter. As we've said, these client-provided values are referred to as "arguments."

Listing 4.2   **Specification for the class *Explorer***

---

explorer
Class Explorer

> **public class** Explorer
> A maze game player.

Constructors

> **public** Explorer (String name, rooms.Room location,
>   **int** hitStrength, **int** stamina)
> Create a new *Explorer*.

Queries

> **public** String name ()
> Name of this *Explorer*.

> **public** Rooms.Room location ()
> *Room* in which this *Explorer* is currently located.

> **public int** strength ()
> Damage (hit points) this *Explorer* does when striking.

> **public int** stamina ()
> Damage (hit points) required to defeat this *Explorer*.

Commands

> **public void** changeName (String newName)
> Change the name of this *Explorer* to the specified *String*.

> **public void** move (rooms.Room newRoom)
> Move to the specified *Room*.

> **public void** takeHit (**int** hitStrength)
> Receive a blow of the specified number of hit points.

> **public void** strike (denizens.Denizen monster)
> Strike the specified *Denizen*.

Assume that e is an *Explorer* object. If a client wants to call e's method takeHit, the client must provide an **int** argument as required by the specification of that method. The call would look something like this:

```
e.takeHit(10);
```

Argument values are included between the parentheses. The general form for invoking a method for a query is

```
objectReference.queryName(arguments)
```

and the general form for a command is

```
objectReference.commandName(arguments);
```

To invoke a constructor, the key word **new** is used:

```
new constructorName(arguments)
```

Thus invoking the constructor to create a new object would look like this:

```
new Explorer("Marjorie",entry,10,100)
```

where we assume that entry is a *Room*. Note that four arguments are provided, in the order indicated by the specification. The arguments are separated by commas.

4.3.4   The class *Denizen*

Before moving to our last example, we give a specification for the class *Denizen*. A *Denizen*'s responsibilities are much like an *Explorer*'s, so we'd expect the specifications to be similar. The specification is given in Listing 4.3.

The query kind is intended to return a simple word describing the monster: "goblin" or "orc" for instance. An obvious difference between a *Denizen* and an *Explorer* is that a *Denizen* does not have strength and stamina features. Undoubtedly a *Denizen* object incorporates such information in some fashion. But it is not part of the specification of the object: it is "hidden" as part of the implementation. A client cannot query a *Denizen* object for *strength* or *stamina*. (Of course, this design decision might be changed at a later date when we have a better idea of how our objects interact.) Finally, note that the same identifier (explorer) is used to name the parameter of the method strike and the package containing the definition of the class *Explorer*. This is fine. Java generally permits different kinds of things to have the same name, as long as there can be no confusion as to what is meant.

Listing 4.3   Specification for the class *Denizen*

denizens
Class Denizen

public class Denizen
   A maze monster.

Constructors

public Denizen (String kind, rooms.Room location)
   Create a new Denizen.

Queries

public String kind ()
   Kind of Denizen.

public rooms.Room location ()
   Room in which this Denizen is currently located.

Commands

public void move (rooms.Room newRoom)
   Move to the specified Room.

public void takeHit (**int** hitStrength)
   Receive a blow of the specified number of hit points.

public void strike (explorer.Explorer explorer)
   Strike the specified Explorer.

We can illustrate the sequence of interactions that occur when an *Explorer* is commanded to strike a *Denizen* with an interaction diagram. In Figure 4.9, some client object gives an *Explorer* object the command `strike`. The client provides a *Denizen* object as argument. In order to accomplish the `strike` command, the *Explorer* gives the *Denizen* the command `takeHit`, which, we assume, causes the *Denizen* to change state.

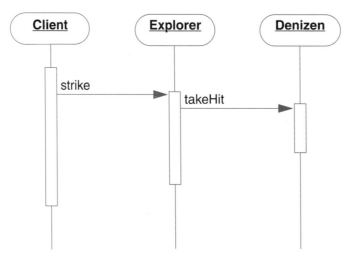

Figure 4.9 An *Explorer* commanded to strike a *Denizen*.

4.4   Another example: class *Student*

As a final example, let's consider the university registration system mentioned above. The functionality we have in mind is a system that allows students to register for courses, assesses fees, prints students' schedules, produces course rolls, *etc*. We ignore inconveniences such as long-term record keeping for now.

Since this is a *student* registration system, it seems reasonable that one of the entities we should model is a "student." There will be a number of students enrolled, each represented by a distinct object. As these objects will have a common set of features, they will all be entities of the same class, which we'll name *Student*. What does a *Student* object need to know? Clearly the student's name and address, and we'll include social security number as well. We want the student's schedule, and since fees are determined by the number of credit hours the student is enrolled in, we'll want that information, too. (Note that the number of credit hours may well be implicitly contained in the student's schedule. However, it seems reasonable that we be able to query the *Student* object directly for credit hours, rather than getting the *Student*'s schedule and computing the credit hours from it. This kind of design decision is difficult to justify completely *a priori*. But we make a reasonable first guess, which we're willing to change as the design progresses.) Finally, we include the fees for the semester, and the amount the student has paid. In summary, we have the following knowing responsibilities for a *Student* object, which we specify as queries directly in Java:

> **public** String name ()
> > This *Student*'s name.
>
> **public** String address ()
> > This *Student*'s address.
>
> **public** String ssn ()
> > This *Student*'s social security number.
>
> **public int** creditHours ()
> > Number of credit hours this *Student* is enrolled in.
>
> **public int** fees ()
> > This *Student*'s fees for the semester (dollars).
>
> **public int** feesPaid ()
> > Amount this *Student* has paid so far this semester (dollars).
>
> **public** courses.CourseList schedule ()
> > This *Student*'s current schedule.

A few observations are in order. We have specified that name and address are simple character strings. But these properties might have some additional structure that we are interested in: we might want to sort a list of *Student*s by last name, for instance, or determine a particular *Student*'s zip code. We have specified the social security number as a *String*, rather than, say, as an **int**. We need to know more about how we intend to use the social security number before we can determine which is more appropriate. For simplicity, we have specified fees as integer dollars. And finally, we have assumed that there is a package courses that contains the definition of the class *CourseList*. Thus the type of the value returned by the method schedule is specified as courses.CourseList.

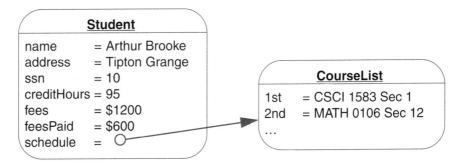

Figure 4.10 A *Student* object.

What should a *Student* object be responsible for doing? As before, we need some idea of how such an object behaves in the system. A typical scenario is as follows. A person enrolls in the university, and a *Student* object is created containing the person's name, address, and social security number. This object models the person. As the person schedules courses, the *schedule*, *credit hours*, and *fees* properties of the object change accordingly. When the person makes a payment, the *fees paid* property of the object is updated. Thus we need a way of creating a new *Student* object with specific *name*, *address*, and *social security number* properties. Once the object is created, it is responsible for changing these properties. It is also responsible for adjusting the *schedule* by adding and removing courses, and for updating *fees paid* when a payment is made. We may ultimately need additional behavior from the *Student* object, but the following set of commands seems a reasonable start:

> **public void** changeName (String newName)
> Change the name of this *Student* to the specified *String*.
>
> **public void** changeAddress (String newAddress)
> Change the address of this *Student* to the specified *String*.
>
> **public void** changeSsn (String newSsn)
> Change the social security number of this *Student* to the specified *String*.
>
> **public void** addCourse (courses.Course course)
> Add the specified *Course*.
>
> **public void** dropCourse (courses.Course course)
> Drop the specified *Course*.
>
> **public void** payFees (**int** amount)
> Pay specified amount of fees (amount paid in dollars).

We have assumed that the package `courses` contains the class *Course* in addition to the class *CourseList*. Also, there are restrictions that at some point we'll want to place on the command arguments. For instance, a student can only drop a course that is on her schedule; a student cannot add a course that conflicts with one she is already enrolled in; and so on. Finally, note that `course` and `Course` are different identifiers: Java, you'll recall, is case sensitive.

We also need a constructor for *Student* objects. When we create a new *Student* object, we must provide name, address, and social security number.

> **public** Student (String name, String address,
>   String ssn)
> Create a new *Student*.

Putting together the specifications for constructor, queries, and commands gives us a complete specification for the class.

4.5   Summary

In this chapter, we saw how to create specifications for a simple class, and how to express the specifications in the programming language Java. We saw that two objects are related in a fundamental way when one object *uses* the other: that is, one object queries and commands the other. We termed this the *client-server* relationship. The client object queries and commands the server object.

We also saw that the definition of an object, or more properly, the definition of the class of which the object is an instance, consists of two parts:

- a *specification*, a precise description of the object's features *as seen by a client*; and

- an *implementation*, the internal mechanisms that enable an object to behave according to its specification.

It is important to appreciate that the client can use only the specification of a server object. Details of the implementation are not available to the client.

Finally, we looked at several examples to see how class specifications are expressed in Java. We noted that methods define both the specifications and implementation of an object's features. A method that defines a query returns a value of a given type. A method that defines a command typically causes the object to change state when it is invoked. Some methods require that the client provide information when the method is invoked. This is indicated by parameters in the method definition. The values the client supplies when invoking the method are called arguments.

In the next chapter, we address the issue of implementing classes. When we add the implementations to the class specifications, we will have completed the class definition.

EXERCISES

4.1   Write a Java specification for a *Counter* command that will set the *Counter* to any specified value.

4.2   Consider a class intended to model rectangles. Write Java specifications for queries to determine a rectangle's width and length.

4.3   Write Java specifications for commands that will change an *Explorer*'s strength and stamina.

4.4   Consider a class intended to model a three-way lamp. Instances can be queried to determine whether the lamp is off, or is on low, medium, or high, and can be commanded to advance to the next setting. Write a Java specification for this class. Be sure to include doc comments that concisely describe your design.

4.5   In the discussion of the class Student above, it is suggested that an address might have structure and not be just a simple character string. Write a Java specification for a class to model addresses.

4.6   In Section 2.3, it is suggested that a class can be used to model dates. Instances of such a class are static objects: once created, they cannot change state. Write a Java specification for a class to model dates.

4.7   Consider the class *Room* of the maze game. Instances of this class represent rooms in the maze. Suppose we want whether or not the *Explorer* is in a *Room* to be a property of the *Room*. Write a Java specification for a *Room* query that reports whether or not the *Explorer* is in the *Room*.

4.8   If a *Room* object is to keep track of whether or not the *Explorer* is in it, it must be informed when the *Explorer* enters and leaves. Write Java specifications for a *Room* command that tells the *Room* that the *Explorer* has entered it and left it.

4.9   Two *Room*s in a maze can be connected by a passageway. Of course, we will define a class to model passageways. Write Java specifications for queries that will determine which *Room*s the passageway connects.

4.10   Write a specification for a class *Course* to be used by the university registration system.

GLOSSARY

argument: a value provided by a client when invoking a method specified with a parameter. The client must provide an argument of the appropriate type for each parameter appearing in the method definition.

class declaration: the Java construct used to define a class. The class definition includes both the specification and implementation of the class.

client: in reference to a given object, a client is another object which uses the given object. The given object is called the server. The client accesses the features of the server; that is, it invokes the server's methods.

constructor: a method used to create a new object.

function: the Java construct used to specify and implement queries and commands. Also called a method.

implementation: the actual internal details that support the specification of an object.

interaction diagram: a diagram that shows the order in which requests between objects are performed.

interface: the collection of features of an object as seen by its clients. Also called the specification of the object.

method: the Java construct used to specify and implement queries and commands. Also called a function.

method or function invocation: the action of a client that causes an object to execute a method.

package statement: the Java construct used to state the package to which a source file belongs.

parameter: in reference to a method, the specification of a value that must be supplied by a client when invoking the method. The corresponding value provided by a client is called an argument.

server: in reference to a given object, a server is another object, which provides a service to the given object. The given object is called the *client*. The client accesses the features of the server; that is, it invokes the server's methods.

specification: the collection of features of an object as seen by its clients. Also called the *interface* of the object.

CHAPTER 5

Implementing a simple class

In the previous chapter, we introduced the client-server relation—the "uses" relation—between objects. To simplify and manage this fundamental interaction, we saw that the definition of a class was divided into two components: a specification, which defines the features of an object available to a client, and an implementation, a detailed description of how the object satisfies its specification.

We have seen how to write a class specification in Java. In particular, we have seen how to specify methods that construct instances of the class, and that provide queries and commands for instances. In this chapter, we complete the class definition by adding an implementation. We see how to store data in an object and how to write method bodies. In the process, we learn the basics of *statements* and *expressions*—two fundamental Java syntactic constructs. We see how one object acts as client to another by invoking queries and commands in the second object. Finally, in order to test an implementation, we learn how to create objects and initiate execution of the system.

5.1   Implementing data descriptions

We've seen how to design a class by specifying the features of objects of the class. Now we need to complete the class definition by adding an implementation. To produce an implementation, we must provide *data descriptions* for the data values an object will contain, and develop *algorithms* that will manipulate these data values and provide the object's functionality.

5.1.1   Instance variables

Recall that an object is in part characterized by its "knowing" responsibilities: specific pieces of information the object is required to know. In many cases, these responsibilities translate into properties whose values can be obtained by querying the object. The simplest way for an object to remember a value is for the object to store the value in a *variable*. A variable is simply a portion of memory reserved for storing a value. The particular value stored in a variable can of course be changed—hence the name "variable." (We can think of a variable as a very simple object with responsibilities only for knowing and changing its value. The features of a variable include one query, to determine its current value, and one operation, to change its value.)

Though different values can be stored in a variable at different times, any given variable can contain values of only one type. An **int** variable contains a single **int** value; a *reference-to-Room* variable (or, simply, a *Room* variable) contains a *reference-to-Room* value, and so on. An **int** variable cannot contain a *reference-to-Room* value, and *vice versa*. We refer to the type of value a variable contains as the "type of the variable."

> **variable:** a portion of memory reserved to hold a single value.
>
> **instance variable:** a variable that is a permanent part of an object; memory space for the variable is allocated when the object is created, and the variable exists as long as the object does.

Consider the class *Counter* specified in the previous chapter. An object of this class has only one property, the *count*, and this property has an integer value. We stipulate that each *Counter* object is to have an **int** variable in which to store the value of its property *count*. That is, a *Counter* object will contain a portion of memory adequate to store an **int** value. This memory space is allocated to the object when the object is created. Such a variable is called an *instance variable*. We will also refer to the variable as a *component* of the object.

We must name the variable with an appropriate identifier. Java permits us to use the same identifier to name both a method and an instance variable, so we could simply name the variable count. (In fact, we'll adopt this as a convention later on.) But to keep things from getting too confusing, we'll use the identifier tally to name the variable. The name of the variable and its associated type (and even the fact that the value is stored in a variable) are part of the object's *implementation* and not part of the *specification*. This information is not directly available to clients. Clients see the object only through its queries and commands.

At the risk of belaboring the point, we note again that a *Counter* object has a property whose associated value (an **int**) can be obtained with the query count. This is part of the object's *specification*. It is included in the view a client has of a *Counter* object. As part of the *implementation* of a *Counter* object, we have decided to store the value of this property in a variable named tally. We'll see examples of variables used for other purposes, and we'll see examples of properties that are not stored in variables. Keeping its value in a variable, however, is a very straightforward way of implementing a property.

Since the variable is part of the implementation, and not available to the object's clients, we define the variable as **private**. The syntax for a private instance variable definition or *declaration* is

private *variableType* *variableName*;

The variable definition is included in the definition of the class:

```
/**
 * A simple integer counter.
 */
public class Counter {

    ...

    private int tally;        // current count


} // end of class Counter
```

Every *Counter* object will now have a component that is an **int** variable named `tally`, containing some **int** value. This is illustrated in Figure 5.1, where the box denotes the variable. (We put implementation details below the double line in the illustrations.)

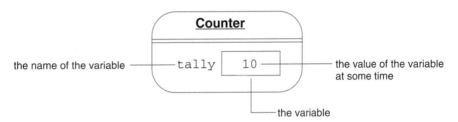

Figure 5.1 **A *Counter* object, showing its instance variable.**

Next let's look at the class *Explorer* specified in the previous chapter. Objects of this class have four properties: *name*, *location*, *strength*, and *stamina*. We use instance variables to store the values of these variables. (Stylistically, we put instance variable definitions at the end of the class definition, in a clearly labeled section.)

```
/**
 * A maze game player
 */
public class Explorer {

    ...

    // Private components:
```

```
        private String playerName;    // name
        private rooms.Room room;      // current location
        private int strengthPoints;   // current strength
                                      // (hit points)
        private int staminaPoints;    // current stamina
                                      // (hit points)
    } // end of class Explorer
```

As before, we could use the same identifiers (name, location, strength, stamina) to name both the methods (queries) and the instance variables. But we again choose different names for clarity in the explanation.

So an *Explorer* object has four components, as shown in Figure 5.2.[1] Note that the value stored in the variable room is a reference value. In fact, it is a value of type *reference-to-Room*.

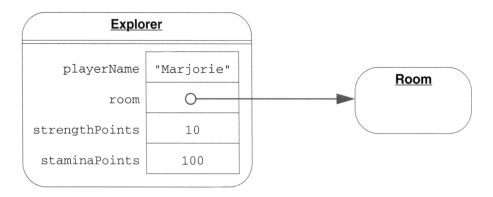

Figure 5.2   An *Explorer* object, showing its instance variables.

Since an instance variable is part of an object's state, it should *always contain a meaningful value*. In particular, *every constructor should ensure that each of a newly created object's instance variables are initialized appropriately*. This is a critical responsibility of a constructor.

When illustrating a class with a diagram, conventional practice is to list the components in a box below the class name. The minus sign preceding the component name emphasizes that the variable is private, part of the implementation, and not accessible by clients. Figure 5.3 shows how the class *Explorer* might be illustrated.

---

1. As we have seen, a *String* is an object; thus, the value of the variable playerName in Figure 5.2 is actually a reference to a *String* object.

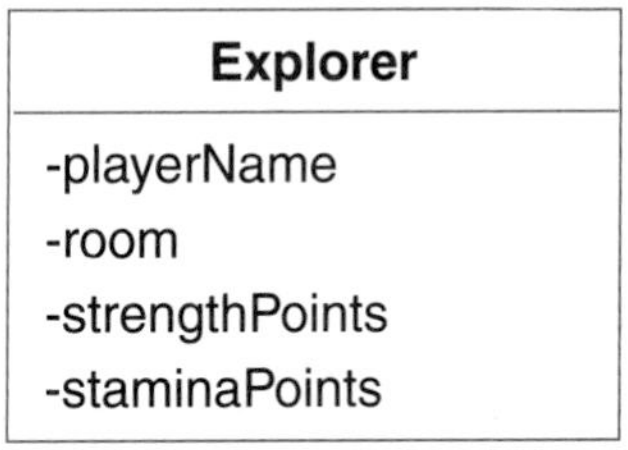

```
          Explorer
-playerName
-room
-strengthPoints
-staminaPoints
```

Figure 5.3 **The class *Explorer*, showing its private instance variables.**

5.1.2 Naming values: named constants

It is sometimes useful when defining a class to give meaningful names to particular values. Suppose we are defining a class *Card* to model playing cards. We may assume that a card has only two attributes of interest: *suit* (spade, heart, diamond, club) and *rank* (2, 3, 4, 5, 6, 7, 8, 9, 10, jack, queen, king, ace). When we create a *Card* instance, we specify the suit and rank, and we can query a *Card* to determine its suit and rank. For simplicity, we assume that instances of the class *Card* are immutable: once created, they do not change state. We sketch the definition:

```
public class Card {

    /**
     * Create a new Card of the specified rank and suit.
     */
    public Card (??? rank, ??? suit) { … }

    /**
     * The rank of this Card.
     */
    public ??? rank () { … }

    /**
     * The suit of this Card.
     */
    public ??? suit () { … }

}
```

The question is, what type of values do we use for suits and ranks? Some languages allow us to define our own types, containing whatever sets of values we want. We could, for instance, define a type *suit* containing values *spade*, *heart*, *diamond*, *club*. Java does not provide such a mechanism. A simple approach is to represent suit and rank values with integers. We might choose 4 to denote spades,

3 for hearts, and so on. Thus we make the parameters to the constructor and the return values of the queries **int**s:

```
public Card (int rank, int suit) { … }
public int suit () { … }
public int rank () { … }
```

The problem is that the particular values we choose to represent suits and ranks are arbitrary. We could just as easily have chosen 5 or 3 to denote spades. In order to make our programs more readable, and more importantly to isolate clients from the particular values we have chosen, it is useful to attach names to these values, and then refer to them by name. We can do this with a *named constant* declaration:

```
public final static int SPADE = 4;
public final static int HEART = 3;
public final static int DIAMOND = 2;
public final static int CLUB = 1;
```

As before, the keyword **public** indicates that this is part of the class specification: it is accessible by a client. The keywords **final static** indicate a constant declaration. The general format is:

```
public final static type identifier =
               constantExpression;
```

We can write "**static final**" or "**final static**." They are equivalent. We'll see precisely what each of these keywords implies later. Furthermore, we won't bother with the details of exactly what constitutes a "constant expression." Essentially, it is an expression that can be evaluated from the program text before the program is executed. By convention, we use uppercase identifiers for named constants.

The above declarations effectively make the identifier SPADE *a name for the value* 4, the identifier HEART a name for the value 3, and so on. SPADE is *not* a variable. It is not the name of a portion of memory that can contain different values at different times.

The point of all this is that a client can refer to these values with names rather than with literals. This makes the client code easier to read, and makes the client independent of the particular arbitrary values chosen by the implementor.

To reference the constant, the client prefixes the class name to the constant name. For example, if discard is a *Card*, we'll see that a client can write

```
if (discard.suit() == Card.SPADE) …
```

to determine if discard is a spade. This is easier to understand and maintain than

```
if (discard.suit() == 4) …
```

and isolates the client from unnecessary dependency on the server. The class *Card* can be changed so that the spade suit is represented by a number other than 4, and as long as the constant SPADE is properly defined, the client code is correct.

Unfortunately, there is nothing in the language syntax or semantics to *prevent* the client from using the literal 4 for the suit rather than the constant Card.SPADE. We can depend only on good programming practice.

With the exception of occasional occurrences of 0 and 1, literals in a program invariably represent some describable concept: the maximum number of students in a class, the speed of light in kilometers per second, the text of a message to be delivered to the user if a file does not exist, the number of shillings in a pound, *etc*. Good programming practice requires that such literals be named, and that the named constants appear in the program rather than the literals. Except for literals like 1 and 0 simply standing for themselves, literals should only appear in constant definitions.

> **named constant:** a value that has an identifier (a name) associated with it; the associated identifier can be used to indicate the value.

5.2 Implementing functionality

The instance variables of an object comprise the object's *data*. We must now see how to provide the object's *functionality* by attaching algorithms to the features of the object.

As we know, an object's features include queries and commands. The object responds to a query by providing the value associated with one of its properties. It responds to a command by performing an action that may change its state. In each case, we must provide an algorithm, a set of instructions, that describes how the processor is to carry out the operation.

5.2.1 Method implementation: simple queries

We've seen that a *method* or *function* implements a feature. The method defines the interface that client must use to invoke or call the method. The definition specifies the name of the method, whether it is a query or command, the type of value returned in the case of a query, and the number and types of the arguments that must be provided by the client. In the last chapter, for instance, we specified the method count for the class *Counter* as

```
public int count () {
    ...
}
```

The keyword **public** indicates that this method is part of the specification: it is available to clients of a *Counter* object. The type name **int** indicates that it is a query and returns a value of type **int** when invoked. The identifier count is the name of the method. The empty parentheses indicate that the method has no parameters: a client does not provide any arguments when invoking the method.

The method definition must also provide an implementation, an *algorithm* that specifies what actions the processor is to perform when the method is invoked. The algorithm, sometimes called the *method body*, is included between the braces in the definition, where we've written the ellipses (…).

The method body consists of a sequence of one or more *statements*:

$$\{ \; statement_1 \; statement_2 \; statement_3 \; … \; statement_N \; \}$$

(When we write the body, we usually start each statement on a separate line for readability—though as we've seen, the end of the line is largely irrelevant in Java.) A statement describes an *action* that the processor is to carry out. When the method is invoked, the processor performs the actions specified by the statements that make up the body of the method. These actions are performed one at a time, in the order in which the statements are written.

The statements that comprise the body of the method express an algorithm that implements the method. The algorithm instructs the processor how to accomplish the task specified by the method. When the method is invoked, the processor performs the required computation as described by the algorithm. Thus implementing the method consists of designing an algorithm.

---

statement: a language construct that describes an action for the processor to perform.

What actions must the processor perform to execute the query count referred to above? It must provide the current value of the property *count* to the client. But this value is stored in the instance variable tally. Thus the processor must simply deliver the value stored in tally to the client. This is done by using a *return* statement:

```
return tally;
```

The return statement tells the processor to furnish a particular value to the client who invoked the method. It is the final action performed in executing the method. When the processor executes the return statement, it is finished with the method and delivers the indicated value to the client. Every query ends with the execution of a return statement.

In our example, this is the only action the processor needs to perform in carrying out the query. Thus the method body consists of only a single statement. The implementation looks like this:

```
/**
 * Current count; the number of items counted.
 */
public int count () {
    return tally;
}
```

It is important to realize that while a client can get the value of the instance variable `tally` by calling the method, the client cannot *directly* access or modify the variable. Only the object itself can directly reference or change its private instance variable.

The implementation of queries for an *Explorer* object are similar. In each case, all that happens is that the value of the appropriate instance variable is returned to the client.

```
/**
 * Name of this Explorer.
 */
public String name () {
    return playerName;
}


/**
 * Room in which this Explorer is currently located.
 */
public rooms.Room location () {
    return room;
}


/**
 * Damage (hit points) this Explorer does when
 * striking.
 */
public int strength () {
    return strengthPoints;
}


/**
 * Damage (hit points) required to defeat this
 * Explorer.
 */
public int stamina () {
    return staminaPoints;
}
```

5.2.2   Arithmetic expressions

The queries defined above all return values stored in an instance variable. Though this is common, it is not always the case. In many situations, the value returned by the query must be computed by the method. For instance, we might have an object representing a rectangle with instance variables `length` and `width`. If we want a query to return the area of the rectangle, it must return the product of `length` and `width`.

The general form of a return statement is

> **return** *expression*;

where *expression* is a language construct that describes how to compute a particular value. Evaluation of an expression produces a value. In the examples we've seen so far, the expression has been very simple: the name of an instance variable. Obviously, such an expression simply denotes the current value of the variable.

> **expression:** a language construct that describes how to compute a particular value. Evaluation of an expression produces a value.

Before we continue with our examination of method implementation, we look at expressions in more detail. For the moment, we limit our attention to expressions of type **int** and type **double**—expressions that produce **int** or **double** values when evaluated.

As we've said, an expression is a construct that describes how to compute a value. When the processor encounters an expression in a statement, the processor *evaluates* the expression. Evaluating the expression produces a value. The type of value produced by evaluating an expression is fixed. That is, one expression might deliver an **int** value and another might deliver a **double**, but a single expression cannot evaluate to an **int** at one time and a **double** later on. Expressions that evaluate to integer and floating point values—that is, expressions of type **byte**, **short**, **int**, **long**, **float**, and **double**—are collectively called *arithmetic expressions*.

Simple expressions

Literals are the simplest form of expressions. (We encountered literals in Section 3.3.) Some **int** and **double** literals are shown below. The values they denote are obvious from our previous discussion:

```
0      7      23      0.5    2.0    3.14159      2.4e-23
```

Variable names are a second simple form of expression. A variable name denotes the value currently stored in the variable. Suppose i1, i2, and i3 are variables of type **int** containing values 10, –20 and 30, respectively; suppose d1 and d2 are variables of type **double** containing values 2.5 and 0.5. Then evaluating these simple expressions produce the values shown. (We use the symbol "⇒" to represent expression evaluation.)

$$i1 \Rightarrow 10 \qquad i2 \Rightarrow -20 \qquad i3 \Rightarrow 30$$
$$d1 \Rightarrow 2.5 \qquad d2 \Rightarrow 0.5$$

Operators

Expressions can be combined with *operators* to form more complicated expressions. *Unary* or *monadic* operators "+" and "–" can be prefixed to an arithmetic expression. Prefixing a "+" has no effect on the expression's value.

$$+7 \Rightarrow 7 \qquad -0.5 \Rightarrow -0.5 \qquad -i1 \Rightarrow -10$$
$$-i2 \Rightarrow 20 \qquad -d1 \Rightarrow -2.5 \qquad +d2 \Rightarrow 0.5$$

Two arithmetic expressions can be combined with *binary* or *dyadic* operators "+", "–", "*", "/", and "%". These operations denote addition, subtraction, multiplication, division, and remainder, respectively. The behavior of the first three operators is straightforward:

$$1 + 2 \Rightarrow 3 \qquad i1 + 10 \Rightarrow 20 \qquad i1 + i2 \Rightarrow -10$$
$$d1 + d2 \Rightarrow 3.0 \qquad i3 - i1 \Rightarrow 20 \qquad i3 - i2 \Rightarrow 50$$
$$i1 * 2 \Rightarrow 20 \qquad d2 * 0.5 \Rightarrow 0.25$$

The division operator "/" denotes division when applied to two **double** operands, but *integer quotient* when applied to two integer operands. For instance

$$d1 / 2.0 \Rightarrow 1.25$$

but

$$i1 / 5 \Rightarrow 2 \qquad i1 / 3 \Rightarrow 3 \qquad i1 / 6 \Rightarrow 1$$
$$i1 / 11 \Rightarrow 0$$

The operator "%" denotes the *remainder* of the first operand divided by the second.

$$i1 \% 5 \Rightarrow 0 \qquad i1 \% 3 \Rightarrow 1 \qquad i1 \% 6 \Rightarrow 4$$
$$i1 \% 11 \Rightarrow 10$$

While this operator is also defined for floating point operands, we'll use it only with integers.

A couple of notes for completeness: integer quotient is "truncated toward 0." So

$$i1 / -3 \Rightarrow -3 \qquad -7 / 2 \Rightarrow -3$$

And since the remainder should satisfy the equation
(*divisor* × *quotient*) + *remainder* = *dividend*,

```
i1 % -3 ⇒ 1              -7 % 2 ⇒ -1
```

(We will only use the remainder operator with positive integer arguments.)

In all the above examples, both operands of a binary operator have been **int**, producing a result of type **int**, or both operands have been **double**, producing a result of type **double**. We might reasonably ask what happens if one operand is **int** and the other **double**, as in the expression

```
7 / 2.0
```

In this case, the **int** operand is converted to a **double** value representing the same mathematical number, and the operation is performed on the two **double** values.

```
7 / 2.0 ⇒ 7.0 / 2.0 ⇒ 3.5
i1 * 0.5 ⇒   10 * 0.5 ⇒   10.0 * 0.5 ⇒ 5.0
```

Operator precedence

We've implied that we can combine two arbitrary arithmetic expressions with a binary operator to build a new expression. If we use the operator "*" to combine the expressions i1 + 10 and 2, we get

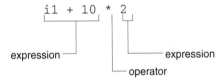

A question arises as to how we are to interpret the above line, given that putting together i1 and 10 * 2 with the "+" operator yields the same expression:

That is, should

```
i1 + 10 * 2
```

be interpreted as

```
(i1 + 10) * 2 ⇒   20 * 2 ⇒ 40
```

or as

$$i1 + (10 * 2) \Rightarrow 10 + 20 \Rightarrow 30$$

Java's *operator precedence* rules give the second interpretation. Java evaluates the expression by first performing the multiplication and then the addition. We say the operators `*`, `/`, and `%` have *higher precedence* than the binary operators `+` and `-`. In particular, the multiplication is done before the addition in an unparenthesized expression like that shown above:

$$i1 + \underbrace{(10 * 2)}_{\text{multiply before adding}} \Rightarrow i1 + 20 \Rightarrow 30$$

A few more examples:

$$i1 * 10 + 2 \Rightarrow 100 + 2 \Rightarrow 102$$
$$10 / 2 + 1 \Rightarrow 5 + 1 \Rightarrow 6$$
$$5 + 6 / 10 \Rightarrow 5 + 0 \Rightarrow 5$$

We should note that *unary* `+` and `-` have higher precedence than the binary operators. Thus

$$-5 + i1 \Rightarrow (-5) + 10 \Rightarrow 5$$

and *not*

$$-5 + i1 \Rightarrow -(5 + 10) \Rightarrow -15$$

Associativity

Suppose our expression contains two operators with equal precedence, such as

$$i1 / 5 * 2$$

or

$$10 - 4 - 3$$

The binary operators in Java are *left associative*: this means that in cases like the above, the operations are performed left to right. Thus

$$\underbrace{(i1 / 5)}_{\text{left operator before right}} * 2 \Rightarrow 2 * 2 \Rightarrow 4$$

$$10 - 4 - 3 \Rightarrow 6 - 3 \Rightarrow 3$$

Expression evaluation can involve both the precedence and associativity rules. For instance

$$i1 - 2 * 5 - i3 \Rightarrow i1 - 10 - i3 \Rightarrow 0 - i3 \Rightarrow -30$$

Finally, we parenthesize expressions to indicate explicitly the order in which we want the operations to be preformed. For instance,

```
(i1 + 10) * 2  ⇒   20 * 2  ⇒  40
       -(5 + i1)  ⇒  -15
i1 / (5 * 2)  ⇒   i1 / 10  ⇒  1
```

Casting

Occasionally we must explicitly convert an **int** value to a **double** or a **double** to an **int**. For instance, if we divide i1 by i3, the result will be the integer quotient 0:

```
i1 / i3  ⇒   10 / 30  ⇒  0
```

If we want the result to be a **double**, we can convert either (or both) **int** operand to a **double** by a *cast operation*. To cast the result of an expression to a different type, we prefix the expression with the new type, in parentheses:

```
(type)expression
```

For example.

```
(double)i1  ⇒ (double)10  ⇒  10.0
```

and so

```
(double)i1 / i3  ⇒  10.0 / 30  ⇒  0.333…
```

We can also cast a **double** to an **int**. The **double** value is truncated to produce the **int**: that is, the fractional part is discarded. If d3 and d4 are **double** variables containing the values 2.9 and –2.9 respectively, then

```
(int)d3  ⇒  2
(int)d4  ⇒  -2
```

Finally, note that the cast operation has higher precedence than the arithmetic operators, so that

```
(double)i1/i3    ⇒    10.0/30  ⇒  0.333…
```

is not the same as

```
(double)(i1/i3)  ⇒  (double)0  ⇒  0.0
```

Concatenation

Before we close this discussion of arithmetic expressions, we should note that the binary operator "+" denotes concatenation when the operands are *Strings*. That is, if *string1* and *string2* are *String* instances, the expression

```
string1 + string2
```

evaluates to a *String* containing the characters of `string1` with the characters of `string2` appended. Thus

`"abc"` + `"def"`   ⇒   `"abcdef"`

Furthermore, if one of the operands of "+" is a *String* and the other isn't, the non-*String* operand will be converted to a *String*, and concatenation performed. For instance, given

> **int** i = 23;

the following expressions evaluate as indicated:

`"abc"` + `i`	⇒	`"abc23"`
`i` + `" "`	⇒	`"23 "`
`"2*i="` + `2*i`	⇒	`"2*i=46"`
`2+i+"!"`	⇒	`"25!"` remember + is left associative!
`"!"+2+i`	⇒	`"!223"`

5.2.3 Method implementation: simple commands

Next let's look at the commands `reset` and `stepCount` of the *Counter* class. A client invokes the command `reset` to change the property *count* to 0, and calls the command `stepCount` to increment *count* by 1. The value of this property is stored in the instance variable `tally`; hence, each of these commands changes the value stored in `tally`. The action of modifying the value stored in a variable is accomplished by an *assignment* statement. An assignment statement has the following general form:

> `variableName = expression;`

When the processor executes an assignment statement, it first computes the value denoted by the expression on the right. It then stores that value into the variable named on the left, replacing the previous value of the variable. The equal sign "=" should be thought of as indicating a "store" operation and **not** denoting mathematical equality. The type of the value produced by the expression must, in general, be the same as the type of the variable. For instance, it would not be legal for the expression to denote a value of type **double** and for the variable to be of type **int**. One cannot put a **double** value into an **int** variable. (We'll see later how to convert one type of value to another, and we'll encounter a few cases in which the value produced by the expression is automatically converted to the required type.)

---

assignment: a statement that instructs the processor to compute a value and store it in a variable.

In the case of the command `reset`, we want to store 0 in the variable `tally`. Thus we write the assignment:

```
tally = 0;
```

Again, we see a very simple form of expression: in this case, the **int** literal 0. When the processor performs the assignment, the value 0 is put into the instance variable `tally`, replacing whatever value was previously stored in the variable. Since this is the only action the processor need take, the implementation of the method `reset` consists of one assignment statement:

```
/**
 * Reset the count to 0.
 */
public void reset () {
    tally = 0;
}
```

Note that there is no `return` statement. This method implements a command, and does not return a value to the client.

When the command `stepCount` is carried out, we again want the value of `tally` to be changed. We again use an assignment statement. What value do we want to put in the variable? Well, we want the value currently in the variable `tally` plus one. This computation is described by the expression

```
tally + 1
```

To evaluate this expression, the processor gets the value stored in `tally` and adds one to it. If `tally` contains the value 3, evaluating the expression gives the value 4; if `tally` contains 4, evaluating the expression gives 5, and so on. Note that evaluating the expression **does not affect** the value stored in the variable. Evaluating an expression does not change the object's state.

The assignment statement instructs the processor to compute this value, and then store it into `tally`, replacing the previous value:

```
tally = tally + 1;
```

In performing the assignment statement, the processor changes the state of the object.

It should be clear from this example that the equal sign "=" does not denote mathematical equality. The assignment statement instructs the processor to compute a value as described by the expression on the right, and then store the value into the variable named on the left.

The action described by the assignment statement is all the processor need do to execute the command `stepCount`.

```
/**
 * Increment the count by 1.
 */
```

```
public void stepCount () {
    tally = tally + 1;
}
```

Note that a named constant, since it is not a variable, can never appear on the left of an assignment. Considering the example of Section 5.1.2, the following would be meaningless:

```
SPADE = 2;  // this is not legal; it is like writing:
            // 4 = 2;
```

Implementing the constructor

We have only to implement the constructor to complete the definition of the class *Counter*. Recall that the constructor creates a new instance of the specified class and initializes instance variables. All the hard work of actually creating the object is done automatically when the constructor is invoked. The critical thing we need to worry about is that the newly created object has a proper initial state. In the present case, we want the *count* property of the newly created object to have a value of 0. So we need to make sure that the variable `tally` contains 0. We already know how to use an assignment statement to do this:

```
/**
 * Create a new Counter.
 */
public Counter () {
    tally = 0;
}
```

Since the `tally` is the only instance variable, the constructor's responsibilities are satisfied by initializing this variable. The complete definition of the class *Counter* is given in Listing 5.1.

5.2.4 Using parameters

Let's return to the class *Explorer*, and look at the command `takeHit`. We specified the command as follows:

```
/**
 * Receive a blow of the specified number of
 * hit points.
 */
public void takeHit (int hitStrength) {
    ...
}
```

Listing 5.1   **The class** *Counter*

===

```
package counters;

/**
 * A simple integer counter.
 */
public class Counter {

    // Constructors:

    /**
     * Create a new Counter.
     */
    public Counter () {
        tally = 0;
    }

    // Queries:

    /**
     * Current count; the number of items counted.
     */
    public int count () {
        return tally;
    }

    // Commands:

    /**
     * Increment the count by 1.
     */
    public void stepCount () {
        tally = tally + 1;
    }

    /**
     * Reset the count to 0.
     */
    public void reset () {
        tally = 0;
    }
```

continued

Listing 5.1   **The class *Counter (continued)***

```
    // Private components:

    private int tally;// current count

} // end of class Counter
```

The client provides an integer argument indicating the strength of the blow. We expect this command to change the state of the *Explorer*: namely, to reduce the *Explorer*'s *stamina* by the strength of the blow. If an *Explorer* has *stamina* of 100, and a client invokes the command `takeHit` with an argument of 5, we expect the *stamina* of the *Explorer* to be reduced to 95.

The *Explorer*'s *stamina* value is stored in the instance variable `staminaPoints`:

```
    private int staminaPoints;    // current stamina
                                  // (hit points)
```

Executing the command `takeHit` should therefore reduce the value of this variable by 5, or by whatever argument value the client supplies. Clearly we need an assignment statement. The only question is how do we denote the argument value provided by the client? This is exactly what the parameter name is for. The method specification stipulates that the client must supply a single **int** argument, and `hitStrength` is the name we use for the argument value. Thus the expression denoting the value to be stored is

```
    staminaPoints - hitStrength
```

and the complete assignment statement is

```
    staminaPoints = staminaPoints - hitStrength;
```

The effective result of this assignment is to reduce the value stored in the variable `staminaPoints` by the amount `hitStrength`, the argument supplied by the client. The complete definition of the method is

```
    /**
     * Receive a blow of the specified number of
     * hit points.
     */
    public void takeHit (int hitStrength) {
        staminaPoints = staminaPoints - hitStrength;
    }
```

Note that there is nothing to prevent the value of staminaPoints from becoming negative. If the method is invoked with an argument that is greater than the current value of staminaPoints, this variable will have a negative value after the assignment.

Let's take a closer look at what happens when this method is invoked or called. Suppose a client invokes the method with an argument of 5. When the client invokes the method, an **int** variable is created for the parameter hitStrength. Such a variable is called an *automatic* variable. It is created when the method is invoked, and is deallocated when execution of the method is completed. When a variable is created, memory space is allocated for it. When the variable is deallocated, the memory space is reclaimed and available for other uses. The lifetime of the automatic variable is the execution of the method body. This is substantially different from an instance variable, whose lifetime is the lifetime of the object.

This automatic variable is initialized with the argument provided by the client. Thus when the processor executes the body of the method takeHit, available variables include the instance variables of the *Explorer* object, and the automatic variable named hitStrength. This is illustrated in Figure 5.4. Execution of the method evaluates the expression staminaPoints - hitStrength, and stores the resulting value in the staminaPoints instance of the object. Upon completion of method execution, the space allocated for the variable hitStrength is released: this variable effectively no longer exists.

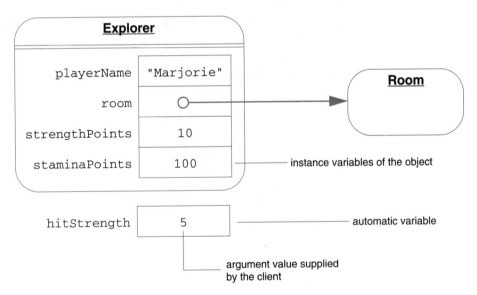

Figure 5.4 **Available variables when *takeHit* is executed.**

> **automatic variable:** a variable that is created when a method is invoked, and de-allocated when the processor finishes executing the method.

The implementation of the *Explorer* command `changeName` is straightforward. We simply store the argument provided by the client in the `playerName` instance variable of the *Explorer* object:

```
/**
 * Change the name of this Explorer to the
 * specified String.
 */
public void changeName(String newName) {
    playerName = newName;
}
```

We need to see a specification for the class *Room* before we can write a reasonable implementation of the *Explorer* command `move`. (For instance, a *Room* object might want to keep track of who's in it.) For the time being, we can implement `move` by simply changing the *Explorer*'s `location`:

```
/**
 * Move to the specified Room.
 */
public void move (rooms.Room newRoom) {
    location = newRoom;
}
```

Note again that the type of the variable on the left of the assignment and the type of the value denoted on the right are identical: both are of type *reference-to-Room*. That is, when a client invokes this method, a reference to a *Room* object is provided as argument and that value is stored in the instance variable `location`.

Implementing the constructor

In the previous chapter, we specified the constructor for an *Explorer* object as follows:

```
/**
 * Create a new Explorer.
 */
public Explorer (String name, rooms.Room location,
                 int hitStrength, int stamina) {
}
```

Invoking the constructor will create a new *Explorer* object and provide a reference to it. As we noted, the client must provide initial values for the newly created *Explorer*'s *name, location, etc*. The implementation of the constructor simply assigns the argument values provide by the client to the instance variables of the object:

```
/**
 * Create a new Explorer.
 */
public Explorer (String name, rooms.Room location,
                 int hitStrength, int stamina) {
    playerName = name;
    room = location;
    strengthPoints = hitStrength;
    staminaPoints = stamina;
}
```

Since there are only four instance variables, this suffices. We'll see how to use constructors to create objects in a later chapter.

5.2.5   Invoking a method: acting as client

We've talked quite a bit about a client accessing the features of a server object by invoking the server object's methods, but we have yet to see how this is done. To see how an object acts as a client, let's consider the command strike of an *Explorer* object. This command is specified as

```
/**
 * Strike the specified Denizen.
 */
public void strike (denizens.Denizen monster) {
    ...
}
```

The command instructs the *Explorer* to strike the *Denizen* provided as argument. We know that in order for this command to be executed, some other object must invoke it. That is, some object must instruct the *Explorer* to perform the command. In this relationship, the other object is client and the *Explorer* object is server: the other object is accessing a feature of the *Explorer*.

When the client invokes the *Explorer*'s method strike, it must provide (a reference to) a *Denizen* object as argument. This argument value is stored in the automatic variable monster. The invocation of this method is illustrated in Figure 5.5.

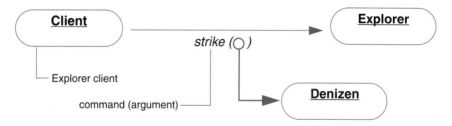

Figure 5.5 *Explorer* is server for a *Client*.

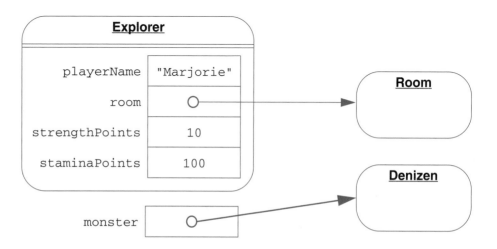

Figure 5.6 **Variables when *Explorer*'s method *strike* is being executed.**

Now the *Explorer* "knows about" the *Denizen* it is to hit: there is a reference to the *Denizen* in the variable monster. We want to change the *Denizen*'s state: to reduce its "stamina." (Figure 4.8 shows the symmetric case of a Denizen hitting the *Explorer*.)

To change an object's state, we must give the object a command. That is, the *Explorer* must give the object monster a command—it must invoke a feature of the *Denizen*. In this case, the *Explorer* is the client, and the *Denizen* the server. If we look at the specification for the class *Denizen* given in the previous chapter, we see exactly the command we need:

```
/**
 * Receive a blow of the specified number of
 * hit points.
 */
public void takeHit (int hitStrength)
```

As we've seen, the syntax for invoking a command is

```
objectReference.commandName (arguments);
```

A command invocation is another form of statement.

To invoke the *Denizen*'s takeHit command, we must provide an integer argument: the strength of the blow. This is just the value of our *Explorer*'s strengthPoints variable. Thus the command invocation looks like this:

```
monster.takeHit(strengthPoints);
```

    object ⌐   feature ⌐   argument ⌐

The only action that the *Explorer* needs to take in responding to a strike command is to call the *Denizen*'s takeHit command. Again the method contains only one statement.

```
/**
 * Strike the specified Denizen.
 */
public void strike (denizens.Denizen monster) {
    monster.takeHit(strengthPoints);
}
```

(You might think that the methods we are building are unrealistically small. This is not the case. It is not uncommon for the methods implementing a substantial class to average less than two statements each.)

Note that in executing the command strike the *Explorer* acts both as server and client. The *Explorer* is a server for whatever object invoked its strike command. To perform the command strike, the *Explorer* invokes the feature takeHit of the *Denizen* object. Here the *Explorer* is client of the *Denizen*, and the *Denizen* is server to the *Explorer*. We repeat in Figure 5.7 the interaction diagram from the last chapter.

Summarizing, when a client invokes the *Explorer*'s method strike, the client supplies a (reference to a) *Denizen* object as argument. This reference value is stored in a newly created automatic variable named monster. The single statement that makes up the body of the method is a call to the *Denizen* object's take-Hit command. This method requires an **int** argument, and we provide one in the value of the *Explorer*'s strengthPoints instance variable. We expect that the takeHit method of the *Denizen* will be similar to that for an *Explorer* object; but of course, we have no specifics as to how this command works. The complete definition of the class *Explorer* is given in Listing 5.2.

We'll see lots more examples in the coming chapters. But a few observations before we conclude this section. First, the arguments provided in a method invo-

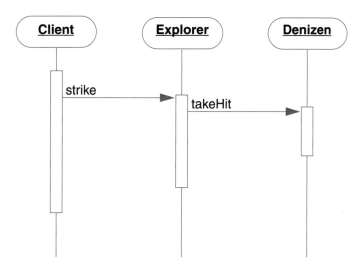

Figure 5.7 **Explorer** is server for **Client,** and client of **Denizen.**

cation are in general *expressions*. Thus we could legally (though perhaps not meaningfully) write

```
monster.takeHit(20);
```

or even

```
monster.takeHit(2*strengthPoints+5);
```

Second, a method invocation must provide an argument of the appropriate type for each parameter. For instance, if a method were specified as

```
public void move(int direction, double distance) {
    ...
}
```

an invocation of that method would need to provide two arguments, an **int** and a **double** in that order. For example,

```
object.move(90, 2.5);
```

Finally, while a command invocation is a form of *statement*, a query, since it produces a value, is a form of *expression*. Recall that the general form of a query is

```
objectReference.queryName (arguments)
```

If ctr is a *Counter* object and i an **int** variable, assignment statements such as the following, which use the value of ctr's property *count*, are legal.

```
i = ctr.count();
i = ctr.count()+10;
```

Listing 5.2   **The class *Explorer***

```
package explorer;

/**
 * A maze game player.
 */
public class Explorer {

    // Constructors:

    /**
     * Create a new Explorer.
     */
    public Explorer (String name, rooms.Room location,
                     int hitStrength, int stamina) {
        playerName = name;
        room = location;
        strengthPoints = hitStrength;
        staminaPoints = stamina;
    }

    // Queries:

    /**
     * Name of this Explorer.
     */
    public String name () {
        return playerName;
    }

    /**
     * Room in which this Explorer is currently located.
     */
    public rooms.Room location () {
        return room;
    }

    /**
     * Damage (hit points) this Explorer does when
     * striking.
     */
    public int strength () {
```

continued

Listing 5.2   **The class *Explorer (continued)***

```
      return strengthPoints;
   }

   /**
    * Damage (hit points) required to defeat this
    * Explorer.
    */
   public int stamina () {
      return staminaPoints;
   }

   // Commands:

   /**
    * Change the name of this Explorer to the specified
    * String.
    */
   public void changeName (String newName) {
      playerName = newName;
   }

   /**
    * Move to the specified Room.
    */
   public void move (rooms.Room newRoom) {
      room = newRoom;
   }

   /**
    * Receive a blow of the specified number of hit
    * points.
    */
   public void takeHit (int hitStrength) {
      staminaPoints = staminaPoints - hitStrength;
   }

   /**
    * Strike the specified Denizen.
    */
   public void strike (denizens.Denizen monster) {
      monster.takeHit(strengthPoints);
   }
```

continued

Listing 5.2   **The class *Explorer* (continued)**

```
// Private components:

private String playerName;     // name
private rooms.Room room;       // current location
private int strengthPoints;    // current strength
                               // (hit points)
private int staminaPoints;     // current stamina
                               // (hit points)


} // end of class Explorer
```

5.2.6   Local variables: another kind of automatic variable

We were introduced to automatic variables in Section 5.2.4. We noted that when a method was invoked, an automatic variable was allocated for each parameter and initialized with the argument value provided by the client. When we implement a method, it is often handy to have additional automatic variables available for storing intermediate results. These are called *local variables*. Their lifetime is essentially the same as the automatic variables seen previously. They are created when the method is invoked, and deallocated when the method completes. However, they are not initialized by client-provided arguments. When a local variable is created, it is "undefined." That is, it does not contain a predetermined value. It must be assigned a value before it can be meaningfully used.

A local variable is created with a variable declaration of the form:

```
type identifier;
```

The declaration is simply written as one of the statements in the method body.

> **local variable:** an automatic variable created as part of a method execution, used to hold intermediate results needed during the computation.

While we can't give a really meaningful example at this point, the following should illustrate the mechanism. Suppose we are writing a method (as part of a *CashRegister* class, for instance) that will produce the net price of an item given gross price, tax rate, and discount rate:

```
public double netPrice (double grossPrice,
                double taxRate, double discountRate) {

    ...
}
```

Since the expression needed to compute the net price is rather complex, we might find it useful to compute the tax and discount amounts separately, and then apply them to the gross price to determine net price. We can use local variables to store these intermediate values.

```
public double netPrice (double grossPrice,
                  double taxRate, double discountRate) {
    double tax;
    double discount;
    tax = grossPrice * taxRate;
    discount = grossPrice * discountRate;
    return grossPrice + tax - discount;
}
```

In the above, `tax` and `discount` are local automatic variables. They are created whenever the method is invoked, and are de-allocated when the method completes. They contain "undefined" values when created, and are used only to hold the tax and discount amounts until they are needed in the final *return* statement. For example, suppose the method is invoked with 10.00, 0.08, and 0.10 as arguments. Five automatic variables would be created, three parameters and two local variables:

grossPrice	10.00
taxRate	0.08
discountRate	0.10
tax	???
discount	???

The parameters are initialized with argument values; the local variables are undefined.

The first assignment statement,

```
tax = grossPrice * taxRate;
```

assigns a value to the local variable `tax`:

grossPrice	10.00
taxRate	0.08
discountRate	0.10
tax	0.80
discount	???

The next assignment,

```
discount = grossPrice * discountRate;
```

assigns a value to `discount`:

grossPrice	10.00
taxRate	0.08
discountRate	0.10
tax	0.80
discount	1.00

Now the values stored in these variables can be used to compute the return value. When the method completes execution, space for these five variables is de-allocated. Note that local variables and instance variables are fundamentally different. An instance variable contains an element of the object's state. It must always contain a meaningful value whether a method of the object is executing or not. A local variable, on the other hand, contains some intermediate value needed only during a particular computation. You should never use an instance variable for this purpose.

Local Variable:

- Defined inside a method.
- Exists only while the method is being executed.
- Can be accessed only from the method.
- Is only meaningful during execution of the method.
- Contains some intermediate value needed only during execution of the method; its value is not part of the object's state.

Instance Variable:

- Defined outside any method.
- Exists as long as the object exists.
- Can be accessed from any method in the class.
- Has a meaningful value at any time during the life of the object, whether the object is actively doing something or not.
- Represents a property of the object; its value is part of the object's state.

Figure 5.8 **Local variables are not components.**

5.3   Testing an implementation

Having implemented a class, we'd like to create an instance and exercise it to make sure that the implementation is correct. We study testing in some detail in Chapter 8. Here, we'll just build a minimal system for creating and exercising an object. As an example, we'll test our *Counter* implementation. For simplicity, the classes defined here will all be in the same package as the class *Counter*.

Of course we need a *Counter* instance to test, but we also need another object to exercise the *Counter*. That is, we need an object that will invoke the *Counter*'s features. We call this object a *CounterInterface*:

> **class** CounterInterface
> A simple interface to test the class *Counter*.

The only function an instance of this class has is to test a *Counter*. So we specify a single command for the class:

> **public void** testCounter (Counter counter)
> Test the specified *Counter*.

Note that the *Counter* to be exercised is provided as a method argument.

Now the *CounterInterface* is going to invoke the queries and commands of the *Counter*. The method testCounter might look something like this:

```
public void testCounter (Counter counter) {
    int value;
    value = counter.count();
    counter.stepCount();
    counter.reset();
    ...
}
```

To know that the *Counter* is behaving correctly, we must somehow "see" the results: we want to know the state of the *Counter* after each command is executed. We'll consider input and output in some detail in later chapters. For now, we use the simplest possible way to produce output.

The predefined object System.out has a method println, specified as

> **public void** println (String s)
> Write a line containing the specified *String* to standard output.

Executing the method results in its argument being displayed, typically in the window in which you run the program.

Using this method, can write testCounter so that it displays the state of the *Counter* at relevant points:

```
public void testCounter (Counter counter) {
    int value;
```

```
// Display the initial value of the Counter.
value = counter.count();
System.out.println("Initial Count: " + value);

// Display the value after two steps.
counter.stepCount();
counter.stepCount();
value = counter.count();
System.out.println("After two steps: " + value);

// Display the value after a reset.
counter.reset();
value = counter.count();
System.out.println("After reset: " + value);
}
```

Note that the operator "+" used in the invocations of `println` is concatenation, as explained on page 104. The left operand in each case is a *String* and the right operand is an **int**. The **int** value is automatically converted to a *String* before being appended to the left operand. The *String* that is printed consists of a message followed by the value of the variable.

Note further that the assignments to the local variable `value` are not necessary. The query `counter.count()` could be incorporated directly in the `println` argument expression. For instance, the last invocation of `println` could have been written:

```
System.out.println("After reset: " + counter.count());
```

When the method `testCounter` is invoked, we expect to see the following three lines displayed:

```
Initial Count: 0
After two steps: 2
After reset: 0
```

If this is not what we get, something must be wrong with the implementation of one of the classes.

5.3.1   Getting it started: invoking constructors

We've defined the classes *Counter* and *CounterInterface*, but we still haven't seen how the system gets started and how the objects get created. We need one more public class, with a method `main` specified as:

public static void main (String[] argv)

We'll ignore the details of this specification. But this is the method that is executed when you start the program. Although the `main` method is defined in a class, it is really outside the object-oriented paradigm. Its only purpose should be to create the top-level objects and get the system started.

***main* method:** the top-level method that initiates execution of a system.

Though it's not essential to do things this way, our convention is that the class containing `main` contains no other method, and is not used to model any other part of the system. We name this class for the application.

What must the method `main` do in our program? It simply creates *Counter* and *CounterInterface* objects, and commands the *CounterInterface* to test the *Counter*.

We saw in Section 4.3.3 that the keyword **new** is used to invoke a constructor. Invoking a constructor creates an object, and returns a reference to the newly created object. We can define the top level class as follows:

```
/**
 * A simple test system for the class Counter.
 */
public class CounterTest {

    /**
     * Create a Counter and CounterInterface,
     * start the test.
     */
    public static void main (String[] argv) {
        Counter counter;
        CounterInterface interface;
        counter = new Counter();
        interface = new CounterInterface();
        interface.testCounter(counter);
    }
}
```

When the program is run, the method `main` is invoked. The method creates a *Counter* instance, creates a *CounterInterface* instance, and gives the *CounterInterface* the command `testCounter`. This is the last statement in the method `main`. When this statement completes, the program terminates.

There are a few items to note:

- In the assignment statement

  ```
  counter = new Counter();
  ```

  the expression on the right is the constructor invocation,

  ```
  new Counter()
  ```

Invoking the constructor creates a *Counter* instance and returns a reference to it, which is stored in the variable `counter`.

- A variable declaration can include an assignment. Thus, we could have written the declaration as:

```
Counter counter = new Counter();
```

- The variables and assignments are not necessary. We could have written the body of `main` to contain the single statement:

```
(new CounterInterface()).testCounter(new Counter());
```

5.4   Summary

In this chapter, we've seen how to write a simple class implementation. Implementing a class involves

- writing data descriptions for data stored in class instances, and
- writing method bodies that define the actions the processor performs when the methods are invoked.

An object's data are stored in instance variables. Instance variables are created when the object is created, and memory space remains allocated as long as the object exists. instance variables are part of the object's implementation, and are not generally accessible by the object's clients. An instance variable is created with a variable declaration, having the form:

```
private variableType variableName;
```

A named constant declaration allows us to associate an identifier with a value. The identifier, rather than a literal, can then be used to denote the value. Using named constants makes programs more readable and maintainable, and helps isolate client code from implementation details of the server.

A method body is made up of a sequence of statements that implement the method algorithm. Statements describe actions the processor performs when executing the method. When the method is invoked, the processor executes the statements one after the other, in the order in which they appear in the method body.

Two elementary kinds of statements are *return* statements and *assignment* statements. A return statement is the last statement executed in a query, and specifies the value to be delivered to the client. It has the form:

```
return expression;
```

An assignment statement stores a value in a variable. Its format is:

```
variable = expression;
```

Both return statements and assignment statements include expressions. An expression describes how a value is to be computed.

When a method with formal parameters is invoked, a variable is allocated for each formal parameter and initialized with the argument provided by the client. These variables are automatic variables. They are created when the method is invoked, and deallocated when the method finishes. Automatic variables are substantially different from instance variables. Instance variables contain data that is permanently maintained as part of the object's state. Automatic variables contain values that are used only for a specific computation. Local variables are automatic variables created as part of a method invocation and used to hold intermediate results needed during the computation.

A command invocation is a form of statement. The format for invoking a command is

```
object.command (arguments);
```

The processor executes the method body associated with the command, which generally results in the object changing state.

A query invocation is a form of expression, since it computes and returns value. The format is similar to a command invocation:

```
object.query (arguments)
```

A constructor invocation creates a new object, and returns a reference to the newly created object. The format is

```
new class (arguments)
```

We concluded the chapter with a brief introduction to the development of a complete program. We specified and implemented a class to be used to test another existing class. Its function is simply to exercise an instance of the existing class in such a way as to verify the correctness of the existing class's implementation. The testing object invokes commands and queries of the object under test, and displays information about its state. By comparing actual results with expected results we can determine if the object under test behaves correctly.

To complete the program, we introduced a class with a single method named main. This is the method that is executed when the program is run. Its only function is to create the initial objects and get the system started. In our example, it creates a testing object, an object to be tested, and commands the testing object to conduct the test. We restrict ourselves to this style of using a "special" class that contains only the method main, and using main only to initialize and start the object-oriented system.

In the examples in this chapter, methods generally contained only a single statement. The algorithms required were very simple, and could generally be expressed with a single *assignment* or *return*. In subsequent chapters we will see other forms of statements which allow us to write more complex algorithms.

EXERCISES

5.1   Given that i and j are variables of type **int**, containing the values 2 and 3 respectively, and that x and y are variables of type **double**, containing the values 4.0 and 5.0 respectively: evaluate the following expressions and state the type for each resulting value.

(a) i*j	(b) i/j	(c) j/i	(d) x/y
(e) x/j	(f) i%j	(g) 12/i+j	(h) j+12/i
(i) 12/(i+j)	(j) -i+2	(k) x+y*3	(l) x+j/i
(m) i-j-2	(n) 12/i*j	(o) 12/i%j	(p) 12/i/j
(q) (x-y)*(i+j)/3		(r) (3+i)+(2-j)*(25%i)	

5.2   Given that i is an **int** variable, write the following in Java:

a.   an expression that evaluates to twice the value stored in i;

b.   a return statement that delivers to the client twice the value stored in i;

c.   an assignment statement that doubles the value stored in i.

5.3   Given that i, j, and k are **int** variables containing the values 2, 4, and 6, respectively, indicate what values i and j will have after each of the following statement sequences:

(a) i = j;	(b) i = j;	(c) k = i;	(d) i = i - j;
j = 5;	j = i;	i = j;	j = j + i;
		j = k;	i = j - i;

5.4   Suppose that i is an **int** variable containing a two-digit number: *i.e.*, a number in the range 0 – 99. Write assignment statements that will store the low-order digit in the **int** variable ones, and the high-order digit in the **int** variable tens. For instance, if i contains 23, the statements should assign 3 to ones, and 2 to tens.

5.5   Assume that pennies, dollars, and cents are **int** variables. The variables pennies contains a value representing a number of pennies. Write assignment statements that will represent this value as dollars and cents, by assigning the dollars to dollars, and the cents to cents. For instance, if pennies contains 298, the statements should assign 2 to dollars, and 98 to cents.

5.6   Do the same as in exercise 5.5, except using the variable `nickels` rather than `pennies`. Assume that the value in `nickels` represents a number of nickels. For instance, if `nickels` contains 23, the statements should assign 1 to `dollars` and 15 to `cents`.

5.7   Do the same as in exercise 5.5, except using both variables `nickels` and `pennies`. For instance, if `pennies` contains 298 and `nickels` contains 23, the statements should assign 4 to `dollars` and 13 to `cents`.

5.8   Add a method to the class *Counter* that will double the *count* of a *Counter*.

5.9   Suppose we want to add to the *Counter* class a command `unReset` that restores the *count* to what it was before the most recent `reset`. For instance, if the *count* is 10 and the command `reset` is performed, the count will be 0. If `unReset` is done, the *count* will again be 10.

Modify the definition of the class *Counter* adding the method `unReset`. This will involve adding an additional instance variable and modifying the `reset` command as well as adding the `unReset` command.

5.10   Write a definition for the class *Date* as specified in exercise 4.6.

5.11   Write a definition of the class modeling a three-way lamp, as specified in exercise 4.4. A lamp has four settings: *off*, *low*, *medium*, and *high*. It has one query, for determining the setting, and one command for advancing the setting: *off* to *low*, *low* to *medium*, *medium* to *high*, *high* to *off*.

5.12   Consider a class modeling rectangles. The class has queries for *length*, *width*, and *area*, and commands for setting *length* and *width*. Write a definition for the class.

5.13   Suppose instances of the class *Room* of the maze game want to keep track of whether or not the *Explorer* is in the *Room*. The class *Room* includes the methods **public void** enter() and **public void** exit() that specify that the *Explorer* has entered or left the *Room*.

   a.   Modify the *Explorer* method `move` so that the *Room*'s are informed of the *Explorer*'s coming and going.

   b.   Illustrate the interaction between an object commanding the *Explorer* to move, the *Explorer*, and the *Room* objects using an interaction diagram.

5.14   Consider the class *Student* specified in the previous chapter.

   a.   Write definitions for instance variables of the class.

   b.   Write definitions for the methods `ssn` and `changeSsn`.

   c.   Assume that fees are $100 per credit hour. Write a definition for the method `fees`.

   d.   Write definitions for the methods `feesPaid` and `payFees`.

The classes *CourseList* and *Course* include the following methods:

public class CourseList
A list of *Courses*

public CourseList()
Create a new empty *CourseList*.

public void add (Course newCourse)
Add specified *Course* to this *CourseList*.

public void remove (Course course)
Remove specified *Course* from this *CourseList*.

public class Course
A university course.

public int creditHours ()
Credit hours for this *Course*.

    e. Write a definition for the class *Student* constructor.

    f. Write a definition of the method addCourse.

5.15   Write a program to test the class Counter defined in this chapter.

5.16   Implement a version of Counter that allows the count to be decremented, and write a program to test the implementation.

5.17   Write a program to test the lamp class of exercise 5.11.

5.18   Write a program to test the rectangle class of exercise 5.12.

GLOSSARY

arithmetic expression: an expression that produces an integer or floating point value when evaluated.

assignment statement: a statement that instructs the processor to compute a value and store it in a variable.

associativity rule: a rule that specifies the order in which un-parenthesized operators of equal precedence are applied in the evaluation of an expression.

automatic variable: a variable that is created when a method is invoked, and de-allocated when the method is completed.

binary operator: an operator that requires two operands; that is, computes a value from two given values. Also called a *dyadic* operator.

cast: an operation in which a value of one type is converted into a value of a different type.

component: an instance variable.

concatenation: an operation in which two *Strings* are joined together to form a longer *String*.

expression: a language construct that specifies how to compute a particular value.

instance variable: a variable that contains data stored as part of an object's state. an instance variable is allocated when the object is created and exists as long as the object does.

local variable: an automatic variable created as part of a method execution, used to hold intermediate results needed during the computation.

main method: the top-level method that initiates execution of the system.

method body: the sequence of statements that comprise the implementation of a method. When the method is invoked, the processor executes the statements that make up the method body.

named constant: a value that has an identifier (a name) associated with it; the associated identifier can be used to refer to the value.

operand: a value given to an operator and used in the computation of another value.

operator precedence rules: rules that specify order in which operators are applied in the evaluation of an expression.

return statement: a statement that specifies the value to be delivered to the client. A return statement is the last statement executed in a query method.

statement: a language construct that describes an action for the processor to perform.

unary operator: an operator that requires one operand; that is, computes a value from one given value. Also called a *monadic* operator.

variable: a portion of memory reserved to hold a single value.

variable decaration: a language construct that causes a variable with specified type and name to be allocated.

variable definition: a variable declaration.[1]

---

1. In some programming languages, definitions and declarations are different.

CHAPTER 6   **Conditions**

In the previous chapter, we saw how to implement methods using simple assignment and return statements. In this chapter, we introduce *conditions* and *conditional statements*. By using conditional statements, a method can behave in different ways depending on state of the object. As we'll see, this is an essential capability if we want to build objects that are at all interesting.

We also introduce the notions of *precondition*, *postcondition*, and *class invariant*. These play a fundamental role in system design and verification of correctness. Preconditions and postconditions form an essential part of a method's specification.

Along the way, we look in detail at *boolean expressions*: expressions that produce a boolean value when evaluated.

6.1   Conditional statements

In the previous chapter, we implemented the classes *Counter* and *Explorer*. Now we'll extend the specifications a bit, and see some new algorithmic constructs to support the extended specification.

Postconditions and invariants

Recall that in Chapter 4, we specified the `count` method for the class *Counter* as

```
/**
 * Current count; the number of items counted.
 */
public int count () {
    ...
}
```

The specification stipulates that a client invoking the method is delivered a value of type **int**. We remarked that we could be more precise in specifying the result of the query: the integer result is nonnegative. That is, for every *Counter* object, the value of the property *count* will always be greater than or equal to zero.

Such an assertion is called a *class invariant*. An *invariant* is a condition that will hold true. A *class invariant* is an invariant concerning properties of class instances. It is a condition that will always be true of all instances of the class.

We include this in the doc comment for the method.

```
/**
 * Current count; the number of items counted.
 *      ensure:
 *          count >= 0
 */
public int count () {
    ...
}
```

(We adhere to a rather rigid convention in formatting comments. Consistency in documentation is quite helpful to the reader. But we are writing comments. The specific notation we use is, of course, not required by the programming language.)

This comment tells the client that the implementor guarantees that the method will deliver a result that is greater than or equal to 0. (">=" means "greater than or equal to"; "≥" is not a standard ASCII character and doesn't generally appear on the keyboard.) Such a commitment is called a *postcondition*. It is a condition that the implementor promises will be satisfied when the method completes execution.

Even though the postcondition is included in a comment, it is an important part of the method specification. The correctness of a client will generally depend on the postcondition being satisfied.

But we can write anything we want in a comment, and it will be ignored by the compiler. In a sense, documentation is little more than advertising. We must make sure that the method implementation satisfies our commitment.

The query count returns the value stored in the private instance variable tally. We need to make sure that this instance variable will never contain a negative value. We document this as well:

```
private int tally;        // current count
                          // invariant: tally >= 0
```

As we mentioned above, the word "invariant" means that the condition always holds. In this case, it says that the value of the variable tally will always be greater than or equal to 0. This is a class invariant, a condition that will always hold true for all instances of the class.

But still, all we've done is advertise. To make sure that the invariant holds, we need to examine every place in the program where the variable is given a value and verify that it can never be given a negative value.

There are three places where tally is set: in the constructor, where it is given an initial value of 0; in the method reset, where it is set to 0; and in the method stepCount, where it is incremented by 1. Clearly a variable that can only be set to 0 and incremented will never contain a negative value. Thus we can conclude that the implementation conforms to the specification; that is, the implementation is correct.

---

postcondition: a condition the implementor guarantees will hold when a method completes execution.

invariant: a condition that always holds true.

class invariant: an invariant regarding properties of class instances; that is, a condition that will always be true for all instances of a class.

Suppose we add a command to decrement the *count*, which we specify and implement as follows:

```
/**
 * Decrement the count by 1.
 */
public void decrementCount () {
    tally = tally - 1;
}
```

Now we have a problem. We can no longer be sure that `tally` will be greater than or equal to 0, and no longer guarantee that a nonnegative value will be returned by the query `count`. For instance, the command `reset` followed by `decrementCount` will set `tally` to -1.

We must first make a design decision as to what we want to happen in a case such as this. If we decide that the property *count* can indeed have a negative value, we must remove the postcondition from the specification of `count`. We no longer guarantee that `count` will return a value greater than or equal to 0. On the other hand, if we decide that *count* should not have a negative value, we must do something to make sure that it never gets one. We adopt the latter approach. Since `count` returns the value of `tally`, we must prevent this variable from being assigned a negative value.

The only way `tally` can *become* negative is if the command `decrementCount` is performed when `tally` has a value of 0. If `tally` is 0, executing the statement

```
tally = tally - 1;
```

assigns -1 to `tally`. If we want to insure that `tally` doesn't become negative, we need to make sure that this assignment statement is done only under the condition that `tally` is greater than 0. We want to *guard* the assignment statement with the condition "`tally > 0`." To do this, we need a new kind of statement called a *conditional* statement. A conditional statement permits us to specify the conditions under which an action is to be performed. That is, it lets us specify that a certain action is to be performed only if appropriate conditions are met. We look at two variants, called *if-then* and *if-then-else*.

6.1.1   The *if-then* statement

An *if-then* statement has the form

```
if (condition)
    statement
```

Note that this is a *composite* statement. It includes another statement as a component. This component statement can be any kind of statement at all, even another *if-then* statement.

The meaning is straightforward. The condition is evaluated, and if it is *true* the included statement is performed. If the condition is *false*, the included statement is not performed. The condition "guards" the included statement. This is illustrated in Figure 6.1.

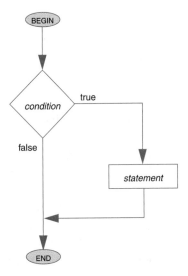

Figure 6.1 An *if-then* statement.

We can use an *if-then* to guard the assignment in the method decrement-Count:

```
/**
 * Decrement positive count by 1.
 */
public void decrementCount () {
    if (tally > 0)
        tally = tally - 1;
}
```

Now the assignment is done only if `tally` is positive. If `tally` is 0, the statement is not done and the value of `tally` remains 0.

(Notice our convention for indenting. The statement that makes up the "body" of the *if-then* is indented a uniform amount from the keyword **if**. Note also that we have slightly modified the comment describing the method to make it more accurate.)

A number of questions remain to be answered. In particular, we need to take a more complete and careful look at conditions. But first, we introduce another variant of the conditional statement, the *if-then-else*.

6.1.2 The *if-then-else* statement

In implementing the *Explorer* command `takeHit`, we noted that the *stamina* value of a *Explorer* could become negative. Let's suppose we want to consider a *Explorer* with a *stamina* of 0 to be defeated, and therefore to restrict the *stamina* value of a *Explorer* to be a non-negative integer. That is, we want the condition that *stamina* is greater than or equal to 0 to be a class invariant.

As before, we document this as a postcondition for the query and as an invariant of the instance variable:

```
/**
 * Damage (hit points) required to defeat
 * this Explorer.
 *     ensure:
 *         stamina >= 0
 */
public int stamina () {
    return staminaPoints;
}
...

private int staminaPoints; // current stamina
                           // invariant: staminaPoints >= 0
```

The variable `staminaPoints` is assigned a value in the constructor, where it is given its initial value, and in the method `takeHit` where it is reduced. We need to insure that the value assigned in each case is not negative.

First consider the `takeHit` method, which we've implemented as:

```
public void takeHit (int hitStrength) {
    staminaPoints = staminaPoints - hitStrength;
}
```

The variable `staminaPoints` will be assigned a negative value if the argument provided by the client, `hitStrength`, is greater than the current value of `staminaPoints`. To prevent this, we can guard the assignment as we did above:

```
public void takeHit (int hitStrength) {
    if (hitStrength <= staminaPoints)
        staminaPoints = staminaPoints - hitStrength;
}
```

Now the assignment is done only if `hitStrength` is less than or equal to the current value of `staminaPoints`. If `hitStrength` is 10 and `staminaPoints` is 15, then `staminaPoints` will be reduced to 5. But if `hitStrength` is 10 and `staminaPoints` is 5, nothing will be done, and `staminaPoints` will remain 5. This is clearly not correct. If `hitStrength` is greater than `staminaPoints`, we want `staminaPoints` to be reduced to 0, its minimum value. We can try to accomplish this by writing two guarded statements:

```
public void takeHit (int hitStrength) {

    if (hitStrength <= staminaPoints)
        staminaPoints = staminaPoints - hitStrength;

    if (hitStrength > staminaPoints)
        staminaPoints = 0;
}
```

Let's be clear about what's happening here. We have written two *if-then* statements that will be done one after the other in the order written. In the first, we decide whether or not to do the assignment

```
staminaPoints = staminaPoints - hitStrength;
```

Then, as a separate and independent decision, we decide whether or not to do the assignment `staminaPoints = 0;`. This is illustrated in Figure 6.2.

We mean these two alternatives to be exclusive; that is, we intend to do one or the other of the assignments, but not both. Is it possible for both conditions to be *true*? The answer is yes, because they are evaluated at different times. Suppose `staminaPoints` is 75, and the method is called with an argument of 50. The first condition is *true*, and the assignment is done setting `staminaPoints` to 25. Now the second *if-then* is done, and since `staminaPoints` has been changed to 25, this condition is also *true*. `staminaPoints` is set to 0. Clearly this is not what we want to happen.

We could correct the problem by reversing the order of the *if-then* statements. A better approach is to use an *if-then-else* statement. The form is

```
if (condition)
    statement₁
else
    statement₂
```

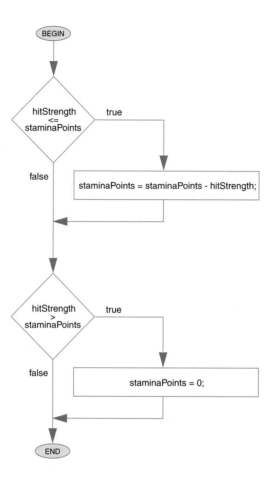

Figure 6.2 **Two consecutive *if-then* statements.**

This is also a composite statement, having two component statements. As with the *if-then*, the included statements can be any kind of statements at all.

If the condition is *true*, *statement₁* is executed; if the condition is *false*, *statement₂* is done. That is, we choose to do either *statement₁* or *statement₂*, but not both, depending on the condition. This is shown in Figure 6.3.

We can now implement the method using an *if-then-else*:

```
public void takeHit (int hitStrength) {
    if (hitStrength <= staminaPoints)
        staminaPoints = staminaPoints - hitStrength;
    else
        staminaPoints = 0;
}
```

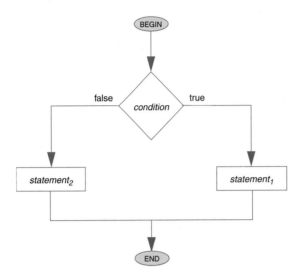

Figure 6.3 **An *if-then-else* statement.**

If the argument (hitStrength) provided by the client is 20, for instance, and the value of staminaPoints is 100, then hitStrength <= staminaPoints is *true*, and first assignment is done: staminaPoints is assigned 80. On the other hand, if hitStrength is 20 and StaminaPoints is 10, then

```
hitStrength <= staminaPoints
```

is *false*, and the "else" part is done: staminaPoints is assigned 0.

Finally, we must examine the constructor. Recall that an initial value is given to staminaPoints in the constructor:

```
public Explorer (String name, rooms.Room location,
                 int hitStrength, int stamina) {
    ...
    staminaPoints = stamina;
    ...
}
```

Suppose the constructor is called with a negative value for the parameter stamina. What should we do in this case? A reasonable approach seems to be to give the *Explorer* the lowest possible stamina value, namely 0. This will do for now. We write the following in the constructor:

```
public Explorer (String name, rooms.Room location,
                 int hitStrength, int stamina) {
    ...
```

```
    if (stamina >= 0)
        staminaPoints = stamina;
    else
        staminaPoints = 0;
    ...
}
```

These changes guarantee that the variable `staminaPoints` will never have a negative value, and thus the value returned by the query `stamina` will be greater than or equal to 0.

6.1.3 Compound statements

Before turning to the question of what conditions look like in general, let's see how we can combine a group of statements into one.

The *if-then* and *if-then-else* constructs allow only a single statement to be given as an option. The *if-then* has the form

```
if (condition)
    statement
```

and the *if-then-else* has the form

```
if (condition)
    statement₁
else
    statement₂
```

In each case, a single statement is to be done if the condition is *true*, and in the *if-then-else*, a single statement is to be done if the condition is *false*.

This seems a bit restrictive. Suppose the alternatives we want to choose from consist of several statements? For instance, suppose we wanted to set both `strengthPoints` and `staminaPoints` to 0 in the event that `takeHit` was called with an argument greater than `staminaPoints`. We could not simply write

```
if (hitStrength <= staminaPoints)
    staminaPoints = staminaPoints - hitStrength;
else
    staminaPoints = 0;
    strengthPoints = 0;
```

Despite the misleading indention, the "else" part of the conditional consists only of the single assignment

```
staminaPoints = 0;
```

The assignment to `strengthPoints` *follows* the conditional: it is an entirely different statement and will be done no matter what the value of the conditional. This is illustrated in Figure 6.4.

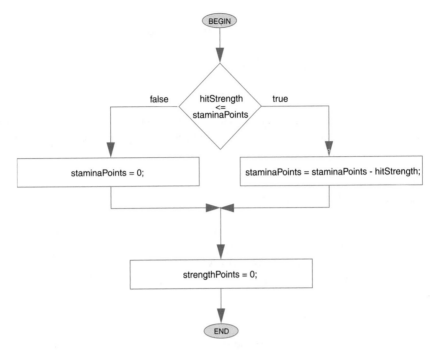

Figure 6.4 **The *else* part consists of a single statement.**

If we put a sequence of statements between a pair of braces:

$$\{ \ statement_1 \ \ statement_2 \ \ldots \ statement_N \ \}$$

the resulting construct is called a *block* or *compound statement*. The statements are simply done one after the other, in the order in which they are written. A compound statement is syntactically considered to be a *single composite statement*. The single statements specified as part of an *if-then* or *if-then-else* construct can be compound statements, as illustrated below:

```
if (condition) {                if (condition) {
    statement₁                      statement1₁
    ...                             ...
    statementN                      statement1N
}                               } else {
                                    statement2₁
                                    ...
                                    statement2M
                                }
```

Note the convention for placement of the braces.

We can now combine the two assignment statements from the preceding example into a single compound statement:

```
if (hitStrength <= staminaPoints)
    staminaPoints = staminaPoints - hitStrength;
else {
    staminaPoints = 0;
    strengthPoints = 0;
}
```

This is shown in Figure 6.5. We'll see many examples of these structures in subsequent chapters. But next we look at conditions in some detail.

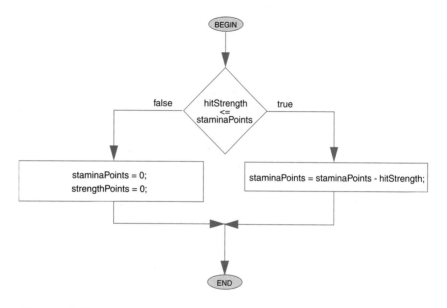

Figure 6.5 **The *else* part is a compound statement.**

6.2   Boolean expressions

A condition, as described above, is either *true* or *false*. You may recall that the type **boolean** introduced in Section 2.2 has two values, *true* and *false*. So when a condition is evaluated, a value of type **boolean** is the result. That is, a condition is a *boolean expression*. Boolean expressions are fundamentally similar to the arithmetic expressions seen in Section 5.2.2. Arithmetic expressions produce arithmetic values when evaluated, that is, values of type **int, double**, *etc*. Boolean expressions produce **boolean** values when evaluated.

6.2.1   Relational expressions

We've already seen several examples of the most common kind of boolean expression, a *relational expression*. A relational expression is composed of two arithmetic expressions joined with a relational or equality operator. These operators are:

    `<` less than
    `<=` less than or equal
    `>` greater than
    `>=` greater than or equal
    `==` equal
    `!=` not equal

For instance, if `i1`, `i2`, and `i3` are **int** variables with values 10, –20, and 30, respectively, then

`i1 < 12` ⟹ **true**		`i1 < 10` ⟹ **false**
`i1 <= 10` ⟹ **true**		`i2 > 0` ⟹ **false**
`i3 == i1` ⟹ **false**		`2*i1 == i2+40` ⟹ **true**
`i1 != 2` ⟹ **true**		`i2*(-1) != i1+i1` ⟹ **false**

Note that "equals" is denoted with the operator `==`. A single equal sign, of course, denotes assignment.

A few further observations. Suppose we wanted to express the condition that the value of `i1` was between 0 and 20. We might be tempted to write something like this:

```
0 < i1 < 20
```

The problem is that the relational operators are *binary* and *left associative*. The above line is equivalent to

```
(0 < i1) < 20
```

which would "evaluate" as

```
(0 < i1) < 20 ⟹ true < 20 ⟹ ???
```

This is not legal. The left operand is a **boolean** value, and the right operand is an **int**. It is not meaningful to compare a **boolean** value with an **int**: "**true** `< 20`" is not syntactically correct. The expression `0 < i1 < 20` does *not* say that `i1` is between 0 and 20. We'll see how to do this in just a bit.

Second, if one of the operands is an **int** and the other is a **double**, the **int** is converted to a **double** before the comparison is made. (This is similar to how arithmetic operators are handled.)

```
i1 < 2.5 ⟹ 10 < 2.5 ⟹ 10.0 < 2.5 ⟹ false
```

Finally, since floating point values are approximations for real numbers (Section 2.2), we must be vary careful comparing floating point numbers for equality or inequality. Values that are mathematically equal may not have identical floating point representations. The following expression, for example, evaluates to *false*:

```
(1.0/6.0+1.0/6.0+1.0/6.0+1.0/6.0+1.0/6.0+1.0/6.0) == 1.0
⇒ false (!)
```

In fact we rarely use the operators == and != with floating point values.

String equality

We've mentioned before that strings are objects, instances of the class *String*. Constructing two strings is likely to produce two different objects, even if the characters that comprise the strings are identical. For instance, if s1 and s2 are *String* variables, and we write

```
s1 = "ab" + "c";
s2 = "a" + "bc";
```

then s1 and s2 will reference two distinct objects. The expression

```
s1 == s2
```

asks if s1 and s2 reference *the same object*, and in this case returns *false*.

To compare strings for equality, we should use the *String* method equals, which returns a **boolean** result. The method invocation

```
s1.equals(s2)
```

return true if s1 and s2 are composed of the same sequence of characters.

We'll have much more to say about this topic in a later chapter.

6.2.2   Boolean variables and assignment

Just as we have **int** literals to denote particular values of type **int**, and **int** variables that contain values of type **int**, we also have **boolean** literals and variables. We have been introduced to the **boolean** literals in Section 3.3; they are **true** and **false** (lower case).

A **boolean** variable can be defined just like any other type of variable. For instance

```
private boolean tooBig;
```

The identifier `tooBig` denotes a portion of memory that holds a **boolean** value. An assignment statement can be used to store a **boolean** value in the variable. For example

```
tooBig = true;
```

or

```
tooBig = i1 > 10;
```

If `i1` is 10, `i1 > 10` is a **boolean** expression yielding *false* when evaluated. The assignment statement stores this value in the variable `tooBig`.

6.2.3   Boolean operators

There are two binary operators and a unary operator for building composite boolean expressions. The unary operator is written ! and read "not." The binary operators are && and ||, and usually read "and then" and "or else" respectively.[1]

```
! booleanExpression
booleanExpression && booleanExpression
booleanExpression || booleanExpression
```

The "not" operator evaluates to *true* if its operand is *false*, and *vice versa*. If, as above, `i1` is an **int** variable with value 10,

```
!(i1 > 9) ⇒ !(true) ⇒ false
!(i1 < 9) ⇒ !(false) ⇒ true
```

Since ! has high precedence (the same as unary + and -), the parentheses are needed in the above expressions. Without them, the expression would not parse correctly.

```
! i1 > 9 ⇒ (!i1) > 9
```

which is not legal.

Liberal use of the "not" operator can make a program difficult to read. For instance

```
i1 >= 9
```

is clearer than

```
!(i1 < 9)
```

A good general rule is to avoid the "not" operator whenever possible.

The "and then" operator evaluates to *true* only if both its operands are *true*; "or else" evaluates to *true* if either (or both) of its operands are *true*. This is usually expressed by a "truth table" as shown in Figure 6.6.

---

1. These operators are sometimes simply called "and" and "or."

b1	b2	b1 && b2	b1 || b2
true	true	true	true
true	false	false	true
false	true	false	true
false	false	false	false

Figure 6.6 **Truth table for the operators && and ||.**

Some examples, again assuming that i1 contains the value 10:

```
(i1 > 10) || (i1 == 10)  ⇒  false || true   ⇒  true
(i1 > 10) || (i1 < 0)    ⇒  false || false  ⇒  false
(i1 > 0) && (i1 < 5)     ⇒  true && false   ⇒  false
(i1 > 0) && (i1 < 20)    ⇒  true && true    ⇒  true
```

As the precedence of the operators && and || is lower than the relational and equality operators, the parentheses are not essential in the above examples. However parentheses usually enhance the readability of boolean expressions, and we often include them even though they are not absolutely essential. (Operator precedence is summarized in Figure 6.7.)

highest

+ (unary) – (unary) !
* / %
+ –
< <= > >=
== !=
&&
||

lowest

Figure 6.7 **Relative precedence of common operators.**

Using the "and then" operator, we can now express the condition that the value of i1 is between 0 and 20:

```
(0 < i1) && (i1 < 20)
```

The first operand is *false* if i1 is 0 or less, and the second is *false* if i1 is 20 or greater. Either situation makes the entire expression *false*. Put another way, mathematically *0 < i1 < 20* if and only if i1 makes both "0 < i1" and "i1 < 20" *true*.

"and-then" and "or-else" are lazy

The operators && and || are somewhat unique in that they evaluate their left operand first, and evaluate the right operand only if necessary. For instance, if i1 is 10, the following expressions are evaluated as shown:

```
(i1 < 10) && (i1 > 0)    ⇒ false && (i1 > 0) ⇒ false
(i1 < 11) || (i1 > 100)  ⇒ true || (i1 > 100)⇒ true
```

The right operands, (i1 > 0) in the first case and (i1 > 100) in the second, are not evaluated.

There might seem little point to this, but consider an example like

```
(x == 0) || (y/x < 10)
```

where x and y are **int** variables. If the left operand is *true*, that is, if x is 0, attempting to evaluate the right operand will result in an attempt to divide by 0 and a run-time error. The rules for evaluating the || operator will not evaluate (y/x < 10) if x is 0. The entire expression will evaluate to *true* without the division being attempted.

One can construct rather baroque expressions with boolean operators. Consider the following, which attempts to determine if the value of the **int** variable year is a leap year:

```
(year % 100 != 0 && year % 4 == 0) ||
(year % 100 == 0 && year % 400 == 0)
```

Such expressions quickly become unreadable. One can accomplish the same result with a more tractable series of steps, as we will see below. Even a relatively simple boolean expression can be misread if sufficient care is not taken. For instance, the expression

```
(i1 != 0) || (i1 != 1)
```

is always *true* no matter what the value of i1.

DeMorgan's laws

As we mentioned above, the use of "not" operator can make an expression particularly difficult to read. For instance, the expression

```
!(i1 > 5 && i1 < 8)
```

is *true* when i1 is less than or equal to 5, or when i1 is greater than or equal to 8. Two equivalences, known as DeMorgan's laws, can simplify such expressions. If b1 and b2 are arbitrary boolean expressions, then

```
!(b1 && b2) ≡ !b1 || !b2
!(b1 || b2) ≡ !b1 && !b2
```

Thus the above expression can be rewritten as

```
!(i1 > 5) || !(i1 < 8)
```

or

```
i1 <= 5 || i1 >= 8
```

6.3 Handling multiple cases

One way of thinking about a conditional statement is that it divides the problem into *cases* that can be considered independently. The *if-then-else* in the method `takeHit`, for instance, separates the problem into the case where

```
hitStrength <= staminaPoints
```
and the case where

```
hitStrength > staminaPoints.
```

takeHit:	

case: hitStrength <= staminaPoints
    staminaPoints = staminaPoints - hitStrength
	case: hitStrength > staminaPoints
	    staminaPoints = 0

In many problems, there are more than two cases, or the cases need to be further divided into subcases. These situations can be handled by nesting conditional statements. That is, the component statements of an *if-then* or *if-then-else* can themselves be conditional statements.

Suppose we are implementing the class *Date*, suggested in Section 2.3. Instances of the class represent calendar dates, and have properties *year*, *month*, and *day*. We would like to implement a query that will tell whether the date occurs in a leap year or not. That is, we want to implement a method specified as

public boolean isLeapYear ()
This *Date* occurs in a leap year.

We can assume the Gregorian calendar rule, which stipulates that a year is a leap year if it is divisible by 4, unless it is also divisible by 100, in which case it is a leap year if and only if it is divisible by 400. For example, 1900 is not a leap year even though it is divisible by 4, but 2000 is a leap year.

Suppose further that the instance variable `year` contains the *year* attribute of the *Date*:

private int year; // the year

Now if we consider the rule given above, it should occur to us to divide the problem into the case where the year is divisible by 4, and the case where it is not:

isLeapYear:	
case: year divisible by 4 ???	case: year not divisible by 4 not a leap year

The "year divisible by 4" case needs to be further divided into subcases depending on whether or not the year is divisible by 100:

isLeapYear:		
case: year divisible by 4		case: year not divisible by 4 not a leap year
case: year divisible by 100 ???	case: year not divisible by 100 a leap year	

We could further subdivide the "year divisible by 100" case, but at this point we'd rather just write the method. We use a local **boolean** variable to store the value we want to return. Note how the subcases are handled by nested conditionals. That is, one of the statements that comprise the outer *if-then-else* is itself an *if-then-else*. This is fine. An *if-then-else* is a kind of statement. The syntactic structure of this method is shown in Figure 6.8:

```
/**
 * This Date occurs in a leap year.
 */
public boolean isLeapYear () {
   boolean aLeapYear;
   if (year % 4 == 0)
      if (year % 100 == 0)
         // if divisible by 100,
         // must also be divisible by 400
         aLeapYear = (year % 400 == 0);
      else
         aLeapYear = true;
   else
      aLeapYear = false;
   return aLeapYear;
}
```

Sometimes a problem naturally splits into more than two equivalent cases. For example, suppose we are building a class to model a traffic signal. Assume the signal cycles from *left-turn-arrow* to *green* to *yellow* to *red*, and that we have named integer constants LEFT, GO, CAUTION, and STOP representing these states. We want to write a method advance that cycles the signal to the next state:

```
public void advance ()
```
           Advance this *Signal* to the next state.

where the signal state is maintained in the instance variable `currentState`:

`private int` `currentState;// the signal state`

There are clearly four cases, depending on the current state of the signal:

advance:			

case: LEFT
    change to GO
	case: GO
	    change to CAUTION
		case: CAUTION
		    change to STOP
			case: STOP
			    change to LEFT

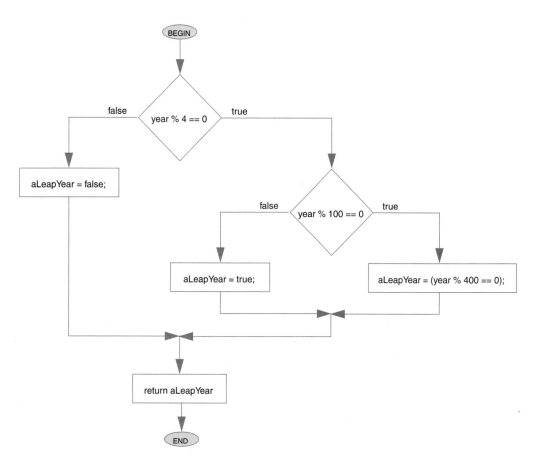

Figure 6.8 **Nested *if-then-else* statements in the method *isLeapYear*.**

One way to handle multiple cases is to "cascade" *if-then-else* statements; that is, write a sequence of nested *if-then-else* statements in which a single case is handled in the "true" branch, and the "false" branch consists of another *if-then-else*:

```
if (case1)
    handleCase1
```

```
else if (case2)
    handleCase2
...
else if (penultimateCase)
    handllePenultimateCase
else
    handleLastCase
```

Even though we think of them as alternatives at the same level, the structure is actually a collection of nested conditionals. We illustrate with the implementation of advance, as shown in Figure 6.9:

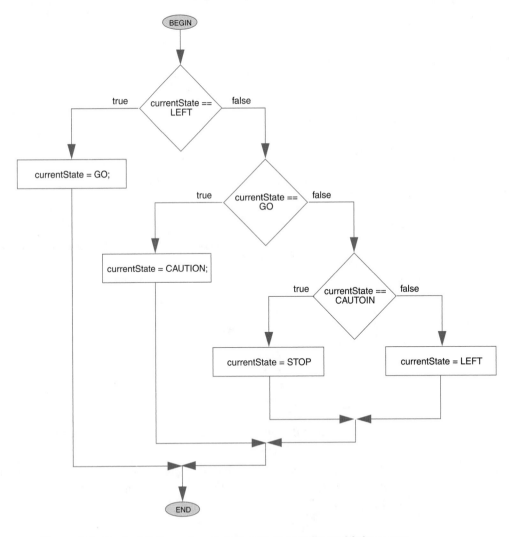

Figure 6.9 **Nested *if-then-else* statements to handle multiple cases.**

```
public void advance () {
    if (currentState == LEFT)
        currentState = GO;
    else if (currentState == GO)
        currentState = CAUTION;
    else if (currentState == CAUTION)
        currentState = STOP;
    else // currentState == STOP
        currentState = LEFT;
}
```

6.3.1 Dangling *else*

Before moving to some further examples, we should mention one additional point for completeness. If we have the following:

```
if (condition1)
    if (condition2)
        statement1
else
    statement2
```

the question arises as to whether we have an *if-then* nested in an *if-then-else*, or an *if-then-else* nested in an *if-then*. That is, which of the following two possible structures do we get?

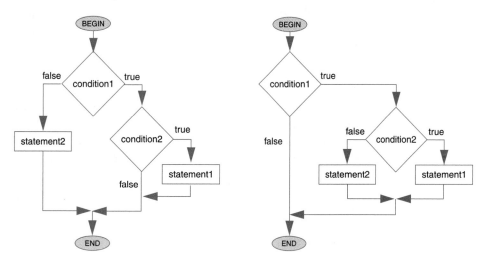

The answer is that an *else* clause is associated with the closest possible *if*. Thus, the figure on the right is correct. If we want an *if-then* nested in an *if-then-else*, *i.e.*, the figure on the left, we must make the *if-then* a compound statement by wrapping braces around it:

```
if (condition1) {
    if (condition2)
        statement1
} else
    statement2
```

6.4 Example: a combination lock

We develop another complete example to get a bit more experience with conditionals. In this example, we model a simple lock with an integer combination. The combination is set into the lock when it is created. To open a closed lock, the client must provide the correct combination.

A lock must know its combination and whether it is locked or unlocked. It must be able to lock and to unlock when provided with the proper combination. Thus the responsibilities of a lock can be summarized as follows.

Combination Lock responsibilities:

Know:
> the combination
> whether open or closed (*i.e.*, unlocked or locked)

Do:
> close (lock)
> open (unlock), when given the proper combination

While the lock must know its combination, this will certainly not be a feature available to clients. (If a client can query a lock for its combination, it is not a very secure lock!) A lock will have only one query, to determine whether it is open or closed. It will have two commands, one to close the lock and one to open it.

Class: *Combination Lock*

Queries:

is open	whether or not the lock is open

Commands:

close	lock the lock
open	unlock the lock (*combination*)

We can write the class specification in Java as follows.

Class CombinationLock

public class CombinationLock
    A lock with an integer combination.

Constructors:

public CombinationLock (**int** combination)
    Create a lock with the specified combination.

Queries:

public boolean isOpen ()
    This lock is unlocked.

Commands:

public void close ()
    Lock this lock.

public void open (**int** combination)
    Unlock this lock; the correct combination must be provided.

Note that the query returns a value of type **boolean**; that is, it returns either *true* or *false*. It is common to name a **boolean** valued query with an adjectival predicate. The name of the query and the doc comment describe the "true" condition, or what it means for the query to return *true*.

Next we consider the implementation. What data should the object contain? We've seen that the lock is responsible for knowing its combination and whether it is open or closed. We create instance variables to store these pieces of information representing properties of the lock:

```
private int combination;  // combination open the lock
private boolean open;      // the lock is unlocked
```

Note that again there is data stored in the object—information known by the object—that is not available to the client. A client cannot query a lock for its combination. A client can only determine whether the lock is open or closed.

open is a **boolean** variable. It contains either the value *true* or the value *false*. We have used the same identifier to name both the variable and query. This causes no problems, since the compiler can determine which we are referring to from the context.

The implementations of the isOpen query and of the close command are straightforward:

```
public boolean isOpen () {
    return open;
}
```

```
public void close () {
    open = false;
}
```

Occurrences of the identifier open in the return and assignment statements refer to the instance variable.

The constructor should set the value of the instance variables combination and open. The combination is provided as an argument, and we'll create locks that are initially unlocked. But we have a slight problem when we try to write the constructor. As specified on page 153, the name of the parameter (and hence of the automatic variable containing the argument value) is the same as the name of the instance variable of the object. This is shown in Figure 6.10.

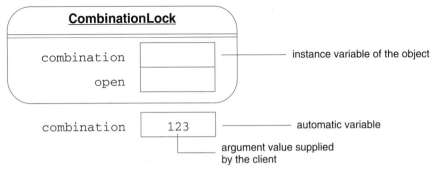

Figure 6.10   A *CombinationLock* being constructed.

When the constructor is being executed, there are two distinct variables with the same name. In the *body of the constructor*, any use of the identifier combination refers to *parameter*, not the lock's instance variable. That is, it refers to the automatic variable containing the argument. For instance, if we wrote

```
public CombinationLock (int combination) {
    combination = 0;
    ...
}
```

the value 0 would be stored in the automatic variable, replacing the argument provided by the client. The instance variable named combination, on the other hand, would be unaffected.

How do we distinguish between the instance variable and the parameter, when both variables have the same name? The keyword **this** refers to the "current" object. In the body of the constructor, **this** refers to the object being constructed. In the body of a method (query or command), it refers to the object performing the query or command. So writing

```
this.combination
```

in the body of the constructor, denotes the instance variable of the newly constructed object, while use of the identifier combination without a prefix refers to
the parameter.

We can write the constructor as follows:

```
public CombinationLock (int combination) {
    this.combination = combination;
    open = false;
}
```

In the first assignment statement above, the identifier combination appearing on
the right refers to the automatic parameter variable containing the argument, while
this.combination refers to the instance variable of the object.

(We could also write the second assignment statement

```
this.open = false;
```

and some programmers would do this just for symmetry of appearance.)

Finally, we must implement the method open. Again, the name of the parameter is the same as the instance variable, and we use the keyword **this** to refer to
the object that is performing the command.

We might be inclined to write something like this:

```
public void open (int combination) {
    open = this.combination == combination;
}
```

The expression on the right of the assignment is a **boolean** expression:

```
this.combination == combination
```

It will be *true* if the value of the instance variable (**this**.combination) is equal
to the argument provided by the client, and *false* otherwise. The variable on the
left, open, is a **boolean** variable. Thus the format of the assignment is correct.
The value *true* will be stored in open if the combination provide by the client is
correct, and the value *false* will be stored if it is not.

But this implementation is not correct, as can be seen by considering what
happens if a client attempts to open an unlocked lock. Giving the command open
to an unlocked lock should have no effect: the lock should remain open. But consider the case illustrated in Figure 6.11, where the client provides an incorrect
combination to an already open lock.

The expression

```
this.combination == combination
```

compares 222 to 123 and evaluates to *false*. This value is then assigned to the
instance variable open, effectively closing the lock.

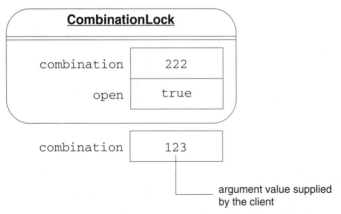

Figure 6.11 ***CombinationLock*** **when the method** *open* **is being executed.**

The correct implementation of the method uses a conditional statement, and avoids the problem of closing an unlocked lock:

```
public void open (int combination) {
    if (this.combination == combination)
        open = true;
}
```

A digit-by-digit lock

Let's refine our model a bit and construct a lock in which the combination is entered one digit at a time. To be specific, we'll assume our lock has a three-digit combination. To open the lock, the client provides digits one at a time. If the client enters the three digits of the combination in order, the lock opens.

There are actually quite a few possible sequences of operations that can happen here, and we need a bit of analysis to make sure we understand the problem. (Analysis of the problem preceding system design is a typical step in the development process, as we will see later.)

To begin with, it doesn't matter how many digits the client provides, as long as the combination is given. For instance, if the combination is 123, we might observe the following:

Digit Entered	Lock Status
4	closed
1	closed
2	closed
4	closed
3	closed
1	closed
2	closed
3	open

Once the lock is open, entering additional digits doesn't close it:

Digit Entered	Lock Status
1	closed
2	closed
3	open
4	open
7	open

What happens if the client gives the command close when the combination has been partly entered, and does it matter if the lock is open or closed at the time?

Client Command	Lock Status
enter 1	closed
enter 2	closed
close	closed
enter 3	?

Client Command	Lock Status
enter 1	open
enter 2	open
close	closed
enter 3	?

We will specify that the command close resets the lock, so that the entire combination must be entered after close. In particular, the lock will not open after the digit 3 is entered in either of the above two cases.

And a final note. If the combination is partly entered correctly, and an incorrect digit is entered, we may or may not have to start over, depending on the combination. For instance, if the combination is 123 and the digits 1-2-2 are entered, we need three digits to open the lock:

Digit Entered	Lock Status	
1	closed	(need 2-3 to open)
2	closed	(need 3 to open)
2	closed	(need 1-2-3 to open)

On the other hand, if the combination is 223 and the digits 2-2-2 are entered, a 3 will still open the lock:

Digit Entered	Lock Status	
2	closed	(need 2-3 to open)
2	closed	(need 3 to open)
2	closed	(still need 3 to open)

Even after entering the third 2, the last two digits entered are still the first two digits of the combination.

We should have a fairly good idea of how the object works now and be able to write the specification. As before, the combination is set when the lock is created, and the only query is to determine whether the lock is open or closed. There will be a command to close the lock, but rather than an open command like we had above, there will be a command to enter a single digit. That is, we expect the lock to be able to accept the combination one digit at a time.

Class CombinationLock

public class CombinationLock
    A lock with a three digit combination.

Constructors:

public CombinationLock (**int** combination)
    Create a lock with a given three digit combination;
    combination values < 100 are assumed to have leading zeros.

    require:
        combination >= 0 && combination <= 999

Queries:

public boolean isOpen ()
    This lock is unlocked.

Commands:

public void close ()
    Lock and reset this lock; partially entered combination is lost.

public void enter (**int** digit)
    Enter a digit of the combination; lock unlocks if the three digits of the
    combination are entered in order.

    require:
        digit >= 0 && digit <= 9

We have introduced a new notation, the "require" clause, in the specification. For instance

    require:
        digit >= 0 && digit <= 9

This is called a *precondition*. It is a requirement placed on the *client*. That is, the client must make sure that the condition is satisfied when the method is invoked.

> **precondition:** a condition the client of a method must make sure holds when the method is invoked.

For the constructor, the precondition requires the client to provide a nonnegative integer less than 1000 as argument:

require:
```
combination >= 0 && combination <= 999
```
(Values less than 100 are treated as having leading zeroes.)

For the method `enter`, the precondition requires that the client provide an integer between 0 and 9; that is, a single-digit number.

For the time being, we'll ignore the question of what happens if a client violates a precondition. But note that this is a condition placed on an *object invoking a method*. It has nothing to do with a user entering data from the console, for instance. We are saying that it is the responsibility of the client object to provide an argument value that satisfied the precondition.

Before we proceed with the implementation, let's carefully specify the lock's responsibilities. What does the object need to know? As before, it needs to know the combination and whether it is open or closed. But it also needs to remember how much of the combination has been successfully entered. That is, if the combination is 456, and the digit 4 is entered, the lock must remember that the first combination digit has been entered and that it should open if the second and third are entered next. If the digit 5 is then entered, it must remember that the first two digits of the combination have been successfully entered, and it should open if the third is entered next. There are any number of ways to accomplish this. Probably the most straightforward is for the lock to remember the three digits last entered. If these match the combination, the lock opens. We summarize:

Combination Lock responsibilities:

Know:
>   the three-digit combination
>   whether open or closed; *i.e.*, unlocked or locked
>   the last three digits entered

Do:
>   close (lock)
>   open (unlock), when given the proper combination
>   accept a digit

We are now ready to develop the implementation. We keep the information as to whether the lock is open or not with a **boolean** instance variable, as before.

But rather than keeping the combination as a single integer, we keep the three digits separately. Thus a lock instance will have the following instance variables.

```
private int comb1;      // 1st combination digit
private int comb2;      // 2nd combination digit
private int comb3;      // 3rd combination digit
                        // invariant:
                        // comb1 >= 0 && comb1 <= 9 &&
                        // comb2 >= 0 && comb2 <= 9 &&
                        // comb3 >= 0 && comb3 <= 9
private boolean open;   // the lock is unlocked
```

We also store the last three digits entered as separate integers. The value –1
will serve to indicate that a particular digit has not been entered, since this value
cannot be a legally entered digit.

```
// entered1, entered2, entered3 are the last three
// digits entered, with entered3 the most recent.
// a value of -1 indicates the digit has not been
// entered.
private int entered1;
private int entered2;
private int entered3;
            // invariant:
            // entered1 >= -1 && entered1 <= 9 &&
            // entered2 >= -1 && entered2 <= 9 &&
            // entered3 >= -1 && entered3 <= 9
```

If the combination is 223, and the digits 2-2 have been entered to a closed
lock, the object will look as shown in Figure 6.12.

CombinationLock	
comb1	2
comb2	2
comb3	3
open	false
entered1	-1
entered2	2
entered3	2

Figure 6.12 **Almost open** *CombinationLock.*

Now let's implement the methods. We start with the constructor. The first question is how do we separate an integer value into its constituent digits? That is, if the client provides the integer 123 as argument, how do we get the 1, 2, and 3 to store into the instance variables? If we look at the operations available for integer values described in Section 5.2.2, integer quotient (/) and remainder (%) look promising. The integer quotient of 123 divided by 10 is 12; the remainder is 3.

$$123 \ / \ 10 \quad \Rightarrow \quad 12 \qquad\qquad 123 \ \% \ 10 \ \Rightarrow \ 3$$

These are exactly the operations we need to separate the number into its component digits:

```
public CombinationLock (int combination) {
    comb3 = combination % 10;
    combination = combination / 10;
    comb2 = combination % 10;
    comb1 = combination / 10;
    open = true;
    entered1 = -1;
    entered2 = -1;
    entered3 = -1
}
```

If the argument is 123, then
    the first assignment assigns 3 to `comb3`;
    the second assignment assigns 12 to `combination`;
    the third assignment assigns 2 to `comb2`;
    the fourth assignment assigns 1 to `comb1`.
The query is the same as before.

```
public boolean isOpen () {
    return open;
}
```

The command `close` has a little more work to do, since it also resets the lock.

```
public void close () {
    open = false;
    entered1 = -1;
    entered2 = -1;
    entered3 = -1;
}
```

Finally, we must implement the command `enter`. This method must set the variables `entered1`, `entered2`, `entered3`, and `open`. The digit being entered becomes the most recent digit entered (`entered3`); the previous most recent becomes the second to last, and so on. Finally, if the three digits match the combination, the lock opens. Note that the first three assignment statements cannot be written in a different order.

```
    public void enter (int digit) {
        entered1 = entered2;
        entered2 = entered3;
        entered3 = digit;
        if (entered1 == comb1 && entered2 == comb2 &&
                entered3 == comb3)
            open = true;
    }
```

The complete class definition is given in Listing 6.1.

Listing 6.1   **The class *CombinationLock***

===

```
/**
 * A lock with a three digit combination.
 */
public class CombinationLock {

    // Constructors:

    /**
     * Create a lock with the given three digit
     * combination; combination values < 100 are assumed
     * to have leading zeros.
     *     require:
     *         combination >= 0 && combination <= 999
     */
    public CombinationLock (int combination) {
        comb3 = combination % 10;
        combination = combination / 10;
        comb2 = combination % 10;
        combination = combination / 10;
        comb1 = combination % 10;
        open = true;
        entered1 = -1;
        entered2 = -1;
        entered3 = -1;
    }

    // Queries:

    /**
     * This lock is unlocked.
     */
    public boolean isOpen () {
        return open;
    }
```

continued

Listing 6.1 **The class *CombinationLock (continued)***

```
// Commands:

/**
 * Lock and reset this lock; partially entered
 * combination is lost.
 */
public void close () {
    open = false;
    entered1 = -1;
    entered2 = -1;
    entered3 = -1;
}

/**
 * Enter a digit of the combination; lock unlocks if
 * the three digits of the combination are entered in
 * order.
 *     require:
 *         digit >= 0 && digit <= 9
 */
public void enter (int digit) {
    entered1 = entered2;
    entered2 = entered3;
    entered3 = digit;
    if (entered1 == comb1 && entered2 == comb2 &&
            entered3 == comb3)
        open = true;
}

// Private Components:

private int comb1;      // 1st combination digit
private int comb2;      // 2nd combination digit
private int comb3;      // 3rd combination digit
                // invariant:
                // comb1 >= 0 && comb1 <= 9 &&
                // comb2 >= 0 && comb2 <= 9 &&
                // comb3 >= 0 && comb3 <= 9
private boolean open;   // the lock is unlocked
```

continued

Listing 6.1   **The class *CombinationLock (continued)***

```
// entered1, entered2, entered3 are the last three
// digits entered, with entered3 the most recent.
// a value of -1 indicates the digit has not been
// entered.
private int entered1;      // the third to last digit
                           // entered

private int entered2;      // the second to last digit
                           // entered
private int entered3;      // the most recent digit
                           // entered
              // invariant:
              // entered1 >= -1 && entered1 <= 9 &&
              // entered2 >= -1 && entered2 <= 9 &&
              // entered3 >= -1 && entered3 <= 9

} // end of class CombinationLock
```

6.5 Summary

We've introduced here boolean expressions and conditional statements. Conditional statements allow us to specify alternative computations and the circumstances under which each is to be performed. The particular action to be done is determined by the processor at execution time, depending on the current data values. It is the conditional statement, and iteration to be introduced later, that enable us to describe a set of computations with a single algorithm as described in Section 1.2.2.

The two forms of conditional statement we've seen are *if-then* and *if-then-else*.

- With an *if-then*, we specify an action that is to be performed only if a given condition is true, that is, a guarded action:

    ```
    if (condition)
        statement
    ```

- With an *if-then-else*, we specify two possible actions, one of which will be done:

    ```
    if (condition)
        statement₁
    else
        statement₂
    ```

Since the syntax of the Java language permits only a single statement as a conditional alternative, we need a way to package a number of statements into one. This is the compound statement. By putting braces around a sequence of statements, we form a single compound statement:

{ *statement₁ statement₂ … statementₙ* }

The condition that is a constituent of a conditional statement is syntactically a boolean expression: an expression that evaluates to a **boolean** value, *true* or *false*.

We also introduced preconditions, postconditions, and invariants. These are not formally part of the Java language but are important in the specification and correctness verification of our designs. Since they are not part of the language *per se*, we include them in comments.

The client of a method is responsible for making sure that all preconditions of the method are satisfied before invoking the method. The method will only work correctly if preconditions are satisfied. Preconditions are documented in a require clause of the method specification.

The implementor of a method is responsible for making sure that all postconditions of the method are satisfied when the method completes. Postconditions are documented in an "ensure clause" of the method specification.

Invariants are conditions that always hold. In particular, class invariants are conditions that are always true of all instances of a class. A class instance is a consistent and coherent model of whatever entity the class represents if the class invariants hold.

EXERCISES

6.1   Given that x, y, and z are **int** variables containing the values 4, 6, and 8, respectively, evaluate each of the following boolean expressions.

(a) x < 4	*(b)* x <= 4
(c) x > 4 || y == 6	*(d)* x > 4 && y == 6
(e) !(x > 4)	*(f)* x != 4 || x != 5
(g) x + 2 != y	*(h)* x == 8 || y == 8 || z == 8

(i) (y < z && y < x) \|\| y >= x
(j) x != 4 && z/(x-4) == 1
(k) z/(x-4) == 1 && x != 4

6.2   Given that i and j are **int** variables. Simplify each of the following.

(a) !(i < 10 && j > 0)	*(b)* !(i < 10 || j > 0)
(c) !(i < 10 && j = 0)	*(d)* !(i <= 10 && i > 0)

(e) !((i <= 10 && i > 0) \|\| j > 0)
(f) !(i != 0 \|\| j != 0)

6.3   For which values of the **int** variable i is the expression

```
(i != 1 || i != 0)
```

true? Compute the negation of this expression, and check against the negation of your original answer.

6.4   Given that x, y, and z are **int** variables, write expressions to accomplish the following.

    a. Determine if x is greater than y.

    b. Determine if x is greater than both y and z.

    c. Determine if x is greater than either y or z.

    d. Determine if x equal to the product of y and z.

    e. Determine if x ends in 0: *i.e.*, if x is divisible by 10.

    f. Determine if x is even.

    g. Determine if x is between y and z, inclusive, where y is known to be less than z.

6.5   On page 143, the observation is made that the operators == and != are rarely used to compare floating point values. How might you compare floating point values for equality?

6.6   Suppose that x and max are **int** variables, and done a **boolean** variable.

    a. Write a statement that will increment x by 1 only if done is *false*.

    b. Write a statement that will increment x by 1 only if x is less than max.

6.7   Given that x, y, and z are **int** variables, write statements to accomplish the following.

    a. Assign to z the larger of x and y.

    b. Assign to x the absolute value of x.

    c. Assign to z the largest of x, y, and z.

6.8   Suppose that value, max, and min are **int** variables. The following code fragment should set value to min if it is smaller than min, and to max if it is larger than max. It is not correctly written. Add braces to make the code correct.

```
if (value >= min)
    if (value > max)
        value = max;
else
    value = min;
```

6.9   Assume that x is an **int** variable. For each of the following code fragments, state which initial values of x will result in x being incremented by 4.

    a. if (x == 1)

```
          x = x + 1;
      else if (x == 2)
          x = x + 2;
      else if (x == 3)
          x = x + 3;
      else
          x = x + 4;
 b. if (x == 1)
          x = x +1;
      if (x == 2)
          x = x + 2;
      if (x == 4)
          x = x + 4;
```

6.10   Consider the class *Student* specified in Chapter 4. Assume that fees are assessed as follows:

0 – 3 credit hours:	$500
4 – 6 credit hours:	$750
7 – 9 credit hours:	$1000
10 or more credit hours:	$1250

Based on this, write a definition of the method `fees`.

6.11   Suppose a class *Employee* contains the following instance variables:

```
private int hours;      // hours worked in the week
private double rate;    // hourly pay rate (dollars)
```

Write a definition of a method `pay` that returns the *Employee*'s pay for the week, where the *Employee* is paid the hourly rate for the first 40 hours worked, and paid time and a half for overtime.

6.12   Rewrite the class modeling a three-digit combination lock. Rather than having the lock explicitly remember the last three digits entered, make the lock remember if the last digit entered was the first digit of the combination, and if the last two digits entered were the first two digits of the combination. That is, replace the instance variables `entered1`, `entered2`, and `entered3` with these:

```
private boolean haveFirst;
    // the last digit entered was comb1
private boolean haveSecond;
    // the last two digits entered were comb1 and comb2
```

GLOSSARY

block: a compound statement.

boolean expression: an expression that yields a value of type **boolean** (*i.e.*, *true* or *false*) when evaluated.

boolean operator: a unary or binary operator that requires **boolean** operands and evaluates to a `boolean` value.

class invariant: an invariant regarding properties of class instances: that is, a condition that will always be true for all instances of a class.

compound statement: a sequence of statements grouped syntactically to form a single statement. The constituent statements are executed in the order in which they are written.

condition: a boolean expression.

conditional statement: a composite statement that describes a number of alternative processor actions. The action performed by the processor depends on the value of a boolean expression (a condition) included as part of the statement. (See *if-then* and *if-then-else* statements.)

guard: a boolean expression associated with an statement, that prevents or allows the statement to be executed. A guarded statement will be executed only if its guard evaluates to *true*. (See *if-then* statement.)

if-then statement: a conditional statement that specifies an action that is to be performed only if a stipulated condition is true.

if-then-else statement: a conditional statement that specifies two alternative actions, one to be performed if a stipulated condition is true, the other if the condition is false.

invariant: a condition that always holds.

postcondition: a condition the implementor of a method guarantees will hold when the method completes execution.

precondition: a condition the client of a method must make sure holds when the method is invoked.

relational expression: an expression composed of two arithmetic expressions joined with a relational or equality operator.

CHAPTER 7

Programming by contract

We've now seen boolean expressions and conditional statements in some detail. Conditional statements allow us to define a number of alternative courses of action. The specific action taken depends on the run-time value of the condition. The same conditional statement might result in different actions being performed at different times in the computation, since the condition can be true at some times, false at others.

We've also introduced the notions of precondition, postcondition, and invariant. These are all conditions, assertions that can be true or false. Preconditions, postconditions, and invariants are not formally part of the Java language. They are not constructs recognized by the compiler or understood by the interpreter. However, they play an important role in the design, specification, and verification of systems. We include them in comments, and they directly influence the implementations we develop.

Since they are not part of Java *per se*, the language syntax does not delimit how we express preconditions, postconditions, and invariants. We have considerable flexibility in specifying these conditions, and can be quite informal if we want. On the other hand, we do not have the compiler and interpreter making sure that what we write is not utter nonsense. We adopt a consistent notational convention when writing these conditions, and use the Java syntax for boolean expressions wherever practical.

In this chapter we elaborate the ideas of precondition and postcondition, and introduce a programming style called *programming by contract*. The point of programming by contract is to clearly delineate in a method's specification the respective responsibilities of client and server. Preconditions and postconditions play a key role in defining these responsibilities.

7.1   Programming by contract

Let's return to an issue raised in the previous chapter: the range of possible values that might be returned from an *Explorer*'s `stamina` query. We have decided that this value has a lower bound of 0, and documented this fact in the specification of the method:

```
/**
 * Damage (hit points) required to defeat
 * this Explorer.
 *      ensure:
 *          stamina >= 0
 */
public int stamina () {
    ...
}
```

In order to guarantee this, we modified the constructor and the `takeHit` method so that they never assign a negative value to the instance variable `staminaPoints`, regardless of the arguments provided by the client. We need to look at these two cases a little more carefully.

In the case of `takeHit`, we protect against the client providing a hit strength that's greater than the current *stamina* of the *Explorer*:

```
public void takeHit (int hitStrength) {
    if (hitStrength <= staminaPoints)
        staminaPoints = staminaPoints - hitStrength;
    else
        staminaPoints = 0;
}
```

This does not at all seem unreasonable. We shouldn't expect a client to worry about the *stamina* of the *Explorer* when striking a blow. We didn't take the stamina of the monster into account, for instance, when we implemented the *Explorer*'s method `strike`:

```
public void strike (Denizens.Denizen monster) {
    monster.takeHit(strengthPoints);
}
```

In fact, no method is provided for obtaining the stamina of a *Denizen*.

In summary, we do not consider it an error for a client to call `takeHit` with an argument greater than `staminaPoints`. It is simply a possibility that the implementation of `takeHit` must account for.

On the other hand, a call to the constructor with a negative initial value for *stamina* seems quite different. This is something that should not happen. It is an error and the fault of the client who makes the call. We document our expectation that the client will provide a non-negative value when invoking the constructor as follows:

```
/**
 * Create a new Explorer.
 *     require:
 *         stamina >= 0
 */
public Explorer (String name, rooms.Room location,
                    int hitStrength, int stamina) {

    ...

}
```

We introduced this notation in the previous chapter. Recall that conditions labeled "require" are called *preconditions*. They are requirements placed on the *client*. We are stating that *client must make sure* that the argument provided (stamina) is nonnegative. Postconditions, labeled "ensure," are requirements on the implementor of the method. Preconditions and postconditions are part of a programming style called *programming by contract*. The basic idea is that use of an object feature (query or command) or constructor is considered to involve a "contract" between the client and server. For an invocation of a feature or constructor to be correct, the client must make sure that the preconditions are satisfied at the time of the call. If the preconditions are satisfied, then the server guarantees that the postconditions will be satisfied when the method completes (*i.e.*, upon "return"). If the preconditions are not satisfied, that is, if the client does not meet his end of the contract, then the server *promises nothing at all*.

---

programming by contract: a programming style in which the invocation of a method is viewed as a contract between client and server, with each having explicitly stated responsibilities.

The point of this approach is to delineate, clearly and explicitly, responsibilities between the client and the server, and ultimately between the user of a method and the implementor of the method. We want to make sure that any possible error that can arise at run time is detected. But we'd like to do as little explicit error checking as possible. Specifically, we'd like to test for every possible error condition only once. One reason is fairly obvious: program efficiency. However, there is a much more important reason for this approach. As we shall see, the most consequential impediment to writing correct, maintainable code is complexity. Adding error checking can make a simple straightforward algorithm unduly convoluted. An approach in which each routine validates all of its arguments—sometimes called *defensive programming*—can result in an excessively high degree of "code pollution." The trick is to maintain a balance between making a program reliable but not so convoluted as to be unmaintainable. Clearly there are many design trade-offs here, and we'll talk more about error handling in Chapter 18. But we'll use preconditions and postconditions to prescribe explicitly who—client or server—is responsible for what.

So we have placed a precondition, `stamina >= 0`, on the constructor. If the client invokes the constructor with a nonnegative `stamina` argument, we are committed to produce a new, well-formed *Explorer* object. If the client invokes the method with a negative argument, *we promise nothing at all*. This is important to realize. If the client does not adhere to his end of the contract, the implementation is not committed to any particular action. But of course *something* must happen. What we do depends to some degree on how much we trust our client. It may be that we are absolutely convinced that the constructor will never be called with a negative second argument—perhaps we're writing the client code ourselves—in which case we need do nothing. But systems change, and initial values are often computed in complex (and error-prone) ways. We can easily imagine, for instance, employing a nontrivial function that determines a random initial value for `stamina`.

The real problem with not verifying the value of the constructor argument is that we can end up violating the invariant condition on the component `staminaPoints`. That is, suppose we simply leave the constructor as we originally wrote it:

```
/**
 * Create a new Explorer.
 *     require:
 *         stamina >= 0
 */
public Explorer (String name, rooms.Room location,
                 int hitStrength, int stamina) {
   playerName = name;
   room = location;
   strengthPoints = hitStrength;
   staminaPoints = stamina;
}
```

If the client violates the precondition, there is no specific requirement on the constructor *with regard to the contract*. However, we have an *internal implementation requirement* in the form of the invariant condition on the component `staminaPoints`:

```
private int staminaPoints;// current stamina
                // invariant:
                        // staminaPoints >= 0
```

Executing the constructor with the precondition violated will result in an *Explorer* object being created that does not satisfy the invariant. For this reason, rather than for the requirements of the contract, the original implementation is not particularly satisfactory.

We can, of course, return to the implementation suggested in the previous chapter, in which the argument value provided for stamina is explicitly checked by the constructor:

```
public Explorer (String name, rooms.Room location,
                 int hitStrength, int stamina) {
    playerName = name;
    room = location;
    strengthPoints = hitStrength;
    if (stamina >= 0)
        staminaPoints = stamina;
    else
        staminaPoints = 0;
}
```

But this is not entirely satisfactory either, since it treats an error condition (violation of the precondition) as a normal, expected, occurrence, and introduces the explicit testing we're trying to avoid.

What would we like to happen if the client violates the precondition? Perhaps the most we could hope for is that the interpreter would recognize that the precondition was violated and generate an informative run-time error. Ideally, we'd like this to happen without having to write anything but the precondition. (Remember a major point of this approach is not to clutter our code with excessive error tests.) That is, we'd like the interpreter to check automatically that preconditions are satisfied whenever a method is invoked. If the preconditions are met, the method executes normally. Otherwise, the computation is interrupted and the user informed of the error condition. Error reporting of this kind is particularly useful while we're developing, testing, and debugging a system. When efficiency is a concern, we might like to tell the interpreter not to do these checks. That is, we want to be able to "turn off" run-time error checking in a mature system, in which we're convinced errors won't occur.

Such a facility is not a built-in part of Java. Any checking that is to be done must be explicitly coded as part of the method implementation. But we can come close to getting what we want by using a library class to do the error checking. We provide a package OOJ.utilities[1] that contains a class named *Require*. This is an unusual class in that it is not meant to be instantiated. No objects of class *Require* are ever created. Rather the class is used to group together a few useful utility methods. These methods are not features of any object but are part of the class itself. Such methods are called *class methods* and are indicated by the keyword **static**.

---

1. This is not a standard Java package but is included in the supporting material for the text. See the preface for details.

One class method included in the class *Require* is `condition`, specified as follows:

static public void condition (**boolean** precondition)

> Verify precondition: raise *RuntimeException OOJ.utiliites.Precondition*
> if `precondition` is *false*.

The keyword **static** indicates that this is a class method, rather than a method associated with an instance of the class. The method requires a single argument of type **boolean**. When the method is invoked, it evaluates its argument and raises an error condition—an *exception*—if the argument is not *true*. This will stop execution of the program and display some information about the cause of the exception to the user. We'll have a lot more to say about exceptions and error handling in general in a later chapter.

To use this method, we first import the package `OOJ.utilties`. That is, we include the following statement in our source file immediately after the **package** statement:

```
import OOJ.utilities.*;
```

This simply allows us to reference classes in the package `OOJ.utilties` without prefixing the package name to the class name. For instance, we can refer to the above mentioned class simply as "`Require`" rather than with its complete name, "`OOJ.utilities.Require`". (One should not be too liberal with the use of **import** statements. Only common, well-known packages should be imported in this way. Excessive use can make a source file unreadable, since they hide the location of a class definition.)

We invoke a class method by writing the class name followed by the method name:

```
Require.condition(stamina >= 0);
```

We can now write the body of the constructor, verifying both initial *stamina* and *strength* values:

```
public Explorer (String name, rooms.Room location,
                 int hitStrength, int stamina) {

    Require.condition(hitStrength >= 0);
    Require.condition(stamina >= 0);

    playerName = name;
    room = location;
    strengthPoints = hitStrength;
    staminaPoints = stamina;
}
```

When the constructor is invoked, it calls the *Require* method `condition` twice, first with `hitStrength >= 0` as argument, and then with `stamina >= 0` as argument. If either of these conditions is *false* (an error), the program is terminated. This might not be as clean as we would like, but at the least we have separated precondition verification from normal behavior of the constructor.

Finally, let's completely specify the behavior of the constructor with preconditions and postconditions. We can define the method like this:

```
/**
 * Create a new Explorer object
 *     require:
 *         hitStrength >= 0
 *         stamina >= 0
 *     ensure:
 *         this.name() == name
 *         this.location() == location
 *         this.strength() == hitStrength
 *         this.stamina() == stamina
 */
public Explorer (String name, rooms.Room location,
                 int hitStrength, int stamina) {
    ...
}
```

While the `ensure` clause may look a bit redundant, the intention is to describe precisely and concisely the relationship between the parameters of the constructor and the properties of the newly created object. The notation means that if the newly created object is queried with the method `name`, for instance, it will return the string provided as the first argument of the constructor. That is, in the condition

```
this.name() == name
```

`this.name()` refers to the value that the newly created object (`this`) will return when the method `name` is invoked. The identifier `name` on the right refers to the first parameter of the constructor.

We have now completely specified the behavior of the constructor for the client. But remember the format we use for writing preconditions and postconditions is a convention intended to convey information to the human reader; it is not part of the programming language. The client must make sure that the preconditions are satisfied *before* the method is invoked, in which case the implementor guarantees that the postconditions will be satisfied *upon completion* of the method.

Next let's take another look at the `takeHit` method, which we have specified as follows:

```
public void takeHit (int hitStrength)
```
    Receive a blow of the specified number of hit points.

We've decided that we won't require `hitStrength` be bounded by our *Explorer*'s current stamina. But we might want to put a lower limit of 0 on the value of this argument. (Unless we decide that some hits can *increase* our *Explorer*'s stamina: hits with a magic wand? hits with a cursed weapon?)

```
public void takeHit (int hitStrength) {
        Receive a blow of the specified number of hit points.
```

require:
```
    hitStrength >= 0
```

In this case, we really need take no specific action if the client violates the precondition. A negative `hitStrength` value won't cause us to destroy the integrity of our object by violating an invariant.

What kind of postcondition can we write to describe to the client the effect of the method? We want to indicate that the *Explorer*'s stamina will decrease: that the value returned by the query `stamina()` after execution of `takeHit` will be less than the value returned by this query before execution of `takeHit`. To do this, we must be able to refer to the state of the *Explorer* when the method is invoked as well as to the state of the *Explorer* when the method completes. (It is common for a command postcondition to describe the state of the object after the command is executed in terms of the object's state when the command is invoked.) When writing a postcondition, we use "`this`" to refer to the state of the object at the time the method completes, and "`old`" to refer to the state of the object *at the time the method is invoked*. The notation "`old`" is not a Java construct; it is a convention used in a comment specifying a precondition.

We might start by writing something like this:

ensure:
```
    this.stamina() == old.stamina() - hitStrength
```

As noted, `this.stamina()` refers to the *stamina* property of the object when the method completes, and `old.stamina()` refers to the *stamina* property when the method begins. What the condition says is that upon completion of the method, the value of the *stamina* will be the *stamina* value when the method is called minus the argument value.

But this postcondition is not correct: if `hitStrength` is greater than *stamina*, *stamina* will end up 0, and not `old.stamina - hitStrength`. We correct the problem by writing:

ensure:
```
    this.stamina() ==
    max (old.stamina() - hitStrength, 0)
```

This says the value of *stamina* upon method completion will be the larger of 0, and the starting *stamina* value minus the argument.

The postcondition is now correct but almost certainly too strong, since it promises the client exactly how the method is implemented. Suppose we decide later in the development that the *Explorer* should be able to do something to lessen the effect of a blow; put on armor, for instance. Not only would the postcondition need to be changed, but any client that invoked the method would need to be reexamined as well. A client's correctness depends on our promises. We don't want a client to depend on irrelevant implementation details.

The following would probably be an adequate postcondition:

ensure:
>   this.stamina() <= old.stamina()

It simply promises that the *Explorer*'s *stamina* after executing the method will be no greater than it was when the method was called.

The definition of `takeHit` can be written as follows:

```
/**
 * Receive a blow of the specified number of
 * hit points.
 *     require:
 *         hitStrength >= 0
 *     ensure:
 *         this.stamina() <= old.stamina()
 */
public void takeHit (int hitStrength) {
    ...
}
```

Note that if the method is invoked with a negative `hitStrength`, `stamina` is increased and the postconditions not satisfied. But if the client violates the preconditions, the sever is under no obligation to comply with the postconditions.

7.1.1 Using preconditions and postconditions

Preconditions

Preconditions must be satisfied by the client when invoking the method. Occasionally, preconditions constrain the order in which methods can be invoked or require that an object be in a certain state before a given method can be invoked. For instance, it might be necessary that a door be unlocked before it can be opened, or that an automobile be started before it can be moved. Most often, however, preconditions constrain values that the client can provide as arguments when invoking the method. This is the case in the `Explorer` constructor and `takeHit` command considered above. The precondition for `takeHit`, for example, requires that the client provide a nonnegative argument.

Query postconditions

When an object responds to a query, it does not change state. It simply provides a value to the client. Thus query postconditions inevitably say something about the value returned. We sometimes use the term "result" to refer to the value returned by the query. For instance, we might specify the *Counter* method `count` in either of the following ways:

> **public int** count ()
>> Current count; the number of items counted.
>
>> **ensure:**
>>> this.count() >= 0
>
> **public int** count ()
>> Current count; the number of items counted.
>
>> **ensure:**
>>> result >= 0

Command postconditions

Commands result in a change of state. Thus command postconditions typically describe the new state of the object, its state after execution of the command. The new state is often compared to the previous state, the state of the object when the command was invoked. For this reason, it is convenient to have a notational convention for referring to the state of the object when the command is invoked. We use "`old`" for this purpose, as illustrated above with the *Explorer* method `takeHit`.

Constructor postconditions

Not surprisingly, constructor postconditions typically describe the initial state of the newly created object. This is the case with the *Explorer* constructor given above.

Preconditions and postconditions are part of the specification

It is important to remember that preconditions and postconditions for public methods are part of an object's specification. As such, they should *never* mention private implementation components. The following specification of the *Counter* method `reset`, for instance, is incorrect. The *Counter* instance variable `tally` is part of the implementation: it is not part of the object's specification, and is meaningless to the client.

> **public void** `reset ()  {  …  }`
>> Reset the count to 0.
>>
>> **ensure:**
>
> ✗   `tally  ==  0`   *This is not correct!!*

Named constants

Named constants should be used in preconditions and postconditions rather than literals. For instance, if we consider the class *Card* introduced in Section 5.1.2, we can specify the constructor and the `suit` query as follows:

> **public** `Card (int rank, int suit)`
>> Create a new *Card* of the specified rank and suit.
>>
>> **require:**
>>> `(2 <= rank && rank <= 10) ||`
>>> `rank == Card.JACK   || rank == Card.QUEEN ||`
>>> `rank == Card.KING   || rank == Card.ACE;`
>>> `suit == Card.CLUB   || suit == Card.DIAMOND ||`
>>> `suit == Card.HEART  || suit == Card.SPADE.`

> **public int** `suit ()`
>> The suit of the *Card*.
>>
>> **ensure:**
>>> `result == Card.CLUB    ||`
>>> `result == Card.DIAMOND ||`
>>> `result == Card.HEART   ||`
>>> `result == Card.SPADE.`

Note that, in the query for instance, the server promises to deliver a meaningful result, but doesn't commit to any *specific* values.

7.2 Summary

In this chapter, we introduced a programming style called programming by contract. The basic idea is to make explicit the respective responsibilities of client and server in a method invocation. To this end, the invocation of a server method by a client is viewed as involving a contract between the client and the server. The server promises to perform the action specified by the method and to ensure that the method's postconditions are satisfied, but only if the client meets the preconditions. Preconditions are the client's responsibility; postconditions are the server's. If the client fails to meet the preconditions, the contract is void: the server is not obligated to behave in any specific way.

Using this approach, it is a programming error for a client to invoke a method without satisfying the method's preconditions. We see how to handle such cases in Chapter 18.

Conversely, if the client satisfies the preconditions, the server must accomplish the action as specified.

EXERCISES

7.1   Suppose that for the *Employee* method `pay` of exercise 6.11, `hours` and `rate` are parameters rather than instance variables. That is, suppose the method is specified as

```
public double pay (int hours, double rate)
```

Write a complete specification, including preconditions and postconditions, for this method.

7.2   Assume that the method `dayOfWeek` takes a day of the year and year as arguments, and returns the day of the week. That is, `dayOfWeek` is specified

```
public int dayOfWeek (int day, int year)
```

and `dayOfWeek(51,1999)` will tell us that the 51st day of 1999 was a Saturday.

Write a complete specification, including preconditions and postconditions, for this method.

7.3   Consider the class *JetCalibrator* partially given below. What this class does is not important.

```
1.    public class JetCalibrator {
2.        ...
3.        /**
4.         * ensure:
5.         *     -5 <= this.jetSetting() &&
6.         *     this.jetSetting() <= 5
7.         */
8.        public int jetSetting () {
9.            ...
10.       }
11.
12.       /**
13.        * require:
14.        *     -3 <= offSet && offSet <= +3
```

```
15.        */
16.        public void adjust (int offSet) {
17.              ...
18.        }
19.
20.        /**
21.         * ensure:
22.         *      this.jetSetting() >= 0
23.         */
24.        public void normalize () {
25.              ...
26.        }
27.        ...
28.        private int jet; // invariant:   -5 <= jet &&
29.                         //                      jet <= +5
30.    }
```

Which of the following statements are true?

a. Ensuring that the condition of line 14 holds is the responsibility of the client.

b. In a correct program, the method `adjust` will never be invoked with an argument of 4.

c. The implementation of the method `adjust` should check the value of `offSet` in case the user enters a value that is out of range.

d. The condition of line 22 implies that the server will never execute the method `normalize` when the property `jetSetting` is negative.

e. The condition of lines 28 and 29 implies that the value of the component variable `jet` will never be 6.

7.4 Let c, i, and j be variables defined as follows:

```
JetCalibrator c = new JetCalibrator (...);
int i;
int j;
```

where *JetCalibrator* is the class sketched in exercise 7.3. Which of the lettered statements are true after the following sequence is executed?

```
i = c.jetSetting();
c.normalize();
j = c.jetSetting();
```

a. i and j are guaranteed to have the same value.

b. i can be -5.

c. j can be -5.

7.5   Given the variable definitions of exercise 7.4, suppose the following statements are executed.

```
i = 4;
c.adjust(i);
j = c.jetSetting();
```

Which of the following are true?

a. j will be 4.

b. It is not possible to tell what will happen.

c. The program will crash.

7.6   Suppose we want to build a maze game in which *Denizens*, when hitting an *Explorer*, sometimes magically increase the *Explorer*'s stamina. We represent a magic stamina-giving hit by furnishing a negative argument to the `takeHit` method. Furthermore, we allow an *Explorer* to have deficit stamina, also represented by a negative value. An *Explorer* with deficit stamina can be revived only by a stamina-giving hit. Can we reuse the class *Explorer* as it exists in this new game? Explain your answer.

GLOSSARY

class method: a method that is a feature of a class itself, rather than of each class instance.

contract: part of a method specification that explicitly states the responsibility of the client and the responsibility of the server.

defensive programming: a programming style in which the server assumes responsibility to check the validity of any arguments provided by the client.

import statement: a statement that permits classes in a different package to be referenced without prefixing the class name with the full package name.

CHAPTER 8   Testing a class

The development of a class involves design, specification, implementation, and testing. The process is iterative in that any of these activities can disclose flaws requiring previous steps to be repeated. We have learned how to specify and implement a simple class. We now address the issue of testing. Testing is fundamental. It validates the implementation of the class, and ultimately the design and implementation of the entire system. But testing can be a difficult topic to get a handle on. While many guidelines have been developed, there are no hard and fast rules that tell us we have devised an adequate series of tests. Nevertheless, it is important to go about testing in a coherent, well-organized way. Every test we conduct should have a clear purpose.

In this chapter, we briefly discuss testing in general, then consider how to test a single class. Every class that we implement should be adequately tested before it is incorporated into a system. We introduce the idea of a test plan, a comprehensive blueprint for ensuring that a method satisfies its specification. Finally, we see how to build a test system, one that allows us to exercise an object to ensure that it behaves correctly.

8.1   Testing

Testing is an activity whose goal is to determine whether or not an implementation functions as intended: succinctly, to determine if the implementation is correct. The purpose of testing is to uncover errors in the implementation. Hence, a successful test is one that reveals some previously undiscovered error. Since it is impossible to exhaustively test any but the simplest system, testing can show that a system contains errors but can never guarantee that a system is completely correct.

Testing consists of two phases: first, test activities are determined and test data selected; and then the test is conducted and test results compared with expected results. Though a system cannot be tested with all possible data, testing needs to be in some sense comprehensive. Test activities and data must be judiciously chosen to thoroughly exercise the system. It is this process of determining test activities and selecting test data that we refer to as *test design*.

Test design generally begin with an analysis of

- the functional specifications of the system, and
- the ways in which the system will be used (referred to as "use cases").

Testing based on these considerations is referred to as *black box testing*. The test designer ignores the internal structure of the implementation in developing the test. The expected external behavior of the system drives the selection of test activities and data. The system is treated as a "black box" whose behavior can be observed, but whose internal structure cannot.

The test is decomposed into several test cases, each addressing a specific use or a specific functionality. A test case is defined by

- a statement of case objectives;
- the data set for the case;
- the expected results.

To help ensure that the test data selected is representative or complete, the set of possible data is partitioned into *equivalency groups*. Test cases are chosen from each equivalency group. The assumption is that if the system behaves correctly for one instance of an equivalency group, it will behave correctly for all instances. Particular attention is paid to data that lie on group boundaries; that is, data that are as close as possible to being in another group.

The result of the design effort is a *test plan*. A test plan is a document that describes the test cases giving the purpose of each case, the data values to be used, and the expected results. The test plan directs the conducting of the test.

Despite the fact that a component cannot be tested until it has been implemented, test design should be carried out concurrently with system development. As the development progresses form analysis and specification to design and implementation, additional cases are uncovered and added to the test plan. Developing and refining test cases based on the implementation of the system is referred to as *white box testing*. (Perhaps "translucent box testing" would be a better name.) For white box testing, knowledge of the implementation is used to select and refine test cases.

System testing is an extensively studied subject. Many strategies and methodologies have been proposed, and many different approaches are used in practice. Developing an adequate test plan for a large system is clearly a complicated, many-leveled business, well beyond the scope of this text. In this chapter, our attention is limited to testing the implementation of an individual class. When we implement a small component such as a class, we are often satisfied with a bit of *ad hoc* testing. But such indiscriminate, haphazard testing is likely to leave critical and problematic cases untested. It is essential that we carefully analyze the specification for the component we are building, and develop a plan that thoroughly tests our implementation. Such a plan need not be formal or elaborate. But careful specification-directed testing is critical at all stages of system development.

A test plan for a class can be based on the class specification only. That is, we can generate test cases based on method specifications, including preconditions and postconditions, without looking at how the methods are implemented. Since we are using the actual class specification rather than specifications of the original problem, this form of test design is sometimes referred to as *gray box testing*.

In the remainder of this chapter, we see how to implement a basic test system and develop a plan for testing for a simple class.

8.2   Testing a class implementation

After designing and implementing a class, we must test the class to determine that the implementation conforms to specifications. Specifically, we need to create an instance of the class and "exercise" it to see that it behaves as expected. Of course, we can't test an object in isolation. We need a test system, sometimes called a *test harness* or *test driver*, that will allow us to interact with the object we want to test. The test system will let us create the object to be tested and then act as a client of the object. Using the test system, we invoke the object's methods and see the resulting behavior of the object. We saw a very simple test system in Section 5.3.

To test one object, we often need others that the object to be tested uses. For example, if we want to test an *Explorer*, we need *Rooms* for the *Explorer* to move between and a *Denizen* for the *Explorer* to battle. To keep our example simple and avoid the need for additional objects, we again test a *Counter* similar to the one introduced in Section 4.2.1. The class is specified as follows:

public class Counter
  A simple integer counter.

public Counter ()
  Create a new *Counter* initialized to 0.

public int count ()
  The current count.

  ensure:
    this.count() >= 0

public void reset ()
  Reset this *Counter* to 0.

public void increment ()
  Increment the count by 1.

public void decrement ()
  Decrement the count by 1. If the count is 0, it is not decremented.

As we've said, a test system must allow us to create a *Counter* instance and invoke its methods in order to verify that it behaves correctly. The test system can be anything from a crude "throw-away," in which the test activities and test data are hard coded, to a sophisticated window-based tool capable of testing a wide range of different classes. We'll develop a straightforward line-oriented test system. Building the test system will afford us the opportunity of seeing a complete program without getting involved in complexities such as event-driven graphical user interfaces.

What we have in mind is a system that will create a *Counter* and provide the user with a choice of methods to invoke. Since a *Counter* has a very simple state and only one query, the test system will show the count after each command. For example, when the system is run, we might see the following dialogue, where the user's input is shown in bold:

```
Enter number denoting action to perform:
Increment..............1
Decrement..............2
Reset..................3
Create a new Counter...4
Exit...................5
Enter choice.
1
The current count is: 1
Enter number denoting action to perform:
Increment..............1
Decrement..............2
Reset..................3
Create a new Counter...4
Exit...................5
Enter choice.
1
The current count is: 2
        .
        .
        .
```

The user is presented with a menu enumerating possible actions. These include invoking commands for the *Counter* and creating a new *Counter* instance. After the selected command is executed, the state of the *Counter* is displayed (the value of count), and the user is again presented with the menu.

Now certainly this system is neither "industrial-strength" nor particularly user-friendly, but it is more than adequate for our purposes. We see how to build the system next.

8.3 Building a test system

The test system will be composed of two objects: a *Counter* to be tested, and a test driver to invoke the *Counter*'s methods. The main purpose of the test driver is to interact with the user. It prompts the user with a menu, gets input from the user (the user's choice of action), and provides output in the form of the count. The test driver provides a *user interface* for the system. In general, a user interface is built from collection of objects whose function is to interact with the user, collecting input or providing output. In our case, we need only a single object.

Implementing a successful user interface is no trivial task. We will have more to say on this topic in later chapters. Here we'll be content with a line-oriented, textual interface. We call the interface object a *CounterTUI*, for "textual user interface." The *CounterTUI* will read input from the user's keyboard, and write output to the user's display. It will be equipped with a *Counter* to exercise, as shown in Figure 8.1.

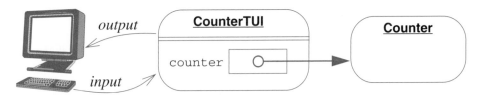

Figure 8.1 A *CounterTUI* provides a user interface for a *Counter*.

8.3.1 Basic input/output classes

Before we can implement the *CounterTUI*, we need some means of reading input and writing output. Although Java has extensive libraries for input and output, we want to keep things as simple as possible for now. Examining Java's comprehensive facilities would take us far afield. We'll use simple classes defined in the local library package OOJ.basicIO. These classes provide minimal facilities for interacting with the user.

The classes we'll instantiate are *OOJ.basicIO.BasicFileReader* and *OOJ.basicIO.BasicFileWriter*. We create an instance of *BasicFileReader* that reads characters from the keyboard, and an instance of *BasicFileWriter* that writes characters to the display window. We limit our presentation to just a few essential features. These classes are discussed in more detail in Appendix A. The complete specification is given in the library documentation.

The *BasicFileWriter* constructor with no parameters creates an instance that writes to the display window:

```
public BasicFileWriter ()
```
        Create a *BasicFileWriter* attached to standard output.

(There is also a constructor requiring a *String* argument that writes output to the file named by the argument. Hence "*BasicFileWriter*.")

The only method we're interested in writes a line of characters to the window:

> **public void** displayLine (String line)
> Write the specified line to the output stream.

A call to displayLine with argument "ABC" for instance, writes a line containing those three characters to the display window. (This behavior is similar to that of the method System.out.println introduced in Section 5.3.)

The *BasicFileReader* constructor with no arguments creates an instance that reads characters from the keyboard:

> **public** BasicFileReader ()
> Create a *BasicFileReader* attached to standard input.

A *BasicFileReader* has a command instructing it to read characters that have the format of an integer literal: that is, a sequence of characters consisting of optional blanks followed by a sequence of digits:

> **public void** readInt ()
> Read a new **int** from standard input. The digit string is interpreted as a decimal integer.
>
> **require:**
> > leading characters in standard input consist of:
> > > zero or more white space characters, followed by
> > > an optional sign, followed by
> > > one or more decimal digits.

For instance, if the user keys

> ····12345abc↵

where "·" represents a space and "↵" represents the "newline" character at the end of the line, execution of readInt causes the *BasicFileReader* to read up through the character "5."

The method will fail (causing the program to terminate) if the leading non-blank characters in the input do not have the form of an integer literal.

Executing the command readInt changes the state of the *BasicFileReader*: it remembers the integer value denoted by the string of characters read. The *BasicFileReader* can then be queried for this value with the method lastInt:

> **public int** lastInt ()
> Last **int** read by readInt.
>
> **require:**
> > this.readInt() has been successfully performed.

A *BasicFileReader* also has a command `readLine` that reads all the characters up to and including the end of line.

    public void `readLine ()`
        Read rest of line from input stream.

In the example above, executing `readInt` causes the *BasicFileReader* to read up through the character "5" leaving "abc\n" in the input stream. Invoking the query `lastInt` will then return the **int** value 12345. Executing `readLine` reads the characters up through the newline, effectively moving to the next line of input.

8.3.2 Implementing the test driver

Specifying the user interface

The specification of the class *CounterTUI* is rather simple. We have a constructor, and a single method to start the test.

    public class `CounterTUI`
        A text-based test driver for the class *Counter*.

    public `CounterTUI ()`
        Create a new test driver with a *Counter* to test.

    public void `start ()`
        Conduct the test.

When the method `start` is invoked, the test driver writes out the menu and prompts the user for a choice. The dialogue continues until the user selects the "exit" option, at which point the method terminates.

Implementing the user interface

A *CounterTUI* needs a *BasicFileReader* for input, a *BasicFileWriter* for output, and a *Counter* to exercise. Thus the implementation will define three instance variables, initialized in the constructor:

```
public class CounterTUI {

    public CounterTUI () {
        input = new OOJ.basicIO.BasicFileReader();
        output = new OOJ.basicIO.BasicFileWriter();
        counter = new Counter();
        ...
    }
    ...
```

```
    private OOJ.basicIO.BasicFileReader input;
    private OOJ.basicIO.BasicFileWriter output;
    private Counter counter;
}
```

If we look at what happens when the test is conducted, we see that the following sequence of actions are repeated over and over:

- display menu to the user and prompt user for input;

- get user's input;

- perform requested action;

- display results.

A pattern such as this is sometimes called a *read-process-write loop*, since the reiterated actions involve getting some data, doing a computation with the data, and displaying the results of the computation (see Figure 8.2).

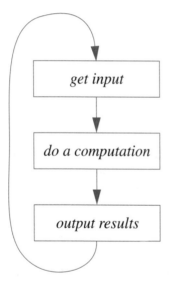

Figure 8.2 **A *read-process-write* loop.**

To make our system easier to read and easier to modify, we define methods to carry out the repeated steps of the test. Specifically, we define methods to display the menu and the prompt, get the user's input, and carry out the requested operation. These methods are not part of the specification of the class *CounterTUI*. They are local, auxiliary methods, to be invoked only in the class itself. Thus we declare them to be *private*.

First we define an instance variable to hold the user's choice.

```
    private int choice;   // the user's most recent choice
```

The local methods we will create are specified as follows.

private void displayMenuPrompt ()
Display the menu to the user.

private void getChoice ()
Get the user's choice.

ensure:
this.choice contains the user's choice.

private void executeChoice ()
Perform the action indicated by this.choice, and display the results to the user.

To perform one iteration of the test, we simply invoke the three methods in order:

```
displayMenuPrompt();
getChoice();
executeChoice();
```

Displaying the menu simply requires writing several lines of output. We invoke the *BasicFileWriter* method displayLine to write each line.

```
private void displayMenuPrompt () {
    output.displayLine(
        "Enter number denoting action to perform:");
    output.displayLine("Increment.............1");
    output.displayLine("Decrement.............2");
    output.displayLine("Reset.................3");
    output.displayLine("Create a new Counter...4");
    output.displayLine("Exit..................5");
    output.displayLine("Enter choice.");
}
```

To get the user's input, we command the *BasicFileReader* to read an integer, and then query it for the integer read:

```
private void getChoice () {
    input.getInt();
    choice = input.lastInt();
}
```

Note that this method is not particularly robust. If the user keys something other than a number, the program will crash. Furthermore, we don't check to make sure that the user keys a legal choice: *i.e.*, a number between 1 and 5. Since we're building a test driver for our own use and not a general purpose interface, we'll not be particularly concerned about these shortcomings.

What action gets performed depends on the user's input. The method executeChoice performs the requested action and displays the results. (Recall that the operator "+" denotes concatenation when one of its operands is a *String*.)

```
private void executeChoice () {
    if (choice == 1) {
        counter.increment();
        output.displayLine(
        "The current count is: " + counter.count());
    } else if (choice == 2) {
        counter.decrement();
        output.displayLine(
        "The current count is: " + counter.count());
    } else if (choice == 3) {
        counter.reset();
        output.displayLine(
        "The current count is: " + counter.count());
    } else if (choice == 4) {
        counter = new Counter();
        output.displayLine(
        "A Counter has been created.");
        output.displayLine(
        "The current count is: " + counter.count());
    } else if (choice == 5)
        output.displayLine("Goodbye.");
}
```

Repeating the actions

In order to get this sequence of actions to happen repeatedly, we need a new statement called a *while* statement. We'll see this statement used extensively when we look at lists in a subsequent chapter. We introduce it briefly here.

A *while* statement is composed of a condition (a boolean expression) and another statement, the body. The syntax is

```
while ( condition )
    body
```

When the *while* statements executed, the condition is first evaluated. If it is true, the body is executed and the process repeated. Thus the body continues to be executed until the condition is false.

Several statements comprise the action that we want to repeat. So we make the body of the while a compound statement:

```
while ( condition ) {
    displayMenuPrompt();
    getChoice();
    executeChoice();
}
```

Now only one issue remains: what is the condition that causes the iteration to continue? When the user keys "5" as a choice, we terminate the repetition. If the choice is anything else, we continue. The condition, then, tests to see if the user's choice is 5. But rather than writing

```
while (choice != 5) {
```

we adhere to the guideline that "except for literals like 1 and 0, literals should appear only in constant definitions." Naming the choices makes the code a little easier to read and maintain. Thus we define

```
private static final int EXIT = 5;
```

and write

```
while ( choice != EXIT ) {
    displayMenuPrompt();
    getChoice();
    executeChoice();
}
```

What value should choice have the very first time the condition is evaluated, before the user has keyed anything? Any value but 5 will do. We let 0 indicate that the user has not yet made a choice, and initialize choice with this value in the constructor. The complete definition of *CounterTUI* is given in Listing 8.1.

Listing 8.1   **The class *CounterTUI***

```
/**
 * A text-based test driver for the class Counter.
 */
class CounterTUI {

    // Constructors:

    /**
     * Create a new test driver with a Counter to test.
     */
    public CounterTUI () {
        input = new OOJ.basicIO.BasicFileReader();
        output = new OOJ.basicIO.BasicFileWriter();
        counter = new Counter();
        choice = NO_CHOICE;
    }
```

continued

Listing 8.1   **The class *CounterTUI (continued)***

```java
// Commands:

/**
 * Conduct the test.
 */
public void start () {
   while (choice != EXIT) {
      displayMenuPrompt();
      getChoice();
      executeChoice();
   }
}

/**
 * Display the menu.
 */
private void displayMenuPrompt () {
   output.displayLine(
      "Enter number denoting action to perform:");
   output.displayLine("Increment..............1");
   output.displayLine("Decrement..............2");
   output.displayLine("Reset..................3");
   output.displayLine("Create a new Counter...4");
   output.displayLine("Exit...................5");
   output.displayLine("Enter choice.");
}

/**
 * Get user's choice.
 */
private void getChoice () {
   input.getInt();
   choice = input.lastInt();
}

/**
 * Execute user's choice.
 */
```

continued

Listing 8.1 **The class *CounterTUI (continued)***

```java
    private void executeChoice () {
        if (choice == INCREMENT) {
            counter.increment();
            output.displayLine(
                "The current count is: " + counter.count());
        } else if (choice == DECREMENT) {
            counter.decrement();
            output.displayLine(
                "The current count is: " + counter.count());
        } else if (choice == RESET) {
            counter.reset();
            output.displayLine(
                "The current count is: " + counter.count());
        } else if (choice == CREATE) {
            counter = new Counter();
            output.displayLine(
                "A Counter has been created.");
            output.displayLine(
                "The current count is: " + counter.count());
        } else if (choice == EXIT)
            output.displayLine("Goodbye.");
    }

    // Private constants:

    private final static int NO_CHOICE = 0;
    private final static int INCREMENT = 1;
    private final static int DECREMENT = 2;
    private final static int RESET = 3;
    private final static int CREATE = 4;
    private final static int EXIT = 5;

    // Private Components:

    private OOJ.basicIO.BasicFileReader input;
    private OOJ.basicIO.BasicFileWriter output;
    private Counter counter;
    private int choice; // the user's most recent choice

} // end of class CounterTUI
```

Getting the system started

We have defined the two classes that we need for the test, and we have a *Counter-TUI* create a *Counter* to test. We need one more piece: a class with a `main` method that creates a *CounterTUI* and gets everything started. As explained in Section 5.3, this is the method that is executed when the program is run.

Recall that the function of `main` is simply to create the initial objects and start execution of the system. In the current case, it need only create a *CounterTUI* instance and give it the command `start`. Our convention is to define the method `main` in a class that contains no other method, and is not used to model any other part of the system. The class can be defined as follows:

```
/**
 * A test system for the class Counter.
 */
public class CounterTest {

    /**
     * Create the user interface, start the system.
     */
    public static void main (String[] argv) {
        CounterTUI theInterface = new CounterTUI();
        theInterface.start();
    }
}
```

8.3.3 Creating a test plan

So what should we do to test a *Counter*? Certainly we want to make sure that the count is correct after a sequence of increments and after a sequence of decrements. We should test sequencing of commands; that is, test increment after decrement, decrement after increment, and make sure that we can increment and decrement after a reset. The minimum value of the count is 0. So we should be sure to test this boundary case. In particular, we should make sure that decrements work as advertised when the count is 0.

To direct the testing, we develop a test plan, as mentioned above. A test plan is a document that describes a number of test cases, giving the purpose of each case, the values to be used in the test, and the expected results. The intent in creating a test plan is to ensure that all possible cases are tested, that the system thoroughly but not inordinately tested.

A *Counter* is very simple object, and there isn't much to testing it. A plan for testing the *Counter* need only make sure that the situations outlined above are tested. It specifies the actions to be performed and expected results. A sample is shown below:

Action	Expected Count	Comment
increment	1	increment from initial state
increment	2	sequence of increments
increment	3	
increment	4	
decrement	3	sequence of decrements
decrement	2	
increment	3	increment follows decrement
reset	0	
increment	1	increment follows reset
decrement	0	
decrement	0	decrement 0 count
reset	0	
decrement	0	decrement follows reset
create	0	initial state
decrement	0	decrement from initial state

8.4 Summary

In this chapter, we briefly examined the process of testing. Well thought out testing is critical to the production of quality software systems. Here, we are concerned with testing the implementation of a class to insure that it conforms to the specifications.

We developed a test system for a simple *Counter*, by constructing a text-based user interface that allowed a user to exercise *Counter* methods. At the heart of the interface is a *read-process-write* loop. The user is presented with a menu of possible *Counter* methods to invoke. The user's choice is read, the requested action performed, and the results reported to the user. This sequence of actions is repeated until the user chooses an "exit" option.

To build the read-process-write loop, we introduced the *while* statement. This statement specifies an action to be repeated until some condition becomes false. We also saw how the `main` method is used to initiate execution of the program. Finally, we illustrated a simple test plan to direct the testing of a *Counter*.

EXERCISES

8.1   Write a test plan for testing the *Explorer* method `takeHit`. The method has a pre-condition requiring that its argument (`hitStrength`) is nonnegative. What is the expected behavior of the method if it is called with a negative argument? Should you include cases in your test plan in which the method is invoked with a negative argument? Why or why not?

8.2   Write a test plan for testing the *Employee* method `pay`, specified in exercise 7.1.

8.3   Implement a test driver for the *CombinationLock* of Section 6.4.

8.4   Implement a test driver and create a test plan for the rectangle class of exercise 5.12.

8.5   Implement a test driver and create a test plan for the three-way lamp of exercise 5.11.

8.6   The method `getChoice` in the class *CounterTUI* does not verify that the user has entered a legal number. Modify the method so that if a user enters a number not in the range 1–5, it prompts for a legal choice.

With the tools you currently have available, you can't handle the case in which a user enters something other than a number in response to the prompt. What kind of facility would be necessary to handle this situation?

8.7   One could make a case that the variable `choice` should be a local variable for the method `start` rather than an instance variable for the class. Modify the class definition making `choice` local to `start`.

GLOSSARY

black box test: a test designed by considering only the expected behavior of a system, without regard for the internal implementation structure of the system.

gray box test: a test in which specification of the component classes is used to develop test cases.

read-process-write loop: a repeated sequence of actions in which input data is read, a computation is performed with the data, and the results of the computation are output.

test driver: a class or collection of classes whose purpose is to allow some other set of classes to be tested.

test harness: a test driver.

testing: an activity whose goal is to determine whether or not an implementation functions as intended.

test plan: a document that details how a system or system component will be tested to insure correctness.

while statement: a statement in which a component statement (the *body*) is repeatedly executed as long as a specified condition remains true. Also called a *while* loop.

white box test: a test designed by taking into account the implementation of the system of component being tested.

CHAPTER 9   Relations

In the last few chapters we've seen how to specify and implement simple classes. We've also observed that objects don't exist in isolation. An *Explorer* object, for instance, is located in a *Room*, and battles *Denizens*; a *Student* enrolls in *Courses*. In general, objects cooperate to solve a problem, and an important part of designing a software system is defining the *relations* between cooperating objects. In this chapter, we look at relations in general and examine some of the fundamental relationships that arise when we structure a system.

9.1   Relations between objects

As we've mentioned several times, objects are not isolated entities. Objects interact to accomplish the goals of the system of which they are a part. They are cooperative players in a system designed with a specific function in mind. A *relation* associates two or more objects in a specific, well-defined way.

> **relation:** specific, well-defined association between two or more objects.

In Section 2.5, we considered an example in which an object of class *Person* had a property *mother*. The value associated with this property was a reference to another *Person* instance. (See Figure 2.9.) Essentially, this property implements a *relation* between the two objects, which we might call *has-as-mother*. One *Person* object *has-as-mother* another *Person* object. This is only one of many relations that can exist between two *Person* instances.

We illustrate relations as shown in Figure 9.1. We call the object on the left (*Elizabeth*) the *source*, and the object on the right (*MrsBennet*) the *target* of the relation.

We often illustrate relations using classes rather than objects. Figure 9.2 shows that an instance of class *Person* is related to another instance of class *Person* by the *has-as-mother* relation. We sometimes draw an arrow to emphasize source and target. (This is particularly handy when several relations are shown in the same diagram.)

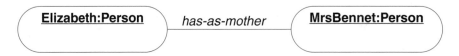

Figure 9.1 **A simple relation between two objects.**

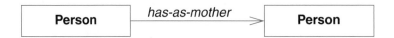

Figure 9.2 **A simple relation between two class instances.**

Note that relations of this kind are bidirectional. That is, if *Elizabeth has-as-mother Mrs. Bennet*, then *MrsBennet is-mother-of Elizabeth*. The relation *is-mother-of* is the *inverse* of the relation *has-as-mother*. Whether we are interested in the inverse of a relation, or whether we are interested in the relation at all, depends of course on the particular problem we are trying to model.

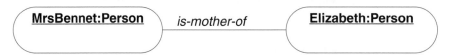

Figure 9.3 **Inverse of the relation illustrated in Figure 9.1.**

We can make a few other observations about these relations: not every *Person is-mother-of* another *Person*, and some *Person*s are related to several other *Person*s by the *is-mother-of* relation. (Not everyone is a mother, and some mothers have more than one child.) On the other hand, every *Person* (well, all but two) is related to a unique other *Person* by the *has-as-mother* relation. (Everyone has exactly one mother).

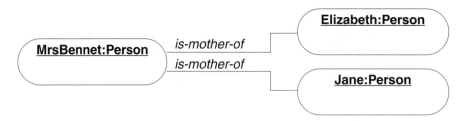

Figure 9.4 **One object related to several others.**

We call a relation in which every source object is related to one target object and in which many source objects can be related to the same target, a *many-to-one* relation. The *has-as-mother* relation is many-to-one: everyone has one mother, but several people can have the same mother. A many-to-one relation is illustrated in Figure 9.5.

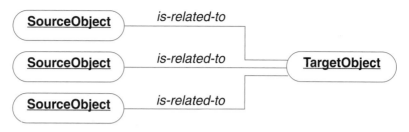

Figure 9.5 **A many-to-one relation.**

The inverse of a many-to-one relation, in which a single source object is related to many target objects, is called, not surprisingly, a *one-to-many* relation. Such a relation is shown in Figure 9.6. The *is-mother-of* relation is one-to-many. (Note that "many" in this case means "zero or more.")

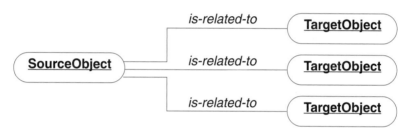

Figure 9.6 **A one-to-many relation.**

If each source object can be related to many targets, and a target can have more than one source object related to it, we have a *many-to-many* relation. Such a relation is illustrated in Figure 9.7.

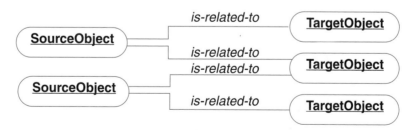

Figure 9.7 **A many-to-many relation.**

In practice, one-to-many and many-to-many relations are treated similarly. When shown as a relation between class instances, an asterisk means "zero or more." Thus the fact that a *Person* instance can be *is-mother-of* a number of other *Person* instances is illustrated as shown in Figure 9.8. To emphasize a many-to-many relation, we put an asterisk at each end of the arrow or line.

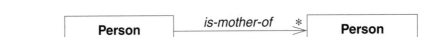

Figure 9.8 Illustrating a source instance related to more than one target.

Of course, objects of one class can be related to objects of a different class. In the registration system discussed in Section 4.4, there are objects representing students, courses, instructors, and so on. *Students* are related to *Courses* by the relation *is-enrolled-in*; *Instructors* are related to *Courses* by the relation *teaches*. If we consider the *Explorer* of the past few chapters, we can identify relations between *Explorers* and *Rooms*, and between *Explorers* and *Denizens*. An *Explorer is-in* a *Room*; an *Explorer hits* and *is-hit-by Denizens*. These relations are illustrated in Figures 9.9 and 9.10.

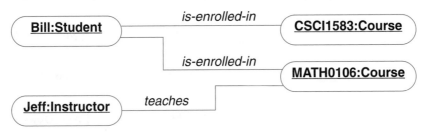

Figure 9.9 Relations in a student registration system.

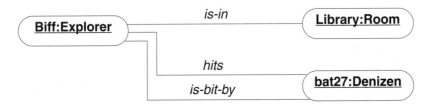

Figure 9.10 Relations in a maze game.

9.2 Responsibilities and relations

There are, of course, many conceivable relations that can be defined between any given collection of objects. Significant relations that need to be modeled in an implementation are identified as we decompose system functionality into constituent objects. Specifically, the responsibilities assigned to each object determine many of the relations that must be implemented.

"Knowing" responsibilities

If we require an object to know about another object it is related to, then clearly the relation must be modeled. For instance, we might require a *Person* to know its mother, an *Explorer* to know its location, a *Course* to know its instructor. In each case, a relation must be implemented. We've already seen the most straightforward way to do this: provide the source object with an instance variable that references the target.

"Doing" responsibilities and the uses relation

When an object is to carry out some functional responsibility, it often needs the help of other objects. When a *Student* enrolls in a *Course*, for instance, the *Student* object requires the assistance of the *Course* object: the *Course* object must add the *Student* to the roll. These other objects, called *collaborators*, are used by the original object to assist in accomplishing its task. This is the client-server interaction we have seen many times before. The original object, the client, invokes features of the collaborator, the server. The relation is called *uses*: the client *uses* the server. The *uses* relation is one of the most fundamental relations that can exist between two objects.

Creation responsibilities

One important relation that can exist between two objects is the *creates* relation. That is, the source object is responsible for creating the target.

9.3 Implementing relations: object composition and arguments

A fundamental method of implementing a relation is simply to provide the source object with a reference to the target. This is an obvious approach for handling a "knowing" responsibility, and a straightforward way to model a *uses* relation. In a client-server interaction, the client must know about, that is, have access to, the server. (The server, on the other hand, generally needs know nothing of the client, and in this sense, is independent of the client.) Providing the client with a reference to the server accomplishes this.

We might mention that a "knowing" responsibility often translates into a *uses* relation. Typically the reason we want one object to know about another is so that the first object can use the second to help accomplish a task.

Furthermore, knowing that a particular object is a server creates a dependency between the client and server. As we'll see in later chapters, we want to minimize this dependency to enhance flexibility as the system evolves.

Object composition

An object can reference another by means of an instance variable. Each instance of the class *Explorer*, for instance, has an instance variable `room` of type *reference-to-Room*:

```
public class Explorer {
    ...
    private rooms.Room room;    // current location
    ...
} // end of class Explorer
```

The *is-in* relation between an *Explorer* and a *Room* is implemented with this instance variable. If an *Explorer is-in* a particular *Room*, then the `room` instance variable of the *Explorer* instance contains a reference to the *Room* object. The *Explorer* object can be queried with the method `location` to determine the target of the *is-in* relation.

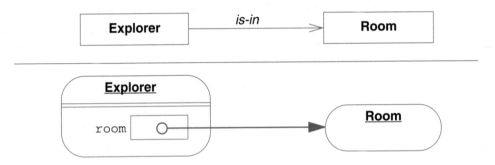

Figure 9.11 **Relation implemented with an instance variable.**

Similarly, we can implement the *has-as-mother* relation by giving a *Person* instance an instance variable that references its mother:

```
public class Person {
    ...
    private Person mother;    // this Person's mother
    ...
} // end of class Person
```

Using instance variables to put objects together is a fundamental mechanism of object design. When designing an object, we determine other objects that are necessary to support the object's responsibilities. We equip the object with assistants by means of instance variables that reference the assistants. The process of constructing an object in this manner is referred to as *object composition*. With object composition, we build an object by collecting auxiliary objects that collaborate with the object and assist it in carrying out its responsibilities. We sometimes refer to the auxiliary objects as *components*. We call the relationship between an object and another

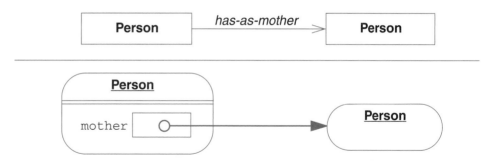

Figure 9.12   **The *has-as-mother* relation implemented with an instance variable.**

object referenced by means of an instance variable the *has-a* relation.[1] For instance, a *Person has-a Person* (as mother), an *Explorer has-a Room* (as location).

> **composition:** the process of constructing an object using instance variables that reference other objects.

Note that *has-a* is an *implementation-level* relation. To say that an *Explorer has-a Room* implies that each instance of the class *Explorer* has an instance variable that references an instance of the class *Room*. The instance variable implements the *is-in* relation, which is effectively part of the object's specification.

(The relation *uses* is also implementation level: to say that one object *uses* another means that the implementation of the first object invokes methods of the second.)

One-to-many and many-to-many relations

While this approach works for many-to-one relations, you may wonder how to handle one-to-many or many-to-many relations. Suppose we want a mother to keep track of all her children. We had a hint when we specified the class *Student* in Section 4.4. There we wanted a *Student* to keep track of the courses he or she was enrolled in. This is a many-to-many relation, since a *Student* can be enrolled in a number of *Course*s, and a number of *Student*s can be enrolled in any *Course* (Figure 9.9).

In the specification for the class *Student*, we included a query for the *Student*'s schedule that returned a *CourseList* object:

```
/**
 * This Student's current schedule.
 */
public courses.CourseList schedule () {
    ...
}
```

---

1. The term *has-a* is sometimes used to refer specifically to the *aggregation* relation, described in Section 9.4.

In the implementation, we expect an instance variable referencing the *CourseList*, as shown in Figure 9.13.

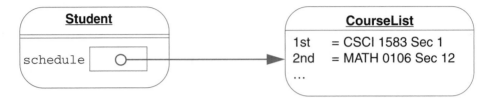

Figure 9.13   A *Student* object references a *CourseList*.

This is actually a rather general method for handling one-to-many and many-to-many relations. We might well implement the *mother-of* relation, for example, with a *PersonList*. A list is a particular form of *container*. A *container* is an object whose purpose is to hold, or contain, a collection of other objects. We must wait until Chapter 12, though, to see the detailed specification for a list object.

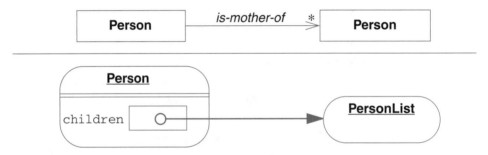

Figure 9.14   Implementing one-to-many with a list.

Establishing the relation

Given that a relation is implemented with an instance variable, we should consider how the relation is established; that is, how the source object gets a reference to the target. The relation can be established when the source object is created, as part of its construction, or it can be established later as a result of some action performed by the source object.

The relation can be established during creation of the source object in two different ways. First, the target object may already exist, in which case it is provided as an argument to the source constructor. If we are establishing the *has-as-mother* relation, for instance, we might require that the mother object exist before the child object is created. When the child is created, it is given a reference to its mother as argument. The relevant parts of the class definition would look something like this:

```
public class Person {

    public Person (…, Person mother, …) {
        …
        this.mother = mother;
        …
    }
    …
    private Person mother; // this Person's mother
    …
} // end of class Person
```

Assuming that `mrsBennet` is a (reference to a) *Person* object, we could create one of her daughters like this, where the ellipses (…) indicate other arguments as appropriate:

```
Person elizabeth = new Person (…, mrsBennet, …);
```

A second case is where the target object does not already exist, but is created by the source constructor. Suppose we are going to create an object to model a window on a computer screen. The object will be an instance of the class *Window*. We want the window to have a slider, modeled by an object of class *Slider*. An obvious way to handle this is to have the *Window* create the *Slider*:

```
public class Window {

    public Window ( … ) {
        mySlider = new Slider ( … );
        …
    }
    …
    private Slider mySlider;
    …
} // end of class Window
```

Relations can also be established between existing source and target objects as the result of some source action. In such cases, the source object is told about the target by some other object, or by the target itself. For instance, a reference to the target can be provided as an argument to a source method. This is how the *is-in* relationship between *Explorer* and *Room* objects is established. The *Explorer*'s method `move` requires a `Room` as argument. The value of the argument is assigned to the *Explorer*'s instance variable `room`, which implements the relation:

```
public class Explorer {
    …
    public void move (rooms.Room newRoom) {
        room = newRoom;
```

```
        }
        …
        private rooms.Room room;    // current location
        …
    } // end of class Explorer
```

A source object can also be informed of a target as the result of a query. Suppose, for example, the *Explorer*'s move method takes a *direction* as argument, rather than a *Room*. That is, the *Explorer* is commanded to move in a specific direction (north, south, *etc.*) from its current location. Assuming that directions are encoded as integers, the specification for move would look something like this:

```
/**
 * Move in the specified direction.
 */
public void move (int direction) { … }
```

How does the *Explorer* determine the new *Room*? It must ask someone whose responsibility it is to know which *Room*s are connected to the *Explorer*'s current location. To keep things simple, let's assume that a *Room* object knows the other *Room*s connected to it. The *Explorer* can then query its current *Room* to determine its new location. If connectedTo is the appropriate *Room* query, we can write

```
/**
 * Move in the specified direction.
 */
public void move (int direction) {
    Room newRoom = room.connectedTo(direction);
    room = newRoom;
}
```

However the relation is established, remember that an instance variable should be initialized when the object is created, even if it is initialized to the *null* value.

Uses implemented with an argument

Relations implemented with instance variables—that is, *has-a* relations—are in a sense persistent. The *Explorer has-a Room* as location throughout its existence. The particular *Room* that the *Explorer* is in may change, of course, but the *Explorer* will always be in a *Room*, regardless of what the *Explorer* is doing, or whether the *Explorer* is doing anything at all.

The *uses* relation, on the other hand, is often transient. That is, the client often need only know about the server for the duration of a method execution. Consider the *Explorer*'s method strike for example. To strike a *Denizen*, the *Explorer* needs the assistance of the *Denizen*. Specifically, the *Denizen* must take the hit and reduce its stamina as appropriate. The *Explorer uses* the *Denizen* by invoking the

Denizen's `takeHit` method. However, the *Explorer* only needs to know the *Denizen* while the *Explorer* is executing its `strike` method. The *Explorer* gets a reference to the `Denizen` by means of an argument to the *Explorer*'s `strike` method:

```
public void strike (denizens.Denizen monster) {
    monster.takeHit(strengthPoints);
}
```

Since this relation is meaningful only during execution of the `strike` method, it would make no sense to use an instance variable. The automatic variable provided by the parameter is perfectly adequate.

9.4 Aggregation

An important relation that commonly occurs in system decomposition is the "whole-part" relation, sometimes called *aggregation*. This book, for instance, is made up of chapters, which are composed of sections, which are made up of paragraphs, and so on; an automobile is made up of engine, drive train, chassis, body, *etc*. A chapter is *part-of* the book; the engine is *part-of* the car. We call the inverse of the *part-of* relation the *includes* relation: the book *includes* a chapter, the car *includes* an engine.

> **aggregation:** the relation between one object and another, in which the second is an integral part of the first.

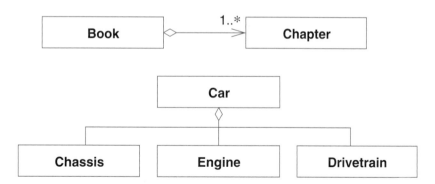

Figure 9.15 **Aggregation**

In our diagrams, we use a small diamond to indicate aggregation, as illustrated in Figure 9.15 and generally show classes rather than objects. The implication is that every instance of the class *Car*, for example, will be related to an instance of the class *Engine* by the *includes* relation. The notation "1..*" used in the *Book* to *Chapter* relation implies "one or more." Thus the diagram indicates that an object of class *Book* will be related to one or more instances of class *Chapter*.

The relation *includes* is an instance of *has-a*, and is implemented by means of instance variables. The *Car* object, for instance, would have instance variables referencing the *Chassis*, *Engine*, and *DriveTrain* objects.

Though there are exceptions, aggregations are typified by several properties. First, it is generally the case that the aggregate and its parts have the same lifetime. That is, the parts are created when the aggregate is, and are "meaningful" only in their role of comprising the aggregate. Often the parts are created by the aggregate constructor. This was the case with the *Window* example given above. The *Window* constructor created the *Slider* component:

```
public Window ( ... ) {
    mySlider = new Slider ( ... );
    ...
}
```

Sometimes, other objects are responsible for creating the parts and putting them together to form the whole. This is often the case when the parts are themselves complicated objects. For instance, we might imagine an assembler object that gets parts from various factories and puts the car together:

```
public class Assembler {
    ...
    public Car createCar () {
        Chassis theChassis;
        Engine theEngine;
        DriveTrain theDriveTrain;
        Car theCar;
        theChassis = chassisFactory.createChassis();
        theEngine = engineFactory.createEngine();
        theDriveTrain =
            driveTrainFactory.createDriveTrain();
        theCar =
            new Car(theChassis,theEngine,theDriveTrain);
        return theCar;
    }
    ...
}
```

The class *Car* will have a constructor that looks something like this:

```
public class Car {
    ...
    // Constructor:
    public Car (Chassis c, Engine e, Drivetrain d) {
        myChassis = c;
        myEngine = e;
        myDriveTrain = d;
        ...
    }
}
```

```
    ...
    // Components:
    private Chassis myChassis;
    private Engine myEngine;
    private DriveTrain myDriveTrain;
    ...
}
```

There are situations in which parts are added to, and even removed from, the aggregate after it is created. Consider a *Book* object that is part of a desktop publishing system. The *Book* will have parts such as *Chapters*, *Table of Contents*, *Index*, *etc*. Such components can be added to the aggregate *Book* at any point in the *Book*'s existence. They can, in fact, be created independently and added to a *Book* at some later time.

Nevertheless, there is a permanence in the *includes* relation that one does not find, say, in the *is-in* relation between *Explorer* and *Room*. Parts are in a strong sense dependent on the whole for their relevance, and rarely have a meaningful existence independent of the aggregate of which they are a part.

Another aspect of aggregation is that clients of the whole are typically not given access to the parts. A client cannot query the aggregate object and obtain a reference to one of the parts. A request for service goes directly to the aggregate. This object may parcel out portions of the job to its parts, as illustrated in Figure 9.16. But the client never deals directly with the components. Note the interaction here between whole and part is client-server, with the whole the client and the part the server.

The decomposition of an object into components proceeds in much the same way, for much the same reasons, as the decomposition of a system into objects. Essentially, dividing an object into parts simplifies the object design. Some aspects of the object's responsibilities can be delegated to the parts. Complicated functions can be broken down into subactions to be accomplished by appropriate components. By breaking the object down into coherent parts, the structure of the object can be considerably simplified.

It is not always obvious whether a relationship is an aggregation or not. For example, is the relationship between a club and its members an aggregation? We'll generally not bother to distinguish between *includes* and *has-a*. Generally, we call any instance of the *has-a* relation with aggregation-like properties "*composition*" and represent it as aggregation in our diagrams.

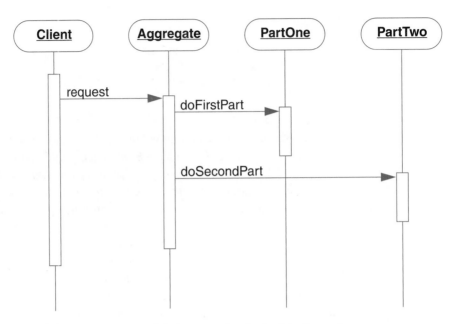

Figure 9.16 **An aggregate delegates parts of a task to its parts.**

9.5   Hierarchical abstraction

As we saw in Chapter 1, abstraction is a key mechanism for managing complexity in a system design. Informally, "to *abstract*" means to eliminate details or distinctions. To categorize both a '68 Datsun 510 and a '98 Lexus 400SC as "cars" is an abstraction; it ignores several differences. To call them "sedans" is less abstract; to call them "vehicles" is more abstract. Clearly the level of abstraction at which we need to model something depends on the problem we are trying to solve. An insurance company is not content to treat these vehicles as "equivalent," while a garage manager is only concerned with the fact that each occupies one parking space.

> **abstraction:** the relation between a class and a more specific, less abstract version of the class.

The process of abstraction typically produces a *hierarchy of classes*. The relationship between a class and a more detailed version is illustrated with a triangle as shown in Figure 9.17.

There is a substantial amount of terminology used to describe hierarchical abstraction. The relation between a class and a more detailed version is sometimes called *generalization*. The inverse relation, between a class and a more abstract ver-

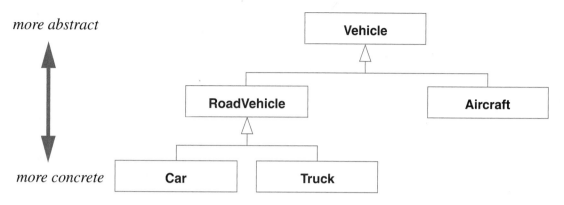

more abstract

more concrete

Figure 9.17 A class hierarchy.

sion, is called *extension*. Thus the class *RoadVehicle* is a *generalization* of the class *Car*; the class *Car* is an *extension* of *RoadVehicle*. The terms *ancestor* and *descendent* refer to generalization and extension across one or more levels of abstraction. The class *Vehicle* is an *ancestor* of *Car*; the class *Car* is a *descendent* of *Vehicle*. The more abstract class is also called a *superclass* of the extension, and the more specific class is called a *subclass* of the generalization. Thus the class *RoadVehicle* is a *superclass* of *Car*, and *Car* is a *subclass* of *RoadVehicle*. (Thinking in terms of subsets will help: the set of *Cars* is a subset of the set of *RoadVehicles*.) Finally, the *extension* relation is commonly called *is-a*: a *Car is-a RoadVehicle*.

Java defines a standard class *Object* that is a superclass of every other class. This class is at the top of the class hierarchy: any instance of any class *is-a Object*.

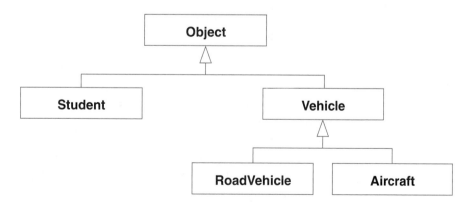

Figure 9.18 Every class is a subclass of *Object*.

As we'll see, abstraction is a powerful tool for identifying and exploiting similarities between classes. For instance, we expect the class *RoadVehicle* to express the commonality between the classes *Car* and *Truck*. Both cars and trucks are

*RoadVehicle*s, and at this level of abstraction they are "equivalent." The features of *RoadVehicle*s are common to both *Car*s and *Truck*s. The class *Object* defines a modest set of features available for all objects.

Conversely, an extension has all the public functionality of its superclass, and perhaps some additional functionality. An object of class *Truck* will have all the features of a *RoadVehicle*, as will an object of class *Car*. Each subclass is said to *inherit* the features of its superclass. A *Truck* object may, of course, have additional features not shared by *Car* objects.

The other relations discussed above, particularly *uses* and *has-a*, are fundamental to decomposing a system into objects and distributing system functionality to objects as responsibilities. Abstraction, on the other hand, has more to do with object design *per se*. The mechanism for implementing abstraction is called *inheritance*. We postpone a detailed discussion of abstraction and the language facilities for implementing inheritance to Chapter 14. We'll see that inheritance and object composition are two fundamental mechanisms for designing objects. And since object design obviously affects the overall structure of the resulting system, these mechanisms must be evaluated with system evolution in mind.

9.6   Summary

In this chapter we introduced the fundamental concepts regarding relations between objects. These relations allow us to view objects in a system as interacting with each other to fulfill the system's functionality. We saw several examples and introduced the "multiplicity" of the relation, that is, the number of source and target objects involved. We distinguished between knowing, doing, and creational responsibilities, and the relations each implied.

At the implementation level, relations are created using composition and object references. We discussed the methods used to initialize a given source object in a relation with its corresponding target object, noticing that this can be done as early as source object construction or as late as the invocation of a service by a client of the source object.

Aggregation was introduced as an important special kind of relation used to design objects as a composition of several sub-objects. The result is a new kind of object that is more than the sum of its parts, in which the components are transparent to its clients. Finally, abstraction was introduced as a relation between two similar objects, where the similarities are designed in a superclass with the distinguishing traits left to the subclasses. Abstraction was also introduced as a object design mechanism along side object composition. Abstraction and object composition play fundamental roles in object design, because of the impact that the resulting objects have in the future maintenance of the system.

EXERCISES

9.1 For each of the following, identify a relation, determine the related objects, name the relation, and categorize it as one-to-one, one-to-many, many-to-one, or many-to-many.

    a. Students get final grades in a course in which they are enrolled.

    b. Students get test and homework grades in a course during a semester.

    c. Students sit in chairs when attending a lecture.

    d. Nations are separated by borders.

    e. Airplanes land at an airport.

    f. Competitors and judges participate in various events in a competition.

9.2 For each of the following sets of objects, identify an abstraction that relates them, and some common features that can be specified in the abstraction.

    a. Objects that are used in a business employee management system: part-time employees, office administrators, janitors, salespersons.

    b. Objects that are used to indicate players with different kinds of expertise in a game: beginner, intermediate, advanced, wizard.

    c. Objects that are used for input by a computer user: mouse, keyboard, optical pen, touch screen.

    d. Objects that are used in a university registration system: undergraduate student, graduate student.

    e. Objects that are used in a word processor: characters, lines, paragraphs, pages.

    f. Objects that are used in a calendar: ordinary day, holiday.

9.3 Categorize the following relations as aggregation, generalization, or simple relation. Justify your answers.

    a. A person uses a toothbrush.

    b. A file contains records.

    c. A file is an ordinary file or a directory file.

    d. A person uses Java in a project.

    e. A student takes a course from an instructor.

    f. The university football team is composed of students.

    g. A triangle is made out of lines.

    h. A person is married or single.

GLOSSARY

abstraction: the relation between a class and a more specific, less abstract version of the class. Also called *generalization*.

aggregation: the relation between one object and another, in which the second is an integral part of the first. The *whole-to-part* relation.

ancestor: the relation between a class and a more specific version, across one or more levels of abstraction. If *A* is a *generalization* of *B*, and *B* is a *generalization* of *C*, then both *A* and *B* are *ancestors* of *C*.

collaborator: an object used by another object to assist it in accomplishing its task.

composition: object composition; the process of constructing an object using instance variables that reference other objects.

descendent: the relation between a class and a more abstract version, across one or more levels of abstraction. If *A* is an *extension* of *B*, and *B* is an *extension* of *C*, then *C* is a *descendent* of both *A* and *B*.

"doing" responsibility: a responsibility of an object to carry out some function or accomplish some task.

extension: the relation between a class and a more abstract version of the class: the inverse of *generalization*. Also called *is-a*.

generalization: the relation between a class and a more specific, less abstract version of the class; the inverse of *extension*.

has-a relation: the relation between an object and another object referenced by means of an instance variable.

includes relation: the relation between one object and another, in which the second is an integral part of the first; the inverse of the *part-whole* relation. Sometimes called *aggregation*.

inheritance: the language mechanism for implementing generalization.

is-a relation: the *extension* relation.

"knowing" responsibility: a responsibility of an object to know some value, or to know about another object it is related to.

many-to-many relation: a relation in which each source object can be related to many target objects, and in which many source objects can be related to the same target.

many-to-one relation: a relation in which every source object is related to one target object, and in which many source objects can be related to the same target.

Object class: the top-level class is the Java class hierarchy; every class *is-a Object*.

object composition: the process of constructing an object using instance variables that reference other objects.

one-to-many relation: a relation in which a single source object can be related to many target objects, and in which each target object has one source object related to it.

part-whole relation: the relation between one object and another, in which the first is an integral part of the second; the inverse of *includes*.

relation: a specific, well-defined association between two or more objects.

source: the "subject" of a relation. If *A is related to B*, then *A* is the source. When illustrating a relation with a diagram, the source object is usually pictured on the left.

subclass: the more specific class in a generalization.

superclass: the more abstract class in a generalization.

target: the "object" of a relation. If *A is related to B*, then *B* is the target. When illustrating a relation with a diagram, the target object is usually pictured on the right.

uses relation: the relation between client and server, in which the source object invokes methods of the target object.

CHAPTER 10

Putting together a complete system

We've seen how to specify, implement, and test a single object, and in the last chapter, we introduced some important relationships that commonly exist between objects. Now we are ready to consider the design of a modest but complete system. Our purpose is to get an idea of what's involved in system design, and to see how a collection of objects work together to solve a problem. We start with an overview of the design and implementation process, outlining the steps involved in producing a complete system. Then, as a case study, we build a system that plays a simple game called "nim." Our example is limited in scope for several reasons. Notably, we want a system we can comprehend in its entirety, and we don't yet have all the tools we need to produce a completely satisfactory design. Consequently we build as small a system as practical, and settle for a less interesting system of limited functionality.

10.1 Software life cycle

System development begins with *problem analysis*, a thorough examination of the problem to be solved. The problem analysis results in a document that carefully and precisely describes *what* the system is intended to do. This description is primarily concerned with the system's *functionality*, and is usually called a *system specification* or *functional specification*. The specification is essentially the contract between the customer—the person who will use the system—and the developer. It explicitly describes for the customer the product to be delivered, and tells the developer what must be produced.

The initial system specification is rarely complete and is often ambiguous and inconsistent. Furthermore, the circumstances in which the system will be used, and hence the customer's requirements, are not static. Accordingly, system specifications must be modified and amended as the design and implementation process proceeds. It is this difficulty in "hitting a moving target" that the object-oriented design process attempts to address.

Once the system is specified, the *design* phase begins. Design involves *defining* a collection of objects (actually classes) and their interactions that will satisfy the specifications. Note that *system design* involves *object specification*.

Following design, *system implementation* can began. This includes actually constructing the (software) modules that will make up the system, using programming languages and other software development tools. This is the coding, or programming, part of system development. It's what we've been dealing with, at a fundamental level, in the first few chapters.

Once modules have been implemented, they must be *tested* to insure that they conform to specifications; *i.e.*, that they behave as expected. This requires the creation of *test plans* to direct the testing process.

The final step in the implementation process is the integration of the modules to produce a complete system. This step also requires testing, called integration testing. The design of an integration test is much more demanding than the design of a unit test. System specification is distributed over many modules, that interact in complicated and often subtle ways. The test design will involve not only black box testing based on system specification and use-cases, but also white box testing checking for unexpected interactions between system components.

The entire process is *iterative* and *incremental*. The design effort often uncovers inadequacies in the specifications which must be addressed before the design can be completed. Testing typically uncovers design and implementation flaws which must be corrected. Test plans must be continually updated as the process proceeds. System integration and integration testing must also be performed incrementally. It is a fatal strategy to leave system integration as one final step.

The process is also *compositional*. That is, the system itself, the objects, and the algorithms implementing each object's features are all composed of simpler pieces, which are themselves composed of pieces, *etc.* The iterative process of design-implement-test occurs at all compositional levels. Consequently the development of a system is not cleanly divided into separate specification-design-implement-test phases: these activities are carried out concurrently in different parts of the system.

Finally, the process is not complete when the system is put into production. As we have mentioned several times, a system's specifications are not fixed, but are constantly evolving. The problem a system is designed to solve inevitably changes over time. *System maintenance* involves modifying the system to meet changing requirements, as well as correcting problems not detected before the system is put into production.

> *The software life cycle involves*
>
> - analysis;
> - specification;
> - design;
> - implementation;
> - testing;
> - maintenance.
>
> *The process is*
>
> - iterative;
> - incremental;
> - compositional.

Figure 10.1 **The software life cycle.**

10.2   Fundamental subsystems

A typical system consists of three fundamental subsystems: *interface*, *data management*, and *model*. We briefly describe each below.

External interface

To be useful, a system must communicate with the external world. A university registration system must provide some means for students to select courses, supply students with schedules, produce class rolls, and so on. A game must create displays for the player and allow the player to input control information. A system controlling a railroad switch yard must sense the presence of rail cars and control the operation of switches. It is generally desirable to isolate these functions into a collection of objects called the *external interface* or *user interface*. The external interface has the responsibility of interacting with the outside world—of obtaining and verifying input, and of formatting and presenting output.

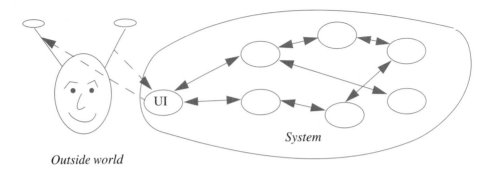

Figure 10.2 **User interface interacts with the user.**

Data management

Many systems need to manage some *external data* that must be maintained whether or not the system is operating and using the data. For instance, a bank needs to keep customer account and transaction records, a student record system needs to maintain student transcripts, and so on, regardless of whether the information is currently being used. Data maintained externally and independently of what the system is doing at the moment is sometimes called *persistent*. The part of the system responsible for storing and retrieving persistent data is the *data management* subsystem.

Model

Finally, there are the components that actually solve particular problems. This part of the system is called the *model* or the *problem domain subsystem*.

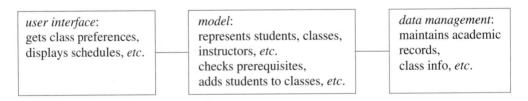

user interface:	model:	data management:
gets class preferences, displays schedules, *etc.*	represents students, classes, instructors, *etc.* checks prerequisites, adds students to classes, *etc.*	maintains academic records, class info, *etc.*

Figure 10.3 **Subsystems in a student registration system.**

The interface and data management subsystems are rather specialized, often built with sophisticated software tools. We'll examine external interfaces in some detail in later chapters, but most of the difficult data management issues are beyond the scope of this text. For our purposes, data management is limited to ordinary sequential files and objects that read and write them. We concentrate on model design at the moment.

10.3   Design of a system

As a case study, we design a system to play the game of "simple nim." In this game there are two players and a pile of sticks. Each player in turn removes one, two, or three sticks from the pile. The player who removes the last stick loses.

Our initial implementation will play a number of games and show the results to the user. The user determines whether to play another game and how many sticks to start with. Later, we'll consider modifications that allow the user to participate in the play, or that allow different strategies to be employed by the players.

There is a fairly easy to determine perfect strategy for the game: one of the players can always win no matter what the other player does, as long as the number of sticks in the pile is known. Which player has the perfect strategy depends on the number of sticks in the pile. This fact is not particularly relevant to our system design.

10.3.1   System functionality

Since we've already determined what we want the system to do, no real problem analysis is required. We can describe the functionality required of the system as follows.

Basic function of the system: Play a number of games of "simple nim," reporting the results to the user.

System functionality:

1. Allow the user to specify the number of sticks the pile contains at the start of the game.
2. For each player in turn, determine what play to make (number of sticks to remove) and make the play.
3. Display the state of the game after each play; *i.e.*, the number of sticks taken, the number of sticks left, whether or not game is over, and if so who won.
4. Allow the user to determine whether another game is to be played.

10.3.2   Preliminary design

Before we begin an extensive design, we should mention that there are many possible approaches and rarely one best solution for any non-trivial problem. Nevertheless specific measures can be applied to proposed solutions, and different approaches can be compared with regard to various criteria. The task of the designer is to explore the solution space—the set of possible solutions—for a problem, and evaluate alternatives.

This kind of detailed evaluation of alternatives is well beyond our experience. Our goal at the moment is to see a collection of objects working together in a complete system. Therefore, we aim for simplicity in the design and try to introduce as few new linguistic constructs as possible. A careful and thorough analysis of the solution presented, though, would identify better alternatives.

Basic subsystems

In terms of the subsystems mentioned above, we clearly need a user interface to interact with the user and a model to play the game. No data management is required.

As we have said, the function of the user interface is interact with the user: to get data from and to the user. Note that in the description we gave of system functionality, we made no mention of *how* the user interacts with the system. That is, we know the user needs to indicate how many sticks to play with, *etc.*, and see the moves being made as the game is played. But we have made no mention at all as to how this is done. How does the user know the system is ready for input? How does he or she provide the input? With the keyboard? With the mouse? What happens if the user gives improper input? What does the output look like? These issues are the responsibility of the user interface. Its purpose is to communicate with and gather appropriate input data from the user, and to format and display results to the user. By identifying this as a separate subsystem we gain flexibility in design. All the details of user interaction, such as how the user provides input, what negotiation is necessary to insure that the user provides acceptable input, and how output is presented, are isolated ("encapsulated") in the user interface. These details can easily be changed without affecting the fundamental function of the system.

Identifying objects

Design involves defining a collection of objects and their interactions to satisfy the specifications. As we saw in Section 2.3.3, we must first identify the objects. This is typically a nontrivial iterative process. While a number of techniques have been suggested for identifying objects in a system, there is no substitute for experience. The broader one's experience, the greater variety of solution patterns one has at hand for attacking a particular problem.

Of course, we really specify *classes* in the design. The objects are created dynamically as required when the system is executed. We can properly describe the first step in design as identifying a potential collection of classes.

There are a number of different kinds of classes that come together in any system design. Some are derived directly from the external system being modeling. A student registration system, for instance, almost certainly needs a class modeling students. These classes are often "there for the picking" and are the kind of classes we have been considering in the preceding chapters.

But these classes that directly model aspects of the external system are not sufficient. Other classes are *architectural* and form the underlying structure of the solution. These structural classes are not directly involved in addressing functional requirements of the system, but are used to define relationships between system components to support maintainability, efficiency, and so on. Although such classes often occur in common patterns, identifying appropriate architectural classes for a system is one of the most difficult problems of design, and one whose successful solution requires considerable experience.

Finally, some classes support the algorithmic implementation of the system. These *implementation classes* are generally well-understood, having been derived from years of algorithmic development. We encounter these classes in later chapters, when we see how to implement some commonly used structures.

An initial collection of potential problem-modeling classes can be developed by carefully examining the required system functionality. Then as responsibilities are allocated to these classes and relationships between them identified, other potential classes, architectural classes, and organizational approaches will suggest themselves. Since this is our first attempt at system design, we present an adequate collection of classes with little more than intuitive justification.

In the discussion above, we concluded that we need a user interface and model. We postpone consideration of the user interface for the moment, and devote our attention to the model. What objects comprise the model? The game is described in terms of two players and a pile of sticks. It seems clear that we want objects modeling the two *players*. The sticks are really not very interesting in themselves. So rather than modeling the individual sticks, we'll define an object to represent the *pile* of sticks. (If our game was poker, however, we'd want objects representing the individual cards, and if we were playing chess we'd want objects representing the individual pieces. Deciding what not to model is as critical to a design as deciding what to model.)

As we proceed with the design, we encounter functions that don't seem to be natural responsibilities of any of these objects. For instance, someone must decide which player's turn it is, when the game is over, and who wins. We might attempt to assign these responsibilities to the *player* or *pile* objects, but the development would become very awkward. It is useful to introduce a structural object responsible for managing the game. Game rules that are independent of the individual players can be encapsulated in this object. We call this object the *game manager*.

Determining responsibilities

Now that we've identified some objects, we can begin to assign responsibilities. We have four model objects: two *players*, the *pile*, and the *game manager*. As we saw in Section 2.3.3, we must determine what each object must know, and what each object must do. Of course, the functionality required of the system determines what should and shouldn't be included. We must take care not to get too concerned with simulating reality rather than modeling system functionality.

Since the design process produces class definitions and not individual objects, we express responsibilities in terms of classes. The two *player* objects behave identically and so are instances of the same class. Consequently we have three classes to consider: *Pile*, *Player*, and *GameManager*.

The *Pile* is a rather simple class that does no more than manage the sticks. The *Pile* need only know how many sticks remain, and be able to remove sticks.

A *Player*'s primary responsibility is to make a play: that is, determine how many sticks to remove and remove them from the pile. We give the *Player* a name so that we can easily identify an individual *Player* to the user. (Note that the only real purpose in naming a *Player* is for the user's benefit.) We also make the *Player* responsible for knowing how many sticks it took on its last turn. (We could equally well argue that knowing how many sticks were taken should be the responsibility of the *GameManager* or even of the *Pile*. There are many situations in which we have little *a priori* reason for choosing one alternative over another.)

The *GameManager* must know the *Player*s and the *Pile*. It must know who is to play next, and who played last. It must know when the game is over, and who the winner is. And since we are thinking of the *GameManager* as a repository of game rules, we assign the *GameManager* the responsibility for knowing how many sticks can be taken on a turn. (Again, we might argue that this knowledge should reside with the *Player* or *Pile*.) The only action we assign to the *GameManager* is to conduct the play of a game. (An alternative here might be to include the responsibility for playing a single "round" rather than an entire game.)

As we identify a specific object's responsibilities, we also try to identify *collaborators*: other objects whose services the specific object requires in order to carry out its responsibilities. The *Pile* is a complete server: it requires no other objects to satisfy its responsibilities. The *Player*, on the other hand, needs the *Pile* in order to make a move. The *Player* must determine from the *Pile* how many sticks are left, and then command the *Pile* to remove a specified number of sticks.

We summarize this information below. For each class, we give a general description of the class, and then enumerate specific responsibilities and collaborators, other classes a given class needs to accomplish its responsibilities.

Class: *Pile*
> the pile of sticks in the simple nim game

Responsibilities:	**Collaborators:**
do:	
remove sticks	
know:	
how many sticks remain in the	
Pile	

Class: *Player*
> a player of the simple nim game

Responsibilities:	**Collaborators:**
do:	
make a play by removing sticks	*Pile*
from the *Pile*	
know:	
Player's name	
how many sticks were removed	
on this *Player*'s most	
recent turn	

Class: *GameManager*
> manager of a simple nim game

Responsibilities:	**Collaborators:**
do:	
play a game of simple nim,	*Players, Pile*
controlling the order of	
play	
know:	
the *Players*	
the *Pile*	
number of sticks that can be	
taken on a turn	
which *Player* plays next	
which *Player* played last	
when the game is over	*Pile*
which *Player* won when game	
is over	

Our class specifications are not yet complete. We have not considered the user interface and how it interacts with the model objects. Nor have we addressed creation responsibilities. Nevertheless, we should be starting to get an idea of how the model objects will work together to satisfy the system requirement.

10.3.3   Relations between objects

Now that we have identified responsibilities and collaborators, we can sketch the relationships that exist between these objects. Considering the *GameManager* first, we can describe the relation between *GameManager* and *Players*, and between *GameManager* and *Pile*, as composition. The *GameManager* has two *Players* and it has a *Pile*. This is illustrated in Figure 10.4.

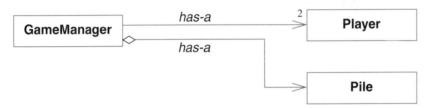

Figure 10.4 *GameManager* **is a composite object.**

The small "2" means that the relation is a "one-to-two" relation: the *Game-Manager* has exactly two *Players*.

We show the relation between *Pile* and *GameManager* as aggregation (part-whole). This implies that the *GameManager* owns and is responsible for the *Pile*. The *Pile* has no meaning independently of the game. We expect the *GameManager* and *Pile* to have identical lifetimes. The *Players*, on the other hand, might well exist independently of the any particular game. We can imagine, for instance, extending our system to one in which the same *Players* engage in a number of different games.

Recall that the relation of an object to a component is typically an instance of the client-server: the object *uses* its components. This is the case here. The *Game-Manager* will be a client of the *Pile* and of the *Players*. The *GameManager* uses these objects by giving them commands and queries. For instance, the *GameManager* will instruct each *Player* in turn to make a move.

The *Player* objects will *use* the *Pile* by removing sticks from it. This is a simple instance of client-server

Figure 10.5 *Player* **is client to** *Pile*.

We must still consider creation responsibilities. Since we have decided that the *Pile* is a part of the *GameManager*, it is appropriate to make the *GameManager* responsible for creating the *Pile*. The *Players* and the *GameManager*, however, exist independently. We do not want to make either responsible for creating the other. We consider the *Players* and *GameManager* top-level objects in the system. We'll see exactly where they come from when we look at the implementation.

To see the interaction of *GameManager*, *Players*, and *Pile*, consider the scenario shown in Figure 10.6. Here we illustrate the situation in which the game is not over (there are sticks remaining in the pile), and *player1* is next to play. To determine if the game is over, the *GameManager* queries the *Pile* to ascertain the number of sticks remaining. As there are sticks remaining, the *GameManager* instructs one of the *Players*—*player1* in this case—to make a move. The *Player* queries the *Pile* to determine how many sticks remain, and then removes some number of sticks from the *Pile*. The process repeats, with *player1* and *player2* alternating moves, until no more sticks remain and the game is over.

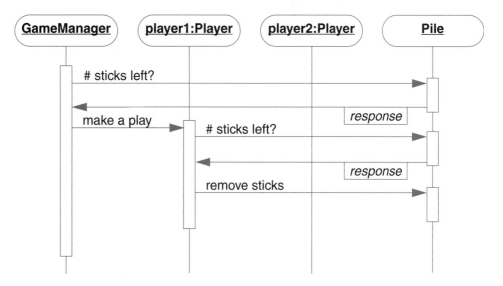

Figure 10.6   **Game not over, *player1*'s turn.**

10.3.4   Integrating the user interface and the model

By this point we have a rather good idea of how the model objects work together. We must now consider the user interface and how it relates to the model.

The interface and model will interact in a client-server relation. We must first decide whether the interface functions primarily as server with the model as client, or *vice versa*. We can, in fact, design the system either way, and with the simple system we're building it's hard to justify either approach over the other *a priori*. However, we want to adopt an approach that will prove to be extensible to larger systems.

If we were experienced with procedural programming, it would probably seem natural to consider the user interface as a server for the model. We'd view the user interface as a sort of sophisticated input/output device, defining a variety of features for getting input and displaying output. In particular, it would have features for obtaining any input value the model might need, and features for reporting various output values to the user. When the model needed an input value or wanted to display an output value, it would invoke an appropriate user interface feature.

The problem with this approach is that dependency is the wrong way around. Recall that in a client-server relationship, the server is independent of the client, but the client is dependent on the server: the client must know about the server, but the server need not know about the client. What we mean by this is that client code explicitly references server features. If the server's specifications are modified, the client must also be modified to conform to the new server specifications. The server, on the other hand, does not directly reference the client. Changes in the client will not affect the server. Put another way, we can imagine the server being *implemented* before the client has been *specified*, but not *vice versa*.

Now the responsibility of the model is to "solve the problem," and the job of the user interface to allow the user to issue commands to the model and report the state of the model to the user. That is, the user interface is a mechanism for viewing and controlling the solution process. From this point of view, the user interface is inherently dependent on the model. On the other hand, it is generally preferable for the model to be as independent of the interface as possible. The reason for this is that the user interface is typically one of the least stable parts of the system, and often among the last to be finalized in system design. Isolating a component that is likely to change makes a system easier to maintain, since required changes don't "propagate" to more stable system elements.

Imagine, for example, an automobile motor as the model, and the surrounding "parts" that allow a person to "use" the motor as the interface. The design of the motor is rather stable, since its primary function does not change. The interface, on the other hand, is constantly modified to meet changing customer demands. If we consider aspects of the interface that let the user view the behavior of the motor, such as an oil pressure gauge or tachometer, the dependency is clear. The functioning of an oil pressure gauge is clearly dependent on a motor, and its design must take into account the motor's specification. The oil pressure gauge is a client of the motor, querying the motor for its oil pressure. The motor, on the other hand, should function perfectly well whether an oil pressure gauge is attached or not. Similarly, the functioning of the motor is independent of whether a digital or analogue tachometer, or any tachometer at all, is connected. It would be a poor design if changes in the design of an oil pressure gauge or tachometer required design modifications in the motor.

Since we want the model to be as independent of the user interface as possible, we define the user interface to model relationship as client to server: the user interface is the client, the model is server. The user interface will query the model to get state information to report to the user, and give the model commands as directed by the user.

There are two distinct functions of the user interface that we will ultimately separate. First, the user interface must display information about the model state to the user. This is essentially an output function. The user interface provides the user with a *view* of the model. Second, the user interface must provide a means by which the user can *control* the model. This is an input function. We briefly examine each of these aspects before continuing with our design.

The paradigm we would like to adopt for control is called *event-driven*. An event-driven system is designed to respond to occurrences—that is, to "events"—external to the system. Exactly what constitutes an event depends on the system, but basically an event is caused by some external agent independent of the system. In an interactive system, such as the one we are designing, events are the result of user actions. The user may move the mouse, click on a menu item, key in a line, *etc.* All of these might be events to which the system must respond.

At the moment, we don't have all the tools we need to build a proper event-driven system. We try to keep as close as possible to the event-driven model, though in this example we'll end up with traditional, algorithm-driven input.

Let's next turn our attention to the output function of the user interface. The user interface must display some aspect of the model state to the user, and so the user interface must query the model to obtain the relevant information. The interface queries the model whenever "something happens" in the model; that is, whenever the model changes state. The question is how does the user interface know when the model state changes? We could have the user interface periodically query the model, but this would not generally prove satisfactory. We could have the model tell the user interface when it changes state, but this seems to negate our goal of keeping the model independent of the user interface. (It is consideration of such issues that results in the introduction of "architectural" classes.)

The pattern emerging here is a variation of a commonly occurring relation called *observes*. We'll see this pattern again in more detail in a later chapter. Essentially, one object (the "observer") needs to know when another object (the "target" or "observed") changes state. But the target should be as independent of the observer as possible. In the case at hand, the user interface needs to know when the model changes state so that the user interface can report to the user.

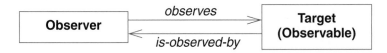

Figure 10.7 **The** *observes* **relation.**

For the observer to know when the target changes state, the target must tell the observer. The target must therefore know something of the observer, but we want to minimize what the target knows about the observer, keeping the target as independent of the observer as possible. The interaction is as follows:

- observer tells the target, "I'm interested in knowing when you change state;"
- whenever the target changes state, it informs the observer "I've changed state;"
- observer then queries the target for any detailed information it needs.

Although the target must know who the observer is, it need not care what kind of object the observer is, nor what the observer plans to do with the information. Consequently the target maintains its essential independence from the observer.

To implement the relation, the target provides a method (*register*) for the observer to use to identify itself to the target, and the observer has a method (*update*) that the target calls to inform the observer of a state change. The sequence of actions is illustrated in Figure 10.8. The observer is first shown registering with the target. Then in the bottom part of the figure, a generic scenario in which the target changes state is depicted. A client gives the target a command, called *change* in the figure, that causes the target to change state. The target lets the observer know that it has changed state by invoking the observer's *update* method. The observer can then query the target to get specific information about the state change.

The "overlapping rectangles" under *Target* in Figure 10.8 indicate that two methods of this object are simultaneously active. That is, the method indicated as *queryState* is invoked before the method *change* has completed. The sequence of events is:

> *Client* invokes *Target.change*;
> > *Target* invokes *Observer.update*;
> > > *Observer* invokes *Target.queryState*;
> > > *Target.queryState* completes and returns control to *Observer*;
> > *Observer.update* completes and returns control to *Target*;
> *Target.change* completes and returns control to *Client*.

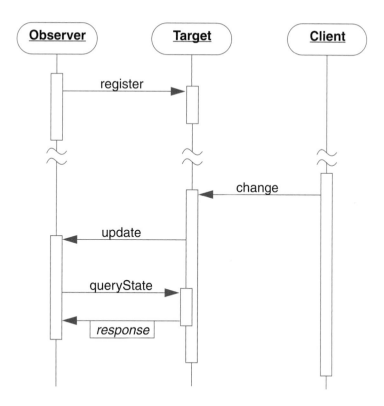

Figure 10.8   Interactions between an *Observer* and a *Target*.

In general, the target should not care whether or not an observer, or even several observers, are registered. We'll see how to handle the general case later. Our present design will require that a single observer be registered with the target.

While a typical user interface is composed of a number of objects, a single *UserInterface* instance will serve our present needs. The *UserInterface* will observe the *GameManager*; the *GameManager* will assume the responsibility of providing all relevant state information about a game.

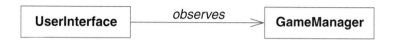

Figure 10.9   *UserInterface* observes *GameManager*.

The fundamental responsibilities of the *UserInterface* are summarized below.

Class: *UserInterface*
              interface for the simple nim system

Responsibilities: **Collaborators**:

   do:

      allow user to specify the num-
         ber of sticks to be used in a
         game
      allow the user to indicate
         whether or not another
         game is to be played
      display each play of a game,
         when the game is over, and
         which player has won

10.3.5   Object specification

We could, and probably should, go back and refine our statement of responsibilities and collaboration. But since our system is fairly simple and we've got a good idea the about the relationships we need to model, we begin specifying the classes.

    We include the class definitions in a package `nim`. Note that there is no need, at least initially, to make most of the classes *public*.

Pile specifications

We start with the specification of the *Pile*, since this object is purely a server and need not know about other objects. The job of the *Pile* is to manage the pile of sticks with which the game is to be played. Its primary responsibilities are to know how many sticks remain, and to remove sticks from the pile.

    In specifying a class, we don't necessarily want to provide the minimal functionality required to solve the problem at hand. We prefer to build a coherent, flexible, and rather complete class. In deciding which features to include, we are concerned more with whether the feature "makes sense" given the purpose of the class, than with whether or not the feature is absolutely necessary in the current problem context.

    We provide two constructors for the class *Pile*: one requires an initial size be specified, and one creates a *Pile* with no sticks. Clearly both are not required. But it is common to provide several constructors, some of which use "default" values in instantiating the class.

```
public Pile (int number)
```
Create a *Pile* with the specified number of sticks.

require:
```
number >= 0
```

ensure:
```
this.size() == number
```

```
public Pile ()
```
Create an empty *Pile*.

ensure:
```
this.size() == 0
```

Of course, we want to be able to query for the number of sticks remaining. We also include a command to set this property.

```
public int size ()
```
Number of sticks in this *Pile*.

ensure:
```
this.size() >= 0
```

```
public void setSize (int number)
```
Set the number of sticks in this *Pile*.

require:
```
number >= 0
```

ensure:
```
this.size() == number
```

The only other feature we need is a command to remove sticks from the *Pile*.

```
public void remove (int number)
```
Remove the specified number of sticks from this *Pile*.

Before we're done, we have a few design decisions to make regarding this last command. As we have written it, we are willing to accept an arbitrary **int** as argument. It's clear what should happen if we have 5 sticks in the *Pile*, and the command specifies that 3 should be removed. But what happens if the argument is 6, or 0, or –2? Will we accept such values as arguments, and if so what will we do with them? We can choose to exclude or accept such values. If we exclude them, we must explicitly say so in the method specification. If we are willing to accept them, we must clearly state what happens in these cases. Our specification for this class is not complete as it now stands.

We stipulate the following, though other alternatives are equally reasonable.

- We accept an argument of 0, since "remove 0 sticks" has a clearly understood meaning.

- We are not willing to accept negative arguments.

- We accept an argument larger than the current pile size, in which case all the sticks are removed from the pile.

The complete specification is as follows. Note that we specify that the resulting size will be 0 if the argument is greater than the current size; that is, if old.size – number is negative.

> **public void** remove (**int** number)
> > Remove the specified number of sticks from this *Pile*. If the specified number is more than the *Pile* size, remove all the sticks.
> >
> > **require:**
> > > number >= 0
> >
> > **ensure:**
> > > this.size == max(0, old.size - number)

We do not define the class to be **public**. Hence, instances of this class will be accessible only from within the package nim. Since this is the case, the keyword **public** specified for each of the methods is extraneous. We could simply have said, for instance,

> **int** size ()

A method not declared **public** is only available to clients defined in the same package. But an object of class *Pile* can only be accessed inside the package anyway, since the class itself is not **public**. If access to an object is restricted, access to its methods is also restricted. Nevertheless, we will continue to mark methods **public** to emphasize that they are part of the object's specification.

Player specification

Next we specify the *Player* class. The main responsibility of a *Player* is to make a play; *i.e.*, to remove sticks from the *Pile*. We also give each *Player* a name, so that the user can easily distinguish the *Players*.

We require that a *Player* be given a name when created, and provide methods for querying the *Player* for its name and for changing its name.

> **public** Player (String name)
> > Create a new *Player* with the specified name.
> >
> > **require:**
> > > name != null
> >
> > **ensure:**
> > > this.name() == name
>
> **public** String name ()
> > This *Player*'s name.

public void setName (String name)
>   Change this *Player*'s name.
>
>   **require:**
>>   name != null
>
>   **ensure:**
>>   this.name() == name

We have also said that a *Player* should know how many sticks were removed on its last turn. We provide a query for this value.

public int numberTaken ()
>   Number of sticks taken on this *Player*'s most recent turn.
>
>   **ensure:**
>>   this.numberTaken() >= 0
>>   if *Player* has not yet had a turn,
>>>   this.numberTaken() == 0

Since a *Player* uses the *Pile*, the *Player* must have access to the *Pile*. Specifically, the *Player* must get a reference to the *Pile* from the *GameManager*. This can be done in two ways: the *Player* can query the *GameManager* for the *Pile*, or the *GameManager* can provide the *Pile* to the *Player* as a method argument. In the first case, the *Player* needs to know the *GameManager*. While this might prove more flexible in general, we choose to have the *GameManager* explicitly provide the *Pile* as a method argument. Again, this can be accomplished in a number of ways. The *GameManager*, for instance, could provide the *Pile* as part of a game initialization process. We simply have the *GameManager* provide the *Pile* as an argument to the *Player*'s makeMove command. The *GameManager* tells the *Player* the maximum number of sticks that can be removed in the same way. The makeMove method is specified as follows.

public void makeMove (Pile pile, **int** maximum)
>   Make a move: remove up to the specified maximum number of sticks from the specified *Pile*.
>
>   **require:**
>>   pile != null
>>   maximum > 0

GameManager specification

The *GameManager* is responsible for playing a game of simple nim and knowing relevant game state information.

We require that the *GameManager* be provided with the *Player*s when it is constructed:

public GameManager (Player player1, Player player2)
> Create a nim *GameManager*, with the specified *Player*s; by default, the first *Player* specified plays first in the first game.

> **require:**
> ```
>     player1 != null
>     player2 != null
> ```

The *GameManager* is responsible for providing state information about the game to the *UserInterface*. State information the interface might be interested in includes:

- the number of sticks left;
- the number of sticks taken on the last play;
- which *Player* made the last play;
- which *Player*'s turn is next;
- whether or not the game is over;
- if the game is over, who won.

We specify a query to provide each of these pieces of information.

public int sticksLeft ()
> The number of sticks in the pile.

> **ensure:**
> ```
>     this.sticksLeft() >= 0
> ```

public int sticksTaken ()
> The number of sticks taken on the last play.

> **ensure:**
> ```
>     this.sticksTaken() >= 0
> ```

public Player nextPlayer ()
> The *Player* whose turn is next.

public Player previousPlayer ()
> The *Player* who last played; returns *null* if no play has been made yet.

public boolean gameOver ()
> The game is over.

public Player winner ()
> The winning *Player*; the one who did not make the last play in the game. Returns *null* if the game is not over.

> **ensure:**
> ```
>     if this.gameOver()
>         this.winner() != this.previousPlayer()
> ```

We include commands for setting the number of sticks in the pile, and for setting which *Player* plays next:

public void setPileSize (**int** number)
Set the number of sticks in the pile.

require:
number >= 0

ensure:
this.sticksLeft() == number

public void setNextPlayer (Player player)
Set which *Player* takes the next turn.

require:
player == one of the *Players* provided as constructor arguments

ensure:
this.nextPlayer() == player

Note that providing a method by which a client can determine who plays next means that previousPlayer() and nextPlayer() are independent. We cannot assume the next *Player* is different from the previous *Player*.

Finally, we provide methods for playing the game and, since a *GameManager* is a target to be observed, for registering an observer. The observer must be a user interface.

public void register (NimUI observer)
Register a user interface; user interface will be notified of *GameManager* state changes.

require:
observer != null

public void play ()
Play a game of simple nim.

UserInterface specification

The *UserInterface* functions almost entirely as a client. When the *UserInterface* is created, we provide a *GameManager* for which it will serve as interface. We include a command update by which the model (the *GameManager*) can report state changes, and a method start to get things going:

public NimUI (GameManager theGame)
Create a new user interface for the specified *GameManager*.

require:
theGame != null

```
public void update (GameManager target)
```
Notify this user interface of a state change in the specified
GameManager.

require:
```
target != null
```

```
public void start ()
```
Start the interface.

10.4   Implementation of the system

Given the specification, implementation of the system is mostly straightforward.
However, we will encounter a few new language constructs essential for completing the implementation.

Each of the classes is included in the package nim and most make use of util-
ities defined in the package OOJ.utilities. Thus we assume that each class
definition is included in a file beginning with

```
package nim;

import OOJ.utilities.*;
```

10.4.1   The top level

As we've seen in Section 5.3, we need a main method to create the top-level
objects and get the program started.

As before, the class containing main contains only no other method and is not
used to model any other part of the system.

```
/**
 * Top-level class for the game "Simple Nim."
 */
public class NimGame {
   /**
    * Create top-level objects, start the system.
    */
   public static void main (String[] argv) {
      GameManager theGame = new GameManager(
                 new Player("Player 1"),
                 new Player("Player 2"));
      NimUI theInterface = new NimUI(theGame);
      theInterface.start();
   }
}
```

10.4.2 The model

Pile implementation

Implementation of the class *Pile* is straightforward and is given in Listing 10.1. Notice that the statement

```
this(arguments);
```

can appear as the first statement of a constructor to invoke another constructor of the class. The constructor with no arguments uses this statement at ❶ to invoke the other constructor, with an argument of 0. This is a conventional way of handling constructors that provide defaults.

Listing 10.1 The class *Pile*

```
/**
 * Pile of sticks for the nim game.
 */
class Pile {

    // Constructors:

    /**
     * Create an empty Pile.
     *     ensure:
     *         this.size() == 0
     */
    public Pile () {
❶      this(0);
    }

    /**
     * Create a Pile with the specified number of sticks.
     *     require:
     *         number >= 0
     *     ensure:
     *         this.size() == number
     */
    public Pile (int number) {
        Require.condition(number >= 0);
        this.size = number;
    }
```

continued

Listing 10.1   The class *Pile (continued)*

===

```java
// Queries:

/**
 * Number of sticks in this Pile.
 *     ensure:
 *         this.size() >= 0
 */
public int size () {
   return this.size;
}

// Commands:

/**
 * Set the number of sticks in this Pile.
 *     require:
 *         number >= 0
 *     ensure:
 *         this.size() == number
 */
public void setSize (int number) {
   Require.condition(number >= 0);
   this.size = number;
}

/**
 * Remove the specified number of sticks from this
 * Pile. If the specified number is more than the
 * Pile size, remove all the sticks.
 *     require:
 *         number >= 0
 *     ensure:
 *         this.size == max(0, old.size - number)
 */
public void remove (int number) {
   Require.condition(number >= 0);
   if (number <= this.size)
      this.size = this.size - number;
   else
      this.size = 0;
}
```

continued

Listing 10.1 **The class *Pile (continued)***

```
    // Private components:

    private int size;// number of sticks in this Pile
                    // invariant: size >= 0

} // end of class Pile
```

Player implementation

This class is shown in Listing 10.2. The strategy of `makeMove` can be as simple or as sophisticated as we want. In this implementation, the method is not particularly clever. Since we attempt to remove no more sticks than are in the *Pile*, the *Pile* promises to remove exactly the number requested.

We introduce the method `notNull` of class `Require`, for example, at ❶. We could have written

```
    Require.condition(name != null);
```

but this is such a common condition that we give it its own method.

Listing 10.2 **The class *Player***

```
/**
 * Player in the nim game.
 */
class Player {

    // Constructors:

    /**
     * Create a new Player with the specified name.
     *    require:
     *        name != null
     */
    public Player (String name) {
❶       Require.notNull(name);
        this.name = name;
        this.numberTaken = 0;
    }
```

continued

Listing 10.2   **The class *Player (continued)***

```java
// Queries:

/**
 * This Player's name.
 */
public String name () {
   return this.name;
}

/**
 * Number of sticks taken on the Player's most
 * recent turn.
 *     ensure:
 *         this.numberTaken() >= 0
 *         if Player has not yet had a turn,
 *             this.numberTaken == 0
 */
public int numberTaken () {
   return this.numberTaken;
}

// Commands:

/**
 * Change this Player's name.
 *     require:
 *         name != null
 *     ensure:
 *         this.name() == name
 */
public void setName (String name) {
   Require.notNull(name);
   this.name = name;
}

/**
 * Make a move: remove up to the specified maximum
 * number of sticks from the specified Pile.
 *     require:
 *         pile != null
 *         maximum > 0
 */
```

continued

Listing 10.2 The class *Player (continued)*

```
public void makeMove (Pile pile, int maximum) {
   Require.notNull(pile);
   Require.condition(maximum > 0);
   int size;   // pile size
   int number; // number to take
   size = pile.size();
   if (size == 0)
      number = 0;
   else if (2 <= size && size <= maximum+1)
      number = size-1;
   else
      number = 1;
   pile.remove(number);
   this.numberTaken = number;
}

// Private Components:

private String name;      // Player's name
private int numberTaken;  // number of sticks taken
                          // on Player's last move
} // end of class Player
```

GameManager implementation

The *GameManager* is given in Listing 10.3. It has components referencing the two *Players* and the *Pile*. The *Pile* is created by the *GameManager*, as part of its constructor action.

There are also components referencing the *Player* to play next (next-Player), and the *Player* who made the previous move (previous-Player). During the normal course of play, these will be different players; *i.e.*, one will reference player1 and the other will reference player2. But as we mentioned above, since we have included a method to set who plays next explicitly (setNextPlayer), we cannot *guarantee* that nextPlayer and previousPlayer will be different. Thus we keep express account of who made the last move.

Most of the queries are obvious. Notice that the queries sticksLeft and sticksTaken are forwarded to the appropriate objects. There is no need to duplicate these data values as *GameManager* components. In order to avoid possible inconsistencies, it's best to store each data value in only one place.

The method `otherPlayer`, defined at ❸, is local to the class. It is not part of the specification of the class *GameManager*. It is simply a handy auxiliary method that can be used in the class, for instance at ❷.

The method `play` employs a *while* statement at ❹. This statement was introduced in Section 8.3.2. When the *while* statement is reached, the condition `!gameOver()` is evaluated. If this condition is *true*—that is, the game is not over—the statements inside the braces are executed. The condition `!gameOver()` is again evaluated and the process repeats. Thus execution of the *while* statement results in players removing sticks until there are no more sticks left in the pile, and the game is over.

Note that the maximum number of sticks that can be taken on a single turn is defined as named constant at ❶. The constant is *public* so that it is available to *GameManager* clients, and is used rather than a literal in the call at ❺.

Finally, note that the *UserInterface* is notified after each play at ❻.

Listing 10.3   **The class *GameManager***

```
/**
 * Manager of the game "Simple Nim."
 */
class GameManager {

   // Constructors:

   /**
    * Create a nim game manager, with the specified
    * Players; by default, the first Player specified
    * plays first in the first game.
    *    require:
    *       player1 != null
    *       player2 != null
    */
   public GameManager (Player player1, Player player2) {
      Require.notNull(player1);
      Require.notNull(player2);
      this.player1 = player1;
      this.player2 = player2;
      this.thePile = new Pile();
      this.nextPlayer = player1;
      this.previousPlayer = null;
   }
```

continued

Listing 10.3 **The class *GameManager* (continued)**

===

```
// Constants:

/**
 * The maximum number of sticks that can be removed
 * on a single turn.
 */
public static final int MAX_REMOVED = 3;

// Queries:
/**
 * The number of sticks in the pile.
 *   ensure:
 *     this.sticksLeft() >= 0
 */
public int sticksLeft () {
   return thePile.size();
}


/*
 * The number of sticks taken on the last play.
 *   ensure:
 *     this.sticksTaken() >= 0
 */
public int sticksTaken () {
   if (this.previousPlayer == null)
      return 0;
   else
      return this.previousPlayer.numberTaken();
}

/**
 * The Player whose turn is next.
 */
public Player nextPlayer () {
   return this.nextPlayer;
}

/**
 * The Player who last played; returns null if no play
 * has been made yet.
 */
```

❶

continued

Listing 10.3   The class *GameManager* (continued)

```
        public Player previousPlayer () {
            return this.previousPlayer;
        }

        /**
         * The game is over.
         */
        public boolean gameOver () {
            return this.thePile.size() == 0;
        }

        /**
         * The winning Player; returns null if the game is not
         * over.
         */
        public Player winner () {
            if (gameOver())
❷              return otherPlayer(this.previousPlayer);
            else
                return null;

        }

        /**
         * The Player who is not the specified Player.
         */
❸      private Player otherPlayer (Player player) {
            if (player == this.player1)
                return this.player2;
            else
                return this.player1;
        }

        // Commands:

        /**
         * Register a user interface; user interface will be
         * notified of game state changes.
         *   require:
         *     observer != null
         */
        public void register (NimUI observer) {
            Require.notNull(observer);
            this.ui = observer;
        }
```

continued

Listing 10.3   **The class *GameManager (continued)***

```
/**
 * Play a game of Simple Nim.
 */
public void play () {
    while (!gameOver()) {
        this.nextPlayer.makeMove(this.thePile,
            this.MAX_REMOVED);
        this.previousPlayer = this.nextPlayer;
        this.nextPlayer = otherPlayer(this.nextPlayer);
        this.ui.update(this);
    }
}

/**
 * Set the number of sticks in the pile.
 *   require:
 *     number >= 0
 */
public void setPileSize (int number) {
    Require.condition(number>=0);
    this.thePile.setSize(number);
}

/**
 * Set which Player takes the next turn.
 *     require:
 *         player == one of the Players provided as
 *             constructor arguments
 */
public void setNextPlayer (Player player) {
    Require.condition(
        player == player1 ||
        player == player2);
    this.nextPlayer = player;
}

// Private components:

private Player player1; // the Players
private Player player2;
private Player nextPlayer;
                // the Player whose turn it is
```

❹
❺

❻

continued

Listing 10.3 **The class *GameManager (continued)***

===

```
    private Player previousPlayer;
                        // the Player who made the last move
    private Pile thePile;    // the pile of sticks
    private NimUI ui;        // the user interface

} // end of class GameManager
```

10.4.3   User interface implementation

Finally, we look at the implementation of the *UserInterface*. As we said above, this is not the kind of event-driven graphical interface we ultimately want to build. But there is something to learn here, and we need some form of interface to complete the system.

We build a text-oriented user interface employing the same *BasicFileReader* and *BasicFileWriter* classes we used to build the test driver in Chapter 8. The interface is extremely simple and not very robust. That is, we ignore the possibility that the user might provide inappropriate input. When we ask the user to key in either a 0 or 1, for example, we assume that's what we get. If the user keys something else, the program simply fails. This approach is adequate for testing the model, but would hardly be suitable for a commercial production system.

The user interface is provided with the *GameManager* when created, and creates a *BasicFileReader* and *BasicFileWriter* in the constructor.

Most of the methods are private, local methods, used to organize the interaction with the user into coherent, easy to understand, pieces. The methods labeled "set" get information from the user, while those labeled "report" provide the user with information about the state of the game. The *UserInterface* class is defined in Listing 10.4.

Notice the use of concatenation, at ❷ for instance, in building output.

Note that local variables do not need to be declared at the beginning of a method. Line ❶ in the method setPlayAgain for example, is a declaration of a local **int** variable code.

The start method contains a *while* statement. This causes the *UserInterface* to run until the user indicates that he or she wants to see no more games. (Recall that the main method invoked start to get the system going.) Before each game, the user can determine how many sticks are to be in the pile.

Finally, look at the method `update`. The *GameManager* that invokes this method provides itself as argument. This is a good idea, since in general an observer might be observing more than one target. It's not absolutely necessary in our case, since the *UserInterface* already knows which *GameManager* is reporting a change of state. That is, the parameter g of the method `update` and the instance variable `myGame` will refer to the same *GameManager* instance. The *UserInterface* queries the *GameManager* to obtain state information to report to the user.

Listing 10.4   **The class *NimUI***

```
/**
 * A NimUI object is a user interface for the nim game.
 * This minimal interface does not validate input.
 */
class NimUI {

   /**
    * Create a new user interface for the specified
    * GameManager.
    *   require:
    *      theGame != null
    */
   public NimUI (GameManager theGame) {
      Require.notNull(theGame);
      myGame = theGame;
      done = false;
      input = new OOJ.basicIO.BasicFileReader();
      output = new OOJ.basicIO.BasicFileWriter();
   }

   /**
    * Notify this user interface of a state change in the
    * specified GameManager.
    */
   public void update (GameManager g) {
      String player = g.previousPlayer().name();
      int taken = g.sticksTaken();
      int left = g.sticksLeft();
      reportPlay(player, taken, left);
```

continued

Listing 10.4   **The class *NimUI (continued)***

=====

```
         if (g.gameOver()) {
             Player winner = g.winner();
             if (winner != null) {
                 String name = winner.name();
                 reportWinner(name);
             } else
                 reportNoGame();
         }
     }

     /**
      * Start the interface.
      */
     public void start () {
         myGame.register(this);
         while (!this.done) {
             setSticks();
             myGame.play();
             setPlayAgain();
         }
     }

     /**
      * Determine if the user wants to play again.
      */
     private void setPlayAgain () {
         output.displayLine("To play again, enter 1;" +
             "to stop, enter 0");
         input.readInt();
❶        int code = input.lastInt();
         input.readLine();
         this.done = code == 0;
     }

     /**
      * Determine the number of sticks to play with.
      */
     private void setSticks () {
         output.displayLine("Enter number of sticks.");
         input.readInt();
         int number = input.lastInt();
         input.readLine();
         myGame.setPileSize(number);
     }
```

continued

Listing 10.4 **The class *NimUI (continued)***

```
/**
 * Report the end of the game.
 */
private void reportWinner (String winner) {
❷     output.displayLine("Game over. " + winner + " won.");
}

/**
 * Report a play.
 */
private void reportPlay (String player, int taken,
    int left) {
    output.displayLine(
        "Player " + player + " takes " + taken +
        " leaving " + left + " sticks.");
}

/**
 * Report no game played.
 */
private void reportNoGame () {
    output.displayLine("No game played.");
}

// Private Components:

private GameManager myGame;     // the game observed
private boolean done;           // user is finished
private OOJ.basicIO.BasicFileReader input;
private OOJ.basicIO.BasicFileWriter output;

} // end of class NimUI
```

10.5 Summary

In this chapter, we have seen how to put together a complete, simple system. We began by considering the life cycle of a system: problem analysis, specification, design, implementation, testing, and maintenance. We then briefly examined the three basic functional subsystems: specifically, the interface, model, and data management components.

As a case study, we carried out the design and implementation of a system to play the simple nim game. System design involved identifying classes, assigning responsibilities to the classes, determining fundamental relationships between classes, and writing detailed class specifications.

As part of the design process, we considered the integration of the user interface with the model. We saw exhibited a common relational pattern, the *observes* relation. In this relation, one object, the *observer*, needs to know when another object, the *target* or *observed*, changes. The observer *registers* with the target, and the target informs the observer of its (the target's) state changes by invoking an observer method (*update*). In our design, the interface acts as the observer and the model as the target.

Finally, we implemented the system and encountered a few new language constructs in the process. We saw how to use a *main* method to get the system started and how to use a *while-loop* to repeat an action a number of times. In building the user interface, we introduced some simple classes for doing input and output, and learned about the concatenation operator for strings.

EXERCISES

10.1   Consider systems to play the following games:

    a. tic-tac-toe;

    b. monopoly;

    c. chess;

    d. poker;

    e. a rogue-like maze-crawling game;

    f. an adventure-like cave exploration game.

For each,

- write a concise statement of the functionality required of the system;
- develop a list of potential model classes;
- specify responsibilities for the fundamental model classes;
- create a set of diagrams that illustrate important relationships between fundamental model classes.

10.2   Do the same fundamental design described in the previous exercise for any of the following systems:

    a. a system to manage inventory in a video store;

    b. a system to schedule classrooms on a campus;

    c. a system to manage windows on a computer desktop;

    d. a system to produce and edit architectural plans for houses.

10.3   There is an easy way to determine perfect strategy for the simple nim game. That is, if the number of sticks is known, one of the players has a winning strategy. Consider the situation from the point of view of the player whose turn it is. One stick left is clearly a losing situation. But 2, 3, or 4 sticks left are winning situations, since by making an appropriate choice, the player can leave the other player with the last stick. If there are 5 sticks left, it is a losing situation since no matter what the player does, the other player is left with a winning situation—that is, the other player is left with 2, 3, or 4 sticks. Continuing in this manner, we see that if there are 6, 7, or 8 sticks left, the player can leave the other player with 5—that is, leave the other player in a losing situation. So 6, 7, or 8 are winning situations. Summarizing:

number of sticks: 1 2 3 4 5 6 7 8 9 10 11 12 13 ...
win/lose: L W W W L W W W L W   W   W   L   ...

Rewrite the `Player` method `makeMove` to use a "perfect" strategy.

(Hint: you will find the remainder operator, `%`, handy in writing this method.)

10.4   It might be more interesting if the user got to determine the plays in the nim game rather than simply observe the play. Rewrite `Player` to include a command `setMove` that tells the `Player` how many sticks to take on its next turn. Modify the user interface so that the user provides the number of sticks each `Player` is to take on each turn.

GLOSSARY

collaborator: an object that assists another object in accomplishing some responsibility of the second object.

compositional process: a procedure for building an entity by combining simpler pieces.

data management: the system component responsible for storing and retrieving persistent data.

event driven system: an interactive system in which system action ("response") is triggered by some external event, such as a user entering text on a keyboard or moving a mouse.

external interface: the system component responsible for interacting with the external world.

functional specification: a description of the functionality required of a system. (See *system specification*.)

iterative process: a procedure for solving a problem by repeated steps.

model: the system component responsible for actually solving the particular problem. (See *problem domain subsystem*.)

observed: the target object in the *observes* relation.

observer: the source object in the *observes* relation.

observes: a relation in which one object (the *observer*) is informed when another object (the *target* or *observed*) changes state.

persistent data: data maintained externally and independently of what the system is doing, and which continues to exist across multiple system runs.

problem analysis: a thorough examination of the problem to be solved, resulting in a *system specification*.

problem domain subsystem: the system component responsible for actually solving the particular problem. (See *model*.)

software life cycle: phases a software system undergoes from its inception to its retirement.

system design: the process of defining a collection of classes and their interactions that will satisfy the system specifications.

system implementation: the process of constructing the (software) modules that will make up the system, using programming languages and other software development tools.

system maintenance: the process of modifying a system to meet changing requirements and correcting problems detected after the system is put into production.

system specification: a description of the functionality required of a system. (See *functional specification*.)

testing: phase of system implementation concerned with verifying that system performs according to the specification.

user interface: an external interface that interacts with a person, the system user.

CHAPTER 11

Software quality

In previous chapters, we mentioned the difficulty involved in dealing with the evolving nature and complexity of a software system. Our approach to software design and construction is largely dictated by the goal of managing complexity while producing a system that can be easily adapted to changing needs. In essence, we want to produce quality software. In this chapter, we step back from our detailed discussion of system development and take a brief look at what we mean by quality software. Specifically, we enumerate some of the important properties we want our systems to have. Of particular importance are the attributes of correctness and maintainability; that is, the system must do what it is supposed to do and be able to be modified easily when necessary. We also identify some of the general characteristics our designs must exhibit if the systems we build are to achieve these standards of quality.

11.1 External qualities

The qualities of a software system that are our ultimate goal—the qualities that the user is concerned with—are sometimes called *external qualities*. The attributes of a system that help achieve these external qualities are *internal qualities*. For example, the external qualities important in an automobile are things like reliability, safety, fuel efficiency, speed, good handling, smooth ride, *etc*. These are what the customer—the user of the automobile—is concerned with. To achieve a smooth ride, the designers might attempt to minimize unsprung weight. Low unsprung weight is an internal quality. The customer is not particularly interested in unsprung weight; the customer wants a smooth ride. Minimizing unsprung weight helps achieve the external quality that the customer wants.

Some of the attributes we want systems to have are quantitative and measurable; others are qualitative. With an automobile, for instance, fuel efficiency is a well-defined, empirically measurable notion. (Of course, what counts as *acceptable* fuel efficiency is relative and qualitative.) On the other hand, safety is a less precise, relative notion. To deal with such qualitative ideas, we generally define a set of measurable attributes that we expect will corellate closely with the qualitative attributes. For example, to "measure" automobile safety, we might design a set of crash tests and carefully specify a measurable set of criteria that constitute acceptable performance in these tests.

What are the important external qualities of a software system—the attributes that are important to the user? Probably the most obvious is *correctness*. A system is correct if it behaves as expected in all cases; that is, if it *conforms to its specifications*. This is not as simple an idea as it first seems. We must first know what it is supposed to do in all possible circumstances, completely and precisely. This is given by the system's *functional specifications*. But developing a complete, precise, and consistent set of specifications for a large system is no trivial matter. Furthermore, assuming we have an adequate specification, how do we tell if the system satisfies it? We can test the system, but we cannot conceivably test all situations. Verifying that a system satisfies a set of specifications is also not an easy matter.

A second quality that usually comes to mind is *efficiency*. By efficiency, we sometimes mean the amount of memory space required to run the system, but more often we mean the time it takes for a system to perform a particular function. For some systems, called *real-time systems*, response time, the time required for a system to respond to some stimulus, is a matter of correctness. Think of a small computer in an anti-lock brake system. When the system detects that a wheel is not rotating, it must respond by releasing the brake. If the time between detecting the wheel lock and releasing the brake is too long, the vehicle will skid. That is, *correctness* requires that the system respond within a specified period of time. As another example, imagine a computer controlling a deceleration thruster on a planetary lander. When the lander comes within a certain distance of a planet's surface, the thruster must be fired to slow the lander. Again, if the system does not respond within a carefully specified amount of time, disaster will result.

For most systems, though, efficiency is a relative matter. If we click a button that instructs the system to balance this month's accounts, it probably doesn't matter to us whether it takes a half second or five seconds. On the other hand, we would not find it acceptable if five seconds elapsed between the time we pressed a key and time the character appeared on the screen.

Another important quality is *ease of use* or *user friendliness*. This is a very relative, hard to measure notion. Indeed, what qualifies as "easy to use" for one person can be annoyingly constraining for another, and impossibly obscure for a third. We will not attempt to discuss the many measures, tests, and principles that have been suggested in this area.

A key aspect of ease of use is *robustness*. A system is robust if it behaves reasonably when encountering unexpected circumstances or incorrect input. Suppose, for instance, a system asks for a user's age (expecting an integer), and the user keys in his name instead. A system that crashes in this situation is not very robust. We would like the system to help the user along, perhaps with a more detailed explanation of what was expected, and give him a chance to try again. (An old adage, however, says that it is impossible to make a system idiot-proof because idiots are too damned clever.)

A system should be *maintainable*. It might seem a bit odd to use the term "maintenance" in regard to software. After all, software doesn't wear out or break down like an automobile or washing machine. Software maintenance generally refers to activities that modify a system after the system has been put into production. Maintenance activities can be classified according to the objective of the modifications:

- *corrective*: taken to correct errors detected in the system;

- *adaptive*: taken to adapt the system to changes in the environment or in the user's requirements;

- *perfective*: taken to improve the quality of the system.

Even with thoroughly tested software, bugs—programming errors—are occasionally discovered after the system is put in use. Some errors go undiscovered for years, showing up only when some very unusual circumstance occurs. One aspect of software maintenance involves tracking down and correcting errors discovered in a production system. A second aspect has to do with the fact that software exists in a dynamic environment. As needs change, the software must be modified and extended. (Software that can be easily adapted to changing circumstances is sometimes called *extendible*.) Modifying production systems to meet evolving specifications is another important part of software maintenance.

We should note that software maintenance is a rather substantive issue. It is generally accepted that about 70% of software cost is due to maintenance, and studies have indicated that upwards of 40% of maintenance costs result from changes in user requirements. The approach to software design we adopt is rooted in the goal of making the system maintainable: in particular, we want to build systems for which a small change in requirements necessitates only a small change in the system.

Though we could extend this list of desirable attributes for many pages, we'll mention just a couple more. *Portability* measures the ease with which a software system can be transferred to run on different kinds of computers and under different operating systems—that is, on "different platforms." The advantage here is that the user is not confined to a particular vendor and can take advantage of price/performance advances in the technology.

Compatibility means that one software system is able to work with others. For instance, if we use a particular computer-aided design (CAD) system to produce technical drawings, a spreadsheet to do cost analysis, and publishing software to create reports, we may well want to incorporate CAD drawings and spreadsheet graphs in a report created with the publishing software. This can be trivial or almost impossible, depending on the compatibility of the three software products.

Note that these qualities are not necessarily implied by the functional requirements of the system. For instance, two distinct implementations of the same set of functional requirements may differ dramatically in efficiency, maintainability, portability, and so on.

11.2   Complexity

Now that we've listed a few of the external qualities we'd like our software to have, we'll take a very brief look at some of the internal qualities that have proven indispensable in achieving these goals. It might be difficult, at this stage, to appreciate the significance of these points fully. In fact, the points themselves may be a bit obscure and hard to comprehend. Nevertheless, we feel obligated at least to sketch the goals toward which so much of our approach is directed, even if their import is not yet completely evident.

As we have emphasized, complexity is the principal obstacle to the creation of correct, reliable, maintainable software. Software systems are, of course, inherently complex. A program performs millions of actions a second, each of which must be specified at some level by system designers. A good design, however, can reduce complexity considerably. We must build our systems from components that are simple enough to be comprehensible. The problem is that the number of possible interactions between components grows as the square of the number of components. Thus an important key to managing complexity is to control the interactions between components. Components should be as self-contained as possible; interactions should be minimal and carefully defined.

11.3   Modularity

To say that a software system is *modular* is simply to say that it is made up of components (*i.e.*, of *modules*). This is somewhat tautological: every piece of software is in some way made up of pieces. To achieve the benefits we seek in managing complexity, modules must be self-contained and coherent. What, specifically, does this mean?

In the first place, we'd like the logical modularity of our design to be supported by the programming language and development system. That is, the logical components of the design should correspond to physically separate syntactic software components. We'd like to be able to manage these software components independently during system development. For instance, we'd like to be able to keep separate components in separate files, have different programmers develop and test them, and so forth. If we are not able to reflect the logical structure of the system with the physical structure of the program, we're starting with a considerable handicap.

Cohesion is a measure of the degree to which a module *completely* encapsulates a *single* notion. Note that there are two aspects to this definition: a module has to do with only one notion, and it in some sense completely represents it. When we say "notion," we mean a facet of the system's functionality or data. If we're designing functionally, we want a module to describe a single function of the system completely—for instance, the operation of producing a student's transcript in a student record system. (This is sometimes referred to as *functional strength*.) If our design is object oriented, we want a module to describe a single kind of data object completely. For instance, an object representing a student in a student record system should completely encapsulate the data and functionality associated with the student, and nothing else.

Coupling is a measure of the degree to which a module interacts with and depends on other modules. That is, it is a measure of intermodule dependency. Clearly, a module that is part of a system must have something to do with other parts of the system. But as we stated above, the number of possible interactions between components grows in proportion to the square of the number of components. If every module in a system can directly affect every other, the complexity of the system is bound to be unmanageable. We want a module to interact with as few other modules as possible, and we want the interaction to be through a minimal, well-defined interface. If two modules need to exchange data, for instance, they should exchange only what is absolutely necessary. Interactions between modules should be clearly defined: one module should not depend on another in subtle and unclear ways. To get a better idea of what we mean, consider a computer workstation and the diesel generator that provides its electrical power. Both of these are very complex physical systems. But their interface is through a simple, well-defined, standard mechanism. The power generator provides electricity with certain well-defined characteristics to a receptacle of specific configuration, and the computer has a power cord that plugs into the receptacle.

Clearly, we want to design modules with *high cohesion* and *weak coupling*. If our modules are well-designed, then effecting a small change in the system should require modification of only a few closely related modules. As we've mentioned, experience has shown that this can be best accomplished by organizing the modular structure of the system around the data rather than around functionality. Furthermore, well-defined modules will localize the effects of run-time errors, simplifying the maintenance process. For example, a module responsible for getting input data might also be responsible for validating that the data is reasonable and has the proper format. Thus bad data doesn't spread through the system, causing hard to trace errors in disparate parts of the system. Problems from the bad data are constrained to the input module, where they can be more easily identified and addressed.

The modular construction of a hardware system, in which extensive use is made of standard components from a parts catalogue, is often contrasted with the construction of a typical software system, where components are hand-crafted from scratch. There would be clear advantages, in terms of cost and reliability, to having a collection of reliably correct software components that could be used in the construction of new systems. Much of the focus of object-oriented methodologies is on creating *reusable software modules*. By this we mean something a little different from prefabricated blocks we can plug together. While it's handy to have a library of standard pieces that can be plugged into commonly occurring situations, a better description of what we want to achieve might be "tailorable software components." Like the basic black shift that we can take up or let down, appoint with a collar or belt, and generally adjust to suit myriad situations, we'd like modules that we can get off the rack and use in our system with only a few minor alterations. Note that the same qualities that make a module easy to adjust for use in a new system also make it easy to adjust to meet changing needs in an existing system.

11.4   Three principles

Before we complete our discussion of software quality, we present three design principles, articulated by Bertrand Meyer in his excellent text *Object Oriented Software Construction* [Meyer 88, 97]. These are the *information hiding principle*, the *principle of continuity*, and the *open-closed principle*. We'll explore these ideas and their consequences thoroughly in the remainder of the text.

Let's suppose that you and I work for a large university in the days when records were kept manually. You work in the Student Records Office, and I work in Financial Aid and Scholarships. In order to determine who should be awarded particular scholarships, I need to get student data from your files. To simplify and standardize this procedure, a form has been devised that I use to request information. For instance, I may request a list of all juniors in Mathematics with a grade point average greater than 3.5. Now whether or not this works well depends on a number of circumstances: how well the form has been designed, how responsive your staff is to my requests, how reasonable I am in my expectations, and so forth. But our interface is simple and well-defined. It doesn't matter if you happen to be out for a day; any clerk in the Records Office can satisfy my request, and I don't particularly care who does. Also if I happen to get a better offer from the school across town and leave, it shouldn't take my replacement long to figure out how to get data from the Records Office.

Now suppose that your files are in an accessible location, and I get tired of using the standard procedures. When I need some information, I rummage through your files myself. The more I use the files, the more details I learn about them. For instance, I discover that there are no files for Math majors in the green cabinet against the wall. I might even begin to make my own notes on your files. What I've done is created a set of rather subtle unspecified dependencies between what I do and your file system. In software terms, I've violated the rule that modules should be weakly coupled: that is, have minimal interaction through a well-defined interface. An innocent change on your part—for instance, you move some Math files to the green cabinet—can cause the system to fail.

A principle that helps minimize the interdependency of modules is the *information hiding principle*. Basically this rule says that the only information one module should be able to obtain about another is that required by the well-defined interface between them. In our example, this means that you shouldn't give me direct access to your files. Then I can't depend on any particular organization of your records. If you change the way you handle student records, it cannot possibly affect me as long as you continue to satisfy my formal requests.

Suppose that a situation arises where cultural considerations need to be taken into account in the awarding of certain scholarships. The Lithuanian Society, for instance, funds several scholarships to encourage students of Lithuanian descent to pursue engineering degrees. It may well be the case that student records do not include information such as national heritage. Adding this kind of information should be a relatively minor change in the system. One would not expect, for instance, that the Accounting Department would have to take notice of such a change. The *principle of continuity* states that a small change in the specifications of a system should result in a small change in the system. In particular, a small change should affect only a few modules in the system, and not the entire structure of the system itself. When each module needs to know details of all the principle data objects, or when knowledge about any specific data item is spread throughout the system, a small change will propagate through the entire system. This is exactly what occurs when the system design is organized around functionality. As we have mentioned a number of times, structuring the system around data rather than around functionality measurably enhances a system's continuity.

A module that can still be modified is said to be *open*. A module that is available for use by other modules is said to be *closed*. We would like to design and build our systems so that the modules are both open and closed. This is the *open-closed principle*. The idea is that we would like to be able to modify or extend a module without affecting other modules—even those that interact with the one being modified—that are not directly concerned with the modification. In the context of our example, we would like to be able to modify student records to include information regarding national heritage without this change affecting the

Accounting Department. That is, the Accounting Department should be able to continue using information from student records without taking notice that the records have been modified to include additional information. Clearly, the open-closed principle is closely related to the continuity principle.

11.5   What is a software system, revisited

We addressed the question of what we meant by a software system in the first chapter. Now that we've taken a look at some of the attributes we want our systems to have, we return to this question and offer three views of what software should be. We want to consider these views as defining criteria for evaluating our software systems and for guiding our developmental efforts.

11.5.1   Software = a temporary solution to an evolving problem

When we build software systems, we cannot simply look for specific solutions to specific problems. We must produce solutions that are amenable to change. Appreciating the fact that malleability must be an essential attribute of our software helps identify fundamental activities that should be part of the design and implementation process. Specifically, we must *design* a system that adequately models the problem as currently perceived, yet *implement* the system in such a way as to minimize dependency on the particularities of the problem at hand.

These two seemingly contradictory goals are addressed through *object design* and *algorithm design*. Object design produces the collection of objects that not only model the problem at hand, but also provide a set of fixed conceptual constituents in terms of which system evolution can be expressed. Object design also defines how the objects interact to solve the problem at hand. Algorithm design involves providing the detailed functionality of the objects. Put simply, as the system changes we expect the behavior of the individual objects to change, and we expect the way in which the objects interact to change. But we expect the set of objects in terms of which the system is defined to remain stable.

You should note that this view of software is intimately related to the principles outlined in the previous section. From this perspective, the quality of a model used to produce a solution depends on how successfully the stable components, as objects, are identified and isolated from those aspects of the problem likely to change. A successful approach segments the most volatile aspects of the system, so that change and modification can be localized.

The term "temporary" is a key one to keep in mind. Problems and their solutions are not rigid, well-defined, well-behaved. Version 1.0 is never the final product. By qualifying a solution as temporary, we intend to encourage a perspective in which emphasis will be placed on identifying those fundamental components, central to the problem, that serve as a supporting framework for an evolving system.

11.5.2   Software = data + algorithms

Niklaus Wirth introduced the formula "Algorithms + Data Structures = Programs" in his 1975 book of that name [Wirth 75]. Wirth's point was that since every program handles data, attention must be paid to how the representation of the data can affect the algorithm. Developments in object-oriented methods have given a twist to Wirth's equation. Experience has shown that data is the fundamental and most stable aspect of a software system. Not only must we isolate data representation as a separate concern, we must carefully design the abstract view of the data and the relationships between component data objects. What we mean to say is that "software = design of data representation followed by algorithm design." The design of an abstract view of the data, followed by the implementation of this abstract view by means of algorithms, is the essence of programming.

11.5.3   Software = English document and a mathematical document

Though software is executed by machines, it is written and maintained by people. This view emphasizes the dual character of software. A software solution must be read and understood by anyone intending to maintain it. As such, it can be seen as a technical document describing the design and implementation of the solution. We can legitimately apply evaluation criteria appropriate to any document, such as readability, ease of accessing pertinent information, and so on. Though at the moment we are necessarily concerned with the details of how to express our problem solutions in a programming language, we should keep in mind that what we write must be clear and comprehensible to a human reader.

Furthermore, the correctness of the solution described by the software should be verifiable in a formal, mathematical sense. That is, the correctness of our solution should follow from the program in much the same sense that the correctness of a mathematical theorem follows from its proof. This is not an easy idea to grasp, and a complete exposition is beyond the scope of this text. But as we describe the software development process in subsequent chapters, we will illustrate how to provide checkpoints in the code to ensure that it performs as specified.

To illustrate how these views help explain the quality of a program, consider the activity of testing a program to detect a possible bug. The quality of the solution is directly related to the ease with which the bug can be isolated and corrected. Ease in identifying and correcting the problem depends on the readability of the code (software as an English document), localization of the affected code (software as structured on data abstractions), and tractability of the code to modification (software as a temporary solution).

Before closing, we again mention that you should not feel uncomfortable if these ideas seem a bit vague and ill-defined. We will spend most of the rest of the book developing methodologies intended to satisfy the goals and principles outlined here.

11.6   Summary

In this chapter, we enumerated some of the important attributes we want our systems to have. Of particular importance are the attributes of correctness—the system conforms to its specifications—and maintainability—the system can be modified with minimum difficulty to meet changing requirements. We noted that it was essential for our systems to be modular constructions, and that the composing modules be

- highly cohesive; that is, completely encapsulating a single notion; and
- weakly coupled, interacting with other modules only through a well-defined minimal interface.

We briefly touched on the importance of constructing reusable—that is, tailorable—modules.

We concluded with three design principles:

- *information hiding*: a module has no access to another module except as explicitly required by the interface;
- *continuity*: a small change in specifications necessitates only a small change in the system; and
- *open/closed*: a module that is available for use by other modules can still be modified;

and three views of software:

- software is a temporary solution to a changing problem;
- software is data design followed by algorithm design;
- software is a technical English document and a formal mathematical document.

EXERCISES

11.1 The discussion of correctness in Section 11.1 states that "we can test the system, but we cannot conceivably test all situations." Suggest some general guidelines for adequately testing a system. Can you think of any other ways of ensuring a system's correctness besides testing?

11.2 Give examples to illustrate the three type of maintenance modifications in each of the following systems:

   a. a university registration system;

   b. the maze game;

   c. a company payroll system;

   d. a university course scheduling system;

   e. a hospital patient management system.

11.3 If system maintenance is as high as 70% of the budget dedicated to system development, why aren't inadequate systems simply abandoned and new systems constructed?

11.4 Each of the statements below refers to a component or functionality of a university registration system. Indicate what property was violated in its development.

   a. The user interface component handles input/output operations to get and display data, and keeps track of the number of times the system is used.

   b. The properties used to model a student include name, social security number, address, courses the student is enrolled in, and the instructors of these courses.

   c. Students who take only occasional courses and are not pursuing a degree need to be accommodated in the registration system. In evaluating the system for this extension, it is determined that about 80% of the system's code needs to be modified.

   d. The component that computes a student's grade point average uses the date the grade point average was last computed, and whether the student has completed any new courses since then.

11.5 Discuss how various system properties affect the ability of a software system to evolve.

11.6 *Correctness* is a software property that overrides any other. Suppose one system is very efficient in producing results, but sometimes the results are not within the required degree of accuracy. Another system is not as fast, but all its results are correct and within the required accuracy. Which system would you prefer and why? How would you respond to someone who argued, "I just need ballpark figures from the system, but I need them quickly"? How would you respond to someone who said "I'll take a system that's fast, even if I have to put up with it crashing once in a while"?

11.7   Assume a set of requirements is implemented via two systems, where one system's source code is twice as large as the other's. What can you infer about the systems with respect to:

    a.   time taken to develop the system;

    b.   correctness of the system;

    c.   maintainability of the system;

    d.   efficiency of the system.

11.8   When we implement a method, what do we do that reflects the fact that we are preparing a mathematical document? What do we do that reflects the fact that we are preparing an English document?

GLOSSARY

cohesion: a measure of the degree to which a module completely encapsulates a single notion.

compatibility: a property exhibited by software systems that can be used in conjunction with each other.

continuity principle: a system should be designed so that a small change in requirements can be accomplished with a correspondingly small change in the system.

correctness: a property exhibited by a system that performs according to its specifications.

coupling: a measure of the degree to which a module interacts with and depends on other modules.

efficiency: a property exhibited by a system that requires a minimal amount of time to accomplish a task.

extendibility: a property exhibited by a system that can be easily modified to meet additional requirements.

functional strength: a property exhibited by a module that performs only one function, and performs that function completely.

information hiding principle: a module should be designed so that only a well-defined, essential subset of the module's features are available to client modules.

maintainability: a property exhibited by a system that can be easily modified to adapt to changing requirements, and in which run-time errors can be easily isolated and corrected.

modularity: a property exhibited by a system that is composed of coherent, self-contained, syntactic components.

open-closed principle: modules should be available for use by other modules (closed) and still available for extension (open).

portability: a property exhibited by a system that can be easily transferred to different platforms.

real-time system: a system whose correctness depends on responding to a stimulus within a well-defined elapsed time.

robustness: a property exhibited by a system that behaves reasonably when encountering unexpected circumstances or incorrect input.

weak coupling: a property exhibited by a module that has minimal interaction with other modules.

CHAPTER 12　　　　**Lists and iteration**

Situations often arise in which we must deal with a *collection* of objects: a *Student*'s schedule, for instance, is a set of *Courses*, a *Course* contains a group of enrolled *Students*, a *PokerHand* contains a number of *Cards, etc*. To manage such collections, objects called *containers* are used. A *container* is simply an object whose purpose is to contain a collection of other objects. Most programming languages provide at least some form of container as a built-in feature, and a variety of containers are generally available as library classes. Programmers can also define their own container classes as needed.

In this chapter, we consider a fundamental container called a *list*. Although several kinds of lists are provided in the standard Java libraries, we introduce a particularly straightforward and simple version here. For the present, we assume that any list classes we need are available in a library and consider only their specification. We'll see various implementation approaches in a later chapter.

We start by defining the fundamental properties of a list, and then develop the specifications for a typical list class. When using a container, we find that we are frequently required to perform some operation on each element in it. This is essentially an iterative process, and we see here how to perform such an iterative process with a list, employing the *while* statement introduced in the previous chapter. Our examples lead to a consideration of exactly what is meant by the "equality" of two objects. We conclude the chapter by introducing another iteration statement, the *for loop*.

12.1　Lists

A *list* is a container that holds a finite sequence of values all of the same type. As usual, we handle objects with reference values. Consequently a list typically contains references to a number of objects that are instances of the same class. In our discussion, we simply refer to a "list of objects" rather than a "list containing references to objects." But we should remember that the list is actually a container, and its components are references to the "contained" objects.

Three important properties of a list are included in this definition:

- A list is *finite*; in particular, a list might contain just one element or it might contain no elements at all. If a list does not contain any elements, it is said to be empty.

- A list is a *sequence*; that is, assuming there are several elements on a list, there is a first element, a second element, and so forth. We access elements of a list by their relative position on the list.

- A list is *homogeneous*: all the elements of a list are of the same type. This might seem unduly restrictive on first glance, but we'll see that we can actually use abstraction to get as much flexibility as we need. Making the elements the same type means that when we get an element from a list, we know exactly what operations we can perform with it.

> **container:** an object whose purpose is to contain other objects.
>
> **list:** a container in which the elements are kept in sequence.

12.2   List specification

Let's look at some of the features we expect a list to have. Just to be specific, we assume a class *StudentList* of *Student* objects:

```
public class StudentList
        A finite list of Students.
```

A *StudentList* instance contains references to *Student* objects, as illustrated in Figure 12.1.

We need a constructor, and we include a trivial one. The list we create will contain no objects initially:

```
public StudentList ()
        Create an empty StudentList.
```

One property we're interested in is how many elements are on the list. We provide a query:

```
public int size ()
        Number of elements in this List.

        ensure:
            this.size() >= 0
```

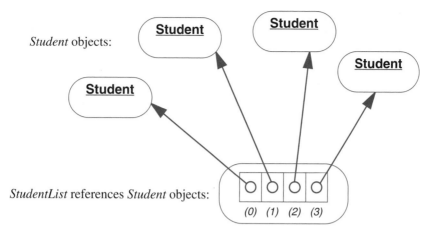

Student objects:

StudentList references *Student* objects:

(0) (1) (2) (3)

Figure 12.1 **StudentList is a composite object containing (references to) Student objects.**

The case in which the list contains no elements is of particular importance. Though it's redundant—saying the list is empty is the same as saying its length is 0—we provide a separate query for this case.

> **public boolean** isEmpty ()
> This *List* contains no elements.
>
> this.isEmpty() == (this.size() == 0)

Observe that an *empty* list is not the same as a *null* value. An empty list *is* an object. If we declare a *StudentList* variable,

> StudentList sl;

the variable will initially contain the *null* value. However, after the assignment,

> sl = **new** StudentList();

sl will contain a reference to a newly created empty list. This is illustrated in Figure 12.2.

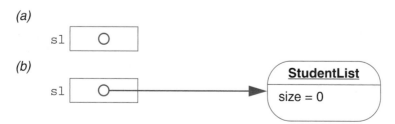

(a)

sl

(b)

sl

StudentList

size = 0

Figure 12.2 **StudentList variable sl contains null (a) and references the empty list (b).**

If the list is not empty, we want to be able to access the individual elements of the list. Since the list is a sequence, we can reference elements by their relative position. For historical reasons, list elements are sometimes indexed by their offset from the beginning of the list rather than by their ordinal position on the list. The first element on the list is at index 0, the second element is at index 1, and so on. Since this convention is adopted in the standard Java libraries, we do the same. Accordingly, the query to access a list element requires that we provide an index as argument.

> **public** Student get (**int** i)
>> The element at the specified position.
>
>> **require:**
>>> `0 <= i && i < this.size()`

Note carefully how this method works. If `enrollees` is an object of class *StudentList*, then

> `enrollees.get(3)`

gives us (a reference to) the fourth element on the list; *i.e.*, the element with index 3. Specifically, it gives us a a reference to a *Student* instance. For this query to be legal, we require there be at least four elements on the list.

If the list is empty (`this.size == 0`), we cannot query `get(i)`. The precondition cannot be satisfied, no matter what value i has: i cannot possibly be greater than or equal to 0 *and* less than 0.

What commands should we provide for modifying the list? It seems clear that we'll want to add and remove elements. We choose a relatively simple form of adding an element: append it to the end:

> **public void** append (Student s)
>> Append the specified *Student* to the end of this *List*.
>
>> **require:**
>>> `s != null`
>
>> **ensure:**
>>> `this.size() == old.size() + 1`
>>> `this.get(this.size()-1) == s`

Read the postconditions carefully. Note that the method `append` appends an element to the end of the list. If a list has five elements, and we append an element, the new element becomes the sixth. The rest of the list remains unchanged. (The underlying assumption in documenting is that anything not mentioned doesn't change.) The postcondition

> `this.size() == old.size() + 1`

means that the list is one element longer after appending than it was before.

We include a method for removing an element at a specified position:

```
public void remove (int i)
```
> Remove the element at the specified position.
>
> **require:**
> ```
> 0 <= i && i < this.size()
> ```
>
> **ensure:**
> ```
> this.size() == old.size() - 1
> for i <= j < this.size()
>     this.get(j) == old.get(j+1)
> ```

The `remove` method allows us to remove an arbitrary element from the list. The postconditions indicate that the list shrinks by one when we delete an element, and the elements after the one deleted move up one position. If a list has six elements, and the command

```
remove(2);
```

is performed, the third element (index 2) is deleted, the old fourth element becomes the new third, the old fifth becomes the new fourth, and the old sixth becomes the new fifth. In this case, the second postcondition says "for each j between 2 and 4, the element with new index j is the element that was previously at index $j+1$."

Finally we include a command that allows us to replace an arbitrary element of the list with another element:

```
public void set (int i, Student s)
```
> Replace the element at the specified position with the specified *Student*.
>
> **require:**
> ```
> 0 <= i && i < this.size()
> s != null
> ```
>
> **ensure:**
> ```
> this.get(i) == s
> ```

We'll add some features in a bit, but what we have is adequate for now.

While we have used a *StudentList* to specify list features, it should be clear that there is nothing particularly unique about the fact that we have a list of *Student*s. We could just as well have a *CourseList*, *CardList*, *RoomList*, *DenizenList*, and so on. The only changes we need to make to the list specification is to replace "Student" with the type of the list elements. For instance, a *CardList* would be specified exactly like the *StudentList*, except for the following:

```
public class CardList
```
> A finite list of *Cards*.

```
public Card get (int i)
    ...

public void append (Card c)
    ...

public void set (int i, Card c)
    ...
```

We won't repeat the specifications for each type of list we deal with.

12.3   Iteration

12.3.1   *while* statement

It is often the case that we need to perform an operation on each element of a list. That is, we need to repeat the operation, once for each list element. This process is called *iteration*.

---

iteration: a process in which an operation is preformed several times.

There are several statements in Java that can be used for performing an iteration. The simplest is the *while* statement, or *while-loop*, which we first encountered in Chapter 8. The *while* statement is a structured statement, as was the *if-then*. It has a condition and another statement as components. The syntax is as follows:

```
while ( condition )
    statement
```

As with the *if-then*, the *condition* is a **boolean** expression. The component *statement* is called the *body* of the *while*. The body can be any kind of statement, and is often a compound statement.

When the *while* statement is executed, the *condition* is evaluated first. If the *condition* is *true*, then the component *statement* is performed, and the entire process is repeated. Thus the *complete* body is repeatedly executed until the *condition* evaluates to *false*, at which point the *while* statement is complete. This is illustrated in Figure 12.3. Because of its structure, the statement is often called a "*while-loop*."

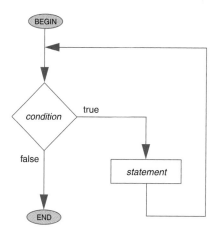

Figure 12.3 **A *while* statement.**

The statement that comprises the loop body might not be executed at all, might be executed once, or might be executed more than once. Note that executing the body should have the potential of changing the value of the condition. For a *while* statement to be correct, we must make sure that if the condition is initially *true*, executing the body a sufficient number of times will cause it to become *false*.

It is possible that the condition of a *while* statement will remain true no matter how many times the body is executed, and the *while* statement will never terminate. Such a situation is called an "infinite loop." Infinite loops are usually the result of programmer error, though there are rare situations where we intend to program an infinite loop.

You should compare the structure of the *while* statement shown in Figure 12.3 with the *if-then* pictured in Figure 6.1. While there is some superficial similarity, these statements exhibit quite distinct behavior, and are used for completely different purposes.

12.3.2 *while* loops and lists

As we've mentioned, a *while* statement is often used to iterate over the elements of a list; that is, to perform some operation on each list element. The general form of such an iteration is

```
while ( more list elements to process )
    process the next element
```

Recall that a list element is accessed by its relative position: that is, we use an integer *index* to identify a particular element. The method `get(i)` delivers the list element with index *i*. If we want to process each element in the list, an obvious approach is to start with the first element (*index* 0), then proceed to the second (*index* 1), and so on, until we're done. Thus we use an index to access an element of the list, and increment the index to get the next element.

If `list` is the list and we define `index` be an **int** variable, we can sketch this approach as follows:

```
int index;
index = 0;
while ( more list elements to process ) {
    process list.get(index);
    index = index + 1;// index of next element
}
```

How do we know whether or not there are more elements to process? Well, the last element on the list has an index one less than the length of the list. We can determine the length with the query `size`. Thus we write

```
int index;
index = 0;
while (index < list.size()) {
    process list.get(index);
    index = index + 1;
}
```

The variable `index` is set to 0. If the list is empty, `list.size()` is 0 and the *while* condition `index < list.size()` is *false*. The loop terminates without executing the body at all. If the list is not empty, the condition is *true*. The element with index 0 is processed, and `index` is incremented to 1. The *while* condition is again evaluated. If the list contains only one element, this condition is now *false* and the loop terminates having processed the one element. Otherwise, the element with index 1 is processed, `index` is incremented to 2, and the process continues.

When we write a *while* loop, we must make sure that the iteration terminates by guaranteeing that the *while* condition will eventually become *false*. Incrementing `index` by 1 each time we execute the loop body ensures that the loop will terminate as long *as the length of the list does not increase*. Thus we must make sure that the operation "*process* `list.get(index)`" does not increase the length of the list.

Note that in the code sketched above, the query `list.size()` is executed for each iteration of the loop. If the length of the list does not change, we can query the list once for its length, and save the value in a local variable:

```
int index;
int length;
length = list.size();
```

```
index = 0;
while (index < length) {
    process list.get(index);
    index = index + 1;
}
```

12.4 Examples

12.4.1 Summing items on a list

As a first example, suppose that we have a list of the students enrolled in a course, a *StudentList*, and we would like to compute the average (mean) of their final exam grades. We write a method that, given the list of students, returns the average final exam grade:

> **public double** finalAverage (StudentList students)
> > The average (mean) of the final exam grades of the specified *Students*.
>
> > **require:**
> > > students.size() > 0

To compute the mean, we must sum up the exam grades and then divide by the number of students. The operation we want to perform on each list element is to get the final exam grade and add it to a sum. For this purpose, assume that we can query an instance of the class *Student* for the student's grade on the final exam:

> **public int** finalExam ()
> > This *Student*'s grade on the final exam.

Using the template for iterating through a list given above, we write

```
int i;      // index of students
int sum;    // sum of grades up to, but not including,
            // the i-th Student
int count;  // number of Students

count = students.size();
sum = 0;
i = 0;
while (i < count) {
    sum = sum + students.get(i).finalExam();
    i = i+1;
}
```

(To simplify documentation, we refer to the element with index *i* as "the *i*-th.")

To make sure we understand what's happening here, let's trace how the variables change as the method is executed. Assume the list students has four elements as illustrated in Figure 12.4.

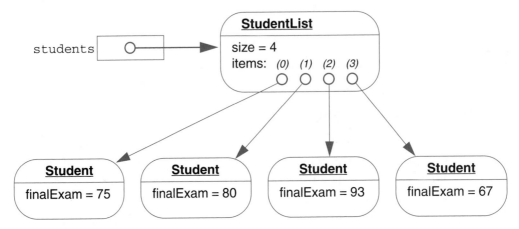

Figure 12.4 The *StudentList*.

After executing the first three assignments, the variables count, sum, and i will have the following values:

i	0
sum	0
count	4

Since the condition is true, the body of the *while* is performed. The first assignment in the body queries students for its first element, queries this *Student* for its final exam grade, and adds it to sum. The second statement increments i. After performing the body of the iteration once, the variables will be

i	1
sum	75
count	4

The condition is still true, so the body is performed a second time. students is queried for its second element (since i is 1), and this *Student*'s final exam grade is added to sum. The variable i is again incremented. After two iterations, we have

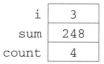

i	2
sum	155
count	4

After a third iteration of the *while*, the variables look like this:

i	3
sum	248
count	4

Once again the condition is true, so the body is done a fourth time:

i	4
sum	315
count	4

Now the condition is false, and the iteration is complete. The body of the *while* statement was performed four times, once for each element of the list.

We still have to compute the average by dividing sum by count. We have one minor problem here: we want a **double**, but sum and count are both **int**s. If we divide sum by count, we get the **int** quotient, which isn't exactly what we want. We need to convert the values of sum and count to **double**, so that we get the **double** quotient. We saw in Section 5.2.2 that we can convert an **int** to a **double** with a cast operation. We write

```
return (double)sum / (double)count;
```

(We actually only need to convert one of the values, since if one operand of the operator is **double**, the other will automatically be converted to **double**.)

The complete method is shown in Listing 12.1.

12.4.2   Summing selected elements of a list

Let's modify the above problem a bit. Assume that some students did not take the test, and are represented in the data by test grades of "-1." These grades should not be included when computing the average.

We have two modifications to make to the method. First, we don't want to add the "-1" grades into the sum. Second, we can't compute the average by simply dividing the sum by the number of elements of the list, since this number includes

---

Listing 12.1 **The method** *average*

```
/**
 * The average (mean) of the final exam grades of the
 * specified Students.
 *     require:
 *         students.size() > 0
 */
public double average (StudentList students) {
    int i;       // index of students
    int sum;     // sum of grades up to, but not
                 // including, the i-th Student
    int count;   // number of Students

    count = students.size();
    sum = 0;
    i = 0;
    while (i < count) {
        sum = sum + students.get(i).finalExam();
        i = i+1;
    }
    return (double)sum / (double)count;
}
```

---

the "–1" grades. We must count the valid test grades on the list to get the divisor. The modified method is given in Listing 12.2.

Note the precondition: we require that there be at least one legitimate test grade on the list. Why is this important?

12.4.3 Finding the minimum

The above examples have used local variables in the *while* condition and in the body of the loop. These variable must be initialized before they are referenced, and must be updated in the body of the loop in such a way as to guarantee that the *while* condition will ultimately become *false*.

Loop variable initialization is critical to the correct execution and termination of a loop. In many cases initialization is straightforward. But there are other cases where careful thought must be given. As an example, let's find the lowest final exam grade for a group of *Students*. Again, we assume that the list provided as argument is not empty.

Listing 12.2 The method *average*, revised

```
/**
 * The average (mean) of the final exam grades of the
 * specified Students. Negative grades are not included.
 *     require:
 *         students.size() > 0
 *         students.get(i).finalExam() >= 0
 *             for some i, 0 <= i < students.size()
 */
public double average (StudentList students) {
    int i;      // index of students
    int sum;    // sum of nonnegative grades up to, but not
                // including, the i-th Student
    int count;  // number of nonnegative grades up
                // to, but not including, the i-th
    int number;// number of Students
    number = students.size();
    sum = 0;
    count = 0;
    i = 0;
    while (i < number) {
        if (students.get(i).finalExam() >= 0) {
            sum = sum + students.get(i).finalExam();
            count = count+1;
        }
        i = i+1;
    }
    return (double)sum / (double)count;
}
```

```
public int minFinalExam (StudentList students)
```
The lowest final exam grades of the specified *Students*.

require:
```
students.size() > 0
```

Essentially, all we have to do is look at the final exam grade of each *Student* on the list, and remember the lowest we see. We need two local variables, one to index the list, and one to remember the lowest grade seen. We can define them as follows:

```
int i;      // index of the next Student to look at
```

```
int low;      // lowest final exam grade of the Students
              // looked at so far; that is, lowest of
              // Students with indexes less than i.
```

The iterative step is clear: look at the final exam grade of the next *Student*, and remember it if it is the smallest so far:

```
while (i < students.size()) {
    if (students.get(i).finalExam() < low)
        low = students.get(i).finalExam();
    i = i+1;
}
```

The only question remaining is how to initialize i and low. It seems reasonable to initialize i to 0, since the first *Student* we need to look at has index 0. But what should low be initialized to? According to the specification, it should be the "lowest final exam grade of the *Students* looked at so far." But what is this when we haven't yet looked at any? We could set low to an initial value that is higher than any anticipated grade. But this is dangerous, since the *Student* method finalExam doesn't specify any upper bound for the value returned. The best approach is to initialize low to the grade of the first *Student* on the list. (We are guaranteed that the list is not empty.) Then to be consistent with the variable specification, we initialize i to 1:

```
low = students.get(0).finalExam();
i = 1;
while (i < students.size()) {
    if (students.get(i).finalExam() < low)
        low = students.get(i).finalExam();
    i = i+1;
}
```

12.4.4 Determining if an object is on a *List*: searching the *List*

For the next example, we again assume that we have a *StudentList*. We want to determine if a given *Student* is on the list. Perhaps the list contains all students enrolled in a certain course, and we want to determine if a particular student is enrolled in the course.

We write the method as a feature of the class *StudentList*:

public boolean contains (Student s)
   This list contains the specified *Student*.

What we need to do is examine each element of the list, and see if it is equal to s. Note that there are now two different conditions that can terminate the iteration: either we examine all the items on the list, or we find the one we're looking for. We make these dual exit conditions explicit when we write the *while* condition:

```
/**
 * This list contains the specified Student.
 */
public boolean contains (Student s) {

    int i;
    int length;

    length = this.size();
    i = 0;
    while (i < length && get(i) != s)
        i = i+1;

    return i < length;
}
```

A few points should be noted about the above implementation:

- Recall that the operator && is lazy: the right operand is evaluated only if the left operand is *true*. The laziness is critical here. If i < length is *false*, we should not invoke the method get(i). If we do, we violate a precondition of the method get, with unpredictable results. Thus the order in which the relational expressions are written is critical in this case.

- If the iteration terminates because s is found, its index i is less than the length of the list. If s is not on the list, the iteration terminates when i == length. Hence, when the iteration terminates, i < length is true if and only if s was found on the list.

12.5 What does "equal" mean?

In the contains method defined above, we used the equality operator == (in the form of its negation, !=) to compare the item we were looking for with the elements on the list. We need to take a more careful look at what we mean when we say two objects are equal, and whether the equality operator always captures our intended meaning.

Suppose we have a class *Date*[1], modeling days of the calendar. An object of this class has integer-valued properties *year*, *month*, and *day*, denoting the

---

1. The class outlined here represents dates somewhat differently than the standard class java.util.Date.

year, the month of the year, and the day of the month. For instance, the class might be specified in part as follows. (We omit obvious preconditions and post-conditions.)

> **public class** Date
>> A calendar date, post 1900.
>
>> **public** Date (**int** day, **int** month, **int** year)
>>> Create a new *Date*, representing the specified day, month, and year.
>
>> **public int** year ()
>>> The year.
>
>> **public int** month ()
>>> Month of the year.
>
>> **public int** day ()
>>> Day of the month.

Suppose further that we have a class representing members of a committee, each of whom has a list of available dates:

> **public class** CommitteeMember
>> A member of a committee.
>
>> **public** DateList availableDates ()
>>> Dates this *CommitteeMember* is available.

If we want to find a day on which two members of the committee are both available, we can look at each *Date* on one of the member's availableDates list, and see if it is on the other member's availableDates list. We expect the method that determines whether or not a *Date* is on a *DateList* to be identical to the method contains given above, with "Student" replaced by "Date." There is, however, one substantive difference.

Remember that a list of objects contains *references* to the objects. The contains method defined above is given a reference to a *Student* object as argument, and compares this reference value to the reference values on the list:

        get(i) != s

Two *reference values* are being compared for *equality*. Two reference values are equal if they refer to the *same object*, as shown in Figure 12.5. This is reasonable, since each student is uniquely represented by a *Student* object: we don't have more than one *Student* object representing the same student.

On the other hand, the situation is a little different with dates. It is easy to imagine a situation in which distinct *Date* objects are created to represent the *same actual date*, as shown in Figure 12.6. The date 9/27/2002 is on both lists pictured, even though the lists do not contain references to the *same object*. That is, Joe's availableDates.get(1) and Sue's availableDates.get(0) are two

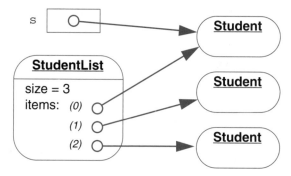

Figure 12.5 s is on the *StudentList*.

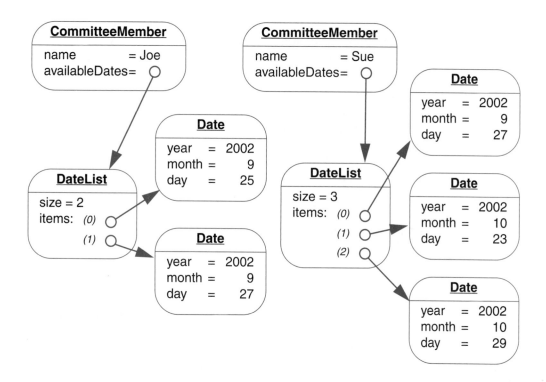

Figure 12.6 Joe and Sue are both available on 9/27/2002.

distinct objects that represent the same date. The reference values identifying these objects are not equal, because they are different objects.

In the case of the *Student* objects, we want to consider two objects to be equal only if they are in fact identical; that is, there are the same object. In the case of the *Date* objects, we want to consider two objects to be equal if their states are equal: that is, their *year*, *month*, and *day* properties are equal.

Every class in Java comes automatically equipped with a method `equals`. The default implementation simply compares references, and is defined as

```
public boolean equals (Object obj) {
    return this == obj;
}
```

The class *Object*, introduced in Section 9.5, is at the top of the Java class hierarchy. As we have seen, every other class is a subclass of *Object*. Thus if `s1` and `s2` are *Student*s, they are also *Object*s, and we can query `s1`

```
s1.equals(s2)
```

to determine if `s1` and `s2` are identical. (We could just as well query `s2`; that is, we could write `s2.equals(s1)`, and the result will be the same.)

The default implementation simply compares references, so writing `s1.equals(s2)` is the same as writing `s1 == s2`.

However, we can provide a different implementation of the method `equals` when we define a class. For instance, we might want to define two *Date*s as equal if they have identical *year*, *month*, and *day* features. To do this, we include the following method definition in the class *Date*:

```
/**
 * This Date is the same as the specified Date.
 *      require:
 *           obj instanceof Date
 */
public boolean equals (Object obj) {
    Require.condition(obj instanceof Date);
❶  Date d = (Date)obj;
    return   this.year()  == d.year() &&
             this.month() == d.month() &&
             this.day()   == d.day();
}
```

Two new Java operations are introduced here. First, **instanceof** is an operator that takes an object as left operand and a class as right operand. It returns *true* if the object is an instance of the class. Second, we have used a *cast* operation to convert the *Object* `obj` to a *Date*. We used the cast above to convert **int** values to **double** values, and have seen that we can convert **double** values to **int** values. Here we see that we can cast an object reference as well. Specifically, `obj` is an *Object* variable. But when we reach line ❶, we know that `obj` in fact contains a reference to *Date*. Since we want to invoke the *Date* methods `year`, `month`, and `day`, we must cast the *reference-to-Object* to a *reference-to-Date*. We'll examine these operations more completely later, when we consider abstraction and inheritance in detail.

Returning to the point, we have redefined the method `equals` so that two *Date* objects are considered equal if they have equal *year*, *month*, and *day* properties.

Identity or referential equality:

- an object is only equal to itself;
- references are equal only if they contain the same reference value: that is, only if they reference the same object;
- the meaning of the equality operator "==;"
- the default meaning of the method `equals`.

State equality:

- two objects are equal if their states are equal;
- must be explicitly defined by the method `equals` in the class definition.

Figure 12.7 **Two meanings of *Equality*.**

We add the following method `indexOf` to our list classes. It determines if an object is on the list, and if so, gives the index of the first instance of the object. If the object is not on the list, it returns –1. (We express the method in terms of locating a *Student* on a *StudentList*, realizing that the same basic approach will work for any kind of list.)

Note that this method is very similar to the method `contains` given above. The basic differences are that here we use the method "`equals`" rather than the operator "==," and return the index of the item if it is on the list.

```
/**
 * The index of the first occurrence of the specified
 * element, or -1 if this List does not contain the
 * specified element.
 *      require:
 *          obj != null
 *      ensure:
 *          if obj equals no element of this List then
 *              indexOf(obj) == -1
 *          else
 *              obj equals get(indexOf(obj)),
 *              and indexOf(obj) is the smallest value for
 *                  which this is true
 */
```

```
public int indexOf (Student obj) {
    int i;
    int length;

    length = this.size();
    i = 0;
    while (i < length && !obj.equals(get(i)))
        i = i+1;

    if (i < length)
        return i;
    else   // item not found
        return -1;
}
```

A couple of points to notice here:

- This method is very similar to the method contains shown on page 287. The differences are the type of value returned, and the use of equals.

- As with the method contains, the loop is followed by a test to determine if the element has been found.

12.5.1 Removing duplicates

As a final example, we write a method that removes duplicates from a specified list. Once again, we use a *StudentList*.

In this method we have two *while-loops*, one contained inside the other. The first outer loop successively selects each element of the list to process. The second inner loop processes the selected element by checking all the elements following it, removing any that are equal.

Note that since the list changes size as we delete elements, we must recompute its length (by invoking the method list.size) for each iteration. Also notice that the index j is not incremented when an element is deleted. The deletion automatically causes the next element in the list to move up to the j-th position, so that the current value of j indexes the next element to be compared:

```
/**
 * Remove duplicate elements from the specified List.
 *     ensure:
 *         for 0 <= i < j < list.size()
 *             !list.get(i).equals(list.get(j)).
 *         for 0 <= i < list.old.size()
 *             list.old.get(i).equals(list.get(j))
 *             for some j
 */
```

```
public void removeDuplicates (StudentList list) {
    int i;          // index of item
    Student item;   // check for duplicates of item
    int j;          // index of element to be compared
                    // to item;
                    // invariant: i < j

    i = 0;
    while (i < list.size()) {
        item = list.get(i);
        j = i+1;
        while (j < list.size())
            if (item.equals(list.get(j)))
                list.remove(j);
            else
                j = j+1;
        i = i+1;
    }
}
```

12.6   Loop structure: a summary

As we have seen in the examples, loops generally have four fundamental parts: initialization, continuation condition, body, and conclusion:

```
initialization
while (condition) {
    body
}
conclusion
```

Initialization statements initialize variables used in the condition and in the body of the loop. This is a critical part of setting up the loop. If loop variables are to be initialized properly, their meaning and behavior must be clearly understood. It is good practice to document the behavior of each loop variable carefully.

The *condition* determines whether or not the body of the loop is to be executed. It is sometimes said to "guard" the loop body: we can be certain that the condition is satisfied when the loop body is reached. The negation of the condition is sometimes referred to as the "exit condition" or "termination condition" of the loop. The exit condition becoming true causes the iteration to terminate.

The loop *body* defines one step in the solution process: executing the loop body brings us one step closer to satisfying the goal of the loop. We must also ensure that executing the loop body brings us one step closer to satisfying the exit condition. That is, we must make sure that the loop condition will ultimately become false, and the loop will terminate.

The *concluding statements* are not always necessary. When we reach the conclusion statements, we know that the loop variables will contain values that make the exit condition true. The concluding statements use the values produced by the loop.

The examples we have seen in this chapter are all instances of counting loops. With a counting loop, we know how many times the body of the loop must be performed. For instance, in the method `average`, the body of the loop must be done once for each student on the list: it is done `students.size()` times. With a counting loop, we simply keep a counter or index that is incremented on each iteration. The loop terminates when the counter indicates that the body has been performed the appropriate number of times. Many loops, such as the loop in the *GameManager* of Chapter 10, are not simple counting loops.

12.7   *for* statement

These patterns for iterating over a list are extremely common. So common, in fact, that the language has a special construct, the *for* statement, primarily intended to be used in exactly these cases. The format of the *for* statement is as follows:

```
for (initializationStatement; condition;
        updateStatement)
    statement
```

The *initializationStatement* and the *updateStatement* are assignment statements stripped of the trailing semicolon. Execution of the *for* statement is equivalent to the following, as illustrated in Figure 12.8:

```
initializationStatement;
while (condition) {
    statement
    updateStatement;
}
```

An iteration processing each element of a list similar to the *while-loop* on page 280 can be written as follows.

```
int index;

for (index = 0; index < list.size(); index = index+1)
    process list.get(index);
```

Note the placement of the semicolons inside the parentheses.

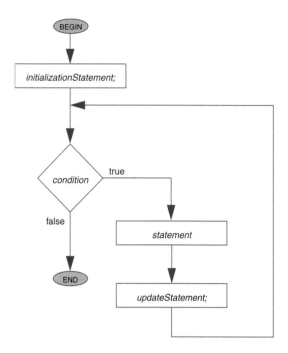

Figure 12.8 **A *for* statement.**

For example, the iteration in the method `average` (Listing 12.2) could be written with a *for* statement as shown below.

```
for (i = 0; i < number; i = i+1) {
    if (students.get(i).finalExam() >= 0) {
        sum = sum + students.get(i).finalExam();
        count = count+1;
    }
}
```

We continue to use *while* statements in our examples, since the order in which things happen is a bit easier to see in this kind of loop.

12.8 Summary

In this chapter, we saw how to use a *list*, a fundamental container object. A list contains a finite sequence of elements, all of the same type. Fundamental list features include queries to determine the number of elements on the list and to access the individual elements, and commands to add, remove, and replace elements.

A common requirement when using a container is to perform some operation on each element in the container. This iterative process can be accomplished when the container is a list by using a *while-loop* and an integer index to successive select each list element. We saw a number of examples, including a method to determine whether a list contained a specified element.

Our examination of this method led us to consider exactly when two objects, or two object references, should be considered equal. In some cases, *equality* means *identity*: two references are equal only if they refer to the same object. This notion of equality is captured by the equality operator == and its negation !=. In other cases, though, we want to consider distinct objects as equal. For this purpose, the language equips each class with a **boolean** method equals. This method is predefined to mean identity, but we can redefine the method to give equality any meaning we want.

We also encountered a new operator, **instanceof**, that can be used to determine if a variable references an object of a specified class. And we saw that a reference to a particular class could be cast to a reference to a subclass. These operations will be examined more completely when we look at inheritance in detail.

Finally, we saw how the loop initialization-test-update operations could be combined in the *for* statement.

In subsequent chapters, we see some more fundamental list operations, how to implement lists, and how to incorporate them into a library.

EXERCISES

12.1 Review the systems considered in the exercises of Chapter 10. Identify some class features that might be implemented with lists.

12.2 Consider the following, where i and sum are **int** variables:

```
i = 1;
sum = 0;
while (i != 10) {
    sum = sum + i;
    i = i + 1;
}
```

a. What is the final value of i? of sum?

b. What does this loop compute?

12.3 Consider the following, where i and sum are **int** variables:

```
i = 1;
sum = 0;
while (i != 10) {
```

```
            sum = sum + i;
            i = i + 2;
        }
```

a. What is the final value of `i`? of `sum`?

b. What does this loop compute?

12.4 Write a method that computes the sum of the integers from 1 to *n*, for any positive integer *n*.

12.5 Write a method that computes the sum of the odd numbers from 1 to *n*, for any positive integer *n*.

12.6 Given the `i` is an **int** variable, indicate the number of times the body of each of the following loops will be performed:

```
a.  i = 1;  while (i <= 10)   { … i = i+1; }
b.  i = 0;  while (i <= 10)   { … i = i+1; }
c.  i = 0;  while (i <= 10)   { … i = i+1; }
d.  i = 0;  while (i <= 10)   { … i = i+2; }
e.  i = 10; while (i > 0)     { … i = i-1; }
f.  i = 10; while (i > 1)     { … i = i-1; }
g.  i = 10; while (i > 0)     { … i = i-2; }
h.  i = 10; while (i != 0)    { … i = i-1; }
i.  i = 9;  while (i != 0)    { … i = i-2; }
j.  i = 0;  while (i != 10)   { … i = i+3; }
```

12.7 Suppose a class *Course* has an instance variable referencing the list of students who are enrolled in the course:

```
        private StudentList enrollees;
```

How will this variable be initialized in the *Course* constructor?

Write a *Course* method for enrolling a specified *Student*:

```
        public void enroll (Student s)
```

How can you handle the case in which the specified *Student* is already enrolled in the *Course*?

Write a *Course* method for dropping a specified *Student*.

12.8 Suppose a *Student* has an instance variable referencing the list of courses he or she is enrolled in, where *Course* is as in the preceding exercise:

```
        private CourseList schedule;
```

Define a *Student* method and modify the *Course* method `enroll` so that the *Student*'s schedule is updated when the student is enrolled in a *Course*.

Is it possible for the system to become inconsistent? If so, can you suggest possible ways of preventing the inconsistencies?

12.9   Assume that the class *Student* defines the query

```
public int finalGrade ()
```

Write a method that takes a *StudentList* as argument, and returns the number of students on the list who have failed, where a final grade of less than 60 is considered failing.

12.10   Using the same assumptions of the previous exercise, write a method that returns a list of the students who have failed. That is, implement

```
public StudentList failingStudents (StudentList sl)
```

12.11   Consider the class *Card* defined below:

```
/**
 * An ordinary playing card.
 */
public class Card {

    // Constants:

    // the suits:
    public final static int CLUB = 0;
    public final static int DIAMOND = 1;
    public final static int HEART = 2;
    public final static int SPADE = 3;
    // the named honors:
    public final static int JACK = 11;
    public final static int QUEEN = 12;
    public final static int KING = 13;
    public final static int ACE = 14;

    // Constructor:

    /**
     * Create a Card with specified value and suit.
     *    require:
     *        2 <= value <= 10 ||
     *        value == JACK || value == QUEEN ||
     *        value == KING || value == ACE;
     *        suit == CLUB || suit == HEART ||
     *        suit == DIAMOND || suit == SPADE
     */
    public Card (int value, int suit) {
        this.value = value;
        this.suit = suit;
    }
```

```
        // Queries:

        /**
         * The value of this Card.
         */
        public int value () {
            return this.value;
        }

        /**
         * The suit of this Card.
         */
        public int suit () {
            return this.suit;
        }

        // Private Components:

        private int value;
        private int suit;


    }
```

Define a method `equals` for this class so that cards with the same value are considered to be equal, regardless of suit.

12.12 Write a method that determines whether all the elements of a specified *CardList* are of the same suit.

12.13 Write a method that determines whether or not a specified *CardList* contains a pair; that is, contains two cards of the same value.

12.14 An instance of the class *java.lang.Integer* wraps a value of type **int** in an object. The class has a constructor that creates an object containing the specified **int**,

        public Integer (**int** value)
            Create an Integer object that represents the primitive **int** argument.

and a query for accessing the **int**:

        public int intValue ()
            The value of this *Integer* as an **int**.

Write a method that will count the number of even values on a specified *IntegerList*.

12.15 Rewrite the method `removeDuplicates` of Section 12.5.1 using *for* statements in place of the *while-loops*. Note that the *updateStatement* in the for loop can be *empty*.

GLOSSARY

container: an object whose main purpose is to contain other objects.

empty: the state of a container that has no elements: an empty container contains 0 elements.

for-statement: a loop statement in which the initialization, test, and update parts are combined in the loop heading.

index: position of a list element relative to the beginning of the list: the first element on a list is at index 0, the second element is at index 1, and so on. Same as *offset*.

iteration: a process in which an operation is performed several times.

list: a container in which the elements are kept in sequence: there is a first element, a second, and so on, depending on the number of elements in the container.

loop: a construct that allows repeated execution of a statement.

offset: position of a list element relative to the beginning of the list; same as *index*.

while-loop: a statement in which a component statement (the *body*) is repeatedly executed as long as a specified condition remains true. Also called a *while* statement.

CHAPTER 13

Sorting and searching

We introduced lists in Chapter 12 and saw how to use their basic features. In this chapter we examine two fundamental list operations: arranging the elements in a specific order, called *sorting*, and determining whether or not a specified element is on a list, called *searching*. Sorting and searching are two of the most common operations performed on lists.

In Chapter 12 we saw that a list contains a finite sequence of elements. We often want to keep these elements ordered in some specific way. For example, we might want a list of students kept in alphabetical order, or ordered by course grade. We might want a list of ball players ordered by batting average or number of home runs. A list in which the elements are maintained in some order is referred to as a *sorted list*. Many methods have been developed for sorting lists. We consider two approaches in this chapter, called *selection sort* and *bubble sort*. These are easy to understand but not particularly efficient. In a later chapter, we'll see a more sophisticated and efficient sorting algorithm known as *quick sort*.

Another common requirement is locating an item on a list. In Chapter 12 we wrote a rather straightforward method indexOf for finding a specified item on a list. The method essentially examined each element of the list in sequence. Here we see a more efficient search algorithm called *binary search*, which requires the list to be sorted.

In the process of developing the algorithms, we introduce the notion of a *loop invariant*. A loop invariant is a condition that remains true as we repeatedly execute the loop body and captures the fundamental intent of the iteration. Loop invariants are indispensable aids in verifying the correctness of the iteration, and hence of the method.

We should note that the primary goal of this chapter is to introduce some standard algorithms and algorithmic techniques. The class structure we use is simply a vehicle for study of the algorithms.

13.1   Ordering lists

If we want to order a list, there must be some ordering on the element class. For instance, the elements of a *StudentList* are *Student* objects. If we want to order a *StudentList*, we must have a way of comparing two *Student* objects to determine which should come first. That is, there must be an *ordering* on the class *Student*. While we don't want to be too formal about what we mean by an ordering, we assume the following.

- There is a **boolean** method lessThan specified for the class whose instances we want to order. This method defines the ordering.

For example, if we are considering the class *Student*, we assume it contains a method

> **public boolean** lessThan (Student s)

Then if s1 and s2 are *Student* objects, the query

> s1.lessThan(s2)

tells us whether or not s1 precedes s2 in the ordering. For convenience, we informally abbreviate this as

> s1 < s2

and use

> s1 >= s2

to mean !s1.lessThan(s2). Of course we can't write such expressions in our programs, except as part of a comment.

- The ordering is *antisymmetric*. That is, it cannot be the case that both s1 < s2 and s2 < s1 are true. (This implies that the ordering is also *irreflexive*. That is, s < s is *false* for every *Student* object s.)

- The ordering is *transitive*. That is, if s1 < s2 and s2 < s3, then s1 < s3.

- The ordering is *total* with respect to some "equivalence" on the class. That is, either s1 < s2, or s2 < s1, or s1 and s2 are "equivalent with respect to the ordering" and only one of these three possibilities holds.

For instance, if we were ordering students by course grade, s1 < s2 means s1 has a lower grade than s2. We would consider two students "equivalent" if they had the same grade. If we were ordering students alphabetically by name, students with identical names would be "equivalent." Notice that we do not insist that two objects be *equal* if neither is less than the other.

Given an ordering on the element class, to say that the list is ordered means that "smaller" elements come before "larger" ones on the list. That is, if s1 and s2 are both on the list, and `s1 < s2`, then `s1` comes before `s2`: the index of `s1` is less than the index of `s2`. We state this a little more precisely:

> for `0 <= i, j < size()`,
>   `get(i).lessThan(get(j))` implies `i < j`.

Let's make sure that we understand exactly what this says. `get(i)` and `get(j)` are two arbitrary elements of the list at positions `i` and `j` respectively. If we are dealing with a *StudentList*, they are objects of class *Student*. If one of the objects, `get(i)`, is less than the other, `get(j)`, in the *Student* ordering, then that object comes before the other on the list; that is, `i < j`.

Equivalently, we could say that for `0 <= i < j < size()`, either `get(i) < get(j)` or `get(i)` is equivalent to `get(j)`.

13.2   Simple sorts

To order a list, we must rearrange the list elements putting them in the proper order. This process is called *sorting*. Sorting is a fundamental and thoroughly studied operation. Many different sorting algorithms have been developed, each having its own distinct advantages. We look at two rather straightforward approaches here. These are among the easiest sort algorithms to understand, but are not particularly efficient. We'll see a more efficient approach in a later chapter.

To be specific, we assume the class *Student* has an ordering `lessThan`, and we want to order a *StudentList*. Clearly, the same techniques work regardless of the kind of list we are dealing with. We will construct a method that requires a *StudentList* as argument, and modifies it so the elements are in the proper order. The method is specified as follows.[1] (For the moment, we won't worry about which class contains the sort method definition.)

> **public void** sort (StudentList list)
>   Sort the specified *StudentList* in increasing order.
>
> **ensure:**
>   for `0 <= i, j < list.size()`,
>   `list.get(i).lessThan(list.get(j)` implies
>   `i < j`.

---

1. Note that the postcondition is not complete. We also ensure that the set of items on the list is not changed. The items are simply rearranged.

"Increasing order" implies that the order of the elements is the same as that of the indexes. Bigger elements have bigger indexes. Again, `list.get(i)` and `list.get(j)` are *Student* objects. `lessThan` is a feature defined for instances of the class *Student*.

13.2.1   Selection sort

The first algorithm we look at is called *selection sort*. Intuitively, it works like this. Find the smallest element on the list, and put it in first; find the second smallest and put it second; and so on, until all elements have been placed in their proper position.

If we write this description down a little more carefully, it's easy to see the iteration. (We illustrate with integers to simplify the pictures.)

1. Find the smallest of all the list elements.

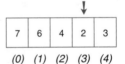

Interchange it with the first (index 0) element.

2. Find the smallest of the list elements, from the second (index 1) to the end.

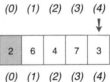

Interchange it with the second (index 1) element.

3. Find the smallest of the list elements, from the third to the end.

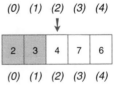

Interchange it with the third element.

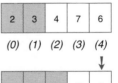

4. Find the smallest of the list elements, from the fourth to the end.

Interchange it with the fourth element.

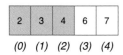

In the first step, we look at elements of the list starting with the first. In the second step, we look at elements starting with the second; *etc.* When the second to last element has been positioned, we are done. The last element is automatically in the right place.

We summarize:

```
int first;     // index of first element to consider
               // on this step
int last;      // index of last element to consider
               // on this step
int small;     // index of smallest of
               // list.get(first)... list.get(last)

last = list.size() - 1;
first = 0;
while (first < last) {
   small = index of smallest of
              list.get(first) through list.get(last)
   interchange list.get(first) and list.get(small)
   first = first+1;
}
```

To accomplish the step

```
small = index of smallest of
           list.get(first) through list.get(last)
```

we examine each element from (index) `first` through (index) `last`, and remember the smallest we see:

```
int next;    // index of next element to examine.
             // small is the index of the smallest of
             // list.get(first)...list.get(next-1).

small = first;
next = first+1;
while (next <= last) {
   if (list.get(next).lessThan(list.get(small)))
      small = next;
   next = next+1;
}
```

The interchange step is also easily accomplished:

```
Student temp;

temp = list.get(first);
list.set(first, list.get(small));
list.set(small, temp);
```

Note that we use a variable `temp` keep a reference to the element at position `first`. If we simply wrote

```
list.set(first, list.get(small));
list.set(small, list.get(first));
```

we'd lose the reference to this element. For example, suppose `first` is 0 and `small` is 3 as illustrated below.

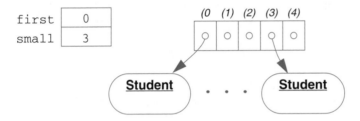

The statement

```
list.set(first, list.get(small));
```

changes `list.get(first)` to `list.get(small)`:

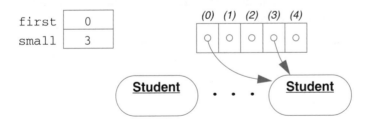

Putting it all together, we make the "find smallest" and "interchange" steps separate methods. This makes the `sort` method a little easier to read. The complete algorithm is given in Listing 13.1.

Listing 13.1   **Selection sort**

```
/**
 * Sort the specified StudentList in increasing order.
 *    ensure:
 *        for 0 <= i, j < list.size(),
 *            list.get(i).lessThan(list.get(j)) implies i < j.
 */
public void sort (StudentList list) {
    int first;        // index of first element to consider
                      // on this step
    int last;         // index of last element to consider
                      // on this step
    int small;        // index of smallest of
                      // list.get(first)...list.get(last)
    last = list.size() - 1;
    first = 0;
    while (first < last) {
        small = smallestOf(list,first,last);
        interchange(list,first,small);
        first = first+1;
    }
}


/*
 * Index of the smallest of
 * list.get(first) through list.get(last)
 *    require:
 *        0 <= first <= last < list.size()
 *    ensure:
 *        for first <= i <= last,
 *            ! list.get(i).lessThan (list.get(result)),
 *            that is, list.get(i) >= list.get(result)
 */
private int smallestOf (StudentList list, int first,
                        int last) {
    int next;        // index of next element to examine.
    int small;       // index of the smallest of
                     // get(first)...get(next-1)
    small = first;
    next = first+1;
    while (next <= last) {
        if (list.get(next).lessThan(list.get(small)))
```

continued

Listing 13.1   **Selection sort (*continued*)**

```
            small = next;
        next = next+1;
    }
    return small;
}


/*
 * Interchange list.get(i) and list.get(j)
 *     require:
 *         0 <= i, j < list.size()
 *     ensure:
 *         list.old.get(i) == list.get(j)
 *         list.old.get(j) == list.get(i)
 */
private void interchange (StudentList list, int i, int j) {
    Student temp;
    temp = list.get(i);
    list.set(i, list.get(j));
    list.set(j, temp);
    }
```

13.2.2   Analysis

We've mentioned that the above algorithm is not particularly efficient. In this section, we try to get a general idea of how many steps are required to sort a list.

If we look at the algorithm, we see that essentially it consists of two **while** loops, one inside the other:

```
        last = list.size() - 1;
        first = 0;
        while (first < last) {
            ...
            next = first+1;
            while (next <= last) {
                if ...
                next = next+1;
            }
            ...
            first = first+1;
        }
```

The statements that get executed most often are the `if` and the assignment to `next` inside the inner loop. Can we determine how many times these statements get performed?

Let's assume there are n elements on the list; that is, `list.size()` equals n. The body of the outer loop is performed $n - 1$ times, with `first` successively taking on the values 0, 2, 3, ..., $n - 2$.

For each iteration of the outer loop, the inner loop body is done with `next` taking on the values `first` + 1, `first` + 2, ..., $n - 1$. That is, the body of the inner loop is done $n -$ `first` times. We can summarize:

value of first	0	1	3	... $n-3$	$n-2$
values of next	1, 2, ..., $n-1$	2, 3, ..., $n-1$	3, 4, ..., $n-1$	... $n-2, n-1$	$n-1$
number of inner loop iterations	$n-1$	$n-2$	$n-3$	... 2	1

So to determine how many times the body of the inner loop is executed, we must sum:

$$(n-1)+(n-2)+...+2+1$$

This sum is well known, and evaluates to $(n^2 - n) / 2$. Thus the number of statements executed by the algorithm, and hence the time required for the algorithm to execute, increases roughly as the square of the length of the list. We say the algorithm is of "order n^2." (The terminology will be explained more fully in Chapter 21.) This is fine for small lists, but might become a problem for lists with upwards of 1,000,000 elements.

n	$\dfrac{n^2 - n}{2}$
10	45
100	4,950
1,000	499,500
10,000	49,995,000
100,000	4,999,950,000
1,000,000	499,999,500,000

To get a bit of perspective, if a step took one second to perform, it would take about 17,000 years to perform 499,999,500,000 steps. If a million steps could be done in a second, it would still take almost 6 days to perform 499,999,500,000 steps.

13.2.3   Bubble sort

In this section, we consider another simple sorting method called *bubble sort*. The method works as follows. Make a pass through the list comparing pairs of adjacent elements. If the pair is not properly ordered, interchange them. At the end of the pass, the last element will be in its proper place. Continue making passes through the list until all the elements are in place. We illustrate, again using a list of integers.

Pass 1

1. Compare first and second elements.

6	4	7	2	3
(0)	(1)	(2)	(3)	(4)

Since they are out of order (the second is less than the first), interchange them.

4	6	7	2	3
(0)	(1)	(2)	(3)	(4)

2. Compare second and third elements. Since they are in order, do nothing.

4	6	7	2	3
(0)	(1)	(2)	(3)	(4)

3. Compare third and fourth elements.

4	6	7	2	3
(0)	(1)	(2)	(3)	(4)

Since they are out of order (the fourth is less than the third), interchange them.

4	6	2	7	3
(0)	(1)	(2)	(3)	(4)

4. Compare fourth and fifth elements.

4	6	2	7	3
(0)	(1)	(2)	(3)	(4)

Since they are out of order (the fifth is less than the fourth), interchange them.

4	6	2	3	7
(0)	(1)	(2)	(3)	(4)

Notice that at the end of this pass, the last element is in place. (The algorithm is called the "bubble sort" because the largest element bubbles to the end of the list.)

The process is now repeated, "bubbling" the second largest element into place:

Pass 2

1. Compare first and second elements.

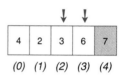

4	6	2	3	7
(0)	(1)	(2)	(3)	(4)

2. Compare second and third elements; interchange.

4	2	6	3	7
(0)	(1)	(2)	(3)	(4)

3. Compare third and fourth elements; interchange.

4	2	3	6	7
(0)	(1)	(2)	(3)	(4)

Two more passes are guaranteed to leave the list sorted.

Pass 3

1. Compare first and second elements; interchange.

2	4	3	6	7
(0)	(1)	(2)	(3)	(4)

2. Compare second and third elements; interchange.

2	3	4	6	7
(0)	(1)	(2)	(3)	(4)

Pass 4

1. Compare first and second elements.

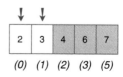

2	3	4	6	7
(0)	(1)	(2)	(3)	(5)

The algorithm is given in Listing 13.2. A little analysis will show that this algorithm takes essentially the same number of steps as the selection sort. That is, the inner loop body is performed $(n^2 - n) / 2$ times for a list of n elements.

Listing 13.2   **Bubble sort**

```
/**
 * Sort specified StudentList in increasing order.
 *     ensure:
 *         for 0 <= i, j < list.size(),
 *             list.get(i).lessThan(list.get(j)) implies i < j.
 */
public void sort (StudentList list) {
    int last;        // index of last element to position
                     // on this pass

    last = list.size() - 1;
    while (last > 0) {
        makePassTo(list, last);
        last = last-1;
    }
}


/*
 * Make a pass through the list, bubbling an element to
 *position last.
 *     require:
 *         0 < last < list.size()
 *     ensure:
 *         for 0 <= i < last,
 *             ! list.get(last).lessThan (list.get(i)),
 *             that is, list.get(last) >= list.get(i)
 */
private void makePassTo (StudentList list, int last) {
        int next;        // index of next pair to examine.
    next = 0;
    while (next < last) {
        if (list.get(next+1).lessThan(list.get(next)))
            interchange(list, next, next+1);
        next = next+1;
    }
}
```

We can improve the algorithm a bit with the following observation. If we make a pass through the list without interchanging any elements at all, then the list is ordered. If the list is ordered or nearly ordered to start with, we can complete the sort in fewer than *n* – 1 passes. For instance, if the list is ordered, we can determine this fact in one pass. If only one element is out of order, one pass sorts the list and a second pass tells us we are done. Thus if we expect to use the algorithm on "mostly ordered" lists, it pays to keep track of whether or not any elements have been interchanged. We modify the methods in a rather straightforward way to handle this. The modified algorithm is given in Listing 13.3.

Note that we have modified the method `makePassTo` so that it reports whether or not any items were swapped. It now behaves like both a command and a query. This is generally not a good idea: we like to keep commands and queries distinct, and in particular, a query should never change an object's state. But as this method is not intended to define an object feature, but just to serve as a utility function for the sort, we are not too concerned with this variance from standard practice.

Listing 13.3 **Bubble sort, modified**

```
/**
 * Sort specified StudentList in increasing order.
 *     ensure:
 *         for 0 <= i, j < list.size(),
 *             list.get(i).lessThan(list.get(j)) implies i < j.
 */
public void sort (StudentList list) {
    int last;        // index of last element to position
                     // on this pass

    last = list.size() - 1;
    done = false;
    while (!done && last > 0) {
        done = makePassTo(list, last);
        last = last-1;
    }
}

/*
 * Make a pass through list, bubbling an element to position
 * last, and report if anything needed to be changed.
 *     require:
 *         0 < last < list.size()
 *     ensure:
 *         for 0 <= i < last,
 *             ! list.get(last).lessThan (list.get(i)),
 *             that is, list.get(last) >= list.get(i)
 *         result == true iff
```

continued

Listing 13.3   Bubble sort, modified (*continued*)

```
*             for 0 <= i, j <= last,
*                list.get(i).lessThan(list.get(j))
*                implies i < j.
*/
private boolean makePassTo (StudentList list, int last) {
    int next;       // index of next pair to examine.
    boolean noItemsSwapped;
                    // no out of order items found

    next = 0;
    noItemsSwapped = true;
    while (next < last) {
        if (list.get(next+1).lessThan(list.get(next))) {
            interchange(list, next, next+1);
            noItemsSwapped = false;
        }
        next = next+1;
    }
    return noItemsSwapped;
}
```

13.3   Binary search

One of the advantages of an ordered list is that it is easier to find an element in an ordered list than in an unordered one. Imagine, for instance, how much more difficult it would be to find a name in the telephone book or a word in the dictionary if they were not ordered alphabetically.

If we are looking up a word in the dictionary, we open the book more or less randomly and compare the first word on the page to the one we're looking for. If we're looking up the word "manciple" and we open the dictionary to a page that begins with "phlogiston," we immediately eliminate the pages after the one we're looking at from consideration. We know "manciple" comes before "phlogiston." We continue by looking at a page somewhat in the middle of those we have left, and again comparing what we see to what we're looking for.

If we formalize this process, we have a search algorithm called *binary search*. The binary search algorithm looks for an item in an ordered list by first looking at the middle element of the list. Depending on how the middle element compares to the item we're looking for, we can eliminate half the list. That is, if the middle element is greater than or equal to the item we're looking for, we forget about the last half of the list. If the middle element is less than the item we're looking for, we forget about the first half of the list. The process is then repeated with the remaining portion of the list.

Suppose, for instance, we want to search for the number 42 in the following 15-element list. (The number happens not to be on the list, but we don't know that until we look.)

2	5	7	12	15	21	25	28	30	33	40	56	64	72	73
(0)	(1)	(2)	(3)	(4)	(5)	(6)	*(7)*	(8)	(9)	(10)	(11)	(12)	(13)	(14)

First, the middle element, the element at index 7, is compared to 42. Since 28 is less than 42, if 42 is on the list, it must be after 28. Thus the first half of the list need not be further examined:

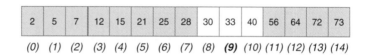

2	5	7	12	15	21	25	28	30	33	40	56	64	72	73
(0)	(1)	(2)	(3)	(4)	(5)	(6)	(7)	(8)	(9)	(10)	*(11)*	(12)	(13)	(14)

The middle element of what's left is the element at position 11. This element, 56, is now compared to 42. Since 56 is greater than 42, the numbers after it in the list can be eliminated as possibilities.

2	5	7	12	15	21	25	28	30	33	40	56	64	72	73
(0)	(1)	(2)	(3)	(4)	(5)	(6)	(7)	(8)	*(9)*	(10)	(11)	(12)	(13)	(14)

Continuing, we next look at the element at index 9, the middle of what's left. This element, 33, is smaller than 42, so any remaining values below it are no longer considered.

2	5	7	12	15	21	25	28	30	33	40	56	64	72	73
(0)	(1)	(2)	(3)	(4)	(5)	(6)	(7)	(8)	(9)	*(10)*	(11)	(12)	(13)	(14)

We're now down to one remaining element, at position 10. But this isn't what we're looking for, so we can conclude that 42 is not in the list.

Note that we have determined that 42 is not on the list by looking at only four elements. If the list were not sorted, we would need to look at all fifteen elements to determine that 42 was not on the list.

Let's develop a search method using the algorithm. As a first step, we write an algorithm that tells us where an item should be if it is on the list. Its specification is as follows:

private int itemIndex (Student item, StudentList list)
> The proper place for the specified item on the specified list, found using binary search.

require:
> list is sorted in increasing order.

ensure:
```
0 <= result <= list.size()
for 0 <= i < result
    list.get(i) < item
for result <= i < list.size()
    list.get(i) >= item
```

Note clearly what this method gives us. It gives a list index such that all the elements prior to the index are smaller than the item searched for, and none of the items from the index to the end of the list are smaller. If the item is smaller than all the list elements, the method returns 0. If it is greater than all the list elements, the method returns list.size().

We now give an implementation.

```
private int itemIndex (Student item,
                       StudentList list) {

    int low;        // the lowest index being examined
    int high;       // the highest index begin examined

    /*
     * list.get(low)...list.get(high) is the segment
     * of the list still to be considered.
     * for 0 <= i < low
     *     list.get(i) < item
     * for high < i < list.size()
     *     list.get(i) >= item
     */

    int mid;        // the middle item between low and
                    // high. mid == (low+high)/2

    low = 0;
    high = list.size() - 1;
    while (low <= high) {
        mid = (low+high)/2;
        if (list.get(mid).lessThan(item))
```

```
            low = mid+1;
        else
            high = mid-1;
    }
    return low;
}
```

It is worth while to take a careful look at this algorithm. Let's first trace the algorithm with the list we used above. (Again, integers simplify the pictures.)

Recall that we are searching for the value 42 in the following list:

2	5	7	12	15	21	25	28	30	40	52	56	64	72	73

(0) (1) (2) (3) (4) (5) (6) (7) (8) (9) (10) (11) (12) (13) (14)

When the method is invoked, list will be the list, item 42. low and high are initialized to 0 and 14, respectively.

item	42
low	0
high	14
mid	?

The first iteration of the loop body sets mid to 7, compares the element at index 7 with item and adjusts low.

item	42
low	8
high	14
mid	7

The second iteration sets mid to 11, compares the element at index 11 with item and adjusts high.

item	42
low	9
high	10
mid	11

The third iteration compares the element at index 9 with item and adjusts low.

item	42
low	10
high	10
mid	9

The final iteration examines the element at index 10 and adjusts `low` again.

item	42
low	11
high	10
mid	10

At this point `low > high`, the iteration terminates, and the value of `low` is returned. Note that the method postcondition is satisfied:

```
for 0 <= i < result
    list.get(i) < item
for result <= i < list.size()
    list.get(i) >= item
```

13.3.1   Completing the search

The method `itemIndex` gives us the index of the first list element that is not smaller than the item we're searching for. We'd like to write a search method using `itemIndex` as follows:

```
/**
 * The index of the specified item on the specified
 * list, located by binary search. Returns -1 if
 * the item is not on the list.
 *      require:
 *          item != null
 *      ensure:
 *          if item equals no element of list then
 *              indexOf(item, list) == -1
 *          else
 *              item equals list.get(indexOf(item, list)),
 *              and indexOf(item, list) is the smallest
 *              value for which this is true
 */
public int indexOf (Student item, StudentList list) {
    i = itemIndex(item, list);
    if (i < list.size() && list.get(i).equals(item))
        return i;
    else
        return -1;
}
```

For this to be correct, the ordering must be complete with respect to equality. For instance, suppose `list` is a *StudentList* ordered by social security number. That is, `s1.lessThan(s2)` means `s1`'s social security number is less than `s2`'s. The method invocation `itemIndex(s,1)` will give us the index of the first *Student* on the list whose social security number is greater than or equal to `s`'s. Since no two *Student*s have the same social security number, if `s` is on the list, it must be at the position returned by `itemIndex`.

On the other hand, suppose the list is ordered by final grade. In this case, `itemIndex(s,1)` will give us the index of the first *Student* on the list whose final grade is greater than or equal to `s`'s. It is possible that `s` is on the list, but other *Student*s with the same final grade precede `s` on the list. We cannot determine whether or not `s` is on the list simply by looking at the element at `itemIndex(s,1)`. We must search the list, starting at this position, until we either find `s` or find a *Student* with a larger grade.

13.3.2 Sequential search and binary search

In Chapter 12 we wrote a search method that simply looked at each list element in order.

```
public int indexOf (Student obj) {
    int i;
    int length;
    length = this.size();
    i = 0;
    while (i < length && !obj.equals(get(i)))
        i = i+1;
    if (i < length)
        return i;
    else  // item not found
        return -1;
}
```

This approach is called *sequential search* or *linear search*. How much better than linear search is the binary search? If the list has n elements, and the element we are looking for is not on the list, the linear search algorithm requires n steps: we need to examine each of the n elements. If the element we are looking for is on the list, we expect to take about $n/2$ steps to find it.

Binary search, on the other hand, is guaranteed to work in $\log_2 n$ steps. If a list contains 1000 elements, binary search will locate an element in 10 steps ($2^{10} = 1024$). If a list contains 1,000,000 elements, binary search still requires only 20 steps ($2^{20} = 1024 \times 1024 \approx 1,000,000$).

The price we pay, of course, is that the list must first be sorted in order to use binary search.

Number of steps required by the algorithm with a list of length n grows proportional to

- Selection sort: n^2

- Bubble sort: n^2

- Linear search: n

- Binary search: $\log_2 n$

Figure 13.1 **Relative efficiency (complexity) of search and sort algorithms.**

13.4   Verifying correctness: using a loop invariant

The iteration in `itemIndex` is one of the first we've encountered that requires more than a casual analysis. In particular, we don't have an index stepping sequentially through the list elements as in the other cases we've seen. We'll use this as an example to illustrate how to verify the correctness of a loop, and to introduce the important idea of a loop invariant.

We repeat the method with numbered lines for easy reference:

```
1.   private int itemIndex (Student item,
                                  StudentList list) {
2.        low = 0;
3.        high = list.size() - 1;
4.        while (low <= high) {
5.            mid = (low+high)/2;
6.            if (list.get(mid).lessThan(item))
7.                low = mid+1;
8.            else
9.                high = mid-1;
10.       }
11.       return low;
12.  }
```

The purpose of the method is to find the index of the first list element (i.e., the list element with lowest index) that is greater than or equal to a specified item. Specifically, the method postcondition states

```
for 0 <= i < result
    list.get(i) < item
```

```
for result <= i < list.size()
    list.get(i) >= item
```

Since the method returns the value of the variable `low`, we want `low` to satisfy this condition when the loop terminates

```
for 0 <= i < low
    list.get(i) < item
for low <= i < list.size()
    list.get(i) >= item
```

Verifying the correctness of the loop, and hence of the method, involves two steps. First we show that if the loop terminates, `low` will satisfy the above condition. This is termed *partial correctness*. That is, demonstrating partial correctness involves demonstrating that the loop is correct *assuming it terminates*. To complete the verification, we demonstrate that the loop will terminate in all cases.

---

partial correctness: the assertion that a loop is correct *if it terminates*.

total correctness: the assertion that a loop is both partially correct, and terminates.

To verify partial correctness, we first find a key *loop invariant*. A loop invariant is a condition that is true before and after each iteration of a loop, as illustrated in Figure 13.2. A key loop invariant captures the essential behavior of the loop. When the loop terminates, at the point labeled *(d)* in the figure, the invariant is true and the *while* condition is false. We want the combination of these two facts to guarantee that the loop has accomplished its purpose.

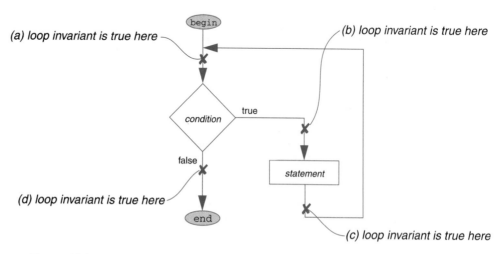

(a) loop invariant is true here

(b) loop invariant is true here

(d) loop invariant is true here

(c) loop invariant is true here

Figure 13.2 A loop invariant.

To show that a condition is a loop invariant, we argue inductively. First we verify that the condition is true when the loop test is reached for the first time: that is, the first time the point labeled *(a)* in Figure 13.2 is reached. (This is the induction base case.) Then assuming that the invariant holds before executing the loop body, we show that it will still hold after executing the loop body. That is, we assume the invariant true at the point labeled *(b)* in Figure 13.2, and show it is still true when the point labeled *(c)* is reached. (This is the induction step.)

> **loop invariant:** a condition that is true at the start of execution of a loop, and remains true no matter how many times the body of the loop is performed.

Preliminaries

Before we verify partial correctness, let's make sure that the reference `list.get(mid)` at line 6 is legal: that is, that the preconditions of `get` are satisfied. We must ensure that `0 <= mid < list.size()`. We know that `low <= high` at line 5, since this is the loop test and must be true to get into the loop. (We sometimes say the condition `low <= high` *guards* the loop body.) This condition insures that the value assigned to `mid` will be between `low` and `high`:

(1)   `low <= mid <= high`

Now *(1)* implies that `low` can only increase as the body of the loop is executed, and `high` can only decrease. Since `low` starts at 0 and `high` at `list.size()-1`, we can conclude that

        `0 <= low <= mid <= high < list.size()`

will hold whenever we reach line 6, and the reference `list.get(mid)` is correct.

The key invariant

The condition

(2)   `for 0 <= i < low`
                `list.get(i) < item`
            `for high < i < list.size()`
                `list.get(i) >= item`

is key to understanding the algorithm. This condition states that everything below `low` is smaller than `item`, and everything above `high` is greater than or equal to `item`:

The operation of the loop is to maintain this relation while moving `low` and `high` closer together. When the loop exits, `low` equals `high+1`, and is the value we want:

Let's informally verify that *(2)* is a loop invariant.

Note that the condition requires something of a set of list elements; specifically, those list elements with indexes less than `low` or greater than `high`. When we first reach the loop test, `low` is 0 and `high` is `list.size()-1`. There are no indexes less than `low` or greater than `high`. Thus the set of list elements of which something is required is empty, and the condition is vacuously true. (Loop invariants are often initially vacuously true.)

Now assume that condition *(2)* holds and we are about to execute the loop body: we have reached point *(b)* in Figure 13.2. We need to show that *(2)* is still true when we reach point *(c)*.

Given that the condition holds before executing the *if* and that the list is sorted in ascending order, it is rather easy to see that condition will remain true after executing the *if*, regardless of which *if* alternative is performed.

Let's consider the case where the *if* condition, `list.get(mid).less-Than(item)` is true, and the assignment

```
low = mid+1;
```

at line 7 is executed. The facts that `list.get(mid) < item` (the *if* condition) and the list is sorted in ascending order guarantees that

```
for 0 <= i <= mid
    list.get(i) < item
```

After the assignment, `low` equals `mid+1` and so

```
for 0 <= i < low
    list.get(i) < item
```

The second part of *(2)*,

```
for high < i < list.size()
    list.get(i) >= item
```

simply follows from the fact that *(2)* was true before the loop body was done. The value of `high` is not changed when the *if* condition is true.

The case in which the *if* condition is false can be argued in a similar manner.

Partial correctness

We have demonstrated that *(2)* is a loop invariant. In particular, it must also be true when the loop is exited: at point *(d)* in Figure 13.2. It is not difficult to determine that when the loop is exited, `low` equals `high+1`. (In fact, this is implied by the invariant.) If the list is empty, the loop body is not executed at all, and point *(d)* is reached with `low == 0` and `high == -1`. If the loop body is performed, we have seen that `low <= mid <= high` at line 6. The only ways the loop exit condition `low <= high` can become false is if either `mid == high` and `low` is set to `mid+1`, or if `low == mid` and `high` is set to `mid-1`. In either case, `low` equals `high+1` when the loop is exited.

Consequently, the following conditions are satisfied on loop exit

```
low == high+1
for 0 <= i < low
    list.get(i) < item
for high < i < list.size()
    list.get(i) >= item
```

which imply

```
for 0 <= i < low
    list.get(i) < item
for low <= i < list.size()
    list.get(i) >= item
```

This tells us that `low` is exactly the value we want to return; that is, `low` satisfies the method postcondition.

Loop termination

We have shown that the method is correct assuming the loop terminates. We must also verify that the loop will indeed terminate. This is also rather easy to see. When the loop body is executed, we have already noted that `mid` will be set to a value between `low` and `high`. That is, condition *(1)* will hold after line 5 is done. So the *if* statement will either cause `low` to be increased or `high` to be decreased (by at least one). Clearly this can only happen a finite number of times before `low` becomes larger than `high`, regardless of their initial values.

13.5 Summary

Sorting and searching are two fundamental list operations. In this chapter, we examined two simple sort algorithms, selection sort and bubble sort. Both of these algorithms make successive passes through the list, getting one element into position on each pass. They are order n^2 algorithms, which means that the time required for the algorithm to sort a list grows as the square of the length of the list. We also saw a simple modification to bubble sort that improved its performance on a list that was almost sorted.

Next, we developed a search method for sorted lists called binary search. This algorithm searches a list in much the same way we would search for a word in the dictionary or a number in the phone book. At each step of the algorithm, the middle of the remaining elements is compared to the element being searched for. This allows half the remaining elements to be eliminated from consideration. A major advantage of the binary search is that it needs to look at only $\log_2 n$ elements to find an item on a list of length n.

In evaluating the binary search algorithm, we saw that two steps were involved in verifying the correctness of the iteration. First, we demonstrated partial correctness: that the iteration is correct if it terminates. To do this, we found a key loop invariant that captured the essential behavior of the iteration. A loop invariant is a condition that remains true no matter how many times the loop body is performed. The key invariant insures that when the loop terminates it has satisfied its purpose. Verification of the key invariant provides a demonstration of partial correctness. Then to complete the verification, we showed that the iteration always terminates.

EXERCISES

13.1 Clearly both the bubble sort and the selection sort will sort a list. If the same list is sorted with the bubble sort and with the selection sort, will the results always be identical?

13.2 Suppose the *if* condition in the bubble sort method `makePassTo` is changes to read

```
if (!list.get(next).lessThan(list.get(next+1))) {
```

Is the result of sorting a list always the same as with the original version? Is the sort still correct?

13.3 Would the binary search algorithm itemIndex still be correct if either of the following modifications are made?

a. The loop exit condition is changed to `low < high`.

b. The assignment to `high` in the loop is changed to `high = mid`.

13.4 A *merge* operation takes two sorted lists and combines them into a single sorted list. For instance

```
/**
 * Merge the specified Lists.
 *      require:
 *          list1 and list2 are ordered.
 *      ensure:
 *          merge(list1, list2) is ordered.
 */
public StudentList merge (StudentList list1,
                                StudentList list2)
```

Implement the method, making sure that any iterations require no more than n_1+n_2 steps, where n_1 is the length of list1 and n_2 is the length of list2.

13.5   An *insertion sort* can be described as follows.

   a.   Each element of the list is "positioned," starting with the second (index 1).

   b.   To position an element *e*, look at the elements preceding *e* on the list. For instance, if *e* is the tenth element, look at the ninth, then the eighth, then the seventh, *etc.* Elements greater than or equal to *e* are shifted one position up, leaving a "vacancy" after the first element encountered that is less than *e*. Put *e* into the vacancy.

   Implement insertion sort.

13.6   A key invariant for loop in the selection sort method smallestOf says that small is the index of the smallest element from first up to, but not including next. A little more formally, it says

```
for first <= i < next,
    list.get(i) >= list.get(small)
```

Verify this invariant.

13.7   A key invariant for the (outer) loop in selection sort says that the elements from 0 up to but not including first are in their proper position:

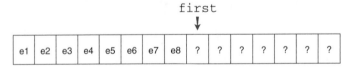

first

That is

list.get(0) through list.get(first-1) are ordered, and
list.get(first) through list.get(last) are all greater than
or equal to list.get(first-1).

Verify this invariant.

13.8   State and verify key loop invariants for the two bubble sort loops.

13.9   State and verify key loop invariants for the methods written in Chapter 12.

13.10   A student attempting to write selection sort makes two mistakes. He starts the inner loop at 0, and reverses the test in the *if* statement. He ends up with the following method:

```
public void sort (StudentList list) {
    int first = 0;
    int last = list.size() - 1;
    while (first <= last) {
        int next = 0;
        while (next <= last) {
            if (list.get(first).lessThan(list.get(next)))
                interchange(l,first,next);
            next = next+1;
        }
        first = first+1;
    }
}
```

Determine what this method does, and verify your hypothesis by finding key invariants for the loops.

GLOSSARY

binary search: a search algorithm that locates an item on a sorted list of n elements in $\log_2 n$ steps. On each step, half of the remaining list elements are eliminated from consideration until only one remains.

bubble sort: a simple sort algorithm that "bubbles" each element into position. On each pass, pairs of successive elements are compared and interchanged if they are out of order.

linear search: a search algorithm that locates an item on a list by examining each list item in sequence. Same as *sequential search*.

loop invariant: a condition that remains true no matter how many times the loop body is executed.

ordering: an antisymmetric, transitive relation on a class.

partial correctness: the assertion that a loop is correct if it terminates.

selection sort: a sort algorithm that operates by repeated finding the smallest item not yet positioned, and putting it in its proper position.

sequential search: a search algorithm that locates an item on a list by examining each list item in sequence. Same as *linear search*.

sort: an algorithm that arranges the elements of a list according to some ordering.

CHAPTER 14

Abstraction and inheritance

In Chapter 9 we introduced the notion of *hierarchical abstraction*. Recall that "to abstract" is to eliminate distinctions: two things considered different at one level are considered to be similar or equivalent at a more abstract level. When applied to classes, the process of abstraction produces a class hierarchy in which upper classes are more abstract, and lower classes are more concrete. In this chapter, we study the language mechanism for implementing abstraction, called *class extension* and *inheritance*. The more concrete subclass *extends* the more abstract superclass, and *inherits* the functionality of the superclass.

We will see a fundamental feature provided by the abstraction mechanism, called *polymorphism* or *dynamic binding*. Essentially, a subclass can redefine the behavior it inherits from its superclass. An instance of the subclass exhibits this modified behavior, even when it is "viewed" at the level of the superclass.

We briefly consider some cases in which the inheritance relation is commonly used, and note that in many instances inheritance is used because of the advantages provided by polymorphism.

We conclude the chapter with a discussion of Java's accessibility and scoping rules. These are the rules which determine from where in the program an object's features, methods, and components, can be accessed.

14.1 Abstraction

As mentioned above, "to abstract" is to eliminate distinctions. Two things considered different at a "more concrete" level are considered to be similar or equivalent at a "more abstract" level. As a relationship between classes, the abstract class *generalizes* or *abstracts* the concrete class. The concrete class *extends* the abstract class. The relation is represented in diagrams by a large arrowhead (hollow white triangle), as shown in Figure 14.1.

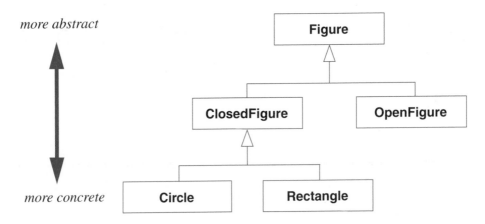

more abstract

more concrete

Figure 14.1 **A class hierarchy.**

Referring to the figure, we say the class *Circle extends ClosedFigure*, a *Circle is-a ClosedFigure*, *Circle* is a *subclass* of *ClosedFigure*, or *Circle* is a *descendent* of *ClosedFigure*. We also say *ClosedFigure generalizes Circle*, *ClosedFigure* is an *abstraction* of *Circle*, *ClosedFigure* is a *superclass* of *Circle*, or *ClosedFigure* is an *ancestor* of *Circle*. The terminology is transitive, so that we can also say that *Circle extends Figure*, *etc.* (If we intend to limit the relation to child-parent, we say "directly extends" or is an "immediate subclass of.")

The critical point is that an instance of a subclass has all the public features of the superclass, and perhaps more. A superclass expresses the common functionality among its subclasses. Of course, there are many possible hierarchies that could be developed from a collection of classes. We define a particular abstraction because we want to use different kinds of objects in the same way.

For an example, let's return to the maze game of earlier chapters. Moving through the maze, an explorer may find various useful items: scrolls, magic wands, rings, weapons, *etc.* Each of these items will be modeled by its own class. But there is a degree of similarity in these items: each is initially located somewhere in the maze, each can be picked up and put down in another location. This similarity might be important to the design. For instance, we might want the explorer to keep a list of the items he's carrying. This list can contain any item that can be picked up and carried. Thus we define a class modeling items than can be picked up and carried, as shown in Figure 14.2

A *Portable* is something that the explorer can pick up, carry, and put down. We can describe the collection of items the explorer is carrying as a *PortableList*. Such a list might contain *Rings*, *Wands*, *Scrolls*, and so on. But all these items share the functionality modeled by the class *Portable*.

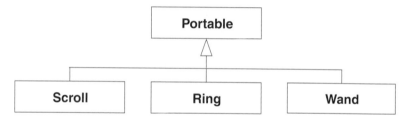

Figure 14.2 Class *Portable* is a superclass of *Scroll*, *Ring*, etc.

14.2 Extension and inheritance

The mechanism provided by the language for implementing abstraction is called *class extension*. Let's look at a simple example in which a class *ClosedFigure* has subclasses *Rectangle* and *Circle*:

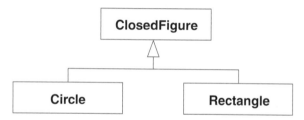

Instances of class *Circle* (and instances of class *Rectangle*) have all the functionality of class *ClosedFigure*. If a *ClosedFigure* can be queried for its *location* and *area*, for example, then so can a *Circle*. We say that the subclass *inherits* the functionality of the superclass.

A *Circle*, however, might have features not shared by other *ClosedFigures*. For instance, we might be able to query a *Circle* for its *radius*. Furthermore, different subclasses might implement common features in different ways. *Circle* and *Rectangle*, for example, will implement *area* differently.

Suppose that a *ClosedFigure* has features to get and set its location. (We don't particularly care what a *Location* is, except to note that it represents the location of a figure. Perhaps it includes coordinates in a Euclidean plane.)

```
public class ClosedFigure {
   public Location getLocation () {
      return this.location;
   }
   public void setLocation (Location newLocation) {
      this.location = newLocation;
   }
   private Location location;
}
```

We make the class *Circle* a subclass of *ClosedFigure* by using the keyword **extends** in the class definition:

```
public class Circle extends ClosedFigure {

    ...
    public int radius () {

        ...
    }

    ...
}
```

Since *Circle* extends *ClosedFigure*, a *Circle* instance will automatically inherit all of the features of a *ClosedFigure*. We can imagine that the *Circle* has a *ClosedFigure* "embedded" in it, as illustrated in Figure 14.3. (Recall that a "plus sign" preceding the feature emphasizes that the feature is public, while a "minus sign" emphasizes that it is private.)

If we have a *Circle* instance, we can query the instance for its location as well as for its radius. Assume the constructor for a *Circle* provides some default *Location* and requires that a radius be specified. If we create a *Circle* c

```
Circle c = new Circle(10);
```

we can query c as follows:

```
Location l = c.getLocation();
int d = c.radius();
```

Technically speaking, a subclass does not "inherit" private features of its superclass.[1] Thus even though a *Circle* has a *ClosedFigure* with instance variable location "embedded" in it, the variable location is *private* to *ClosedFigure*. It can't be directly accessed as a *Circle* feature, even in the definition of the class *Circle*. That is, we can't write a statement like

```
this.location = null;
```

in the class *Circle*, though we can write

```
this.setLocation(null);
```

---

1. This is according to Java's definition of the term "inherit." Informally, we would like to say that private features are inherited by the subclass, but not directly accessible from the subclass.

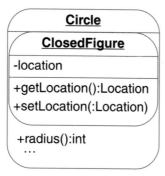

Figure 14.3 Class *Circle* extends class *ClosedFigure*.

We'll examine this situation more carefully later in the chapter, when we study feature accessibility.

> **inheritance:** a mechanism by which a subclass automatically possesses all of the nonprivate features of its superclass.

14.2.1   Generalization and subtyping

An important aspect of generalization is illustrated by the fact that since a *Circle is-a ClosedFigure*, a reference to a *Circle* is also a reference to a *ClosedFigure*. We say that the type *reference-to-Circle* is a *subtype* of the type *reference-to-ClosedFigure*: the set of *reference-to-Circle* values is a subset of the *reference-to-ClosedFigure* values. Specifically, this means that we can supply a *Circle* in any context requiring a *ClosedFigure*. For instance, a *reference-to-ClosedFigure* variable can contain a *reference-to-Circle* value.

```
        Circle c = new Circle(10);
        ClosedFigure f;
✓       f = c;                  // This is ok since a Circle is-a
                                // ClosedFigure.
```

After the assignment, both f and c reference the same *Circle* instance:

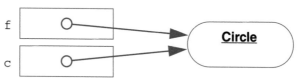

On the other hand, we cannot expect to be able to treat a *ClosedFigure* as a *Circle*. In the above example, since f is a *ClosedFigure* variable, we can invoke f.getLocation() to obtain the location of the *ClosedFigure* referenced by f, but we cannot query f.radius(). The variable f can reference an instance of any concrete subclass of *ClosedFigure*. It might be referencing a *Circle*, but it might also be referencing a *Rectangle* or some other *ClosedFigure*. In fact, it can reference a *Circle* at one time and a *Rectangle* at another.

```
     int d;
     Location l;
✓    l = f.getLocation();      // This is ok; getLocation is
                               // a ClosedFigure feature.
✗    d = f.radius();           // This is not ok; radius is
                               // not a ClosedFigure feature.
```

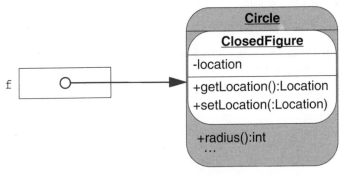

Figure 14.4 The view from *f* shows only a *ClosedFigure*.

For the same reason, an assignment like

```
✗    c = f;    // A ClosedFigure is not necessarily a Circle
```

where c and f are declared as above, is not permitted. The variable c can only reference a *Circle*, and the value contained in f might not be a reference to a *Circle*. A *Circle* is a *ClosedFigure*, but a *ClosedFigure* is not necessarily a *Circle*.

There are occasions when there is no doubt as to the kind of object a variable references. For example, the operator **instanceof**, introduced in Section 12.5, can be used to determine the class of a referenced object. Recall this operator has a reference value as left operand and a class as right operand:

reference-value **instanceof** *class*

It returns *true* if the object referenced by the left operand is an instance of the class named on the right, or of a subclass of the class named on the right. For example, the expression

f **instanceof** Circle

returns *true* if the value of f references a *Circle* (or a subclass of *Circle*). If we write a statement like

```
if (f instanceof Circle) {
    // f guaranteed to reference a Circle here
    ...
}
```

we can be certain that f will refer to a *Circle* in the body of the *if-then,* and not, say, a *Rectangle*. Inside the body of the *if-then* we can safely query f for its radius. (The operator **instanceof** returns *false* if its left operand is *null*. Thus requiring f **instanceof** Circle implicitly requires that f is not *null*.)

Knowing that f references a *Circle*, we must convert or *cast* the variable to the type *Circle* in order to treat the referenced object like a *Circle*. (We first saw the cast operation in Section 5.2.2, where it was used to convert one type of arithmetic value to another. We briefly encountered it again in Section 12.5, when we discussed the method equals.) In the present case, the cast has the form

```
(Class)reference-value
```

for instance

```
(Circle)f
```

This says that we are certain that f contains a reference to a *Circle*, and we want to treat the object referenced by f as a *Circle*. If f does not in fact reference a *Circle*, the cast operation will result in a run-time error.

We can safely write

```
int d;
if (f instanceof Circle) {
    d = ((Circle)f).radius();
    ...
}
```

or

```
if (f instanceof Circle) {
    Circle c = (Circle)f;
    d = c.radius();
    ...
}
```

since the body of the **if** will not be performed unless f references a *Circle*.

Note that since feature selection, ".", has higher precedence than casting, the outer parentheses are necessary in the query ((Circle)f).radius(). Writing

```
(Circle)f.radius()
```

is equivalent to writing

```
(Circle)(f.radius())
```

which says that the *result* of the query `f.radius()` should be treated as a reference to a `Circle`. This is nonsense, since `f` is a *ClosedFigure* and can't be queried for its radius, and even if it could, the method `radius` returns a **int**, which can't be cast to a reference to a *Circle*.

> **subtyping:** a mechanism by which an instance of a subclass can be used in any context specifying the superclass.

14.2.2   Abstract classes and abstract methods

If we look at the classes shown in Figure 14.2, it should occur to us that while we expect to have instances of *Ring*, *Scroll*, and so on, we will not encounter any instances of *Portable per se*. That is, any *Portable* will in fact be a *Ring*, or a *Scroll*, or some other specific kind of thing. The reason for introducing the class *Portable* is to capture the commonality in a set of other classes, so that we can handle instances of these other classes in a uniform manner. The same might also be true of the class *ClosedFigure*, introduced in the previous section. That is, a *ClosedFigure* might always be either a *Circle* or a *Rectangle* or some other specific kind of figure.

A class that we don't intend to instantiate should be declared as *abstract*. No instances of an abstract class can be created. Its purpose is to serve as a foundation on which to build subclasses, allowing us to manipulate dissimilar but related objects in the same way; through the specification of a common superclass. In contrast, a class that is not abstract is called *concrete*. The purpose of concrete classes is to provide the run-time instances that collaborate in the problem solution. We prefer extending abstract classes to extending concrete classes, since this tends to cause fewer problems as the system evolves.

A class is declared abstract by use of the keyword **abstract**:

```
public abstract class ClosedFigure {
```

and denoted in diagrams by a slanted font:

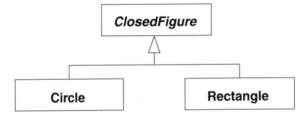

Even though we can't instantiate an abstract class, we can still define variables that reference the class. As we've seen, since *reference-to-Circle* is a subtype of *reference-to-ClosedFigure*, a *ClosedFigure* variable can contain a reference to a *Circle*.

```
      ClosedFigure f;
✗     f = new ClosedFigure();  // no -- can't instantiate
                               // an abstract class
✓     f = new Circle(10);      // ok -- a Circle is a
                               // ClosedFigure[
```

An abstract class can contain *abstract methods*. An *abstract method* is one that is specified, but not implemented. Since a concrete class cannot contain an abstract method, any concrete subclass must provide an implementation for any abstract method it inherits. For example, we can define an abstract method area for the class *ClosedFigure*:

```
public abstract class ClosedFigure {

    public abstract int area();
    ...
}
```

No method body is given for area. Each concrete subclass must implement the method in its own way. The class *Circle*, for example, will implement this method differently from the class *Rectangle*. However, we can be sure that whatever kind of *ClosedFigure* we encounter, it will have a method area. Consequently, if f is defined as a *ClosedFigure* variable and is not *null*, we can legally write

```
int d = f.area();
```

without concern for the kind of *ClosedFigure* f actually references when the statement is executed. If f references a *Circle* when the statement is executed, the query f.area() is directed to a *Circle*. The method that will be executed is the method area as defined for a *Circle*. If f references a *Rectangle* when the statements executed, the query is directed to a *Rectangle*, and the area method as implemented in *Rectangle* is done. This mechanism is called *polymorphism*, *dynamic binding*, or *dispatching*. We discuss it in more detail later in the chapter.

> **abstract class:** a class that cannot be instantiated, but is used as a foundation on which to build other classes by extension.

14.2.3   Constructors and subclasses

Constructors are not inherited; each class must define its own constructors. A constructor is responsible for initializing instance variables defined in a superclass as well as those expressly defined in the class itself. Hence the first thing a constructor does is invoke, either explicitly or implicitly, a constructor of its parent class, or explicitly invoke another constructor of the same class. In any case, the parent class constructor is ultimately invoked.

For instance, *Circle* is a subclass of *ClosedFigure*, and we have suggested above that a constructor for a *Circle* require a radius as argument:

```
public class Circle extends ClosedFigure {

    public Circle (int radius) {
        ...
```

But *ClosedFigure* has an instance variable location, and this variable must be properly initialized when a *Circle* instance is created. To do this, the *Circle* constructor invokes the *ClosedFigure* constructor with the keyword **super**. The format is

```
super(arguments);
```

For instance we can write

```
public class Circle extends ClosedFigure {

    public Circle (int radius) {
        super();
        myRadius = radius;
    }
    ...
    private int myRadius:
}
```

Of course, for this to be legal the superclass *ClosedFigure* must *have* a constructor requiring no arguments, and this constructor must properly initialize *ClosedFigure* features.

We have already seen that the keyword **this** can be used in a constructor to invoke another constructor of the same class. Suppose we want to equip the class *Circle* with a second constructor that creates an instance with a default radius of 1. The second constructor can invoke the first as follows:

```
public class Circle extends ClosedFigure {

    public Circle (int radius) {
        super();
        myRadius = radius;
    }
```

```
public Circle () {
    this(1);          // invoke above constructor
                      // with argument 1.
}
...
private int myRadius;
}
```

Note that even though we can't instantiate an abstract class, an abstract class will nevertheless be equipped with one or more constructors. This is essential, since instantiating a concrete subclass of an abstract class will result in a constructor for the abstract class being invoked.

Suppose we extend *Circle* with a class *ColoredCircle*:

```
public class ColoredCircle extends Circle { ...
```

A constructor for *ColoredCircle* invokes a *Circle* constructor to initialize *Circle* features. For example

```
public class ColoredCircle extends Circle {

    public ColoredCircle (int radius, Color c) {
        super(radius);
        myColor = c;
    }
    ...
    private Color myColor;
}
```

If we write a constructor that neither calls a superclass constructor explicitly nor calls another constructor of the same class, it is assumed to begin with

```
super();
```

That is, the constructor begins with an invocation of the superclass constructor requiring no arguments. For instance, the *ColoredCircle* constructor

```
public ColoredCircle (Color c) {
    myColor = c;
}
```

is equivalent to

```
public ColoredCircle (Color c) {
    super();
    myColor = c;
}
```

Notice that invocation of a class constructor results in invocation of a constructor for each of the class's ancestors. For instance, an invocation of a *ColoredCircle* constructor

```
new ColoredCircle(c)
```

will call a *Circle* constructor which will call a *ClosedFigure* constructor which will call an *Object* constructor.

If a class doesn't contain a constructor definition, a default constructor requiring no arguments is automatically provided. This default constructor is provided whether or not the class is abstract, and for a *public* class, is equivalent to

```
public Class () {
    super();
}
```

Finally, note that the key words **this** and **super** as constructor invocations can appear only as the first statement of another constructor.

14.3   Overriding and polymorphism

We have seen that a subclass inherits all the (public) features of its parent class. For instance, in Section 12.5, we noted that every Java class comes equipped with a method `equals`, effectively defined as

```
public boolean equals (Object obj) {
    return this == obj;
}
```

The reason every class has this method is that the method is defined for the class *Object*, and as we observed in Section 9.5, every class is a subclass of *Object*.

A class can redefine a method that it inherits. Such a redefinition is called *overriding*. The redefined method must have the same return type and the same number and type of parameters as the inherited method. For instance, we might redefine `equals` in the class *Circle* so that two *Circle*s with the same radius are considered equal:

```
public class Circle extends ClosedFigure {
    ...
    public boolean equals (Object c) {
        if (c instanceof Circle)
            return this.radius() == ((Circle)c).radius();
        else
            return false;
    }
    ...
}
```

Note the use of the operator **instanceof**, and the cast of the *Object* c to *Circle*. We could not simply write c.radius(), because c is an *Object*, and *Object*s do not have a radius feature.

We can also redefine equals for the class *Rectangle*, so that two *Rectangles* with the same length and width are equal. The classes *ClosedFigure*, *Circle*, and *Rectangle* now each have a different implementation of the equals method. (*ClosedFigure* inherits the method from *Object*.)

Consider the following:

```
    ClosedFigure f1;
    ClosedFigure f2;
    int n;
❶   // n is given a value here
    if (n == 0) {
        f1 = new Circle();
        f2 = new Circle();
    } else {
        f1 = new Rectangle();
        f2 = new Rectangle();
    }
❷   boolean b = f1.equals(f2);
```

f1 and f2 are *ClosedFigure* variables. When ❷ is reached, they will both reference *Circles* or will both reference *Rectangles*, depending on the value computed for n at ❶. Which equals method is executed at ❷ depends on the object f1 references when the statement is reached. If f1 references a *Circle*, the equals defined in *Circle* will be invoked; if f1 references a *Rectangle*, the equals defined in *Rectangle* will be invoked. This behavior is referred to as *dynamic binding*, *dispatching*, or *polymorphism* (since f1 can "take the form of" a *Circle* or a *Rectangle*). Note that even though f1 is a *ClosedFigure* variable, the *ClosedFigure* version of equals will not be used.

A class that overrides a method can call its parent's overridden method with the key word **super**. For instance, assuming the query color() is defined for *Colored-Circles*, we might define the method equals for the class *ColoredCircle* as follows:

```
    public class ColoredCircle extends Circle {
        ...
        public boolean equals (Object c) {
            if (c instanceof ColoredCircle)
                return super.equals(c) &&
                        this.color().equals(c.color());
            else
                return false;
        }
        ...
    }
```

The method first checks to make sure that the argument is a *ColoredCircle*, and then invokes the `equals` method as defined for the class *Circle*. For two *ColoredCircle*s to be equal, they must be equal as *Circle*s, and their *Color*s must be equal.

---

overriding: providing an alternative implementation of an inherited method.

polymorphism: dynamic behavior by which the method performed as the result of a call to a given object is determined at run-time by the class of the object.

Method overloading

There is an aspect of the language called *method overloading* that appears similar to overriding, but in fact has quite different semantics. A class can contain distinct methods with the same name as long as these methods differ in number or type of parameters. For instance, a class could contain three methods specified as:

```
public int m (int x);
public int m (Object obj);
public void m (int x, int y);
```

Note that these are completely separate, independent methods. They simply all happen to be named m. Which method is invoked is determined, obviously enough, by the number and types of arguments. For example, the call `m(2,3)` would invoke the third of the three methods, while the call `m(2)` would invoke the first.

A class cannot contain two methods with the same name and the same number and type of parameters, even if the methods have different return types. For example, a class could not contain two methods specified as

```
public void m (int x);
public Object m (int i);
```

even though one is a query returning an *Object*, and the other is a command.

Giving different methods in the same class the same name is called *overloading*. This is in fact what we did when we defined several constructors for a class. Overloading appears similar to overriding, since in both cases there are "different" methods with the same name. However, overloaded methods are different *methods* in the *same* class, while overriding involves providing different *implementations* for a method in two *different* classes.

Suppose we modified the definition of `equals` in the class *Circle* to read as follows:

```
public class Circle extends ClosedFigure {
    ...
    public boolean equals (Circle c) {
        return this.radius() == c.radius();
    }
    ...
}
```

This method now *overloads* the `equals` method inherited from *ClosedFigure*, and does not override it. That is, the class *Circle* now has two methods named `equals`, one inherited from *ClosedFigure* and specified as

```
public boolean equals (Object obj);
```

and the other explicitly defined in the class, and specified as

```
public boolean equals (Circle c);
```

The reason that the method defined in *Circle* overloads rather than overrides the inherited method is that its parameter has a different type from that of the inherited method.

Overloading inherited methods, as in the above example, can lead to confusing situations. Consider the following:

```
       ClosedFigure f = new Circle();
       Circle c = new Circle();
❶      boolean b1 = f.equals(c);
❷      boolean b2 = c.equals(f);
```

At ❶, f is a *ClosedFigure* variable that contains a reference to a *Circle*. But in terms of functionality, the view we have of the object through f is as a *ClosedFigure*. As illustrated in Figure 14.5, a *ClosedFigure* does not have an `equals`-with-*Circle*-parameter method. Thus the inherited `equals`-with-*Object*-parameter method is invoked at ❶, since it is not overridden in *Circle*.

The question at ❷ is which of c's `equals` methods gets invoked: f is a *ClosedFigure* variable, but actually references a *Circle* instance when we reach ❷. The issue is resolved according to the type of f, not the object that f references during execution. We look for an `equals` method that accepts a *ClosedFigure* argument rather than one that accepts a *Circle* argument. Again, it is the inherited `equals`-with-*Object*-parameter method that is invoked. A *ClosedFigure* is-a *Object*, and can be supplied when the context requires an *Object*. A *ClosedFigure* cannot be supplied in a context requiring a *Circle* without an explicit cast.

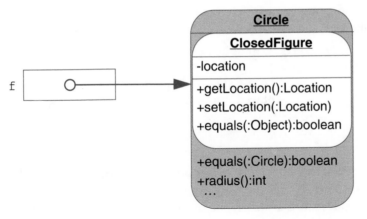

Figure 14.5 **The view from *f* shows only *ClosedFigure* functionality.**

Finally, if we write

boolean b3 = c.equals((Circle)f);

the *Circle*-defined equals-with-*Circle*-parameter method is invoked, since the type of the expression (Circle)f is *Circle*.

14.4 Subclasses and contracts

We have seen that because of subtyping, an instance of a subclass can be provided in any context requiring the superclass. For instance, a method

public void invert (ClosedFigure f)

with a *ClosedFigure* parameter can be invoked with a *Circle* as argument, assuming that *Circle* is a subclass of *ClosedFigure*.

Now the invocation of a method involves a contract between the client and the server. The method specification defines preconditions that the client is required to meet when invoking the method, and postconditions that the server guarantees will be satisfied when the method completes. For instance, the class *ClosedFigure* might contain a method fill specified as follows:

public void fill (Color c)
    Paint this *ClosedFigure* with the specified *Color*.

require:
    c != null

ensure:
    this.backgroundColor().equals(c)

The only requirement on the client is that the argument be a non-*null* value. (We actually don't need to require this explicitly, since the phrase "the specified *Color*" implies that a non-*null* value must be provided. The value *null* doesn't qualify semantically as a *Color*.) The server promises to paint the figure with the specified *Color*, and set the *backgroundColor* attribute of the figure to the specified *Color*.

This specification defines the contract between a *ClosedFigure* client invoking the method `fill` and the *ClosedFigure* instance executing the method.

Suppose that we extend *ClosedFigure* with class *MonochromeFigure*:

```
public class MonochromeFigure extends ClosedFigure …
```

A *MonochromeFigure* can now be supplied wherever a *ClosedFigure* is required. In particular, a client invoking the *ClosedFigure* method `fill` may actually be referencing a *MonochromeFigure*. Thus while the subclass *MonochromeFigure* can override the method `fill`, it is still bound to the contract *as specified in ClosedFigure*.

Suppose, for instance, *MonochromeFigure* overrode `fill` as follows:

```
/**
 * Paint this MonochromeFigure black or white.
 *     require:
 *         c.equals(Color.white) ||
 *         c.equals(Color.black)
 *     ensure:
 *         this.backgroundColor().equals(c)
 */
public void fill (Color c) {
   Require.condition(
      c.equals(Color.white) || c.equals(Color.black);
   …
```

A *ClosedFigure* client that innocently tries to fill a *ClosedFigure* with gray, for instance, will unexpectedly fail if the *ClosedFigure* happens to be *MonochromeFigure*.

This leads us to postulate the following general rule:

- When overriding a method, preconditions can be weakened but cannot be strengthened.

There would be no harm if, for instance, an overriding version of `fill` were willing to accept a *null* argument and treat it as black.

A complementary problem results from strengthening postconditions. Suppose, for example, the *MonochromeFigure* method `fill` decided to treat any color other than white as if it were black. It might be specified as follows.

```
public void fill (Color c)
```
Paint this *MonochromeFigure* white or black.

require:
```
c != null
```

ensure:
```
if c.equals(Color.white)
    this.backgroundColor().equals(c)
else
    this.backgroundColor().equals(Color.black)
```

Here we've weakened the postcondition. Instead of guaranteeing that the background color will be the one specified, we guarantee that it will be the one specified or black. Again, this can cause problems for the *ClosedFigure* client that expects the `fill` postconditions as specified in *ClosedFigure* to be met.

The general rule is:

- When overriding a method, postconditions can be strengthened but cannot be weakened.

We allow ourselves one exception to these rules. When we define generalized abstract containers in later chapters, we specify only that the containers hold *Objects*. We will feel free to extend these container classes to homogenous versions that are guaranteed to contain objects of some specific class: a container restricted to hold *ClosedFigures*, for instance. This violates the first of the two rules stated above. However, we are really forcing the extension mechanism into inappropriate duty here. If our language provided features such as genericity or polymorphic types, we could avoid this exception.

14.5   Using inheritance

Understanding the extension mechanism is not particularly difficult. The challenge is in learning how to apply inheritance to build flexible, reusable systems. There are many situations in which inheritance can be used to structure a solution. We mention just a few here, and expand a bit on these ideas in the next chapter. When to use inheritance, and when to use another structuring technique is generally not clear-cut. Choosing the best approach to a particular problem requires careful analysis and substantial design experience.

Identifying common functionality among a collection of classes

As we have stated several times, the process of abstraction identifies commonality in different objects. We use inheritance when we want to exploit this commonality: that is, we want to treat a collection of instances from different classes in the same way, to exploit polymorphism. For instance, suppose all the items that a maze game explorer can carry have weight. We can capture this similarity by making *weight* a feature of the class *Portable*, which is a superclass of the classes denoting the different kinds of items an explorer can carry. (See Figure 14.2.)

```java
public abstract class Portable {
    ...
    public int weight ()
    ...
}
```

Now as was suggested above, the collection of things the explorer is carrying can be modeled by a *PortableList*. The actual objects on the list will be *Rings*, *Scrolls*, and so on, but they are all similar in that they are all *Portables*. If class *Pack* represents the *Explorer*'s pack, we can define a method that computes the total weight of the items in the pack. For instance

```java
public class Pack {
    ...
    public int totalWeight () {
        int sum = 0;
        int i = 0;
        while (i < items.size()) {
            sum = sum + items.get(i).weight();
            i = i + 1;
        }
        return sum;
    }
    ...
    private PortableList items;   // items in this Pack
}
```

All this method needs to know is that each item on the list is a *Portable*, and so has a method `weight`. The method `totalWeight` treats all the different kinds of *Portable* objects in the same way. Additionally, the method does not need to be revised if the class *Portable* is extended with new subclasses at a later time. Any object can show up on a *PortableList*, as long as it is an instance of a subclass of *Portable*, and hence defines a method `weight`.

This is an illustration of the *open-closed principle* defined in Chapter 11. The class *Pack* can be closed, that is, specified, compiled, and available for use by other modules. But it is open for extension in that it can accommodate new kinds of *Portable* items not yet defined when *Pack* is implemented. The class specifies only that items must be *Portable,* allowing it to deal with new *Portable* items by default through polymorphism.

Providing an alternative implementation for a method

A common use of inheritance takes advantage of polymorphism to provide differ-ent implementations for a method. For example, consider the class *Player* defined as part of the nim game in Chapter 10. The class defines a method makeMove that determines how many sticks to take and removes them from the pile:

> **public void** makeMove (Pile pile, **int** maximum)
> > Make a move: remove up to the specified maximum number of sticks from the specified *Pile*.

The method uses a rather simple-minded strategy for making a move. As out-lined in exercise 10.3, we can build a *Player* with a perfect strategy: a *Player* who will win whenever possible. One way to do this is to extend the class *Player* with a class *PerfectPlayer* (Figure 14.6). *PerfectPlayer* overrides the makeMove method with a method using a more clever strategy. The classes are otherwise identical. The only difference is the implementation of makeMove.

Note that the creation of a new subclass does not require changes in a *Player* client. For instance, the method play of the *GameManager* invokes the *Player* method makeMove:

```
public void play () {
    while (!gameOver()) {
        nextPlayer.makeMove(thePile, MAX_REMOVED);
        ...
    }
}
...
private Player nextPlayer;
```

It does not matter to the *GameManager* whether nextPlayer references a *Player*, *PerfectPlayer*, or an instance of some other subclass of *Player*. In fact, during execution, nextPlayer might sometimes reference a *Player*, and some-times a *PerfectPlayer*. Each will execute its own makeMove method in response to the command from the *GameManager*.

Refining the implementation of a method

When we *refine* a method, we override the method so that the subclass performs some action in addition to what is done in the superclass. The subclass overrides the method, but invokes the superclass method in the overriding definition. As an example, assume that the class *Explorer* includes a method by which an *Explorer* can pick up an item and add it to his pack:

> **public void** addToPack (Portable item)

Figure 14.6 **PerfectPlayer** *extends* **Player**.

Suppose further that some items are cursed. It is a bad thing to put cursed items in your pack. Perhaps we would like a special grade of *Explorer*, a *Wizard*, who can remove curses. We can define *Wizard* by extending *Explorer* and refining the implementation of the method addToPack:

```
public class Wizard extends Explorer {
    …
    public void addToPack (Portable item) {
        item.removeCurses();
        super.addToPack(item);
    }
    …
}
```

To add an item to its pack, a *Wizard* calls the *Explorer* addToPack method after first removing any curses from the item.

The general format of the overriding method is

```
do something before
call the superclass method
do something after
```

As with the above case, the advantage is derived from polymorphism. Creation of the subclass does not require modification of an *Explorer* client.

Extending functionality of an existing class

Another common use of inheritance is to extend the functionality of a class. For example, we might decide that the nim game would be more interesting if the players could bet. We can add this functionality—the ability to place and collect bets—to the class *Player* by extending it. The extended class defines additional methods, for placing and collecting bets, and has additional instance variables, such as the value of the player's stake.

Sometimes providing additional functionality involves overriding existing methods. For instance, an exercise of Chapter 10 suggested defining a nim *Player* whose move is set by a client, so that the user can control the *Player*. Again, we can achieve this by extending the original class *Player*. In this case, we add additional functionality, a command to set the number of sticks the *Player* will take on its next turn, and override the `makeMove` method so that it simply takes the number of sticks specified:

```
class DummyPlayer extends Player {

    /**
     * Set the number of sticks this Player is to take
     * on its next turn.
     */
    public void setNumber (int n) …

    /**
     * Take the number of sticks previously specified
     * by setNumber.
     */
    public void makeMove (Pile pile, int maximum) …

}
```

14.6   Feature accessibility

To this point, all the features defined for a class—methods, instance variables, named constants—have been labeled either *public* or *private*. Public features are part of the class specification and are visible to clients of the class. Private features are part of the implementation and are not available to clients. We now take a more careful look at the issue of "feature accessibility," and introduce two more possibilities, *protected* and *restricted* features. We touch only the most significant points, and make no claim of completeness.

Accessibility is a static issue

The first thing to note is that the issue of feature access has to do with the structure of the *program text* and not with the run-time state of the system. Specifically, the question to be answered is "From where in the program text can this feature be accessed?" and not "Which objects can access this feature?"

To see what this means, observe that a feature labeled *private* is accessible from within the class in which it is defined. Consider the following example:

```
public class Circle {

    public Circle (int radius) {
        myRadius = radius;
    }

    public boolean equals (Object obj) {
        if (obj instanceof Circle) {
            return myRadius == ((Circle)obj).myRadius;
        else
            return false;
    }

    public int radius() {
        return myRadius;
    }

    private int myRadius;
}
```

❶

At ❶, the private instance variable myRadius of the argument obj is being accessed. If we write

```
Circle c1 = new Circle(10);
Circle c2 = new Circle(12);
```

c1 and c2 are two distinct instances of the class *Circle*, each with its own private instance variable myRadius. If we query c1 with

```
c1.equals(c2)
```

c1 will execute the *Circle* method equals, and legally access the private myRadius component of c2 at line ❶. The reason is that the *Circle* component myRadius can be referenced from anywhere in the text of the class *Circle*.

Suppose we again consider extending *Circle* with a class *ColoredCircle*:

```
public class ColoredCircle extends Circle {

    public ColoredCircle (int radius, Color c) {
        super(radius);
        myColor = c;
    }

    public boolean equals (Object obj) {
        if (obj instanceof ColoredCircle) {
```

```
                    // the following line is not legal!
❶✘                 return myRadius == ((Circle)obj).myRadius &&
                       myColor == ((ColoredCircle)obj).myColor;
               else
                   return false;
          }

          public Color color () {
              return myColor;
          }

          private Color myColor;
      }
```

Now even though a *ColoredCircle* instance executing the `equals` method and the method argument `obj` are both *Circles*, and *Circles* have `myRadius` instance variables, *neither* of the references to `myRadius` at ❶ is legal. Since *ColoredCircle* does not *inherit* the private component `myRadius` from *Circle*, the instance variable cannot be directly accessed from a *ColoredCircle*. Even if we cast an object to a *Circle*, its `myRadius` instance variable can be accessed only from within the definition of the class *Circle*, where the private variable `myRadius` is defined.

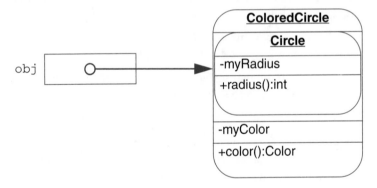

Figure 14.7 **A *ColoredCircle* is-a *Circle*.**

The method can be written legally as follows:

```
          public boolean equals (Object obj) {
              if (obj instanceof ColoredCircle) {
                  return this.radius() == ((Circle)obj).radius()
                     && myColor == ((ColoredCircle)obj).myColor;
              else
                  return false;
          }
```

The method `radius` is public, inherited by *ColoredCircle*, and available in the class *ColoredCircle*.

Of course, just because a construct is possible does not mean that it is proper. We prefer to view private features as part of the implementation of an object that should not be directly accessed by a client, even if the client happens to be of the same class.

Feature accessibility is limited by class accessibility

We saw early on that a class might or might not be labeled *public*. A class that is not labeled public can be accessed only from within its own package. Rather obviously, if the class is not visible outside its package, neither are any of its features. That is, access to features of a nonpublic class, even if the features are labeled public, is limited to the package containing the class definition.

Though we haven't seen any examples yet, it is also possible for a class to be defined inside of another class. Such a class is called an *inner class*. The accessibility of an inner class is determined by the same rules as the accessibility of other class features. In most cases, however, use of an inner class is limited to the class in which it is defined. We won't consider other situations here.

14.6.1   Protected features

Private features of a class are not directly accessible in a subclass. Occasionally, though, we want class features to be available to class extensions without making these features public. Consider for instance the class *Player* defined as part of the nim game in Chapter 10. Omitting comments, constructor, and methods for dealing with the *Player*'s name, the class was essentially defined as follows:

```
class Player {
    ...
    public int numberTaken () {
        return this.numberTaken;
    }

    public void makeMove (Pile pile, int maximum) {
        int size;               // pile size
        int number;             // number to take
        size = pile.size();
        if (size == 0)
            number = 0;
        else if (2 <= size && size <= maximum+1)
            number = size-1;
```

```
        else
            number = 1;
        pile.remove(number);
        this.numberTaken = number;
    }

    private int numberTaken;    // number of sticks
                                // taken on Player's
                                // last move

}
```

As we've seen, we can build players with different move strategies by extending *Player* and overriding the method `makeMove`.

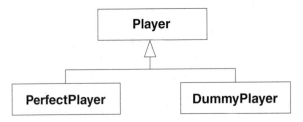

Let's try to write *DummyPlayer*, modeling a player whose move is set by a client.

```
class DummyPlayer extends Player {

    public DummyPlayer (String name) {
        super(name);
    }

    public void setNumberToTake (int n) {
        numberToTake = n;
    }

    public void makeMove (Pile pile, int maximum) {
        int size = pile.size();
        int number;
        if (numberToTake <= size &&
            numberToTake <= maximum)
            number = numberToTake;
        else if (size <= maximum)
            number = size;
        else
            number = maximum;
        pile.remove(number);
        this.numberTaken = number; // illegal access
    }
```

❶✗

```
private int numberToTake;

}
```

There is one problem with this method. At ❶ we want to remember the number of sticks taken on this turn. But the instance variable `numberTaken` is a private feature of *Player*, and cannot be accessed here.

We don't want to make `numberTaken` public, because it could then be accessed from anywhere, in particular by clients of *Player*. One possibility is to declare the *Player* instance variable `numberTaken` *protected*:

```
protected int numberTaken;// number of sticks taken
                          // on Player's last move
```

A class inherits a feature specified as *protected*, and the feature is accessible in the class. Thus if is it declared protected, the instance variable `numberTaken` is accessible at ❶ above.

A better approach is to allow controlled access to the instance variable through a *protected method*. For instance,

```
protected void setNumberTaken (int number) {
    numberTaken = number;
}
...
private int numberTaken;
```

Accessing component data by queries and commands limits class coupling, and localizes the effects of change.

The accessibility of a protected feature, though, is rather broad. The definition of a class can reference a protected feature in instances of the class. But it can also reference that protected feature in instances of subclasses that inherit the feature. For example, suppose *AClass*, *BClass*, and *CClass* are defined in separate packages, and *CClass* extends *BClass*, and *BClass* extends *AClass*:

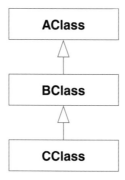

A protected feature f defined in *AClass*,

```
protected int f;
```

is inherited by *BClass* and *CClass*. From the definition of *AClass*, the feature f of an *AClass*, *BClass*, or *CClass* instance can be accessed. From *BClass*, the feature f of a *BClass* or *CClass* instance can be accessed. Thus the following method

```
void setF (CClass c) {
    c.f = 0;
}
```

can be contained in the definition of *AClass*, *BClass*, or *CClass*.

However, the feature f of a *CClass* instance is accessible from neither *CClass* descendents nor from *AClass* ancestors. Thus, assuming all classes are in different packages, the method setF could appear in any of the following unshaded classes but could not appear in any of the shaded classes:

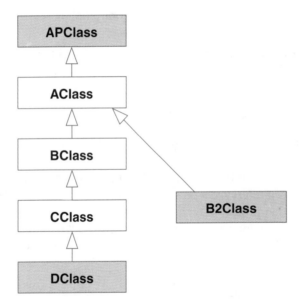

Furthermore, a protected feature is accessible from the package containing the class in which the feature is defined. So the setF method shown above could also appear in any class defined in the same package as *AClass*.

Defining a feature *protected* extends its accessibility considerably. Returning to the *Player* example, note that the class *Player* is not labeled *public*. Thus access to the class itself, and hence to all of its features, is limited to its package. Since declaring a feature *protected* exposes it to the entire package (at least), there is no effective difference in this case between declaring a feature *protected* and declaring it *public*. In either case, the feature is accessible throughout the package.

14.6.2   Restricted features

Sometimes a situation arises in which we want to permit certain classes that are not subclasses to have access to a feature. For example, consider the classes *Explorer* and *Room* from the maze game.The *Explorer* must know which room he is in, and the *Room* must know its contents:

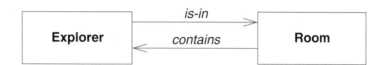

Explorer has a command move, and in the process of executing this command an *Explorer* might leave one *Room* and enter another. If the system is to remain consistent, the command move must inform a *Room* that the *Explorer* is entering or leaving it. To this end, we equip a *Room* with methods for adding and removing an *Explorer*:

void add (Explorer e)
> The specified *Explorer* has entered this *Room*, and should be added to this *Room*'s contents.

void remove (Explorer e)
> The specified *Explorer* has left this *Room*, and should be removed from this *Room*'s contents.

How should we label these methods? We can't declare them *private*, because they must be invoked from the class *Explorer*. We don't want to make them *public*, because they should only be invoked by an *Explorer* when he leaves or enters the *Room*. If they are invoked from anywhere else, we could easily end up with inconsistencies in the system.

A possibility is to make them *restricted*. If a feature is not declared *public*, *protected*, or *private*, it is by default *restricted*. (Note there is no reserved word **restricted**.) A restricted feature is accessible anywhere in the package containing the class in which the feature is defined. Therefore if the *Room* features add and remove are restricted, and if *Room* and *Explorer* are in the same package, then an *Explorer* can invoke the features.

Certainly this allows only very coarse control over access to the feature. A class can be in only one package, and a restricted feature can be accessed from anywhere in the package. Declaring a feature, particularly an instance variable, protected or restricted weakens encapsulation and compromises the integrity of the class. (Recall the information hiding principle discussed in Chapter 11.) A restricted feature introduces a possible point of interaction with every current and future member of the package. This can lead to increased system complexity particularly during system maintenance. Maintenance programmers often have very subtle problems to solve, little time to solve them, and no clear understanding of the overall system architecture. Thus they are likely to exploit the kind of encapsulation weaknesses created by protected and restricted features. The result is a system in which modules are related in obscure and complex ways: a system whose maintainability is significantly diminished.

The misuse of feature accessibility as specified by the system architecture leads to what is termed *architectural drift* or *architectural erosion*. The system becomes *brittle*, frustrating further maintenance efforts. If a feature is neither public nor private, it is incumbent upon the maintenance programmer to determine why this is so, and to make sure that any new use of the feature does not compromise the system structure.

14.7   Java scoping rules

At this point, we digress a bit to take a look at Java's scoping rules. As with the feature access rules discussed in the previous section, scoping rules are static, having to do with the program text and not with the run-time state of the system. In fact, the rules regarding feature access are part of the language scoping rules. Again, we touch only the most significant points and do not attempt a complete presentation.

An identifier may occur many times in a program in many different contexts. An identifier can be introduced as the name of a variable, method, or parameter in a variable definition, method definition, or parameter specification. Such an occurrence is referred to as a *defining* or *naming occurrence* of the identifier. For instance, the following are defining occurrences of the identifiers `takeHit`, `hitStrength`, `tally`, and `temp`.

```
public void takeHit (int hitStrength)
private int tally;
int temp;
```

A defining occurrence establishes the identifier as the name of some entity. (Of course, identifiers are also used to name packages, classes, and so on. Here we're concerned only with identifiers that name variables and methods.)

Other occurrences, for instance occurrences of an identifier in an expression, are called *applied occurrences*. An applied occurrence is simply the use of an identifier to refer to the thing it names. For instance, both occurrences of the identifier `tally` in the assignment

```
tally = tally + 1;
```

are applied occurrences. They refer to a particular **int** variable created by a definition such as the one shown above.

An applied occurrence is sometimes prefixed with an object reference. For instance, in the assignment statement

```
this.room = monster.location();
```

the applied occurrences of the identifiers room and location are prefixed with object references **this** and monster. (An identifier can also be prefixed with a package or class name, but we ignore those cases here.)

Scoping rules, sometimes referred to as *static scoping rules*, are language rules that associate applied identifier occurrences with defining occurrences. For instance, if a class is defined as

```
public class Counter {
    ...
    public void increment () {
❶      tally = tally + 1;
    }
    ...
❷   private int tally;
    ...
}
```

scoping rules specify that the applied occurrences of the identifier tally at ❶ are associated with the defining occurrence at ❷. We say the applied occurrence "refers to" or "references" the defining occurrence. Thus we say the applied occurrences of tally at ❶ "refer to" the instance variable defined at ❷.

Now certainly the run-time semantics of the program are intimately connected to the static program syntax. If line ❶ above is performed during program execution, the variable incremented will be an instance variable of an instance of the class *Counter*, created because of the definition at line ❷. But during execution of the program, there might be no *Counter* instance created, or there might be thousands of *Counters*. Thus at any point, there might be many variables named tally or none at all. The scoping rules refer to the text, and not directly to entities created dynamically during program execution.

The *scope* of a definition is the section of program text in which applied occurrences of an identifier refer to the identifier introduced by the definition. For instance, in the above example, the scope of the variable definition at ❷ is the definition of the class *Counter*. Applied occurrences of the identifier tally in this segment of the program refer to the definition at ❷. (Technically it is a *definition* that has scope, though we informally refer to the "scope of an identifier.")

We've already looked at scoping issues regarding instance variables and methods. Here we consider automatic variables—local variables and parameters.

The scope of a local variable definition is from the definition to the end of the compound statement (or method body) containing the definition. A parameter is treated like a local variable defined just inside the method body. Thus the scope of parameter definition is the method body. For instance, in the method

```
public boolean smallerThan (Rectangle r) {

    double myArea;
    double yourArea;
    myArea = pi*radius*radius;
    yourArea = r.length() * r.width();
    return myArea < yourArea;
}
```

the scope of the parameter r is the body of the method smallerThan; the scopes of the local variable myArea and yourArea extend from the variable definitions to the end of the method smallerThan. Applied occurrences of these identifiers in the body of the method refer to automatic variables created when the method is invoked. Furthermore, these definitions have no effect outside of the method. One cannot write a reference to the variable myArea, for instance, except inside the body of smallerThan.

Note that the scope of a local variable begins with its definition. It cannot be referenced prior to its definition:

```
public class C {
    // can't reference x or y here
    public void m (int x) {
        // can reference x here, but
        // can't reference y
        int y;
        // can reference both
        // x and y here
    }
    // can't reference x or y here
}
```

scope of int y

scope of int x

For example, this would be legal

```
    public boolean smallerThan (Rectangle r) {
        double area1 = 100.0;
✓       double area2 = area1;  // in the scope of area1
```

but this would not

```
        public boolean smallerThan (Rectangle r) {
✗       double area1 = area2;  // not in the scope of area2
        double area2 = 100.0;
```

A local variable definition can appear almost anywhere in a method body. The scope extends to the end of the compound statement containing the definition:

```java
public void m (int x) {
    if (x > 0) {
        int i = 1;                    scope of int i
        ...
    }
    ...
}
```

Though a method can contain definitions of several distinct variables with the same name, the scopes of these definitions cannot overlap. For instance, the following method contains legitimate definitions for two variables named sum, one a **double** and one an **int**:

```java
public double m (int x) {
    double result;
    if (x > 1) {
        int sum = x;
        result = sum/2;              scope of int sum
    }
    else {
        double sum = x;
        result = sum/2;              scope of double sum
    }
    return result;
}
```

But the following is not legal, since the scopes of the **int** sum and the **double** sum overlap:

```java
public double m (int x) {
    double result;
    double sum = x;
    if (x > 1) {
        int sum = x;
        result = sum/2;              scope of int sum
    }                                                     scope of double sum
    else {
        result = sum/2;
    }
    return result;
}
```

Finally, we note that an automatic variable can "hide" an instance variable with the same name, but an automatic variable cannot be prefixed with an object reference. For instance, at line ❶ of the following,

```
public class Circle {
    ...
    public void setRadius (int radius) {
❶        this.radius = radius;
    }
    ...
❷    private int radius;
}
```

the identifier `radius` on the right of the assignment denotes an automatic variable (the parameter), while **this**.`radius` denotes an instance variable defined at ❷.

14.8   Summary

This chapter introduced one of the fundamental methods of modeling with objects: abstraction via class extension. Using extension, we can build subclasses of a class that automatically inherit all of the public functionality of the original class. The subclasses can extend the functionality of the parent class and can define alternate implementations for inherited methods.

Subtyping permits us to supply an instance of a subclass in any context specifying the parent class. For example, a method can specify a base class parameter, and the method can be invoked with an argument that is an instance of a subclass of the base class. Thus we take advantage of polymorphism, since the argument's behavior is dependent on its run-time class.

We saw several uses of inheritance including identifying and taking advantage of commonality in a set of cases, refining and providing alternative implementations of an inherited method, and extending the functionality of a base class.

Finally, we examined the possible qualifications of a feature's accessibility provided by Java. Public features are part of the class's specification and available to all clients. Private features are part of the class's implementation, and are hidden from clients. Protected features are accessible in extensions of the class. Restricted features are accessible to clients in the same package. We concluded with a brief discussion of scope and of the scoping rules of Java.

EXERCISES

14.1 Indicate whether each of the following statements is true or false:

a. If class *A* extends class *B*, class *A* is a subclass of class *B*, and class *B* is a superclass of class *A*.

b. An instance of a superclass can be treated as if it were an instance of any of its subclasses.

c. Public features of a public class are accessible from any other class of any other package.

d. Access to restricted features of a class is limited to classes in the same package only if the the class is not public.

e. If a method is qualified as abstract, the class that contains it must also be qualified as abstract.

f. Polymorphism implies that the method actually invoked at run-time is dependent on the run-time classes of the method's arguments.

14.2 Consider the following three classes:

```
public class AClass {
    public AClass () {
        System.out.println("AClass");
    }
}

public class BClass extends AClass {
    public BClass () {
        System.out.println("BClass");
    }
}

public class CClass extends BClass {
    public CClass () {
        System.out.println("CClass");
    }
}
```

The method System.out.println writes a line to the user's terminal.

a. What is the parent class of *AClass*?

b. What will be written to the user's terminal when a new instance of *CClass* is created?

14.3   The *Explorer* in the maze game has a query to determine its location, and a command to change location. However, it can only move between *Room*s that are connected by a passage:

```
public Room location ()
```
This *Explorer*'s current location.

```
public void move (Room newLocation)
```
Move to the specified *Room* if it is connected to this *Explorer*'s current location.

```
protected Room location;
```
This *Explorer*'s current location.

Some rooms in the maze are enchanted, and there is a special kind of explorer, a wizard, who can move into an enchanted room even if it is not connected to the wizard's current room.

Enchanted rooms and wizards are modeled by subclasses of *Room* and *Explorer*. Implement the wizard's method move. (Assume that a *Room*'s state doesn't change when someone enters.)

14.4   Design a class to model a bag of items that an explorer can carry around in the maze. Include functionality that provides the total weight of the bag of items and a *String* describing the items in the bag.

14.5   Assume that an explorer can lose his bag in the maze, and another explorer can find it. How can you model a bag of items so that an explorer can pick it up and add it to his bag?

14.6   Consider a class *Room* that models a room that can be used for different kinds of events. The class is partially specified as follows:

```
public class Room {
    public Room (…) {…}
    public int capacity () {…}
    public double rentalPrice () {…}
    ...
}
```

and is extended by *ConferenceRoom*:

```
public class ConferenceRoom extends Room {
    public ConferenceRoom (…) {…}
    public int capacity () {…}
    public double rentalPrice (double discount) {…}
    ...
}
```

a.   Which features are inherited by *ConferenceRoom*?

> **b.** Which methods are overridden by *ConferenceRoom*?
>
> **c.** Which methods are overloaded by *ConferenceRoom*?

14.7 Consider the two classes defined below:

```
public AClass {
    public int method (Object obj) {
        return 1;
    }
    public int method (AClass a) {
        return 2;
    }
}

public AXClass extends AClass {
    public int method (AClass a) {
        return 3;
    }
    public int method (AXClass ax) {
        return 4;
    }
}
```

> **a.** What are the features of *AXClass*?
>
> **b.** What methods does *AXClass* override?
>
> **c.** Given the definitions:
>
> ```
> Object o1 = new AClass();AClass a1 = new AClass();
> AClass a2 = new AXClass();AXClass ax = new AXClass();
> ```
>
> what do the following method invocations return?
>
> *(a)* a1.method(o1)   *(b)* a2.method(a1)
> *(c)* a2.method(o1)   *(d)* a2.method(ax)

14.8 Given the definitions of the classes *Circle* and *ColoredCircle* suggested in Section 14.2.3, can the following method legally appear in th e class *Circle*? Why or why not?

```
public ColoredCircle cloneWithColor (Color c) {
    ColoredCircle cc = new ColoredCircle(c);
    ((Circle)cc).myRadius = this.myRadius;
    return cc;
}
```

14.9   Each of the classes *A*, *B*, and *C* is defined in a different package:

```
package Apackage;
public class A {

    ...

    protected int x;
}


package Bpackage;
public class B extends Apackage.A {

    ...

}


package Cpackage;
public class C extends Bpackage.B {

    ...

}
```

Consider the following method:

```
public void setX (Bpackage.B aB) {
    aB.x = 1;
}
```

Can this method definition appear in the class *A*? in the class *B*? in the class *C*? in some other `Apackage` class? in some other `Bpackage` class?

14.10   A board game has different kinds of game pieces—squares, circle, and triangles— each with its own rules as to how to move on the board. Each piece has a color and board location. How might you design classes to model these pieces?

Suppose it is possible for a piece to mutate to a different shape during the game. What difficulties does this present to your design?

14.11   Assume the class *Employee* models employees of a company, as part of a payroll system. Among the attributes are year-to-date pay, year-to-date tax withholding, *etc.* There are several kinds of employees, such as part-time, hourly, sales, management, and so on, and the pay for each class is computed differently. Evaluate each of the following approaches, with respect to flexibility and system maintainability.

    a.   The class *Employee* defines an integer instance variable `employeeType` that denotes the kind of employee an instance represents. The method that computes the employee's pay uses the value of this variable to determine how the pay should be computed.

    b.   Each of the different kinds of employee is modeled by a subclass of the class *Employee*. The subclass overrides the method that computes the employee's pay.

    c.   The class *PayComputer* has a method for computing an employee's pay. An *Employee* has a *PayComputer* component. Different methods of computing an employee's pay are modeled by subclasses of *PayComputer*.

14.12 The class *IntVector* models finite, immutable, integer sequences. An *IntVector* can be empty, or it can be constructed from an integer and another *IntVector*, by prefixing the integer to the front of the *IntVector*. For instance, by prefixing the integer *3* to the empty *IntVector ( )*, we get the one-element *IntVector (3)*. By prefixing *4* to this *IntVector*, we get the two-element *IntVector (4, 3)*.

We model the two kinds of *IntVector*, empty or constructed, by subclassing *IntVector*:

```
class ConstructedVector extends IntVector ...
```

Invoking the *IntVector* constructor will produce a new empty *IntVector*. Invoking the *ConstructedVector* constructor will produce a new, nonempty *IntVector*.

We want a method that produces a new *IntVector* by prefixing an integer to an existing one:

```
public IntVector prefix (int i)
```

and methods to retrieve the two pieces used to build a constructed *IntVector*:

```
public int head ()
public IntVector tail ()
```

For instance, if `iv` is an *IntVector*, then

```
iv.prefix(2).head() == 2, and
iv.prefix(2).tail().equals(iv)
```

Clearly, the methods `head` and `tail` can only be legitimately invoked for a *ConstructedVector*.

We also want a method `isEmpty` that tells us what kind of *IntVector* we have.

a. Implement *IntVector* and its subclass.

b. Write a method that, given an *IntVector*, will produce the sum of the integers.

14.13 Design and implement classes *Course* and *Student* intended to be part of a grading system. A *Student* object should keep track of the *Courses* the *Student* is enrolled in, and a *Course* object should keep track of the enrolled *Students*. (Try to make sure that *Courses* and *Students* remain consistent with each other. For instance, the system is inconsistent if a *Student* thinks he or she is enrolled in a *Course*, but the *Course* doesn't know about the *Student*.)

Each *Student* has two grades for each *Course*, midterm and final. An instance of the class *TestRecord* contains a *Student*'s grades for a *Course*. A *TestRecord* should be created whenever a *Student* enrolls in a *Course*. (Who should be responsible for creating and maintaining *TestRecords*?)

A *Student*'s final average is determined by averaging the two grades. A *Student* can be queried for his or her final average in a specified *Course*, and a *Course* can be queried for the final average of a specified *Student*.

Consider the fact that it is likely that in the future, final grades will be computed differently for different *Courses*. Suggest possibilities for handling this situation in your system.

Consider the fact that it is likely that in the future, different *Courses* will have different kinds of grades used in computing the final average. Some may have several exams, some may include homework scores, and so on. How might this situation be handled in your system?

GLOSSARY

abstract class: a class that can't be instantiated. The purpose of an abstract class is to serve as a foundation on which to build subclasses.

abstract method: a method in an abstract class which is specified but not implemented in the class.

abstraction: the process in which distinct entities are considered equivalent, by identifying commonalities and ignoring differences.

applied occurrence: an occurrence of an identifier that is not a defining occurrence. The identifier is being used to refer to some entity (*e.g.*, method, variable) that it names.

base class: a class that is extended to define a subclass.

concrete class: a class that is instantiated to provide run-time objects that participate in the problem solution.

defining occurrence: an occurrence of an identifier in a variable definition, method definition, or parameter specification, in which it is introduced as the name of a method or variable.

dispatching: another name for polymorphism.

dynamic binding: another name for polymorphism.

extends: the relationship of a class to a more abstract class. Also called *is-a*.

extension: the language mechanism for implementing abstraction.

generalizes: the relationship of a class to a more concrete class.

hierarchy: the structure of relationships that results from reiterated abstraction or extension.

inheritance: the mechanism by which a class automatically gets all of the non-private features of its superclass.

is-a: the relationship of a class to a more abstract class. Also called *extends*.

overloading: providing a class with several distinct methods having the same name.

overriding: redefining the implementation of a method that a class inherits from its superclass.

polymorphism: dynamic behavior by which the method performed as the result of a call to a given object is determined at run-time by the class of the object.

protected: attribute of a feature that makes it accessible in subclasses.

restricted: attribute of a feature that makes it accessible to all class members of the same package.

scope: the section of program text in which applied occurrences of an identifier refers to the identifier introduced by a particular definition.

scoping rules: language rules that associate applied identifier occurrences with defining occurrences.

subclass: the relationship of a class to the class it extends. The more concrete class is a *subclass* of the more abstract class.

superclass: the relationship of a class to a class that extends it. The more abstract class is a *superclass* of the more concrete class.

subtype: the subset relation between the values of type *reference-to-a* and the values of type *reference-to-b*, when *a* is a subclass of *b*.

CHAPTER 15   Modeling with abstraction

In the previous chapter, we examined class extension and inheritance, the language mechanisms for implementing abstraction. We also saw several common situations in which constructing classes by extension might prove useful. In this chapter, we consider the use of abstraction in class design a little more carefully.

We start by reviewing the role of abstract classes in system design and implementation, and then introduce Java interfaces. Interfaces provide a mechanism of pure specification, separated from any implementation issues. Interfaces play a role similar to abstract classes in system design but offer some distinct advantages over abstract classes.

We next compare the two fundamental mechanisms for constructing classes: extension and composition. We note that these two approaches are not as obviously distinct as they first seem. There are many situations in which either can be applied to a particular design problem.

We conclude by offering some guidelines on class design and implementation. As usual, we are concerned with developing designs that are coherent, flexible, and maintainable.

15.1   Abstract classes and interfaces

15.1.1   Abstract classes

We encountered abstract classes in the previous chapter. We cannot instantiate an abstract class, but an abstract class can contain abstract methods: methods that are only specified, without implementation. Otherwise, an abstract class works just like an ordinary concrete class. In particular, an abstract class can be a superclass or a subclass of a concrete class. (In fact, all classes are subclasses of the concrete class *Object*.) An abstract class has constructors, which are invoked when its concrete subclasses are instantiated. We can define variables and specify parameters that reference an abstract class. (Of course, at run-time, the actual objects referenced by such variables will be instances of some concrete subclass of the abstract class.)

In developing a system design, however, abstract classes are used in ways that are quite different from the ways in which concrete classes are used. Specifically, abstract classes are used as a basis from which to build extensions. They serve to structure the system design rather than provide the run-time objects that actually participate in problem solution. Concrete classes, on the other hand, provide the run-time objects, and are not particularly well-suited as bases for extension.

Though they are difficult to justify *a priori* at this point, we suggest the following guidelines in the use of abstract classes.

- An abstract class should be used to model a generalized object, not simply to capture common functionality. That is, the class abstracts a set of classes that share features, though perhaps with different implementations, and are related in what they model. The public specification of the abstract class reflects the commonality of the subclasses. The abstract class may also contain common data components found in these subclasses.

- The decision to use generalization must be made with care. A concrete subclass is closely dependent on its abstract parent class; the classes are strongly coupled. The features defined in an abstract class must not be susceptible to change, as any changes in the abstract class will propagate to its descendants and their clients. In other words, the specification of an abstract class must be stable.

- An abstract class should "factor out" common implementation details of its concrete subclasses. These common implementation details may be in the form of method implementations or data components. If no sharing of implementation is possible, an interface (described below) should be used rather than an abstract class.

- Abstraction provides opportunities to exploit polymorphism. Common functionality specified in the parent abstract class can be given implementations appropriate to the concrete subclass. However, since a class can explicitly extend only one other class, care should be taken in using an abstract class purely to exploit polymorphism.

15.1.2   Interfaces

An *interface* in Java is much like an abstract class, but with no constructors, method bodies, or instance variables. That is, there is no trace of an implementation in an interface. An interface can be used to define a restricted view of a group of objects, or to specify a minimal set of features a group of objects is expected to have for some particular purpose.

Interface definition

An interface can contain only method specifications (abstract methods) and named constant definitions. As with an abstract class, instances of an interface cannot be created. Like a class, an interface is an element of a package. For instance, the package `java.awt` contains an interface *LayoutManager*, defined as follows:

```
public interface LayoutManager {
    Dimension minimumLayoutSize (Container parent);
    Dimension preferredLayoutSize (Container parent);
    void addLayoutComponent (String name,
                                       Component comp);
    void removeLayoutComponent (Component comp);
    void layoutContainer (Container parent);
}
```

This looks very much like an abstract class definition, with the keyword **interface** replacing the keywords **abstract class**. Since all the methods and constants specified in an interface are implicitly public, and the methods are implicitly abstract, they need not be labeled "**public**" or "**public abstract**."

As stated above, an interface does not have constructors. If the interface `LayoutManager` were made an abstract class, it would be equipped with a default constructor if none were explicitly defined. The interface does not have a constructor, default or otherwise.

Interface implementation

A class *implements* an interface in much the same way it extends an abstract class. A class that implements an interface must implement the methods specified in the interface. For example, the definition

```
public class FlowLayout implements LayoutManager { ... }
```

requires that the class *FlowLayout* implement methods `minimumLayoutSize`, `preferredLayoutSize`, *etc.*, as specified by the interface *LayoutManager*. Of course, *FlowLayout* can define additional features as well.

A class must specifically declare that it implements an interface. It is not sufficient that the class happens to implement the methods specified by the interface. However, a class also implements an interface that its superclass implements. That is, the relation *implements* is transitive.

In our diagrams, we represent the *implements* relation exactly like the *extends* relation, and denote an interface by placing the word "interface" in guillemets:

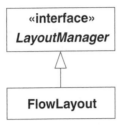

Extending interfaces

One interface can extend another interface in much the same way that one class can extend another class. (Notice that a class *implements* an interface, but an interface *extends* an interface.) For instance, the `java.awt` interface *LayoutManager2* extends *LayoutManager*:

```
public interface LayoutManager2
    extends LayoutManager {
    void addLayoutComponent (Component comp,
                                Object constraints);
    Dimension maximumLayoutSize (Container target);
    float getLayoutAlignmentX (Container target);
    float getLayoutAlignmentY (Container target);
    void invalidateLayout (Container target);
}
```

Any class that implements *LayoutManager2* must implement these five methods in addition to the five methods specified by *LayoutManager*.

Multiple inheritance

An important difference between interface and class hierarchies is that an interface can extend more than one parent. This is sometimes termed *multiple inheritance*. For instance, given that *DataInput* and *DataOutput* are interfaces, we could define an interface *DataIO* as follows:

```
public interface DataIO extends DataInput, DataOutput
{ }
```

This interface includes specifications from both *DataInput* and *DataOutput*. A class that implements *DataIO* must implement the methods specified by *DataInput* and those specified by *DataOutput*. Note that the interface *DataIO* does not specify any additional methods, though it could.

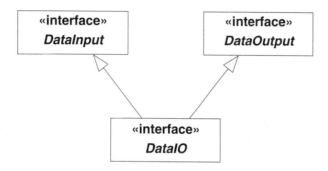

Figure 15.1 **An interface can extend more than one parent.**

Interface hierarchies are not particularly common and tend to be very shallow. Of more significance is the fact that a class can implement more than one interface. That is, a class can have several parents as long as all but one of its parents are interfaces. For example

```
public class RandomAccessFile implements DataInput,
     DataOutput { … }
```

specifies that the class *RandomAccessFile* implements both of the named interfaces. *RandomAccessFile* in fact has three parents: the two interfaces and the class *Object*.

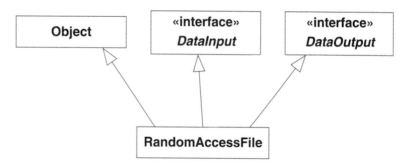

Figure 15.2 **A class can have more than one parent.**

Reference-to-interface types

An interface, like a class, defines a reference type. Even though we cannot directly create *LayoutManager* instances, for example, we can create variables of type *reference-to-LayoutManager*:

```
private LayoutManager mgr;
```

This variable can reference an instance of any class, such as *FlowLayout*, that implements *LayoutManager*.

```
mgr = new FlowLayout();
```

> instance of class implementing *LayoutManager*
>
> reference-to-*LayoutManager* variable

The same subtyping rules that hold for classes also hold for interfaces. For instance, given the definition

```
LayoutManager2 mgr2 = new BorderLayout();
// BorderLayout implements LayoutManager2
```

this assignment is legal

```
mgr = mgr2;     // a LayoutManager2 is a LayoutManager
```

while this one is not, without an explicit cast of `mgr` to *LayoutManager2*:

✗   `mgr2 = mgr;     // Not legal! a LayoutManager is not`
                        `// necessarily a LayoutManager2`

15.1.3   Interfaces vs. abstract classes

How do we use interfaces in system design? Clearly interfaces and abstract classes are similar in many ways. Both are tools for abstraction, permitting commonality between distinct classes to be identified and exploited. But their functions as elements of a design differ substantially.

From the earliest chapters we have emphasized the distinction between an object's specification and its implementation. The purpose of a class is to provide an implementation. A class, even an abstract class, carries an implementation part in that it defines instance variables and includes method implementations. If we are careful, we can design abstract classes with no implementation aspect. But in general, we consider a class definition as framing an implementation for some object specification. An abstract class should be used to implement the generalization relationship, factoring out common implementation details from the subclasses. Concrete subclasses implement specific differences and extend functionality.

Classes related by inheritance are tightly coupled semantically. Subclasses share the structure of their parent class, and often share a common implementation of common functionality. Thus class inheritance produces a family of closely related classes.

An interface, on the other hand, defines only a specification. Neither the structure nor implementation-level behavior of an object satisfying the interface is prescribed. Two classes that implement the same interface are related only in that they support the same abstract functionality defined by the interface. A hierarchical family of closely tied classes is not created, as is the case with class inheritance.

The advantage of interfaces over classes lies in the following:

- Interfaces are by definition abstract; they do not fix any aspect of an implementation.

- A class can implement more than one interface.

- Interfaces allow a more generalized use of polymorphism, in that instances of relatively unrelated classes can be treated identically for some specific purpose. (See the example below.)

Interfaces, abstract classes, and modification

Both interfaces and abstract classes form bases for hierarchies. We have mentioned that the features found in an abstract class should be stable, as a change in the specification filters down through the hierarchy and to clients of the classes in the hierarchy. The result is substantial code modification and recompilation, often for even a small change. The exception is that the addition of a feature to an abstract class, with a default implementation provided in the abstract class, does not affect the subclasses and clients. Thus abstract classes support "incremental programming." This is not the case with interfaces. Interfaces are impossible to modify without requiring modifications of all their implementations as well.

Interfaces and the software life cycle

The use of interfaces promotes higher reusability and thus makes the development cycle more efficient.

- *Design*: Interfaces are an important method for abstraction and serve as a stabilizing element in specifying and implementing classes.

- *Implementation*: The compiler verifies that in a class implementing an interface, all methods of the interface are implemented with the correct specification. Any changes to an interface are thus immediately visible to developers building implementations. The fact that an interface cannot be modified without modification of any class implementing the interface can be useful in maintaining the consistency of an implementation.

- *Integration*: Well-established interfaces act as the "glue" for composed classes and subsystems.

- *Testing*: Testing is enhanced, as logical errors are limited to a subset of methods.

In summary, abstract classes are used to form hierarchies of implementations. Abstract classes generalize concrete class features and provide common default implementations, and the resulting hierarchy is amenable to incremental programming. The use of interfaces promotes abstraction and reuse across class hierarchies. Interfaces specify only functionality and can extend one or more existing interfaces. A class can implement multiple interfaces, but an interface cannot be modified without affecting its implementations.

15.1.4   An example

As an example, suppose we want to specify that a figure appearing in a diagram has a *Location* and *Dimension*. Though we don't particularly care about the details, a *Location* might be given in terms of the Cartesian coordinates of the upper left corner of the figure, and a *Dimension* might include length and width. Omitting comments, we define the following interface:

```
/**
 * A figure that can be depicted in a diagram.
 */
public interface Depictable {

    ...

    public Location getLocation ();
    public Dimension getDimension ();

    ...

}
```

and define classes that implement the interface, such as:

```
public abstract class GeometricalFigure
    implements Depictable {

    ...

    public abstract Location getLocation ();
    public abstract Dimension getDimension ();

    ...

}


public class Rectangle extends GeometricalFigure {

    ...

    public Location getLocation () { ... }
    public Dimension getDimension () { ... }

    ...

}
```

Now a client of the interface *Depictable* includes methods that manipulate references to *Depictables*. For instance, a client might contain a method that determines whether an arbitrary point is contained within a diagram figure, which is modeled as a *Depictable*:

```
public boolean isIn (Location point,
                     Depictable figure) {
    Location l = figure.getLocation();
    Dimension d = figure.getDimension();
    ...
}
```

If we later decide to expand the kinds of things that can appear in a diagram, for example by extending an existing class *ArtClip*,

```
public abstract class ArtClip { ... }
```

```
public class WordBalloon extends ArtClip
     implements Depictable { ... }
```

we can pass instances of the newly created class to the isIn method without modifying either the method or its clients.

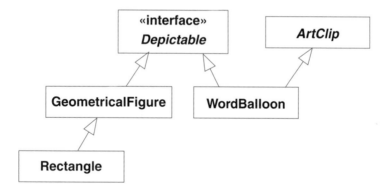

Figure 15.3 **An interface allows relatively unrelated classes to be treated identically.**

Using classes and single inheritance, we'd either have to somehow merge the *ArtClip* and *Depictable* hierarchies so that *WordBalloons* could be passed to *Depictable* client methods like isIn, or overload these client methods to accept other *WordBalloon* arguments. Such methods would be mostly rewritten code, accommodating a different type of argument. By specifying the parameter of a method like isIn as an interface, any class in any family can be tailored to provide suitable arguments for the method.

The primary intent of an interface is to separate an object's implementation from its specification. There are substantial benefits to be gained from manipulating objects solely in terms of the specifications defined in an interface. Clients remain independent of the specific types of the objects they manipulate, and independent of the classes that implement these objects. New classes can be created that implement an interface, or existing implementations modified, without affecting clients that depend solely on the interface. This greatly reduces the interdependencies between subsystems, and produces more flexible and manageable code. The benefits are so consequential that the adage "program to an interface, not to an implementation" is often stated as a fundamental principle of object-oriented design. This means that developers should not write code that interacts with an object *per se*. Rather, client code should be able to interact with any implementation of the interface of that object.

15.2   Extension and composition

Two fundamental ways of building classes are by means of extension (inheritance) and composition. Extension implements the *is-a* relation, and composition implements the *has-a* relation. We use extension to build a subclass from an existing superclass. When we use composition, we construct a class (a *composed* class) from one or more component or core classes. Both are sometimes referred to as instances of "code reuse" since we're reusing the code from the superclass in creating the subclass, and reusing the code from a component class in building the composed class.

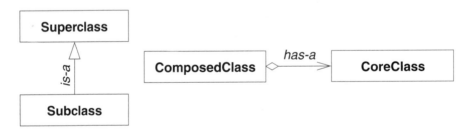

Figure 15.4 **A class can be constructed by extension or composition.**

Though *is-a* and *has-a* are fundamentally different relations, we are often faced with situations in which either could be employed in the development of new classes. For example, consider the nim *Player* class and its extensions discussed in Chapter 14. It seems perfectly straightforward to say that a *PerfectPlayer is-a Player*, and to model the relation between these classes with inheritance. *PerfectPlayer* inherits all the features of *Player*, and overrides the move method.

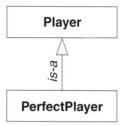

But we can also view a player as *having* a move strategy. Different players have different strategies, and so make their moves in different ways. A player might even change strategies during its lifetime. In this case, the move strategy that differentiates player behavior is a *Player* component.

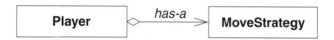

The purpose of a *MoveStrategy* is to determine the move to be made on the *Player*'s turn. An instance of a *MoveStrategy* class is sometimes called a *function object*. Its only purpose is to provide the functionality implemented by the `numberToTake` method.

WARNING!! Saying that the purpose of an object is to *do* something is often the sign of a faulty design. Specifically, it's often a case of a function masquerading as an object, when the function should properly be one of the responsibilities of some other more coherent object. The structure discussed here, though, is commonly used and considered acceptable practice. The basic responsibility for making a move rests with the *Player*. The *Player* delegates the responsibility of determining the move to its *MoveStrategy* component.

Let's see how this approach could be developed. We want a *MoveStrategy* instance to determine the number of sticks to be removed. Different *MoveStrategy* instances will determine which move to make in different ways. We define *MoveStrategy* as an interface, which specific concrete strategies implement. Omitting the obvious documentation,

```
interface MoveStrategy {
    int numberToTake (Pile pile, int maximum);
}
```

The *Player* has methods for setting and querying for its *MoveStrategy*. The *Player* method `makeMove` queries the *MoveStrategy* to determine the number of sticks to take.

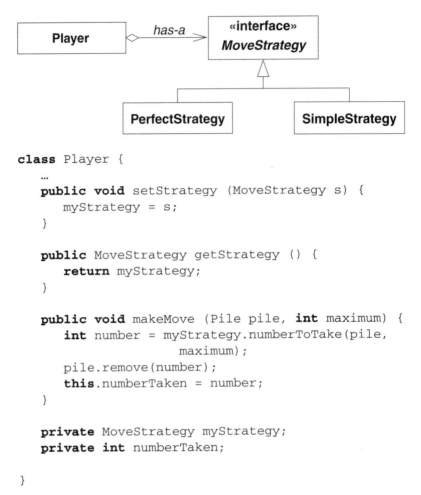

```
class Player {
    ...
    public void setStrategy (MoveStrategy s) {
        myStrategy = s;
    }

    public MoveStrategy getStrategy () {
        return myStrategy;
    }

    public void makeMove (Pile pile, int maximum) {
        int number = myStrategy.numberToTake(pile,
                        maximum);
        pile.remove(number);
        this.numberTaken = number;
    }

    private MoveStrategy myStrategy;
    private int numberTaken;

}
```

It might seem that we are still really using abstraction here to achieve different *Player* behaviors, and to some extent that is true. The interface *MoveStrategy* abstracts the various concrete strategies. But the implementation hierarchy is very shallow, and completely separate from any class hierarchy that *Player* might be a part of. One *Player* behaves differently from another because it *has* a different strategy, rather than because it is an instance of a different class.

It is sometimes the case that a degree of reuse can be achieved by using the same core class in the construction of new composed classes. However, this is not likely to be the case here. It is hard to imagine the strategy classes being employed as a component of anything other than a nim *Player*. The best we can do is specify an interface *MoveStrategy* for game implementations that use the *Pile* class.

Inheritance, composition, and reuse

There are no absolute guidelines for determining whether we should employ inheritance or composition in building a specific class. Different situations call for different approaches, and there is no substitute for experience. Nevertheless, it will be useful to compare the advantages and disadvantages of each, so that we can begin to understand which technique is appropriate in various circumstances. In making this comparison we should highlight the classes being reused and the classes resulting from reuse.

	reused class:	*resulting class*:
inheritance:	superclass	subclass
composition:	core class	composed class

Two advantages often mentioned regarding inheritance are code reuse and polymorphism. Since a subclass inherits the features of its superclass, inheritance provides a substantial degree of code reuse. Furthermore, polymorphism is a powerful tool for extending an application. If client code uses an instance of a particular class, this code can be applied to a subclass instance without modification. In the nim game, for example, no modifications to the *GameManager* are required if one of the *Player*s is a *PerfectPlayer*. Inheritance allows us to extend the functionality of class without affecting the clients of the original class.

On the other hand, a superclass and subclass are strongly coupled. A change to a superclass specification (reused class) affects its subclasses and their clients as well as its own clients. It propagates outward to clients, and downward to subclasses and their clients. Encapsulation is broken in that changes to the superclass implementation also propagate to subclasses. Further, a subclass by definition is committed to maintain the specifications inherited from its superclass. No changes can be made to a subclass specification that affect the specification of a superclass.

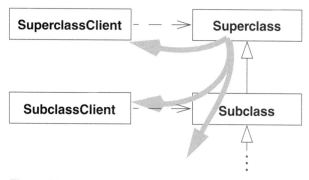

Figure 15.5 **Changes to a superclass specification propagate to clients and subclasses.**

Composition also offers opportunities for code reuse, in that core classes can be used in the construction of different composed classes. A principal advantage of composition is that it is possible to change an object's behavior dynamically, at run time. For example, the behavior of a nim *Player*-with-*MoveStrategy* is determined by the *Player*'s *MoveStrategy* component. This component can be set and changed dynamically during execution of the program. With inheritance, on the other hand, the *Player*'s behavior depends on the particular *Player* subclass that is instantiated, and is fixed when the *Player* is created.

Composition also supports stronger encapsulation than does inheritance. Changes to the core class (reused class) need not result in changes to the specification of the composed class. Thus core class changes do not affect clients of the composed class. Furthermore, it is generally easy to change the specification of the composed class without affecting the core class. With inheritance, changes in a superclass propagate to subclasses and their clients, and it is difficult to change the specification of a subclass without breaking the specification of its superclass.

Figure 15.6 **Changes to a core class need not affect clients of the composed class.**

In summary, modifying the reused class with inheritance is likely to affect more of the system than modifying the reused class with composition. Modifying the resulting class with composition will not affect the reused class. On the other hand, modifying the resulting class with inheritance may not be feasible if the modification changes the specification of inherited features. The resulting class can be modified if changes are limited to adding new data or methods to the superclass. We conclude that reuse through composition produces more flexible code. However, we must not ignore the advantages of polymorphism. On the surface, we lose polymorphism with composition, but we can gain it back by composing with interfaces and defining core classes that implement them.

Inheritance, composition, and modifying functionality

Inheritance is sometimes used to model *roles* that class instances can perform, or as we have seen in the previous chapter, to provide alternate implementations of the same functionality. The former can result in awkward constructions in which detailed knowledge of an object's possible roles is spread throughout the application. The latter can lead to a combinatorial explosion in the class hierarchy as the system evolves through cycles of maintenance. Suppose we are modeling a card game in which a player takes on the roles of dealer or dummy. It seems natural to model dealer and dummy functionality by extending *Player*; that is, by defining classes *Dealer* and *Dummy* that are extensions of *Player*. But difficulties arise when we want a given *Player* to change roles. One approach to handling this situation is to make *Player* a component of *Dealer* and *Dummy*. That is, to *wrap* the additional functionality around the *Player*. This can be done dynamically, during run time, by setting the *Player* component of the *Dealer* or *Dummy* instance.

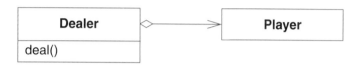

Figure 15.7   Composition can wrap additional functionality around an object.

If we use inheritance to provide alternate implementations of some functionality, problems may arise if we later want to extend the base class to add new features. For example, we saw how we could use inheritance to provide nim *Player*s with different move strategies, by extending the class *Player* and overriding the makeMove method. If we later decide that we want to create *Player*s with some additional functionality, *Player*s who can wager for instance, we can't simply extend *Player*, since we already have a family of classes that differ in how makeMove is implemented. We must extend each of the different *Player* subclasses. The problem here is that we are trying to make *Player* part of two distinct hierarchies: an implementation hierarchy that captures makeMove implementation differences, and an "application" hierarchy that extends the functionality of *Player*.

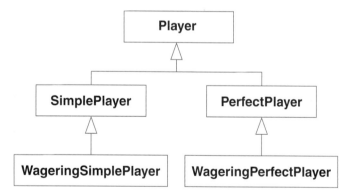

Figure 15.8   Using inheritance for implementation can lead to *class explosion*.

In summary, we suggest favoring composition over inheritance. Inheritance should not be used simply for code reuse or to take advantage of polymorphism. We must keep in mind the life cycle of the system: it's harder to maintain inheritance-based code than composition-based code. Inheritance should be limited to cases where there is a legitimate, permanent *is-a* relation between classes, and where the specification of the superclass is stable. Interfaces can be employed to maintain separation between specification and implementation, and to provide reuse and polymorphism across class hierarchies. Composition can be used to provide alternate implementations of some specific functionality.

15.3   Extension and state

The "kind" of thing an object models and the "state" of an object are closely related semantic notions. For instance, in a university registration system we might have several categories of students: junior division students, undergraduates, post baccalaureates, graduates, nondegree students. (Perhaps students are classified as "junior division" until they complete some specified number of credit hours.) We could differentiate among the various kinds of student by making the classification part of the state of a *Student* object:

```
public class Student {

    ...
    // Student classifications:
    public static final int JUNIOR_DIVISION = 0;
    public static final int UNDERGRADUATE = 1;
    public static final int GRADUATE = 2;

    ...
    public int classification () { ... }

    ...
    public void setClassification (int class) { ... }

    ...
    private int classification;
}
```

Some of the functionality of a *Student* is state dependent. That is, how the *Student* object behaves in response to a command or query depends on the *Student*'s state; in particular, it depends on the *Student*'s classification. Code that depends on a student's classification is structured with a conditional to do a case analysis. For instance, a method to register someStudent might look like this:

```
int classification = someStudent.classification();
if (classification == Student.JUNIOR_DIVISION) {
    // handle JUNIOR_DIVISION case
} else if (classification == Student.UNDERGRADUATE) {
    // handle UNDERGRADUATE case
} else if (classification == Student.GRADUATE)
    ...
```

The problem with this approach is that a method containing such code is dependent on the set of possible student classifications. Furthermore, we are likely to find identically structured conditional statements scattered through the implementation. Adding a new classification requires modifications in a number of places, complicating maintenance. Long conditionals are generally undesirable in an object-oriented system. Large monolithic structures are hard to understand, and the resulting code is difficult to modify and extend.

An obvious alternative is to model different classifications by subclassing *Student* rather than including classification as part of a *Student*'s state. Classification-dependent behavior is handled by providing different implementations to common methods in each subclass. Adding a new classification is handled by defining a new subclass. Clients depend on polymorphism to supply the appropriate behavior. The conditional case analysis disappears. The selection is handled by the polymorphism dispatching mechanism at run time.

The approach using inheritance introduces more classes, and is less compact than a state-based approach. However, experience has shown that the distribution of behavior over different classes is particularly beneficial if there are a substantial number of alternatives, which would otherwise necessitate large conditionals.

State as an object

There is one difficulty with subclassing, though, that must be addressed. The class of an object is fixed when the object is created. It cannot be changed dynamically during program execution. For example, suppose *JuniorDivisionStudent* and *Undergraduate* are subclasses of *Student*. An instance of *JuniorDivisionStudent* is created to represent an individual student when he or she is first admitted to the university. At some point, the student is admitted to a college and becomes an undergraduate. However, there is no way to convert the *JuniorDivisionStudent* object to an *Undergraduate* object. The best that can be done is to create a new *Undergraduate* object to represent the student and copy information from the old *JuniorDivisionStudent* object. The problem is that other elements of the system reference the old object. (A *Course*, for instance, might have a list of *Student*s enrolled.) Making sure that all references to the old object are updated to the new one is difficult, error-prone, and complicates the system structure considerably.

An approach similar to that seen above with the "strategy" interface can be used to avoid this difficulty. Rather than employing extension directly, we use composition. That is, we define an interface (or abstract class) that isolates state-dependent behavior, and equip an object with a state-defining component that implements the interface. Different behaviors are achieved by providing different subclasses for this component, each with its own implementation. State-dependent requests are simply forwarded to the state component.

For instance, the *Student* class can be structured as follows:.

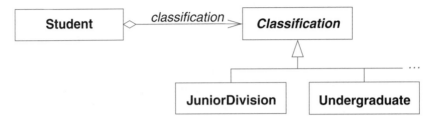

Classification-dependent behavior is specified in the interface or abstract class *Classification*. *Student* forwards responsibility for functions like registration to the *Classification*:

```
public class Student {
    ...
    public void register () {
        classification.register();
    }
    ...
    private Classification classification;
}
```

An additional advantage to this approach is that state transitions—the change from one state to another—become explicit, and can be delegated to the state subclasses. This approach can produce an extremely flexible and easily modifiable design.

15.4 Summary

In this chapter, we considered in some detail how to use abstraction in the structure of a system design. We took a careful look at abstract classes, and introduced interfaces. Specifically, an abstract class should be used to model a generalized object, and to factor out common implementation details from its subclasses. Abstract classes also support "incremental programming," since a functionality with a default implementation can be added to an interface without affecting existing subclasses. Interfaces, on the other hand, provide for multiple inheritance. Thus any class in any hierarchy can be extended to implement an interface.

Next we compared the two primary means of constructing new classes from existing ones, composition and extension. We noted that we could achieve alternate implementations of a specified functionality either by extending the class, or by providing the class with a "strategy" component. We observed that, furthermore, composition led to fewer maintenance problems than extension. In general, we concluded that composition produced a more flexible and maintainable structure than extension. Inheritance should be limited to cases where there is a legitimate, permanent *is-a* relation between classes, and where the specification of the superclass is stable.

We concluded by noting that the state of an object could be modeled with extension. In cases where an object can dynamically change state, combining composition and inheritance—by providing an object with a state component that is subclassed to define specific state-dependent behavior—produces a flexible maintainable system.

EXERCISES

15.1   An application requires two kinds of counters: a standard step-counter that starts at 0 and can be incremented and decremented by 1, and a "cell-division" counter that starts at 1, is doubled by the increment operation, and decremented by 1. Model these counters with an abstract class and two concrete classes.

15.2   As part of a retail sales system, a class is needed to model a payment.

   a.   Specify the data components of a payment.

   b.   A payment can be made in any combination of check, cash, or credit card. Specify an abstract class *FormOfPayment* and three concrete subclasses, handling the three possible kinds of payment.

   c.   Implement the class *Payment*.

15.3   A *binary operation* on a set is an operation that, given two elements of the set (*left* and *right operands*), produces a result in the set. For instance, *addition* is a binary operation on the set of integers.

A binary operation o is *associative* if it satisfies the rule

$$(s1 \; o \; s2) \; o \; s3 = s1 \; o \; (s2 \; o \; s3)$$

where $s1$, $s2$, and $s3$ are arbitrary elements of the set. For instance, *addition* is associative on the integers:

$$(s1 + s2) + s3 = s1 + (s2 + s3)$$

An *identity* for a binary operation o is an element i such that

$$i \; o \; s = s \; o \; i = s$$

for any element s of the set. For instance, 0 is an identity for addition on the integers.

$$0 + s = s + 0 = s$$

A set along with an associative binary operation that has an identity is called a *monoid*.

Write the definition of an interface *Monoid* that models a monoid.

15.4   Suppose a method is written to perform an operation based on the time, and is structured as follows:

```
void dailyOperation (int timeOfDay) {
    if (timeOfDay == BEFOREHOURS)
        doOpeningActivity();
    else if (timeOfDay == MORNING)
        doMorningActivity();
    else if (timeOfDay == AFTERNOON)
        doAfternoonActivity();
    else if (timeOfDay == EVENING)
        doEveningActitivity();
    else if (timeOfDay == AFTERHOURS)
        doClosingActivity();
}
```

Show how to restructure the code to eliminate the conditional case analysis.

15.5   Consider the class *Student* outlined in Section 15.3. Assume that there are only three classifications for a *Student*: junior division, undergraduate, and post baccalaureate. A *Student* changes classification when earned credit hours reaches or exceeds a predetermined value. Using abstraction and composition, implement a simplified version of *Student*. The only functionality you need consider is change of classification.

15.6   The class *Room* models a room in the maze game. A *Room* is initially *undiscovered*. When the *Explorer* enters the *Room*, it becomes *known*. A *Room* can be *occupied* (the *Explorer* is in the *Room*) or *unoccupied*, and it can also be *lighted* or *dark*. Design a set of classes (or interfaces) to model a room and its state. Define the possible state transitions, and what causes them. Sketch the implementation.

15.7   Consider the classes *Course* and *Student* of exercise 14.13. Recall that a *Course* keeps track of the *Students* enrolled, and can be queried for the final average of any enrolled *Student*. The *Course* also keeps a *TestRecord* for each enrolled *Student*. The *TestRecord* contains the raw test scores, homework, *etc.*, for the *Student* in the *Course*.

To accommodate the fact that different *Courses* are graded in different ways, each course will be equipped with a *Grader*. *Grader* is an interface with the responsibility of computing the final averages.

Since the data maintained by a *TestRecord* will also be different for different *Courses*, *TestRecord* will be an interface or abstract class. *TestRecords* and *Graders* are closely related. A specific, concrete *Grader* will compute final averages from a specific kind of concrete *TestRecord*. To maintain consistency, the *Grader* is given the responsibility for creating *TestRecords*. Thus at run time, the concrete *Grader* instance will create the appropriate kind of *TestRecord*.

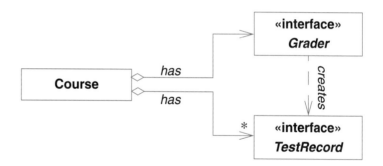

Design and implement *Student, Course, Grader, TestRecord*. Implement at least two distinct concrete subclasses of *Grader* and *TestRecord*.

Do you think that the responsibility for computing final averages is properly placed in *Grader*?

GLOSSARY

code reuse: use of an existing class definition to construct a new class, either by extending the existing class or by employing the existing class as a component.

composed class: a class constructed by putting together existing classes as components.

core class: a class that is used as a component to construct a composed class.

function class: a class whose primary purpose is to provide an implementation of some functionality. A function class elevates a method to class status. The class contains the method as its unique public functionality.

interface: a language structure that encapsulates a collection of method specifications. An interface defines a restricted view of a collection of mostly unrelated classes, by specifying a set of functionalities supported by all the classes in the collection

multiple inheritance: the ability of a class to have more than one parent. In Java, every class (except *Object*) has a single class parent but can have multiple interface parents.

CHAPTER 16   **Organizing Lists**

We introduced lists as container objects in Chapter 12, and in Chapter 13 saw algorithms for sorting and searching lists. Now that we have a basic understanding of abstraction, we want to use this idea to give some structure to our list classes. We first use inheritance to factor out common feature implementations. Then we see how we can write generalized sort methods by passing the order as an argument to the method. We conclude the chapter by sketching the specification of a sorted list—a list whose elements are maintained in a specified order.

16.1   Using abstraction to organize lists

When a client obtains an element of a container, there should be no question as to what type of element it is. That is, we want containers, and specifically lists, to be homogenous—to contain only one type of object. To this end, we make a list class depend upon its component class. We have class *StudentList* whose instances contain *Student* objects, class *RoomList* whose instances contain *Room* objects, and so on. Note that this does not hinder our ability to make a list as general as we care to. As we've seen in Chapter 14, if we want a list that can contain *Ring*s, *Scroll*s, and *Wand*s, we create a *Portable* list, where *Portable* is a superclass of *Ring*, *Scroll*, and *Wand*.

There is clearly a great deal of similarity among the different kinds of lists. The basic functionality provided by a list—the ability to add and remove items, and to access an item by index—is independent of the kind of items the list contains. This common functionality is something we would like to exploit. When we wrote the sorting and searching algorithms in Chapter 13, for instance, we assumed we were dealing with a *StudentList*, but the algorithms clearly did not depend on the fact that the list items were *Student*s. We would write the same algorithms to sort a list of ball players by batting average, a list of properties by assessed value, a list of employees by salary. The sort algorithms depend only on the fact that we have a list and an ordering on the list elements. We want to implement these algorithms once and use them to sort all kinds of lists.

Furthermore, when we consider how to implement a list, we expect that the structures and algorithms that constitute the implementation will be independent of the type of elements the list contains.

This is clearly a case in which we can make effective use of abstraction. We define an abstract class *List* to capture the essential idea of list structure. Specific concrete list classes extend *List*, as shown in Figure 16.1.[1]

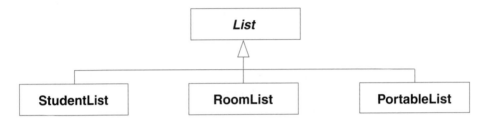

Figure 16.1   *List* is a superclass of concrete list classes.

We define the class *List* to be abstract. We do not want to create instances of the class but use it as a basis from which other classes are derived. (As we've said, we want lists to be homogeneous. When we get an element from a list, we want to know exactly what kind of element we are getting. The decision to make *List* an abstract class is difficult to justify *a priori*; we are always willing to change if a better alternative presents itself.[2])

How should we specify the features of the class *List*? *StudentList* methods append and set, for example, require a *Student* argument:

```
public void append (Student s);
public void set (int i, Student s);
```

and get provided a *Student* as result:

```
public Student get (int i);
```

If *List* is to abstract all possible concrete list classes, the only thing we know about list elements is that they are *Objects*. We therefore specify the class *List* as shown in Listing 16.1. We include a method add that allows us to insert an element into an arbitrary position of the *List*, shifting back the element at that position and any subsequent elements. We also include a method toString that provides a *String* representation of the *List*.

---

1. *Generalization* is one of the few structuring tools available to us in Java. Other languages have powerful facilities known as *genericity* and *polymorphic types* that are more appropriate ways of handling this situation.
2. *List* is defined as an *interface* in the library package java.util.

Listing 16.1 **The class *List***

OOJ.lists
Class List

> **public abstract class** `List`
> A finite list of *Objects*.
>
> **Warning:** the class of elements a *List* can contain may be restricted by a *List* subclass.

Constructors

> **public** `List ()`
> Create an empty *List*.
> **ensure:**
> > `this.isEmpty()`

Queries

> **public int** `size ()`
> Number of elements in this *List*.
> **ensure:**
> > `this.size() >= 0`
>
> **public boolean** `isEmpty ()`
> This *List* contains no elements.
> > `this.isEmpty() == (this.size() == 0)`
>
> **public** `Object get (`**int** `i)`
> The element at the specified position.
> **require:**
> > `0 <= i && i < this.size()`
>
> **public int** `indexOf (Object obj)`
> The index of the first occurrence of the specified element, or –1 if this *List* does not contain the specified element.
> **require:**
> > `obj != null`

continued

Listing 16.1 **The class *List (continued)***

> **ensure:**
>> if obj equals no element of this *List* then
>>> indexOf(obj) == -1
>>
>> else
>>> obj.equals(get(indexOf(obj))),
>>> and indexOf(obj) is the smallest value for
>>> which this is true
>
> **public** String toString ()
>> *String* representation of this *List*.

Commands

> **public void** set (**int** i, Object s)
>> Replace the element at the specified position with the specified *Object*.
>
>> **require:**
>>> 0 <= i && i < this.size()
>>> s != null
>>
>> **ensure:**
>>> this.get(i) == s
>
> **public void** append (Object s)
>> Append the specified *Object* to the end of this *List*.
>
>> **require:**
>>> s != null
>>
>> **ensure:**
>>> this.size() == old.size() + 1
>>> this.get(this.size()-1) == s
>
> **public void** add (**int** i, Object s)
>> Insert the specified *Object* at the specified position.
>
>> **require:**
>>> s != null
>>> 0 <= i <= this.size()

continued

Listing 16.1   **The class *List (continued)***

> **ensure:**
>> ```
>> this.size() == old.size() + 1
>> this.get(i) == s
>> for i < j < this.size()
>>     this.get(j) == old.get(j-1)
>> ```

> **public void** remove (**int** i)
>> Remove the element at the specified position.
>
> **require:**
>> ```
>> 0 <= i && i < this.size()
>> ```
>
> **ensure:**
>> ```
>> this.size() == old.size() - 1
>> for i <= j < this.size()
>>     this.get(j) == old.get(j+1)
>> ```

There are no abstract methods. All the methods are implemented for the class *List*. (An abstract class containing a complete implementation is not typical.)

Next we must build concrete extensions, such as *StudentList*. Since *StudentList* extends *List*, the features of *List* are inherited by *StudentList*. And since there are no abstract methods, there is not much that we need to do to build the class *StudentList*. We don't inherit the constructor, but we can settle for the default constructor for now. Since we want to guarantee that a *StudentList* contains only *Students*, we explicitly check that anything put on the list is an instance of this class.[1] A rather minimal definition of *StudentList* is as follows:

```
/**
 * A finite list of Students.
 * Required: any item placed on the list is an instance
 * of Student.
 * Ensured: any item on the list is an instance of
 * Student.
 */
public class StudentList extends List {

    /**
```

---

1. Note that we are violating the principle stated in Section 14.4 that preconditions cannot be strengthened in an overriding method.

```
 *  Append the specified Student to the end of this
 *  List.
 *      require:
 *          s instanceof Student
 *      ensure:
 *          this.size() == old.size() + 1
 *          this.get(this.size()-1) == s
 */
public void append (Object s) {
   Require.condition(s instanceof Student);
   super.append(s);
}


/**
 *  Replace the element at the specified position
 *  with the specified Student.
 *      require:
 *          0 <= i && i < this.size()
 *          s instanceof Student
 *      ensure:
 *          this.get(i) == s
 */
public void set (int i, Object s)
   Require.condition(s instanceof Student);
   super.set(i,s);
}


} // end of class StudentList
```

There is one significant difference between this version of *StudentList* and the version given in Chapter 12 that affects how we use the class. Even though we are guaranteed that every item on a *StudentList* is an instance of the class *Student*, the method get delivers an *Object*. Before we can use the item as a *Student*, we must explicitly cast it to *Student*. For instance, if sl is a (nonempty) *StudentList*, sl.get(0) is syntactically an *Object*, even though we can be certain that this *Object* is an instance of *Student*. If we want to query for the *Student*'s name for example, we must write

```
((Student)sl.get(0)).name()
```

If we do not explicitly cast the *Object* to *Student*, the run-time system will complain that the class *Object* does not have a method name.

(Note that this problem does not occur when we add a *Student* to a *StudentList*, since *Student* is a subclass of *Object*. A *Student* can be supplied in a context requiring an *Object*.)

16.1.1   Generalizing *sort*

Now that we've generalized lists, we'd like to rewrite the sort methods so that they take *List* arguments. Then we can use them to sort any kind of list. But the sort algorithms need an ordering `lessThan` defined on the list components. The components of a *List* are only known to be *Object*s, and the class *Object* doesn't have a feature `lessThan`. Furthermore, we might want to sort the same kind of list, or even the same list, in different ways at different times: we might want to sort a *StudentList* alphabetically by name, numerically by final grade, *etc.* To do this, we need to be able to specify the ordering as well as the list. That is, both the ordering and the list should be arguments to the sort method.

We can provide the ordering as an argument if the *ordering itself is an object.* What kind of object is an ordering? It is an object with one feature: a method for comparing two objects. We specify this with an interface:

```
/**
 * An ordering on some class.
 * The ordering "lessThan" (<) is transitive,
 * antisymmetric, and total with respect to some
 * class equivalence.
 */
public interface Order {

    /**
     * x < y
     */
    boolean lessThan (Object x, Object y);

}
```

A concrete order will implement this interface by defining the relation `lessThan` for some particular class. We are not particularly interested in the individual instances of the concrete order class. We need instances only so that we can pass the ordering as an argument to a sort method. The instances really have no distinguishing "properties" or semantic structure. They simply carry the method `lessThan`. Like the *Strategy* objects of the last chapter, instances of classes that implement *Order* are *function objects.*

Let's consider an example. Suppose *Student* objects have a property:

```
public int finalGrade()
```

and we want to order a *StudentList* by final grade. We can define a class:

```
/**
 * Order Students by finalGrade
 */
class GradeOrder implements Order {
```

```
/**
 * finalGrade of first Student < finalGrade of
 * second.
 *     require:
 *         x instanceof Student
 *         y instanceof Student
 */
public boolean lessThan (Object x, Object y) {
    Student sx = (Student)x;
    Student sy = (Student)y;
    return sx.finalGrade() < sy.finalGrade();
}
}
```

Note that we don't explicitly define a constructor for the class. Since there are no data to initialize, the default constructor is adequate. Also notice that we must explicitly cast the *Object* arguments to *Student* before we can invoke the *Student* method `finalGrade`. If an argument is not a *Student*, a run-time error will result from the attempted cast.

Now we are ready to specify the method `sort`. We require two arguments: a *List* and an *Order*, where the *Order* is a relation on the *List* elements.

> **public void** sort (List list, Order compare)
> Sort the specified *List* according to the specified *Order*.
>
> **require:**
> if x and y are items of `list`,
> `compare.lessThan(x,y)` is defined.

The sort algorithms given in Chapter 13 need to be slightly modified. When we wrote those algorithms, we assumed that `lessThan` was a list element feature. We wrote expressions like

```
list.get(next).lessThan(list.get(small))
```

to compare two elements. Now we must write

```
compare.lessThan(list.get(next), list.get(small))
```

since `lessThan` is a feature of the *Order* instance `compare`. This feature requires two *Objects* as arguments, and returns a **boolean**.

If `roster` is a *StudentList*, the invocation

```
sort(roster, new GradeOrder());
```

will invoke the method with parameters `list` and `compare` initialized as shown below. The list will be sorted according to the *Student* property `finalGrade`.

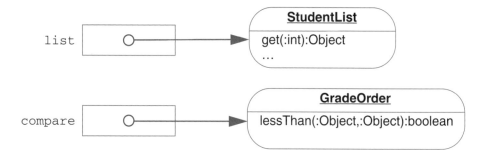

Anonymous classes

A class like *GradeOrder* really has no structural purpose in the design of a system. Its only function is to permit us to treat the ordering as an object so that we can use it as a method argument. Java has a facility called an *anonymous* class that allows simultaneous class definition and instantiation.

In the above example, we had need of an instance of a class that implements the interface *Order*. We first defined a class (*GradeOrder*) implementing the interface. The class provided the implementation of the method `lessThan`. We were then able to instantiate the class and obtain the required object. With an anonymous class, we define the class and instantiate it in one expression. The syntax looks something like a combination of a constructor invocation and a class definition:

```
new InterfaceName () {
    // definitions
}
```

The class being defined has no name, and hence is called an *anonymous class.*

For example, we can create an object like the one used as a `sort` argument above by writing

```
new Order() {
    boolean lessThan(Object x, Object y) {
        return    ((Student)x).finalGrade() <
                  ((Student)y).finalGrade();
    }
}
```

Note that this expression both defines an anonymous class that implements the interface *Order*, *and* instantiates the class.

Now rather than explicitly defining a class *GradeOrder* and then instantiating it in the call to `sort`, we can write the call to `sort` like this:

```
sort(roster,
   new Order() {
      boolean lessThan(Object x, Object y) {
         return   ((Student)x).finalGrade() <
                  ((Student)y).finalGrade();
      }
   }
);
```

An anonymous class can be a class extension rather than an interface implementation. We see an example of this when we extend the class *WindowAdpater* in
Chapter 19.

Interface Sorter

We've seen two simple sort methods so far, and will see another later; but we still
haven't said where the sort methods are defined. We will handle sorts with an
approach similar to that used for orderings. We define an interface whose implementations realize various sort algorithms:

```
/**
 * A sorter for a List.
 */
public interface Sorter {

   /**
    * Sort the specified List according to the
    * specified Order.
    *     require:
    *         if x and y are items of list,
    *             compare.lessThan(x,y) is defined.
    *     ensure:
    *         for 0 <= i, j < list.size(),
    *             compare.lessThan(list.get(i),
    *                              list.get(j))
    *             implies i < j.
    */
   void sort (List list, Order compare);
}
```

The implementation of selection sort, for instance, will look like this:

```
/**
 * A selection sort for a List.
 */
public class SelectionSorter implements Sorter {
```

```
/**
 * Sort the specified List according to the
 * specified Order, using selection sort.
 */
public void sort (List list, Order compare) {
    ...
}
} // end of class SelectionSorter
```

We include a number of sort algorithms in our library, in the package OOJ.lists.utilities.

16.2   Ordered lists

While we occasionally sort a list for some singular purpose, it is more typical that we want to maintain the list in a specific order. Moreover, we tend to treat ordered and unordered lists in different ways. For instance, we may add an element to the end of an unordered list but want to put the element in the "right place" when adding to an ordered list. Because we tend to use them differently, we add *OrderedList* to our library as a distinct container class:

> **public abstract class** OrderedList
> > A finite ordered list.

For the most part, *OrderedList* will have the same features as *List*:

> **public int** size ()
> **public boolean** isEmpty ()
> **public** Object get (**int** i)
> **public int** indexOf (Object obj)
> **public void** remove (**int** i)

The method add inserts an element at the proper place rather than at the end of the list, and we don't include the method set since it may break the ordering.

> **public void** add (Object obj)
> > Add the specified item to the proper place in this *OrderedList*.
> >
> > **require:**
> > > obj != null
> >
> > **ensure:**
> > > this.size() == old.size()+1
> > > for some i, 0 <= i < this.size()
> > > > this.get(i) == obj

Since we've isolated the notion of an order in an interface, we make the ordering a property of an *OrderedList*, and require that an *Order* be provided when an *OrderedList* is created:

public OrderedList (Order ordering)
>   Create a new *OrderedList*, ordered by the specified *Order*.

>   **ensure:**
>>   this.isEmpty() == true

public Order ordering ()
>   The *Order* used to order this *OrderedList*.

We include a constructor for initializing an *OrderedList* from a *List*, and a method for constructing a *List* from an *OrderedList*:

public OrderedList (Order ordering, List list)
>   Create a new OrderedList from the specified List.

>   **require:**
>>   if x and y are items of list,
>>>   ordering.lessThan(x,y) is defined.

>   **ensure:**
>>   this.size() == list.size()
>>   for 0 <= i < list.size()
>>>   list.get(i) == this.get(j), for some j

public List toList ()
>   Create a new *List* containing the elements of this *OrderedList*.

>   **ensure:**
>>   toList.size() == this.size()
>>   for 0 <= i < this.size(),
>>>   toList.get(i) == this.get(i)

Qualified invariant

We can define a class invariant for an *OrderedList* that states that the items are, in fact, ordered:

public abstract class OrderedList
>   A finite ordered list.

>   class invariant:
>>   for 0 <= i, j < size(),
>>>   ordering().lessThan(get(i),get(j)) implies
>>>   i < j.

But we must qualify the invariant. The items on the list exist, and can be manipulated, independently of the list. For instance, if we have a list of *Student*s ordered alphabetically by name, the *Student* objects can be accessed directly by clients, without using list methods. In particular, it's possible that a client might change the name of one of the *Students* on the list. Changing the name of a *Student* on a list ordered by name can, of course, invalidate the ordering, and the list has no control over this. Thus the list invariant must be qualified. It holds as long as no list item changes state in a way that affects the `lessThan` relation.

> **public abstract class** OrderedList
> > A finite ordered list.
>
> > class invariant:
> > > for 0 <= i, j < size(),
> > > > ordering().lessThan(get(i),get(j)) implies i < j.
> > >
> > > Subject to no list item changing properties which determine the relation ordering().lessThan.

Finally we include a command to make sure the list is properly ordered, and reorder it if necessary:

> **public void** validateOrder ()
> > Validate ordering, and reorder if necessary.
>
> > **ensure:**
> > > for 0 <= i, j < size(),
> > > > ordering().lessThan(get(i),get(j)) implies i < j.

16.3 Summary

In this chapter, we saw how to use abstraction to provide a common abstract superclass for lists. This class captures the essential structure of a list. Since implementation of a list is independent of the kind of items the list contains, this structure will allow us to factor out implementation details from the application-dependent concrete list subclasses. Furthermore, it allows us to write methods that manipulate list structures independently of the class of the list components.

We saw how to generalize sort methods by providing an ordering as well as a list as method arguments. To do this, we need a class instance to carry the ordering. We defined an interface *Order* that specifies that an implementing class must define an ordering method and observed that the Java anonymous class mechanism allows us to implement the interface and instantiate the implementing class in one syntactic expression.

Finally, we outlined the specification for a class *OrderedList*. Instances are lists whose elements are maintained in some specified order.

EXERCISES

16.1   Rewrite the search and sort methods of Chapter 13 using the class *List* and the interface *Order* as defined in this chapter.

16.2   Redo exercise 13.4 using the class *List* and the interface *Order* as defined in this chapter.

16.3   Redo exercise 13.5 using the class *List* and the interface *Order* as defined in this chapter.

GLOSSARY

anonymous class: a nameless concrete class that implements an interface or extends an abstract class. Java syntax allows for the definition and instantiation of the class to be done in a single expression.

CHAPTER 17   **Recursion**

In this chapter, we examine an algorithmic technique know as *recursion*. As in Chapter 13, we are concerned here primarily with algorithmic design. The objects and class structures we develop are principally intended to support our study of algorithmic technique.

Recursion is a technique related to iteration. Every programming language must provide facilities for at least one of these two techniques. Recursion is a powerful tool that can be effectively used by following a few simple guidelines. With recursion, a solution is developed by repeatedly performing an operation on simpler and simpler cases of the problem, until a trivial case is reached. The process then unwinds until the solution to the original problem is produced.

We conclude the chapter with a simple example illustrating how a recursive solution can be developed using class structure to control the recursion, rather than algorithm design.

17.1   Recursion and iteration

17.1.1   Iteration

Recursion is an algorithmic method closely related to iteration. When we develop an iterative solution to a problem, we describe a single step toward the solution. We then repeat the step until the problem is solved. If we consider selection sort or bubble sort, for example, a single step is *put one element of the list in its proper position*. This action is repeated until all the elements are in position.

The sorts differ in which element they choose to position, and how the element is determined. Selection sort can be described as

```
first = 0;
last = list.size()-1;
while (first < last) {
```

```
            //Find the smallest of elements first through last,
            //and put it in position first.
            first = first+1;
        }
```

while bubble sort can be expressed as:

```
        last = list.size()-1;
        while (last > 0) {
            Bubble the largest of elements 0 through last into
            position last.
            last = last-1;
        }
```

Both approaches are clearly iterative. The algorithm specifies a step in the solution process that is to be repeated or iterated. After each iteration, we are measurably closer to the desired solution, and we are certain that we will reach the solution after a finite number of iterations.

17.1.2   Recursion

With recursion, the idea is to provide a solution to a trivial, basic case of the problem, and then design a solution to the general case by showing how to "reduce" the general case to one that is a step closer to the basic case. That is, the solution is built on a strategy for reducing the general case of the problem so that repeated reduction ultimately ends with the basic case.

The algorithm is implemented so that it handles the trivial case of the problem directly. Given an instance of the general case, the algorithm *invokes itself* to solve a slightly reduced case. The solution is constructed from the solution of the slightly reduced case. Executing the algorithm results in a chain of self-calls ultimately resulting in an invocation with the trivial case, for which the algorithm can provide a direct solution. To insure correctness, we must guarantee that the general case will eventually reduce to the basic case.

Essential design of a recursive algorithm:

- Find one or more base cases for which there is a direct solution.

- Give a solution to the general case in terms of a slightly simpler case; that is, in terms of a case slightly closer to a base case.

Figure 17.1   **Structure of a recursive algorithm.**

Let's consider selection sort as an example. We want to separate the problem into trivial and nontrivial instances, which we call "base" and "general" cases, respectively. What are the trivial cases? If the list to be sorted is empty or contains only a single element, sorting is certainly easy. We need, in fact, do nothing at all. This gives us base cases.

- *Base cases*: sort a list that is empty or contains only a single element.

The general case is to sort a nontrivial list. That is, sort a list not covered by the base case:

- *General case*: sort a list containing n elements, where $n > 1$.

We express the problem in terms of the number of elements to be sorted, because that is the basis on which we separate the problem into base and general cases.

Next we need to reduce the general problem to one that is slightly closer to the base case. That is, we describe a solution to the general problem in terms of a slightly simpler problem. What is slightly simpler than sorting a list of n elements? Sorting a list with fewer elements: specifically, sorting a list of $n - 1$ elements. So we need to describe how to sort a list of n elements, *assuming we know how to sort a list of n – 1 elements*. That is, we reduce the problem of sorting a list of n elements to the problem of sorting a list of $n - 1$ elements.

If we're thinking in terms of selection sort, the solution to the general case can be described as follows.

1. Find the smallest element and put it first;
2. Sort the remaining $n - 1$ elements.

Notice how closely this resembles the iterative solution. The problem that we reduce the general case to is exactly the problem we are left with after one step of the iteration.

When we implement the algorithm with a method, the step "sort the remaining $n - 1$ elements" will be accomplished by an invocation of the method itself. Thus a call to the method with five elements results in a call to the method with four elements, which results in a call to the method with three elements, and so on, ending in a call with one element. Consequently the chain of self calls is terminated by a call to the method for the base case.

Now let's write a method that implements the recursive approach to selection sort. Thinking about the problem a bit, it is clear that we are manipulating a single list. The "remaining $n – 1$ elements" is simply a segment of the original list. It will be convenient to use arguments to specify the portion of the list we are concerned with, just as we did when writing binary search. We specify the method as follows—we'll see in a bit why we make it **private**. (To eliminate some clutter, we won't write out all the preconditions and postconditions.)

```
private void sort (List list, int first, int last,
    Order compare)
        Sort list from index first through index last according to the
        Order compare.
```

First, we must distinguish cases. A simple *if-then* will serve, since we need do nothing at all in the base case:

```
private void sort (List list, int first, int last,
    Order compare) {
    if (last > first) {
        // the general case:
        // Find the smallest element and put it first;
        // sort the remaining n-1 elements.
    }
}
```

We know how to find the smallest element and put it first. This was a well-defined step of selection sort (see Section 13.2.1):

```
private void sort (List list, int first, int last,
    Order compare) {
    int small;      // index of smallest of
                    // list.get(first)...list.get(last)

    if (last > first) {
        small = smallestOf(list,first,last,compare);
        interchange(list,first,small);
        // sort the remaining n-1 elements.
    }
}
```

All that is left is to sort the remaining $n - 1$ elements: that is, sort l.get(first+1) through l.get(last). But we have a method that will do this—the one we're writing. So we invoke the method itself:

```
private void sort (List list, int first, int last,
    Order compare) {
    int small;      // index of smallest of
                    // list.get(first)...list.get(last)

    if (last > first) {
        small = smallestOf(list,first,last,compare);
        interchange(list,first,small);
        sort(list,first+1,last,compare);
    }
}
```

At first glace, it may seem that we are cheating. But notice that the method works by the exact strategy described above. In the trivial case, the method does nothing. In the general case, the method invokes itself with a slightly simpler case:

the solution to the general case is built by reducing the problem to one that is a step closer to the trivial case.

Verification of correctness can be done with a straightforward induction. The base cases of the induction are obviously the base cases of the algorithm. The general case of the induction handles the general case of the algorithm.

We'll trace an example through to illustrate the underlying mechanism. But you should understand that you need not consciously step through the mechanism to use recursion effectively.

Assume we have a list of *Student* objects, and an ordering that compares them alphabetically by name. When the method `sort` is called, the list is provided as first argument, something like this:

```
sort(theStudentList,0,theStudentList.size()-1,
    alphaOrder);
```

Automatic variables are allocated for the parameters, and initialized with the argument values. (The arrow shows the next step to be performed. We don't show the order `compare` to reduce clutter in the illustrations.)

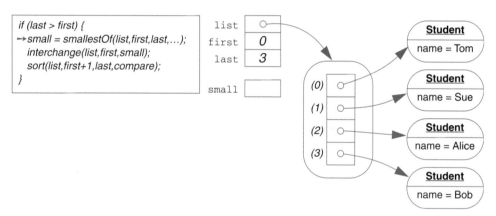

The local variable `small` is assigned the index of the smallest element

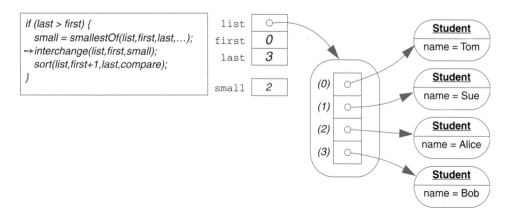

and that element is interchanged with the `first`.

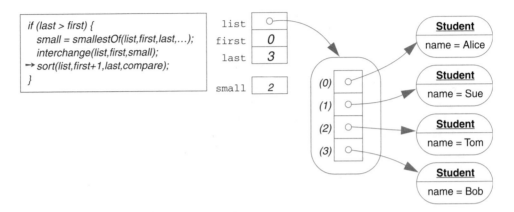

Now the method `sort` is invoked again, with the list as first argument, but with 1 (`first+1`) and 3 (`last`) as second and third arguments. The mechanism is exactly the same as in the original method invocation: automatic variables are created, and the parameters are initialized with the argument values.

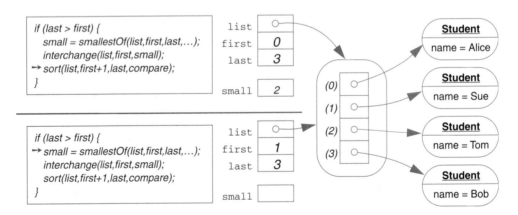

We now have two sets of local variables, one for each invocation of the method `sort`. This is no different than if we had invoked two different methods. The first invocation has not yet completed, so its automatic variables have not yet been deallocated. But the second invocation of the method is completely independent of these variables: they are local variables for some other invocation. The fact that it happens to be an invocation of the same method is irrelevant.

The method finds the smallest of elements 1 through 3, and interchanges it with element 1 (since `first` has value 1).

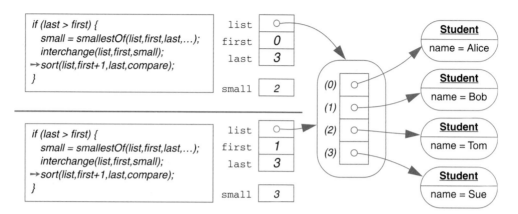

The method `sort` is called once again, this time with 2 (`first+1`) as second argument,

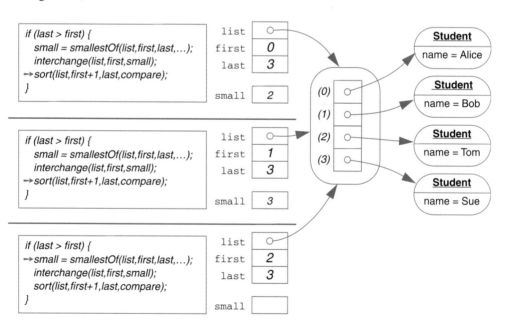

The smaller of elements 2 and 3 is interchanged with item 2.

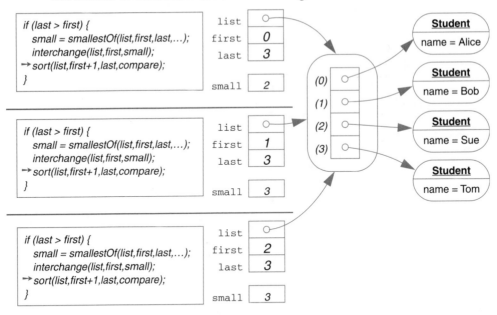

The method `sort` is invoked one more time:

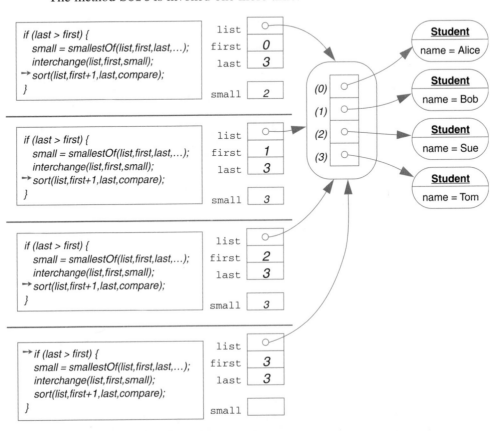

The condition `last > first` is now *false*, so the method returns to its caller without further ado. The call, of course, was from the previous invocation of the method `sort`. When the method returns, its automatic variables are freed.

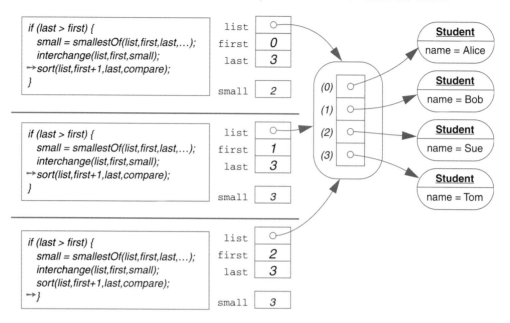

This completes the third invocation, and so it also returns. Each invocation in turn returns to its caller, completing the original call to the method.

To put this procedure into a *Sorter*, we provide a public method that simply calls the recursive method with the appropriate arguments:

```
/**
 * A recursive selection sort for a List of objects.
 */
public class RecursiveSelectionSorter
    implements Sorter {

    /**
     * Sort the specified List according to the
     * specified Order, using recursive selection sort.
     */
    public void sort (List list, Order compare) {
        sort(list,0,list.size()-1,compare);
    }

    /*
     * Sort list from index first through index last
     * according to the Order compare.
     */
```

```
        private void sort (List list, int first, int last,
            Order compare) {
            ...
        }

        private int smallestOf (List list, int first,
            int last, Order compare){
            ...
        }

        private void interchange (List list, int i,
            int j) {
            ...
        }

    } // end of class RecursiveSelectionSorter
```

Note the overloading of the method name `sort`. One `sort` defines the public interface, and the other is a private auxiliary method that actually does the work. As we have seen, overloading is permitted as long as the number and/or types of the parameters are different.

The recursive selection sort uses a very simple form of recursion, called *tail recursion*. The recursive and iterative versions of the algorithm are essentially identical. But there are many problems for which the recursive solution is conceptually simpler, as we shall see next.

17.2   Example: the towers puzzle

We next look at a standard example, sometimes called the "Towers of Hanoi" puzzle. The puzzle consists of a set of different-sized disks and three pegs. The disks are stacked on one of the pegs in order of size, with the largest disk on the bottom, as illustrated in Figure 17.2.

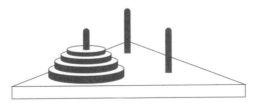

Figure 17.2 **A four-disk Towers of Hanoi puzzle.**

The point is to move the stack of disks from the starting peg to one of the other pegs. The disks are moved one at a time, and a disk can never be placed on top of a smaller one.

For instance, the following sequence of moves will move a stack of three disks. We label the pegs 1, 2, and 3 for easy reference.

Assume the disks start on peg 1, and we want to move them to peg 2.

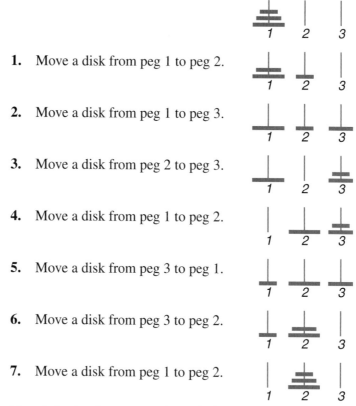

1.   Move a disk from peg 1 to peg 2.

2.   Move a disk from peg 1 to peg 3.

3.   Move a disk from peg 2 to peg 3.

4.   Move a disk from peg 1 to peg 2.

5.   Move a disk from peg 3 to peg 1.

6.   Move a disk from peg 3 to peg 2.

7.   Move a disk from peg 1 to peg 2.

Now let's develop a recursive solution to the puzzle. First, we must separate the problem into base case and general case. The situation in which we have only one disk to move is clearly trivial, and will serve as the base case.

The general case requires us to move a stack of n disks, where $n > 1$. Moving a stack of one fewer disks is a bit simpler—a step closer to the base case. Thus we need to describe how to move a stack of n disks, assuming we know how to move a stack of $n - 1$ disks. That is, we want to build a solution to the problem of moving n given a solution to the problem of moving $n - 1$ disks.

Notice that if we have a stack of n disks, we can ignore the largest disk when considering the $n - 1$ smaller disks. The largest disk won't get in the way when moving the others. Hence we can reduce the problem of moving n disks to the problem of moving $n - 1$ as follows.

1. Move $n - 1$ disks from the starting peg to the "other" peg.
2. Move a disk from the starting peg to the destination peg.
3. Move $n - 1$ disks from the "other" peg to the destination peg.

We have the essential form of a solution, but the structure is not yet complete. We must report the solution to a client. Keeping this in mind, there are several ways we could organize our approach. If we want to maintain separation between server and client, we can build the server to provide a list of moves solving the specified puzzle. On the other hand, we might want to interlace the server's generation of a sequence of moves with the client's use of the moves. In this case, we can structure the server so that it provides the next move on demand, or we make the client an observer of the server, as we did with the nim game user interface in Chapter 10. This last alternative is the approach we'll use in the example.

Recall that in the *observes* relationship, the client is the *observer* and the server is the *observed* or *target*. The observer makes itself known to the target by registering with the target. The target then calls a predetermined method in the observer (update) to let the observer know that it, the target, has done something worthy of notice.

Figure 17.3 **The *observes* relationship.**

In our case, the puzzle solver will be the target; it will inform the observer when it has computed the next move to be performed in solving the puzzle.

Before we start building the solver, we need to decide how to model a move. We take a straightforward approach and model a move as a class instance. Since the top disk on a peg is the only one that can be moved, a move is completely characterized by the peg the disk is moved from and the peg the disk is moved to.

public class Move
  A move in the Towers puzzle. Pegs are numbered 1, 2, 3.

 public Move (**int** from, **int** to)
  A move of a disk from the first peg specified to the second.

 public int from ()
  Peg the disk is moved from.

 public int to ()
  Peg the disk is moved to.

Since the observer and the problem solver are rather tightly coupled and to simplify the structure a bit, the observer identifies itself to the solver when requesting a solution, rather than through a separate registration method. That is, the puzzle solver offers a method specified as follows:

```
public void moveTower (int n, int from, int to,
    SolverObserver o)
```
> Report to the specified observer the moves required to move a tower of the specified number of disks, from the specified starting peg to the specified destination peg.

> **require:**
> ```
> n >= 1
> 1 <= from <= 3 && 1 <= to <= 3
> from != to
> ```

Furthermore, the solver provides the observer with each successive move as an argument to the observer's update method. Hence, a *SolverObserver* must implement the method

```
public void update (Move m)
```

The relationship between solver and observer is illustrated in Figure 17.4.

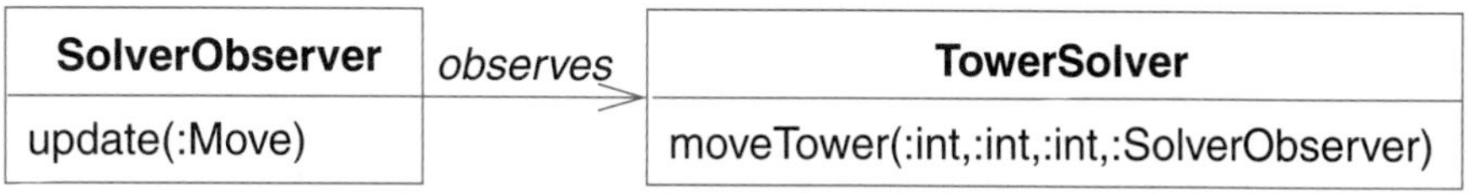

SolverObserver	*observes*	**TowerSolver**
update(:Move)		moveTower(:int,:int,:int,:SolverObserver)

Figure 17.4 **The *observes* relationship for the Towers of Hanoi puzzle.**

Now let's write the recursive method moveTower. As we have noted, the case in which we have only one disk to move will serve as the base case. In this case, we need only report the move to the observer:

```
public void moveTower (int n, int from, int to,
    SolverObserver o) {
    if (n == 1) {
        o.update(new Move(from,to));
    } else {
        // the general case
    }
}
```

The general case requires us to move a stack on n disks, where $n > 1$. To do this, we move $n - 1$ disks to the "other" peg, move the big disk to the target peg, and then move the $n - 1$ smaller disks to the target peg. Note that the "other" peg can easily be determined by subtracting source peg number (from) and target peg number (to) from 6 (= 1 + 2 + 3):

```
public void moveTower (int n, int from, int to,
    SolverObserver o) {
    if (n == 1) {
        o.update(new Move(from,to));
    } else {
        int other = 6-from-to;    // the peg that is not
                                  // from or to
        // move n-1 disks to other peg
        moveTower(n-1,from,other,o);
        // move big disk to the target
        o.update(new Move(from,to));
        // move n-1 disks to the target
        moveTower(n-1,other,to,o);
    }
}
```

We'll do one more trace to emphasize the underlying mechanism. In the illustrations, we don't show the parameter o. It is unchanged throughout the execution, and always references the client that originally called the method.

Suppose the method is called as follows.

```
MoveTower(2,1,2,this)
```

This invocation should produce a sequence of moves to move two disks from peg 1 to peg 2. We illustrate the key steps below. The arrows indicates which step of the method is being executed. Automatic variables, for the parameters n, to, and from, and for the local other, are shown to the right. (The parameter o is not shown, since in all cases it contains a reference to the same observer instance.)

Notice that a set of automatic variables are allocated each time the method is invoked, and deallocated when the invocation terminates. This calling mechanism is the same whether the method invokes itself of is invoked by some other client.

step 1		
→ *if (n == 1)*	n	2
...	from	1
else {	to	2
...		
}		

Method has been called by the original client with arguments 2, 1, and 2. (Parameter o not shown.) Variables for the parameters have been allocated and initialized with the argument values.

▬▬▬ *step 2* ▬▬▬

```
if (n == 1)
    ...
else {
    int other = 6- from- to;
→   moveTower(n- 1,from,other,o);
    o.update(new Move(from,to));
    moveTower(n- 1,other,to,o);
}
```

n	2
from	1
to	2
other	3

Local variable other *has been created and initialized. Method is about to call* moveTower *with arguments 1, 2, 3, and* o.

▬▬▬ *step 3* ▬▬▬

```
if (n == 1)
    ...
else {
    int other = 6- from- to;
→   moveTower(n- 1,from,other,o);
    o.update(new Move(from,to));
    moveTower(n- 1,other,to,o);
}
```

n	2
from	1
to	2
other	3

Method is executing call moveTower *with arguments 1, 2, 3, and* o.

_____

```
if (n == 1)
→   o.update(new Move(from,to));
else {
    ...
}
```

n	1
from	1
to	3

Method has been called a second time with arguments 1, 1, and 3. (Parameter o *not shown.)* o.update *is invoked, with a 1-to-3 move as argument.*

▬▬▬ *step 4* ▬▬▬

```
if (n == 1)
    ...
else {
    int other = 6- from- to;
    moveTower(n- 1,from,other,o);
→   o.update(new Move(from,to));
    moveTower(n- 1,other,to,o);
}
```

n	2
from	1
to	2
other	3

Call to moveTower *has completed.* o.update *is invoked with a 1-to-2 move as argument.*

▬▬▬ *step 5* ▬▬▬

```
if (n == 1)
    ...
else {
    int other = 6- from- to;
    moveTower(n- 1,from,other,o);
    o.update(new Move(from,to));
→   moveTower(n- 1,other,to,o);
}
```

n	2
from	1
to	2
other	3

Method is about to call moveTower *with arguments 1, 3, 2, and* o.

━━━━━ *step 6* ━━━━━

```
if (n == 1)
    ...
else {
    int other = 6-from-to;
    moveTower(n-1,from,other,o);
    o.update(new Move(from,to));
→   moveTower(n-1,other,to,o);
}
```

n	2
from	1
to	2
other	3

Method is executing call moveTower with arguments 1, 3, 2, and o.

```
if (n == 1)
→   o.update(new Move(from,to));
else {
    ...
}
```

n	1
from	3
to	2

Method has been called a third time with arguments 1, 3, and 2. (Parameter o not shown.) o.update is invoked, with a 3-to-2 move as argument.

━━━━━ *step 7* ━━━━━

```
if (n == 1)
    ...
else {
    int other = 6-from-to;
    moveTower(n-1,from,other,o);
    o.update(new Move(from,to));
    moveTower(n-1,other,to,o);
→ }
```

n	2
from	1
to	2
other	3

Call to moveTower has completed. Original invocation of moveTower is about to complete. Note that o has been informed: move-1-to-3, move-1-to-2, move-3-to-2.

17.3 Quick sort

For our next example of recursion, we return to the sort problem and present another classic algorithm called *quick sort*. Quick sort's advantage over those previously seen is efficiency. While selection sort and bubble sort take on the order of n^2 steps to sort a list of n elements, quick sort typically takes on the order of $n \cdot \log_2 n$ steps.

n	n^2	$n \cdot \log_2 n$
10	100	33
100	10,000	64
1,000	1,000,000	9,966
10,000	100,000,000	132,877
100,000	10,000,000,000	1,660,964
1,000,000	1,000,000,000,000	19,931,569

Like bubble sort and selection sort, quick sort starts by putting one element into position. But rather than positioning the largest or smallest element, quick sort puts an arbitrary element in proper position, with smaller elements below and larger elements above. The two sublists—the elements below the positioned element and the elements above it—are then (recursively) sorted. The algorithm is essentially the following:

1. Put an element in its proper sorted position, with smaller elements below and larger elements above. (The positioned element is referred to as the "pivot element.")
2. Sort the sublist of smaller elements below the positioned element.
3. Sort the sublist of larger elements above the positioned element.

Since we reduce the problem of sorting a list to the problem of sorting a shorter list, the approach is clearly recursive.

As with recursive selection sort, we implement a private method to sort a list segment. The public `sort` simply calls this method with the entire list:

```
/**
 * A quick sort for a List.
 */
public class QuickSorter extends Sorter {

    /**
     * Sort specified List according to the specified
     * Order, using quick sort.
     */
    public void sort (List list, Order compare) {
        sort(list,0,list.size()-1,compare);
    }

    /**
     * Sort list elements indexed first through last.
     */
    private void sort (List list, int first, int last,
        Order compare) {
        ...
    }

} // end of class QuickSorter
```

The base case is the same as for recursive selection sort: an empty list or a list with a single element. The general case is handled by the three steps described above. The only complexity is in the first step, sometimes called the *pivot step*. We separate this step out into a private method called `partition`. The method `partition` will position an element (the *pivot element*) as described in step 1 above, and report where it was placed.

Like the method `makePassTo` of the modified bubble sort (Section 13.2.3), the method `partition` is neither a proper command nor a proper query. It changes the state of the list like a command, and returns a value like a query. Since this is an ancillary method and not an object feature, we are willing to employ it without too much concern:

```
private int partition (List list, int first, int last,
    Order compare)
```
    Partition `list` elements indexed `first` through `last` for quick sort; return the pivot position.

require:
```
    0 <= first < last < list.size()
```

ensure:
```
    first <= result <= last
    for first <= i < result,
            list.get(i) < list.get(result)
            i.e., compare.lessThan(
                    list.get(i),list.get(result))
        for result <= i <= last,
            list.get(i) >= list.get(result)
            i.e., !compare.lessThan(
                    list.get(i),list.get(result))
```

Suppose, for example, `list` is the following list, `compare` is simply numeric "less than," and the method `partition` is called with second and third arguments of 0 and 14.

```
partition(list,0,14,compare)
```

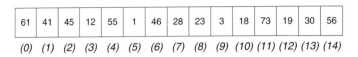

61	41	45	12	55	1	46	28	23	3	18	73	19	30	56
(0)	(1)	(2)	(3)	(4)	(5)	(6)	(7)	(8)	(9)	(10)	(11)	(12)	(13)	(14)

The method can position any of the 15 elements of the list. Suppose the element 28 is chosen to be positioned. (This is the pivot element.) The proper position for this element in the list is position 6. (There are 6 elements smaller than 28, 8 elements larger.) The method will put 28 in the sixth position, with the smaller 6 elements—in any order—in positions 0–5, and the larger 8 elements, again in any order, in positions 7–14. For instance, the list might be rearranged as follows.

12	1	23	3	18	19	**28**	56	45	61	55	73	41	30	46
(0)	(1)	(2)	(3)	(4)	(5)	(6)	(7)	(8)	(9)	(10)	(11)	(12)	(13)	(14)

The method returns the value 6, the index of the pivot element.

Using the method `partition`, we can easily implement quick sort:

```
/*
 * Sort list elements indexed first through last.
 */
private void sort (List list, int first, int last,
    Order compare) {
    int position;// the pivot index
    if (first < last) {
        position = partition(list,first,last,compare);
        sort(list,first,position-1,compare);
        sort(list,position+1,last,compare);
    }
}
```

We need only write the method `partition`, and we are done. There are many possible approaches. We adopt one that is straightforward, though perhaps not the most efficient.

We choose the middle element of the sublist as pivot element. For instance, if we are to partition all 15 elements in the following list, we choose the seventh element, 28, as pivot element.

61	41	45	12	55	1	46	**28**	23	3	18	73	19	30	56
(0)	(1)	(2)	(3)	(4)	(5)	(6)	(7)	(8)	(9)	(10)	(11)	(12)	(13)	(14)

First, we move the pivot element in the last position to "get it out of the way," interchanging it with the last element:

61	41	45	12	55	1	46	56	23	3	18	73	19	30	**28**
(0)	(1)	(2)	(3)	(4)	(5)	(6)	(7)	(8)	(9)	(10)	(11)	(12)	(13)	(14)

Then we examine each element of the list, shuffling smaller elements to the front. To do this, we keep two indexes into the list. The first index, which we'll call *i*, simply steps through the list, identifying each element in turn to be examined. The second index, which we'll call *pi*, separates elements found to be smaller than the pivot element from those found to be larger.

For instance, as illustrated below, if *i* is 8, then the first 8 (items 0–7) have already been examined and the next element to examine is item 8. If *pi* is 3, elements 0–2 are less than the pivot element, and elements 3–7 are greater than or equal to the pivot element.

s	s	s	L	L	L	L	L	?	?	?	?	?	?	28
(0)	(1)	(2)	(3)	(4)	(5)	(6)	(7)	(8)	(9)	(10)	(11)	(12)	(13)	(14)

↑ pi (at index 3)   ↑ i (at index 8)

In the partition operation, both indexes start at the element 0.

61	41	45	12	55	1	46	56	23	3	18	73	19	30	28
(0)	(1)	(2)	(3)	(4)	(5)	(6)	(7)	(8)	(9)	(10)	(11)	(12)	(13)	(14)

↑ pi ↑ i (both at index 0)

Elements are examined until one is found that is smaller than the pivot element.

61	41	45	12	55	1	46	56	23	3	18	73	19	30	28
(0)	(1)	(2)	(3)	(4)	(5)	(6)	(7)	(8)	(9)	(10)	(11)	(12)	(13)	(15)

↑ pi (at index 0)   ↑ i (at index 3)

The items at the two indexes are interchanged, the smaller one moving down and the larger one up

12	41	45	61	55	1	46	56	23	3	18	73	19	30	28
(0)	(1)	(2)	(3)	(4)	(5)	(6)	(7)	(8)	(9)	(10)	(11)	(12)	(13)	(14)

↑ pi (at index 0)   ↑ i (at index 3)

and the indexes are incremented.

12	41	45	61	55	1	46	56	23	3	18	73	19	30	28
(0)	(1)	(2)	(3)	(4)	(5)	(6)	(7)	(8)	(9)	(10)	(11)	(12)	(13)	(14)

↑ pi (at index 1)   ↑ i (at index 4)

Note that the elements below *pi* are less than the pivot element, and the elements from *pi* up to (but not including) *i* are greater than or equal to the pivot element.

The process is repeated, until all the elements have been examined.

12	41	45	61	55	1	46	56	23	3	18	73	19	30	**28**

Find next element smaller than pivot

(0) (1) (2) (3) (4) (5) (6) (7) (8) (9) (10) (11) (12) (13) (14)

↑pi (at 1) ↑i (at 5)

12	1	45	61	55	41	46	56	23	3	18	73	19	30	**28**

Interchange elements

(0) (1) (2) (3) (4) (5) (6) (7) (8) (9) (10) (11) (12) (13) (14)

↑pi (at 1) ↑i (at 5)

12	1	45	61	55	41	46	56	23	3	18	73	19	30	**28**

Increment indexes

(0) (1) (2) (3) (4) (5) (6) (7) (8) (9) (10) (11) (12) (13) (14)

↑pi (at 2) ↑i (at 6)

12	1	45	61	55	41	46	56	23	3	18	73	19	30	**28**

Find next element smaller than pivot

(0) (1) (2) (3) (4) (5) (6) (7) (8) (9) (10) (11) (12) (13) (14)

↑pi (at 2) ↑i (at 8)

12	1	23	61	55	41	46	56	45	3	18	73	19	30	**28**

Interchange elements

(0) (1) (2) (3) (4) (5) (6) (7) (8) (9) (10) (11) (12) (13) (14)

↑pi (at 2) ↑i (at 8)

12	1	23	61	55	41	46	56	45	3	18	73	19	30	**28**

Increment indexes

(0) (1) (2) (3) (4) (5) (6) (7) (8) (9) (10) (11) (12) (13) (14)

↑pi (at 3) ↑i (at 9)

12	1	23	61	55	41	46	56	45	3	18	73	19	30	**28**

Find next element smaller than pivot

(0) (1) (2) (3) (4) (5) (6) (7) (8) (9) (10) (11) (12) (13) (14)

↑pi (at 3) ↑i (at 9)

12	1	23	3	55	41	46	56	45	61	18	73	19	30	**28**

Interchange elements

(0) (1) (2) (3) (4) (5) (6) (7) (8) (9) (10) (11) (12) (13) (14)

↑pi (at 3) ↑i (at 9)

Increment indexes

12	1	23	3	55	41	46	56	45	61	18	73	19	30	**28**
(0)	(1)	(2)	(3)	(4)	(5)	(6)	(7)	(8)	(9)	(10)	(11)	(12)	(13)	(14)

↑ pi (4)   ↑ i (10)

Find next element smaller than pivot

12	1	23	3	55	41	46	56	45	61	18	73	19	30	**28**
(0)	(1)	(2)	(3)	(4)	(5)	(6)	(7)	(8)	(9)	(10)	(11)	(12)	(13)	(14)

↑ pi (4)   ↑ i (10)

Interchange elements

12	1	23	3	18	41	46	56	45	61	55	73	19	30	**28**
(0)	(1)	(2)	(3)	(4)	(5)	(6)	(7)	(8)	(9)	(10)	(11)	(12)	(13)	(14)

↑ pi (4)   ↑ i (10)

Increment indexes

12	1	23	3	18	41	46	56	45	61	55	73	19	30	**28**
(0)	(1)	(2)	(3)	(4)	(5)	(6)	(7)	(8)	(9)	(10)	(11)	(12)	(13)	(14)

↑ pi (5)   ↑ i (11)

Find next element smaller than pivot

12	1	23	3	18	41	46	56	45	61	55	73	19	30	**28**
(0)	(1)	(2)	(3)	(4)	(5)	(6)	(7)	(8)	(9)	(10)	(11)	(12)	(13)	(14)

↑ pi (5)   ↑ i (12)

Interchange elements

12	1	23	3	18	19	46	56	45	61	55	73	41	30	**28**
(0)	(1)	(2)	(3)	(4)	(5)	(6)	(7)	(8)	(9)	(10)	(11)	(12)	(13)	(14)

↑ pi (5)   ↑ i (12)

Increment indexes

12	1	23	3	18	19	46	56	45	61	55	73	41	30	**28**
(0)	(1)	(2)	(3)	(4)	(5)	(6)	(7)	(8)	(9)	(10)	(11)	(12)	(13)	(14)

↑ pi (6)   ↑ i (13)

Now there are no more elements less than the pivot element. The last step is to put the pivot element into position by swapping it with the element at *pi*.

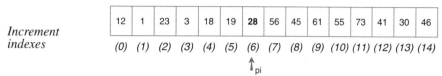

Increment indexes

The index *pi* identifies the proper location of the pivot element.

(You should note that this operation takes *n* steps if there are *n* elements in the sublist to be partitioned. Each element in the sublist is examined once.)

We give the implementation next:

```
private int partition (List list, int first, int last,
   Order compare) {

      int pi;         // pivot index; pivot element goes
                      // here;
                      // everything below pi is < item
      int i;          // index of the next item of 1
                      // to examine
      int mid;        // middle index: (first+last)/2

      Object item;    // pivot item

      mid = (first+last)/2;
      item = list.get(mid);

      // put pivot item at end of list for now
      interchange(list,mid,last);

      pi = first;
      i = first;      // haven't examined anything yet

      /* loop invariant:
       *     for first <= j < pi
       *         list.get(j) < item
       *     for pi <= j < i
       *         list.get(j) >= item
       */
      while (i != last) { // list.get(last) is pivot item
         if (compare.lessThan(list.get(i),item)) {
            interchange(list,pi,i)
            pi = pi+1;
         }
         i = i+1;
      }
```

```
                interchange(list,pi,last); // put pivot item in
                                           // place
            return pi;
        }
```

A few observations:

- The loop invariant given at ❶ is key. It says that smaller items will be in positions first ... pi-1, and larger elements will be in positions pi ... i-1.

  Note that when line ❷ is reached for the first time, the clauses of the invariant are vacuously true. Since first == pi == i, there is no value j such that first <= j < pi, and there is no value j such that pi <= j < i.

- When the loop terminates, i == last, all the elements have been examined, pi points at the first element greater than or equal to the pivot, and the pivot item is at position last.

We should mention why we choose the middle element of the sublist as pivot, rather than, say, the last element. After all, the algorithm will work regardless of which element we choose as pivot. As noted above, quick sort takes about $n \cdot \log_2 n$ steps to sort a list of n elements in almost all cases. There are, however, a few pathological cases for which the algorithm requires n^2 steps. Essentially, these are situations where each partition operation leaves the pivot element at one end or the other of the sub-list. If we choose the last (or first) element as pivot, then situations that might well occur in practice, such as a list that is already ordered, can require n^2 steps. The pathological cases that occur if we choose the middle element as pivot are much less likely actually to be encountered.

17.4   An inefficient algorithm

While recursion is a powerful problem solving tool, we need to be a little careful in analyzing the work required by a recursive algorithm. For example, the Fibonacci numbers can be defined as the sequence of integers beginning with 0 and 1, and in which each successive number is the sum of the previous two:

    0, 1, 1, 2, 3, 5, 8, 13, 21, 34, ...

We can write a very straightforward recursive algorithm to compute the nth Fibonacci number. (We consider 0 to be the "0-th" number in the sequence.)

```
/**
 * The nth Fibonacci number.
 *     require:
 *          n >= 0
 */
```

```
public int fib (int n) {
   if (n == 0)
      return 0;
   else if (n == 1)
      return 1;
   else
      return fib(n-1)+fib(n-2);
}
```

The problem with this algorithm is that it is notoriously inefficient. Each level of the recursion essentially duplicates work done at the previous level. For instance, computing *fib*(6) requires computing *fib*(5) and *fib*(4). But the computation of *fib*(5) also computes *fib*(4), repeating the work of the previous level. In fact, since the work required to compute *fib*(n) is the sum of the work required to compute *fib*(n–1) and the work required to compute *fib*(n–2), it is not difficult to see that the time required to compute *fib*(n) is roughly proportional to *fib*(n)! A simple iterative approach solves the problem in computational time proportional to n.

Of course, one can write an efficient recursive algorithm to compute the Fibonacci numbers, and inefficiencies due to unnecessarily repeated work can be found in iterative algorithms as well. But the inefficiency is often more obvious in an iterative algorithm, since we control the steps in an iterative process more directly than in a recursive process. We will consider exactly what we mean by efficiency and how it is measured in Chapter 21.

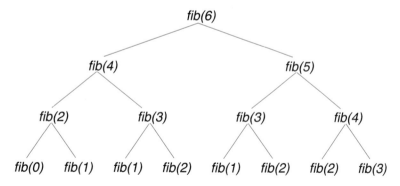

Figure 17.5   **Repeated work in the simple Fibonacci algorithm.**

17.5   Indirect recursion

The previous examples have all involved a method invoking itself: direct recursion. A method can also invoke itself *indirectly*: for instance, a method m_1 invokes

m_2 which invokes m_3 ... which invokes m_n which invokes m_1. We consider a rather contrived example to see how this works.

Assume we have two methods `head` and `tail`, each requiring a non-empty *String* as argument. `head` gives us the first character of the argument, and `tail` gives us a *String* that is equal to the argument with the first character removed:

> **public char** head (String s)
>> The first character of the specified non-empty *String*.

> **public** String tail (String s)
>> A *String* equal to the specified non-empty *String* with its first character removed.

For instance, `head("abc")` produces the character `'a'`, and `tail("abc")` produces the *String* `"bc"`.

Now let's write a recursive method that gets a balanced string of parentheses as argument and removes the first balanced substring. For instance, the method might be given any of the following arguments:

```
"()"
"()()()()"
"((()))"
"(()()(()()))()(())"
```

and would produce the following results:

```
""
"()()()"
""
"()(())"
```

(Clearly we could do this in a straightforward, nonrecursive manner!)

> **public** String removeSet (String s)
>> A *String* equal to the specified *String* with the first balanced substring of parenthesis removed.
>
>> **require:**
>> s is a balanced string of parentheses.

Note that if we remove the first open parenthesis, we must then remove a string that contains one more closed parenthesis than open parentheses. We specify an auxiliary method to do this:

> **private** String reduceClosed (String s)
>> A *String* equal to the specified *String* with the first substring containing one more closed parenthesis than open parentheses removed.
>
>> **require:**
>> s is a string of parentheses that would be balanced if an open parenthesis were appended to the front; in particular, s contains one more closed parenthesis than open parentheses.

There are two cases to consider for this method:

1. The head of s is a closed parenthesis, in which case we simply return the tail of s.
2. The head of s is an open parenthesis, in which case we must first remove the initial balanced substring from s.

We can implement these methods in a mutually recursive manner:

```
public String removeSet (String s) {
    if (s.equals(""))
        return "";
    else
        // head(s) is '('
        return reduceClosed(tail(s));
}

private String reduceClosed (String s) {
    if ( head(s) == ')' )
        return tail(s);
    else
        // head(s) == '('; first remove a balanced set
        return reduceClosed(removeSet(s));
}
```

Note that an invocation of removeSet may call reduceClosed, which may again call removeSet. This is an example of indirect recursion. Indirect recursion typically involves a set of mutually recursive methods, as is the case here.

17.6   Object recursion

In this section, we examine another form of recursion. The previous examples have all involved algorithms implemented by recursive methods, methods that invoked themselves. In this section, we consider structural recursion, using object structure in a recursive manner to derive problem solutions. An object tasked with solving a problem gets assistance from a similar object which solves a simpler instance of the problem. The object then constructs a solution by extending the solution of the simpler problem. Structurally, the similar object that provides the solution to the simpler problem is a component of the original object:

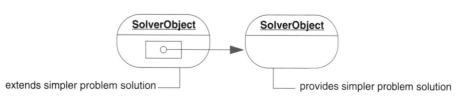

In modeling solver objects, we have two flavors corresponding to the two cases of a recursive algorithm. One is the general problem solver, and the other is the trivial problem solver. We make these subclasses of a common abstract parent:

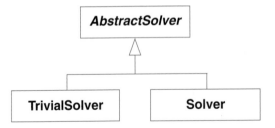

Since we want to concentrate on the structure of the objects, we use a rather trivial example. Suppose we want to construct an odometer-like counter that consists of a sequence of digits, in which one digit turning over from 9 to 0 causes its left neighbor to increment.

| 0 | 0 | 5 | 0 | 4 |

Figure 17.6 **Five-digit counter.**

A *solution state* is simply a stable state of the counter, in which all digits are set. We can tell the counter to find the first solution state; that is, reset all digits to 0. And we can tell the counter to find the next solution; that is, increment the counter by 1. There is a final solution state, in which all digits are 9. We specify that attempting to find the next solution after the final state will fail; *i.e.*, a counter that is all 9s will not turn over to all 0s.

We name the solver class *Digit*, and the trivial solver class *NullDigit*. Each *Digit* instance is responsible for a single digit of the solution. Each *Digit* has an *associate*, the *Digit* to its left. A *Digit* will extend the solution provided by its associate. Thus the *Digit*s are "linked together" to form the counter. The high-order (left-most) *Digit* has a *NullDigit* as its associate. The high-order *Digit* really needs no associate. The logic in the *NullDigit* will simply end the recursion. We have the following fundamental class structure:

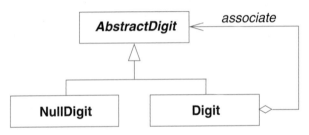

Essentially, a *Digit* finds a solution by extending the partial solution provided by its associate. A *Digit* that is right-most in a four-digit number, for example, has an associate that is right-most in a three-digit number. The four-digit number is built by extending the three-digit number. Notice that the right-most *Digit* in a 1-digit number has a *NullDigit* as associate.

Now let's see how this all works. If we want a three-digit counter, we need to create three *Digit* instances and one *NullDigit*, structured as shown below. Notice that a *Digit* and its associate component have the same structure; hence, the term "structural recursion." We call the top-level object that contains the structure a *DigitCounter*.

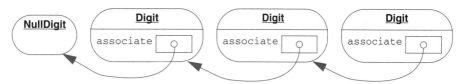

Figure 17.7 **Objects comprising a three-digit counter.**

Recall that a class can be defined inside another class. Such a class is called an *inner class* and follows the same accessibility rules of other class members. We make *AbstractDigit*, *Digit*, and *NullDigit* inner classes of the *DigitCounter*.

When we build the *DigitCounter*, we start with a *NullDigit*, and create one *Digit* instance for each digit in the counter.

```
/**
 * A counter containing the specified number of
 * digits.
 */
public class DigitCounter {

    /**
     * Create a new DigitCounter with the specified
     * number of digits.
     *     require:
     *         digits >= 1
     */
    public DigitCounter (int digits) {
        int i;
        AbstractDigit d = new NullDigit();
        for (i = 1; i <= digits; i = i+1)
            d = new Digit(d);
        lowDigit = d;
    }
    ...
```

```
        private AbstractDigit lowDigit; // right-most digit

        private abstract class AbstractDigit {
           ...
        } // end of class AbstractDigit

        private class NullDigit extends AbstractDigit {
           ...
        } // end of class NullDigit

        private class Digit extends AbstractDigit {

           public Digit (AbstractDigit associate) {
              this.associate = associate;
              ...
           }
           ...
           private AbstractDigit associate;
                                        // left neighbor

        } // end of class Digit

     } // end of class DigitCounter
```

Now what features should *DigitCounter* have? We provide commands for finding the first solution and for finding the next. That is, the command `first` sets the counter to all 0s, and the command `next` increments the counter. We should use the counter by giving the command `first`, and then repeatedly giving the command `next`. We have a query `solved` to determine whether a solution was found. We expect `solved` to return *false* initially, and then return *true* after we have given the command `first`. It should continue to return *true* until we try to increment a counter consisting of all 9s. Finally, we have a method `toString` that returns the value of the counter as a *String*. For example, a two-digit counter would behave as follows:

command:	solved:	toString:
—	*false*	—
first	*true*	00
next	*true*	01
next	*true*	02
...		
next	*true*	99
next	*false*	—

These *DigitCounter* methods simply forward the request to the *DigitCounter* component, `lowDigit`, right-most digit of the counter:

```java
public class DigitCounter {
    ...
    /**
     * Find the first number: i.e., set this
     * DigitCounter to all 0.
     */
    public void first () {
        lowDigit.first();
    }

    /**
     * Find the next number: i.e., increment this
     * DigitCounter by 1 if possible.
     */
    public void next () {
        lowDigit.next();
    }

    /**
     * This DigitCounter contains a legitimate count.
     * That is, first() or next() has been successfully
     * performed.
     */
    public boolean solved () {
        return lowDigit.solved();
    }

    /**
     * The number contained in this DigitCounter.
     *     require:
     *         this.solved()
     */
    public String toString () {
        return lowDigit.toString();
    }

    private AbstractDigit lowDigit; // right-most digit

    private abstract class AbstractDigit {
        public abstract boolean solved ();
        public abstract void first ();
        public abstract void next ();
        public abstract String toString ();
    } // end of class AbstractDigit
    ...
} // end of class DigitCounter
```

Now how does a *Digit* work? When given the command `first`, it instructs its left neighbor to find the first number, and then tacks on its own 0. When given the command `next`, it increments its digit if it's not 9. If it is, it instructs its left neighbor to increment, and then tacks on a 0. In each case, we check to make sure that the neighbor was successful. Omitting documentation, *Digit* is defined as follows:

```java
private class Digit extends AbstractDigit {

    public Digit (AbstractDigit associate) {
        this.associate = associate;
        this.digit = 0;
        this.solved = false;
    }

    public boolean solved () {
        return solved;
    }

    public void first () {
        associate.first();
        if (associate.solved()) {
            digit = 0;
            solved = true;
        } else
            solved = false;
    }

    public void next () {
        if (digit < 9) {
            digit = digit + 1;
            solved = true;
        } else {
            associate.next();
            if (associate.solved()) {
                digit = 0;
                solved = true;
            } else
                solved = false;
        }
    }

    public String toString () {
        return associate.toString() + digit;
    }
```

```
    private AbstractDigit associate;  // left neighbor
    private boolean solved;            // a valid number
    private int digit;                 // my digit

} // end of class Digit
```

A little analysis would show the test in `first` and many of the assignments to `solved` to be unnecessary. Still, we include them to give the flavor of the general approach. Notice how the recursive nature of the solution is evident from object recursion. The digit structure is traversed, with each object delegating the job to its associate. This logic is particularly clear in the method `toString`, in which an object delegates building the *String* representation to its associate, and then adds its digit. We can also see this logic in the methods `first` and `next`, where the object is delegating responsibility to its associate.

We have only to complete the definition of *NullDigit*. Remember that `first` and `next` are called by an element's right neighbor. `first` is called when the right neighbor is has its initial piece of the solution, and needs only to get the first solution from its associate. On the other hand, `next` is called when the right neighbor can no longer extend the current partial solution on its own and needs a new partial solution from its associate. *NullDigit* represents the solution to the empty problem. It always solves the problem vacuously, and therefore has a "first" solution; but does not have a "next" solution. *NullDigit* rather clearly should be built as follows:

```
    private class NullDigit extends AbstractDigit {

        public boolean solved () {
            return solved;
        }

        public void first () {
            solved = true;
        }

        public void next () {
            solved = false;
        }

        public String toString () {
            return "";
        }

        private boolean solved;

    } // end of class NullDigit
```

Structurally we do not need the class *NullDigit*. Its purpose is to permit all object entries in the structure to be treated uniformly. If we do not give the left-most *Digit* an associate, the methods of the *Digit* class will be polluted with tests to determine whether or not the associate component is *null*. Thus every *Digit* instance is given a non-*null* associate. But what kind of associate should the left-most *Digit* be given? An instance of *NullDigit*, a class whose method logic is straightforward. By making the type of the associate component *AbstractDigit*, a *Digit* can be equipped with a *Digit* or *NullDigit* as an associate. Polymorphism distinguishes the two classes, allowing us to write simpler methods for the class *Digit*.

17.7 Summary

In this chapter we introduced the problem solving technique of recursion. We've seen two forms of recursive computation: *algorithmic recursion*, in which a method invokes itself directly or indirectly, and *object recursion*, based on the creation of composite object structure in which the structure of a component is the same as that of the composite object.

With algorithmic recursion, the solution logic depends on identifying simple base cases that can be easily solved directly, and on describing how to reduce the general case to one that is slightly simpler: that is, slightly closer to a base case. The method that actualizes this logic invokes itself to solve the slightly simpler case to which the general case is reduced.

Using object recursion, a solver object is structured with a similar solver object as a component. A solver object delegates the responsibility of solving a simpler version of the problem to its component, and then extends the solution provide by the component. The recursive nature of the approach is seen here as well: a solution to the general case is found by using a solution to a simpler case, in this instance given by the component.

EXERCISES

17.1 Write a recursive version of the binary search algorithm of Section 13.3.

17.2 Write a recursive version of insertion sort as described in exercise 13.5.

17.3 Recall from exercise 13.4 that a *merge* operation takes two similarly sorted lists and combines them into a single sorted list. *Merge sort* can be described informally as follows:

a. Break the list into two halves.

b. Sort each half.

c. Merge the two sorted halves into a sorted list.

Implement merge sort.

17.4 Write a recursive method `reverse` that takes a *String* argument and produces a *String* that is the reverse of the argument as result. For instance, `reverse("abc")` should produce the *String* `"cba"`.

17.5 Write a recursive method reverse that takes a *List* as argument and produces a *List* that is the reverse of the argument as result.

17.6 Write a recursive method `palindrome` that takes a *String* argument, and determines whether or not the *String* is a palindrome. (A *palindrome* is a string that reads the same forward as backward: for instance "amanaplanacanalpanama.")

17.7 An *integer expression* is either an integer, a unary operator and operand, or a binary operator and left and right operands. Unary operators are + and −. Binary operators are +, −, *, and /. An operand is another integer expression.

Design a class to model integer expressions. The class should include a method `evaluate` that returns the integer value of the expression.

17.8 The *queens problem* is to place *n* queens on an *n* × *n* chessboard in such a way that no queen can capture any other in one move. Implement a solution to the queens problem using object recursion. The value for *n* is specified when the problem instance is created. If the problem cannot be solved, `solved` will return *false* after the method `first` is invoked. Otherwise, `first` produces a solution and successive invocations of `next` produce successive solutions to the problem.

Consider creating a *Solver* instance for each row or the board. A *Solver* instance is responsible for extending the partial solution provided by its neighbor by adding a queen to its row.

GLOSSARY

direct recursion: an algorithmic technique in which a method directly invokes itself.

indirect recursion: an algorithmic technique in which a method calls another method, resulting in a chain of calls that ultimately includes a call to the original method.

object recursion: a recursive technique in which an object builds a solution by obtaining a solution to a simpler version of the problem from a component that is similar to itself.

recursion: a problem solving technique in which a general case problem solution is built from a solution to a slightly simpler version of the problem.

structural recursion: a structure in which an object has a component of the same class as itself.

CHAPTER 18

Failures and exceptions

Though we would probably like to ignore the issue, we must admit that even the most carefully designed system may fail. In this chapter, we address the issue of failure: what it means for a system to fail, what are the possible causes of failure, and how a system failure can be handled.

We must first understand the mechanism provided by the language for detecting and dealing with failure. This is the *exception mechanism*. Exceptions are the means by which a method detects and reports failure, and are modeled by the class *Exception* and its subclasses.

Once we understand how the mechanism works, we must consider how to use it appropriately. What are the possible causes of failure, and what actions can a method legitimately take in the event of failure?

We conclude by noting that an application can define and generate its own exceptions, and by briefly considering what can be done about failures caused by logical errors in the program.

18.1 Failures

By *failure* we mean the inability of a system, at run-time, to accomplish its intended purpose. Since failure of a system ultimately is caused by failure of a method, we focus our discussion on method failure. We must consider what can cause a method to fail, and what we can do about it.

A method can fail for two fundamental reasons. It can fail because of

- a logical error in its implementation (a programming "bug"); or
- its inability to obtain some needed resource from the environment.

If a program contains an error, there is rarely anything that the program itself can do about it at run-time. The most we can hope for is a helpful error message that will assist in identifying and locating the problem.

The second situation includes a wide range of possibilities. A system may need resources from the hardware, the operating system, the file system, the network, a data base, and a user to achieve its purpose. For instance, it may need to acquire additional virtual memory, access to a particular file, or get input data in a particular format. In each case, the environment in which the system is running may be unable to provide the needed resource.

The occurrence of a detectable, abnormal situation that may lead to system failure is termed an *exception*. In many instances of program error, and in most instances of unavailable resources, exceptions are detected by the interpreter or run-time system. For example, if a program attempts to execute a query s.name() when s is *null*, the run-time system will detect the error. Similarly, if a program attempts to access a file that does not exist, the file system will report the problem to the run-time system. Clearly, we cannot expect the run-time system to detect every, or even most, logical errors. In some cases though, we can design the program so that the program itself will detect some logical errors.

Which exceptions we expect to occur and what we want to do about them depend on the circumstances in which the system is run. For instance, we may not expect program bugs in a mature, thoroughly tested system, but we are likely to encounter a number of logical errors during program development, and be actively concerned with their detection. Similarly, the kinds of resource acquisition problems we anticipate depend on the specific environment in which the system is used. Thus we can rarely give a definitive answer as to how to handle a particular possible failure.

> **exception:** the occurrence of a detectable, abnormal situation which may lead to system failure.

18.2   The Java exception mechanism

The facilities provided by the language for detecting, reporting, and handling exceptions are collectively referred to as the *exception mechanism*. Before we examine it in detail, we must emphasize that the exception mechanism is not just another control structure. Its purpose is to deal with abnormal conditions: specifically, with conditions that lead to failure. You should *never use the exception mechanism to handle normal, expected events*.

As we mentioned above, an exception can be detected by the run-time system or by the program itself. We consider run-time system detected exceptions first.

The Java run-time system or interpreter detects certain run-time errors, such as attempts to divide by zero or to use a *null* reference when an object is required.

The run-time system notifies the program of the error by *throwing an exception*. An exception is said to be thrown from the point in the program at which the error occurred. (A program can also explicitly throw an exception, as we'll see shortly.)

A thrown exception involves a *transfer of control*: the processor stops executing the current sequence of statements, and begins executing statements at a different point in the program. The exception is said to be *caught* or *handled* at the point to which control is transferred.

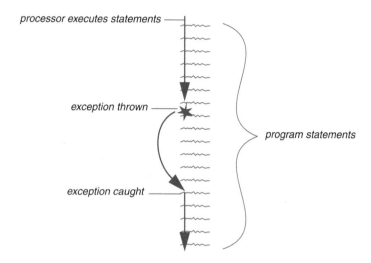

18.2.1   Exceptions as objects

An exception is modeled by an instance of the Java class *Throwable*. An object of this class carries information about the exception from the point at which the exception occurs to the point at which it is caught. The fundamental Java exception class hierarchy is shown in Figure 18.1.

The class *Error* and its subclasses represent conditions from which an ordinary program is not generally expected to recover. It includes linking and loading errors, and errors resulting from system resource limitations. We will not consider it further. Exceptions that an ordinary program might be interested in are instances of *Exception* and its subclasses.

A few of the standard exception classes defined by Java and detected by the run-time system are given below. They are all subclasses of *RuntimeException*.

- *ArithmeticException*: an exceptional arithmetic situation has arisen, such as an integer division with zero divisor.

- *ClassCastException*: an attempt has been made to cast a reference to an inappropriate type.

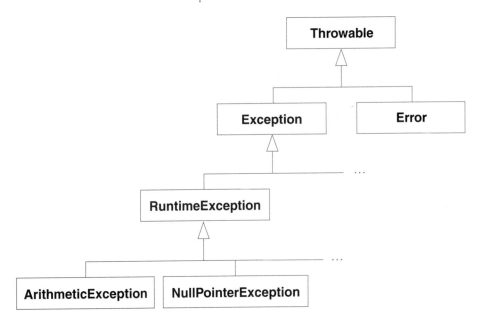

Figure 18.1 **Java Exception Hierarchy.**

- *IllegalArgumentException*: a method was invoked with an invalid or inappropriate argument, or invoked on an inappropriate object.
- *NullPointerException*: an attempt was made to use a null reference in a case where an object reference was required.
- *SecurityException*: a security violation was detected.

18.2.2 Catching exceptions

Exceptions are caught or handled with a *try-catch* statement. The somewhat baroque syntax is as follows:

```
try {
    statements₁
} catch ( exception parameter₁ ) {
    statements₂
} catch ( exception parameter₂ ) {
    statements₃
} …
```

The statement begins with the key word **try**, followed by a sequence of statements (possibly including local variable definitions) called the *try block*. The *try* block is followed by one or more *catch clauses*, which are also called *exception handlers*.

Each *catch* clause has a parameter of type *Exception* or one of its subclasses. For instance:

```
try {
    statements₁
} catch ( ArithmeticException e ) {
    statements₂
} catch ( NullPointerException e ) {
    statements₃
} catch ( Exception e ) {
    statements₄
}
```

As noted above, *ArithmeticException* and *NullPointerException* are subclasses of *Exception*. The run-time system throws an *ArithmeticException* if there is an attempt to divide by zero and throws a *NullPointerException* if there is an attempt to use a *null* reference when a reference to an object is needed.

To execute the *try-catch* statement, the processor first performs the statements of the *try* block—labeled *statements₁* in the above example. If no exceptions occur, the *try-catch* is complete, and the *catch* clauses are ignored.

If an exception is thrown during execution of the *try* block, an attempt is made to match the exception to the *catch* clause parameters. The first *catch* clause whose parameter type is the same class as the exception or is a superclass of the exception, catches the exception. The mechanism for executing a *catch* clause is very much like the mechanism for invoking a method. An automatic variable is allocated for the parameter of the *catch* clause, and the variable is initialized with a reference to the thrown *Exception* instance. Then the body of the *catch* clause is performed.

In the above example, if an *ArithmeticException* (or a subclass of *ArithmeticException*) is thrown during execution of *statements₁*, the exception is caught by the first *catch* clause, and *staments₂* are executed. A *NullPointerException* is caught by the second *catch* clause (*statements₃* executed). An *IllegalArgumentException* is caught by the third *catch* clause: *IllegalArgumentException* is neither a subclass of *ArithmeticException* nor of *NullPointerException*, but is a subclass of *Exception*. In each case, the parameter e references an object that models the exception.

Let's fill out the example a bit, to make sure we understand the mechanism. Suppose i and j are **int** variables, name a *String*, and s a *Student* variable. Consider the following:

```
1.  try {
2.      i = i/i;
3.      j = 0;
4.      name = s.name();
```

```
5.        j = 1;
6.    } catch (ArithmeticException e) {
7.        j = 3;
8.    } catch (NullPointerException e) {
9.        j = 4;
10.   } catch (Exception e) {
11.       if (e instanceof IllegalArgumentException)
12.          j = 6;
13.       else
14.          j = 5;
15.   }
16.   System.out.println("The value of j is " + j);
```

The *try-catch* statement starts at line 1 and ends at line 15. The command invocation System.out.println at line 16 follows the *try-catch* statement. It writes out the value of the variable j.

Note that the *try-catch* is set up to catch an *ArithmeticException* or a *NullPointerException* explicitly. The *catch* clause at line 10 will catch any other exception.

In each *catch* clause, e is a formal parameter, an automatic variable, allocated and initialized when an exception is caught by the handler. It will contain a reference to the thrown *Exception* instance.

When the *try-catch* is executed, line 2 is first done. If i is 0, this statement causes an *ArithmeticException*, and control is transferred to the exception handler at line 6. Line 3 is never reached. The variable j is set to 3 at line 7, and the *try-catch* statement is finished. The remaining *catch* clauses are ignored. Line 16 writes out the number 3.

If i is not 0, line 2 completes successfully and line 3 and 4 are then done. If s happens to contain the *null* reference, attempting to query s.name() will generate a *NullPointerException*. Control is transferred to the exception handler at line 8. The variable j is set to 4, and the *try-catch* statement is finished. Line 16 writes out the number 4.

It is possible that execution of line 4 will result in an exception that is neither an *ArithmeticException* nor a *NullPointerException*. Such an exception will be caught by the handler at line 10. The formal parameter e will reference the object representing the exception. Line 11 checks to see if the exception is an instance of *IllegalArgumentException*. (Exactly what causes a *IllegalArgumentException* is not particularly relevant here; it is simply another subclass of *Exception*. Of course, the *IllegalArgumentException* could have been caught with a separate *catch* clause.) The variable j is set to 5 or 6 accordingly.

Otherwise, if the query s.name() completes successfully, j is set to 1 at line 5, and the *try-catch* statement is finished. The *catch* clauses are ignored. Line 16 write out the number 1.

18.2.3 Propagated exceptions

What happens if a method does not catch an exception? That is, what happens if an exception is thrown by the execution of a statement that is not part of a *try-catch*, or if an exception is generated that does not match any of the *catch* clauses? In such a case, the exception is *propagated* to the calling method.

For instance, suppose an exception is thrown during execution of the *Student* method name, invoked from line 4 of the above example. If the method name does not handle the exception, the exception is propagated to the caller. In effect, the exception is thrown again at line 4. It will then be caught either by the handler at line 6, or by the handler at line 8, or by the handler at line 10, depending on the class of the exception.

An uncaught exception propagates up the *call chain* from each method to its caller. If no method in the call chain catches the exception, the program terminates with an error message. Suppose method nim.NimGame.main invokes method nim.NimUI.start which invokes method nim.GameManager.play which invokes method nim.Player.makeMove which attempts to divide by zero. If the *ArithmeticException* generated is not caught by makeMove, it will be propagated to play, and then to start, and then to main until a handler is found. (See Figure 18.2.) If none of the four methods catches the exception, the program terminates with an error message that might look something like this:

```
java.lang.ArithmeticException: / by zero
        at nim.Player.makeMove(Player.java:36)
        at nim.GameManager.play(GameManager.java:114)
        at nim.NimUI.start(NimUI.java:29)
        at nim.NimGame.main(NimGame.java:11)
```

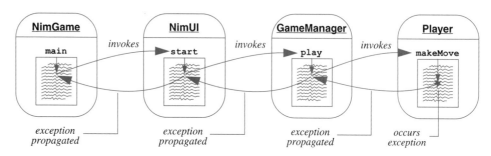

Figure 18.2 **Propagation of an exception up the call chain.**

18.2.4 Checked and unchecked exceptions

The class *RuntimeException* and its subclasses are referred to as *unchecked exception classes*. Other exception classes are *checked exception classes*. The compiler verifies that checked exceptions are appropriately handled by analyzing which checked exceptions can result from execution of a method or constructor. If it is possible for a method to throw a *checked* exception to its caller, the method's specification must explicitly express this possibility with a *throws* clause. That is, a *throws* clause must be included in a method specification if it is possible for a checked exception to be thrown in the method, and the method does not catch the exception. On the other hand, a method's specification need not document the possibility that an *unchecked* exception may be thrown and propagate to the caller.

For instance, the class *IOException* is not a subclass of *RuntimeException*, and so is a checked exception class. The method readLine defined in the class *java.io.BufferedReader* can throw the exception *IOException*. (It's not important what this method does, though you can probably make a good guess.) The method readLine is specified as:

```
public String readLine() throws IOException
```

An *IOException* that occurs in readLine is propagated to readLine's caller. A method that invokes readLine and does not explicitly handle a resulting *IOException* propagates the exception to its caller—that is, it also throws an *IOException*. Such a method must also specify that it can throw an *IOException*. Consider the following, where input is a *java.io.BufferedReader*:

```
public void skip () throws IOException {
    String s;
    s = input.readLine();
}
```

As you can see, this method does not catch an *IOException* that might be generated by the call to readLine. Such an exception is simply propagated to skip's caller. Thus the specification of the method skip must include the **throws** IOException clause.

If the method can throw several different checked exceptions, the classes are simply enumerated in the method specification. For example

```
public void skip () throws EOFException,
    FileNotFoundException {
    ...
}
```

Since *RuntimeExceptions* can occur almost everywhere, Java's designers thought it pointless to require documenting their possible occurrences.

18.3   Dealing with failure: using exceptions

Now that we understand generally how Java's exception mechanism works, we need to consider how to use the mechanism to deal with failure. We will examine how a method can fail, and what we can do in each case.

A method fails if it is not able to accomplish its intended purpose. In Chapter 7, we introduced the notion of programming by contract. A method invocation is viewed as a "contract" between the client and the server, specified by method preconditions and postconditions. The client must make sure that the preconditions are satisfied when the method is called, in which case the server guarantees that the postconditions will hold when the method completes. The server promises to fulfill the contract only if the client satisfies the preconditions. The server has no obligation with regard to the contract if the client fails to meet the preconditions. As we have observed, the primary reasons for this approach are to simplify code and to make each component's responsibilities explicit.

Note that whether a method fails depends on what it promises to do. For instance, in Chapter 12 we specified a search method something like this:

public int indexOf (Object item)
> The index of the first occurrence of the specified item on this *List*, or – 1
> if this List does not contain the specified item.

This method does not guarantee to return a legal list index. The possibility that the argument is not on the list is treated as normal. If the argument is not on the list, the method returns –1, and the client must be prepared to deal with this result.

Suppose the method was specified like this:

public int indexOf (Object item)
> The index of the first occurrence of the specified item on this *List*.

Now the method guarantees to find the item and return a legal index. If the item is not on the list, the method fails. This would not be a very good specification, since in general we have no way of knowing *a priori* whether or not the requested item is on the list.

Finally, we could make it the client's responsibility to ensure that the item searched for was on the list:

public int indexOf (Object item)
> The index of the first occurrence of the specified item on this *List*.
>
> **require:**
> this.get(i).equals(item), for some i.

Here, the method *requires* that the item be on the list. It is a program error if the method is called with an argument not on the list, but not a failure of *this* method. Again, this is not a particularly good specification, since it puts an unreasonable burden on the client. The work involved in determining whether or not a particular item is on a list is almost surely equivalent to what is required to locate the item. Essentially, the client is asked to find the item on the list before calling this method to find the item on the list.

Specifically then, a method fails if it is unable to complete a contract even though its client has satisfied all preconditions. If a method detects that it will fail, it *must report failure* to its client. A method must *never* simply return to its caller, knowing that it has not satisfied the terms of the contract.

We can distinguish three cases in which a method may not be able to accomplish its purpose, even though its client has satisfied all preconditions.

- There is a logical error in the method. This is the most problematic case: we cannot in general expect an erroneous program to recognize correctly the fact that it is erroneous.

- The method is not able to obtain necessary resources from its environment. We have mentioned a few examples above, such as an inaccessible file.

- The method invokes another method (a "subcontractor") which fails.

18.3.1 Dealing with exceptions

Let's consider the latter two cases first. We can assume that the method is notified of the failure by an exception. In order to get a resource, the method performs some action, such as invoking a system library method. If the resource is not available, this results in an exception. If the method calls a server and the server fails, the server should notify the method by throwing an exception. (Of course, it is possible that a server fails because of an undetected programming error, and returns without throwing an exception. We'll worry about this case later.)

In terms of the mechanism, we have seen that we can deal with an exception by catching the exception or by letting the exception propagate to the caller.

In terms of logical structure, there are two ways of dealing with a failure:

- clean up and report the failure to the caller (by throwing an exception); or

- try to correct the situation that caused the exception, and try again.

There are no other possibilities. A method *must not* return to its caller without either satisfying the contract or reporting failure.

Notice that there is no mention of writing "error messages." "Reporting failure" means throwing an exception. If necessary, the production of error messages can be allocated as a specific responsibility to some object. It is almost never the responsibility of the failing method.

An example should help explain the point. One of the constructors for the class *java.io.FileReader* requires a *String* argument denoting a file to be accessed. The constructor creates a *FileReader* instance that gets input from the named file. (Specifics of the class *FileReader* are not important to the example.)

```
public FileReader (String fileName)
    throws FileNotFoundException, SecurityException
```

This constructor throws a *FileNotFoundException* if the named file does not exist in the file system, and throws a *SecurityException* if the program does not have permission to read the file. (*SecurityException* is a subclass of *RuntimeException*, and so is an unchecked exception. Therefore it need not be explicitly mentioned in the method specification. We include it simply to clarify the example.) The constructor reports failure to its caller by throwing the appropriate exception.

Suppose we are writing a method that creates a *FileReader* by invoking this constructor. How do we handle failure of the constructor? Probably the most typical approach is to give up and report to our client that we have failed. Generally if our server fails, we have no choice but to fail also.

To report failure means to throw an exception. If we simply do not catch the exception thrown by the *FileReader* constructor, it will be propagated to our caller. Our method might look something like this:

```
public void getSomeData ()
    throws FileNotFoundException, SecurityException {
    FileReader in;
    in = new FileReader("DataFile");
    ...
}
```

If the *FileReader* constructor fails and throws, say, a *FileNotFoundException*, the exception is propagated to the caller of getSomeData, since getSomeData doesn't catch the exception. (Again, *SecurityException* does not need to be mentioned explicitly in the method specification, since it is an unchecked exception.)

We can also catch the exception, do some cleanup, and then throw either the same exception or a different one to our caller.

We use a *throw* statement to throw an exception explicitly. Its format is

```
throw exception;
```

For instance:

```
public void getSomeData ()
    throws FileNotFoundException, SecurityException {
    FileReader in;
    try {
        in = new FileReader("DataFile");
        ...
    } catch (FileNotFoundException e) {
        // cleanup
        throw e;
    } catch (SecurityException e) {
        // cleanup
        throw e;
    }
}
```

Here, the method `getSomeData` catches a *FileNotFoundException* or a *SecurityException*, does some cleanup, and throws the same exception to its caller.

Before we go on, we should briefly mention what we mean by "cleanup." A method cannot know how its caller will respond to the exception. The caller might be able to recover from the method's failure and continue. In that event, it is important that the method leave its object in a consistent state; that is, a state in which all class invariants are satisfied. Therefore upon discovering that it will fail, a method should make sure that the object is consistent before reporting failure to its caller.

Occasionally, it is possible to attempt recovery from a server failure. To concoct an example, suppose we expect the file `DataFile` to be occasionally locked by another program, and that we get a *SecurityException* if we attempt to access the locked file with the *FileReader* constructor. Suppose further that this is likely to be a transient situation: if we wait a few seconds, the lock will be removed. We can write our method so that if we get a *SecurityException* when we try to create the *FileReader*, we wait a bit and then try one more time to access the file. For instance:

```
1.  public void getSomeData ()
2.      throws FileNotFoundException, SecurityException {
3.      FileReader in;
4.      boolean success = false;      // DataFile opened
5.                                    // successfully
6.      int tryNumber = 0;            // number of tries to
7.                                    // open DataFile
8.      int delay = 5*1000;           // wait in millisecs
9.                                    // between tries
10.     while (!success)
11.        try {
12.            tryNumber = tryNumber + 1;
13.            in = new FileReader("DataFile");
14.            success = true;
15.            ...
16.        } catch (SecurityException e) {
17.            if (tryNumber == 1)
18.                try {
19.                    Thread.sleep(delay);
20.                } catch (InterruptedException e) {}
21.            else
22.                throw e;
23.        }
24.  }
```

A few things to note in the above implementation:

- The *FileReader* constructor can generate two different exceptions: *FileNotFoundException* and *SecurityException*. The first is not caught, and is propagated to the caller. The second is caught by the *catch* clause at line 16.

- The actual body of the method is the *try* block of lines 12–15. The *while* loop is wrapped around the *try* statement to permit a "re-try" in case the *FileReader* constructor fails. Note that the body of the *while* loop consists of a single *try-catch* statement.

- The variable `success` indicates whether or not we have successfully opened the file `DataFile`. If invocation of the *FileReader* constructor of line 13 is successful, `success` is set to **true** at line 14, and the rest of the method, indicated by line 15, is performed. Completing line 15 completes the *try* statement, which is the body of the loop. The *while* condition (`!success`) is again evaluated, and evaluates to *false*. This terminates the loop, and the method is complete.

- The variable `tryNumber` indicates how many times we have tried to open the file `DataFile`. If the *FileReader* constructor throws a *SecurityException* when we first reach line 14, the exception is caught at line 16. Since `tryNumber` is 1, the process waits about five seconds (that's what the `sleep` invocation does). This completes the *catch* clause, which completes the *try* statement. Since `success` is still *false*, a second iteration of the *while* loop is begun. If the *FileReader* constructor succeeds this time, everything proceeds normally. If the constructor again throws a *SecurityException*, it is again caught at line 16. But this time `tryNumber` is 2. We give up and report failure to the caller by throwing at line 22 the same *SecurityException* we caught.

18.3.2 Application defined exceptions

It is sometimes useful to define our own exception classes. For instance, a client of the `getSomeData` method may only be interested in the fact that data was not obtained, and not in the specific reason we couldn't access the file. We could handle this by defining our own exception class, say *NoDataException*, and throwing this exception if we fail to get data for any reason.

We define our own exception classes by extending the class *Exception* or one of its subclasses. Exception classes typically provide two constructors, one requiring no argument and the other requiring a *String* error message. The definition of a program-defined exception class is often as simple as the following:

```
public class NoDataException extends Exception {
    public NoDataException () {
        super();
    }
    public NoDataException (String s) {
        super(s);
    }
} // end of class NoDataException
```

We can now write a variation of `getSomeData` that throws a *NoDataException* as follows. Note that we explicitly create a new instance of *NoDataException* to throw.

```
public void getSomeData () throws NoDataException {
    FileReader in;
    try {
        in = new FileReader("DataFile");
        ...
    } catch (FileNotFoundException e) {
        // cleanup
        throw new NoDataException(
            "File does not exist");
    } catch (SecurityException e) {
        // cleanup
        throw new NoDataException(
            "File cannot be accessed");
    }
}
```

Another reason for defining an exception class is to pass state information from the method detecting the exception to the method that will handle it. Such information can be essential in determining the course of a retry or useful in providing a more informative error message before the program is aborted. For example, if incorrectly formatted data is encountered while reading a file, we may want to report the location of the bad data. Such information can be packaged in an exception by the method discovering the error and passed along to the method responsible for reporting the error. It can be included in the *String* argument or as an explicit component of a program defined exception. For instance, an exception that reports which line in a file contains badly formatted data might be defined as follows:

```
public class BadDataException extends Exception {

    public BadDataException (int lineNumber) {
        super();
        this.lineNumber = lineNumber;
    }

    /**
     * Line containing bad data
     */
    public int lineNumber () {
        return this.lineNumber;
    }

    private int lineNumber;

} // end of class BadDataException
```

The method detecting the error creates an instance of *BadDataException* containing the number of the line with the bad data. The method handing the exception can query the *BadDataException* to determine line number.

Note that the purpose of an exception object is to carry information from the point where the error was detected to the point where the error is handled or reported. Thus exception objects are structured as immutable objects; their interface includes no state-changing commands.

18.3.3 Dealing with logical errors

As we mentioned above, detecting logical errors is an inherently difficult problem. A logical error often results in the run-time system throwing an exception, such as a *NullPointerException* or *ArithmeticException*. There is generally very little to do in this situation except fail. Sometimes a logical error causes a method to produce reasonable but incorrect results. In such cases, it may be virtually impossible to detect the error mechanically.

There are some instances, however, when we can get a good handle on the source of a logical error. Specifically, we can check preconditions, postconditions, and invariants. If a client invokes a method without preconditions being satisfied, it is an error. We have defined an exception and simple verification method to handle this case:

```
public class PreconditionException
    extends RuntimeException
        Failure because a precondition is not satisfied.

public class Require {
    static public void condition (boolean precondition)
    {
        if (!precondition)
            throw new PreconditionException(
                "Precondition not satisfied.");
    }
    static public void notNull (Object reference) {
        if (reference == null)
            throw new PreconditionException (
                "Null reference.");
    }
} //end of class Require
```

The method `condition` simply checks to see if its argument is *true* and throws a newly created *PreconditionException* if it is not. Since `condition` does not catch this exception, it is propagated to its caller.

We can use this mechanism to catch precondition violations without seriously complicating the structure of the method. For instance

```
/*
 * Interchange l.get(i) and l.get(j)
 *    require:
 *        0 <= i, j < l.size()
 *
 *    ...
 */
private void interchange (List l, int i, int j) {
   Require.condition(0 <= i && i < l.size());
   Require.condition(0 <= j && j < l.size());

   ...
```

If a client invokes the method without satisfying the preconditions, an exception is thrown reporting the nature and location of the error.

A method that does not satisfy its postconditions is also an error, and we can devise a similar method for checking that case.

```
public class PostconditionException
    extends RuntimeException
        Failure because a postcondition is not satisfied.


public class Ensure {
   static public void condition (
      boolean postcondition) {
      if (!postcondition)
      throw new PostconditionException(
          "Postcondition not satisfied.");
   }
} //end of class Ensure
```

Postconditions tend to be a bit trickier to handle than preconditions, since they often involve comparing the object's state *after* method execution to the object's state *prior* to execution. Such a condition can only be verified if previous state information has been saved.

Finally, invariants tell us what conditions must hold at various points in the program. We define one more exception for reporting violated invariants:

```
public class AssertionException
    extends RuntimeException
        Failure because an assertion is not satisfied.


public class Assert {
   static public void condition (boolean condition) {
      if (!condition)
         throw new AssertionException(
            "Assertion not satisfied.");
   }
} //end of class Assert
```

As with postconditions, invariants are often too complex to verify with a simple condition. Nevertheless, we can sometimes identify conditions worth validating at key points in the program.

Whether to include such checks depends to a large degree on where we are in the development process. We are much more concerned with logical errors early in the implementation, when the system is relatively unstable and has not been thoroughly tested and verified.

18.4 Summary

In this chapter, we addressed the issue of failure and examined the exception mechanism provided by Java to deal with failures. We saw that a method can fail for two fundamental reasons. It can fail because of:

- a logical error in its implementation (a programming "bug"); or

- its inability to obtain some needed resource from the environment.

An *exception mechanism* is provided by the language for detecting, reporting, and handling failure. An exception is a detectable, abnormal situation which may lead to system failure, and is modeled by an instance of the Java class *Exception*. An instance of this class carries information about the exception from the point at which the exception occurred (is thrown) to the point at which it is handled (is caught).

The language structure for handling exceptions is the *try-catch* statement. Exceptions thrown in the statements that comprise the *try* block can be handled in one of the *catch* clauses. An exception thrown in a method and not caught in the method is propagated to the method's caller.

A method fails if it cannot satisfy its contract even though the client has satisfied the method's preconditions. A method that fails must not simply return to its client. It must inform the client of the failure by throwing an exception.

When a client is notified of a server's failure (by the server's throwing an exception), there are only two possible courses of action the client can take. The client can

- attempt to correct the situation that caused the failure, and try again; or

- report failure to its caller, by throwing or propagating an exception.

Most often, the second alternative is the only one practical.

An application can define its own exception classes, by extending the class *Exception* of one of its subclasses. Program defined exceptions can be useful in providing more specific information about the cause of the failure.

Finally, logical errors, by their very nature, can be difficult to detect. Nevertheless, it can be useful, particularly during program development, to verify explicitly conditions such as preconditions that must hold in a correct program.

EXERCISES

18.1   Suppose a search method is specified as:

> **public int** indexOf (Object item) **throws** ItemNotFound
>> The index of the first occurrence of the specified item on this *List*; throws
>> *ItemNotFound* exception if this *List* does not contain the specified item.

and client code is written like this:

```
try {
    i = 1.indexOf(item);
    // handle the case in which item is on list 1.
} catch (ItemNotFound e) {
    // handle the case in which time is not on list 1.
}
```

Comment on the reasonableness of the method specification and the method use.

18.2   Section 18.3.1 illustrates how to try again by means of a *while* loop. Sketch how
this could be accomplished with a recursive call instead.

18.3   As part of a user interface, the user is required at one point to key in either 'Y' or
'N' indicating "yes" or "no." The method responsible for getting the user's input
promises to deliver either 'Y' or 'N' and fails (by throwing an exception) if it cannot. Sketch how the "try-again" response to failure can be used to prompt the user
continually until an appropriate response is given. Comment on the reasonableness of this approach.

GLOSSARY

catch clause: a syntactic part of a *try-catch* statement that handles one class of
exceptions.

checked exception: an exception that is not an instance of *RuntimeException* or of
one of its subclasses. Methods that can throw checked exceptions must document this face with a *throws* clause in the method heading.

exception: the occurrence of a detectable, abnormal situation that may lead to system failure. Also, an instance of the class *Exception* that carries information
about the cause of an abnormal situation.

failure: the inability at run time of a system or method to accomplish its intended
purpose.

try block: the syntactic part of a *try-catch* statement that defines the "normal"
execution of the statement.

try-catch statement: a Java statement used to detect and handle exceptions.

unchecked exception: an exception that is an instance of *RuntimeException* or of one of its subclasses. Unchecked exceptions can occur almost anywhere in a program.

CHAPTER 19

Building the user interface

In this chapter, we look at the fundamental classes used for implementing a graphical user interface. In Java, these classes are provided primarily in a user interface library known as *Swing*. Swing is an enhancement of a library called the *Abstract Window Toolkit*, or AWT. The AWT has been available as long as the language itself and has undergone substantial evolution since its original design. Swing is the most recent extension of the AWT, intended to provide the functionality and flexibility necessary to develop substantial commercial applications.

The Java user interface libraries are large and complex, containing several hundred classes and interfaces. This complexity is probably unavoidable in any set of tools capable of supporting the degree of customization required in building sophisticated, portable, extensible graphical user interfaces. Furthermore, the Swing components are built as an extension of previous AWT library elements. The designers likely had in mind maintaining some degree of compatibility between Swing and existing applications built with the AWT and providing a relatively straightforward path for upgrading applications to Swing. Maintaining compatibility between versions of a software system almost inevitably leads to increased complexity in the later versions.

A comprehensive discussion of the Swing components and their use would require thousands of pages and is clearly beyond the scope of this text. Our intention is not to develop proficiency in designing user interfaces with Swing. Rather, we want to understand some of the more fundamental concepts and take a brief look at a few of the most central classes. This will serve our purpose, which is to see how an event-driven, window-based application is structured.

Swing will also serve as a case study of how a large library is organized. However, many Swing design decisions were influenced both by the existing AWT libraries and by the need to provide a degree of flexibility well beyond the scope of this discussion. As a result, we cannot always offer a convincing justification for the underlying structures of the user interface libraries. Fortunately, there are several good reference texts available to the reader who needs detailed information regarding Swing and its use.

19.1   The system interface

As we have seen, the *interface* and the *model* are two of the principal components of a software system. The model is the basic problem representation and problem-solving component; the interface handles interaction with the external world. When the external world is a person, we refer to the interface as a *user interface*. We have concentrated previously on design and implementation of the model. Now we take a closer look at the user interface.

In order to distinguish it from the underlying computational environment, we refer to the program or software system we are building to solve a specific problem as an *application*.

19.1.1   Algorithm-driven interfaces

There are two fundamental models for describing how an application interacts with its environment, that we'll call *algorithm-driven* and *event-driven*. While these two approaches are not truly different semantically, an application's structure will be markedly influenced by the approach adopted.

In an algorithm-driven approach, the application determines exactly what information it needs from the environment, and when it needs it. The application has access to several *streams* of data. A stream is essentially just a sequence of bytes. If the bytes denote characters, in the ASCII character set for instance, we refer to the stream as a *character stream*. Otherwise, we refer to the stream as a *binary stream*. Some of these streams are *sources* of data, and are called *input streams*; others are *destinations*, called *output streams*. If, during execution, the application determines that it needs data from a particular input stream, it explicitly *reads* the data from the stream. Similarly, the application explicitly determines what and when to *write* to an output stream.

Figure 19.1 Input and output streams.

The actual source of the data in an input stream can be a user's keyboard, a file, another program, an external device, *etc*. Similarly, the target of an output stream can be a user's display screen, a file, another program, and so on. The Java compiler is an example of an application with an algorithm interface. It has one input character stream, and two output streams. Input stream characters come from the source file being compiled. The compiler writes the binary compiled byte code to a "class" file, and writes error messages and warnings, as a character stream, to the user's display.

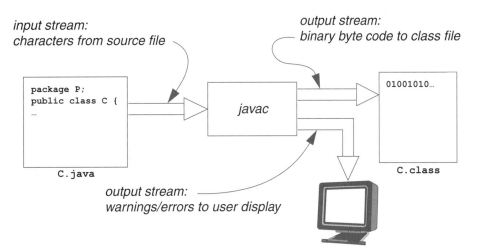

Figure 19.2 **Input and output streams for *javac*.**

The user interface for simple nim game developed in Chapter 9 read information such as the number of sticks to play with from the user's keyboard and wrote the results of each game as an output character stream to the user's display. Running the game results in a dialogue like the following on the user's display, with the user's response indicated by italics:

```
Enter number of sticks.
3
Player Player 1 takes 2 leaving 1 sticks.
Player Player 2 takes 1 leaving 0 sticks.
Game over. Player 1 won.
To play again, enter 1; to stop enter 0
1
Enter number of sticks.
```

Note that the application specifically performs input and output actions. It prompts the user (writes output) when it needs data, and then reads the user's response (reads input).

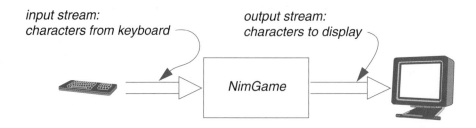

Figure 19.3 **Input and output streams for** *NimGame*.

Exactly where input data comes from and where output data goes is often not important to the application. There are many applications known as "filters" that read input from a single input stream called *standard input*, write output to an output stream called *standard output*, and write error messages to a stream called *standard error*.

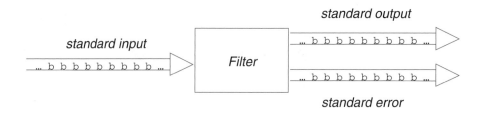

Figure 19.4 **Input and output streams for a** *filter*.

The actual source and destination of the input and output is irrelevant to the filter. Input can come from and output go to a user, a file, or another program. The source of input and destination of output is determined by the operating system when the program is run.

We used simple library classes in Chapter 10 to read and write character streams. We will not further consider Java's extensive facilities for stream-based input and output. For the remainder of this chapter we concentrate on event-driven interfaces.

19.1.2   Event-driven interfaces

While the application is active in an algorithm-driven interface, it is passive in an event-driven system. In an event-driven system, the application waits for something to happen in the environment: that is, it waits for an *event*. When an event occurs, the application responds to the event, and then waits for the next event.

> **event-driven:** an input-output model in which the application waits for an event to occur, responds to the event, and waits for the next event.

Real-time systems are typically event driven, and applications with a graphical, window-based user interface (usually called simply a *graphical user interface*, or GUI) are almost always event driven. We are concerned with the latter here.

An application with a window-based interface provides the user with a graphical "control panel" containing a range of options. There may be menus, buttons, text fields, *etc*. After displaying the interface, the application waits for the user to do something. The user can press a button, choose a menu item, enter text in a text field, or exercise any other option provided. When the user performs an action, the application responds to this event, and then waits for the next user action.

Figure 19.5 **A graphical user interface window, offering a number of options.**

In a window-based system, we assume that there is a native windowing system (such as Windows NT™ or Motif®) that actually detects events like mouse clicks, mouse movement, key strokes, *etc*., and manages the display. (There are operating systems, managing embedded systems in consumer products for instance, that do not have native windowing systems.) A Java application interacts with the native windowing system through AWT components.

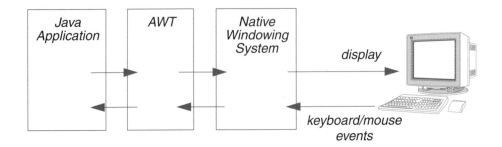

Figure 19.6   **Java applications interact with the native widowing system through the AWT.**

The application communicates with the native windowing system (through AWT classes) to create a display. Events are detected by the native windowing system and *delivered* to the application. The application performs some action in response to the event (possibly changing the display), and then waits for notification of the next event.

19.2   An introduction to Swing

19.2.1   Components

A graphical user interface is made up of *components* (sometimes called *widgets*). Components are things like windows, buttons, checkboxes, menus, scroll bars, text fields, labels, and so on. A component occupies display screen real estate: it has location, size, shape, color, *etc*.

The Java Swing components are defined in a class library contained in the package `javax.swing` and its subpackages. An application uses these classes to build and manage a graphical user interface. One of the fundamental classes in `javax.swing` is the abstract class *JComponent*. Most of the components created by an application are instances of some *JComponent* subclass. A few of the more elementary subclasses of *JComponent* are as follows.

JButton   a simple push button that can be "pushed" with a mouse click.

JCheckBox   a button that can be toggled on or off, and displays its state to the user.

JComboBox   a drop-down list with an optional editable text field. The user can either key in a value or select a value from the drop-down list.

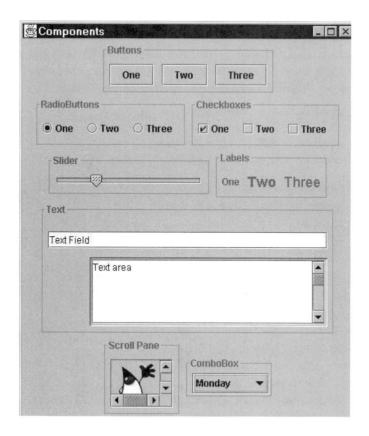

Figure 19.7 **Some Swing** *components.*

JFileChooser	a component providing a simple mechanism for selecting a file.
JLabel	a component containing a short text string, an image, or both. A label does not react to input events.
JList	a component that allows a user to select one or more items from a list.
JRadioButton	a button that can be toggled on or off, and displays its state to the user. Only one radio button in a group can be on.
JScrollPane	a component that manges a scrollable view.
JSlider	a component that lets the user graphically select a value by sliding a knob within a bounded interval.
JTextArea	an area for multiple lines of text; can be editable, or read-only.
JTextField	an area for entering a single line of input.

Some component attributes

JComponent is a subclass of the AWT class *java.awt.Component*, and inherits many of its most obvious properties from that class. Component properties include foreground and background colors, location, and size. (We'll see more as we go along.) The values of these properties can be obtained with queries:

```
public Color getForeground ();
public Color getBackground ();
public Point getLocation ();
public Dimension getSize ();
```

and can be set with methods:

```
public void setForeground (Color fg);
public void setBackground (Color bg);
public void setLocation (Point p);
public void setSize (Dimension d);
```

Many of the methods are overloaded. For instance, there are versions of setLocation and setSize that take two **int** arguments rather than a *Point* or *Dimension*.

Color, *Point*, and *Dimension* are AWT classes (defined in java.awt) that model the obvious notions. Instances of the class *Color* are immutable: once the instance is created, it cannot be changed. The class *Color* defines a number of constant references, such as Color.red, Color.blue, Color.green.

An instance of the class *Point* represents a (relative) position in an x-y coordinate space. Units are pixels[1], and the origin (0,0) is in the upper left. Attributes of a *Point* can be accessed through *public*(!) instance variables x and y:

```
public int x;
public int y;
```

(The methods getX and getY return the coordinates as **double**s. There are no setX and setY methods.)

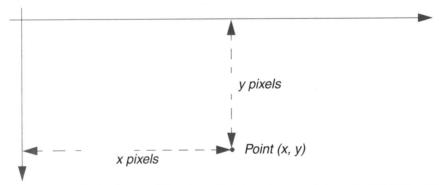

Figure 19.8 **An instance of the class *Point* models a point on the display screen.**

---

1. A pixel is the smallest dot that can be independently colored on a display screen.

An instance of the class *Dimension* encapsulates width and height, again in pixels. Attributes are accessed directly through public instance variables as was the case with Point:

```
public int height;
public int width;
```

(As with *Point*, methods `getHeight` and `getWidth` return the values of the attributes as **double**s.)

19.2.2 Containers

An object that contains components is a *container*. Containers are modeled by the `java.awt` abstract class *Container*. An important simplifying aspect of the library structure is that a *Container* is just another kind of component. That is, the class *Container* is a subclass of the class *Component*. This means that a *Container* can contain another *Container*. Furthermore, the Swing class *JComponent* is a subclass of *Container*. So any *JComponent* can contain other components. This relationship is illustrated in Figure 19.9. In this and subsequent figures, shaded rectangles denote AWT classes, and unshaded rectangles Swing classes.

> **component:** a distinct element of a graphical user interface, such as a button, text field, and so on.
>
> **container:** a graphical user interface component that can contain other components.

The simplest, garden-variety, no-frills container is a *JPanel*. A *JPanel* is generally used just as a place for putting a collection of other components. Components

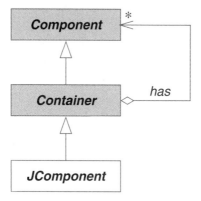

Figure 19.9 **A *JComponent* is-a *Container* is-a *Component*.**

are added to a *Container* with the method add. (There are, in fact, five overloaded versions of add.) For instance, the following creates a *JPanel* and adds two buttons, labeled "on" and "off."

```
JPanel p = new JPanel();
p.add(new JButton("on"));
p.add(new JButton("off"));
```

The class *Container* defines an extensive set of methods for manipulating its contents. For example:

public int getComponentCount()
>   The number of *Components* in this *Container*.

public Component getComponent (**int** n)
>   The *Component* with the specified index.

>   **require:**
>>   0 <= n < this.getComponentCount()

public void remove (Component comp)
>   Remove the specified *Component*.

public void remove (**int** index);
>   Remove the *Component* with the specified index.

>   **require:**
>>   0 <= index < this.getComponentCount()

Top-level containers

A *top-level container* is one that is not contained in any other container. Swing classes *JApplet, JDialog, JFrame*, and *JWindow* are commonly used to provide top-level containers. The standard top-level container for an application's user interface is a *JFrame*. We do not consider the others here.

A *JFrame* is a window with title and border. It can be moved, resized, iconified, *etc.* like any other native system window. A *JFrame* can also have a menu bar. There are two things to note about the class *JFrame*. First, though it is a subclass of *java.awt.Container*, it is not a subclass of *JComponent*. Second, it delegates the responsibility of managing its components to another object, a *JRootPane*.

A *JRootPane* is a *JComponent* whose principal responsibility is to manage the contents of some other container. It is a composite object, including among other things a *content pane*[1]. The content pane is usually a *JPanel*, and is the working area of the *JFrame*, excluding the title, border, and menu.

---

1. A *JRootPane* has a *JLayeredPane,* which actually contains the content pane and an optional *JMenuBar.*

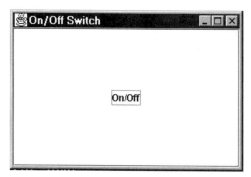

Figure 19.10 **A *JFrame* is a top-level application window.**

The details of a *JRootPane* are not particularly relevant here, and the rationale for the structure are beyond the scope of the present discussion. What is important to remember is that a *JFrame* has a *JRootPane*, which has a content pane. Components are not added directly to the *JFrame*, but to the content pane. The *JFrame*'s content pane can be obtained with the method `getContentPane`, which returns a *Container*. Thus we add a button to a *JFrame* like this:

```
JFrame f = new JFrame("A Frame");
JButton b = new JButton("Press");
Container cp = f.getContentPane();
cp.add(b);
```

JApplet, JDialog, JWindow and *JInternalFrame* also use a *JRootPane* to manage their components. These classes implement the interface *RootPaneContainer*.

> **Aside**: Our discussion is centered on *applications*: that is, self-contained programs. Java is also commonly used to write *applets*. Applets are small programs intended to be run within another program, typically within a web browser such as *Netscape Navigator*™. The top-level container for an applet is an instance of the class *JApplet*.

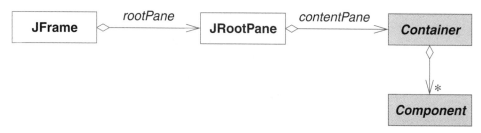

Figure 19.11 **A *JFrame* delegates responsibility for managing components to a *JRootPane*.**

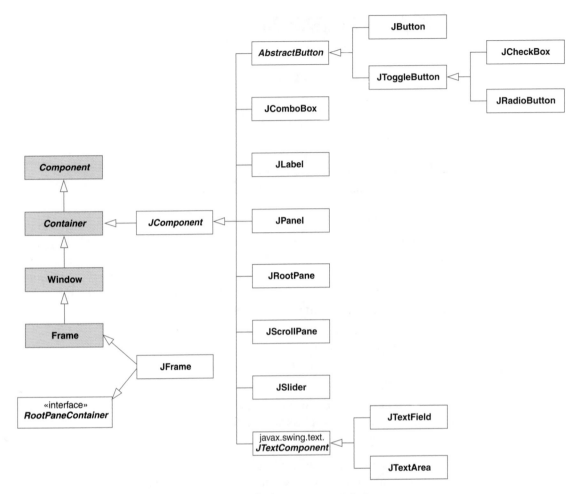

Figure 19.12 **Some of the Swing component classes.**

Heavyweight components and component peers

Instances of the classes *JApplet*, *JDialog*, *JFrame*, and *JWindow* are called *heavy-weight* components. Other Swing components, in particular instances of subclasses of *JComponent*, are *lightweight* components. When a heavyweight component is created, an associated native GUI component called a *peer* is also created. For instance, if the application creates a *JFrame*, a frame peer will also be created. The peer is part of the native windowing system, and does the actual work of capturing user input and managing the screen area in which the component is displayed.

Lightweight components, on the other hand, are completely implemented by Java. They are not associated with peer objects in the native windowing system. Lightweight components are essentially drawn on the space provided by their heavyweight parent containers. Since all the underlying details are handled behind the scenes by AWT-related classes, we usually don't have to worry about peer objects.

19.3 Creating components

19.3.1 The top-level frame

To get an idea of how things work, let's look at some trivial programs that create displays. For simplicity, we do everything at first in the method `main`. In an actual system, of course, building and managing the display is the job of the user interface.

First, we need to create a *JFrame* instance:

```
import javax.swing.*;

public class DisplayFrame {

    public static void main (String[] args) {
        JFrame f = new JFrame("A Frame");
        ...
```

The *String* argument to the *JFrame* constructor gives the frame a title, and can be omitted.

The *JFrame* instance has an initial width and height of 0 when created. We'll set its size a little bigger, to make it easier to deal with:[1]

```
f.setSize(300,200);
```

This sets the width of the *JFrame* to 300 pixels and the height to 200. The exact physical size of the *JFrame* and how much display real estate it will occupy depend on the size and resolution of the display screen.

If we look up the class *JFrame* in the Swing documentation, we won't find the method `setSize`. *JFrame* inherits `setSize` from *Component*.

---

1. How a 0×0 window actually looks is system dependent.

The *JFrame* has been created and sized, but is not yet visible on the display screen. In effect, the native windowing system which actually manages the display knows nothing about the *JFrame*. To show the *JFrame*, we must set its *visible* property to *true*:

```
f.setVisible(true);
```

This command does considerably more than change the state of the object. A peer is created, and the *JFrame* is displayed on the screen, as shown in Figure 19.10.

The top-level *JFrame* has a lifetime that is independent of the application's `main` method.[1] Suppose these are the only statements in the method `main`:

```
public static void main (String[] args) {
    JFrame f = new JFrame("A Frame");
    f.setSize(300,200);
    f.setVisible(true);
}
```

The automatic variable `f` is local to `main`, and when `main` completes, this variable is deallocated. However, the *JFrame* remains and the *application does not terminate*, even though `main` has completed.

You can resize, move, and iconify the *JFrame*, just as with any other native GUI window. As things stand, choosing *"Close"* from the *JFrame* window menu generally closes the window, but does not terminate the application. The only way that you can terminate the application is by an explicit signal from the operating system. (`Ctrl-C` works on many systems, but if you don't know how to get the operating system to kill a process, don't run this application!)

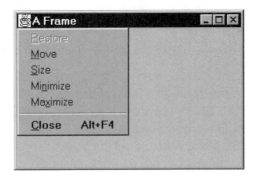

Figure 19.13   **Closing the top-level *frame* does not automatically terminate the application.**

---

1. Unfortunately, as far as the authors can determine, the AWT's run-time semantics are not formally specified at present. Thus it is not possible to separate standard behavior from implementation-dependent behavior.

19.3.2 Adding components: layout

As we've seen, even though a *JFrame* is a container, it delegates responsibility for managing its components to a content pane. To add a button to a *JFrame*, for instance, we add it to the *JFrame*'s content pane. The following

```
JButton b = new JButton("Hello");
Container cp = f.getContentPane();
cp.add(b);
```

creates a new *JButton* object, and effectively adds it to the *JFrame* f. The argument to the *JButton* constructor specifies the label that will appear on the button.

Simply adding a component to the frame won't cause the component to appear suddenly on the display, however. Things are a bit more complicated than that. We must first address the question of where the component should be positioned in the container. To handle this problem, each container is equipped with a *layout manager*. A layout manager is an object with the responsibility of positioning and sizing components in a container. The container delegates responsibility for positioning and sizing the components to the layout manager. A layout manager must implement the interface *java.awt.LayoutManager*. This interface specifies the methods all layout managers must provide. Some layout managers additionally implement the interface *java.awt.LayoutManager2*, which extends *LayoutManager*.

A *Container* has query `getLayout` and command `setLayout` for accessing and setting its layout manager:

```
public LayoutManager getLayout();
public void setLayout (LayoutManager manager);
```

Java provides several classes that implement *LayoutManager*: Among them are *FlowLayout*, *BorderLayout*, *GridLayout*, *CardLayout*, *GridBagLayout*, *BoxLayout*, and *OverlayLayout*. *BoxLayout* and *OverlayLayout* are defined in the package `javax.swing`. The others are defined in `java.awt`. You can, of course, implement your own layout manager. Some layout manager classes are designed so that a single layout manager instance can mange the layout of several containers. In other cases, each container requires its own layout manager instance.

Discussing layout in detail is well beyond the scope of this chapter. We briefly summarize, though, the standard layout managers.

FlowLayout   lays out components left to right, top to bottom. *FlowLayout* is the default layout for a *JPanel*.

BorderLayout   lays out up to five components, positioned "north," "south," "east," "west," and "center." *BorderLayout* is the default layout for a *JFrame*'s content pane.

GridLayout	lays out components in a two-dimensional grid.
CardLayout	components are displayed one at a time from a deck of preset components.
GridBagLayout	lays out components vertically and horizontally according to a specified set of constraints; the most complex and flexible of the Java-provided layout mangers.
BoxLayout	lays out components in either a single horizontal row or single vertical column. *BoxLayout* is the default layout for the Swing lightweight container *Box*.
OverlayLayout	lays out components so that specified component alignment points are all in the same place. Thus components are laid out on top of each other.

Figures 19.14, 19.15, and 19.16 show *JFrames* laid out by a *FlowLayout* layout manager, a *BorderLayout* manger, and a *GridLayout* layout manager. The code to produce each of the figures is given in Listings 19.1, 19.2, and 19.3, respectively.

FlowLayout

Note that the windows in Figure 19.14 are the same *JFrame* shown at different times. The second was obtained by manually resizing the first. When the window is resized, the layout manager repositions the components.

Since the content pane manages the components for the *JFrame*, we set the content frame's layout manager at ❶, not the *JFrame*'s. Even though the content pane is a *JPanel*, the default layout manager for a *JFrame* content pane is *BorderLayout*. If we want *FlowLayout*, we must explicitly set the layout manager.

Figure 19.14 Two instances of a *JFrame* laid out with *FlowLayout*.

Listing 19.1 **FlowLayout**

```
import java.awt.*;
import javax.swing.*;
public class DisplayFrame {
public static void main (String[] args) {
      JFrame f = new JFrame("A Frame");
      JButton b1 = new JButton("1");
      JButton b2 = new JButton("2");
      JButton b3 = new JButton("3");
      JButton b4 = new JButton("4");
      JButton b5 = new JButton("5");
      JButton b6 = new JButton("6");
      JButton b7 = new JButton("7");
      JButton b8 = new JButton("8");
      JButton b9 = new JButton("9");
      JButton b10 = new JButton("10");
      Container cp = f.getContentPane();
❶    cp.setLayout(new FlowLayout());
      cp.add(b1); cp.add(b2);
      cp.add(b3); cp.add(b4);
      cp.add(b5); cp.add(b6);
      cp.add(b7); cp.add(b8);
      cp.add(b9); cp.add(b10);
      f.setSize(300,200);
      f.setVisible(true);
   }
} // end of class DisplayFrame
```

BorderLayout

The default layout manager for a *JFrame* content pane is *BorderLayout*. We do not need to set it explicitly at ❶.

JButton constructor is called directly in the add argument list. This avoids the extraneous *JButton* variables of the previous example.

The version of add we use here requires two arguments. (Recall that *Container* has five overloaded versions of add.) It is specified as:

```
public void add (Component comp, Object constraints);
```

The second argument is a named constant defined in the class *BorderLayout*, and tells the layout manager where to position the component. (The default is CENTER.)

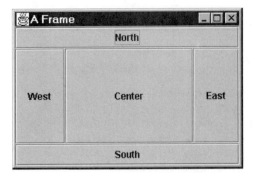

Figure 19.15 **A *JFrame* laid out with *BorderLayout*.**

Listing 19.2 **BorderLayout**

```
import java.awt.*;
import javax.swing.*;
public class DisplayFrame {
      public static void main (String[] args) {
          JFrame f = new JFrame("A Frame");
          Container cp = f.getContentPane();
❶         cp.setLayout(new BorderLayout());// not needed!
          cp.add(new JButton("North"), BorderLayout.NORTH);
          cp.add(new JButton("South"), BorderLayout.SOUTH);
          cp.add(new JButton("East"), BorderLayout.EAST);
          cp.add(new JButton("West"), BorderLayout.WEST);
          cp.add(new JButton("Center"), BorderLayout.CENTER);
          f.setSize(300,200);
          f.setVisible(true);
      }
} // end of class DisplayFrame
```

GridLayout

When we create the *GridLayout*, we specify that we want a grid of three rows and two columns. Since we have more than six components, *GridLayout* expands the number of columns, while keeping the number of rows at three.

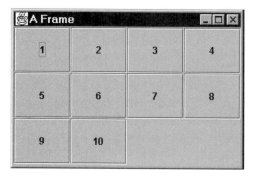

Figure 19.16   A *JFrame* laid out with *GridLayout*.

Listing 19.3   **GridLayout**

```
import java.awt.*;
import javax.swing.*;
public class DisplayFrame {
    public static void main (String[] args) {
        JFrame f = new JFrame("A Frame");
        Container cp = f.getContentPane();
        cp.setLayout(new GridLayout(3,2));
        cp.add(new JButton("1")); cp.add(new JButton("2"));
        cp.add(new JButton("3")); cp.add(new JButton("4"));
        cp.add(new JButton("5")); cp.add(new JButton("6"));
        cp.add(new JButton("7")); cp.add(new JButton("8"));
        cp.add(new JButton("9")); cp.add(new JButton("10"));
        f.setSize(300,200);
        f.setVisible(true);
    }
} // end of class DisplayFrame
```

Container validity

We mention one further *Container* property before moving on to other things. A *Container* is *valid* if it does not need to be laid out. That is, if its size is known to the system, and its layout manager knows about all of its components and has laid them out properly. A *Container* is invalid if its state is inconsistent with its appearance. For instance, adding a component to a *Container* does not automatically cause the *Container* to be laid out again. A *Container* to which a component has been added after it was last laid out is invalid.

Depending on the particular layout manager, any number of things can cause it to lay out the *Container*. Layout managers typically notice a change in *Container* size, for example, and lay out the *Container* again in this case. The command validate explicitly sets the *Container*'s *valid* property to *true*, and instructs the layout manager to lay out the *container*. The query isValid returns the value of this property. The features are specified (for the class *Component*) as follows:

```
public boolean isValid ();
public void validate ();
```

There are, of course, many *Container* and *LayoutManager* features we have not mentioned. We'll see a few more as we go along, but, as always, you should consult the documentation if you need details.

19.4   Events: programming the user interface

As we've said above, an event-driven system waits for and responds to external events. In a system with window-based graphical user interface, external events are user actions such as moving the mouse, pressing a key, *etc*. We must now see how to capture and handle events.

Some events are low-level: pressing or releasing a key on the keyboard, moving the mouse, pressing a mouse button. Other events are high-level: selecting an item from a menu, pressing a button, entering text in a field. Note that a high-level event usually involves one or more low-level events. For example, to enter text in a text field, the user moves the mouse cursor, clicks a mouse button, and presses and releases several keyboard keys.

We summarize some of the different categories of events below. We limit our attention in the examples, however, to high-level events:

key event:	keyboard key has been pressed or released.
mouse event:	mouse button has been pressed or released; mouse has been moved or dragged; mouse cursor entered or left component.
component event:	component has been hidden, shown, resized, or moved.
container event:	component has been added to or removed from a container.
window event:	window has been opened, closed, iconified, de-iconified, activated, deactivated.
focus event:	component has gained or lost focus.
action event:	high-level event indicating a component-defined action (*e.g.*, a button has been pressed, a checkbox selected, RETURN/ENTER pressed in a *JTextField*).
adjustment event:	high-level event representing scrollbar motions.

| *item event*: | high-level event that occurs when a user selects a checkbox, choice, or list item. |
| *document event*: | generated by a *TextComponent* when its content changes in any way. |

An important aspect of *Component*s is that they are the *source* of events: events occur within *Component*s. The *Component* in which an event occurs is said to *generate* the event, or to be the *source* of the event.

> **event:** the occurrence of an action, typically external to the system, that the system is aware of and must respond to.

Many events are modeled by subclasses of the abstract class *java.awt.AWTEvent*, which is itself a subclass of *java.util.EventObject*. Some are shown in Figure 19.17.

We can determine the source of an event with the query getSource, defined on the class *EventObject*:

```
public Object getSource();
```

Note that the method returns a *reference-to-Object*. If we know that the source is, say, a *JButton*, and want to treat it as such, we must cast the return value to the type *reference-to-JButton*. We'll see examples below.

An object that is interested in knowing when an event occurs is called a *listener*. To be notified of an event, a listener must *register* with the event's source. When an event occurs, any listeners registered with the event's source are notified. The relation between a listener and an event source is the *observes* relation that we've seen several times before.

19.4.1   An example

Let's develop a simple example to get an idea of how this works. First, we create a *JFrame* containing a single large black and white button. (The button will occupy the entire available space in the *JFrame*, as shown in Figure 19.18.)

```
import java.awt.*;
import javax.swing.*;
import java.awt.event.*;

public class OnOffTest {
    public static void main (String[] args) {
        OnOffSwitch sw = new OnOffSwitch();
    }
} // end of class OnOffTest
```

```
class OnOffSwitch extends JFrame {

    public OnOffSwitch () {
        super("On/Off Switch");
        JButton button = new JButton("On/Off");
        Container cp = this.getContentPane();
        button.setForeground(Color.black);
        button.setBackground(Color.white);
        cp.add(button,BorderLayout.CENTER);
        this.setSize(300,200);
        this.setVisible(true);
    }

} // end of class OnOffSwitch
```

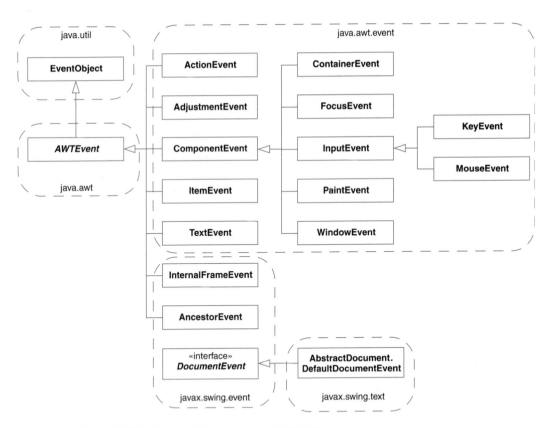

Figure 19.17 Some of the Java event classes.

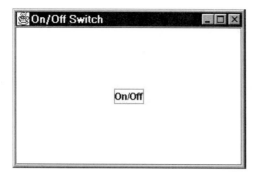

Figure 19.18 OnOffSwitch: a big JButton in a JFrame.

We've organized things a little differently this time. Specifically, we've extended the class *JFrame* with *OnOffSwitch*, and given its constructor the responsibility for adding components, and so on.

Adding an ActionListener

If the user presses the button (*i.e.*, clicks with the mouse in the button), the *JButton* object generates an *ActionEvent*. Let's now create a listener object that is interested in being notified of this event.

First, the listener—we'll call it a *Switcher*—must implement the interface *java.awt.event.ActionListener*. Java defines an interface for each category of event, and an object interested in being notified of a particular kind of event must implement the appropriate interface. This insures that the listener object defines the methods that will be called when an event occurs.

There is only one method specified in the interface *ActionListener*:

```
public void actionPerformed (ActionEvent e);
```

This method is invoked to inform the listener that an event has occurred. A minimal implementation of the *Switcher* class looks like this:

```
class Switcher implements ActionListener {

    public void actionPerformed (ActionEvent e) {
    }

} // end of class Switcher
```

Of course with this minimal implementation, a *Switcher* does nothing about the event after being informed of it. We'll take care of that in a bit. First, though, let's add code to create a listener and register it with the *JButton* component:

```
public OnOffSwitch () {
    super("On/Off Switch");
    JButton button = new JButton("On/Off");
```

```
        Switcher control = new Switcher();
        button.addActionListener(control);

        Container cp = this.getContentPane();
        cp.add(button,BorderLayout.CENTER);
        this.setSize(200,300);
        this.setVisible(true);
    }
```

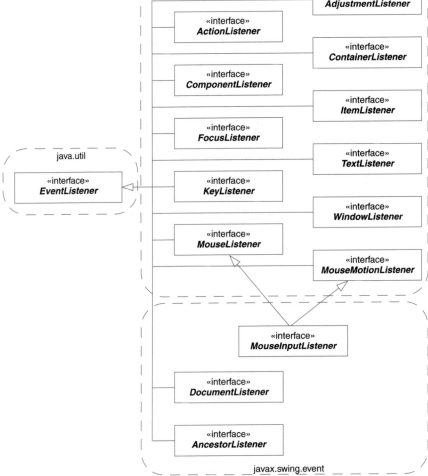

Figure 19.19 The interface *EventListener*, and some extensions.

We create a new *Switcher* instance, which the variable `control` references, and register it with the *JButton* component by calling the *JButton*'s `addActionListener` method. This tells `button` that the listener referenced by `control` wants to be informed of any *ActionEvent*s it generates.

Finally, let's make the *Switcher* do something in response to the event. We'll just have it invert the foreground and background colors of the button.

```
public void actionPerformed (ActionEvent e) {
    Component source = (Component)e.getSource();
    Color oldForeground = source.getForeground();
    source.setForeground(source.getBackground());
    source.setBackground(oldForeground);
}
```

Note that we query the event to determine the source. Since the query `getSource` returns an *Object*, we must coerce the result to a *Component* in order to invoke *Component* methods.

Let's review this program before moving on. There are three objects involved: the top-level *JFrame*, an *OnOffSwitch*; a component *JButton*; and an event handler, the *ActionListener*. The `main` method simply creates the top-level *JFrame*—an *OnOffSwitch*—and exits.

The *OnOffSwitch* constructor creates a *JButton* component and a *Switcher* "action event" listener. It then registers the *Switcher* with the *JButton*, so that any *ActionEvents* generated by the *JButton* will be delivered to the *Switcher*.

Finally, it adds the *JButton* to itself as a component (by adding the *JButton* to its content pane), and displays itself on the screen by setting its *visible* attribute to *true*.

Figure 19.20   *Container*, *Component*, and *Listener*.

When the user presses the button, an *ActionEvent* is generated by the button. This event is delivered to all of the button's *ActionListeners*, by means of an invocation of their `actionPerformed` method. In this case, there is only one listener and its `actionPerformed` method inverts the button's foreground and background colors.

Notice that since the listener explicitly determines the source of the event, it could handle events from several sources without modification. For instance,

```
public OnOffSwitch () {
    super("On/Off Switch");
```

```
JButton button1 = new JButton("On/Off");
JButton button2 = new JButton("On/Off");
Switcher control = new Switcher();
button1.addActionListener(control);
button2.addActionListener(control);
...
```

Of course, the listener responds to each button in the same way. We need to do a little more work if we want the listener to perform a different action for each button.

Adding a WindowListener

Next, let's look at how we can terminate the application cleanly, without explicitly requesting the operating system to kill it.

We would like to terminate the application when the user selects the "*Close*" option from the top-level window menu. Selecting "*Close*" generates a *WindowEvent* in the *JFrame*, specifically a window-closing event. So we must first create a listener for *WindowEvent*s. The *WindowListener* interface is a bit more complicated than the *ActionListener* interface. *WindowListener* specifies seven methods, while *ActionListener* specifies only one. Each of these methods handles a different kind of *WindowEvent*. Specifically, *WindowListener* specifies the following methods:

void windowActivated (WindowEvent e)
> Invoked when the window is set to be the user's active window, which means the window (or one of its subcomponents) will receive keyboard events.

void windowClosed (WindowEvent e)
> Invoked when a window has been closed as the result of calling dispose on the window.

void windowClosing (WindowEvent e)
> Invoked when the user attempts to close the window from the window's system menu.

void windowDeactivated (WindowEvent e)
> Invoked when a window is no longer the user's active window, which means that keyboard events will no longer be delivered to the window or its subcomponents.

void windowDeiconified (WindowEvent e)
> Invoked when a window is changed from a minimized to a normal state.

void windowIconified (WindowEvent e)
> Invoked when a window is changed from a normal to a minimized state.

void windowOpened (WindowEvent e)
> Invoked the first time a window is made visible.

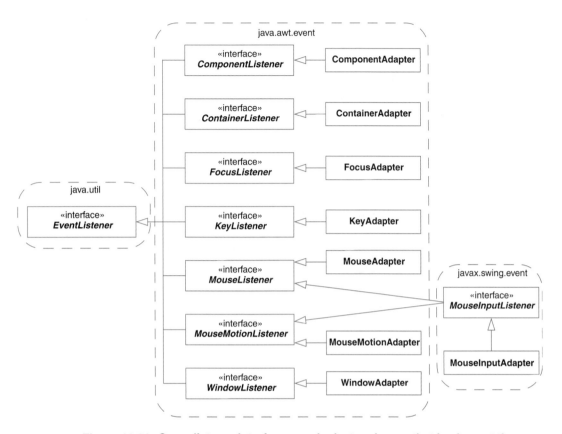

Figure 19.21 **Some listener interfaces, and adapter classes that implement them.**

But we are not interested in most of these *WindowEvents*; we're only interested in events associated with the user closing the window and terminating the application. To simplify implementation of a listener, Java provides a collection of abstract event adapter classes. These adapter classes implement listener interfaces with null methods. Thus to implement a listener class, we can extend one of the adapter classes and override only the methods we are interested in.

We'll call our *WindowListener* class *Terminator*:

```
class Terminator extends WindowAdapter {
    ...
} // end of class Terminator
```

The class *WindowAdapter* implements *WindowListener*, and since *Terminator* is a subclass of *WindowAdapter*, it also implements *WindowListener*. *Terminator* inherits the seven *WindowListener* methods from *WindowAdapter*. These are all null "do-nothing" methods. We must override the methods relating to the events we're interested in: namely, the events that are generated when the user tries to close the window and terminate the application.

A window-closing event occurs, as we have said, because the user wants to close a window. This event results in an invocation of the listener's `windowClosing` method. Thus one of the inherited *WindowAdapter* methods we must override is `windowClosing`:

```
class Terminator extends WindowAdapter {

    public void windowClosing(WindowEvent e) {
        ...
    }

} // end of class Terminator
```

What should we do when a window-closing event is delivered? We could simply terminate the application. But there is a slightly better approach, since we do not know if there are other listeners also interested in this event. What we'll do is release the window's resources, close it, and remove its peer. This is accomplished by the *Window* method `dispose`:

```
class Terminator extends WindowAdapter {

    public void windowClosing(WindowEvent e) {
        Window w = e.getWindow();
        w.dispose();
    }

} // end of class Terminator
```

The *WindowEvent* method `getWindow` is essentially the same as the *EventObject* method `getSource`, except that it returns a *Window* rather than an *Object*. Thus we are saved the trouble of casting the result.

Disposing of the window causes it to generate one more event, a window-closed event. We handle this event with the method `windowClosed`, and here is where we finally terminate the application:

```
class Terminator extends WindowAdapter {

    public void windowClosing(WindowEvent e) {
        Window w = e.getWindow();
        w.dispose();
    }
    public void windowClosed(WindowEvent e) {
        System.exit(0);
    }

} // end of class Terminator
```

The call to System.exit causes the application to terminate. By convention, an argument of 0 indicates normal termination, and a nonzero argument indicates abnormal termination—typically because of some error condition.

Of course, we still must create a *Terminator* instance and register it with the top-level *JFrame*. This is straightforward:

```
public OnOffSwitch () {
    super("On/Off Switch");
    JButton button = new JButton("On/Off");
    Switcher control = new Switcher();
    Terminator arnold = new Terminator();
    button.addActionListener(control);
    this.addWindowListener(arnold);
    ...
```

Before we conclude this section, we should note that a class like *Terminator* is an ideal candidate for being made an anonymous inner class, as introduced in Section 16.1.1. That is, rather than naming the class in a full-fledged independent class definition and then instantiating it, we can create an instance of an anonymous class:

```
this.addWindowListener(
    new WindowAdapter() {
        public void windowClosing(WindowEvent e) {
            e.getWindow().dispose();
        }
        public void windowClosed(WindowEvent e) {
            System.exit(0);
        }
    }
);
```

Here we create a new unnamed class that extends *WindowAdapter*, with methods windowClosing and windowClosed overridden, and at the same time creating an instance of this class.

19.5   Some class features

We conclude this chapter by summarizing a few features of the classes we have been studying. There is no attempt at completeness. We simply want to give a flavor of some of the class features. Recall that all the Swing component classes are extensions of the java.awt classes *Component* and *Container*. Furthermore, *JFrame* is a subclass of the java.awt classes *Window* and *Frame*.

19.5.1 *Component*

Some of the properties of *Component* instances, and features for accessing and changing them, are as follows:

Background color

```
public Color getBackground ()
public void setBackground (Color c)
```

Foreground color

```
public Color getForeground ()
public void setForeground (Color c)
```

Location

The *Component*'s position in its parent's coordinate space. The *Point* returned is the upper left corner of the bounding box around the *Component*; that is, of the smallest rectangle containing the *Component*. The layout manager may make it impossible to change the location of a Component:

```
public Point getLocation ()
public void setLocation (int x, int y)
public void setLocation (Point p)
```

Location on screen

The *Component*'s position in the screen's coordinate space. Throws *Illegal-ComponentStateException* if the *Component* is not showing:

```
public Point getLocationOnScreen ()
```

Size

The width and height of the *Component*. The layout manager may make it impossible to change the size of a *Component*:

```
public Dimension getSize ()
public void setSize (int height, int width)
public void setSize (Dimension d)
```

Preferred size

The preferred size of the *Component*. This attribute can be used by the layout manager to size the *Component*. The method `getPreferredSize` is sometimes overridden to force a particular size for a *Component*:

```
public Dimension getPreferredSize ()
```

Minimum size

The minimum size of the *Component*. This attribute can be used by the layout manager to size the *Component*. The method `getMinimumSize` is sometimes overridden to force a particular size for a *Component*:

```
public Dimension getMinimumSize ()
```

Parent

The *Container* that contains the *Component*. The method `getParent` returns *null* if the *Component* is a top-level window:

```
public Container getParent ()
```

Enabled

If the *Component* is enabled, the user can interact with it and it can generate events. If it is disabled, the user cannot interact with it:

```
public boolean isEnabled ()
public void setEnabled (boolean enabled)
```

Valid

The *Component* is valid if the system knows its size, and in the case of a *Container*, if it's properly laid out. If the size of the *Component* has changed since it was last displayed, the *Component* is invalid. A *Container* is also invalid if one of its *Components* is invalid, or if a *Component* has been added or removed since the *Container* was last laid out. A layout manager typically notices an event such as *Container* resizing, and lays out the *Container* again.

```
public boolean isValid ()
public void validate ()
public void invalidate ()
```

Visible and Showing

Visible and *showing* can be somewhat confusing. A *Component* is *showing* if the user can find it on the display screen. It does not matter if the *Component* or window containing the *Component* is iconified or hidden behind another window.

If a *Component* is *visible*, then it should be showing when its parent is. A *Component* can be *visible* without appearing on the display screen. For a *Component* to be *showing*, it must be *visible* and be contained in a *Container* that is *visible* and *showing*. It is possible for *visible* to be *true*, and *showing* to be *false*, but not *vice versa*.

A top-level window is either *showing* and *visible*, or *not showing* and *not visible*. That is, the *visible* and *showing* properties for a top-level window always have the same value. Top-level windows are not visible when created. They must be explicitly made visible. Other *Components* are *visible* when they are created.

(There must certainly be a reason behind this distinction, but we admit to being at a loss.)

```
public boolean isVisible ()
public boolean isShowing ()
public void setVisible (boolean visible)
```

Font

The class *java.awt.Font* models character fonts. Each *Component* has a *Font* instance associated with it. The *Font* instance determines the character font used to display text associated with the *Component*. Details of fonts and their manipulation are beyond the scope of this discussion.

```
public Font getFont ()
public void setFont (Font f)
```

Graphics

The abstract class *java.awt.Graphics* defines a "graphics context" and provides mechanisms for drawing, displaying images, and so on. The method `getGraphics` can be invoked to provide a graphics context for showing *Components*. Details of the abstract class *Graphics* are beyond the scope of this discussion.

```
public Graphics getGraphics ()
```

Listeners

```
public void addComponentListener (
    ComponentListener listener)
public void removeComponentListener (
    ComponentListener listener)
```

```
public void addFocusListener (FocusListener listener)
public void removeFocusListener (
   FocusListener listener)
public void addKeyListener (KeyListener listener)
public void removeKeyListener (KeyListener listener)
public void addMouseListener (MouseListener listener)
public void removeMouseListener (
   MouseListener listener)
public void addMouseMotionListener (
   MouseMotionListener listener)
public void removeMouseMotionListener (
   MouseMotionListener listener)
```

19.5.2 *Container*

Component Manipulation

The number of Components in the *Container*:

```
public int getComponentCount ()
```

The *Component* at the specified position. (Note: the first *Component* is at position 0.)

```
public Component getComponent (int position)
   require:
      0 <= position <= this.getComponentCount() - 1
```

The *Component* containing a given point. These methods return the *Container* itself if the point is in the *Container*, but not in any of the *Container*'s *Components*. They return *null* if the point is not in the *Container*:

```
public Component getComponentAt (int x, int y)
public Component getComponentAt (Point p)
```

Add a *Component* to the *Container*. The first method adds the *Component* as the "last" object, the second adds the *Component* at the indicated position. How position is handled depends on the layout manager. The third method is used when the layout manager requires additional information, as seen with *BorderLayout*. There are several other variants of the method add.

These methods return the *Component* added; the return value is usually ignored:

```
public Component add (Component component)
public Component add (Component component,
   int position)
public Component add (Component component,
   Object constraints)
```

Remove a *Component* from a *Container*:

```
public void remove (Component component)
public void remove (int position)
```

Layout Manager

```
public LayoutManager getLayout ()
public void setLayout (LayoutManager manager)
```

Listeners

```
public void addContainerListener (
    ContainerListener listener)
public void removeContainerListener (
    ContainerListener listener)
```

19.5.3   *Window*

The following are some general *Window* commands.
Resize the *Window* to the preferred size of its *Components*, and validate it.

```
public void pack ()
```

Bring the *Window* to the display foreground.

```
public void toFront ()
```

Send the *Window* to the display background.

```
public void toBack ()
```

Release a *Window*'s resources, and remove its peer.

```
public void dispose ()
```

Listeners

```
public void addWindowListener (
    WindowListener listener)
public void removeWindowListener (
    WindowListener listener)
```

19.5.4   *Frame*

Title

```
public String getTitle ()
public void setTitle (String title)
```

Resizable

The *resizable* attribute determines whether or not the user can resize the Frame. It muse be set before the Frame's peer is created and the Frame made visible.

```
public boolean isResizable ()
public void setResizable (boolean resizable)
```

19.5.5   *JComponent*

JComponent overrides many *Component* methods, but with the same basic functionality. Some additional features provided by *JComponent* include the following.

Borders

A *border* is an object capable of rendering a border around the edges of a component. Borders are modeled by the javax.swing.border interface *Border*. Several standard classes implementing this interface are defined in the package:

```
public Border getBorder ()
public void setBorder (Border border)
```

Ancestors

Get the *JRootPane* ancestor for the component, or the top-level ancestor of the component:

```
public JRootPane getRootPane ()
public Container getTopLevelAncestor ()
```

Transparency

A component is opaque if its background will be filled with the background color. Otherwise, it its transparent:

```
public void setOpaque (boolean isOpaque)
public boolean isOpaque()
```

19.5.6   *JFrame*

Components

These methods return or set the content pain, menu bar, or root pane of the *JFrame*:

```
public Container getContentPane ()
public JMenuBar getJMenuBar ()
public JRootPane getRootPane ()
public void setContentPane (Container contentPane)
public void setJMenuBar (JMenuBar menubar)
```

Default close operation

When a user attempts to close a window representing a *JFrame*, after the WINDOW_CLOSING event has been delivered to any listeners, the *JFrame* may hide or dispose of itself of its own accord. The default action is that the *JFrame* will hide itself: that is, it will become *not visible*. In this case, the program could later make the frame *visible* again.

The default response taken by a *JFrame* to a close action can be determined or set with these methods:

```
public int getDefaultCloseOperaton ()
public void setDefaultCloseOperation (int operation)
```

The argument passed to setDefaultCloseOperation must be one of the following constants:

```
WindowConstants.DO_NOTHING_ON_CLOSE
WindowConstants.HIDE_ON_CLOSE
WindowConstants.DISPOAE_ON_CLOSE
```

19.6   Summary

In this chapter, we took a first careful look at building a user interface. We briefly examined algorithm-driven interfaces, in which the application determines what data is to be input or output, and when input and output is to occur. In an algorithm driven interface, the application typically prompts the user for input, reads the input, and then provides results as output.

Most of the chapter was devoted to studying Java's facilities for constructing event-driven, graphical user interfaces. In an event-driven interface, the application responds to an external event such as a mouse click or key press, and then waits for the next event.

A graphical user interface is constructed from components, such as buttons, text fields, and so on. These components are the source of user-generated events that provide input to the system, and are used to deliver output to the user. The components are organized into containers, which are themselves components. The responsibility for arranging components in a container is delegated to the container's layout manager.

The top-level window in a Java application is a container called a *JFrame*. The graphical display is created by adding components to the *JFrame*'s content pane. When the user performs some action such as pressing a mouse button, the component in which the action takes place generates an event. An event listener is an object that is to be informed when a particular kind of event occurs in a particular component. The listener is informed when the event occurs, and responds with an appropriate action.

EXERCISES

These exercises involve building a simple accumulator that lets users add numbers to a running total. The application interface will be through a simple window that looks something like the following:

The user enters a summand by keying into the text field and pressing ENTER or RETURN key. Pressing the large button labeled "+" adds the summand to a running sum, which is displayed in the text field after the button is pressed.

19.1   First, we will build the model for the application. The model is a very simple class specified as follows:

class simpleAccumulator.Accumulator
> A simple object that maintains a running integer sum.

> **public** Accumulator ()
>> Create a new *Accumulator*, with sum set to 0.

> **public int** sum ()
>> The running sum.

> **public void** add ()
>> Add summand to sum.

> **public void** setSummand (**int** val)
>> Set the value of the summand.

Implement this class.

19.2   The interface will be defined by a class *SimpleAccumulatorUI*. For simplicity, this
class will extend *JFrame*. An instance of *SimpleAccumulatorUI* will be given a
reference to a model when it is created. Thus we will have

```
package simpleAccumulator;
import javax.swing.*;
import java.awt.*;
import java.awt.event.*;

/**
 * Simple user interface for an Accumulator
 */
class SimpleAccumulatorUI extends JFrame {

    /**
     * Create a new interface for the specified
     * Accumulator.
     */
    public SimpleAccumulatorUI (Accumulator model) {
        ...
```

The top level simply creates the interface and the model:

```
package simpleAccumulator;

/**
 * A simple accumulator.
 */
public class SimpleAccumulator {

    public static final void main (String[] main) {
        SimpleAccumulatorUI ui =
            new SimpleAccumulatorUI(new Accumulator());
    }
}
```

Complete a preliminary implementation of *SimpleAccumulatorUI* as follows:

a. Title the frame "Simple Accumulator."

b. Add three components to the content pane:

- a *JLabel*, that reads "Enter a number:" –

```
new JLabel ("Enter a number:")
```

- a *JTextField* 40 characters wide –

```
new JTextField(TEXT_FIELD_SIZE)
```

where

```
static final int TEXT_FIELD_SIZE = 40
```

- a *JButton* labeled with a "+" –

```
new JButton("+")
```

Use the content pane's default *BorderLayout* layout manager, and add the components in the NORTH, CENTER, and SOUTH positions, respectively.

c. Pack the frame and set its *visible* attribute to *true*.

At this stage, you should be able to compile and run the application, though of course nothing happens when you enter data or press the button. Furthermore, closing the window doesn't terminate the application. Note how the layout manager distributes space in the window when you manually resize it.

19.3 Add a *WindowListener* that terminates the application when the window is closed.

19.4 Add *ActionListeners* for the *JButton* and the *JTextField*.

The button listener should do the following when the button generates an *ActionEvent*.

a. Command the model to do an addition.

b. Query the model for the current sum.

c. Display the current sum in the text field.

The *Integer* method toString can be used to convert an **int** value to a *String*:

```
public static String toString (int i)
```
> Returns a new *String* object representing the specified integer.

The *JTextField* method setText can be used to set the text in the text field:

```
public void setText (String t)
```
> Sets the text of this *JTextField* to the specified text. If the text is null or empty, has the effect of simply deleting the old text.

The text field listener should do the following when the text field generates an *ActionEvent*.

a. Get the number entered by the user in the text field.

The following methods should be useful for this.
From *JTextField*:

```
public String getText ()
```
> Returns the text contained in this *JTextField*.

From *Integer*:

```
int intValue ()
```
> Returns the value of this *Integer* as an **int**.

```
static Integer valueOf (String s)
    throws NumberFormatException
```
> Returns a new *Integer* object initialized to the value of the specified *String*.
>
> **throws:**
> > *NumberFormatException* if the *String* cannot be parsed as an integer.

b. Set the summand in the model to the value entered by the user.

Make sure that the case in which a user enters some text other than an integer is handled reasonably.

19.5   Suppose that the text field listener in the above exercise responds to *TextEvent*s rather than *ActionEvent*s. How will the behavior of the application change?

19.6   The interface built above is awkward to use because the same text field is used for user input and to display output. Modify the interface to improve its user friendliness.

19.7   Implement a graphical user interface for the nim game of Chapter 10.

GLOSSARY

application-driven: an input-output model in which the application explicitly determines when to get input and when to produce output.

character stream: a data stream whose elements are characters encoded in some standard character set.

component: a distinct element of a graphical user interface, such as a button, text field, and so on.

container: a graphical user interface component that can contain other components.

data stream: a sequence of bytes being read or written by an application.

event: the occurrence of an action, typically external to the system, that the system is aware of and must respond to.

event-driven: an input-output model in which the application waits for an event to occur, responds to the event, and waits for the next event.

event listener: an object that will be notified when a particular event occurs in a particular component, and that will then take appropriate action in response to the event.

filter: a program that reads input form a particular data stream called standard input, writes output to a particular data stream called standard output, and writes error messages to a data stream called standard error. The actual source an destination of these data streams is generally determined by the operating system when the program is initiated.

heavyweight component: a graphical user interface component that has a corresponding (peer) component in the native windowing system of the machine.

input stream: a data stream from which the application can read input.

layout manager: an object responsible for positioning and sizing components in a container.

lightweight component: graphical user interface component that is implemented entirely in Java. It has no corresponding (peer) component in the native windowing system of the machine.

output stream: a data stream to which the application can append output.

Swing: a particular collection of library classes and interfaces used to build graphical user interfaces in Java.

top-level container: a graphical user interface container that is not an element of any other container.

CHAPTER 20

Designing the GUI front-end: the Model-View-Controller pattern

The *Model-View-Controller* (MVC) pattern is often used to structure graphical user interfaces. In this approach, the interface or an interface element is partitioned into two components, view and controller. The view is responsible for displaying some aspect of the model, and the controller is responsible for capturing input events and effecting appropriate state changes in the model.

In this chapter, we consider MVC and its implementation in Java. In the process, we will see the standard Java library facilities for implementing the *observes* relation. Finally, we will see that the basic Swing components we encountered in the last chapter are themselves structured along the lines of the MVC pattern.

20.1 Model-View-Controller

The *Model-View-Controller* (MVC) pattern is commonly used in designing event-driven, window-based applications. With this approach, graphical user interface components are partitioned into *view* and *controller*. Thus an application is composed of

- *model components*—the objects that model and solve the problem at hand;
- *view components*—the objects that determine the manner in which the model components are to be displayed; and
- *controller components*—the objects that handle user input.

The advantages of this structure are rather obvious:

- input processing is separated from output processing;
- controllers can be interchanged, allowing different user interaction modes (expert or novice, for instance);
- multiple views of the model can be easily supported.

The fundamental relationship between components is shown in Figure 20.1. The view and controller explicitly know about the model. But the model does not require details of the other components. The model need not know how it is being displayed or precisely how the user interacts with the application. While the controllers and views directly depend on the model, the model does not depend in any essential way on the views and controllers. Thus the model can be readily retrofitted with a new look and feel.

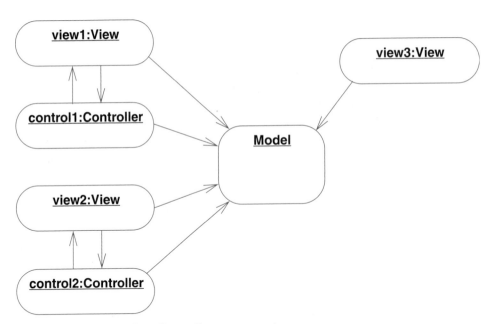

Figure 20.1 ***Model-View-Controller*** *components.*

The view must ensure that the display accurately reflects the current state of the model. Thus the view must be notified when the model state changes. We have seen previously that the *observes* relation allows an observer to be notified of state changes in a target, while maintaining the target's independence of the observer. The relationship between view and model is therefore generally implemented as the *observes* relation. The controller must effect changes in the model as determined by user input. The controller is simply a model client.

The controller defines how the view responds to user input. A view essentially uses a controller to implement a particular response strategy. The relation between view and controller is often *has-as-strategy* as discussed in Section 15.2. The controller, on the other hand, generally captures events generated by view components. Thus the controller typically *listens to* the view or its components.

Finally, we note that a view is often a composite built of simpler views. For instance, a complex control panel might be a view composed of views of the individual controls, or a view of a maze in a maze game might be composed of views of the maze rooms and passages. The structure exhibited here is identical to the graphical user interface *Container* seen in the previous chapter.

20.2   Implementing MVC in Java

To see how we might implement the MVC pattern in Java, we'll consider a simple example in which the model is a right triangle. We'll develop three different views of the triangle and one controller. One view will simply describe the triangle by displaying the lengths of its three sides. A second view will display the triangle graphically. Finally, a third view will log changes in the triangle state to a file.

The controller will be associated with the first view, and allow a user to modify the sides of the triangle.

20.2.1   The model

The model will be a very simple object modeling a right triangle. We permit the lengths of two of the sides, called the *base* and the *height*, to be modified. The length of the third side, the *hypotenuse*, is determined by the lengths of the base and the height.

The methods `round` and `sqrt` are static functions defined in *java.lang.Math*. They perform the obvious operations of rounding a **double** to an integer, and computing the square root of a number.

Listing 20.1   **The model class *RightTriangle***

```
/**
 * A right triangle. Units assumed to be pixels.
 */
public class RightTriangle {
```

continued

Listing 20.1   The model class *RightTriangle (continued)*

===

```
// Constructor:

/**
 * Create a right triangle with the specified base
 * and height.
 *     require:
 *         base >= 0; height >= 0
 */
public RightTriangle (int base, int height) {
   this.base = base;
   this.height = height;
   setHypotenuse();
}

// Queries:

/**
 * The base.
 *     ensure:
 *         result >= 0
 */
public int base () {
   return this.base;
}

/**
 * The height.
 *     ensure:
 *         result >= 0
 */
public int height () {
   return this.height;
}


/**
 * The hypotenuse.
 *     ensure:
 *         result >= 0
 */
```

continued

Listing 20.1   **The model class *RightTriangle (continued)***

```java
public int hypotenuse () {
   return this.hypotenuse;
}

// Commands:

/**
 * Change base.
 *    require:
 *        newBase >= 0
 */
public void setBase (int newBase) {
   this.base = newBase;
   setHypotenuse();
}

/**
 * Change height.
 *    require:
 *        newHeight >= 0
 */
public void setHeight (int newHeight) {
   this.height = newHeight;
   setHypotenuse();
}

// Private Methods:

/*
 * Adjust hypotenuse.
 */
private void setHypotenuse () {
   this.hypotenuse = (int) Math.round(
      Math.sqrt(base*base + height*height));
}

// Private Components:

// the sides of the triangle
private int base;
private int height;
```

continued

Listing 20.1   The model class _RightTriangle (continued)_

```
    private int hypotenuse;
} // end of class RightTriangle
```

20.2.2   The class _Observable_ and interface _Observer_

To support the _observes_ relation, Java provides a class _Observable_ and an interface _Observer_ in the package `java.util`. The _Observer_ is client and the _Observable_ is server. The _Observer_ registers with the _Observable_, and the _Observable_ informs the _Observer_ when it (the _Observable_) changes state.

Figure 20.2   The _Observer_ pattern in Java.

The most important methods provided by the class _Observable_ are

```
    public void addObserver (Observer o);
    protected void setChanged ();
    public void notifyObservers ();
    public void notifyObservers (Object arg);
```

The first method is used by an _Observer_ to register with a target; that is, with an _Observable_. The remaining three are used by a target to notify all the registered observers that it has changed state.

To be more specific, the method `setChanged` sets the target object's _hasChanged_ attribute to _true_. When `notifyObservers` is called, if _hasChanged_ is _true_, all of the registered observers are notified, and _hasChanged_ is reset to _false_. Thus an object takes note of the fact that it has changed and it must notify its observers by setting its _hasChanged_ attribute. It then actually notifies observers by calling one of its `notifyObservers` methods.

The target can provide information to the observers by supplying an argument to `notifyObservers`. This argument typically includes details about exactly what changed in the target, so that the observers can conduct their response more efficiently.

To continue our example, we make the class _RightTriangle_ an extension of _Observable_:

```
    public class RightTriangle extends Observable
```

A client registers as an observer by calling the method `addObserver`. For instance, if a client (perhaps a view) wants to register with a *RightTriangle* `rt`, it executes the call

```
rt.addObserver(this);
```

When the *RightTriangle* changes state, it calls its methods `setChanged` and `notifyObservers`:

```
setChanged();
notifyObservers();
```

to notify all the registered observers of the event.

A *RightTriangle* changes state only in response to a `setBase` or `setHeight` command. Therefore, observers should be informed when these commands are executed:

```
public void setBase (int newBase) {
    this.base = newBase;
    setHypotenuse();
    setChanged();
    notifyObservers();
}

public void setHeight (int newHeight) {
    this.height = newHeight;
    setHypotenuse();
    setChanged();
    notifyObservers();
}
```

Since the state of the model is so simple, we just inform observers that something has changed without providing additional information in the form of an argument to the `notifyObservers` method.

We are finished with the model. Note that the model does not need to know who its observers will be, or what they intend to do about changes in its state.

20.2.3 An *Observer*

Let's first take a look at how an observer is structured. We sketch a class *RTObserver* that implements the interface *Observer*, and observes a *RightTriangle*.

An observer must know the target object. In this case, the observer is told about the target *RightTriangle* when it, the observer, is created. The observer then registers itself with the target. The fact that the target extends *Observable* ensures that it will support an `addObserver` method.

```
/**
 * RightTriangle observer.
 */
class RTObserver implements Observer {

    /**
     * Create an observer of RightTriangle rt.
     */
    public RTObserver (RightTriangle rt) {
       target = rt;
       target.addObserver(this);
    }
    ...
    private RightTriangle target;

} // end of class RTObserver
```

The interface *Observer* specifies only one method:

```
void update (Observable o, Object arg);
```

This is the method that the target calls to notify the observer of a state change. The first parameter references the target object reporting the change, and the second is the argument provided by the target to `notifyObservers`. That is, if a target object invoked the method

```
notifyObservers(info);
```

the `update` method of each of its observers would be called, with a reference to the target as first argument, and `info` as second. The second argument to `update` is *null* if the target invokes `notifyObservers` with no argument.

The observer implements the method `update`, defining what it wants to do about the target state change.

```
public void update (Observable o, Object arg) {
    // do something about o's state change.
}
```

To summarize, an *Observable* has a property *hasChanged* and maintains a list of *Observer*s. The method `addObserver` adds an object to the list. The method `notifyObservers` calls the `update` method of each *Observer* on the list. We could implement a minimal version of *Observable* as follows:

```
public class Observable {

    public Observable () {
        observers = new ObserverList();
        hasChanged = false;
    }
```

```
public void addObserver (Observer o) {
    observers.append(o);
}

public void setChanged () {
    hasChanged = true;
}

public void notifyObservers (Object arg) {
    if (hasChanged) {
        int i;
        int len = observers.size();
        for (i = 0; i < len; i = i+1)
            ((Observer)observers.get(i)).update(
                this, arg);
        hasChanged = false;
    }
}

public void notifyObservers () {
    this.notifyObservers(null);
}

private boolean hasChanged;
private ObserverList observers;

}
```

20.2.4 A simple view and controller

Now that we've seen how an observer is structured, let's build a simple user interface for a *RightTriangle*. We opt for simplicity over flexibility and elegance in constructing the GUI.

The model is an instance of the class *RightTriangle* given above. We build a view that shows the three components of the triangle in text fields, as shown in Figure 20.3.

A controller will capture input from the text fields labeled *Base* and *Height*, and modify the state of the *RightTriangle* appropriately. (We won't let the user change *Hypotenuse*.)

For simplicity, we put everything in the same package.

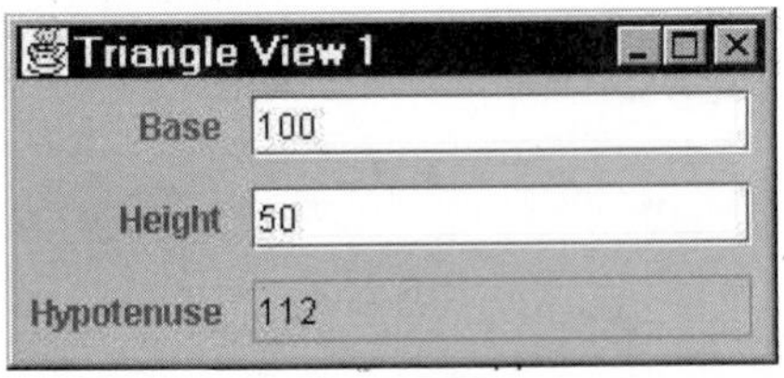

Figure 20.3 **View of a *RightTriangle*.**

The View

The view extends *JPanel* and implements *Observer*. We'll make the *JPanel* the content pane of a top level *JFrame*. The *RightTriangle* to display is provided as a constructor argument:

```
class TextView extends JPanel implements Observer {

    public TextView (RightTriangle model) {
        super();
        ...
```

The fundamental components of the view are the three text fields. They will be referenced by instance variables and created in the *TextView* constructor. We'll see how to handle the layout later. The text fields are created to be FIELD_SIZE characters wide, and are each assigned an *action command*. The *action command* is incorporated in any *ActionEvent* generated by the text field. By looking at the *action command* of an *ActionEvent*, we can determine which text field generated the *ActionEvent*. The *editable* property of the hypotenuse text field is set to *false*, so that it cannot be changed by the user. Since hypotenuse will not generate any *ActionEvents*, its *action command* need not be set:

```
class TextView extends JPanel implements Observer {

    public TextView (RightTriangle model) {
        super();
        ...
        base = new JTextField(FIELD_SIZE);
        base.setActionCommand("Base");
        ...
        height = new JTextField(FIELD_SIZE);
        height.setActionCommand("Height");
        ...
        hypotenuse = new JTextField(FIELD_SIZE);
        hypotenuse.setEditable(false);
        ...
    }
```

```
...
    private final static int FIELD_SIZE = 16;
    private JTextField base;
    private JTextField height;
    private JTextField hypotenuse;
}
```

Since *TextView* implements *Observer*, it must implement the method `update` specified by the interface. As we've seen, this method is invoked by the model whenever it changes state. When the model changes state, the text fields must be updated with new model state information. Thus `update` queries the model for the new state information, and writes it to the text fields:

```
public void update (Observable model, Object arg) {
    int side;
    RightTriangle rt = (RightTriangle)model;
    side = rt.base();
    base.setText(String.valueOf(side));
    side = rt.height();
    height.setText(String.valueOf(side));
    side = rt.hypotenuse();
    hypotenuse.setText(String.valueOf(side));
}
```

Note that since the *RightTriangle* invokes the `notifyObservers` method with no arguments, the second argument to `update` (`arg`) will be *null*. The *JTextField* method `setText` writes a text string into the text field. The *String* method `valueOf` with an **int** argument returns a *String* representation of the integer value.

The Controller

We're not quite finished with the view, but let's now look at the controller. The controller captures user input from the `base` and `height` text fields, and updates the model. It must therefore know about both the view's text fields, and the *RightTriangle* the view is displaying.

The controller and the view are very closely related. Because of this tight coupling, and to simplify the design, we make the controller class an inner class of *TextView*. Therefore we define the controller class, which we call *TVController*, inside *TextView*. The controller will then have direct access to the view's text field components. We'll also provide a reference to the model when the controller is constructed.

The controller needs to know when the user enters a value in the `base` or `height` text fields. Specifically, it must respond to *ActionEvents* generated by these text fields. (A text field generates an *ActionEvent* when the user presses RETURN or ENTER in the text field.) To respond to the appropriate *ActionEvents*, the controller must be an *ActionListener* and must be added as a listener to the base and height text fields of the view. As an *ActionListener*, it must implement the method actionPerformed.

```
private class TVController implements ActionListener {

    /**
     * Create a new controller for the TextView of the
     * specified RightTriangle.
     */
    public TVController (RightTriangle model) {
        this.model = model;
        TextView.this.base.addActionListener(this);
        TextView.this.height.addActionListener(this);
    }

    /**
     * Update the model in response to user input.
     */
    public void actionPerformed (ActionEvent e) {
        // do something when user has entered text in a
        // text field
    }

    private RightTriangle model;

} // end of class TVController
```

❶

The notation TextView.**this**.base seen in line ❶ specifies that base is a feature of the *TextView* associated with this *TVController*: that is, of the *TextView* instance enclosing the definition of this *TVController*. We could just as easily have written

```
base.addActionListener(this);
```

but the additional syntax emphasizes that base is a *TextView* component.

When the user enters text, the controller gets the value of the text field and instructs the model to update the appropriate component, either *base* or *height*. As we've seen, *ActionEvents* generated by the text fields have an *action command* property. By examining this property, the controller can determine which text field generated the event.

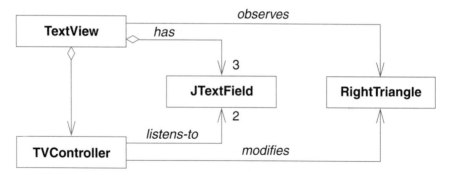

Figure 20.4 **View, Controller, and Model.**

The `actionPerformed` method can be written as follows:

```
/**
 * Update the model in response to user input.
 */
public void actionPerformed (ActionEvent e) {
❶     JTextField tf = (JTextField)e.getSource();
       try {
❷         int i = Integer.parseInt(tf.getText());
❸         String which = e.getActionCommand();
           if (which.equals("Base"))
               model.setBase(i);
           else
               model.setHeight(i);
❹     } catch (NumberFormatException ex) {
           TextView.this.update(model, null);
       }
   }
```

A few notes:

❶ The *ActionEvent* query `getSource` returns a reference to the *Object* that was the source of the event.

❷ The *JTextField* query `getText` returns the text in the text field, as a *String*. The method `parseInt` of the class *Integer* converts the *String* to the **int** that it denotes. This method will throw a *NumberFormatException* if the its argument does not represent an **int**—that is, if the user keyed something besides a sequence of digits in the text field.

❸ The *ActionEvent* query `getActionCommand` returns action command of the event. In this case, either `"Base"` or `"Height"`.

❹ If the user keys gibberish, we catch the *NumberFormatException* and explicitly tell the view to update itself. This results in the view getting the current state of the model and updating the display, replacing the gibberish keyed by the user with correct values from the model.

View layout

Now let's finish the view by seeing how to do the layout. The view will be composed of three labels and three text fields. The components will be laid out in a 3×2 grid, using a *GridBagLayout* layout manager.

cell (0,0)	cell (1,0)
cell (0,1)	cell (1,1)
cell (0,2)	cell (1,2)

Figure 20.5 **Components are laid out in a 3×2 grid of cells.**

GridBagLayout is a flexible but somewhat complicated layout manager. Complete details are beyond the scope of this presentation. We only remark on features necessary for our example.

A *GridBagLayout* layout manager uses a *GridBagConstraints* object to position each component. The constraints object specifies things like which grid cells the component is to occupy, how the component should be positioned in its cell or cells, how extra space is to be allocated to the cells, and so on.

We set the layout manager for the *TextView* to *GridBagLayout*, and create a *GridBagConstraints* instance. (We can use the same constraint instance to position each component.)

```
public TextView (RightTriangle model) {
    super();
    setLayout(new GridBagLayout());
    GridBagConstraints constraints =
        new GridBagConstraints();
```

Now we set the attributes of the constraints object to position the labels. The labels all appear in column (*x*-position) 0. We set the row (*y*-position) to the special value RELATIVE. The effect of this is to place each component below the previous one.

```
constraints.gridx = 0;
constraints.gridy = GridBagConstraints.RELATIVE;
```

We set the `anchor` attribute so that the labels are right-justified in their cells.

```
constraints.anchor = GridBagConstraints.EAST;
```

Finally, we use an *Insets* instance to place a 5-pixel border around the label.

```
constraints.insets = new Insets(5,5,5,5);
```

Now that the constraints object has been created and set, it can be used to position the labels.

```
add(new JLabel("Base"),constraints);
add(new JLabel("Height"),constraints);
add(new JLabel("Hypotenuse"),constraints);
```

Note that we use the version of `add` that requires two arguments. In this case, the component is the first argument, and the constraints object is the second.

If we change the column position to 1, we can use the same constraints object for positioning the text fields that we used for the labels:

```
constraints.gridx = 1;

base = new JTextField(FIELD_SIZE);
base.setActionCommand("Base");
add(base,constraints);

height = new JTextField(FIELD_SIZE);
height.setActionCommand("Height");
add(height,constraints);

hypotenuse = new JTextField(FIELD_SIZE);
hypotenuse.setEditable(false);
add(hypotenuse,constraints);
```

We conclude the constructor by registering with the model, creating a controller, and getting the initial model state.

```
model.addObserver(this);
controller = new TVController(model);
update(model,null);
}
```

The complete definition, including the class that creates the view and model, is given in Listing 20.2.

Listing 20.2   **The class *TextView***

```java
import java.util.*;
import java.awt.*;
import java.awt.event.*;
import javax.swing.*;

/**
 * View for a RightTriangle, as three text fields.
 */
class TextView extends JPanel implements Observer {

    /**
     * Create a view for the specified RightTriangle.
     */
    public TextView (RightTriangle model) {
        super();
        setLayout(new GridBagLayout());
        GridBagConstraints constraints =
            new GridBagConstraints();

        constraints.gridx = 0;
        constraints.gridy = GridBagConstraints.RELATIVE;
        constraints.anchor = GridBagConstraints.EAST;
        constraints.insets = new Insets(5,5,5,5);

        add(new JLabel("Base"),constraints);
        add(new JLabel("Height"),constraints);
        add(new JLabel("Hypotenuse"),constraints);

        constraints.gridx = 1;

        base = new JTextField(FIELD_SIZE);
        base.setActionCommand("Base");
        add(base,constraints);

        height = new JTextField(FIELD_SIZE);
        height.setActionCommand("Height");
        add(height,constraints);

        hypotenuse = new JTextField(FIELD_SIZE);
        hypotenuse.setEditable(false);
        add(hypotenuse,constraints);
```

continued

Listing 20.2   The class *TextView (continued)*

```
      model.addObserver(this);
      controller = new TVController(model);
      update(model,null);
   }

   /**
    * Update the view with current model state.
    */
   public void update (Observable model, Object arg) {
      int side;
      RightTriangle rt = (RightTriangle)model;
      side = rt.base();
      base.setText(String.valueOf(side));
      side = rt.height();
      height.setText(String.valueOf(side));
      side = rt.hypotenuse();
      hypotenuse.setText(String.valueOf(side));
   }

   // Private components:

   private final static int FIELD_SIZE = 16;
   private TVController controller;
   private JTextField base;
   private JTextField height;
   private JTextField hypotenuse;

   /**
    * RightTriangle controller for a TextView.
    */
   private class TVController implements ActionListener {

      /**
       * Create a new controller for the specified TextView
       * of the specified RightTriangle.
       */
      public TVController (RightTriangle model) {
         this.model = model;
         TextView.this.base.addActionListener(this);
         TextView.this.height.addActionListener(this);
      }
```

continued

Listing 20.2 **The class *TextView (continued)***

```
    /**
     * Update the model in response to user input.
     */
    public void actionPerformed (ActionEvent e) {
        JTextField tf = (JTextField)e.getSource();
        try {
            int i = Integer.parseInt(tf.getText());
            String which = e.getActionCommand();
            if (which.equals("Base"))
                model.setBase(i);
            else
                model.setHeight(i);
        } catch (NumberFormatException ex) {
            TextView.this.update(model, null);
        }
    }

    // Private components:

    private RightTriangle model;
  } // end of class TVController

} // end of class TextView

/**
 * Create an editable RightTriangle and View it.
 */
public class RightTriangleViewer {

    public static void main (String[] args) {
        JFrame f = new JFrame("Triangle View 1");
        RightTriangle model = new RightTriangle(1,1);
        TextView view = new TextView(model);
        f.getContentPane().add(view);
        f.pack();
        f.addWindowListener(
            new WindowAdapter() {
                public void windowClosing(WindowEvent e) {
                    e.getWindow().dispose();
                }
```

continued

Listing 20.2   The class *TextView (continued)*

```
        public void windowClosed(WindowEvent e) {
            System.exit(0);
        }
    }
);
f.setVisible(true);
}
}
```

20.2.5   A graphic view

We implement another view of the *RightTriangle*, this one without a controller. This view simply shows a graphic rendition of the triangle. The basic structure is the same as the previous view. We define the view as an extension of *JPanel* that we can pack into a top-level frame. For convenience, we include a local method for retrieving the current model state:

```
/**
 * Graphical view for a RightTriangle.
 */
class GraphicView extends JPanel implements Observer {

    /**
     * Create a graphic view for the specified
     * RightTriangle.
     */
    public GraphicView (RightTriangle model) {
        super();
        model.addObserver(this);
        update(model,null);
    }

    /**
     * Update the view with current model state.
     */
    public void update (Observable model, Object arg) {
        ...
    }
```

```
/*
 * Get the properties of the model.
 */
private void getModelState (RightTriangle model) {
   modelBase = model.base();
   modelHeight = model.height();
}

// Private Components:

private int modelBase;
private int modelHeight;

} // end of class GraphicView
```

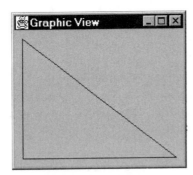

Figure 20.6 Graphic View of a *RightTriangle*.

We've used *JPanels* previously as containers for other components. But a *JPanel* is also useful as a blank canvas on which to draw. The actual rendering of a component is a rather involved process. Probably the simplest way to draw on a *JPanel* is to override its `paintComponent` method. This method is called to allow the component to update its display representation. It gets a *Graphics* object as argument. Every component has a *graphics context* that gives access to the displace space occupied by the component. The graphics context is modeled by an instance of the abstract class *java.awt.Graphics*. Since this is an abstract class, it can't be instantiated. The only way we can get an instance is from a component.

The *Graphics* object provides a large number of methods for drawing on components. In particular, it includes a method

```
public void drawLine (int x1, int y1, int x2, int y2)
```

that draws a one-pixel wide line from the point (*x1*, *y1*) to the point (*x2*, *y2*) in the component's coordinate space.

We define `paintComponent` as follows:

```java
public void paintComponent (Graphics g) {
    super.paintComponent(g);
    g.setColor(getForeground());
    g.drawLine(
        BASE_X,BASE_Y+modelHeight,
        BASE_X+modelBase,BASE_Y+modelHeight);
    g.drawLine(
        BASE_X,BASE_Y,
        BASE_X,BASE_Y+modelHeight);
    g.drawLine(
        BASE_X,BASE_Y,
        BASE_X+modelBase,BASE_Y+modelHeight);
}
```

The first statement of the method calls the *JPanel* `paintComponent`, which draws the background. The next statement sets the color that the *Graphics* object will use to draw with. The final three statements draw the three lines of the triangle: the bottom line, then the vertical line, then the hypotenuse. The constants BASE_X and BASE_Y are offsets from the left and top edges of the panel:

```java
private final static int BASE_X = 10;
// offset of drawing from left edge of panel (pixels)
private final static int BASE_Y = 10;
// offset of drawing from top of panel (pixels)
```

Preferred size and *minimum size* are component properties accessed by the methods

```java
public Dimension getPreferredSize ();
public Dimension getMinimumSize ();
```

`getPreferredSize` returns the "preferred" size of the component, and `getMinimumSize` returns the smallest reasonable size for displaying the component. (They can be identical.) These values are often used by the layout manager when laying out the component containing the component. We override these methods to make sure that the panel is big enough to contain the drawing of the triangle and a 10-pixel border:

```java
/*
 * Define preferred and minimum size so that the
 * triangle fits.
 */
public Dimension getPreferredSize () {
    return new Dimension(
        2*BASE_X+modelBase, 2*BASE_Y+modelHeight);
}

public Dimension getMinimumSize () {
    return getPreferredSize();
}
```

Finally, we implement update:

```
/**
 * Update the view with current model state.
 */
public void update (Observable model, Object arg) {
    getModelState((RightTriangle)model);
    repaint();
    Container w = getTopLevelAncestor();
    if (w instanceof Window)
        ((Window)w).pack();
}
```

This method first gets the current state of the model. The invocation of the method repaint then causes the component to be redrawn as soon as possible. This method can be invoked when we want the component to be redrawn. Finally, we force the top-level window containing the *JPanel* to be resized to fit the preferred size of the *JPanel*. The complete class definition is given in Listing 20.3.

Listing 20.3   **The class *GraphicView***

```
/**
 * Graphical view for a RightTriangle.
 */
class GraphicView extends JPanel implements Observer {

    /**
     * Create a graphic view for the specified RightTriangle.
     */
    public GraphicView (RightTriangle model) {
        super();
        model.addObserver(this);
        update(model,null);
    }

    /**
     * Update the view with current model state.
     */
    public void update (Observable model, Object arg) {
        getModelState((RightTriangle)model);
        repaint();
        Container w = getTopLevelAncestor();
        if (w instanceof Window)
            ((Window)w).pack();
    }
```

continued

Listing 20.3   **The class *GraphicView (continued)***

```
/**
 * Draw the triangle on this JPanel.
 */
public void paintComponent(Graphics g) {
    super.paintComponent(g);
    g.setColor(getForeground());
    g.drawLine(
        BASE_X, BASE_Y+modelHeight,
        BASE_X+modelBase, BASE_Y+modelHeight);
    g.drawLine(
        BASE_X, BASE_Y,
        BASE_X, BASE_Y+modelHeight);
    g.drawLine(
        BASE_X, BASE_Y,
        BASE_X+modelBase, BASE_Y+modelHeight);
}

/*
 * Define preferred and minimum size so that the triangle
 * fits.
 */
public Dimension getPreferredSize () {
    return new Dimension(
        2*BASE_X+modelBase, 2*BASE_Y+modelHeight);
}

public Dimension getMinimumSize () {
    return getPreferredSize();
}

/*
 * Get the properties of the model.
 */
private void getModelState (RightTriangle model) {
    modelBase = model.base();
    modelHeight = model.height();
}

// Private Components:
```

continued

Listing 20.3 **The class *GraphicView (continued)***

```
    private int modelBase;// base of model (pixels)
    private int modelHeight;// height of model (pixels)
    private final static int BASE_X = 10;
        // offset of drawing from left edge of panel (pixels)
    private final static int BASE_Y = 10;
        // offset of drawing from top of panel (pixels)

} // end of class GraphicView
```

20.2.6   A logger as a view

We give one more example of a view, to illustrate that a view need not be part of a graphical interface. This view simply logs changes in the model's state to a file. It is shown in Listing 20.4. Note the following:

❶ The constructor creates an output stream, with the named file as destination. An *IOException* is thrown if the file cannot be created.

❷ The method `println` writes a line of output to the output stream, containing the values of the variables `modelBase` and `modelHeight`, as *String*s separated by a space.

Listing 20.4 **The class *RTLogger***

```
import java.io.*;

/**
 * RTLogger logs changes in a RightTriangle to an
 * output file.
 */
class RTLogger implements Observer {

    /**
     * Create a RightTriangle logger, to log changes in the
     * specified model to the specified log file.
     */
```

continued

Listing 20.4   **The class *RTLogger (continued)***

```
   public RTLogger (RightTriangle model, String fileName)
      throws java.io.IOException {
❶     this.logFile = new PrintWriter(
         new FileOutputStream(fileName));
      getModelState(model);
❷     logFile.println(modelBase + " " + modelHeight);
      model.addObserver(this);
   }

   /**
    * Log when model changes state.
    */
   public void update (Observable model, Object arg) {
      getModelState((RightTriangle)model);
      logFile.println(modelBase + " " + modelHeight);
   }

   // Private methods:

   /*
    * Get the properties of the model.
    */
   private void getModelState (RightTriangle model) {
      modelBase = model.base();
      modelHeight = model.height();
   }

   // Private Components:

   private PrintWriter logFile;

   // Model state:
   private int modelBase;
   private int modelHeight;

} // end of class RTLogger
```

20.3   The MVC pattern and Swing components

Up to now we've treated Swing components as if they were monolithic entities. In fact, the components themselves are structured along the Model-View-Controller pattern. Though a detailed discussion is well beyond the scope of the text, we can get at least an elementary idea as to how Swing components are built.

The model

Each Swing *JComponent* has an associated model object that is responsible for maintaining the component's state. A *JButton* or *JCheckBox* has a *ButtonModel*, for instance, while a *JTextArea* or *JTextField* has a *Document*. *ButtonModel* and *Document* are interfaces defined in `javax.swing` and `javax.swing.text` respectively.

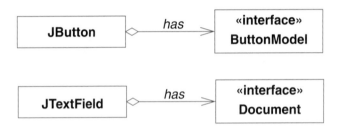

Figure 20.7 **JComponents have models.**

The state of a button is rather simple. It can be *enabled* (only an enabled button can be pressed), it can be *pressed*, and, in the case of a check box or radio button, it can be *selected*. (There are a few more aspects of a button's state that we'll ignore.) Different states of the button are typically reflected in the view. A button that is not enabled might be grayed-out, for instance. The *ButtonModel* is responsible for managing the button state; the interface specifies methods for setting and getting the button's state. For example

> **public boolean** isPressed()
> > This button is pressed.
>
> **public boolean** isEnabled()
> > This button can be pressed or selected by an input device.
>
> **public void** setPressed (**boolean** b)
> > Set this button to pressed or unpressed.
>
> **public void** setEnabled (**boolean** b)
> > Enable or disable this button.

The state information maintained by a *Document* is much more complex. It includes the actual text of the document plus structural information about the text. Support is provided for editing the text and manipulating text attributes, and for notifying listeners when changes are made to the *Document*.

In the case of an ordinary button, the model is usually provided by an instance of the `javax.swing` class *DefaultButtonModel*. Applications don't generally interact directly with the model. Rather, the component itself provides methods that manipulate the model. For example, the class *JButton* has methods `isEnabled` and `setEnabled` that simply invoke the corresponding *ButtonModel* methods.

The default model in the case of a *JTextField* is an instance of the `javax.swing.text` class *PlainDocument*. A *JTextField* can be customized by changing or extending the model. For example, the *Document* method `insertString` inserts characters into the *Document*. In particular, it is invoked every time the user enters a character into the text field. If we want the text field to ignore any characters that are not digits, we can extend the model overriding the `insertString` method.

```
/**
 * A PlainDocument that will contain only digits.
 */
class NumberDocument extends PlainDocument {

    public void insertString (int offset, String str,
        AttributeSet a) throws BadLocationException {
        if (str.length() > 0)
            if (Character.isDigit(str.charAt(0)))
                super.insertString(offset,str,a);
    }
}
```

Now a text field equipped with this model will only accept digits keyed as input. For instance, if *JTextFields* `base` and `height` are the *TextView* components, we can restrict input to digits as follows:

```
base.setDocument(new NumberDocument());
height.setDocument(new NumberDocument());
```

Though default model implementations are provided for Swing components, the basic intention is to allow the programmer to wrap implementation data by constructing the appropriate model interface.

The UI delegate

Since the view and controller for a component are very closely related, they are combined into one object for many Swing components.The component delegates the view and control responsibilities to its *UI delegate*. The package `javax.swing.plaf` ("pluggable look-and-feel") contains an abstract delegate class for each Swing component. For instance the abstract class *ButtonUI* provides the "look-and-feel" interface for a button.

Allocating the view and controller responsibilities to a UI delegate makes it possible to change the look-and-feel of the component, and even define a custom look-and-feel. The package `javax.swing.plaf.basic` contains a set of classes that can be used as the basis for building custom look-and-feel components. The `javax.swing.plaf.basic` class *BasicButtonUI*, for instance, extends *ButtonUI* and provides a basic button drawing facility. Other subpackages of `javax.swing.plaf` provide sets of classes defining specific look-and-feel implementations. For example, the package `javax.swing.plaf.metal` contains a custom look-and-feel designed to give a Java application the same appearance across all platforms. For a button, the `javax.swing.plaf.metal` class *MetalButtonUI* extends *BasicButtonUI* and draws a button with the standard Java "metal" look.

A Swing component such as a *JButton* has several constituents. In the case of a *JButton*, the standard look-and-feel implementations separate view and controller functions into different classes. Thus a standard *JButton* implementation consists of:

- a model, that implements the interface *ButtonModel* and is usually a *DefaultButtonModel*;

- a look-and-feel specific view element that knows how to draw the button; for instance, a *MetalBasicButtonUI*;

- an element that responds to user input, and functions as a controller. This is generally an instance of the `javax.swing.plaf.basic` class *BasicButtonListener*.

(A button also has an object responsible for drawing its border: an instance of the `javax.swing.plaf.metal` class *MetalButtonBorder*, for example.)

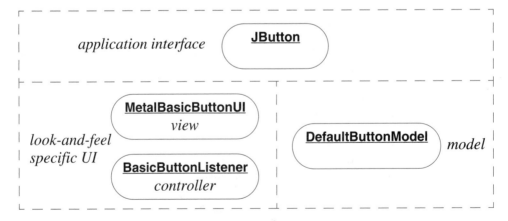

Figure 20.8 **Fundamental elements of a *JButton*.**

20.4 Summary

In this chapter, we saw the basic format of the *Model-View-Controller* pattern, commonly used to structure event-driven graphical user interfaces. With MVC, interface responsibilities are partitioned into two segments: the *view* has display responsibilities, while the *controller* modifies the model in accordance with user input.

As an example, we developed three views of a right triangle. In the process, we noted the facilities provided by the standard Java library for implementing the *observes* relationship. The fundamental relationship between the view and the model is *observes*, and can be easily implemented by making the model object an extension of the class *Observed*, and having the view implement the interface *Observer*.

Finally, we discovered that the Swing components are themselves structured along the lines of MVC. Each Swing component has an associated model object that is responsible for maintaining the component's state. It also has a UI delegate, to which view and control responsibilities are delegated. One advantage of this structure is that it is possible to change the look-and-feel of an application in a system-independent way.

EXERCISES

20.1 The exercises of the preceding chapter developed a graphical user interface for a simple accumulator. Modify the interface to conform to the MVC structure. Display the summand and the running sum in separated text fields.

20.2 Build a graphical user interface for the nim game of Chapter 10, using the MVC structure. Add an additional view that displays the state of the model but has no controller.

GLOSSARY

Model-View-Controller: a pattern for structuring a graphical user interface or graphical user interface component, in which display responsibilities for a model are delegated to a separate *view*, and input responsibilities are delegated to a separate *controller*.

CHAPTER 21   Computational complexity

We interrupt our study of object-oriented design for a brief, informal look at the important topic of algorithmic efficiency. Measuring the efficiency of a program is in general a complicated issue. In this chapter, we try to get a handle on determining how the time required for a program to compute a solution depends on the algorithm chosen. We introduce a commonly used measure, computational complexity, that allows us to compare the efficiency of algorithms in a very fundamental way. We will apply this measure to algorithms developed in subsequent chapters.

After defining the measure, we apply it to some simple algorithms, and conclude with an example that develops three different methods for solving the same problem. These algorithms have dramatically different complexities, and should give us considerable insight into the effects of algorithm choice on program execution time.

21.1 Measuring program efficiency

When we speak of the efficiency or cost of a program, there are many issues we might be considering. We might be concerned with the time it takes for the program to produce a result, the amount of memory or other system resources required by the program, the programmer effort required to maintain the program, and so on. Here we specifically limit our attention to the execution time required for a program to solve a problem.

There are, of course, many factors that affect execution time:

- the hardware—the type and speed of the processor, size and speed of memory, disk transfer rate, network speed, *etc.*

- the operating system;

- the system environment—number of active processes, *etc.*

- the programming language and compiler;
- the run-time system or interpreter;
- the algorithms that constitute the program;
- the data on which the program is run.

We want to isolate the effects on execution time due to algorithm and data, ignoring hardware speed, operating system, *etc.* To this end, we define a measure of program efficiency called *computational complexity* or *time complexity.* This is a coarse but extremely important gauge of a program's execution time. While the definition may seem less than intuitive at first, the concept has proven to be of considerable benefit in comparing and evaluating problem solutions.

We will not attempt a complete or rigorous treatment. We give some fundamental definitions, and apply them rather informally to a few examples. Our intention is simply to gain some familiarity with the notions so that we can infer the time-cost of algorithms examined in subsequent chapters.

21.2   Time complexity for a method

Since complexity is an algorithmic notion, we limit our attention to determining the complexity of a method. We want to determine the time-cost of a method that solves a particular problem.

First of all, we assume that each instance of a problem has some inherent size, and that the execution time required by a method to solve a problem instance depends on its size. For example, if we are considering one of the sort algorithms of Chapter 13, the problem size is the length of the list to be sorted. We expect that the time required to sort the list will depend on the length of the list. If we have a method that determines whether or not a particular integer is prime, the problem size is the size of the integer. We expect the method to take longer to determine whether 9907 is prime than to determine whether 7 is prime.

Of course, a method may require a different amount of time to solve two different problem instances of the same size. For example, a sort method might be able to sort a list of 100 items that is already nearly sorted more quickly than it can sort a list of 100 items that is thoroughly scrambled. Though we are sometimes interested in an "average" time required by a method to solve a problem of a given size, for the most part we want to know the worst case behavior of an algorithm. That is, we want the maximum time-cost over all problems of a given size.

It would seem natural to compute the time-cost of a method in units of time, such as seconds, microseconds, *etc.* But the actual clock time required by a method clearly depends on a number of factors other than the algorithm. Rather than using units of time, we'll measure the time-cost by counting the number of primitive steps the algorithm performs in solving the problem. This measure is easier to calculate and will be perfectly adequate for comparing the relative time cost of various algorithms. In fact, we don't even care to specify exactly what a primitive step is, except to say that it takes a fixed amount of time to perform regardless of the problem. For instance, we can consider it to be a single instruction executed by the Java interpreter.

We now define the *time-cost* or *time complexity* of a method M to be a non-decreasing function t_M from the natural numbers $\mathbf{N}$ (*i.e.*, $\{0, 1, 2, \ldots \}$) to the positive reals $\mathbf{R}^+$

$$t_M : \mathbf{N} \rightarrow \mathbf{R}^+$$

such that $t_M(n)$ is the maximum number of steps for method M to solve a problem of size n, over all problems of size n. For example, if M is the selection sort of Chapter 13, $t_M(100)$ is the maximum number of steps required by the method to sort a list of 100 elements.

21.3   Comparing method costs

We want to compare different algorithms for solving a problem according to their time efficiency. This amounts to comparing their corresponding cost functions. How should we do this? The following approach to comparing cost functions has proven most useful for our purposes. The definition may not seem entirely intuitive, but with a little experience it will become familiar.

Note the relation $\sqsubseteq$ defined in this section is not standard notation. It is given here to simplify the definitions of the standard class constructors O, Ω, and Θ given in the next section.

Let f and g be non-decreasing functions from the natural numbers to the positive reals

$$f, g : \mathbf{N} \rightarrow \mathbf{R}^+$$

We say f is O-*dominated by* g, and write $f \sqsubseteq g$, provided

there is a positive integer n_0, and
there is a positive real c, such that
for all $n \geq n_0, f(n) \leq c \cdot g(n)$.

This says that f is O-dominated by g if some multiple of g dominates f for all large integers, and is illustrated graphically in Figure 21.1.

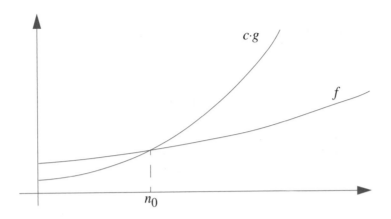

Figure 21.1 *f* is O-dominated by *g*.

Now let's see how to use this definition to compare methods. Suppose M and N are two different sort methods (selection sort and bubble sort, for instance), with time-cost functions t_M and t_N respectively. What does it mean to show that $t_M \sqsubseteq t_N$? First, we can throw out as many specific problems as we want by choosing n_0 sufficiently large. For instance, if we choose n_0 to be 100, we only look at lists that have more than 100 elements. It doesn't matter how they compare on smaller lists. Next, we can "slow down" N as much as we want by choosing an appropriate value of c. For example, if we choose c to be 10, we compare t_M with $10 \cdot t_N$. We can imagine running method N on a machine that is 10 times slower than the machine M is running on. Under these conditions, M must perform as well as N.

Note that we need only demonstrate that the third line of the definition holds for *one* n_0 and *one* c. But $t_M(n)$ must be less than or equal to $c \cdot t_N(n)$ for *all* $n \geq n_0$.

This may seem like a very weak condition. In fact, it may seem that any method can be made to run faster than any other if we slow the second down enough! To get a better handle on the definition, consider what it means if t_M is *not* O-dominated by t_M. In this case, no matter how much we slow down the machine running N, we can always find arbitrarily large problems for which N will run faster than M. Clearly, M is not as efficient as N in some very fundamental way.

We make a few observations about the relation $\sqsubseteq$, without proof. In the following, we assume f, g, h, f', and g' are non-decreasing functions from the natural numbers to the positive reals.

- The relation is *reflexive*: that is, for any function f, $f \sqsubseteq f$.

- The relation is *transitive*: that is, for functions f, g, and h, $f \sqsubseteq g$ and $g \sqsubseteq h$ imply $f \sqsubseteq h$.

- The relation is *not anti-symmetric*: there are functions f and g such that $f \sqsubseteq g$ and $g \sqsubseteq f$, but $f \neq g$.

- The relation is *not total*: there are functions f and g such that neither $f \sqsubseteq g$ nor $g \sqsubseteq f$.

If $f \sqsubseteq g$ and $g \sqsubseteq f$, we say f and g are said to *have the same magnitude*, and we write $f \equiv g$.

If $f \sqsubseteq g$ but it is not the case that $g \sqsubseteq f$, we write $f \sqsubset g$.

(If *exp(n)* is an expression whose value depends on n, we use *exp(n)* to denote the function f defined by $f(n) = exp(n)$. For instance, we denote the function f defined by $f(n) = n^2$ simply as n^2, and denote the constant function $f(n) = 1$ as 1.)

The *pointwise sum, f+g, pointwise product, f·g,* and *pointwise max, max(f, g)* of two functions f and g are defined as follows.

$$[f + g](n) = f(n) + g(n))$$
$$[f \cdot g](n) = f(n) \cdot g(n)$$
$$[max(f, g)](n) = max(f(n), g(n))$$

The following items are easy to show.

<21.1>   If c_1 and c_2 are positive real constants, then $f \equiv c_1 \cdot f + c_2$.

<21.2>   If f is a polynomial function, $f(n) = c_k n^k + c_{k-1} n^{k-1} + \ldots + c_0$, where $c_k > 0$, then $f \equiv n^k$.

<21.3>   If $f \sqsubseteq g$ and $f' \sqsubseteq g'$, then $f \cdot f' \sqsubseteq g \cdot g'$.

<21.4>   If $f \sqsubseteq g$ and $f' \sqsubseteq g'$, then $f + f' \sqsubseteq max(g, g')$. Furthermore, $f + g \equiv max(f, g)$.

<21.5>   If a and b are > 1, $\log_a n \equiv \log_b n$.[1]

<21.6> $1 \sqsubset \log_a n \sqsubset n \sqsubset n \cdot \log_a n \sqsubset n^2 \sqsubset n^3 \sqsubset n^4 \sqsubset \ldots \sqsubset 2^n$.

21.4   Complexity classes

Suppose f is a non-decreasing function from the natural numbers to the positive reals. We define the following sets of functions:

O(f) is the set of functions that are O-dominated by f. That is,

$$O(f) = \{ \ g \ | \ g \sqsubseteq f \ \}.$$

$\Omega(f)$ is the set of functions that O-dominate f. That is,

$$\Omega(f) = \{ \ g \ | \ f \sqsubseteq g \ \}.$$

1. Of course, we fudge a bit with logarithmic functions and eliminate 0 from the domain.

$\Theta(f)$ is the set of functions that have the same magnitude as f. That is,
$$\Theta(f) = \{ \ g \ | \ g \equiv f \ \} = \{ \ g \ | \ f \sqsubseteq g \text{ and } g \sqsubseteq f \ \} = O(f) \cap \Omega(f).$$

$O(f)$ is pronounced "oh of f" or "big oh of f." $\Omega(f)$ is "omega of f," and $\Theta(f)$ is "theta of f."

If M is a method with time-cost t_M, then we say "M is in $O(f)$," or simply "M is $O(f)$," if $t_M \in O(f)$. Similar statements are made for Ω and Θ.

If M is a method with complexity $t_M(n) = c$, for some constant c, then M is $\Theta(1)$ and we say M is *constant*. If M is $\Theta(n)$, we say that M is *linear*. If M is $\Theta(n^2)$, M is *quadratic*. If M is not $O(n^k)$ for any k, then M is *exponential*. Most exponential methods encountered in practice are $\Omega(2^n)$. If a method is linear, we expect the run-time to increase proportionally with the size of the input; if it's quadratic, we expect run-time to increase as the square of the input; and so on.

In subsequent chapters, we categorize the methods in terms of the hierarchy shown in <21.6>. That is, we will categorize methods as being $\Theta(1)$, or $\Theta(\log n)$, or $\Theta(n)$, etc. The table below shows the values of a few complexity functions for several values of n.

To get some idea of the implications, Table 21.1 gives the number of microseconds in several time units. If we are counting steps that take a microsecond, a method with complexity n^3 will take about 17 minutes for a problem of size 1,000, and over 300 centuries for a problem of size 1,000,000. The implications of this are clear. If a method is to be used on large cases, it almost surely needs to be quadratic or better. A method that is exponential can be applied in practice only to very small problem instances.

Table 21.1 **Values of Some Complexity Functions**

n	$\log_2 n$	$n \cdot \log_2 n$	n^2	n^3	2^n
10	3.32	33.2	100	1,000	1,024
100	6.64	664	10,000	1,000,000	1.27×10^{30}
1,000	9.97	9,966	1,000,000	10^9	1.07×10^{301}
1,000,000	19.93	19,931,569	10^{12}	10^{18}	10^{301030}

21.4.1   Complexity of a problem

To this point, our discussion has concerned the complexity of a *method*. Sometimes we are interested in the complexity of a *problem*. That is, we want to know the complexity of the best possible method for solving the problem. If we say that the complexity of a problem is t, we mean that every method for solving the problem is $\Omega(t)$, and some method is $\Theta(t)$. That is, the best possible method for solving

Table 21.2 **Microseconds per Unit of Time.**

Unit	Number of μsecs
second	10^6
minute	6×10^7
hour	3.6×10^9
day	8.64×10^{10}
year	3.15×10^{13}
century	3.15×10^{15}

the problem is $\Theta(t)$. For instance, it is known that the complexity of the general sorting problem using comparison is $n \cdot \log n$. That is, there are methods that can sort any list of length n with $n \cdot \log n$ time-cost, and it is not possible to write a method capable of sorting every list of length n and having time-cost better than $n \cdot \log n$.

Some problems are known to be exponential, and are called *intractable*. (Some problems have no algorithmic solution at all, and are called *unsolvable*.)

Determining the complexity of a method involves analyzing the method and is often straightforward. Determining the complexity of a problem is generally much more difficult, since it involves proving something about all possible methods for solving the problem.

21.4.2 Determining the complexity of a method

We now sketch a few ideas on analyzing methods to determine their time-cost. As we have said, we do not intend to give a thorough, formal presentation.

Methods encountered in practice generally have a cost that fits into the hierarchy of <21.6>. Since complexity is a function of problem size, any method that in the worst case must examine all of its data is at least linear. For instance, a method that finds the largest element on an arbitrary list must examine each element of the list. If the list has n elements, at least n steps are required to examine the elements. A method with constant time complexity, $\Theta(1)$, needs to use only a fixed amount of its data. For instance, a method to remove the first element of a list might require the same number of steps to complete regardless of the length of the list. Methods with complexity better than linear typically require that the problem data have some specific organization or structure. For instance, the binary search algorithm seen in Section 13.3 is $\Theta(\log n)$, but requires the list to be sorted. It is this property of the list that enables the method to find an item without examining each list element.

To determine the time-cost of a method, we must count the steps performed in the worst case. Considering the possible kinds of statements that can comprise a method, we observe the following.

- A simple, elementary statement, like a simple assignment, requires a constant number of steps. Similarly, evaluation of a simple expression requires a constant number of steps.

- To determine the number of steps required by a statement that invokes a method, we must determine the number of steps required by the method that is invoked.

- The worst case number of steps required by a conditional such as an *if-then-else* is the maximum of the number of steps required by each alternative. For instance, if statements A and B have time-costs t_A and t_B respectively, then

```
if (simpleCondition)
    A
else
    B
```

has time-cost $max(t_A, t_B)$.

- To determine the number of steps required by a sequence of statements, we sum the number of steps required by each statement. Here, **<21.4>** simplifies our task considerably. For example, if statements A, B, and C have time-costs t_A, t_B, and t_C respectively, then

```
A; B; C;
```

has time-cost $t_A + t_B + t_C \equiv max(t_A, t_B, t_C)$.

- To determine the time-cost of a loop, we determine the number of steps required by the loop body and multiply by the number of times the loop body is executed.

- To determine the number of steps required by a recursive call, we must determine the depth of the recursion.

A little consideration of the above points should make it clear that loops and recursive calls are the syntactic elements likely to determine the complexity of a method.

An example containing a loop

As a first example, consider the method to compute the average final grade of a list of *Students*, as seen in Section 12.4. The problem size here is rather clearly the length of the argument list, students.

```
public double average (StudentList students) {
    int i;
    int sum;
    int count;
    count = students.size();
    sum = 0;
    i = 0;
    while (i < count) {
        sum = sum + students.get(i).finalExam();
        i = i+1;
    }
    return (double)sum / (double)count;
}
```

If we assume that the method `size` requires constant time independent of the length of the list, then all of the statements in the method except for the *while-loop* contribute only a constant amount to the time-cost. Clearly the complexity of the method depends on the loop. If we further assume that the *Student* method `finalExam` and the *StudentList* method `get` are constant, then the body of the loop requires constant time to execute, and we need only count the number of times the body of the loop is performed. But the body of the loop is performed once for each element of the list. If the length of the list `students` is n, the loop body is done n times. (The test `i < count` is actually done $n+1$ times, but this does not change the complexity of the method.) Thus the method is linear, $\Theta(n)$.

Now suppose that the method `get` is linear in its argument: in particular, suppose that `get(i)` requires ic_1+c_0 steps to complete, where c_1 and c_0 are constants. The body of the loop is no longer constant, and we need to do a little more work to determine the complexity of the method.

We can list the number of steps required by `get(i)` for each value of `i` as follows:

value of `i`:	0	1	2	...	$n-1$
steps of `get(i)`:	c_0	c_1+c_0	$2c_1+c_0$	...	$(n-1)c_1+c_0$

We sum the n terms to determine the total number of steps required by the invocations of `get`:

$$\sum_{i=0}^{n-1} (ic_1 + c_0) = nc_0 + c_1 \sum_{i=1}^{n-1} i$$

It is easy to see by induction that

(1)
$$\sum_{i=1}^{k} i = \frac{k(k+1)}{2} = \frac{1}{2}(k^2 + k)$$

Thus the total number of steps required by invocations of get is

$$nc_0 + \frac{1}{2}c_1(n^2 - n)$$

and the method is quadratic.

To simplify calculations, we assume for the remainder of this chapter that *List* methods such as size and get require constant time.

An example containing nested loops

As a second example we consider a method containing a pair of nested loops: a method that will determine if a List contains duplicate elements. (This is similar to the method that removed duplicate elements from a list presented in Section 12.5.1.) We can probably guess that a method containing nested loops, each of which depends on problem size, will be at least quadratic. The method is defined as follows:

```
boolean hasDuplicates (List list) {
    int i;
    int j;
    int n;
    boolean found;
    n = list.size();
    found = false;
    for (i = 0; i < n-1 && !found; i = i+1)
        for (j = i+1; j < n && !found; j = j+1)
            found = list.get(i).equals(list.get(j));
    return found;
}
```

We consider the case where the list has no duplicates. This case requires the longest execution time, since the method must examine every pair of elements.

The outer loop is performed $n - 1$ times, with i successively taking on the values 0, 1, 2, …, $n-2$. The number of iterations of the inner loop depends on i:

value of i:	0	1	2	…	$n - 3$	$n - 2$
iterations of the inner loop	$n - 1$	$n - 2$	$n - 3$	…	2	1

To compute the number of times the assignment

```
found = list.get(i).equals(list.get(j));
```

is done, we must compute the sum:

$$1 + 2 + \ldots + (n - 3) + (n - 2) + (n - 1).$$

From equation *(1)*, this is to equal to $\frac{n^2 - n}{2}$. Thus the method is $\Theta(n^2)$.

21.5   An example: three methods

In this section, we analyze three different methods for solving the same problem. This will give us a good idea of what is involved in analyzing both iterative and recursive methods. The problem is based on [Weiss 92].

Define a *sublist* of a list *l* to be a list containing 0 or more contiguous elements of *l*. For instance, the list (1, 2, 3) has seven sublists: the empty sublist; three sublists of length 1: (1), (2), and (3); two sublists of length 2: (1, 2) and (2, 3); one sublist of length 3: (1, 2, 3).

The problem we want to solve is this: given a list of integers, find the maximum sum of the elements of a sublist. For example, the following lists have sublists with maximum sum as shown.

list	sublist with max sum	max sum
(-2, 4, -3, 5, 3, -5, 1)	(4, -3, 5, 3)	9
(2, 4, 5)	(2, 4, 5)	11
(-1, -2, 3)	(3)	3
(-1, -2, -3)	()	0

Note that the sum of the elements of the empty list is 0. Thus if a list contains only negative integers, the empty sublist is the sublist with maximum sum. Furthermore, any method to solve this problem must be at least linear, since each element of the list must be examined.

To simplify the code, assume that *IntegerList* has a method `getInt`, where

```
getInt(i)  ==  ((Integer)get(i)).intValue()
```

We can then specify the method we want to write as follows:

> **int** maxSublistSum (IntegerList list)
>   The maximum sum of a sublist of the given list.
>
>   if list.getInt(i) > 0 for some i, 0 <= i < list.size(), then
>   *max* { list.getInt(i) + ... + list.getInt(j) |
>   0 <= i <= j < list.size() }
>   else
>   0

The problem is admittedly artificial. But it admits several easy to understand and quite distinct solutions. We consider three methods for solving the problem, each with different time-cost.

21.5.1   A naive method

The first method we consider uses a straightforward, brute force approach. Simply sum the elements of each possible sublist, and remember the maximum. The method is given in Listing 21.1.

Listing 21.1   **A naive approach**

```
int maxSublistSum (IntegerList list) {
    int n = list.size();
    int maxSum;// max of all values of sum
    int sum;// list.getInt(i) + … + list.getInt(j)
    int i;// starting index of sublist being summed
    int j;// ending index of sublist being summed
    int k;// index of summand, i <= k <= j

    maxSum = 0;
    for (i = 0; i < n; i = i+1)
        for (j = i; j < n; j = j+1) {
            // compute list.getInt(i) + … + list.getInt(j)
            sum = 0;
            for (k = i; k <= j; k = k+1)
                sum = sum + list.getInt(k);
            if (sum > maxSum)
                maxSum = sum;
        }

    return maxSum;
}
```

The outer index i determines the starting point of the sublist, and the second index j determines the ending point. The inner loop then sums the elements list.getInt(i) + … + list.itmeAt(j).

Since we have three nested loops, each of which depends on the length of the list, we expect the method to be $\Theta(n^3)$. We'll do the arithmetic this once to verify our conjecture.

The body of the inner loop (k-loop) is executed the most often. To determine the complexity of the method, we count the number of times this is done.

The outer loop is done n times, with i taking on the values 0, 2, ..., $n-1$. For each value of i, j iterates through the values i through $n-1$. For each value of i and j, k iterates from i through j. For each value of k, the body of the inner loop is done once. Thus we must compute the sum:

$$\sum_{i=0}^{n-1} \sum_{j=i}^{n-1} \sum_{k=i}^{j} 1$$

This requires just a little arithmetic, given equation *(1)* on page 543 and the following:

(2)
$$\sum_{i=1}^{k} i^2 = \frac{k(k+1)(2k+1)}{6}$$

The inner summand

$$\sum_{k=i}^{j} 1$$

obviously equals the number of integers k such that $i \le k \le j$; *i.e.*, equals $j-i+1$. Now moving to the middle sum,

$$\sum_{j=i}^{n-1} \sum_{k=i}^{j} 1 = \sum_{j=i}^{n-1} (j-i+1);$$

substituting $j = i, i+1, \ldots, n-1$, we get

$$= 1 + 2 + \ldots + (n-i)$$

$$= \frac{(n-i+1)(n-i)}{2}, \text{ by equation (1) above;}$$

$$= \frac{1}{2}i^2 - \left(n + \frac{1}{2}\right)i + \frac{1}{2}(n^2 + n), \text{ after expansion.}$$

Finally, using equations *(1)* and *(2)* and a little algebra, we compute:

$$\sum_{i=0}^{n-1} \sum_{j=i}^{n-1} \sum_{k=i}^{j} 1 = \sum_{i=0}^{n-1} \left(\frac{1}{2}i^2 - \left(n + \frac{1}{2}\right)i + \frac{1}{2}(n^2 + n)\right)$$

$$= \frac{1}{2}\sum_{i=0}^{n-1} i^2 - \left(n + \frac{1}{2}\right)\sum_{i=0}^{n-1} i + \frac{1}{2}(n^2 + n)\sum_{i=0}^{n-1} 1$$

$$= \frac{1}{2}\left(\frac{(n^2 - n)(2n - 1)}{6}\right) - \left(n + \frac{1}{2}\right)\left(\frac{n(n-1)}{2}\right) + \frac{1}{2}(n^2 + n)n$$

$$= \frac{1}{6}n^3 + \frac{1}{2}n^2 + \frac{1}{3}n$$

Is this method satisfactory? It is certainly easy to understand and to write correctly. If we intend only to use it a few times on relatively small lists, it is adequate. It is not critical to spend time trying to find a better approach. But if the method is part of critical operating system code or if we want to use it for large lists, we need something better.

It is relatively straightforward to improve this method to $\Theta(n^2)$ by summing in the second loop and eliminating the third. We'll leave this as an exercise, and look at two rather different approaches.

21.5.2   A recursive method

The next method we consider uses a recursive "divide and conquer" approach. Lists of length 0 and 1 are obvious base cases. If we have a longer list, we divide it in half and consider the possible cases. For the discussion, assume the list is $(x_0, \ldots, x_{n-1})$ with left half $(x_0, \ldots, x_{mid})$ and right half $(x_{mid+1}, \ldots, x_{n-1})$:

$x_0 \ \cdots \ x_{mid}$	$x_{mid+1} \ \cdots \ x_{n-1}$

There are three possible cases:

1. the sublist with the max sum is in the left half of the list, *i.e.*, in $(x_0, \ldots, x_{mid})$;

2. the sublist with the max sum is in the right half of the list: *i.e.*, in $(x_{mid+1}, \ldots, x_{n-1})$;

3. the sublist with max sum "overlaps" the middle of the list: in particular, it includes both x_{mid} and x_{mid+1}.

As is commonly the case with recursive methods, we write an auxiliary method that takes as arguments the starting and ending indexes of the portion of the list to consider:

```
private int maxSublistSum (IntegerList list,
    int first, int last)
```
    The maximum sum of a sublist in the given range. That is, the maximum
    sum of a sublist of (list.get(first), ..., list.get(last)).

    require:
        0 <= first <= last < list.size()

The principle method handles the empty list explicitly, and otherwise calls the auxiliary method:

```
int maxSublistSum (IntegerList list) {
    if (list.size() == 0)
        return 0;
```

```
            else
                return maxSublistSum(list,0,list.size()-1);
    }
```

The auxiliary method cannot be called with an empty range, since `first <= last` is required. The base case of a single element is explicitly handled. If there is more than one element, the maximum sums of sublists in the left and right half are recursively obtained, and the maximum sum of a sublist that overlaps the middle is computed.

To determine the maximum sum of a sublist overlapping the middle, the maximum sum of a sublist ending with x_{mid}, and the maximum sum of a sublist beginning with x_{mid+1} are computed and then added.

The largest of the three values—maximum sum of sublist in the left half, maximum sum of sublist in the right half, and maximum sum of a sublist that overlaps both halves—is then returned. The method is shown in Listing 21.2.

Listing 21.2 **A divide-and-conquer approach**

```
/*
 * require:
 *    0 <= first <= last < list.size()
 */
private int maxSublistSum (IntegerList list, int first,
    int last) {
    int maxSum;// return value
    int mid = (first + last)/2;
            // index of middle element;
            // first <= mid <= last
    int maxLeftSum;
            // maxSublistSum of left half of list: i.e., of
            // (list.get(first), …, list.get(mid))
    int maxRightSum;
            // maxSublistSum of right half of l: i.e., of
            // (list.get(mid+1), …, list.get(last))
    int maxMidSum;
            // max sum of a sublist containing both
            // list.get(mid) and list.get(mid+1)
    int maxEndMid;
            // max sum of a sublist ending with
            // list.get(mid)
    int maxStartMid;
            // max sum of a sublist starting with
            // list.get(mid+1)
    int endMidSum;
            // list.getInt(i) + … + list.getInt(mid)
```

continued

Listing 21.2*   A divide-and-conquer approach *(continued)

```
int startMidSum;
      // list.getInt(mid+1) + ... + list.getInt(i)
int i;// index for summing

if (first == last)
   if (list.getInt(first) < 0)
      return 0;
   else
      return list.getInt(first);
else {
   // first <= mid < last
   maxLeftSum = maxSubList(list, first, mid);
   maxRightSum = maxSubList(list, mid+1, last);

   maxEndMid = list.getInt(mid);
   endMidSum = list.getInt(mid);
   for (i = mid-1; i >= first; i = i-1) {
      endMidSum = endMidSum + list.getInt(i);
      if (endMidSum > maxEndMid)
         maxEndMid = endMidSum;
   }

   maxStartMid = list.getInt(mid+1);
   startMidSum = list.getInt(mid+1);
   for (i = mid+2; i <= last; i = i+1) {
      startMidSum = startMidSum + list.getInt(i);
      if (startMidSum > maxStartMid)
         maxStartMid = startMidSum;
   }

   maxMidSum = maxEndMid + maxStartMid;

   maxSum = maxMidSum;
   if (maxLeftSum > maxSum)
      maxSum = maxLeftSum;
   if (maxRightSum > maxSum)
      maxSum = maxRightSum;

   return maxSum;
}
```

This method is much more involved than the previous, and care must be taken to ensure correctness. For instance, we must make sure that preconditions are satisfied for each of the recursive calls.

The analysis of this recursive method is a little different from those that we've looked at previously. We give a very informal analysis.

The complexity of the method is clearly the complexity of the auxiliary method. Let t be the time-cost function of the recursive auxiliary method. If there is only one element to consider, the method requires a fixed amount of time, which we'll call c_0.

(3) $$t(1) = c_0$$

If there are $n > 1$ elements to consider, the method twice recursively calls itself, with half as many elements each time:

$$t(n) = 2 \cdot t(n/2) + \ldots$$

It then performs two loops, iterating each essentially $n/2$ times. If we let c_1 be the time required for an iteration, we have:

$$t(n) = 2 \cdot t(n/2) + c_1 \cdot n + \ldots$$

Finally, there are a number of other steps requiring constant time independent of n. Call this time c_2:

(4) $$t(n) = 2 \cdot t(n/2) + c_1 \cdot n + c_2$$

An equation like *(4)* that describes a function at one point in terms of its value at another point is called a *recurrence relation*. Recurrence relations are often the key to analyzing recursive methods.

If we substitute $n/2$ for n in *(4)*, we get:

(5) $$t(n/2) = 2 \cdot t(n/4) + c_1 \cdot (n/2) + c_2$$

Substituting the right side of *(5)* for $t(n/2)$ in *(4)*, we have:

(6) $$t(n) = 2 \cdot (2 \cdot t(n/4) + c_1 \cdot (n/2) + c_2) + c_1 \cdot n + c_2$$
$$= 4 \cdot t(n/4) + 2 \cdot c_1 \cdot n + 3 \cdot c_2$$

Repeating the process for $n/4$ gives:

$$t(n/4) = 2 \cdot t(n/8) + c_1 \cdot (n/4) + c_2$$

and from *(6)*:

$$t(n) = 8 \cdot t(n/8) + 3 \cdot c_1 \cdot n + 7 \cdot c_2$$

It is not hard to show that this generalizes to

$$t(n) = 2^k \cdot t(n/2^k) + k \cdot c_1 \cdot n + (2^k - 1) \cdot c_2$$

We can solve the equation if we can determine $t(n/2^k)$ for some particular k. But we know

$$t(1) = c_0,$$

and $n/2^k = 1$ when $n = 2^k$, or when $k = \log_2 n$. Thus for $k = \log_2 n$, $n/2^k = 1$ and

$$t(n) = 2^k \cdot t(1) + k \cdot c_1 \cdot n + (2^k - 1) \cdot c_2$$
$$= 2^{\log_2 n} \cdot c_0 + \log_2 n \cdot c_1 \cdot n + (2^{\log_2 n} - 1) \cdot c_2$$
$$= n \cdot c_0 + c_1 \cdot n \cdot \log_2 n + (n - 1) \cdot c_2$$

and the complexity of the method is $\Theta(n \cdot \log_2 n)$. This is a considerable improvement over the previous method, but we can do even better.

21.5.3   An iterative method

Finally, we consider an iterative approach. Suppose we have examined the first i elements of the list, $(x_0, \ldots, x_{i-1})$, and have found the sublist with maximum sum in the first i elements. We now look at the $i + 1$st element.

x_0 ... x_{i-1}	x_i

There are two possibilities for the maximum sum sublist of the first $i + 1$ elements:

1. it doesn't include x_i, in which case it is the same as the maximum sum sublist of the first i elements; or

2. it includes x_i.

If we look at the maximum sum sublist ending with x_i, there are again two cases:

1. it consists only of x_i; or

2. it includes x_{i-1}, in which case it is x_i appended to the maximum sum sublist ending with x_{i-1}.

It is, in fact, rather easy to distinguish these two cases. Let l_{i-1} denote the maximum sum sublist ending with x_{i-1}, l_i the maximum sum sublist ending with x_i. If l_{i-1} has a negative sum, then l_i consists of just x_i. Otherwise, l_i is l_{i-1} with x_i appended.

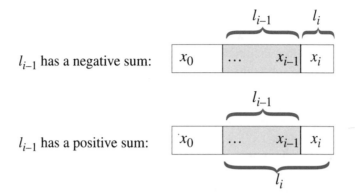

l_{i-1} has a negative sum:

l_{i-1} has a positive sum:

This suggests that we write a method that iterates through the list, keeping track of the maximum sublist sum, and the maximum sum of a sublist ending with the current element. The method is shown in Listing 21.3. The method is $\Theta(n)$, which is the best we can hope for. It is also rather straightforward and easy to understand.

Listing 21.3 **An iterative approach**

```
int maxSublistSum (IntegerList list) {
    int n = list.size();
    int i;// index for the list
    int maxSum;// max sum of a sublist of
           // (list.get(0), …, list.get(i-1))
    int maxTail;// max sum of a sublist ending with
           // list.get(i-1)

    maxSum = 0;
    maxTail = 0;
    for (i = 0; i < n; i = i+1) {
        if (maxTail > 0)
            maxTail = maxTail + list.getInt(i);
        else
            maxTail = list.getInt(i);
        if (maxTail > maxSum)
            maxSum = maxTail;
    }

    return maxSum;
}
```

21.6   Summary

In this chapter, we considered a fundamental measure of algorithm efficiency called time complexity. We will use this measure to evaluate algorithms introduced in subsequent chapters.

The time-cost of a method is a function that specifies the maximum number of steps required by the method to solve a problem of a specified size. Time-cost functions can be compared with a relation O-*dominated by*. If f and g are time-cost functions, f is O-dominated by g when there exist positive numbers n_0 and c such that $f(n) \leq c \cdot g(n)$ for all $n \geq n_0$. If f is O-dominated by g, then $f \in O(g)$ and $g \in \Omega(f)$. If $f \in O(g)$ and $f \in \Omega(g)$, then f and g have the same magnitude, and $f \in \Theta(g)$. Comparing the time-cost of a method to a collection of standard functions enables us to categorize efficiency of the method in a very fundamental way.

We saw how to compute the time-cost for some simple examples, and noted that loops and recursive invocations played a principle role in determining the complexity of a method. Finally, we did a case study in which three different methods were presented to solve the same problem, with substantially different complexities.

EXERCISES

21.1   Compute the time-cost of the selection sort and bubble sort algorithms of Chapter 13.

21.2   How many steps are required by the modified bubble sort algorithm (Listing 13.3) to sort a list of length n in the best possible case?

21.3   Modify the "naive" algorithm for maximum sum of a sublist (Listing 21.1) so that it is $\Theta(n^2)$.

21.4   Compute the time-cost of the insertion sort algorithm of exercise 13.5.

21.5   Compute the time-cost of the recursive binary search algorithm of exercise 17.1. Compute the time-cost of the binary search algorithm of Section 13.3.

21.6   Compute the time-cost of the towers puzzle-solving algorithm given in Section 17.2.

21.7   Compute the time-cost of the merge-sort algorithm of exercise 17.3.

21.8   Compute the time-cost of the *String*-reversing method of exercise 17.4.

21.9   Verify that the relation $\sqsubseteq$ introduced in Section 21.3 is transitive.

21.10   Verify assertions <21.1> through <21.6> from page 539.

GLOSSARY

O-*dominated by*: a relation between time-cost functions; f is O-dominated by g provided there is a positive integer n_0 and a positive real c, such that $f(n) \leq c \cdot g(n)$ for all $n \geq n_0$.

$O(f)$: the set of functions that are O-dominated by f.

$\Omega(f)$: the set of functions that f is O-dominated by.

$\Theta(f)$: the set of functions that have the same magnitude as f; that is $\Theta(f) = O(f) \cap \Omega(f)$.

intractable: a problem for which the best possible algorithm is exponential.

time-complexity: the time-cost of a method.

time-cost: a function that gives the maximum number of steps required by a method to solve a problem of a specified size.

CHAPTER 22

Implementing lists: array implementations

In the next few chapters, we consider the problem of implementing the class *List*. We look at two fundamentally different approaches. In this chapter, we build implementations on a primitive language-provided structure called an *array*. In the next chapter, we consider explicitly linked implementations. These approaches to implementing structure are fundamental, and are used to build many kinds of structural relationships between problem components. As we proceed, we will also encounter several important relationships between classes used to effect various implementations. These relational patterns solve commonly occurring specific design problems, and can be applied to many different applications.

22.1 Arrays

An *array* is a contiguous sequence of variables all of the same type. The individual variables are identified by *index values* or *indexes*. In Java, index values are integers, beginning with 0. See figure 22.1.

The variables that comprise an array are called the *components* or *elements* of the array, and can have a primitive type (**char**, **int**, **boolean**, **double**, *etc.*) or a reference type (*reference-to-*Student, *reference-to-*Object, *etc.*) The *length* of the array is the number of component variables that comprise the array. Note that just as with a *List*, if the length of an array is *n*, the component variables are indexed 0 through *n* - 1.

> **array:** a structure composed of a contiguous sequence of variables, all of the same type.

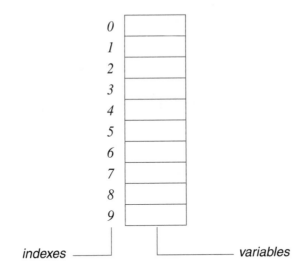

Figure 22.1 *A 10-element array.*

There are two important aspects of an array. First, the length of an array is fixed when the array is created. Second, since contiguous memory is allocated for the variables, accessing a particular variable in the array requires a constant amount of time independent of the array length. For example, suppose the variables comprising a particular array each occupy four bytes, and the array is allocated memory starting at location 100:

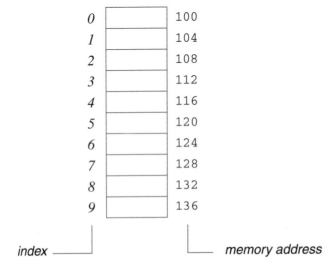

The address of the variable with index i is $100 + 4\cdot i$: the address of the variable with index 6, for instance, is $100 + 4\cdot 6 = 124$. In general, the address of an array element can be computed as (*starting address of the array*) + (*variable size*) · (*element index*). This computation requires a fixed amount of time, and is independent of either the index or the length of the array. (Many kinds of computer processors have specialized instruction formats designed for doing exactly this calculation very efficiently.)

Arrays in Java are encapsulated in objects, called surprisingly enough, *array objects* or simply *arrays*. In addition to the component array variables and features inherited from the class *Object*, array objects have a public **int** component `length`.

The class of an array is determined by the type of the component variables: an array with **int** components is an "*array-of-***int**," and an array with *reference-to-Student* components is an *array-of-Student*, and so on. The class is written as the component type followed by a pair of brackets. Thus, **int**`[]` denotes the class *array-of-***int**, and `Student[]` denotes the class *array-of-Student*. (Note these are brackets, not braces or parentheses.)

Arrays of primitive values are often used explicitly, particularly in complex numeric algorithms where run-time efficiency is critical. Arrays, however, are rather low-level structures. We will limit our use of arrays, specifically the class *array-of-Object*, to the implementation of other higher-level structures.

Defining arrays

As with any class, variables can be defined to reference instances of an array class. For example, the definitions

```
int[] grades;
Student[] cs2125;
```

create two variables, one of type *reference-to-array-of-***int** named `grades` and the other of type *reference-to-array-of-Student* named `cs2125`.

(These definitions can also be written

```
int grades[];
Student cs2125[];
```

but we will not use this syntax.)

While we might refer to a variable like `grades` as an **int**-array variable or an **int**-array, it is important to remember that the variable contains a *reference* to an *array object*. In particular, creating the variable *does not* create an array. Creating a variable never automatically creates an object. Arrays are no different from other objects in this way.

The above definitions result in the creation of two *null*-valued variables:

grades	○
cs2125	○

As with any other object, we use a constructor to create an array object. The constructor requires a single integer argument, the length of the array. The argument, however, is written inside the brackets that are part of the array class name. For instance, the assignments

```
grades = new int[5];
cs2125 = new Student[5];
```

create two arrays of length 5, and assign references to these arrays to the specified variables:

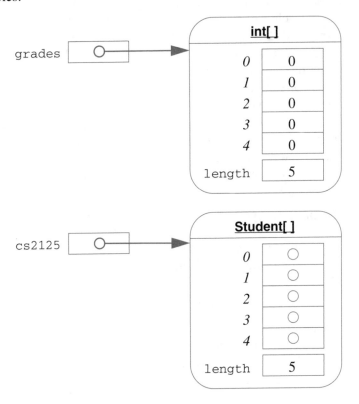

The component variables of the arrays are initialized with standard default values: for example, 0 for **int**, *null* for references. The length given in the constructor is simply an argument. It need not be a literal. (In fact, it generally *shouldn't* be a literal!) Any integer expression will do. For instance, the following are correct, assuming studentCount is an **int**:

```
cs2125 = new Student[studentCount];
grades = new int[4*cs2125.length];
```

(The astute reader may wonder if we can create an array whose component variables are themselves array variables. The answer is yes, though we shall not build such structures in this text. If we define a variable `matrix` as

```
int[][] matrix;
```

then `matrix` references an array whose component variables are of type `int[]`. That is, the component variables reference `int` arrays. The syntax for constructor invocation (and component access) is perhaps not quite as expected. For example,

```
matrix = new int[3][];
```

creates an array with 3 components, each of type `int[]`. The statement

```
matrix = new int[3][4];
```

also creates three `int` arrays of 4 elements each.)

Accessing array components

To access a component of an array, a reference to the array is followed by an index value in brackets. For example

```
grades[3]
```

is an `int` variable—the one with index 3 in the array referenced by the variable `grades`. This is an ordinary `int` variable, and can be used like any other `int` variable. For instance, we can write:

```
grades[3] = 100;
grades[4] = grades[3]/2;
```

and so on. Similarly, we can write:

```
cs2125[0] = new Student(…);
cs2125[0].payFees(100);
```

The expression in brackets that denotes a particular array element need not be a literal. It can be an arbitrary integer expression, as long as the value is nonnegative and less than the length of the array. For instance, we can assign each component of the array `grades` the value 100 with the following iteration:

```
int i;
for (i = 0; i < grades.length; i = i+1)
    grades[i] = 100;
```

The assignment

```
grades[i] = 100;
```

is performed a number of times, with i having a different value each time. The first time i has value 0 and the variable `grades[0]` is assigned 100. The second time, i is 1 and `grades[1]` is assigned. The variable i successively gets the index value of each array component, and that component is then assigned 100.

If an array is referenced with an index that is negative or not less than the array length—that is, if a nonexistent component is referenced—an *ArrayIndex-OutOfBoundsException* is thrown. For example, the following will store the value 100 in all components of the array `grades`, and then throw an *ArrayIndexOutOf-BoundsException* on the last iteration of the loop, when i equals `grades.length`.

```
int i;
for (i = 0; i <= grades.length; i = i+1)
    grades[i] = 100;
```

22.2   An array-based list implementation

Now that we know what an array is, we can use arrays to implement lists. The idea is very straightforward: we allocate an array to hold (references to) the elements of the list. Array component 0 references the first element of the list element, component 1 references the second, and so on.

Note that the length of the list is bounded by the length of the array, and the array length is fixed when the array is created. To emphasize this fact, we'll call the class *BoundedList*, and require that a maximum list size be specified when an instance is created. Otherwise, it will have the same functionality as the class *List*.

> **public abstract class** BoundedList
> A list of objects with a fixed maximum size.
>
> **protected** BoundedList (**int** maxSize)
> Create a new *BoundedList* with a specified maximum size.
>
> > **require:**
> > maxSize >= 0
> >
> > **ensure:**
> > isEmpty(new BoundedList(n))

Recall that an abstract class constructor will only be invoked by a subclass constructor, and thus is generally declared *protected*. For instance

```
public class BoundedStudentList extends BoundedList {

    public BoundedStudentList (int maxSize) {
        super(maxSize);
    }
    ...
}
```

The data components of a *BoundedList* include the array containing the list elements, and an **int** variable containing the list length. (Note that the length of the *array* is the *maximum* list length.)

```
private Object[] elements; // elements of the list
private int size;          // size of the list
// elements[0] … elements[size-1] are valid;
// elements[size] … elements[elements.length-1]
// are not.
```

These variables are initialized by the constructor:

```
protected BoundedList (int maxSize) {
    Require.condition(maxSize >= 0);
    elements = new Object[maxSize];
    size = 0;
}
```

A *BoundedList* is illustrated in Figure 22.2.

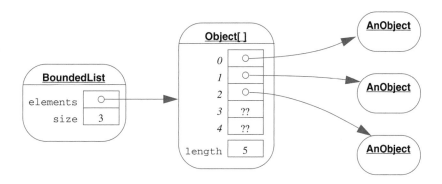

Figure 22.2 **A *BoundedList*.**

Most other features can be implemented in a very straightforward fashion. We omit comments to simplify the presentation, though methods add and append must now have preconditions requiring that the size of the list be less than the maximum size.

```
public int size () {
    return this.size;
}

public Object get (int i) {
    Require.condition(0 <= i && i < size);
    return elements[i];
}
```

```
public void append (Object obj) {
    Require.notNull(obj);
    Require.condition(size < elements.length);
    elements[size] = obj;
    size = size+1;
}

public void add (int i, Object obj) {
    Require.notNull(obj);
    Require.condition(0 <= i && i <= size);
    Require.condition(size < elements.length);
    int index;
    for (index = size-1; index >= i; index = index-1)
        elements[index+1] = elements[index];
    elements[i] = obj;
    size = size+1;
}

public void remove (int i) {
    Require.condition(0 <= i && i < size);
    int index;
    for (index = i; index < size-1; index = index+1)
        elements[index] = elements[index+1];
    size = size-1;
}

public void set (int i, Object obj) {
    Require.notNull(obj);
    Require.condition(0 <= i && i < size);
    elements[i] = obj;
}

public void clear () {
    size = 0;
}
```

Note that the methods `add` and `remove` must shuffle a portion of the array up or down. For instance, to insert a new element at position `i` in the list, the `i`-th through last elements of the list must each be moved up one place in the array. If the list contains six elements, for example, and a new element is to be inserted at index position 2, then the last four elements in the array must be moved up to make room for the new element:

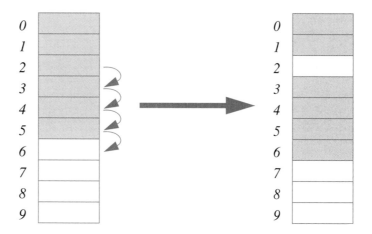

Elements must be moved starting with the last, or else elements will get over-written. For instance, if we wrote

```
for (index = i; index < size; index = index+1)
    elements[index+1] = elements[index];
```

the result would be as shown in Figure 22.3, assuming `size` is 6 and `i` is 2.

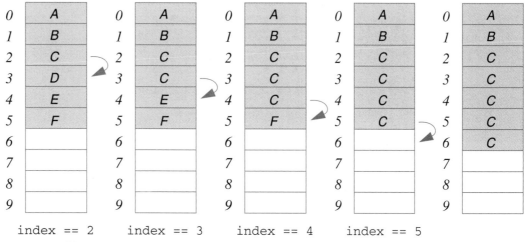

Figure 22.3 **Elements overwritten by an incorrect algorithm.**

Also note that when elements are deleted with `clear` or `remove`, there is no need to set array components to *null*. Array components index from `size` through `elements.length` are considered invalid. It does not matter what values they contain.

The methods isEmpty, indexOf, and toString can be defined in terms of the above methods:

```
public boolean isEmpty () {
    return this.size() == 0;
}

public int indexOf (Object obj) {
    int i;
    int n = this.size();
    i = 0;
    while (i < n && !obj.equals(get(i)))
        i = i+1;
    if (i == n)
        return -1;
    else
        return i;
}

public String toString () {
    String s = "[";
    int n = this.size();
    if (n > 0) {
        s = s + this.get(0).toString();
        int index;
        for (index = 1; index < n; index=index+1)
            s = s + ", " + this.get(index).toString();
    }
    s = s + "]";
}
```

We also add a query for the maximum size of the list:

```
public int maxSize () {
    return elements.length;
}
```

22.2.1   The method *copy*

We must still implement the method copy, which produces a (shallow) copy of the list. By "shallow copy" we mean that the list object is copied, but the elements on the list are not copied. That is, the original list and the copy reference the same list elements.)

We might be tempted to write something like this:

```
public BoundedList copy () {
    int i;
    BoundedList theCopy = new BoundedList(
        elements.length);
```

```
        for (i = 0; i < size; i=i+1)
            theCopy.elements[i] = this.elements[i];
        theCopy.size = this.size;
        return theCopy;
    }
```

The problem with this, of course, is that *BoundedList* is an *abstract* class, and so we cannot create a new instance of *BoundedList*. To make a copy of a *BoundedList*, we must create a new object. But we don't know what kind of object to create. That's determined by concrete subclass of the instance being copied. For example, if a *BoundedCardList* instance is executing the method, we want to create a new *BoundedCardList*. If a *BoundedStudentList* instance is executing the method, we want to create a new *BoundedStudentList*. But we don't want each subclass to have to implement copy. A subclass should simply inherit this method, just as it inherits other list methods.

We outline two approaches to the problem: one takes advantage of the Java object hierarchy; the other is more generally applicable to related problems.

Java interface Cloneable

The class *Object* defines a method clone specified as

```
        protected Object clone ()
            throws CloneNotSupportedException
                Create a copy of this Object.
```

The idea is that a clone of an object is an exact duplicate of, and of the same run-time class as, the original object. For instance, if s is *Student*, executing s.clone() should create a new *Student* object, distinct from s, but whose components are identical to s; that is, same name, same address, and so on. In particular, we typically expect

```
        s != s.clone()
        s.equals(s.clone())
        s.clone() instanceof Student
```

assuming equals compares components and is not simply identity. In fact, even if the static type of s is a superclass of *Student*, for example

```
        Object s = new Student(…);
```

we expect

```
        s.clone() instanceof Student
```

if s is referencing a *Student* when the method clone is executed at run-time.

Note that since clone returns an *Object*, it is often necessary to cast the result:

```
        Student s2 = (Student)s.clone();
```

The standard package `java.lang` defines an interface *Cloneable*, which specifies *no methods*:

```
public interface Cloneable { };
```

This interface should be implemented by any class that supports (or overrides) the method `clone`. The method `clone` as defined in the class *Object* first checks to see if the object executing the method is an instance of a class that implements *Cloneable*. If so, a shallow copy of the object is produced. If not, a *CloneNotSupportedException* is thrown.

For instance, suppose class *AClass* doesn't override the method `clone` it inherits from *Object*. If an *AClass* instance executes `clone`

```
AClass a = new AClass();
... a.clone()...
```

the method first checks to see if the class of a—*i.e.*, *AClass*—implements the interface *Cloneable*. If it doesn't, a *CloneNotSupportedException* is thrown. Otherwise, a new instance of class *AClass* is created, and its components are initialized with the values of the corresponding components of a. That is, `clone` works essentially as follows:

```
if (this instanceof Cloneable) {
    Object copy = new instance of this class;
    for each component variable v of this
        copy.v = this.v;
    return copy;
} else
    throw CloneNotSupportedException;
```

Cloneable is a rather unusual interface. Implementing the interface does not require a class to implement any methods. Rather, it specifies that the class wants to "inherit" the method `clone` implemented in the class *Object*. Ideally, the method `clone` would be defined and implemented in a class other than *Object*. Then a class that wanted the functionality could simply extend this class. But this would not be practical in Java, where a class is limited to a single parent class. Rather, implementing the interface "turns on" the method inherited from *Object*.

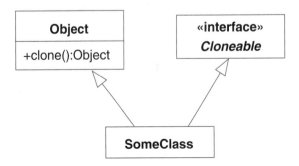

Figure 22.4 **Implementing a cloneable class in Java.**

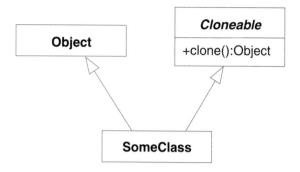

Figure 22.5 **Implementing a cloneable class with multiple class inheritance.**

While this approach can be regarded as something of a general technique, its use leads to classes that are not particularly cohesive and structures that can become ungainly. We recommend using it rarely if at all.

Now by specifying that *BoundedList* implements *Cloneable* and using the method `clone` of *Object*, we can write a `clone` method for *BoundedList*. We start by creating a shallow copy of the *BoundedList*:

```
public abstract class BoundedList implements Cloneable
{
    ...
    public Object clone () {
        BoundedList theCopy =
            (BoundedList) super.clone();
```

This gives us a structure like that shown in Figure 22.6. But we don't want a copy that is quite this shallow. We don't want the object and its copy to share a common array object, because we want to be able to manipulate the list and its clone independently. The structure we want after we clone a *Boundedlist* is as shown in Figure 22.7.

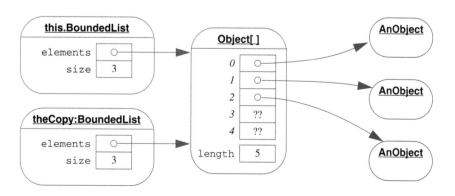

Figure 22.6 **A very shallow copy of a *BoundedList*.**

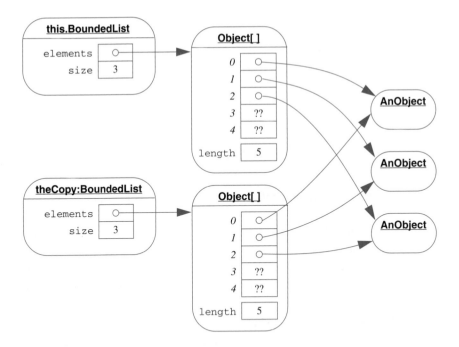

Figure 22.7 **A shallow copy of a *BoundedList*.**

Array classes implement *Cloneable*, so we can accomplish our purpose by cloning the array as well as the *BoundedList*. Here, then, is an implementation.

```
public Object clone () {
    try {
        BoundedList theCopy =
            (BoundedList) super.clone();
        theCopy.elements =
            (Object[]) this.elements.clone();
        return theCopy;
    } catch (CloneNotSupportedException e) {
        return null;
    }
}
```

A few items should be noted about the implementation.

- Since method `clone` returns an *Object*, we explicitly cast the result to *BoundedList* or *Object[]* as appropriate.

- Since the method we are implementing appears in the definition of the class *BoundedList*, Java's scoping rules allow private components of the *BoundedList* `theCopy` to be accessed directly in the method.

- Since the *Object* method `clone` (invoked by the call **super**.clone()) is specified as possibly throwing a *CloneNotSupportedException*, we must either include a *try* statement that catches the exception or include a *throws* clause in the specification of our method. We know that the exception will never actually be thrown, because *BoundedList* implements *Cloneable*. (The class *Object[]* overrides the `clone` of *Object*; the method throws no exceptions.) Thus we can safely ignore the possibility that the *catch* clause will ever actually be performed.

Finally, recall that the original problem was to write a statement in the abstract class *BoundedList* that creates a new object, but have the class of the object created be determined by the concrete instance that executes the statement at run-time. This is accomplished, since, as explained above, the object created by the call `super.clone()` will be of the same run-time class as the object executing the call.

The method `copy` can be implemented in terms of `clone`:

```
public BoundedList copy () {
    return (BoundedList)this.clone();
}
```

Abstract constructor

The problem of defining a method in an abstract superclass that creates an object while letting subclasses decide exactly which class to instantiate, is in fact a rather generally occurring problem. A common, straightforward approach is to define an *abstract constructor*, sometimes called a *factory method*. The superclass specifies an abstract *create* method that is implemented by the subclasses. For example, the abstract class *BoundedList* might define an abstract `createList` method, specified as follows:

```
public abstract BoundedList createList (int maxSize)
```
        Create a new *BoundedList* with a specified maximum size.

   require:
   ```
   maxSize >= 0
   ```
   ensure:
   ```
   isEmpty(createList(n))
   ```

Each concrete *BoundedList* subclass then implements this method to create the appropriate kind of list. For instance,

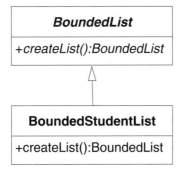

Figure 22.8   A factory method.

```
public class BoundedStudentList extends BoundedList {
    ...
    /**
     * Create a new BoundedStudentList with a specified
     * maximum size.
     *      require:
     *          maxSize >= 0
     *      ensure:
     *          isEmpty(createList(n))
     *          createList(n) instanceof
     *              BoundedStudentList
     */
    public BoundedList createList (int maxSize) {
        return new BoundedStudentList(maxSize);
    }
    ...
} // end of class BoundedStudentList
```

The class *BoundedList* or any of its clients can call the abstract constructor to create an instance. The `copy` method can now be implemented in a fashion similar to our first attempt:

```
public BoundedList copy () {
    int i;
    BoundedList theCopy = createList(
        this.elements.size);
    for (i = 0; i < this.size; i=i+1)
        theCopy.elements[i] = this.elements[i];
    theCopy.size = this.size;
    return theCopy;
}
```

22.2.2   Advantages and limitations of an array implementation

The principal advantage of an array implementation is that elements of the list can be accessed efficiently, in constant time independent of the length of the list. Note in particular that the methods `get`, `append`, and `set` all operate in constant time.

The limitations are also fairly obvious. The client must have a good idea of the ultimate size of a list when the list is created. Choosing a size that is too large will waste space; choosing a size too small will cause the program to fail.

Additionally, the operations `remove` and `add` are linear. On average, half the list needs to be shifted up or down. (Note, though, that `remove` deletes the last element of the list in constant time, independent of the list length.) The method `indexOf` is also linear.

From these observations, it seems than an array-based implementation might not be a good choice for a very dynamic list—one where elements are constantly being added and removed—but would be a good choice for a static list where accessing arbitrary elements by index was the most common operation.

22.3 Dynamic arrays

The abstract class *List*, as originally specified, has no limit on the number of elements that can be added to an instance. There are no preconditions for methods add and append preventing a client from adding an element to a full *List*. An instance of the class *BoundedList*, on the other hand, has a fixed maximum size, determined when the instance is created. We can distinguish between implementations with a maximum size, which we call *bounded*, and those with no upper bound, which we call *dynamic*.

A fairly obvious solution to the fixed size limitation is simply to create a larger array when necessary. That is, every time an item is added to the list, we can check to see if there is room in the array. If not, we create a larger array, and copy the contents of the original one into the new one. For example

```
public void append (Object obj) {
    Require.notNull(obj);
    if (this.size == elements.length) {
        // need a bigger array, so
        // make one twice as big
        Object[] newArray =
            new Object[2*elements.length];
        // copy contents of old array to new
        int i;
        for (i = 0; i < elements.length; i = i+1)
            newArray[i] = elements[i];
        // replace old array with new
        elements = newArray;
    }
    elements[size] = obj;
    size = size+1;
}
```

The disadvantage is that the append operation can now become expensive. But this operation shouldn't happen too often; in practice, we can't double a list all that many times. Also as we have sketched the approach, we never replace a larger array with a smaller one, even if the list shrinks.

Java defines a container class *Vector* in java.util that encapsulates just such a dynamic use of arrays. An instance of the class contains an *Object* array. If an element is added to the *Vector* and there is no more room in the array, the array is automatically replaced with a larger one.

The class includes three constructors:

```
public Vector ();
public Vector (int initialCapacity);
public Vector (int initialCapacity,
    int capacityIncrement);
```

The argument `initialCapacity` specifies the initial size of the *Object* array; `capacityIncrement` specifies how much larger to make the array when it needs to grow. For instance

```
new Vector(100,20)
```

creates a *Vector* instance containing a 100 element array. One hundred elements can be added to the *Vector*; but if a 101st element is added, the array is automatically replaced with one that is 120 elements in length.

A `capacityIncrement` of 0 means that the array should be doubled in size when it needs to grow larger. The default `initialCapacity` is 10; while default `capacityIncrement` is 0.

The class *Vector* has all of the functionality and most of the methods that we defined for lists. A class that provides required functionality but lacks the required interface can be easily tailored to fit our needs by wrapping the class in a *wrapper* or *adaptor* class. That is, we define a new class that contains an instance of the original as a component. The new class has the desired specification, and simply delegates[1] its responsibilities to the instance of the original class.

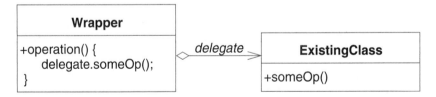

Figure 22.9 *A wrapper class.*

To see how this works, we'll implement a version of *List* using the following *Vector* methods.

> **public** Object elementAt (**int** index)
>   The element at the given array index.

> **public int** indexOf (Object elem)
>   Index of the given element in the array; −1 if the array does not contain the element.

---

1. Some designers would object to the use of the term "delegate" here, since the term can be used with a narrower, more technical meaning.

```
public int size ()
        The number of elements in the Vector.
```

```
public Object clone ()
        A new copy of the Vector.
```

```
public void addElement (Object elem)
        Add the element to the end of the Vector; size is increased, and capacity
        is incremented if necessary.
```

```
public void insertElementAt (Object obj, int index)
        Add the given element at the given array index, shifting elements up as
        necessary.
```

```
public void removeElementAt (int index)
        Remove the element at the given index, and shift higher indexed ele-
        ments down.
```

```
public void setElementAt (Object obj, int index)
        Replace the element at the specified array index with the Object provided.
```

```
public String toString()
        A string representation of this Vector, containing the String representa-
        tion of each element.
```

```
public void removeAllElements()
        Remove all components from this Vector and set its size to zero.
```

The class *Vector*, of course, contains many more methods than these. We name the wrapper class *DynamicList*, and give it without documentation in Listing 22.1.

Listing 22.1 **The class *DynamicList***

```java
public abstract class DynamicList implements Cloneable {

    public DynamicList () {
        elements = new Vector();
    }

    public int size () {
        return elements.size();
    }

    public boolean isEmpty () {
        return this.size() == 0;
    }
```

continued

Listing 22.1   **The class *DynamicList (continued)***

```java
public Object get (int i) {
    return elements.elementAt(i);
}

public int indexOf (Object obj) {
    return elements.indexOf(obj);
}

public String toString () {
    return elements.toString();
}

public Object clone () {
    try {
        DynamicList theCopy =
            (DynamicList)super.clone();
        theCopy.elements =
            (java.util.Vector)this.elements.clone();
        return theCopy;
    } catch (CloneNotSupportedException e) {
        return null;
    }
}

public DynamicList copy () {
    return (DynamicList)this.copy();
}

public void append (Object obj) {
    Require.notNull(obj);
    elements.addElement(obj);
}

public void add (int i, Object obj) {
    Require.condition(0 <= i && i <= this.size());
    Require.notNull(obj);
    elements.insertElementAt(obj, i);
}
```

continued

Listing 22.1 **The class *DynamicList (continued)***

═══

```
public void remove (int i) {
    Require.condition(0 <= i && i < this.size());
    elements.removeElementAt(i);
}

public void set (int i, Object obj) {
    Require.condition(0 <= i && i < this.size());
    Require.notNull(obj);
    elements.setElementAt(obj, i);
}

public void clear () {
    elements.removeAllElements();
}

private java.util.Vector elements;

} // end of class DynamicList
```

───

Note that the time complexity of the methods is the same as with
BoundedList. For instance, the method `remove` might appear to be constant at
first glance. But the method calls `removeElement` from the class *Vector*, which is
linear: it is essentially the same as *BoundedList* `remove`.

22.4 Summary

In this chapter, we examined Java's array classes. An array is a primitive structure
that consists of a contiguous sequence of variables, all of the same type. The component variables of an array can be of a primitive type or of a reference type.
Since the components of an array are allocated in contiguous memory, access to
an element requires only constant time, independent of the size of the array. An
array constructor requires an integer argument that specifies the size of the array.
The size is fixed once the array is created.

We then used *Object* arrays to implement a version of the class *List*. Simply, the array was used to store the elements of the list. Since the maximum
size of the list must be specified when the list is created, we named the class
BoundedList.

In considering how to implement the *BoundedList* method `copy`, we saw the *Object* method `clone` and how a class "turns on" the cloning facility by implementing the interface *Cloneable*. We also saw how to use abstract constructors or factory methods. A factory method provides an abstract mechanism for creating objects in a superclass; subclasses implement the method and determine which actual concrete class to instantiate.

Next, we considered a straightforward approach to solve the fixed size limitation of *BoundedList*. The idea is simply to create a new, larger array to hold list elements when the existing array is filled. The Java class *java.util.Vector* in fact takes this approach. Elements are stored in an array. When an element is added to the Vector and there is no room in the array, a new, larger array is created. Elements are copied form the old array to the new. We defined a class *DynamicList* that implementing list functionality by wrapping a *Vector* and delegating responsibilities to its *Vector* component.

Finally, we noted that with an array-based implementations methods such as `get`, `set`, and `append` are constant time. Methods `add` and `remove`, however, are linear.

EXERCISES

22.1 Write a method that takes an *array-of-***int** as argument, and returns the number of negative values in the array.

22.2 Write a method that takes an *array-of-***int** as argument, and reverses the values in the array. For instance, if a is the argument and has 5 elements, with a[0] through a[4] containing the values 1, 3, 7, 9, 4, respectively, before the method is executed, then a[0] though a[4] should contain, respectively, the values 4, 9, 7, 3, 1 after execution.

22.3 Write a method that takes an *array-of-***int** as argument, and shifts the values in the array up by one, moving the last value into the 0-th position. For instance, if a is the argument and has ten elements, the value in a[0] is moved into a[1], the value in a[1] is moved into a[2], *etc.* The value in a[9] is moved into a[0].

22.4 Write a method that takes two *array-of-***int** arguments with the same length and computes the inner product assuming that the arrays represent vectors. The inner product of vectors *v*1 and *v*2 is given by the formula

$$\sum_{i=0}^{m-1} v1[i] \times v2[i]$$

where *m* is the length of the vectors.

22.5 The class *Matrix* models an integer matrix. Constructor arguments specify the number of rows and columns of the matrix:

> **public** Matrix (**int** rows, **int** columns)
>> Crate a matrix with the specified number of rows and columns.
>
>> **require:**
>>> rows > 0 && columns > 0

A *Matrix* has an array component whose elements are the rows of the matrix. That is, a component

> **private int**[][] elements;

where elements[n] is the *n*-th row of the matrix. (Note that elements[n] is an *array-of-***int**.)

Implement the constructor, and methods for accessing and setting an arbitrary matrix element.

22.6 Let *A* be a matrix with *n* rows and *p* columns, and *B* a matrix with *p* rows and *m* columns. Denote the *A* element in row *r* column *c* by $a_{r,c}$, and denote the *B* elements in row *r* column *c* by $b_{r,c}$. Then the product *A·B* is the matrix with *n* rows and *m* columns, whose row *r* column *c* entry $p_{r,c}$ is defined as

$$p_{r,c} = \sum_{i=0}^{p-1} a_{r,i} \cdot b_{i,c}$$

Implement a *Matrix* method that takes a *Matrix* instance as argument, and returns the product of the *Matrix* and the argument.

22.7 The class *IntSet* models a set of small, nonnegative integers. A constructor argument specifies the maximum element of the set.

> **public** IntSet (**int** maxElement)
>> A subset of the integers 0, ..., maxElement.
>
>> **require:**
>>> maxElement >= 0

An *IntSet* has a **boolean** array component that indicates which numbers are in the set. That is, a component

> **private boolean**[] isIn;

where isIn[n] is *true* means that *n* is in the set.

Implement the constructor, methods for adding and removing elements, and a method for determining whether an arbitrary nonnegative integer is in the set.

22.8 Implement an *IntSet* method that takes an *IntSet* instance as argument, and returns the set union of the *IntSet* and the argument.

22.9   Implement an *IntSet* method that takes an *IntSet* instance as argument, and returns the set intersection of the *IntSet* and the argument.

22.10 Implement an *IntSet* method that takes an *IntSet* instance as argument, and returns the set difference of the *IntSet* and the argument.

GLOSSARY

abstract constructor: an abstract method for creating objects in a superclass; subclasses implement the method and determine which actual concrete class to instantiate.

array: a structure composed of a contiguous sequence of variables, all of the same type.

clone: a copy of an object that is distinct from the original object, equals the original object, and is of the same class as the original object.

factory method: an abstract constructor.

wrapper: a class that adds functionality to or modifies the specification of another wrapped class. The wrapper contains the wrapped class as component, and delegates much functionality to the wrapped class.

CHAPTER 23

Implementing lists: linked implementations

In the previous chapter, we saw two *List* implementations based on arrays. In this chapter, we explore a number of linked implementations. With an array, the structure is derived from the sequential relationship among the array elements. With a linked implementation, the structure is explicitly built through object references. As we shall see, a linked implementation provides another approach to building dynamic lists introduced in the previous chapter. Furthermore, linked implementations can be used in a natural way to implement more complex structures than a simple sequence.

23.1 A linked *List* implementation

A list has a particularly simple structure. The elements are arranged in a linear sequence: if the list is not empty, there is a first element and a last element; every element (except the last) has one following it; and every element (except the first) has one preceding it. In an array implementation, the structure is modeled by positioning variables referencing the list elements sequentially in memory. A references to the first list element is stored first in memory, followed by a reference to the second list element, and so on. In a linked implementation, a structure is explicitly built from a collection of *nodes* that reference each other. A node contains a variable referencing an element of the list, and one or more variables referencing other nodes in the structure. In our first version, each node will reference the node containing the next list element. That is, each node references the next one in sequence. Thus the sequential list structure is explicitly constructed by "gluing" nodes together.

Array implementation

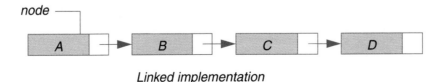

Linked implementation

Figure 23.1 Alternate list implementations.

We name the list class *LinkedList*,[1] and define class *Node* to model the nodes that a list comprises. Since node structure is purely implementation detail, the class *Node* is defined local to *LinkedList*.

The structure of a *Node* is straightforward. A *Node* has two responsibilities: it must know an element of the *List*, and it must know the next *Node* in sequence. Hence a *Node* has two data components, one referencing the list element, and the other referencing the next *Node*. Since *Node* is a private inner class of *LinkedList*, we omit methods for accessing and setting these variables, and manipulate them directly.

```
public abstract class LinkedList implements Cloneable
{
    ...
    private class Node {

        /**
         * Create a Node containing the specified
         * element.
         */
        public Node (Object element) {
            this.element = element;
            this.next = null;
        }
```

---

1. The standard library package `java.util` includes a concrete class *LinkedList*.

```
        private Object element;
        private Node next;

    } // end of class Node
}
```

A *LinkedList* instance contains an instance variable `size`, and an instance variable `first` that references the first *Node* of the list, as illustrated in Figure 23.2.

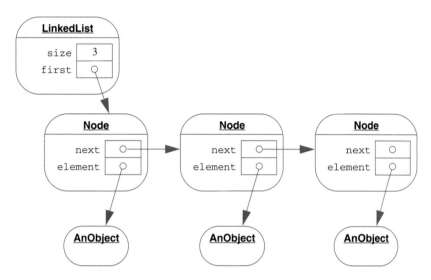

Figure 23.2 **A linked list.**

```
public abstract class LinkedList implements Cloneable {

    /**
     * Create an empty LinkedList.
     */
    protected LinkedList () {
        size = 0;
        first = null;
    }
    ...
    private int size;
    private Node first;

} // end of class LinkedList
```

Note that the `next` component of the last *Node* is always *null*, and the *LinkedList* component `first` is *null* if the list is empty. An empty list is shown in Figure 23.3.

Figure 23.3 An empty list.

23.1.1 Implementing *LinkedList* methods

Let's take a look at some of the methods that depend on the linked structure. In particular, we'll look at `get`, `append`, `remove`, and `add`. Note that there is a similarity of approach in all of these methods.

get

To find the element with a given index, we start at the front and traverse the list.

```
public Object get (int i) {
    Node p = first;
    int pos = 0;
    while (pos < i) {
        p = p.next;
        pos = pos + 1;
    }
    return p.element;
}
```

Carefully examine how this method works. In particular, note the relationship between the variables `p` and `pos`. The variable `p` is initialized with a reference to the 0-th *Node* of the list:

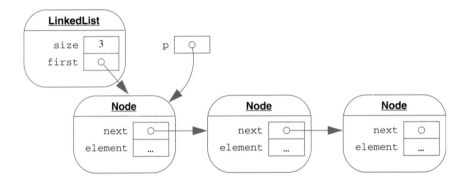

Each iteration of the loop assigns p a reference to the next element of the list, and increments pos. For instance, after one iteration, p references the element at index 1:

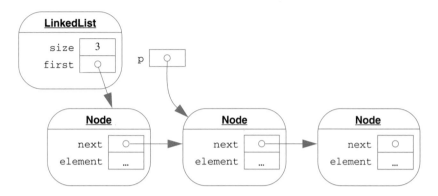

In particular, the fact the p references the *Node* containing the element with index pos is an invariant of the loop. When the loop terminates, pos == i, and p references the *Node* containing the element we are looking for.

append

To append an element, we must find the last element of the list. This can be done by traversing the list and counting as with get, or by traversing the list until we reach a *Node* with a *null* next component:

```
Node p = first;
while (p.next != null)
    p = p.next;
```

When this loop terminates, p references the last element of the list:

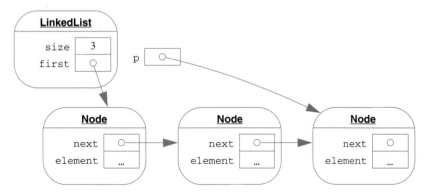

We create a new *Node* containing the element to be appended, and set the old last *Node*'s next component to reference it:

```
p.next = new Node(obj);
```

However, we need to be a bit more careful. If the list is empty, p is *null* initially, and the reference p.next is an error. We must explicitly test for the case in which we are appending an element to an empty list. Taking care of this special case, we can write the method as follows:

```
public void append (Object obj) {
    if (this.isEmpty())
        first = new Node(obj);
    else {
        Node p = first;
        while (p.next != null)
            p = p.next;
        p.next = new Node(obj);
    }
    size = size + 1;
}
```

remove

Implementing the method remove requires similar care. Basically, we need to find the *Node* in front of the one we want to delete: that is, we need to find a *Node* p such that p.next is the *Node* to be removed. Assuming i is the index of the element to be deleted, we find the *Node* in front of it as follows:

```
Node p = first;
int pos = 0;
while (pos < i-1) {
    p = p.next;
    pos = pos + 1;
}
```

For instance, if i is 2, the iteration will leave p referencing the element with index 1:

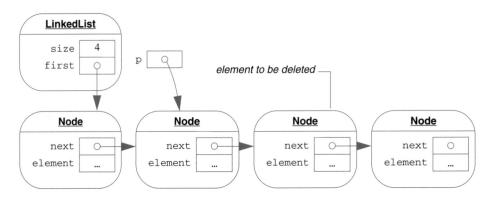

Now we must make index 1 *Node*'s next component reference the *Node* with index 3, effectively eliminating the element with index 2 from the list:

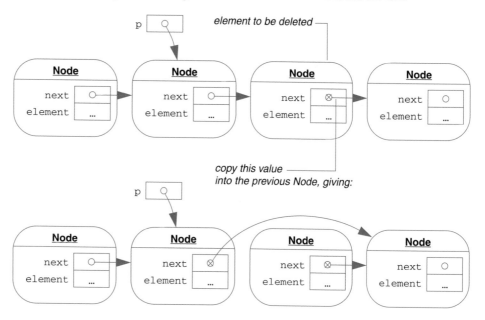

The value we need to copy is next of p.next: that is, p.next.next. This value should be set to the next component of the *Node* referenced by p:

```
p.next = p.next.next;
```

Note that since p.next is the *Node* to be deleted, p.next cannot be *null*. Thus the reference p.next.next is legal.

This operation may seem confusing at first, and you should make sure that you understand what is happening. Such operations are very typical of linked structure manipulation.

Again, we have a special case to consider: the case in which we remove the first element of the list. In this case, the first component of the *LinkedList* object must be modified. The complete method is as follows:

```
public void remove (int i) {
    if (i == 0)
        first = first.next;
    else {
        Node p = first;
        int pos = 0;
        while (pos < i-1) {
            p = p.next;
            pos = pos + 1;
        }
```

```
        p.next = p.next.next;
    }
    size = size - 1;
}
```

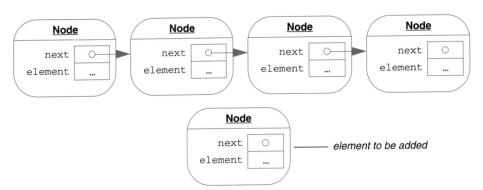

to add a new element with index 2,
the new Node must be made to reference
the old Node with index 2

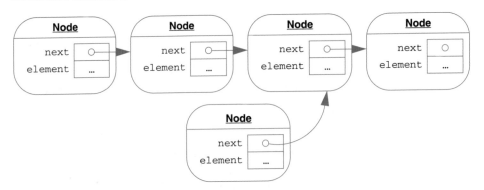

and the Node with index 1 must
be made to reference the new Node

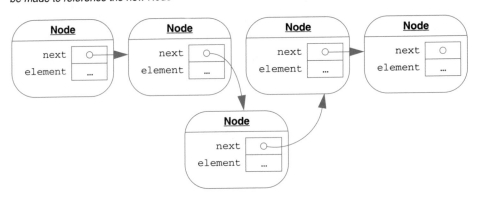

add

Finally, we sketch add. As with remove, if we want to add an element at the *i*-th position, we must find the element with index *i*–1. And as with remove, we have a special case to consider when *i* is 0.

```
public add (int i, Object obj) {
    Node newElement = new Node(obj);
    if (i == 0) {
        newElement.next = first;
        first = newElement;
    } else {
        Node p = first;
        int pos = 0;
        while (pos < i-1) {
            p = p.next;
            pos = pos + 1;
        }
        newElement.next = p.next;
        p.next = newElement;
    }
    size = size + 1;
}
```

A few observations on the implementation so far:

- get, append, remove, and add all require linear time on average. On the other hand, deleting the first element and inserting a new first element are constant time operations.

- We must be particularly careful of boundary cases: those involving the empty list, a list with one element, the first or last element of a list. These may well require explicit handling.

23.2   Linked list variations

A simple change to our model will make append a constant time operation. If we keep references to both the first and last elements in the *LinkedList*, we don't have to traverse the list in order to append.

```
public append (Object obj) {
    Node newElement = new Node(obj);
    if (this.isEmpty())
        first = newElement;
```

```
      else
          last.next = newElement;
      last = newElement;
      size = size + 1;
  }
```

However, there are now additional special cases to handle in other methods. For instance, remove must explicitly check for the case in which the last element is deleted:

```
public void remove (int i) {
    if (size == 1) {
        // remove the only element
        first = null;
        last = null;
    } else if (i == 0) {
        // remove the first element
        first = first.next;
    } else {
        Node p = first;
        int pos = 0;
        while (pos < i-1) {
            p = p.next;
            pos = pos + 1;
        }
        p.next = p.next.next;
        if (i == size-1)
            // last element removed
            last = p;
    }
    size = size - 1;
}
```

We could also make append constant time by having the *LinkedList* object reference the last *Node* in the list, and each *Node* reference the *preceding Node* rather than next. We leave this as an exercise.

Header nodes

One way to eliminate special cases is by employing a *header* node. This is a dummy node that contains no element but is always present at the front of the list. The *LinkedList* component first always references the header node, and is never *null*. In particular, the empty list contains only a header.

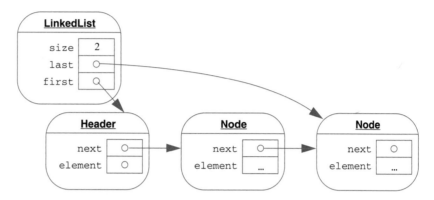

Figure 23.4 **A linked list with header.**

We extend the class *Node* to produce headers:

```
private class Header extends Node {

    public Header () {
        super(null);
    }



}
```

The *LinkedList* constructor creates the header:

```
protected LinkedList () {
    size = 0;
    first = new Header();
    last = first;
}
```

Note how this simplifies many methods. The method append, for instance, need not explicitly check for the empty list:

```
public append (Object obj) {
    Node newElement = new Node(obj);
    last.next = newElement;
    last = newElement;
    size = size + 1;
}
```

Circular lists

There are many variations on the linked list theme. In a circular linked list, for instance, the last node references the first. We show a circular list without header in Figure 23.5, though of course a header could also be used.

An advantage of a circular list is that it is possible to traverse the entire list starting from any node. (Clearly care must be taken with this kind of structure to avoid infinite iterations or recursions.) This additional structure would not be of particular advantage in implementing the functionality we have defined for the class *List*. But we can easily imagine other abstractions where such a structure would prove useful. We won't consider details here.

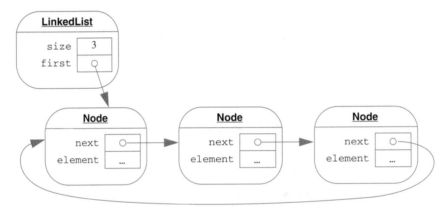

Figure 23.5 **A circular linked list without header.**

23.3 Doubly-linked lists

A common linked list variation is a *doubly-linked list*. In this structure, each node references the preceding as well as the following node. We sketch the construction of a class *DoublyLinkedList*, whose instances are doubly-linked circular lists with header. Such a structure is illustrated in Figure 23.6.

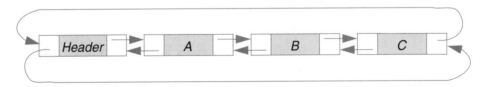

Figure 23.6 **Doubly-linked circular list with header.**

A *Node* in a doubly-linked lists contains three components: the list element, and references to its two neighbor *Node*s. A *DoublyLinkedList* has a size and a reference to the header *Node*. As was the case with the class *LinkedList*, we make the *Node* class local to the abstract class *DoublyLinkedList*:

```
public abstract class DoublyLinkedList
    implements Cloneable{
    ...
    private int size;
    private Node header;

    private class Node {
        public Node (Object element) {
            this.element = element;
            this.next = null;
            this.previous = null;
        }
        Object element;
        Node next;
        Node previous;
    } // end of class Node
}
```

Assuming that *Header* extends *Node* as before, the DoublyLinkedList constructor creates the header *Node*, and links it to itself:

```
protected DoublyLinkedList () {
    size = 0;
    header = new Header();
    header.next = header;
    header.previous = header;
}
```

Note that, as shown in Figure 23.7, the empty list contains only the header, which references itself.

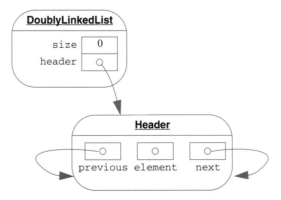

Figure 23.7 **An empty *DoublyLinkedList*.**

Operations on a *DoublyLinkedList* are a bit more complicated since we have two references in each *Node* to deal with. But the combination of a circular structure and a header eliminate the need for handling most boundary cases explicitly.

Let's consider the `append` method for this structure. The `previous` component of the header references the last element in the list, and the `next` component of the last element references the header.

To append a new element, we must set:

- the `previous` component of the new *Node* to reference the old last *Node*;

- the `next` component of the new *Node* to reference the header;

- the `previous` component of the header to reference the new *Node*;

- the `next` component of the old last node to reference the new *Node*.

Note that no special test is required to handle the empty list. The method can be written as follows:

```java
public void append (Object obj) {
    Node newElement = new Node(obj);
    Node last = header.previous;
    newElement.next = header;
    newElement.previous = last;
    last.next = newElement;
    header.previous = newElement;
    size = size + 1;
}
```

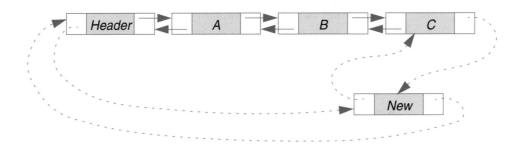

Figure 23.8 **Appending a new *Node* to a *DoublyLinkedList*.**

23.4 Limitations of linked structures

The principal disadvantage of a linked implementation compared to an array-based implementation is that accessing elements by index is a linear time operation. That is, the method `get` is constant time in an array-based implementation, but is $\Theta(n)$ in a linked implementation. Thus we would not likely use a linked implementation if the primary operation is to access elements randomly by index.

Of course, to this point we have used indexes as our primary means for accessing list elements. For instance, to determine if an element is on a list, we obtain each element of the list by means of its index:

```
public boolean contains (List list, Object obj) {
    int n = list.size();
    int i = 0;
    while (i < n && !obj.equals(list.get(i)))
        i = i+1;
    return i < n;
}
```

If the implementation is array-based, this method is linear. However, if the implementation is linked, it is $\Theta(n^2)$ since `get(i)` is $\Theta(i)$.

The only reason we use item indexes in the above method is to obtain each element of the list successively. We can do this for a linked list without invoking the method `get`. For instance, the following linear method determines if a given object is on a *LinkedList*:

```
public boolean contains (LinkedList list, Object obj)
{
    Node p = list.first;
    while (p != null && !obj.equals(p.element))
        p = p.next;
    }
    return p != null;
}
```

Of course, the above method uses private members of the class *LinkedList*. It could only be legally written within the definition of *LinkedList*. We'll see how to develop a more general solution to this problem in the next chapter, by means of objects called *iterators*.

23.5 Dynamic storage allocation

Though details are beyond the scope of this text, we briefly review issues of storage allocation and deallocation, particularly as they apply to linked structures.

Recall that memory space for automatic variables—method parameters and local method variables—is allocated when the method is invoked, and reclaimed (deallocated) when the method completes. This is sometimes called *automatic* allocation and deallocation. Space for an object's instance variables is allocated when the object is created. This is sometimes called *dynamic* allocation.

In an array-based list implementation, memory space for the elements of the array is allocated when the array is created; that is, when the list object is created. In a linked implementation, space required for a node is allocated when the node is created; that is, whenever an item is added to the list. But when is this space deallocated?

The Java run-time system or interpreter implements a facility called *garbage collection*. Dynamically allocated space that can no longer be accessed is termed *garbage*. If we create an object and then lose all references to the object, the memory space occupied by the object becomes garbage. For instance, a node deleted from a linked list is garbage.

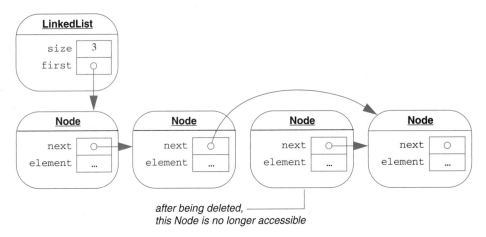

after being deleted,
this Node is no longer accessible

The run-time system continuously looks for garbage and reclaims the space; that is, it "collects the garbage." Of course there is some overhead involved, but this is generally not a problem unless we are writing an extremely time-critical real-time application.

Many programming languages do not include garbage collection as part of their run-time systems. These languages require programs to *deallocate explicitly* dynamically allocated space. The problem with this is that in an object-oriented environment, it is often difficult to know when an object is no longer accessible and can be safely deallocated. Subtle errors can easily lead to some garbage not being recognized and reclaimed (sometime called a *memory leak*), or to space that is still accessible being mistakenly reclaimed as garbage. A reference to space that has been mistakenly reclaimed is called a *dangling reference*. Dangling references result in errors that are often extremely difficult to track down.

The effect is that memory space still being used for an accessible object is reclaimed and used for something else. Thus two independent objects end up using the same memory space for unrelated purposes.

```
p = new SomeObject();
q = p;
// p and q reference the same object
```

```
free(p);
// The object p references is explicitly
// deallocated; space will be used for something
// else, but the original object is still accessible
// through q
```

Figure 23.9 **A dangling reference.**

23.6 Summary

With linked structures, structural relationships between objects in a container are explicitly modeled by references between nodes that contain the objects. In this chapter, we saw several approaches to implementing lists with linked structures. In the simplest approach, each node contains an element of the list and references the node containing the next element. We noted that the addition of a header node simplified the implementation by eliminating some of the special cases that would otherwise need to be explicitly handled.

We considered several variations including a doubly-linked circular list with header. In this structure, each node references both the preceding and the following node. The structure is circular: the header follows the last node in the list, and the last node in the list precedes the header.

One shortcoming with the linked list implementations we constructed is that `get`, `remove`, and `add` are all linear. In each case, we must start at the beginning of the list and traverse the list iteratively to locate the node with a particular index. We will see how to overcome this difficulty in the next chapter.

Finally, we briefly considered dynamic storage allocation. In Java, the runtime system recognizes when an object is no longer accessible and reclaims the storage space used by that object. This mechanism is called garbage collection. In some programming languages, the application must explicitly free storage space that is no longer needed. This can lead to subtle errors in a program. On the one hand, space might become inaccessible without being explicitly freed; on the other, space might be freed which it is still accessible.

EXERCISES

23.1   Write a *LinkedList* method that will reverse a *LinkedList* by reversing the nodes. The method should not allocate any new nodes and should not change the element a particular node contains.

23.2   Consider a *LinkedList* implementation in which the *LinkedList* object references the last element of the list, and each *Node* references the preceding *Node*, rather than the following *Node*. Implement the methods append and remove for this structure.

23.3   Implement the method append for a circular list without header.

23.4   Implement methods remove and add for the class *DoublyLinkedList*.

23.5   Define a linked implementation of the class *IntVector* described in exercise 14.12.

23.6   A careful examination of *LinkedList* methods reveals repeated code for finding the *Node* containing the *i*-th list element. Write a private *LinkedList* method similar to get but that returns the *Node* containing the *i*th element, rather than the *i*-th element itself.

23.7   Implement the *LinkedList* method

private Node find (Object obj)

that returns the *Node* immediately before the first occurrence of the specified *Object*. If the specified *Object* is first on the list, or is not contained on the list, the method returns *null*.

23.8   Implement a version of the method find of the previous exercise for linked lists with headers.

23.9   Use the method find from exercise 23.7 or exercise 23.8 to implement the method

public void remove (Object obj)

which removes the first occurrence of the specified *Object* from a list.

23.10   Implement the method

public void removeAll (Object obj)

which removes all occurrences of the specified *Object* form a list.

23.11   Consider the abstraction *CircularList*. A *CircularList* is a finite collection of elements, one of which is designated the *current element*. A *CircularList* has a feature get for accessing the current element, and a feature next for changing the current element to the next element in the list. If the *CircularList* has *n* elements, then performing next *n* times will iterate "current" through all elements, and leave the current element the same as when the process began. Note that there is no notion of "first" or "last" element.

A *CircularList* should also have features for adding and removing elements.

Write a complete specification for the class *CircularList*. Define two implementations, one based on an array and the other on a linked structure.

23.12   Consider a recursive list implementation as follows. The class *RecursiveList* has a *ListState* component, to which it forwards all service requests.

ListState is implemented by classes *EmptyList* and *NonEmptyList*. *EmptyList* has no components. *NonEmptyList* has components *head* and *tail*; *head* is the first element on the nonempty list; *tail* is the *ListState* denoting the "rest" of the list.

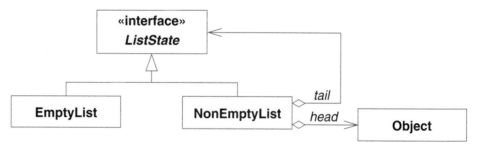

RecursiveList provides the following functionality, with the obvious semantics:

```
public boolean isEmpty ()
public int size ()
public Object get (int i)
public int indexOf (Object obj)
public void append (Object obj)
public void set (int i, Object obj)
public void add (int i, Object obj)
public void remove (int i)
```

As mentioned above, *RecursiveList* simply forwards all responsibility to its *state* component. For example, size is implemented as:

```
public int size () {
    return state.size();
}
```

The interface *ListState* specifies the following methods:

```
boolean isEmpty ()
int size ()
Object get (int i)
int indexOf (Object obj)
void set (int i, Object obj)
ListState add (int i, Object obj)
ListState remove (int i)
```

The methods add and remove return a modified state.

The implementation of these methods for *EmptyList* is straightforward. For instance, size simply returns 0, while set throws an exception.

A *NonEmptyList* generally must decide whether to handle the request itself, or forward the request to its *tail*. For example, *NonEmptyList* might implement set as follows:

```
public void set (int i, Object obj) {
    if (i == 0)
        head = obj;
    else
        tail.set(i-1,obj);
}
```

Complete the implementation of *RecursiveList*.

Why would it not be a good idea to eliminate the class *RecursiveList* and make *ListState* directly available to clients?

GLOSSARY

automatic allocation: variable allocation strategy in which space for variables is allocated when a method is invoked, and deallocated when the method completes.

circular list: a list structure in which the node containing the last element references the first node of the list.

dangling reference: an erroneous situation arising form reclaiming storage that is still accessible.

doubly linked list: a linked list structure in which nodes reference both the following and preceding nodes.

dynamic allocation: variable allocation strategy in which space is explicitly allocated, for instance when an object is created.

garbage collection: memory reclamation strategy in which the run-time system notes when variables are no longer accessible and reclaims the allocated storage space.

header: a node that does not carry an element, but serves the purpose of always being present even in an empty list.

linked list: a list implementation in which the sequential relationship between list elements is explicitly modeled by references between nodes.

memory leak: an erroneous situation resulting from inaccessible storage not being reclaimed.

node: a member of a linked structure that carries an element of the structure and references other nodes of the structure.

CHAPTER 24

Organizing list implementations

In the previous two chapters we have seen several list implementations, both link structured and array based. It remains to organize these classes into a reasonable library structure. Additionally, we noted in the last chapter that accessing the elements of a linked list by index does not always result in optimal code. We introduce the notion of an *iterator*: an object that allows us to access the elements of a list efficiently regardless of its structure.

We conclude the chapter with a brief look at the standard Java library interface *Collection*, and some of its related classes.

24.1 A library structure

We have now seen a number of classes that implement the notion of a list, including *BoundedList*, *DynamicList*, *LinkedList*, and *DoublyLinkedList*. But we've defined these as independent classes, and have not specified that they extend our original class *List*. Clearly we don't want these classes isolated. We would like to apply methods, such as the searches and sorts, to instances of any of these implementation classes, and in general use any implementation where a *List* is required. As we have seen in Section 14.5, when there are several alternative implementations of the same abstraction, a common approach is to define the implementations as subclasses of the class defining the abstraction. Thus we could make *BoundedList*, *DynamicList*, *etc.* subclasses of *List*, as illustrated in Figure 24.1.

In Chapter 15, though, we noted a difficulty with this approach. If we use inheritance to provide alternate implementations of class functionality, we encounter problems when we try to extend the base class for other purposes, such as adding new functionality. In the case of *List*s, we have used extension to ensure homogeneity of *List* components. That is, we construct *StudentList*s guaranteed to contain only *Student*s, *PortableList*s that contain only *Portable*s, *etc.*

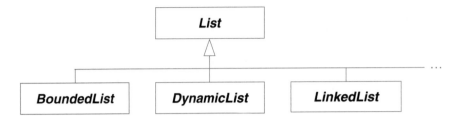

Figure 24.1 **Implementations as subclasses.**

(As we mentioned in Chapter 16, this is not an ideal solution to the problem. It would be preferable if, for instance, we could parameterize the class *List* with the type of *List* components. As Java does not provide such facilities, we make do with extension.) We want these classes to be extensions of *List* as well, so that we can use standard *List* algorithms on them. With the structure shown in Figure 24.1, we are forced to extend the implementation classes:

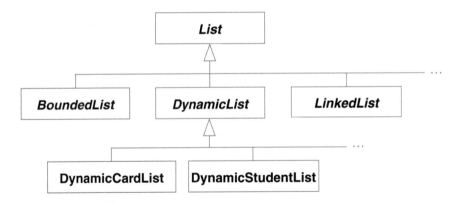

This is exactly the kind of class explosion mentioned in Chapter 15, hardly an attractive situation. We end up instantiating each kind of list for each kind of implementation. The problem is that the class *List* is a participant in two distinct hierarchies: an implementation hierarchy and a concrete application hierarchy. In the above picture, we have tried to merge the two hierarchies into one. As suggested in Chapter 15, we get a cleaner, more manageable structure if we use composition rather than extension to handle different implementation strategies. That is, we build a separate implementation hierarchy and provide each *List* with an implementation as a component. This kind of structure is called a *bridge* and is shown in Figure 24.2.

The interface *ListImplementation* defines implementation-dependent methods, and the class *List* forwards responsibility for implementation-dependent operations to its *ListImplementation*. For instance, the method `get` is constructed

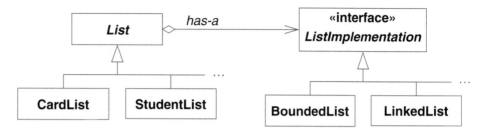

Figure 24.2 **Implementing** *List* **with a bridge.**

differently for different implementations. *List* therefore forwards this responsibility to its *ListImplementation*:

```
public abstract class List implements Cloneable {
    ...
    public Object get (int i) {
        return imp.get(i);
    }
    ...
    private ListImplementation imp;
    ...
} // end of class List

public interface ListImplementation
    extends Cloneable {
    ...
    Object get (int i);
    ...
} // end of interface ListImplementation
```

Note that the *ListImplementation* subclasses are now concrete classes. Each concrete *ListImplementation* subclass must provide an appropriate definition of the method `get`. A *BoundedList*, for example, returns the appropriate array element:

```
class BoundedList implements ListImplementation {
    ...
    public Object get (int i) {
        return elements[i];
    }
    ...
} // end of class BoundedList
```

Specifying the implementation

A *ListImplementation* is created when a *List* is created. We make the client responsible for determining which implementation to use when creating the *List*. This seems reasonable, since the client is likely to know best which implementation is most appropriate for a specific purpose. Note that this provides considerable flexibility, since the decision as to which implementation to use for a particular *List* is not made until run time. We show the *List* constructors in Listing 24.1.

Putting implementation selection in the *List* constructor complicates maintenance of the *List* class, since adding a new library implementation requires modification of this class. However, we expect the set of List implementations in the library to be rather stable.

We also include a constructor that takes an *implementation instance* as argument. This allows a client to define his own *ListImplementation*.

Listing 24.1 **List constructors**

```
public abstract class List implements Cloneable {

    // Codes for various library implementations

    public static final int BOUNDED = 1;
    public static final int DYNAMIC = 2;
    public static final int LINKED = 3;
    public static final int DOUBLY_LINKED = 4;

    /**
     * Create a List with the specified implementation, and
     * specified capacity.
     * If LINKED or DOUBLY_LINKED, capacity is ignored.
     * If DYNAMIC, capacity is doubled when necessary.
     *     require:
     *         implementation == List.BOUNDED ||
     *         implementation == List.DYNAMIC ||
     *         implementation == List.LINKED ||
     *         implementation == List.DOUBLY_LINKED
     *         capacity >= 0
     *     ensure:
     *         this.isEmpty()
     */

    protected List (int implementation, int capacity) {
        if (implementation == BOUNDED) {
            imp = new BoundedList(capacity);
```

continued

*Listing 24.1   List **constructors** (continued)*

```
      else if (implementation == DYNAMIC)
         imp = new DynamicList(capacity);
      else if (implementation == LINKED)
         imp = new LinkedList();
      else if (implementation == DOUBLY_LINKED)
         imp = new DoublyLinkedList();
   }

   /**
    * Create a List with the specified implementation.
    * If BOUNDED, capacity is 10.
    * If DYNAMIC, initial capacity is 10, and capacity is
    * doubled when necessary.
    *    require:
    *        implementation == List.BOUNDED ||
    *        implementation == List.DYNAMIC ||
    *        implementation == List.LINKED ||
    *        implementation == List.DOUBLY_LINKED
    *    ensure:
    *        this.isEmpty()
    */
   protected List (int implementation) {
      this(implementation, DEFAULT_CAPACITY);
   }

   /**
    * Create a List with the default implementation.
    * Default implementation is DYNAMIC, with initial
    * capacity 10; capacity is doubled when necessary.
    *    ensure:
    *        this.isEmpty()
    */
   protected List () {
      this(DEFAULT_IMPLEMENTATION, DEFAULT_CAPACITY);
   }

   /**
    * Create a List with the specified implementation.
    *    ensure:
    *        this.isEmpty()
    */
```

continued

---

*Listing 24.1   **List** constructors (continued)*

```
protected List (ListImplementation implementation) {
    Require.notNull(implementation);
    imp = implementation;

}
...

private static final int DEFAULT_IMPLEMENTATION =
    DYNAMIC;
private static final int DEFAULT_CAPACITY = 10;

} // end of class List
```

24.2   Iterators

We have seen many cases in which we need to access each element of a list. In the previous chapter, we noted that accessing by index was fine for array-based implementations, but not entirely satisfactory for linked implementations. The reason is that get(i) is $\Theta(i)$ for linked implementations, and so a loop like

```
for (i = 0; i < list.size(); i = i+1)
    do something with list.get(i);
```

is $\Theta(n^2)$.

Furthermore, the reason we locate an element in a container so that we can do something with it: delete it, copy it, modify it, insert another element in front of it, *etc*. Again, indexes are not efficient for all implementations. For instance, if we write

```
i = list.indexOf(item);
list.remove(i);
```

both statements are linear for a linked implementation. In the first statement, we search the list sequentially to find the item. Then, having obtained its index, we invoke list.remove(i) which starts at the beginning of the list and counts through the list elements to locate the *i*-th item. This seems particularly pointless, since we're needlessly doing the same work twice.

(Both statements are linear for an array-based implementation as well, but for a different reason. The `remove` method is linear for an array-based implementation since elements need to be shuffled up in the array.)

The problems of examining each element of a container and of obtaining a "handle" on a particular container element are very general. The element's index is the only way we have so far for accessing a list element. As we have seen, this is not always satisfactory.

An *iterator* is an object associated with a particular container that provides a means of sequentially accessing each element in the container. Use of an iterator removes responsibility for access and traversal from the container. We specify the following interface for iterators.[1]

> **public interface** Iterator **extends** Cloneable
>> Iterator for accessing and traversing elements of a container.
>
>> **public void** reset ()
>>> Initialize this *Iterator* to reference the first item.
>
>> **public void** advance ()
>>> Advance this *Iterator* to the next item.
>>>
>>> **require:**
>>>> !this.done()
>
>> **public boolean** done ()
>>> No more items to traverse in the container.
>
>> **public** Object get ()
>>> Container item this *Iterator* currently references.
>>>
>>> **require:**
>>>> !this.done()
>
>> **public boolean** equals (Object obj)
>>> The specified *Object* is an *Iterator* of the same class as this, and references the same relative item of the same container.

Assuming that `c` is a container of some sort and `i` an iterator associated with it, we can access each item in the container as follows:

```
i.reset();
while (!i.done()) {
    do something with i.get();
    i.advance();
}
```

---

1. The standard package `java.util` also includes an interface named *Iterator*.

For instance, we can see if an item `obj` is in the container:

```
i.reset();
while (!i.done() && !obj.equals(i.get())) {
    i.advance();
}
```

When this loop terminates, if `i.done()` is *true*, the item `obj` is not in the container. If `i.done()` is *false*, the iterator `i` references it.

An **int** variable used to index a list is a simple form of iterator. It is reset by assigning it 0 and advanced by incrementing. It is done when it equals the length of the list.

Note that for two *Iterators* to be equal, they must reference the same relative item of the same container. This implies that equal *Iterators* remain equal if each is advanced. For instance, suppose the same object appeared more than once on a *List*, perhaps with indexes 3 and 5. An *Iterator* that referenced the item with index 3 would not be equal to an *Iterator* that reference the item with index 5, even though the two *Iterators* in fact happen to reference the same object.

24.2.1   Iterator classes

If an interface is to traverse a container efficiently, it must be closely linked to the container implementation. It is the responsibility of an implementation to know how to traverse itself. We define an appropriate iterator class for each different list implementation.

The class *ListIterator* uses an index value to reference a list element, and is adequate for array-based implementations. It will also serve as a suitable default. Classes *LinkedListIterator* and *DoublyLinkedListIterator* define iterators for traversing *LinkedList* and *DoublyLinkedList* structures respectively.

Let's first look at the class *ListIterator*, given in Listing 24.2. When a *ListIterator* is created, it is given a reference to the *ListImplementation* it will traverse. The current element referenced by the iterator is represented simply as an integer index. Since indexing is efficient for arrays, we use this class to provide iterators for array-based implementations.

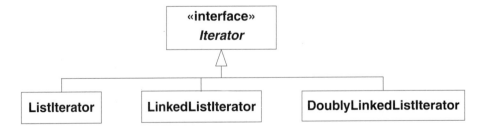

Figure 24.3   **Iterator classes for *Lists*.**

Listing 24.2 The class *ListIterator*

```
class ListIterator implements Iterator {

   /**
    * Create a new iterator for the specified List.
    */
   public ListIterator (ListImplementation list) {
      theList = list;
      current = 0;
   }

   /**
    * Initialize this Iterator to reference the first item.
    */
   public void reset () {
      current = 0;
   }

   /**
    * Advance this Iterator to next item.
    *    require:
    *       !this.done()
    */
   public void advance () {
      current = current + 1;
   }

   /**
    * No more items to traverse in the container.
    */
   public boolean done () {
      return current >= theList.size();
   }

   /**
    * Container item this Iterator currently references.
    *    require
    *       !this.done()
    */
```

continued

Listing 24.2   **The class *ListIterator (continued)***

===

```
public Object get () {
    return theList.get(current);
}

/**
 * The specified Object is an Iterator of the same class
 * as this, and references the same relative item of
 * the same container.
 */
public boolean equals (Object obj) {
    if (obj instanceof ListIterator) {
        ListIterator other = (ListIterator)obj;
        return this.current == other.current &&
                this.theList == other.theList;
    } else
        return false;
}

/**
 * This Iterator traverses the specified
 * ListImplementation.
 */
public boolean traverses (ListImplementation imp) {
    return imp == theList;
}

/**
 * Index of the element this Iterator currently
 * references.
 *     require:
 *         !this.done()
 */
public int indexOf () {
    return this.current;
}

// Components:

private int current;            // index into the List
private ListImplementation theList;
            // the List this Iterator references

} // end of class ListIterator
```

Advancing an integer index, though, is not an efficient way to traverse a *LinkedList*, as we have seen. It is preferable to keep a reference to a *Node*, which can be efficiently advanced to reference the next *Node* in the list. To do this, the *Iterator* must have access to the implementation structure of the *LinkedList*. That is, it must be tightly coupled to the class *LinkedList*. Thus we make *LinkedListIterator* an inner class, local to *LinkedList*. A *LinkedListIterator* can then directly access the implementation structure both of the *LinkedList* and of the component list *Node*s. A *LinkedListIterator* simply keeps a reference to the *Node* containing the current item. The class is given in Listing 24.3.

Listing 24.3 **The *LinkedList* class *LinkedListIterator***

```
private class LinkedListIterator implements Iterator {

    /**
     * Create a new Iterator for the specified LinkedList.
     */
    public LinkedListIterator (LinkedList list) {
        theLinkedList = list;
        reset();
    }

    /**
     * Initialize this Iterator to reference the first item.
     */
    public void reset () {
        current = theLinkedList.first;
    }

    /**
     * Advance this Iterator to next item.
     *     require:
     *         !this.done()
     */
    public void advance () {
        current = current.next;
    }

    /**
     * No more items to traverse in the container.
     */
    public boolean done () {
        return current == null;
    }
```

continued

Listing 24.3   The *LinkedList* class *LinkedListIterator (continued)*

```
  /**
   * Container item this Iterator currently references.
   *     require
   *         !this.done()
   */
  public Object get () {
     return current.element;
  }


  /**
   * The specified Object is an Iterator of the same class
   * as this, and references the same relative element of
   * the same container.
   */
  public boolean equals (Object obj) {
     if (obj instanceof LinkedlistIterator)
        return this.current ==
           ((LinkeListIterator).obj).current;
     else
        return false;
  }


  /**
   * This Iterator traverses the specified
   * ListImplementation.
   */
  public boolean traverses (ListImplementation imp) {
     return imp == (ListImplementation)theLinkedList;
  }

  // Components:

  private Node current;        // Node of theLinkedList
  private LinkedList theLinkedList;
                 // the LinkedList this Iterator references.

} // end of class LinkedListIterator
```

24.2.2 Creating an iterator

Since an *Iterator* is intimately bound to the *List* it is traversing, we add functionality for creating an *Iterator* to the class *List*. Since this is an implementation-dependent operation, a *List* forwards the responsibility to its *ListImplementation*:

```
public abstract class List implements Cloneable {
    ...
    /**
     * Create a new Iterator for this List.
     */
    public Iterator iterator () {
        return new imp.iterator();
    }
    ...
} // end of class List
```

ListImplementation defines a factory method that produces the appropriate kind of *Iterator*:

```
interface ListImplementation extends Cloneable {
    ...
    /**
     * Create a new Iterator for this List.
     */
    Iterator iterator ();
    ...
} // end of interface ListImplementation
```

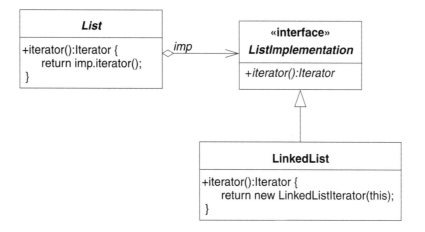

Concrete implementation classes implement the factory method to produce an appropriate iterator. For instance

```
class LinkedList extends ListImplementation {
    ...
```

```
/**
 * Create a new Iterator for this LinkedList.
 */
public Iterator iterator () {
    return new LinkedListIterator(this);
}
...
} // end of class LinkedList
```

As the relationships are a bit involved, let's review the events involved in creation of an *Iterator*. To obtain an iterator for a *List*, a client invokes the *List* method `iterator`. The *List* forwards the responsibility to its *ListImplementation*, by calling the implementation's `iterator` method. If the implementation is, say, a *LinkedList*, a *LinkedListIterator* is created and returned to the client.

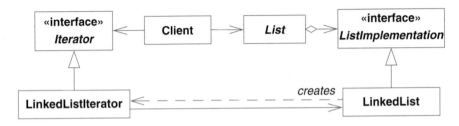

The iterator references the implementation, and has access to the underlying structure of the implementation. The client can then use the iterator to traverse the list efficiently, without concern for the implementation structure, as shown above. The events in creation and use of an iterator are summarized in the following interaction diagram:

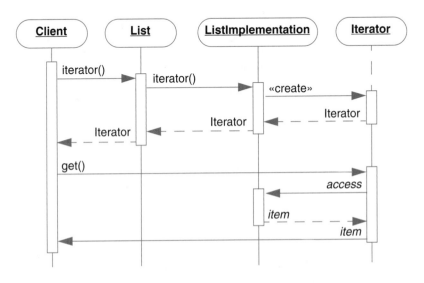

24.3 *List* methods with iterators as arguments

Now that we have iterators, we want to use them in much the same ways we've been using indexes. Like an index, an iterator identifies a particular element of a list. We'd like to be able to delete the element identified by an iterator, change it, insert an element in front of it, *etc.*

We overload the *List* methods that take index arguments with methods taking iterators as argument. In particular, we add the following methods to *List*:

public Object get (Iterator i)
> The element referenced by the specified *Iterator*.

> **require:**
>> ```
>> this.traversedBy(i)
>> !i.done()
>> ```

public Iterator iteratorAt (Object obj)
> An *Iterator* referencing the first occurrence of the specified element in this *List*; *Iterator* is done if this *List* does not contain the specified element.

> **require:**
>> ```
>> obj != null
>> ```

> **ensure:**
>> if obj equals no element of this *List* then
>>> iteratorAt(obj).done()
>>
>> else
>>> obj.equals(iteratorAt(obj).get()),
>>> and iteratorAt(obj) references the first position in a traversal for which this is true

public void add (Iterator i, Object obj)
> Insert the specified *Object* at the specified position.

> **require:**
>> ```
>> this.traversedBy(i)
>> !i.done()
>> obj != null
>> ```

> **ensure:**
>> ```
>> this.size() == old.size() + 1
>> i.get() == obj
>> (i.advance(); i.get()) == old.i.get()
>> ```

public void remove (Iterator i)
> Remove the element at the specified position.

require:
```
this.traversedBy(i)
!i.done()
```

ensure:
```
this.size() == old.size() - 1
i.get() == (old.i.advance(); old.i.get())
```

public void set (Iterator i, Object obj)
Replace the element at the specified position with the specified *Object*.

require:
```
this.traversedBy(i)
!i.done()
```

ensure:
```
this.get(i) == obj
```

public boolean traversedBy (Iterator i)
This *List* is traversed by the specified *Iterator*.

The final postconditions for add and remove indicate a sequence of method calls. The add postcondition

```
(i.advance();i.get()) == old.i.get()
```

indicates that advancing the iterator followed by a get gives the same element get would have returned before the add. That is, the new element is added in front of the old current element, and the iterator references the new element. Note that this is the same behavior as that exhibited by an integer index.

The remove postcondition

```
i.get() == (old.i.advance(); old.i.get())
```

indicates that the element referenced by the iterator after the remove is the one following the element that was removed.

The implementation of these methods is straightforward. For instance, the get operation can be forwarded to the *Iterator*:

```
public Object get (Iterator i) {
    Require.condition(this.traversedBy(i));
    return i.get();
}
```

Most other operations are forwarded to the *ListImplementation*. For example

```
public void remove (Iterator i) {
    Require.condition(this.traversedBy(i));
    imp.remove(i);
}
```

24.3.1   Improving *LinkedListIterator*

In Section 24.2.1 we defined a *LinkedListIterator* that referenced the "current" node of a *LinkedList*, as shown below.

This works fine for `get` and `set`. But when we try to implement `remove` and `add`, we notice that we need a reference to the *Node preceding* the current *Node*. We are forced to traverse the list to find the *Node* that we need.

This problem can be avoided in a number of ways. We could keep a pair of references in the iterator, one to the current *Node* and one to the preceding *Node*. Or we could just keep a reference to the *Node* preceding the current one. In either case, it will simplify things if a *LinkedList* has a header.

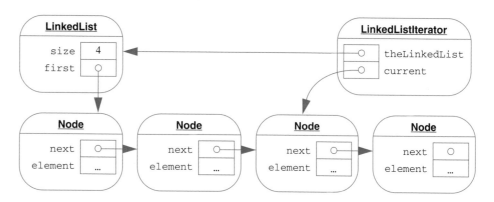

24.3.2   *Iterator* extensions

If we look at the implementation of the class *DoublyLinkedList*, we note that since such a list is circular, it is easy to move from the last element to the first, and since each node contains both forward and backward pointing references, it is possible to move forward or backward through the list. This suggests that we might want to extend the capabilities of iterators that reference *DoublyLinkedLists*.

We define *Iterator* extensions that capture the notion of a circular list, and that permit forward and backward traversal of a list. We can ensure that an *Iterator* created by a *DoublyLinkedList* implements the interface *CircularIterator*. That is, the iterator can be moved backward and forward through the list in a circular fashion.

> **public interface** WrappingIterator **extends** Iterator
> An *Iterator* that returns to the beginning of the enumeration when advanced past the last element of the container. done is *true* if the *Iterator* is referencing the first item of the enumeration, having been advanced from the last item, or if the container is empty.

public void advance ()
> Advance this *Iterator* to the next item. Advance to the first item if this *Iterator* is currently referencing the last item in the enumeration.
>
> **require:**
>> The container this *Iterator* is referencing is not empty.

public boolean done ()
> This *Iterator* currently references the first item of the enumeration having been advanced from the last, or the container is empty.

public Object get ()
> Container item this *Iterator* currently references.
>
> **require:**
>> The container this *Iterator* is referencing is not empty.

public interface BiDirectionalIterator
extends Iterator
> An *Iterator* that can move to previous as well as next item. offRight is *true* if the *Iterator* has been advanced past the last element, or if the container is empty. offLeft is *true* if the *Iterator* has been backed up past the first element, or if the container is empty.
>
> If offRight, backup positions the *Iterator* to the last element. If offLeft, advance positions the *Iterator* to the first element. done is equivalent to offRight.

public boolean done ()
> This *Iterator* has been advanced past the last element, or the container is empty. Equivalent to offRight.

public boolean offRight ();
> This *Iterator* has been advanced past the last element, or the container is empty. Equivalent to done.

public boolean offLeft ();
> This *Iterator* has been backed up past the first element, or the container is empty.

public void backup ()
> Move this *Iterator* back to the previous item.
>
> **require**
>> !this.offLeft()

public interface CircularIterator
    extends WrappingIterator, BiDirectionalIterator

> An *Iterator* can move to next or previous item in the container, and wraps at the ends of the enumeration. That is, moves to the first element when advanced past the last element, and moves to the last element when backed up from the first element.
>
> If the container is not empty, the *Iterator* references the first element of the enumeration when offRight (done) is *true*.
> If the container is not empty, the *Iterator* references the last element of the enumeration when offLeft is *true*.

public void advance ();

> Advance this *Iterator* to the next item. Advance to the first item if this *Iterator* is currently referencing the last item in the enumeration.
>
> **require:**
>> The container this *Iterator* is referencing is not empty.

public void backup ();

> Move this *Iterator* back to the previous item. Move to the last item if this *Iterator* is currently referencing the first item in the enumeration.
>
> **require:**
>> The container this *Iterator* is referencing is not empty.

24.3.3 Iterators and list modification

We now have two ways of modifying a list: by specifying an index, or by using an *Iterator*. Furthermore, several *Iterators* can be traversing the same list. We must explicitly describe an *Iterator*'s behavior when the *List* it is traversing is modified.

Suppose an *Iterator* i is referencing a particular element of a *List* list, for instance the element with index 2:

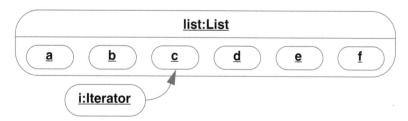

The specifications promise that if we delete the element referenced by the *Iterator*, the *Iterator* will reference the next element. That is, after

```
list.remove(i);
```

the *List* will look like this:

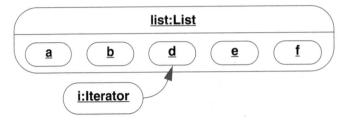

Furthermore, the specifications promise that if we next do

```
list.add(i, x);
```

for some object x, the *List* will be modified as shown:

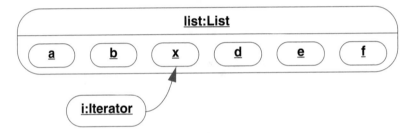

The question arises as to how an *Iterator* behaves if the *List* is modified by means of another *Iterator*, or by means of an index. For instance, suppose i and j are distinct *Iterators* referencing the same element:

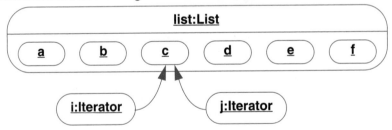

If we do

```
list.remove(j);
```

or

```
l.remove(2);
```

what will the state of i be? The specifications don't tell us.

We could build *Iterators* that are *Observers* of an *Observable List*. The *Iterators* register with the *List*, and the *List* informs all its *Iterators* whenever it is structurally modified. In this case, the specifications could clearly promise how the *Iterator*s behave in event of *List* modification.

Rather than add this additional structure, we simply assume that if a *List* is modified by index, all *Iterator*s that reference the *List* become invalid. Furthermore, if a *List* is modified by an *Iterator*, all other *Iterator*s that reference the *List* become invalid.

This may seem a very limiting assumption—in particular, it appears to make method verification difficult, since we generally can't account for all the possible objects that might be referencing a given object at some point. In practice, *Iterator*s typically have very local scope and short lifetimes, so the assumption does not present serious practical problems.

We might decide to add methods to the class *List* that take several *Iterator*s as arguments. For instance, we could define a method that deletes all the elements between two given *Iterator*s:

> **public void** remove (Iterator i1, Iterator i2)
>> Delete all the elements of this *List* from the element specified by the first *Iterator* through the element specified by the second, inclusive.

In such a case, the method postconditions would describe the state of the *Iterator*s after the method is executed.

24.3.4   Internal or passive iterators

With the iterator mechanism we have defined, a client is responsible for controlling the iteration. That is, a client obtains an iterator for a list and explicitly steps the iterator through the list. There is another flavor of iterator, sometimes called an *internal* or *passive* iterator, that shifts this responsibility from the client to the iterator. Using a passive iterator, a client provides an operation and the iterator applies the operation to each element of the container.

We illustrate the idea by defining a simple internal iterator for *List*s. When the iterator is created, it is provided with a *List*, a condition, and an operation. The iterator can then be commanded to apply the operation to each *List* element that satisfies the condition.

Since we need to package a condition and a command as objects so that we can pass them as arguments to the iterator, we define the following interfaces.

```
public interface Predicate {
    public boolean evaluate (Object obj);
}

public interface Operation {
    public void execute (Object obj);
}
```

The internal iterator constructor takes a *List*, *Predicate*, and *Operation* as arguments. It has only one command, which applies the *Operation* to all *List* elements that satisfy the *Predicate*.

> **public class** ListTraverser
>> Internal iterator that performs a specified operation on each *List* element that satisfies a given condition.
>
> **public** ListTraverser (List list, Predicate p, Operation op)
>> Create new iterator with specified *List*, *Predicate*, and *Operation*.
>
> **public void** traverse () {
>> Apply the *Operation* to each element of the *List* that satisfies the *Predicate*.

For example, here's how we might build an iterator to print out all students on *StudentList* courseList who have a final average greater than 90:

```
ListTraverser listA = new ListTraverser (
    courseList,
    new Predicate () {
        public boolean evaluate (Object obj) {
            return ((Student)obj).finalAve() > 90;
        }
    },
    new Operation () {
        public void execute (Object obj) {
            System.out.println(((Student)obj).name());
        }
    });
```

Note the use of anonymous class instantiation (introduced in Section 16.1.1) in providing the first two constructor arguments. The first argument, for instance, is specified as

```
new Predicate () {
    public boolean evaluate (Object obj) {
        return ((Student)obj).finalAve() > 90;
    }
}
```

This defines an anonymous class that implements the interface *Predicate* with the method evaluate as specified, and creates an instance of this class.

To perform the iteration, we give the iterator the traverse command:

```
listA.traverse();
```

24.4   Comparing implementations

We summarize the complexity of features for array-based and linked *List* implementations in Table 24.1.

Table 24.1 **Complexity of *List* Features**

feature	array-based	linked
`get(int)`	$\Theta(1)$	$\Theta(n)$
`get(Iterator)`	$\Theta(1)$	$\Theta(1)$
`indexOf(Object)`	$\Theta(n)$	$\Theta(n)$
`iteratorAt(Object)`	$\Theta(n)$	$\Theta(n)$
`append(Object)`	$\Theta(1)$	$\Theta(1)$
`remove(int)`	$\Theta(n)$	$\Theta(n)$
`remove(Iterator)`	$\Theta(n)$	$\Theta(1)$
`add(int, Object)`	$\Theta(n)$	$\Theta(n)$
`add(Iterator, Object)`	$\Theta(n)$	$\Theta(1)$
`set(int, Object)`	$\Theta(1)$	$\Theta(n)$
`set(Iterator, Object)`	$\Theta(1)$	$\Theta(1)$

24.5   The java.util *Collection* hierarchy

The standard Java package `java.util` defines a set of interfaces and classes rooted at the interface *Collection*, and referred to as the *collection hierarchy*. This hierarchy contains a number of members closely related to the classes and interfaces described in this chapter. While a detailed presentation is beyond the scope of this text, we briefly introduce some of the fundamental members.

The interface *Collection* models a rather generalized container. Some *Collection*s allow duplicate elements, while others do not. Some *Collection*s impose an ordering on the elements; some are unordered. Some of the principal methods specified by the interface are:

public boolean contains (Object o)
    This collection contains the specified element.

pubic boolean isEmpty()
    This collection contains no elements.

public int size ()
    The number of elements in this collection.

public java.util.Iterator iterator()
    An iterator over the elements in this collection.

Operations to add and remove elements are optional. An implementing class can choose to support them or not. For instance, the method `add` is specified as follows:

```
public boolean add (Object o) throws
    UnsupportedOperationException,
    ClassCastException,
    IllegalArgumentException
```

Note that the method returns a **boolean**. It returns *true* if the specified object is successfully added to the *Collection*, and return *false* if the element is already in the *Collection* and the *Collection* does not allow duplicates. That is, the **boolean** result indicates whether or not the *Collection* has changed state as a result of the operation.

If the operation `add` is not supported by the implementing class, an *UnsupportedOperationException* is thrown. A *Collection* client cannot, therefore, assume that method `add` is available for a *Collection*—which may cause the reader to wonder why it is specified here.

*ClassCastException*s and *IllegalArgumentException*s can also be thrown by the method `add`. This warns a *Collection* client that a specific implementing class may not be willing to add an arbitrary *Object*. If the class of the argument prevents it from being added to the *Collection*, a *ClassCastException* is thrown. (This is much the same situation we have with our homogeneous *List*s. The *List* method `append`, for instance, specifies an *Object* argument. But a concrete *List* subclass such as *StudentList* limits the class of elements it is willing to append, and throws an exception if a client attempts to append an unacceptable element.) If any aspect of the object other than its class prevents it from being added to the *Collection*, an *IllegalArgumentException* is thrown.

In `java.util`, *List* is an interface that extends *Collection*. This interface models a sequential collection in which elements can be accessed by index. The interface *List* specifies, for example, the familiar method `get`:

```
public Object get (int index)
```
The element at the specified position in this *List*.

A *List* can contain duplicate elements, but operations to add and remove elements are still specified as optional. The interface *java.util.Set*, on the other hand, extends *Collection* and specifies a *Collection* that does not contain duplicate elements.

Corresponding to the interfaces *Collection*, *List*, and *Set* are abstract classes *AbstractCollection*, *AbstractList*, and *AbstractSet*. These classes provide skeletal implementations of the interfaces. *AbstractList*, for instance, extends *AbstractCollection* and implements *List*.

Concrete implementation classes typically extend these abstract classes. Array-based list implementations such as *java.util.Vector* extend *AbstractList* directly. Linked implementations, such as *java.util.LinkedList*, extend the abstract class *AbstractSequentialList*, which extends *AbstractList*.

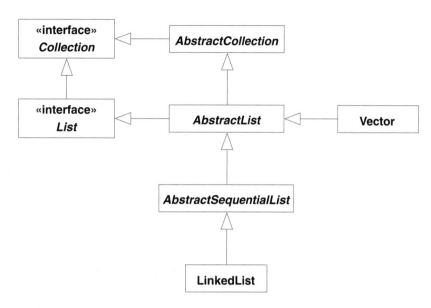

Figure 24.4   **Lineage of *java.util.LinkedList* and *java.util.Vector*.**

Iterators

The `java.util` interface *Iterator* specifies three methods:

> **public boolean** hasNext ()
>> The iteration has more elements.next
>
> **public** Object next () **throws** NoSuchElementException
>> The next element in the iteration. Throws *NoSuchElementException* if
>> hasNext() is *false*.
>
> **public void** remove () **throws**
>> UnsupportedOperationException,
>> IllegalStateException
>>> Removes from the underlying collection the last element returned by the
>>> iterator (optional operation). This method can be called only once per
>>> call to next.

The query `hasNext` is essentially the converse of our *Iterator* method `done`. Note that the method `next` is not a proper query since it changes the state of the iterator. We could implement `next` by accessing the current element and then advancing the iterator:

```
public Object next () {
    Object temp = this.get();
    this.advance();
    return temp;
}
```

The `java.util` interface *ListIterator* extends *Iterator*. Using a *ListIterator*, it is possible to traverse a list in either direction, and modify the list during iteration. It includes a method `previous` that serves as a companion to `next` and optional methods for adding, removing, and setting list elements.

24.6 Summary

In this chapter, we considered how we might organize list classes into a coherent library structure. We separated the *List* abstraction hierarchy from the implementation hierarchy by use of a bridge. That is, we equipped a *List* with a component that provides the implementation. The library provides a collection of different implementations from which a client can choose at run time. The abstract *List* class delegates responsibility for implementation dependent operations to its implementation. By using a bridge, the abstraction and the implementation hierarchies can be developed independently, allowing the abstraction hierarchy access to any available implementation. As a consequence we gain great flexibility, since the *List* abstraction is not tightly coupled to any particular implementation.

Providing both array-based and linked implementations for *List* raises the question of method performance. While elements in an array-based implementation can be accessed by index in constant time, accessing an element of a linked implementation by index requires linear time. Thus simple operations that iterate through each *List* element become $\Theta(n^2)$ for linked implementations when elements are accessed by index. Abstracting the notion of index, we introduced external iterators. Iterators allow us to iterate through each element of a *List* in linear time, regardless of the implementing structure. The iterator abstraction provides the operations for traversing a *List* while examining each *List* element in turn. The structure of each *List* implementation dictates the algorithms used to traverse it; thus iterator implementations are tightly coupled to the structure they traverse. Having noted this, we provide each implementation with an inner class that implements an appropriate iterator. A client of the *List* abstraction is provided with a factory method to create iterators suitable for a chosen implementation.

List operations that take an index were overloaded with operations that take *Iterator* instances, providing a richer *List* abstraction. Care must be taken in specifying *Iterator* behavior with regard to *List* modification. We chose to mimic the behavior of indexes as closely as possible. For instance, deleting an element with a given index "moves" the next element of the *List* up to that index position. We define deletion with an iterator similarly: after the deletion, the iterator references the "next" *List* element.

We must also be careful when modifying a *List* referenced by an *Iterator* by a means other than with the *Iterator*. For instance, if we delete a *List* element by index, we assume that any *Iterators* referencing the *List* become invalid.

We extended the *Iterator* interface to define iterators for circular lists and iterators that can traverse a list in either direction.

External iterators give rise to the internal iterator abstraction, where the implementor is in full control of the traversal. As an example, we defined an internal iterator in which the client provided a condition and a method to execute on those *List* elements meeting the condition.

We concluded the chapter with a small tour on the *Collection* interfaces and abstractions found in the standard Java package `java.util`. The *Collection* interface provides a very rich abstraction with several implementations. *List* is an interface that extends *Collection* and models a sequential collection in which elements can be accessed by index. The package `java.util` also provides iterators for *Collections*.

EXERCISES

24.1   Rewrite the bubble sort and selection sort of Chapter 13 using iterators.

24.2   Using *CircularIterators*, write a method that reverses a *List*. Assume that the *List* method `iterator` returns a *CircularIterator*.

24.3   Implement the merge operation, described in exercise 13.4, using iterators.

24.4   Write a method `concatenate` that takes two *Lists* as arguments and returns a new *List* in which the elements of the second *List* appear after the elements of the first *List*.

24.5   Extend the class *List* by adding a *cursor*. A cursor identifies a *List* element much like an *Iterator*, but it is not a separate object. Rather, it is part of the list functionality. Call this abstraction *ListWithCursor*.

24.6   Implement the class *DoublyLinkedListIterator*.

24.7   A *List* is a *palindrome* if it appears to be the same when traversed in either directions. Assume that the *List* method `iterator` returns a *CircularIterator*. Write a method that determines whether or not the *List* is a palindrome.

24.8   Implement the class *ListTraverser*.

24.9   Extend the interface *Iterator* defining operations for modifying the underlying container directly with the *Iterator*.

24.10 Define and implement a class *RobustIterator*. A *RobustIterator observes* the *List* it is referencing and maintains a well-defined state when the *List* is modified.

GLOSSARY

bridge: a design pattern that allows for loose coupling between two hierarchies. For instance, loosely coupling an abstraction hierarchy and an implementation hierarchy permits each to be developed independently.

external iterator: an iterator that traverses a container under the control of a client.

internal iterator: an object that will perform a specified operation with each element of a container. Traversal of the container is controlled by the iterator implementation rather than by the client.

iterator: an object used to access each element in a container.

passive iterator: an internal iterator.

CHAPTER 25

Dispensers and dictionaries

To this point, the only containers we have seen have been lists. We conclude with a brief look at two additional kinds of containers: *dispensers* and *dictionaries*. A *dispenser* is a container to which we can freely add items but restricts item access and removal.

Figure 25.1 **A gumball dispenser.**

A *dictionary* is a container in which elements are accessed by *key*. For instance, a telephone directory is a dictionary in which items are accessed by name. The name serves as a key to access the telephone number.

We specify dictionaries and three very commonly used dispensers: stacks, queues, and priority queues. We consider straightforward implementations and see how *ListImplementation* classes can be adapted to provide dispenser implementations. Efficient implementations of priority queues and dictionaries, however, are beyond the scope of the text.

25.1 Dispensers

As we've said, a dispenser is a container that restricts access to its elements. In particular, there is one element in the container that we will call the *current element*. This is the only element that can be accessed or removed from the container. Removing the current element, of course, causes another element to become current. Adding an element to the dispenser may or may not change the current element, depending on the type of dispenser.

We assume that a dispenser has three essential features: a method for adding items to the container, a method for removing items, and a method for accessing items. Different kinds of dispensers use different names for these operations, but we'll refer to them generically as add, remove, and get:

void add (Object obj)
> Add the specified element to this dispenser.

void remove ()
> Remove the current element from this dispenser.

Object get ()
> The current element of this dispenser.

The query get allows us to access the current item, and the command remove removes the current item from the dispenser.

There are many ways to define and implement dispensers. One common approach combines access and removal into one operation. That is, there is a method

```
Object dispenseItem ()
```

that removes an item from the dispenser, and returns the removed item. That is,

```
obj = dispenser.dispenseItem();
```

is equivalent to

```
obj = dispenser.get();
dispenser.remove();
```

While dispenseItem may capture the intuitive semantics of the word "dispenser"—a dispenser gives us one of its items, thereby removing it from the dispenser—we adopt the former approach. We prefer to differentiate commands from queries, and not unnecessarily introduce public queries that change an object's state.

As we did with *Lists*, we specify and implement dispenser classes having *Object* instances as elements. A dispenser for a specific type of element can be derived via inheritance, where the subclass adds *Require* condition checks for the type of element added, and delegates the actual implementation of the methods to the superclass.

25.2   Stacks

A *stack* is a simple dispenser in which the current item is the container item that has been added most recently. That is, it is the youngest or newest item in the container. Stacks can be implemented efficiently, and are used in many diverse applications.

An obvious model of a stack is a list in which items are added, accessed, and removed from one end only:

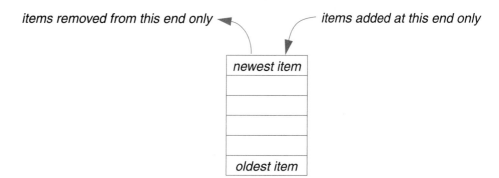

The name "stack" derives from the image conveyed by this model. A stack is sometimes called a *last-in first-out*, or *LIFO*, list. The end to which items are added and from which they are removed is referred to as the *top*. (The other end is obviously the *bottom*.)

---

stack: a dispenser in which the current element is the container element most recently added to the container.

In the context of a stack, the features get, add, and remove are traditionally named top, push, and pop. The specification is given in Listing 25.1. The following illustrates adding items to and removing items from a stack.

Assume s is an initially empty Stack:

```
s.push(A);   // s.top() is A
```
A

```
s.push(B);   // s.top() is B
```
B
A

```
s.push(C);   // s.top() is C
```
C
B
A

```
s.pop();     // s.top() is B
```
B
A

```
        s.pop();      // s.top() is A
```

A

D
A

```
        s.push(D);    // s.top() is D
```

Listing 25.1   **The class *Stack***

Class Stack

public abstract class Stack
  Dispenser adhering to a last-in/first-out discipline.

  Warning: the class of elements a *Stack* can contain may be restricted by a *Stack* subclass.

Constructors

protected Stack ()
  Create a new empty *Stack*.

  ensure:
    this.isEmpty()

protected Stack (**int** maxSize)
  Create a new empty *Stack* with the specified maximum size.

  require:
    maxSize >= 0

  ensure:
    this.isEmpty()

protected Stack (StackImplementation imp)
  Create a new empty *Stack* with the specified implementation.

  ensure:
    this.isEmpty()

Queries

public boolean isEmpty ()
  This *Stack* contains no elements.

public boolean isFull ()
  This *Stack* contains a maximum number of elements.

continued

Listing 25.1 **The class *Stack (continued)***

---

public Object top ()
> The element of this *Stack* that was most recently added.

> **require:**
>> !this.isEmpty()

public String toString ()
> *String* representation of this *Stack*.

Commands

---

public void push (Object obj)
> Add the specified element to this *Stack*.

> **require:**
>> !this.isFull()
>> obj != null

> **ensure:**
>> !this.isEmpty()

public void pop ()
> Remove the element of this *Stack* that was most recently added.

> **require:**
>> !this.isEmpty()

public void clear ()
> Remove all the elements from this *Stack*.

> **ensure:**
>> this.isEmpty()

25.2.1 *Stack* implementations

We use the same bridge pattern for implementing dispensers as we did for implementing lists. That is, we provide the container with an implementation component so that we can extend the class to meet the needs of an application, independently of its implementations.

We can clearly build stacks in the same ways that we built lists, with arrays or linked structures. In fact, we could simply use a *List* to implement a *Stack*. But in order to insure that the *Stack* methods are constant time and not linear, we use *ListImplementation*s to build *Stack*s.

In an array-based implementation, we make the element with highest index the top. This allows adding and removing to be done in constant time, without the need to shuffle the entire array:

0	A	—— bottom element
1	B	
2	C	
3	D	—— top element
4		
5		
6		

With a linked implementation, we make the first element the top. Again this allows us to add and remove elements in constant time:

Now we have already developed classes for manipulating array-based and linked lists: specifically, *BoundedList* and *LinkedList*. These classes have features for adding, removing, and accessing arbitrary elements. But the specifications of these features are not exactly as we want them. For instance, there is no command push to add an element obj to the front of a *LinkedList* list. We must use the command

```
list.add(0,obj);
```

How can we translate *Stack* features into *BoundedList* or *LinkedList* features? In Chapter 22, when we built the class *DynamicList* using the class *Vector*, we saw that we could use an *adapter* class to translate the specifications of an existing class to those required. In that situation, we wrapped the existing class in the new class. That is, we made the existing class a component of the new class, and simply forwarded responsibilities to the component. We can do exactly the same here. For instance, we can define a class *LinkedStackImplementation* with a *LinkedList* component as shown in Figure 25.2.

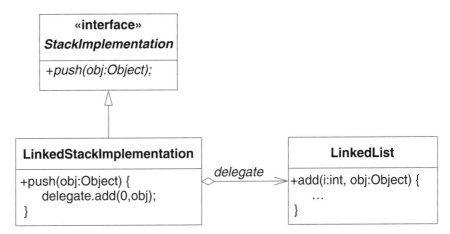

Figure 25.2 A *StackImplementation* adapter wrapping the adapted class.

It is also possible to adapt an existing class by extending it. For example, as illustrated in Figure 25.3, we can define an adapter class extends *LinkedList* and implements *StackImplementation*. *Stack* features are implemented by calls to appropriate *LinkedList* methods.

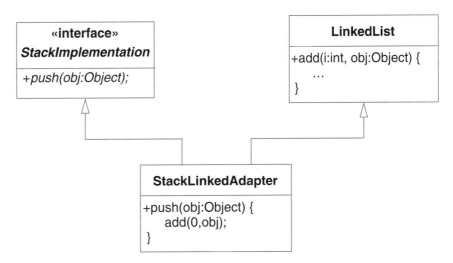

Figure 25.3 A *StackImplementation* adapter extending the adapted class.

We can easily construct similar adapters for other *ListImplementations* such as *BoundedList*. As with the class *List*, we allow the client to choose a predefined implementation or provide one of its own.

25.3   Queues

A *queue* is a simple dispenser in which the current item is the one least recently added to the container; that is, the oldest item in the container. Queues are also commonly used in many applications.

An obvious model of a queue is a list in which items are added to one end, and accessed and removed from the other end:

| | oldest | | | | newest | |

items removed from this end only   *items added at this end only*

A queue is sometimes called a *first-in first-out*, or *FIFO*, list. The end at which items are added is the *rear* of the queue, and the end from which items are removed is the *front*.

> **queue:** a dispenser in which the current element is the container element least recently added to the container.

In the context of a queue, the features `add` and `remove` are often called *enqueue* and *serve*. We name the fundamental dispenser features `front`, `append`, and `remove`, and give a specification in Listing 25.2.

Listing 25.2   **The class *Queue***

Class Queue

public abstract class Queue
    Dispenser adhering to a first-in/first-out discipline.

    Warning: the class of elements a *Queue* can contain may be restricted by a *Queue* subclass.

Constructors

---

protected Queue ()
    Create a new empty *Queue*.

    ensure:
        this.isEmpty()

continued

Listing 25.2 The class *Queue (continued)*

protected Queue (**int** maxSize)
    Create a new empty *Queue* with the specified maximum size.

    require:
```
maxSize >= 0
```

    ensure:
```
this.isEmpty()
```

protected Queue (QueueImplementation imp)
    Create a new empty *Queue* with the specified implementation.

    ensure:
```
this.isEmpty()
```

Queries

public boolean isEmpty ()
    This *Queue* contains no elements.

public boolean isFull ()
    This *Queue* contains a maximum number of elements.

public Object front ()
    The element of this *Queue* that was least recently added.

    require:
```
!this.isEmpty()
```

public String toString ()
    String representation of this *Queue*.

Commands

public void append (Object obj)
    Add the specified element to this *Queue*.

    require:
```
!this.isFull()
obj != null
```

    ensure:
```
!this.isEmpty()
```

continued

Listing 25.2   **The class *Queue* (continued)**

---

public void remove ()
        Remove the element of this *Queue* that was least recently added.

        require:
            !this.isEmpty()

public void clear ()
        Remove all the elements from this *Queue*.

        ensure:
            this.isEmpty()

25.3.1   *Queue* implementations

Linked implementations

As for stacks, we can develop array-based and linked implementations for queues. If a *LinkedList* maintains references to both ends of the list, elements can be added to either end in constant time.

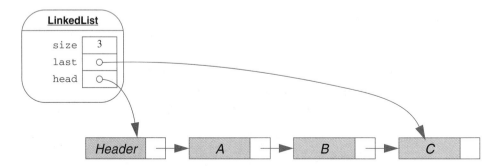

However, constant time deletes can be done only from the front of the list. This implies that we should make the front of the queue be the front of the *LinkedList*. An adapter class can easily be defined in much the same way as was done for *Stacks*.

Circular arrays

If we attempt to use the class *BoundedList* to implement queues, we encounter a problem. While we can add and remove elements from one end of the list in constant time, adding and removing elements from the other end requires shuffling the list, and takes linear time. Thus if we implement queues with *BoundedLists*, we can make either `append` or `remove` constant time (by appropriately choosing which end of the list is the front of the queue), but the other command will be linear.

An array-based approach that permits all queue methods to operate in constant time is to view an array logically as a circular structure, in which the element with index 0 follows the highest indexed element. This is illustrated in Figure 25.4.

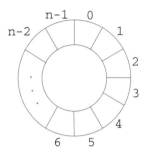

Figure 25.4 **A circular array of size *n*.**

The queue occupies a set of contiguous array elements, and "circulates" through the array as items are added and removed.

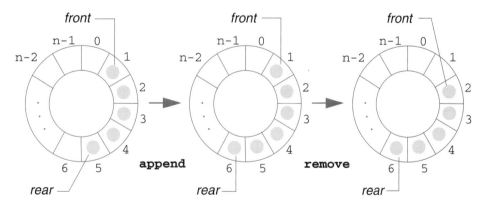

The implementation maintains two indexes, `front` and `rear`, identifying the front and rear elements of the queue; `front` is advanced when an item is removed from the queue, and `rear` is advanced when an item is added.

Note that when the queue has one element, `front == rear`. Removing an element increments `front`. Thus the relationship between these indexes is the same for both the full queue and the empty queue. That is, `(rear+1)%n ==` `front` for both the empty and full queue, where `n` is the length of the array. The implementation is straightforward and is given in Listing 25.3.

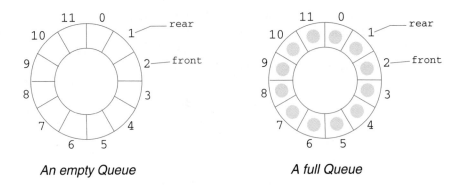

An empty Queue   A full Queue

Figure 25.5   **Empty and full *Queues*, implemented with a circular array.**

Listing 25.3   **The class *CircularQueue***
===

```
/**
 * Circular array implementation of the class Queue
 */
class CircularQueue implements QueueImplementation,
    Cloneable {

    /**
     * Create a CircularQueue with specified maximum size.
     *      require:
     *          maxSize >= 0
     *      ensure:
     *          this.isEmpty()
     */
    public CircularQueue (int maxSize) {
        elements = new Object[maxSize];
        size = 0;
        front = 0;
        rear = maxSize-1;
    }

    /**
     * The maximum size of this Queue.
     *      ensure:
     *          this.maxSize() >= 0
     */
    public int maxSize () {
        return elements.length;
    }
```

continued

Listing 25.3 **The class *CircularQueue (continued)***

```
/**
 * The number of elements in this Queue.
 *    ensure:
 *        this.size() >= 0
 *        this.size() <= this.maxSize()
 */
public int size () {
    return this.size;
}


/**
 * This Queue contains no elements.
 */
public boolean isEmpty () {
    return this.size == 0;
}


/**
 * This Queue contains a maximum number of elements.
 */
public boolean isFull () {
    return this.size == elements.length;
}


/**
 * The element of this Queue least recently added.
 *    require:
 *        !this.isEmpty()
 */
public Object front () {
    return elements[front];
}


/**
 * A String representation of this Queue.
 */
public String toString () {
    String s = "[";
    if (size > 0) {
        s = s + elements[front].toString();
```

continued

Listing 25.3 **The class *CircularQueue (continued)***

```java
        int i;
        for (i = front; i != rear; i = next(i))
            s = s + ", " + elements[next(i)].toString();
    }
    s = s + "]";
    return s;
}

/**
 * Add a new element to this Queue.
 *     require:
 *         obj != null
 *         !this.isFull()
 *     ensure:
 *         !this.isEmpty()
 */
public void append (Object obj) {
    rear = next(rear);
    elements[rear] = obj;
    size = size+1;
}

/**
 * Remove the element of this Queue that was least
 * recently added.
 *     require:
 *         !this.isEmpty()
 */
public void remove () {
    front = next(front);
    size = size-1;
}

/**
 * Remove all the elements from this Queue.
 *     ensure:
 *         this.isEmpty()
 */
```

continued

Listing 25.3 **The class *CircularQueue (continued)***

```
public void clear () {
    size = 0;
    front = 0;
    rear = maxSize-1;
}

// Private methods

/**
 * The next index, mod length of the array.
 */
private int next (int index) {
    return (index+1) % elements.length;
}

// Components

private Object[] elements;
private int front;    // index of the front Queue item
private int rear;     // index of the rear Queue item
private int size;     // size of the Queue

} // end of class CircularQueue
```

25.4 Priority queues

Suppose there is an ordering on the component class of a container, and we want to retrieve the items based on the ordering. The container contains instances of the class *Student*, for example, and we want to retrieve *Student*s in order of final grade. In such a situation, a *priority queue* is an appropriate structure to use.

A *priority queue* is a dispenser in which the current item is a largest item in the container with respect to some given ordering. The ordering is called a *priority*, and a largest item with respect to the ordering is referred to as a *highest priority* item. We name the dispenser features highest, add, and remove, and give a specification in Listing 25.4.

> **priority queue:** a dispenser in which the current element is a largest container element with respect to some given ordering.

Listing 25.4   The class *PriorityQueue*

Class PriorityQueue

public abstract class PriorityQueue
> Dispenser adhering to a priority-out discipline.

> **Warning:** the class of elements a *PriorityQueue* can contain may be restricted by a *PriorityQueue* subclass.

Constructors

---

protected PriorityQueue (Order priority)
> Create a new empty *PriorityQueue*, ordered with the specified *Order*.

> **ensure:**
> > this.isEmpty()

protected PriorityQueue (Order priority, **int** maxSize)
> Create a new empty *PriorityQueue* with the specified *Order* and maximum size.

> **require:**
> > maxSize >= 0

> **ensure:**
> > this.isEmpty()

protected PriorityQueue (Order priority,
   PriorityQueueImplementation imp)
> Create a new empty *PriorityQueue* with the specified *Order* and implementation.

> **ensure:**
> > this.isEmpty()

Queries

---

public boolean isEmpty ()
> This *PriorityQueue* contains no elements.

continued

Listing 25.4 **The class *PriorityQueue (continued)***

public boolean isFull ()
:   This *PriorityQueue* contains a maximum number of elements.

public Object highest ()
:   An element of this *PriorityQueue* with highest priority.

> **require:**
>> !this.isEmpty()
>
> **ensure:**
>> for each element e in this *PriorityQueue*
>>> !priority.lessThan(highest(),e)

public Order priority ()
:   The priority used to order this *PriorityQueue*.

public String toString ()
:   *String* representation of this *PriorityQueue*.

Commands

public void add (Object obj)
:   Add the specified element to this *PriorityQueue*.

> **require:**
>> !this.isFull()
>> for each element e in this *PriorityQueue*
>>> priority.lessThan(e,obj) and
>>> priority.lessThan(obj,e) are defined.
>
> **ensure:**
>> !this.isEmpty()

public void remove ()
:   Remove an element of this *PriorityQueue* with highest priority.

> **require:**
>> !this.isEmpty()

public void clear ()
:   Remove all the elements from this *PriorityQueue*.

> **ensure:**
>> this.isEmpty()

25.4.1   *PriorityQueue* implementations

An obvious way to implement a priority queue is with the class *OrderedList*, introduced in Chapter 16. Recall that an ordering is provided when an *OrderedList* is created, and the elements on the list are maintained in increasing order. Otherwise, the features of an *OrderedList* are similar to those of a *List*.

An *OrderedList* can be built with any of the *ListImplementations* used to construct *Lists*. With an array-based implementation, we can find an element's position in *log n* time using binary search. But inserting an element takes linear time, since following elements in the array have to be shuffled down. Binary search requires that an element be accessed by index in constant time. Hence binary search cannot be used effectively with a linked list, and locating an element's position on a linked list requires linear time. If we base a *PriorityQueue* implementation on either an array-based or linked implementation of *OrderedList*, add will be linear, though operations highest and remove can be made constant time.

There are a number of different and very efficient approaches to implementing *PriorityQueues*. A discussion of these structures, however, is beyond the scope of this text.

25.5   Dictionaries

A *dictionary*, sometimes called a *key-value table*, is a container in which elements are accessed by *key*. We think of the entries in a dictionary as having two components, a *key* and an associated *value*—a *key-value pair*. In a dictionary of the English language, for instance, an English word is the key and the definition is the value. In a telephone directory, a name is the key and the telephone number is the value. When we use a dictionary, we have a key and are interested in obtaining the associated value.

We can also consider the key to be an attribute of the entry, rather than a separate component. For instance, we can view the telephone directory as containing records that consist of name, address, and telephone number. The key—the name—is simply one of the record attributes. We adopt the former point of view, though, as it is more consistent with standard Java library classes.

The features of a dictionary are similar to those of a dispenser. The fundamental difference is that a key must be provided to access or delete an item. A question that arises is whether there can be several elements in the dictionary with the same key. We assume keys are unique. That is, we assume there can be at most one element in the dictionary with any given key. We give an elementary specification in Listing 25.5.

Listing 25.5   **The class *Dictionary***

Class Dictionary

public abstract class Dictionary
Container in which elements are uniquely accessed by key.

Warning: the classes of keys and values a *Dictionary* can contain may be restricted by a *Dictionary* subclass.

Constructors:

public Dictionary ()
Create a new empty *Dictionary*.

ensure:
    this.isEmpty()

Queries:

public boolean isEmpty ()
This *Dictionary* contains no entries.

public Object get (Object key)
The element of this *Dictionary* associated with the specified key. *null* if there is no entry with the specified key.

public String toString ()
String representation of this *Dictionary*.

Commands:

public void add (Object key, Object value)
Add an entry with the specified key and value to this *Dictionary*. If this *Dictionary* already contains an entry with the specified key, the value associated with this entry is replaced by the specified value.

ensure:
    !this.isEmpty()

continued

Listing 25.5 **The class *Dictionary (continued)***

---

public void remove (Object key)
>   Remove the entry specified by the given key from this *Dictionary*. If this
>   *Dictionary* does not contain an entry with the specified key, this method does
>   nothing.

public void clear ()
>   Remove all the entries from this *Dictionary*.

>   **ensure:**
>   this.isEmpty()

We can build a straightforward implementation of a dictionary with a *List* whose elements are key-value pairs. The methods get and remove simply search the *List* to locate the item with the given key. However, there are much better ways to implement dictionaries. As with priority queues, a discussion of the implementing structures are beyond the scope of the text.

Finally, we mention that the standard package java.util defines an interface *Map* that serves as a superclass for dictionary variants.

> **dictionary:** a container in which the elements are accessed by key.

25.6   Summary

With this chapter we conclude an introductory overview of containers by briefly discussing the abstraction dispenser. We discussed the fundamental notion of a dispenser and its principal variants, stacks, queues, and priority queues. We also considered dictionaries. For each of these we presented a specification, and discussed elementary implementations using existing list implementations such as *BoundedList* and *LinkedList*.

These last few chapters dealing with containers should be viewed as an introduction to data structuring within the context of object orientation and the methodology used in this text. Our intention has been to use these topics as a case study for presenting design choices for class and library design, and also to suggest how the methodology might be continued to subsequent topics.

EXERCISES

25.1 Complete a *Stack* implementation based on the class *BoundedList*.

25.2 Complete a *Stack* implementation based on the class *LinkedList*.

25.3 Implement the class *PriorityQueue*.

25.4 Implement the class *Dictionary*.

25.5 Carefully read the specifications for the class *java.util.Hashtable*. Define an implementation of *Dictionary* based on this class.

25.6 A *prefix integer expression* can be defined to be either an integer, or two prefix integer expressions preceded by a binary operator:

> *prefixIntegerExpression* =
>   *integer* or
>   *binaryOperator prefixIntegerExpression prefixIntegerExpression*

For instance, the following are prefix integer expressions:

```
  1       2      + 1 2        * + 1 2 4        * + 1 2 + 1 2
```

To evaluate an expression, evaluate the subexpressions and then apply the operator. For instance,

```
  * + 1 2 + 1 2  ⇒  * 3 + 1 2  ⇒  * 3 3   ⇒ 9
```

Class *Operator* models binary operators, and class *Operand* modes integers. Both are subclasses of class *Token*.

A *TokenList* can now be interpreted as a prefix integer expression.

Define classes *Operator*, *Operand*, and *Token*. Implement a method that uses a stack to evaluate prefix integer expressions.

GLOSSARY

dictionary: a container in which elements are accessed by key. Also known as a *key-value table*.

dispenser: a container that allows access and removal of elements in a predetermined way. A current element is distinguished as the element that can be accessed and removed.

priority queue: a dispenser in which the current element is the largest item in the container with respect to some given ordering.

queue: a dispenser in which the current element is the container element least recently added to the container.

stack: a dispenser in which the current element is the container element most recently added to the container.

APPENDIX A   Stream i/o

Data streams for input and output were introduced in Chapter 19. In this appendix, we take a closer look at facilities for manipulating data streams.

Recall that a data stream is essentially a sequence of bytes. If the stream is a source of data for an application, it is an *input stream*. If it is a destination (or sink), it is an *output stream*. An application *reads* data, removing it from an input stream, and *writes* data, appending it to an output stream.

The actual source of the data in an input stream might be a user's keyboard, a file, another program, a network connection, an external device, *etc*. Likewise, the destination of an output stream could be a terminal window, a file, another program, a network connection, and so on.

A data stream can be finite—for instance, if the source of an input stream is a file—or conceptually unbounded—for instance, if the source of an input stream is a sensor that continually reports temperature every ten seconds. An application generally has a way of determining that an input stream is exhausted—that all the data has been read and no more data will appear in the stream—and a way of indicating that an output stream is complete.

The bytes that comprise a data stream can be interpreted in many ways. If they are to be interpreted as characters, the stream is usually referred to as character stream. Otherwise, the stream is a binary stream. For example, if the source of an input stream is a text file, the stream is a character stream. If the source is a file in which each group of four bytes is a two's complement binary integer, the stream is a binary stream.

We need to be a little careful with our terminology in regard to Java. Specifically, Java represents characters with the 16-bit Unicode character set. In Java, the term *character stream* refers to a data stream whose elements are Unicode characters. Any other data stream—even one whose elements are ordinary 8-bit ASCII characters—is a *byte stream*.

A.1   OOJ library classes

The libraries that support this text, available at

```
http://www.cs.uno.edu/~fred/OOJ/
```

include some very basic classes for manipulating simple data streams. This is not so unusual. Everyone has his or her own basic classes for stream i/o. The standard `java.io` package is rather formidable, and not easily digestible. Our classes are based on a version of Bertrand Meyer's libraries for the programming language *Eiffel* [Meyer 88, 97].

Aside: Some programmers staunchly oppose using libraries that are not either standard or home grown. Considering the amount of vendor and third-party software we trust, this seems to us a little narrow minded. After all, a major thrust of the paradigm is producing reusable software and building on the work of others.

The fundamental classes in the package `OOJ.basicIO` are *Basic-FileReader* and *BasicFileWriter*. A *BasicFileReader* instance is associated with an input stream, and a *BasicFileWriter* instance is associated with an output stream. The data streams are assumed to contain characters represented with the default system encoding: *e.g.*, ASCII characters. Constructors allow a file name to be specified as the source or sink of the data streams. (What constitutes a legal file name, of course, is system dependent.) Defaults are the streams "standard input" and "standard output."

public `BasicFileReader ()`
 Create an input stream for standard input.

public `BasicFileReader (String fileName)`
 Create an input stream for the named file.

public `BasicFileWriter ()`
 Create an output stream for standard output.

public `BasicFileWriter (String fileName)`
 Create an output stream for the named file.

BasicFileReader

BasicFileReader has commands for reading one or more bytes from the input stream:

public void readChar ()
    Read a new character from this input stream.

public void readInt ()
    Read a new integer from this input stream.

public void readDouble ()
    Read a new double from this input stream.

public void readLine ()
    Read the rest of the line from this input stream.

public void readWord ()
    Read a new word from this input stream.

The methods readInt, readDouble, and readWord skip any white space at the beginning of the input stream. White space consists of spaces, tabs, end of lines, *etc*. readInt requires that the characters following the white space denote an optionally signed decimal integer. Similarly, readDouble requires that the characters following the white space have the format of an optionally signed double literal. readWord reads a sequence of non-white characters. The methods can throw the following *RuntimeExceptions*:

OOJ.basicIO.EOFException	end of file encountered in read attempt.
OOJ.basicIO.DataException	malformed token (readInt or readDouble).
OOJ.basicIO.IOException	any other kind of input error.

Suppose, for example, that the input stream is as follows, where "•" represents a space and "⏎" represents the line separator ("newline" character) at the end of the line:

    •••+12345a••⏎•bac••xyz⏎••⏎•••12.3e+2••⏎zzz⏎

After each of the specified commands the input stream will be as shown:

readInt();	a••⏎•bac••xyz⏎••⏎•••12.3e+2••⏎zzz⏎
readChar();	••⏎•bac••xyz⏎••⏎•••12.3e+2••⏎zzz⏎
readChar();	•⏎•bac••xyz⏎••⏎•••12.3e+2••⏎zzz⏎
readWord();	••xyz⏎••⏎•••12.3e+2••⏎zzz⏎
readLine();	••⏎•••12.3e+2••⏎zzz⏎
readDouble();	••⏎zzz⏎

Note that reading effectively changes the state of the *BasicFileReader*. Queries are used to determine the results of the reading. Thus queries and commands are distinguished as usual. (Asking a question shouldn't change the answer.)

public char lastChar ()
> Character most recently read by readChar.

public int lastInt ()
> **int** most recently read by readInt.

public double lastDouble ()
> **double** most recently read by readDouble.

public String lastString ()
> *String* most recently read by readWord or readLine.

After the previously shown six read commands have been executed, the following queries return the indicated values:

```
lastInt()      ⇒ 12345      (int value)
lastChar()     ⇒ ' '        (space character)
lastString()   ⇒ "  xyz"    (five character String from readLine)
lastDouble()   ⇒ 12.3e3     (double value)
```

Finally, there is a method for determining whether or not the stream is exhausted:

public boolean eof ()
> End of input stream has been reached.

BasicFileWriter

The methods available for *BasicFileWriter* are straightforward. The displayLine methods append an implementation dependent line separator ("newline" character) to the output stream. The method flush makes sure that any output that may be temporarily buffered in memory is actually written to the output stream. The methods for displaying an *Object* simply call the *Object*'s toString method:

public void blankLine (**int** n)
> Write the specified number of blank lines to the output stream.

public void close ()
> Close the output stream.

public void display (**char** ch)
> Write the specified char to the output stream.

public void display (**int** value)
>   Write a decimal representation of the specified int to the output
>   stream.

public void display (**double** value)
>   Write a decimal representation of the specified double to the output
>   stream.

public void display (Object obj)
>   Write a *String* representation of the specified *Object* to the output
>   stream.

public void display (String st)
>   Write the specified *String* to the output stream.

public void displayLine (**char** ch)
>   Write the specified char to the output stream, followed by a line sepa-
>   rator.

public void displayLine (**int** value)
>   Write a decimal representation of the specified int to the output
>   stream, followed by a line separator.

public void displayLine (**double** value)
>   Write a decimal representation of the specified double to the output
>   stream, followed by a line separator.

public void displayLine (Object obj)
>   Write a *String* representation of the specified *Object* to the output
>   stream, followed by a line separator.

public void displayLine (String st)
>   Write the specified *String* to the output stream, followed by a line
>   separator.

public void flush ()
>   Flush the output buffer: write any buffered data tot he output stream.

A.2   The *java.io* library

The standard package java.io is a menagerie containing, at last count, ten interfaces, fifty classes, and sixteen exceptions. The functionality can be categorized as

- facilities for reading and writing data streams;
- facilities for manipulating files; and
- facilities for serializing objects.

File manipulation facilities include the class *File*, which models a file in the
local file system, and the class *RandomAccessFile*, which provides mechanisms

for reading and writing a file in a nonsequential manner. Object serialization provides a means for writing objects to a byte stream, and later re-creating the objects from the byte stream. We will not consider these facilities in this appendix.

The classes that support reading and writing from data streams can be organized into four categories:

- classes for reading byte streams;
- classes for writing byte streams;
- classes for reading character streams; and
- classes for writing character streams.

(Recall that a Java character stream is a data stream whose elements are Unicode characters.)

Each category has an abstract class at the top of its hierarchy: *InputStream* and *OutputStream* for byte streams, and *Reader* and *Writer* for character streams.[1] Other classes in the hierarchies extend the functionality of the base classes in two ways: some add functionality by extending the base classes; others add functionality by wrapping an instance of another class. The benefits of composition (wrapping) were explained in Chapter 15. Principally, composition allows the extended functionality to be applied dynamically, at run-time. We briefly consider some of the central classes in each category.

A.2.1   Input byte streams

Abstract class InputStream

The top of the hierarchy is the abstract class *InputStream*. Fundamental methods for reading the stream are specified in this class, including:

> **public abstract int** read () **throws** IOException
> Read and return the next byte of data from the input stream. Return −1 if the end of the stream is encountered (the stream is exhausted).
>
> **ensure:**
> 0 <= this.read() <= 255 || this.read() == -1

> **public void** close () **throws** IOException
> Close the input stream and release associated resources.

---

1. The character stream classes were developed after the byte stream classes. Although similarities exist, byte stream and character stream classes are not entirely symmetric.

Note that the method `read` is neither a proper command nor a proper query. It changes the state of the stream *and* returns a value. Most of the `java.io` input methods are of this flavor.

Class FileInputStream

FileInputStream is a straightforward concrete extension of *InputStream*:

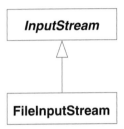

FileInputStream specifies a file as the source of the input stream, but otherwise adds no functionality to that specified by *InputStream*. A *FileInput-Stream* is generally wrapped with a *DataInputStream*, *BufferedInputStream*, or *InputStreamReader* to provide a richer interface.

The file is identified—with a *String* file name, a *File* object, or a system-specific file descriptor—in the *FileInputStream* constructor. The file is implicitly opened when the *FileInputStream* instance is created. The constructors are:

```
public FileInputStream (String name)
    throws FileNotFoundException, SecurityException
public FileInputStream (File file)
    throws FileNotFoundException, SecurityException
public FileInputStream (FileDescriptor fd)
    throws FileNotFoundException, SecurityException
```

Class FilterInputStream

FilterInputStream provides no additional functionality, but serves as a base class for *InputStream* wrappers:

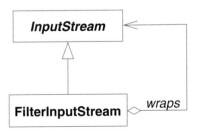

Note that *FilterInputStream* is also a subclass of *InputStream*. This allows one *FilterInputStream* to wrap another *FilterInputStream*.

Two commonly used subclasses of FilterInputStream are *DataInputStream* and *BufferedInputStream*:

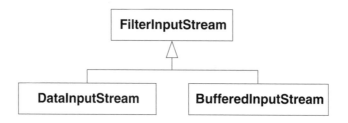

DataInputStream provides methods for reading values of primitive Java data types from the input stream. Included are the following:

public boolean readBoolean () **throws** IOException
> Read one byte and return *true* if the byte is non-zero, *false* if the byte is zero.

public char readChar () **throws** IOException
> Read two bytes and return the value as a Unicode character.

public double readDouble () **throws** IOException
> Read eight bytes and return the value as a **double**.

public int readInt () **throws** IOException
> Read four bytes and return the value as an **int**.

public byte readByte () **throws** IOException
> Read and return one input byte. The byte is treated as a signed value in the range—128 through 127, inclusive.

Note that these methods do *not* read character representation of the values, but binary representations. They throw an *java.io.EOFException* if the end of the input stream is encountered during the read attempt.

A *BufferedInputStream* uses an in-memory buffer to store input from the stream. That is, a large number of bytes are read from the input stream and stored in an internal buffer. Bytes are then read directly from the internal buffer. When the buffer is exhausted, it is filled again with another chunk of data form the input stream. Of course, the operating system also buffers input data in memory if possible. Using a *BufferedInputStream*, however, reduces the number of calls to the operating system. The operating system need only be accessed occasionally to fill the buffer.

As we've said, these subclasses of *FilterInputStream* wrap an *InputStream*. The *InputStream* component is provided as a constructor argument:

public DataInputStream (InputStream in)
   Create a *DataInputStream* that reads from the given *InputStream*.

public BufferedInputStream (InputStream in)
   Create a *BufferedInputStream* that buffers input from the given
   InputStream in a buffer with the default size of 2048 bytes.

As an example, suppose the file noise.dat contains a sequence of 32-bit integer values. The file can be opened and wrapped with a *DataInputStream* as follows:

```
FileInputStream in = new FileInputStream("noise.dat");
DataInputStream data = new DataInputStream(in);
```

The integer values can be read by using the *DataInputStream* method readInt:

```
int i;
try {
   while (true) {
      i = data.readInt();
      process(i);
   }
} catch (EOFException e) {
   data.close();
}
```

Using exceptions to detect the expected end of input condition is nauseating.

We mentioned that since *FilterInputStream* is a subclass of *InputStream*, one *FilterInputStream* can wrap another. If we wanted to buffer input from the above file, we could first wrap the *FileInputStream* in *BufferedInputStream*:

```
FileInputStream in = new FileInputStream("noise.dat");
BufferedInputStream bf = new BufferedInputStream(in);
DataInputStream data = new DataInputStream(bf);
```

Of course, there is really no need to name all these instances. We could just as easily write:

```
DataInputStream data =
   new DataInputStream(
      new BufferedInputStream(
         new FileInputStream("noise.dat")));
```

A.2.2   Input character streams

Abstract class Reader

The top level of the input character stream hierarchy is the abstract class *Reader*. *Reader* is similar in purpose and structure to *InputStream*, but *Reader* reads a stream of Unicode characters rather than bytes. Its basic `read` method is specified as follows:

public int read () **throws** IOException
> Read and return the next character of data from the input stream. The character is returned as an integer in the range 0 to 65535 (0 to $2^{16}-1$). Return -1 if the end of the stream is encountered (the stream is exhausted).

> **ensure:**
> ```
> 0 <= this.read() <= 65535 ||
> this.read() == -1
> ```

Note that the method returns a value of type **int**, not of type **char**. (Why? So that there is a convenient "non-character" value that can be returned if the end of the stream has been reached.) The postcondition guarantees that the **int** can be safely cast to a **char**:

```
int i = reader.read();
if (i != -1)
    char c = (char)i;
```

Class *BufferedReader*

BufferedReader is used to buffer character stream input in much the same way that *BufferedInputStream* is used to buffer byte stream input.

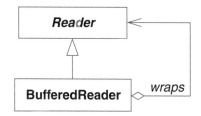

BufferedReader has a handy method for reading a line of input:

public String readLine () **throws** IOException
> Read and return a line of text. Return *null* if the end of the stream is encountered. Line terminating characters are not included in the *String*.

Class *InputStreamReader*

InputStreamReader is an adapter class that wraps an *InputStream* and provides the functionality of a *Reader*.

The *InputStreamReader* converts each byte of the *InputStream* to a Unicode character using an encoding scheme that can be specified when

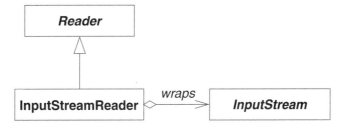

the *InputStreamReader* is created. If no encoding scheme is specified, a
system default is used.[1]

> **public** InputStreamReader (InputStream in)
>> Create an *InputStreamReader* that reads from the given *InputStream* and
>> translates bytes to characters using the system default encoding.

> **public** InputStreamReader (InputStream in, String enc)
>>   **throws** UnsupportedEncodingException
>> Create an *InputStreamReader* that reads from the given *InputStream* and
>> translates bytes to characters using the specified encoding.

Class *FileReader*

FileReader extends *InputStreamReader*. In effect, a *FileReader* is an
InputStreamReader using the system default encoding and wrapped around a
FileInputStream. The constructors are similar to those of *FileInputStream*:

> **public** FileReader (String name)
>>   **throws** FileNotFoundException, SecurityException

> **public** FileReader (File file)
>>   **throws** FileNotFoundException, SecurityException

> **public** FileReader (FileDescriptor fd)
>>   **throws** FileNotFoundException, SecurityException

Class *StreamTokenizer*

We still have no mechanism for reading character sequences that look like decimal integers, look like double literals, and so on. One possibility is to use a
StreamTokenizer. A *StreamTokenizer* can be wrapped around a *Reader*, and used
to parse the input stream into tokens that look like those used in Java. The details

---

1. A typical default is ISO-8859-1 (Latin 1). This is an 8-bit character set that covers most Western
European languages. The first 128 characters (characters 0 to 127) are identical to ASCII. It is
denoted in Java by the String "ISO8859_1".

of the class are beyond the scope of this appendix. The interested reader should consult the standard documentation.

A.2.3   Output byte streams

The collection of output stream classes mirrors the input classes. At the top of the output byte stream hierarchy is the abstract class *OutputStream*. Fundamental methods are:

> **public abstract void** write **(int** b) **throws** IOException
>> Write the specified byte (low order 8 bits of the **int** provided) to the output stream.

> **public void** close **() throws** IOException
>> Close the output stream and release any associated resources.

> **public void** flush **() throws** IOException
>> Write any buffered bytes to the output stream.

FileOutputStream extends *OutputStream* by allowing a file to be specified as the destination of the output, in much the same way that *FileInputStream* extends *InputStream*.

FilterOutputStream provides a base class for *OutputStream* wrappers, again in a way similar to its input counterpart, *FilterInputStream*. *BufferedOutputStream* and *DataOutputStream* extend *FilterOutputStream*, and provide functionality symmetric to their input stream counterparts. (The class *PrintStream* also extends *FilterOutputStream*. However, *PrintWriter*, discussed below, should be used instead of *PrintStream*.) Details on these classes can be obtained from the standard documentation.

A.2.4   Output character streams

The abstract class *Writer* is at the top of the output character stream hierarchy. It is similar in functionality to *OutputStream*, but of course its write method writes a Unicode character rather than a byte:

> **public abstract void** write **(int** c) **throws** IOException
>> Write a character consisting of the low order 16 bits of the **int** provided to the output stream.

The wrapper class *BufferedWriter* extends *Writer* and is symmetric to the *Reader* class *BufferedReader*.

OutputStreamWriter adapts an *OutputStream* to a *Writer* and is symmetric to *InputStreamReader*. *FileWriter* extends *OutputStreamWriter* in a manner similar to *FileReader*'s extension of *InputStreamReader*.

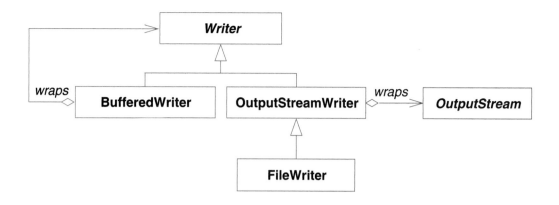

Class PrintWriter

The class *PrintWriter* is one of the most useful output stream classes. *PrintWriter* extends *Writer* and wraps either an *OutputStream*[1] or a *Writer*.

    PrintWriter provides functionality for writing string representations of primitive values and objects. If an *OutputStream* is wrapped, characters are converted to bytes using the system default encoding scheme.

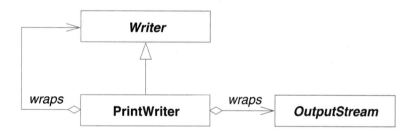

The four constructors are specified as follows:

public PrintWriter (OutputStream out)
        Create a *PrintWriter* that sends output to the specified *OutputStream*. An
        intermediate *OutputStreamWriter* that converts characters to bytes using
        the system default encoding is also constructed.

---

1. If an *OutputStream* is specified in the *PrintWriter* constructor, an intermediate *OutputStreamWriter*
   wrapping the *OutputStream* is automatically created. Thus properly *PrintWriter* wraps a *Writer*
   which might be an *OutputStreamWriter*.

public PrintWriter (OutputStream out,
    boolean autoFlush)

> Create a *PrintWriter* that sends output to the specified *OutputStream*. An intermediate *OutputStreamWriter* that converts characters to bytes using the system default encoding is also constructed.

> If autoFlush is true, the *PrintWriter* calls its flush method after every invocation of println.

public PrintWriter (Writer out)

> Create a *PrintWriter* that sends output to the specified *Writer*.

public PrintWriter (Writer out, **boolean** autoFlush)

> Create a *PrintWriter* that sends output to the specified *Writer*.

> If autoFlush is true, the *PrintWriter* calls its flush method after every invocation of println.

Among the methods provided are these.

public void print (**boolean** b)

> Write "true" or "false" to the output stream depending on the value specified.

public void print (**char** c)

> Write the specified character to the output stream.

public void print (**double** d)

> Write a string representation of the specified **double** to the output stream.

public void print (Object obj)

> Write a string representation of the specified *Object* to the output stream, using the *Object*'s toString method.

public void print (String s)

> Write the specified *String* to the output stream.

public void println ()

> Write a (system dependent) line separator to the output stream

public void println (**boolean** b)

> Write "true" or "false" to the output stream depending on the value specified, followed by a line separator.

public void println (**char** c)

> Write the specified character to the output stream, followed by a line separator.

public void println (**double** d)

> Write a string representation of the specified **double** to the output stream, followed by a line separator.

public void println (Object obj)
>   Write a string representation of the specified *Object* to the output stream, using the *Object*'s `toString` method, followed by a line separator.

public void println (String s)
>   Write the specified *String* to the output stream, followed by a line separator.

System constants

Finally, we should mention that the data streams standard input, standard output, and standard error are accessible through constants defined in the class *java.lang.System*. Standard input is specified as an *InputStream*, while standard output and standard error are specified as *PrintStreams*:

```
public static final PrintStream err;// standard error
public static final PrintStream out;// standard out
public static final InputStream in; // standard in
```

Thus it is rather easy to write a line to standard output:

```
System.out.println("Goodbye for now.");
```

APPENDIX B   **Applets**

B.1 Applets

We have been concerned in this text with the development of independent software applications and the libraries to support them. Java is also used to write *applets*. Applets are small programs intended to be run by another program, typically a web browser such as Netscape Navigator. In a typical scenario, a compiled applet is downloaded by a browser as part of an HTML[1] document and executed by the client system.

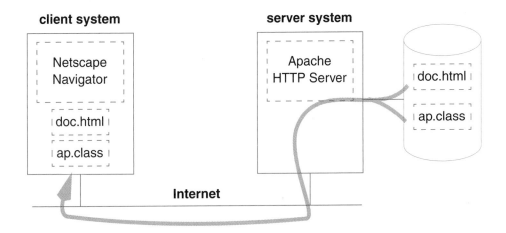

The HTML document identifies an applet to be loaded with either an `<applet>` tag[2] or an `<object>` tag. Though a discussion of HTML is well beyond the scope of this text, a minimal HTML document that loads an applet `Hello.class` might look like this:

---

1. HyperText Markup Language, the standard notation for writing Web documents.
2. Deprecated in HTML 4.0.

```
<html>
<head>
<title>Simple HTML document</title>
</head>
<body>
<applet code="Hello.class" height=100 width=300>
</applet>
</body>
```

After downloading and displaying the HTML document, the browser downloads and executes the applet. Execution of the applet continues until the applet code terminates or the user stops viewing the document containing the applet. The browser sets aside a region in the document display space for the applet, exactly as it would for an in-line image. The size and position of the display area is controlled by the browser and the HTML code. The applet controls what is displayed inside the area. A single document can contain several applets, in which case they are run in parallel, and can communicate with each other.

The contextual structure and run-time environment required for executing the applet is provided by the browser. For obvious security reasons, an applet's access to the client computing system is restricted. Applets can get user input through the mouse and keyboard and can read and write data on the originating server system. However, the browser will generally prevent the applet from accessing files on the client system or connecting to other third-party systems.

Applets can be used for more than simple web page decoration. One can build a web-based user interface for an application, in which the interface is presented by a browser. Applets running as part of the interface can communicate across a network with an application running on a server, sending and receiving data. A discussion of web-based applications is beyond the scope of this appendix.

B.1.1   The class *JApplet*

Applets are instances of *javax.swing.JApplet*, a Swing class with a lengthy lineage. *JApplet* extends *java.applet.Applet*, which extends *java.awt.Panel*, which extends *java.awt.Container*. We were introduced to *Container* in Chapter 19.

JApplet has the same structure as *JFrame* (Section 19.2.2), and serves as the top-level container for an applet in much the same way that a *JFrame* serves as the top-level container for an application's user interface.

JApplet inherits some fundamental methods from *java.applet.Applet*. In particular, there are four methods invoked by the browser that control overall execution of the applet. These methods are commonly overridden in classes that extend *JApplet*.

public void init ()
> Called once by the browser after the applet has been first loaded. It should be used for initialization functions that need to be done only once. Subclasses of *JApplet* generally do not provide a constructor. Functions that would otherwise be preformed in a constructor are done in init.

public void start ()
> Called after init and each time the browser revisits the page containing the applet. May be called when the browser is deiconified. This is the "main" method of the applet.

public void stop ()
> Called whenever the browser leaves the page containing the applet, and just before the applet is to be destroyed. May be called when the browser is iconified. This method should stop or suspend everything the applet is doing.

public void destroy ()
> Called when the browser determines it will no longer keep the applet in its cache. The applet should release any resources it has allocated. In practice, most applets don't need to override destroy.

Here's an example of a very simple applet.

```
import javax.swing.*;
import java.awt.*;

public class Hello extends JApplet {

    public void start () {
        Container cp = getContentPane();
        cp.add(new JLabel("Hello, World."));
    }


}
```

This applet can be tested by loading the HTML file shown on page 670 with the Java Development Kit *appletviewer*. If the HTML file is named Hello.html, the command is

```
appletviewer Hello.html
```

and the resulting display is shown in Figure B.1.

Just as with a *JFrame* (Chapter 19), a *JApplet*'s content pane is a *JPanel* with *BoarderLayout*. Every time the applet is started, the label "Hello, World" is added to the *JPanel*'s center component, replacing any previous center component.

Since this applet is completely static, we could achieve the same effect by adding the label in the init method rather than overriding the start method:

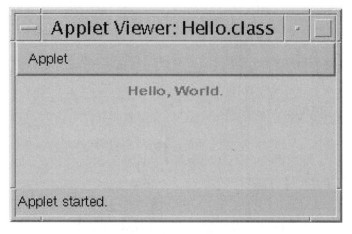

Figure B.1 "**Hello, World.**"

```java
import javax.swing.*;
import java.awt.*;

public class Hello extends JApplet {
    public void init () {
        Container cp = getContentPane();
        cp.add(new JLabel("Hello, World."));
    }
}
```

We can get a better picture of what's happening by giving the content pane a *FlowLayout*. With a FlowLayout, add will append the new label rather than replace the previous one. With the applet defined as follows:

```java
import javax.swing.*;
import java.awt.*;

public class Hello extends JApplet {
    public void init () {
        cp = getContentPane();
        cp.setLayout(new FlowLayout());
        cp.add(new JLabel("init."));
    }
    public void start () {
        cp.add(new JLabel("start."));
    }

    private Container cp;    // the content pane
}
```

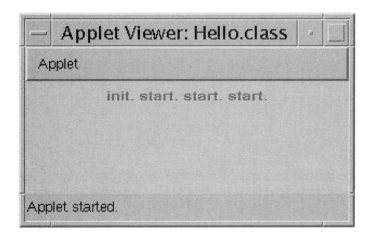

Figure B.2 **"Hello, World," initialized and started three times.**

the display after the *appletviewer* has been iconified and deiconified twice is shown in Figure B.2.

B.1.2   Applets as applications

There are a number of ways of writing an applet so that it can either execute from within a browser or run as a stand-alone application. (We must admit that it is not clear *why* one would want to do this.) In particular, an applet can be equipped with a main method. A browser ignores this method when it runs the applet. The main method can create a *JFrame* to display the applet, and invoke the applet methods init, start, stop, and destroy just as a browser would.

As an example, we show in Listing B.1 how the applet Hello can be written to run as an application. Note the following:

- A main method has been added to the applet class. This method creates a *JFrame* to contain the applet.

- The *JFrame* constructor creates an instance of the applet, and adds it to its content pane.

- The *JFrame* constructor initializes and starts the applet, in much the same way that a browser does.

- The *JFrame WindowListener* stops and starts the applet as appropriate. After restarting the applet, the *JFrame*'s layout manager is prompted (validate) to lay out the *JFrame* again.

Listing B.1   **The class *Hello***

```java
import javax.swing.*;
import java.awt.*;
import java.awt.event.*;

public class Hello extends JApplet {

    public static void main (String[] args) {
        AppletAppFrame f =
            new AppletAppFrame("Hello, World.");
    }

    public void init () {
        cp = getContentPane();
        cp.setLayout(new FlowLayout());
        cp.add(new JLabel("init."));
    }

    public void start () {
        cp.add(new JLabel("start."));
    }

    private Container cp;

} // end of class Hello

class AppletAppFrame extends JFrame {

    public AppletAppFrame (String title) {
        super(title);
        applet = new Hello();
        this.getContentPane().add(applet);
        this.setSize(300,100);
        applet.init();
        applet.start();
        this.setVisible(true);
        this.addWindowListener(
            new WindowAdapter() {

                public void windowClosing(WindowEvent e) {
                    e.getWindow().dispose();
                }
```

continued

Listing B.1   The class *Hello* (continued)

```java
        public void windowClosed(WindowEvent e) {
            applet.destroy();
            System.exit(0);
        }

        public void windowIconified(WindowEvent e) {
            applet.stop();
        }

        public void windowDeiconified(WindowEvent e) {
            applet.start();
            AppletAppFrame.this.validate();
        }
    });
}

    private Hello applet;

} // end of class AppletAppFrame
```

B.1.3   An example: a simple clock

As an example of a dynamic applet, we illustrate a simple clock. The applet uses a text field to display the current time. Approximately every 30 seconds, the applet gets the current time and updates the text field.

If we run the applet from an HTML document similar to that shown on page 670, the display will appear as in Figure B.3.

As with most dynamic applets, this applet creates a new *thread*. A thread is an independent sequence of actions. Creating a new thread specifies a sequence of statements that can be executed in parallel with, and independently of, the original sequence of statements. A detailed discussion of threads is beyond the scope of this appendix.

The code for the applet is given (without comments) in Listing B.2. Note the following:

- The method `init` adds the text field to the content pane. The text field needs to be at least eight characters wide to display the time.

- The method `start` creates and starts a new thread. This thread will actually get and write the time. The argument "`this`" to the *Thread* construc-

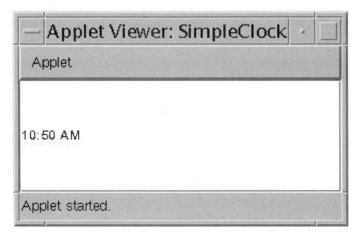

Figure B.3 **A simple clock.**

tor specifies that the new thread will execute the `run` method of the current object.

- The method `run` contains the sequence of statements that will be executed by the timer thread. *Date* and *SimpleDateFormat* are classes defined in `java.util`. A *Date* object represents an instant in time, with millisecond precision. The *SimpleDateFormat* can produce a *String* representation of a *Date*. The constructor argument specifies that the format will be "hours:minutes AM/PM."

- The body of the infinite loop in the method `run` first creates a new *Date* object containing the current time. The formatter converts this to a *String* in the specified format. This *String* is written to the text field. Finally, the thread waits for about 30 seconds before continuing.

Listing B.2   **The class *SimpleClock***

```
import javax.swing.*;
import java.awt.*;
import java.util.*;
import java.text.*;

public class SimpleClock extends JApplet
    implements Runnable {

    public void init () {
        cp = getContentPane();
```

continued

Listing B.2   **The class *SimpleClock (continued)***

```
        clock = new JTextField(TEXT_SIZE);
        cp.add(clock);
    }

    public void start () {
        timer = new Thread(this);
        timer.start();
    }

    public void stop () {
        timer = null;
    }

    public void run () {
        Date currentTime;
        SimpleDateFormat formatter =
            new SimpleDateFormat("h:mm a");
        while (true) {
            currentTime = new Date();
            clock.setText(formatter.format(currentTime));
            try {
                Thread.currentThread().sleep(DELAY);
            } catch (InterruptedException e) {}
        }
    }

    private final static int TEXT_SIZE = 8;
    private final static int DELAY = 30*1000; // milliseconds
    private Container cp;
    private JTextField clock;
    private Thread timer;
}
```

B.1.4   An example: an animated box

We conclude with one final example. In this applet, a box moves randomly around the display. A snapshot of the running applet is shown in Figure B.4.

A *timer* is used to control the animation. A timer is a thread that periodically generates action events. Each time the timer generates an event, the applet randomly computes a new position for the box and redraws the display. The code (again, without documentation) is shown in Listing B.3.

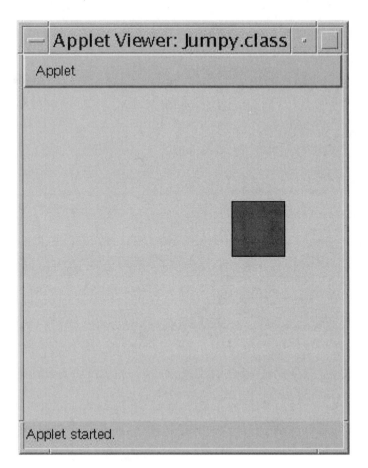

Figure B.4 **An animated box.**

Listing B.3   **The class *Jumpy***

```
import java.awt.*;
import java.util.*;
import java.awt.event.*;

public class Jumpy extends JApplet
    implements ActionListener {

    public void init () {
        Container cp = getContentPane();
```

continued

Listing B.3   The class *Jumpy (continued)*

```
    canvas = new Canvas();
    cp.add(canvas);
    cp.validate();    // so we can get width and height of
                      // canvas
    random = new Random();
    timer = new Timer(DELAY,this);

    // Start the rectangle in the middle of the canvas.
    x = (canvas.getWidth()-REC_WIDTH)/2;
    y = (canvas.getHeight()-REC_HEIGHT)/2;
    canvas.repaint();
}

public void start() {
    timer.start();
}

public void stop() {
    timer.stop();
}

public void actionPerformed (ActionEvent e) {
    // When the timer clicks, randomly update rectangle
    // coordinates and repaint the canvas.
    if (random.nextBoolean())
        x = x+random.nextInt(MAX_MOVE);
    else
        x = x-random.nextInt(MAX_MOVE);
    if (random.nextBoolean())
        y = y+random.nextInt(MAX_MOVE);
    else
        y = y-random.nextInt(MAX_MOVE);

    canvas.repaint();
}

private class Canvas extends JPanel {

    public void paintComponent(Graphics g) {
        super.paintComponent(g); // paint background
```

continued

Listing B.3   The class *Jumpy (continued)*

```
            g.drawRect(x, y, REC_WIDTH-1, REC_HEIGHT-1);
            g.setColor(Color.red);
            g.fillRect(x+1, y+1, REC_WIDTH-2, REC_HEIGHT-2);
        }

    }

    private final static int REC_WIDTH = 50;
                            // width of the rectangle
    private final static int REC_HEIGHT = 50;
                            // height of the rectangle
    private final static int DELAY = 1000;
                            // elapsed time between timer
                            // events (microseconds)
    private final static int MAX_MOVE = 20;
                            // max pixels the rectangle
                            // will move in either direction
                            // on one move
    private Timer timer;    // generates action events
    private Canvas canvas;  // JPanel in which the action
                            // takes place
    private Random random;  // pseudo random number generator
    private int x,y;        // coordinates of upper left
                            // corner of the rectangle
}
```

Note the following:

- The class *Timer* is defined in the package `javax.swing`. The constructor requires two arguments: a delay *d* (milliseconds) and an action listener. The *Timer* notifies its listener (by generating an action event) every *d* milliseconds.

- The class *Random* is defined in `java.util`. An instance is used to produce a stream of pseudorandom numbers. A method invocation such as

  `random.nextInt(MAX_MOVE)`

  produces a nonnegative pseudorandom integer that is less than MAX_MOVE. The method invocation

  `random.nextBoolean()`

  produces a pseudorandom `boolean` value.

- The *JPanel* method `repaint` invokes the method `paintComponent`, providing it with a graphics context. `paintComponent` is overridden in *Canvas* to draw the box and fill it with the color red.

Readers who would like more examples of applets are referred to Sun's Java tutorial. The tutorial can be found at

```
http://java.sun.com/docs/books/tutorial/
```

A list of applets can be found at

```
http://java.sun.com/docs/books/tutorial/
    listofapplets.html#swing
```

APPENDIX C

Java syntactic summary

In this text we use Java as a tool for implementing software designs and make no attempt to cover the Java programming language comprehensively. This appendix summarizes most of the fundamental Java syntactic structures. Again, there is no attempt at completeness. The reader interested in the full story should consult [Joy 00] or the *Java Language Specification* available for downloading or browsing at `http://java.sun.com/docs/`.

In naming and categorizing syntactic structures, we do not rigorously adhere to the terminology of the *Java Language Specification*. The Java semantics informally described here has also been simplified and is not rigorously accurate.

C.1 Lexical structures

Literal

Integer Literal

An integer literal may be expressed in decimal (radix 10), octal (radix 8), or hexadecimal (radix 16).

A decimal literal is a sequence of digits either beginning with a non-zero digit, or consisting of the single digit 0:

```
    0    2    1234
```

An octal literal starts with 0. For example

```
    07    012    0123
```

denote the values 7, 10 (= $1 \times 8 + 2$), and 83 (= $1 \times 64 + 2 \times 8 + 3$).

A hexadecimal literal starts 0x or 0X. For example

```
    0xFF    0xff    0X123
```

denote the values 255 (= $15 \times 16 + 15$), 255, and 291 (= $1 \times 256 + 2 \times 16 + 3$).

These literals all denote values of type **int**. Suffixing the letter L or 1 denotes a value of type **long**:

        21   0xffL

Floatingpoint Literal

A floating point literal is a sequence of digits containing a decimal point, such as

        0.2   2.5   .3   7.

or a sequence of digits optionally containing a decimal point and followed by an exponent indicator. For example,

        1e1   2.5e+10.4E-4

denote the values 1.0×10^1, 2.5×10^{10}, and 4.0×10^{-4}.

These literals all denote values of type **double**. Suffixing the letter F or f denotes a value of type **float**.

        0.5f   2e-2F

Boolean Literal

A boolean literal is one of

        true   false

Character Literal

A character literal is any single character (except \ or ') enclosed in single quotes, such as

        'a'   '2'   ' '   (the space character)

or an escape sequence enclosed in single quotes, for example

        '\\'   '\''   '\t'   '\n'   '\u03a9'

These escape sequences denote the characters backslash, single quote, horizontal tab, newline, and the Unicode character with hex value 0x03a9, respectively.

Escape sequences include:

\b	backspace
\t	horizontal tab
\n	linefeed
\f	formfeed
\r	carriage return
\"	quotation (double quote)
\'	apostrophe (single quote)
\\	backslash

Since Unicode escapes are processed very early, it is not correct to write '\u000a' for the linefeed character or '\u000d' for the carriage return character.

The escapes `\u000a` and `\u000d` become *line terminators* early in the scan, making the character literal invalid. See [Joy 00] for details.

String Literal

A *String* literal is a possibly empty sequence of characters enclosed in quotations. Examples are:

> `"ABC"`   `"123"`   `""` (the empty *String*)

String literals can contain escape sequences. The characters `"` and `\` must be escaped in a string literal:

> `"abc\ndef"`   `"He said, \"Let's go!\""`

String literals cannot extend across more than one line. Concatenation can be used to construct a long *String*:

> `"bababadalgharaghtakamminarronnkonnbronntonner"` +
> `"ronntuonnthunntrovarrhounawnskawntoohoohoorde"` +
> `"nenthurnuk!"`

Null Literal

There is only one null literal:

> **null**

Identifier

An identifier is a sequence of one or more letters, digits, underscores, and dollar signs that does not begin with a digit. The `$` should be used only in mechanically generated code. Examples are:

> `heartOfGold`   `MAX_VALUE`   `B29`

Identifiers are case sensitive. Thus `X` and `x` are distinct identifiers. (In fact, any Unicode letter can be a constituent of an identifier. Thus αμαθια is an identifier, and is distinct from ΑΜΑΘΙΑ.)

Keywords and identifier literals are excluded from the set of identifiers. Keywords and identifier literals are the following:

abstract	**default**	**goto**	**null**	**synchronized**
boolean	**do**	**if**	**package**	**this**
break	**double**	**implements**	**private**	**throw**
byte	**else**	**import**	**protected**	**throws**
case	**extends**	**instanceof**	**public**	**transient**
catch	**false**	**int**	**return**	**true**
char	**final**	**interface**	**short**	**try**
class	**finally**	**long**	**static**	**void**
const	**float**	**native**	**super**	**volatile**
continue	**for**	**new**	**switch**	**while**

Comment

A multiline comment begins with the character pair "/*" and ends with the character pair "*/". For example:

```
/* This is a multi
line comment. */
```

A multiline comment that begins /** is a doc comment. Documentation software takes note of doc comments.

```
/** This is a doc comment. */
```

A single line comment begins with the character pair // and extends to the end of line:

```
// This comment extends to the end of line only.
```

C.2   Names

A name can denote a variable, method, constructor, class, or interface. A name can be simple or qualified.

Simple Name

A simple name is an identifier.

Qualified Name

A qualified name is a sequence of identifiers separated by periods. A qualified name can include the keywords **this** or **super**:

```
Require.condition      this.base              super.equals
TextArea.this.base     java.util.Observable.hasChanged
```

C.3   Types

A type is a collection of values and associated operations. Every value is an element of one or more type. Every variable has a type, and can contain only values of that type. Every expression has a type, the type of the value it will produce when evaluated.

We sometimes distinguish between the static and run-time type of a variable or expression. For instance, a variable f declared

```
Figure f;
```

has static type Figure. However at run-time, the variable can contain a reference to an instance of a Figure subclass. For example, if Circle is a subclass of Figure, after the assignment

        f = **new** Circle();

the variable f references a Circle, though its (static) type remains Figure.

Type

Primitive Type

Primitive types are **byte**, **short**, **int**, **long**, **char**, **float**, **double**, and **boolean**. All but **boolean** are numeric types. The first five numeric types are integral types. **float** and **double** are floating point types.

Value ranges for the integral types are:

byte	–128 to 127;
short	–32,768 to 32,767;
int	–2,147,483,648 to 2,147,483,647;
long	–9,223,372,036,854,775,808 to 9,223,372,036,854,775,807;
char	0 to 65,535.

Values of type **float** and **double** are stored as 32-bit single precision and 64-bit double precision floating point numbers respectively. Values of type **float** have about seven decimal places of accuracy, and values of type **double** about sixteen.

Reference Type

Each class and interface defines an associated type. A reference type for a class consists of all references to instances of the class or to instances of any subclasses of the class. A reference type for an interface consists of all references to instances of any class that implements the interface. Note that if class *Second* extends class *First*, then the set of reference-to-*Second* values is a subset of the reference-to-*First* values. The type *Second* is said to be a subtype of *First*.

C.4 Packages

A package is the highest level syntactic component of a Java application. Members of a package are classes, interfaces, and other packages (subpackages).

Compilation Unit

Source files that contain a package's class and interface definitions are called compilation units. A compilation unit has three parts, each of which is optional:

- a package declaration, giving the fully-qualified name of the package to which the compilation unit belongs:

      package OOJ.basicIO;

- **import** declarations, that allow classes and interfaces form other packages to be referred to with simple, rather than fully qualified, names;

- declarations of classes and interfaces.

import declarations are of two kinds. The first specifies a single class or interface:

      import java.util.Vector;

The specified class or interface can then be referred to in the compilation unit by its simple name rather than its qualified name. Thus

      Vector v = **new** Vector();

rather than

      java.util.Vector v = **new** java.util.Vector();

The second form of **import** specifies a package followed by ".*":

      import java.util.*;

In this case, any visible class or interface in the package can be referred to by its simple name.

A class or interface declared in a package can be specified **public**, in which case it has global scope. Otherwise, the scope is the package.

Subpackage

The name of a subpackage is formed by prefixing the name of the parent package to an identifier:

      OOJ.basicIO.utilities

The package to subpackage relationship has no semantic significance.

C.5   Classes

A class can be a member of a package (an outer class) or a member of another class (an inner class).

A class that is a member of a package can be specified **public**, in which case its scope is global; that is, the entire program. Otherwise its scope is limited to the package of which it is a member.

A class that is a member of another class can have its scope modified just as any other class member. (See below.)

The fully-qualified name of an outer class is composed of the class name prefixed with the package name; for example

```
java.util.Vector
```

An inner class is named as any other class member.

Class Member

A class definition is composed of members that are constructors[1], methods, variables, named constants, and other classes. Class members are defined in the class body. The class body is enclosed in braces, and follows the class heading:

```
class Hero {
    // class body consists of member declarations
}
```

Methods, variables, constants, and classes defined in a class can be *static members*, in which case they are associated with the class itself rather than with any instance of the class; or they can be *instance members*, in which case each instance of the class has the defined feature.

Member Name

A member that is not static is associated with an instance of the class. The member is generally accessed by prefixing its name with a reference to the class instance. For instance, given the definition

```
public class Bag {
    ...
    public void setLength (int length) { ... }
    ...
}
```

the instance member setLength is accessed through a reference to the instance:

```
Bag b = new Bag(...);
b.setLength(0);
```

Within its class, a member can generally be accessed by its simple name. The exception is that a member variable cannot be accessed by its simple name within the scope of a local variable of the same name. For example:

```
public class Bag {
    ...
```

---

1. Technically, constructors are not considered class members.

```java
        public void setLength (int length) {
            // here the simple identifier "length" refers to
            // the parameter, not to the instance variable.
        }
        ...
        private int length;
        ...
    }
```

An instance member can always be accessed within its class by prefixing the simple name with the reserved word **this**:

```java
    public void setLength (int length) {
        this.length = length;
    }
```

A member of an instance of a textually enclosing class can be accessed by qualifying the keyword **this**. For example, suppose *Node* is an inner class of *Bag*:

```java
    public class Bag {
        ...
        private class Node {
            ...
            private Node first;
            ...
        }
        ...
        private Node first;
        ...
    }
```

Within the class *Node*, the *Bag*'s instance variable first can be referenced as Bag.**this**.first. The class *Node* might contain a statement such as

```java
    this.first = Bag.this.first;
```

A member that is static is associated with the class itself. (See below.) The member can be accessed by prefixing the member name with the class name. For example, the class *Require* contains the static method condition, specified as:

```java
    static boolean condition (boolean preCondition)
```

The method can be referenced, for example, by

```java
    Require.condition(i >= 0);
```

A member defined in an immediate superclass can be accessed in the subclass by prefixing the member name with the keyword **super**. This is useful for referencing overridden methods or hidden variables. For example:

```
public class Bag {
   ...
   public boolean equals (Object obj) { ... }
   ...
   protected int length;
   ...
}

public class GrabBag extends Bag {
   ...
   public boolean equals (Object obj) {
      // invoke overridden equals
      if (super.equals(obj)) {
         ...
         // access hidden int length
         if (super.length > 0)
         ...
      }
   ...
   private double length;// hides inherited length
}
```

A variable, method, and class defined in the same class can all have the same simple name. A class can define several methods with the same name as long as the methods differ in number and/or types of parameters. For example, a class can contain the following three methods:

```
public void m (Object obj) { ... }
public void m (Circle c) { ... }
public void m (Object obj, Circle c) { ... }
```

but not these two:

```
public void m () { ... }
private Object m () { ... }
```

Scope Modifier

A member can be specified as **public**, **protected**, or **private**. Otherwise, the member is restricted.

```
public void reset () { ... }
protected int numberTaken;
int updateEnrollment (Student s) { ... }
private class Node { ... }
private int count;
```

Public members have the same scope as the class. For example, if size is a public member of public class *Bag*

```
public class Bag {
    ...
    public int size () { ... }
    ...
}
```

then a reference to the `size` method of a *Bag*, such as

```
Bag b = new Bag(...);
if (b.size() > 0) ...
```

can occur anywhere in the program.

The scope of a private member is limited to the class declaration. For example, if `length` is a private member of the class *Bag*,

```
public class Bag {
    ...
    private int length;
    ...
}
```

then the reference `b.length`, where b is a *Bag*, can occur only in the definition of the class *Bag*.

The scope of a restricted member is the package. If `verify` is a restricted *Bag* member

```
public class Bag {
    ...
    void verify () { ... }
    ...
}
```

the reference `b.verify()`, where b is again a *Bag*, can occur anywhere in the package of which *Bag* is a member.

Protected members are accessible in the package containing the class and are available in subclasses of the defining class. For example, suppose `limit` is a protected member of *Bag*, and *GrabBag* is a subclass:

```
public class Bag {
    ...
    protected int limit;
    ...
}

public class GrabBag extends Bag {
    ...
}
```

If b is a *GrabBag*, the reference b.limit is legal in *Bag*, *GrabBag*, and the package of which *Bag* is a member. But it is not otherwise legal in a subclass of *GrabBag*.

Note that scope rules always refer to the outer class containing the definition. For example, if *Node* is an inner class of *Bag* defined as follows

```
public class Bag {

    ...

    private class Node {

        ...

        private Node next;

        ...

    }

    ...

    private int length;

    ...

}
```

b a *Bag* and n a *Node*, then references b.length and n.next can occur anywhere within the definition of *Bag*.

We suggest the following use of scope specification:

- **public** – for members that are part of the class specification;

- **private** – for members that are part of the class implementation;

- **protected** – for members that are part of the implementation, but are to be available to subclasses;

- restricted – for members that are to be accessed from only a few, specific, closely related classes.

Static Modifier

Class members can be specified as **static**. A member that is static is associated with the class itself, rather than with an instance of the class. Examples are

```
static void main (String[] args) { ... }
static boolean condition (boolean preCondition) { ... }
```

Static members can be referenced by prefixing the member name with the class name. If the method condition specified above is defined in the class *Require* it can be invoked, for instance, as

```
Require.condition(i >= 0);
```

Nonstatic members are associated with each class instance; static members are associated with the class itself, independently of any specific instance. For example, suppose a class defines a static variable `global` and an instance variable `local`:

```
class Monitor {
    ...
    private static int global = 0;
    private int local;
}
```

Then exactly one variable named `global` is created, but any number of variables named `local` might be created, since each *Monitor* instance has one.

Clearly, static members cannot reference non static members. For example, if the class *Monitor* sketched above has a static method `update`, that method could not reference the variable `local`.

Final Modifier

Class members can be specified as **final**. A method that is final cannot be overridden in a subclass. A "variable" that is final is, in fact, a named constant. The value associated with the name cannot be modified after creation. For example,

```
static final int CLUB = 1;
```

Abstract Modifier

A method can be specified as **abstract**. An abstract method declaration includes the heading, but no body. A semicolon replaces the body in the declaration:

```
abstract void move (int direction);
```

A class containing an abstract method declaration must be an abstract class. Any concrete subclass must provide an implementation of the abstract method.

Class Specialization

Every class (except *java.lang.Object*) is a subclass of exactly one other class. If the parent class is not *java.lang.Object*, it must be specified by an **extends** clause in the class heading:

```
class Orc extends Monster { ... }
```

A class can implement any number of interfaces. These are identified in an **implements** clause in the class heading:

```
class Leather extends Armor
    implements Wearable, Buyable { ... }
```

A class inherits all public and protected members of its parent superclass and super interfaces. It inherits restricted members if it is in the same package as the superclass or super interface.

Scope Modifier

A class that is not a member of any other class can be labeled **public**, in which case it is global. Otherwise, its scope is the package of which it is a member.

A class that is a member of another class has its scope specified exactly as any other class member.

Abstract Modifier

A class can be specified as **abstract**, in which case it cannot be instantiated. An abstract class can contain abstract members, and can be a superclass of abstract or concrete classes.

```
public abstract class OutputStream { … }
```

C.6 Interfaces

The syntactic structure of an interface is similar to that of a class, with the keyword **interface** used in place of the keyword **class**:

```
interface Portable {
    // member declarations
}
```

An interface cannot be instantiated. Members of an interface can be only abstract methods and constants. A method that is an interface member is implicitly **abstract** and **public**. A constant is implicitly **static** and **final**.

```
public interface Switchable {
    int state ();
    void flip ();
    int ON = 1;
    int OFF = 0;
}
```

An interface can extend any number of interfaces:

```
public interface Wearable extends
    Portable, Buyable { … }
```

An interface cannot extend a class.

C.7 Methods

A method specifies a sequence of actions to be performed. A method declaration consists of a heading and a body. The heading specifies the name, return type, and parameters of the method. The body is composed of statements that describe the actions to be performed when the method is executed.

Method Header

A method header specifies the type of value returned by the method, the name of the method, and a list of method parameters. The parameter list is a possibly empty sequence of automatic variable declarations, separated by commas and enclosed in parentheses. Examples are

```
int firstInstance (Object obj, List list)
int length ()
```

If the method is specified as **void**, it does not return a value when executed. For instance

```
void setLength (int length)
```

Scope Modifier, Static Modifier, Final Modifier

Since a method is a member of a class or interface, it can be declared as **private**, **public**, **protected**, **static**, and/or **final**.

```
public static void main (String[] args)
```

See Section C.5 for details.

Abstract Modifier

A method can be declared **abstract**, in which case its body is replaced by a semicolon:

```
public abstract void move (int direction);
```

Throws Clause

If it is possible for a checked exception to be thrown in a method, and the method does not catch this exception, a **throws** clause must be included after the parameter list. (A *checked exception* is an instance of the class *Exception* that is not a *RuntimeException*.) Thrown exceptions are comma separated in the clause. For example

```
public void appendToFile (File f, char c)
    throws IOException, FileNotFoundException { ... }
```

Method Body

A method body is a block; that is, a possibly empty sequence of statements and local variable declarations enclosed in braces:

```
public int count () {
    // the statements that make up the method body
}
```

In an abstract method, the body is replaced with a semicolon:

```
public abstract void move (int direction);
```

C.8 Constructors

A constructor declaration is similar in format to a method declaration. A constructor is named with the class name and does not have a return type. (By default, it returns a reference to an instance of the class.) For example:

```
public Hero (String name) { … }
```

Except for the class *Object*, every constructor begins with an implicit or explicit invocation of another constructor of the same class or of a constructor of the parent superclass.

A constructor of the same class is invoked with the keyword **this**:

```
public Circle () {
    this(0,0,1);
    …
```

A constructor of the parent class is invoked with the keyword **super**:

```
public Circle (int x, int y, int radius) {
    super(x,y);
    …
```

A constructor that does not explicitly call another constructor of the same class or a parent constructor implicitly begins with the invocation:

```
super();
```

A class that does not contain an explicit constructor definition implicitly contains the default constructor:

```
public ClassName () {
    super();
}
```

Constructors cannot be **static**, **abstract**, or **final**.

C.9 Variables

A variable is declared by specifying the type of the variable, an identifier that names the variable, and, except for a parameter, an optional initializer. Except for parameters, variable declarations are terminated by a semicolon.

For a variable of primitive type, the type specified is the type of the value the variable contains. For a variable of a reference type, the name of a class or interface is specified. The variable will contain either a null value or a value that references an instance of the specified class, an instance of a subclass of the specified class, or an instance of a class that implements the specified interface. Examples are

```
int count;
List schedule;
Observer watcher;
```

To declare a variable that will reference an instance of an array class, the array component type is followed by a pair of brackets. For instance

```
double[] vector;
Portable[] contents;
String[] args;
double[][] matrix;
```

The variable `matrix` as declared above will reference an array whose components are arrays of **double**s.

An initializer is an assignment operator followed by an expression, such as

```
int count = 0;
Observer watcher = new ClockWatcher();
```

An array variable can be initialized by a sequence of comma separated expressions or array initializers enclosed in braces. For example

```
double[] vector = { 1.0, 2.0, 3.0, 4.0 };
double[][] matrix = { {1.0,2.0}, {0.0,0.0,0.0} };
```

An array initializer implicitly creates a new array instance, with its size determined by the number of expressions in the initializer. Note that in the initialization of the variable `matrix` shown above, three objects are created: a two-element **double** array containing the values 1.0 and 2.0; a three-element **double** array containing three zero values; a two-element array whose components are of type **double**[].

Except for parameters, several variables can be declared in one declaration. The individual variable declarations are separated by commas:

```
int i = 0, j, k = 1;
```

Instance Variable, Class Variable

A variable that is not defined in a method or constructor is a member of a class. If the variable is specified as **static**, it is a class variable associated with the class itself:

```
static int generation = 0;
```

Otherwise, the variable is an instance variable: each instance of the class has a variable conforming to the declaration specification.

As with any member, the scope of the variable can be **private**, **public**, **protected**, or restricted. Examples are

```
private int count;
public int length;
Node next;
```

A "variable" specified as **final**, such as

```
static final int CLUB = 1;
```

is in fact a named constant.

Local Variable

A variable that is declared in the body of a method or constructor is a local variable. It is created when the method or constructor is invoked, and deallocated when the method or constructor terminates. The scope of the variable is the block containing the definition. A local variable can have an initializer, but cannot have a scope modifier, static modifier, or final modifier. For instance:

```
int index = 0;
```

A local variable can have the same name as a class member.

A method can have several local variables with the same name as long as their scopes do not overlap. The following method, for example, contains definitions of two local variables named i:

```
public int sum (int x) {
    int sum = 0;
    if (x%2 == 0) {
        int i = 0;
        while (i <= x) {
            sum = sum + i;
            i = i + 2;
        }
    } else {
        int i = 1;
        while (i <= x) {
            sum = sum + i;
            i = i + 2;
        }
    }
    return sum;
}
```

(Note: we do not recommend the structure illustrated by this example.)

Parameter Variable

A parameter is a variable declared in a method or constructor parameter list. A parameter is essentially a local variable initialized with an argument value when the method or constructor is invoked. Its scope is the method body.

A parameter cannot have an initializer, and its definition is not terminated with a semicolon:

```
int firstInstance (Object obj, List list)
```

C.10   Statements

A statement describes an action to be performed by the processor.

Simple Statement

A simple statement has no constituent substatements.

Empty Statement

An empty statement consists only of a semicolon. It has no effect.

```
;
```

Assignment Statement

An assignment statement is composed of a variable name, assignment operator (=), an expression, and semicolon:

```
i = 2*i;
hero.location = this.connectingRoom(NORTH);
contents[i] = item;
```

The variable name is referred to as the "left-hand side of the assignment," the expression as the "right-hand side." The expression is evaluated, and its value replaces the previous value of the variable.

The type of the expression must be compatible with the type of the variable. If the variable is of type reference to class C, the expression must denote an instance of class C or an instance of a subclass of C. If the variable is of type reference to interface I, the expression must denote an instance of a class that implements I. For variables of primitive type, the following expression types are allowed:

left-hand side:	right-hand side:
boolean	boolean
char	char
byte	byte
short	byte, short

int	byte, short, char, int
long	byte, short, char, int, long
float	byte, short, char, int, long, float
double	byte, short, char, int, long, float, double

There are eleven additional assignment operators. See the section labeled *Assignment Expression* on page 713.

Method Invocation, Constructor Invocation

A method invocation followed by a semicolon constitutes a statement. A method invocation consists of a method name and argument list. The argument list is a possibly empty sequence of expressions, separated by commas, and enclosed in parentheses:

```
count.reset();
hero.move(north);
schedule.set(i+2, new Course("1583"));
```

Arguments must correspond to method parameters in number and type. Arguments must be compatible with corresponding parameters in generally the same way that assignment right-hand sides must be compatible with assignment left hand sides.

A method invocation is executed by initializing the method parameters with the argument values, and then executing the statements that make up the method body.

A constructor invocation followed by a semicolon constitutes a statement. A constructor invocation consists of the reserved word **new**, a class name, and an argument list:

```
new CheckTimer();
```

Such constructor usage is not common.

Constructor invocations consisting of the keyword **this** or the keyword **super** followed by an argument list and ending with a semicolon are permitted as the first statement in a constructor:

```
this(0);
super();
```

Increment Statement, Decrement Statement

An increment statement is a numeric variable name prefixed or suffixed with ++, followed by a semicolon:

```
i++;
++i;
```

An increment statement increments the value of the variable by 1.

A decrement statement is a numeric variable name prefixed or suffixed with $--$, followed by a semicolon:

```
i--;
--i;
```

A decrement statement decrements the value of the variable by 1.

Return Statement

A return statement consists of the keyword **return** optionally followed by an expression, ending with a semicolon:

```
return;
return count+1;
```

Executing a return statement terminates execution of the method. The value of the expression is the value returned by the method.

The first form of return statement can occur only in a **void** method. The type of the expression in the second form of return statement must be compatible with the return type of the method.

Break Statement

A break statement

```
break;
```

exits the innermost containing switch or loop statement.

The following method, for example, returns a *String* equal to its argument with trailing spaces, tabs, and newlines removed. The **break** causes the loop to be exited when the rightmost non-blank, non-tab, non-newline is encountered. *String* method length returns the length of the *String*, getChar(n) the character with index n, and substring(start, end) a new *String* that contains the characters from index start through index end-1:

```
/**
 * A String equal to the specified String with trailing
 * blanks, tabs, and newlines removed.
 */
String trim (String s) {
   int n;
   for (n = s.length()-1; n >= 0; n--) {
      char c = s.getChar(n);
      if (c != ' ' && c != '\t' && c != '\n')
         break;
   }
   return s.substring(0,n+1);
}
```

(Note: we do not recommend the structure illustrated by this example.)

Continue Statement

A continue statement

```
continue;
```

terminates the current iteration of a loop statement.

For example, the following loop skips repeated items in a list:

```
int i;
for (i == 0; i < list.size(); i=i+1) {
    if (i>0 && list.get(i).equals(list.get(i-1)))
        continue;
    // process list.get(i)
    ...
}
```

(Note: we do not recommend the structure illustrated by this example.)

Throw Statement

A throw statement causes an exception to be thrown. The expression following the keyword **throw** must denote an exception. For example

```
throw new RuntimeException();
throw e;
```

Conditional Statement

If-then Statement

An if-then statement is composed of a boolean expression and statement:

```
if ( BooleanExpression ) Statement
```

The boolean expression is evaluated, and if true, the statement is executed. The following statement increments i if i is negative:

```
if (i<0)
    i = i+1;
```

If-then-else Statement

An if-then-else statement is made up of a boolean expression and two statements:

```
if ( BooleanExpression ) Statement1 else Statement2
```

The boolean expression is evaluated, and if true, the first statement is executed. If false, the statement following the **else** is executed. The following assigns max the larger of a and b:

```
if (a > b)
    max = a;
else
    max = b;
```

Note that because of a possible ambiguity, an if-then cannot be the "true" alternative of an if-then-else. That is, in

```
if (a > b)
    if (a > c)
        n = a;
    else
        n = c;
```

the "else" goes with the inner if: the if-then-else is nested in the if-then. If the outer statement is to be an if-then-else, the inner if-then must be converted to a block by enclosing it in braces:

```
if (a > b) {
    if (a > c)
        n = a;
} else
    n = c;
```

A cascade of if-then-else statements is often used to select one of several alternatives. For instance,

```
if (suit == 1)
    clubCount = clubCount + 1;
else if (suit == 2)
    diamondCount = diamondCount + 1;
else if (suit == 3)
    heartCount = heartCount + 1;
else if (suit == 4)
    spadeCount = spadeCount + 1;
else
    invalidCount = invalidCount + 1;
```

Switch Statement

A switch statement consists of an integer, character, or boolean valued expression and a switch block:

> **switch** (*Expression*) *SwitchBlock*

A switch block consists of labeled statement groups enclosed in braces:

> { *LabeledStatementGroup* … }

A labeled statement group consists of a possibly empty sequence of statements preceded by one or more labels, where a label has one of the following forms:

> **case** *ConstantExpression* :
> **default** :

The label **default** can appear at most once in a switch block, and must be the last label in the block. For example

```
switch (suit) {
case 1:   clubCount = clubCount + 1;
          break;
case 2:   diamondCount = diamondCount + 1;
          break;
case 3:   heartCount = heartCount + 1;
          break;
case 4:   spadeCount = spadeCount + 1;
          break;
default:  invalidCount = invalidCount + 1;
}
```

The expression is evaluated, and execution continues with the statement following the label that matches the value of the expression. If no label matches the value of the expression, execution continues at the **default** label. If there is no **default** label, execution of the switch statement is complete. The above example increments a count depending on the value of suit.

Note that execution of the switch is not terminated by reaching another label. Execution is complete only if no label matches the value of the expression and there is no **default** label, a **break** statement is executed, or end of the switch block is encountered. Also note that a labeled statement group can have more than one label. For instance:

```
switch (suit) {
case 2:
case 3:   redCardCount = redCardCount + 1;
          break;
case 4:   spadeCount = spadeCount + 1;
case 3:   blackCardCount = blackCardCount + 1;
          break;
default:  invalidCount = invalidCount + 1;
}
```

If the value of suit is 4, three statements are executed: the assignment to spadeCount, the assignment to blackCardCount, and finally the **break**.

Loop Statement

While Statement

A while statement is composed of a boolean expression and a statement, the loop body:

```
while ( BooleanExpression ) Statement
```

The boolean expression is evaluated and if true, the statement is executed and the process repeated. The expression and the statement are repeatedly executed until the expression evaluates to false. For example, the following loop doubles i until it's greater than `limit`:

```
while (i <= limit)
    i = 2*i;
```

The body of while statement is often a block or other structured statement, as illustrated by the following examples.

This method computes the greatest common divisor of two positive integers. The body of the **while** statement is an if-then-else:

```
/**
 * Greatest common divisor of the specified integers.
 *      require:
 *          a > 0 && b > 0
 */
int gcd (int a, int b) {
    while (a != b)
        if (a > b)
            a = a-b;
        else
            b = b-a;
    return a;
}
```

The (partial) correctness of the above method can be seen by observing that:

- gcd(a,b) = gcd(b,a), and
- if a > b, gcd(a,b) = gcd(a-b,b).

Termination follows from the invariance of max(a,b) > 0, and the fact that max(a,b) is decremented by each iteration.

This method computes the *n*-th Fibonacci number. The body of the while statement is a block:

```
/**
 * The nth Fibonacci number, where the "1st" is 1,
 * the "2nd" is 1, etc.
 *      require:
 *          n >= 1
 */
int fib (int n) {
    int n1 = 0;
    int n2 = 1;
    int i = 1;
```

```
    while (i < n) {
        n2 = n2 + n1;
        n1 = n2 - n1;
        i = i + 1;
    }
    return n2;
}
```

Do Statement

Like a while statement, a do statement is also composed of a boolean expression and a statement:

do *Statement* **while** (*BooleanExpression*)

The statement is executed, and then the boolean expression is evaluated. If true, the process is repeated. The statement and the expression are repeatedly executed until the expression evaluates to false. Note that the body of the do statement is always executed at least once. For instance, the following loop doubles i at least once:

```
do
    i = 2*i;
while (i <= limit)
```

The do statement is not very common. The following method builds a *String* representation of an integer value. Digits are obtained, right to left, by successively dividing the integer by 10 and converting the remainder to a character. The method depends on the fact that the character code for '1' is one more than the code for '0', the code for '2' is two more than '0', *etc.* A do statement is useful here, since at least one character must always be generated, even if the integer argument is 0:

```
/**
 * Representation of the specified integer as a String
 * of decimal digits.
 *     require:
 *         n >= 0
 */
String intToString (int n) {
    String s = "";
    do {
        char digit = (char)(n%10+'0');
        s = digit + s;
        n = n/10;
    } while (n != 0);
    return s;
}
```

For Statement

A for statement consists of a for clause and a body statement. The for clause contains an initialization component, a boolean expression, and an update component, separated by semicolons. Any of these can be empty:

```
for ( Initialization ; BooleanExpression ; Update )
    Statement
```

- The initialization consists of a possibly empty comma separated sequence of assignment statements, increment statements, decrement statements, and/or local variable declarations. The scope of any local variable declared in the initialization is the for statement.

- The update consists of a possibly empty comma separated sequence of assignment statements, increment statements, and/or decrement statements.

The ending semicolon is omitted from any statement in the initialization or update.

When the for statement is executed, the initialization statements are done first. Then the boolean expression is evaluated. If true, the body statement and then update statements are executed, and the boolean expression is again evaluated. The boolean expression, body statements, and update statements are repeatedly executed until the boolean expression evaluates to false. The for statement is roughly equivalent to

```
Initialization;
while ( BooleanExpression ) {
    Statement;
    Update;
}
```

As an example, the following method determines whether or not a specified *String* is a palindrome. (A *palindrome* is a string that reads the same forward or backward, such as "amanaplanacanalpanama".)

```
/**
 * The specified String is a palindrome.
 */
boolean isPalindrome (String s) {
    boolean isPalindrome;
    for (int i=0, int j=s.lenght()-1,
         isPalindrome=true; i<j; i=i+1, j=j-1)
        if (s.getChar(i) != s.getChar(j))
            isPalindrome = false;
    return isPalindrome;
}
```

The body of a for statement is sometimes an empty statement, as in

```
/**
 * The specified char is in the specified String.
 */
boolean isIn (char c, String s) {
    int i;
    for (i=0; i<s.length() && s.getChar(i)!=c; i=i+1) ;
    return i<s.length();
}
```

The above method would not be correct if the for statement was written:

```
for (int i=0; …
```

In this case, the scope of the local variable i is the for statement, and i cannot be referenced in the return statement.

Try Statement

A try statement consists of a block and one or more catch clauses. A catch clause consists of a parameter and block.

```
try {
    // statements and/or declarations of the try block
} catch ( ParameterDeclaration) {
    // statements and/or declarations of a catch clause
} catch ( ParameterDeclaration) {
    // statements and/or declarations of a catch clause
} // possibly other catch clauses
```

Catch clause parameters are exceptions. To execute a try statement, the statements of the try block are first executed. If they complete normally, the try statement is complete. If an exception is thrown during execution of the try block, control is transferred to the first catch clause whose parameter is compatible with the thrown exception. If the catch clause completes normally, the try statement is complete. If the statements of the catch clause throw an exception, the exception is propagated to the method caller.

In the following example, data is an input stream reader, and its method readInt throws an EOFException if end of file has been reached. The try statement processes data from the input stream until the end of file exception is thrown, and then closes the stream:

```
try {
    while (true) {
        data.readInt();
        int i = data.lastInt();
        process(i);
    }
```

```
    } catch (EOFException e) {
        data.close();
    }
```

(Note: we do not recommend the structure illustrated by this example.)

A try statement can be optionally followed by a **finally** clause:

```
finally { // statements and declarations of the
    finally clause

}
```

A finally clause is executed upon normal completion of the try block or of a catch clause.

Block

A block consists of a possibly empty sequence of statements and/or local variable declarations enclosed in braces. A block is often a component statement of an if-then statement, an if-then-else statement, or a loop:

```
{
    int temp;
    temp = a;
    a = b;
    b = temp;
}
```

The scope of a variable defined in a block is from the definition to the end of the block.

Labeled Statement

A statement can be prefixed with a label, consisting of an identifier followed by a colon. For instance

```
outerLoop: while ( … ) …
```

A **break** or **continue** statement can include a label

```
break outerLoop;
continue outerLoop;
```

Execution of a break statement with a label causes termination of the labeled statement. The break statement must be included in the labeled statement.

Execution of a continue statement with label causes termination of the current iteration of the labeled statement. The labeled statement must be a loop, and the continue statement must be included in the labeled statement.

The following method determines whether or not two *Strings* have a character in common. The break statement is used to terminate the outer loop when a character common to both *Strings* is found:

```
/**
 * The specified Strings have a character in common.
 */
boolean haveCommonChar (String s1, String s2) {
    int i, j;
    outerLoop:
    for (i = 0; i < s1.length(); i++)
        for (j = 0; j < s2.length(); j++)
            if (s1.getChar(i) == s2.getChar(j))
                break outerLoop;
    return i < s1.length();
}
```

(Note: we do not recommend the structure illustrated by this example.)

C.11   Expressions

An expression produces a value when executed.

Simple Expression

Literal

A literal simply evaluates to the value it denotes.

Variable Name, Constant Name

A variable name denotes the value stored in the variable. A named constant denotes the value it is initially bound to.

A variable or constant name can be an identifier:

```
i    count    first
```

a member selection:

```
this.start
super.size
anteroom.next
rogue.utilites.Direction.NORTH
```

or an array component selection:

```
contents[size-1]
list[0]
matrix[0][1]
```

The keyword **this** in a member selection refers to the currently executing object. The keyword **super** refers to the currently executing object treated as an instance of its parent (super) class.

An array component selection consists of the array name followed by an integer index expression in brackets. Note that given the definition

```
double[][] matrix;
```

the expression `matrix[0]` is of type `double[]`, while the expression `matrix[0][0]` is of type `double`.

Method Invocation

A method invocation consists of the method name followed by an argument list. An argument list is a possibly empty sequence of expressions, separated by commas and enclosed in parentheses:

```
count()                 super.equals(x)
courseList.sublist(first,mid)
```

A method invocation executes the method body, and returns a value of the type specified by the method header.

Invocation of a method specified as **void** does not return a value and is not an expression.

The keyword **super** specifies that the method to be executed is as defined in the immediate superclass of the executing class. This construct is useful for executing an overridden method implementation.

Constructor Invocation

A constructor invocation consists of the keyword **new** followed by a class name and argument list:

```
new Room(length, width, location)
new java.util.Date()
```

A constructor invocation evaluates to a reference to the newly created object.

A constructor invocation for an array class consists of the keyword **new**, the type of array components, and an argument specifying the array size in brackets.

```
new int[100]
new Room[count]
```

Note that there is a historical inconsistency when creating arrays whose components are arrays. For instance,

```
new double[3][]
```

creates an array of three components, each of which is of type **double[]**, while

```
new double[3][4]
```

creates an array of three components and also creates each of the three components. Each component is an array of four **double**s. Thus the statement

```
double[][] matrix = new double[3][4];
```

creates four objects, one of type **double[][]** and three of type **double[]**, as shown in Figure C.1. The variable matrix[0] references an array of four **doubles**, and matrix[0][0] is a variable of type **double**:

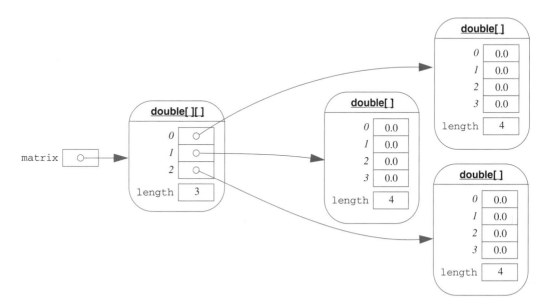

Figure C.1 **An array whose components are arrays.**

Parenthesized Expression

An expression can be enclosed in parentheses (but not braces or brackets) without changing its value.

Assignment Expression

An assignment expression consists of a variable name, an assignment operator (=), and an expression. The value of an assignment expression is the value of the right-hand side expression. Evaluation has the side effect of changing the value of the variable to the value of the expression.

```
i = 2*i
hero.location = anteroom
contents[i] = item
i = (j = 2*j)
```

Note that in the last of the above examples, the value 2*j is assigned to j, and this value is also the value of the expression j = 2*j. For instance, if j is initially 2, the value 4 is assigned to j and then to i.

There are eleven other assignment operators that incorporate binary operators. They are:

```
*=    /=    %=    +=    -=    <<=   >>=   >>>=   &=    ^=    |=
```

The effect of executing

```
i *= 2
```

is essentially the same as executing

```
i = i*2
```

Other assignment operators work in a similar way.

We recommend that assignment expressions, and other expressions that result in a change of state, not be used as a constituent of a larger expression.

Increment Expression

An increment expression is a numeric variable name prefixed or suffixed with ++:

```
i++
++i
```

An increment expression has the side effect of incrementing the value of the variable by 1. If the operator ++ is a suffix, the value of the increment expression is the value of the variable before it is incremented. If the operator ++ is a prefix, the value of the increment expression is the value of the variable after it is incremented. For example

```
int i = 0;
int j = i++;
// j is 0; i is 1
j = ++i;
// j and i are both 2
```

We recommend that increment expressions, and other expressions that result in a change of state, not be used as a constituent of a larger expression.

Decrement Expression

A decrement expression is a numeric variable name prefixed or suffixed with --:

```
i--
--i
```

A decrement expression has the side effect of decrementing the value of the variable by 1. If the operator -- is a suffix, the value of the decrement expression is the value of the variable before it is decremented. If the operator -- is a prefix, the value of the decrement expression is the value of the variable after it is decremented.

We recommend that decrement expressions, and other expressions that result in a change of state, not be used as a constituent of a larger expression.

Arithmetic Expression

An arithmetic expression denotes a value of a numeric type. Arithmetic expressions can be combined with the binary operators *, /, %, +, -, denoting multiplication, division, remainder, addition, and subtraction, and can be prefixed with the unary operators + and -. See the discussion of precedence and associativity below.

Integer division truncates toward 0. Thus

```
11/3          ⇒        3
(-11)/3       ⇒        -3
```

Integer remainder satisfies the equation

$$(divisor \times quotient) + remainder = dividend.$$

Thus

```
11%3          ⇒        2
11%-3         ⇒        2
(-11)%3       ⇒        -2
(-11)%(-3)    ⇒        -2
```

String Expression

The binary operator + denotes catenation when the operands are *Strings*. If one operand is a *String* and the other is not, the non-*String* operand is converted to a *String*. Thus

```
"abc"+"def" ⇒       "abcdef"
6+"abc"       ⇒       "6abc"
"abc"+2*3     ⇒       "abc6"
```

If the non-*String* operand is an object, the object's toString method is invoked to provide the argument:

```
"abc"+obj    ⇒       "abc"+obj.toString()
```

Boolean Expression

Relational Expression

Expressions denoting numeric values can be combined with the binary operators <. <=. >, >=, denoting less than, less than or equal to, greater than, greater than or equal to. The result of evaluating the expression is a boolean value.

Equality Expression

The value of two expressions of compatible types can be compared for equality or inequality with the binary operators == and !=. The result of evaluating the expression is a boolean value.

Note that these operators compare reference *values* for equality. For instance, if o1 and o2 refer to objects,

```
Object o1, o2;
```

then o1 == o2 is true if and only if o1 and o2 refer to the *same object*.

Instanceof Expression

If the value of an expression is a reference to an object, the type of the reference value can be tested with the operator **instanceof**. The left operand of the operator evaluates to a reference value, and the right operand names a reference type. The result of evaluating the expression is a boolean value. For example

```
opponent instanceof Orc
```

evaluates to true if the object referenced by opponent is an instance of the class *Orc* or of a subclass of *Orc*.

Note that **instanceof** tests set membership. The left operand denotes a reference *value*, and the right operand denotes a reference *type* which is effectively a set of values.

Conditional And Expression

Two boolean expressions can be combined with the binary operator &&. For instance

```
0 < i && i < 10
```

The left operand is evaluated first. If false, the result of the conditional-and expression is false. If the left operand is true, the right operand is evaluated, and its value is the value of the conditional-and expression. The fact that the right operand is only evaluated if the left operand is true can be used to guard against attempts to evaluate invalid expressions. For instance

```
i != 0 && j/i > 10
```

guards against division by 0, while

```
0 <= i && i < list.size() && !list.get(i).equals(item)
```

guards against a reference to a non-existent list item.

Conditional Or Expression

Two boolean expressions can be combined with the binary operator ||. For instance

```
i < 0 || i > 10
```

The left operand is evaluated first. If true, the result of the conditional-or expression is true. If the left operand is false, the right operand is evaluated, and its value is the value of the conditional-or expression.

Logical Expression

A boolean expression can be prefixed with the unary operator !, representing the logical operation NOT. Two boolean expressions can be combined with the binary operators &, ^, and |, representing the logical operations AND, exclusive OR, and inclusive OR respectively.

- ! *be* evaluates to true if and only if *be* evaluates to false.

- *be1* & *be2* evaluates to true if and only both *be1* and *be2* evaluate to true.

- *be1* ^ *be2* evaluates to true if and only if either *be1* or *be2*, but not both, evaluates to true.

- *be1* | *be2* evaluates to true if and only if either *be1* or *be2* or both evaluate to true.

The operators && and || are generally preferred to & and |.

Bitwise Expression

The operands for bitwise operators must be integer expressions.

Shift Expression

The operations are preformed on the two's complement integer representation of the value of the left operand.

- The value of n<<s is n left-shifted s bit positions.

- The value of n>>s is n right-shifted s bit positions with sign extension.

- The value of n>>>s is n right-shifted s bit positions with zero extension.

Examples are

```
0x12345678<<4    ⟹  0x23456780
0x87654321>>4    ⟹  0xF8765432
0x87654321>>>4   ⟹  0x08765432
```

Bitwise Logical Expression

The operator ~ is a unary operator. The result of applying this operator is the bitwise complement of the operand value.

Bitwise logical binary operators are &, ^, and |. The result of & is the bitwise AND of the operand values. The result of ^ is the bitwise exclusive OR of the operand values. The result of | is the bitwise inclusive OR of the operand values.

Examples are

```
~0x00FF00FF    ⟹  0xFF00FF00
0x00FF00FF & 0x0F0F0F0F   ⟹  0x000F000F
0x00FF00FF ^ 0x0F0F0F0F   ⟹  0x0FF00FF0
0x00FF00FF | 0x0F0F0F0F   ⟹  0x0FFF0FFF
```

For details of the shift and bitwise logical operators, see [Joy 00].

Cast Expression

A cast expression consists of a parenthesized type followed by an expression.

(*Type*) *Expression*

A cast expression converts a value of one numeric type to a similar value of another numeric type, or converts the (static) reference type of an expression to a compatible type. The (static) type of the cast expression is the type specified in parentheses.

For example, if length is of type **int**, then

(**double**) length

is of type **double** and evaluates to the **double** equivalent of the **int** length.

Note that converting a value of one numeric type to another may result in loss of information regarding the magnitude of the number or its precision. For instance, a value of type **int** (32 bits) is converted to a value of type **short** (16 bits) by discarding the high-order 16 bits. Converting an **int** or **long** to **float** or a **long** to **double** may result in the loss of precision—that is, may lose some of the least significant bits of the value. Also note that floating point values are truncated toward 0 when being converted to integer values. The following examples illustrate some of these points:

```
int i = 0x12345678;
double d = 1.9;
(short)i             ⟹  0x5678
(int)((float)i)      ⟹  0x12345680
(int)d               ⟹  1
```

The type of a reference-valued expression can be cast to a supertype or a subtype. For example, suppose *Second* is subclass of *First*, *Third* a subclass of *Second*, and aSecond a variable of type *Second*:

```
class Second extends First { … }
class Third extends Second { … }
Second aSecond;
```

Then the (static) type of the expression

(First)aSecond

is (reference to) *First*, and the (static) type of

(Third)aSecond

is (reference to) *Third*.

Note that the run-time type of the object denoted by (First)aSecond is not affected by the cast. For instance, if the class *First* has a method m overridden in *Second*, ((First)aSecond).m() still invokes the overriding implementation defined in *Second*. That is, given the definitions

```
class First {
   public int m () {
      return 1;
   }
}
class Second extends First {
   public int m () {
      return 2;
   }
}

Second aSecond = new Second();
First aFirst = new Second();
```

the expressions `((First)aSecond).m()` and `aFirst.m()` both return 2, even though the static types of `(First)aSecond` and `aFirst` are both *First*. These are both cases of polymorphism.

Furthermore, casts to a subtype are checked for correctness at run time. For instance, evaluation of the expression

```
(Third)aSecond
```

involves a run-time check that the object referenced by `aSecond` is in fact an instance of the class *Third*, or an instance of a subclass of *Third*.

Conditional Expression

A conditional expression is composed of a boolean expression and two component expressions.

```
BooleanExpression ? Expression1 : Expression2
```

The boolean expression is first evaluated. If true, the expression following the `?` is evaluated and is the value of the conditional expression. If false, the expression following the `:` is evaluated and is the value of the conditional expression.

The following expression, for example, evaluates to the absolute value of the integer `i`:

```
i>0 ? i : -i
```

Precedence, associativity

All binary operations are left associative, with the exception of the assignment operators which are right associative. Conditional expressions are right associative. Unary operations are performed right to left. Selection proceeds left to right.

The precedence hierarchy, high to low, is as follows:

14.	array component selection	[]	left to right
	member selection	.	
	method or constructor invocation	()	

13.	`!` `~` `++` `--` unary `+` unary `-` cast `()`	right to left
12.	`*` `/` `%`	left to right
11.	`+` `-`	left to right
10.	`<<` `>>` `>>>`	left to right
9.	`<` `>` `<=` `>=` **`instanceof`**	left to right
8.	`==` `!=`	left to right
7.	`&`	left to right
6.	`^`	left to right
5.	`|`	left to right
4.	`&&`	left to right
3.	`||`	left to right
2.	conditional `? :`	right to left
1.	`=` `*=` `/=` `%=` `+=` `-=` `<<=` `>>=` `>>>=` `&=` `^=` `|=`	right to left

The following examples illustrate some of the associativity and precedence rules:

```
-2+2                ⟺  (-2)+2
i/2*j               ⟺  (i/2)*j
i=j=k               ⟺  i=(j=k)
(Circle)c.area()    ⟺  (Circle)(c.area())
a?b:c?d:e           ⟺  a?b:(c?d:e)
```

Numeric promotion

Numeric operands of binary and unary operators are automatically converted to similar values of a different type when necessary.

- **byte**, **short**, or **char** operands of a unary operator are converted to **int**.
- If either operand of a binary operator is **double**, the other is converted to **double**.
- Otherwise, if either operand of a binary operator is **float**, the other is converted to **float**.

- Otherwise, if either operand of a binary operator is **long**, the other is converted to **long**.

- Otherwise, both operands of a binary operator are converted to **int**.

String conversion

If either operand of the binary operator + is a *String*, the other is converted to a *String*. See the discussion on *String* expressions, page 715.

REFERENCES

[Arnold 00]

Ken Arnold, James Gosling, and David Holmes. *The Java Programming Language*, Third Edition. Addison-Wesley, 2000.

[Booch 01]

Grady Booch, Robert Martin, and James W. Newkirk. *Object-Oriented Analysis and Design with Applications,* Third Edition. Addison-Wesley, 2001.

[Budd 00]

Timothy Budd. *Understanding Object-Oriented Programming with Java:* Updated Edition. Addison-Wesley, 2000.

[Coad 98]

Peter Coad, Mark Mayfield, and Jonathan Kern. *Java Design: Building Better Apps and Applets. Second Edition.* Prentice Hall, 1998.

[Cooper 00]

James W. Cooper. *Java Design Patterns: A Tutorial*. Addison-Wesley, 2000.

[Deitel 99]

H. M. Deitel and P. J. Deitel. *Java: How to Program, Third Edition.* Prentice Hall, 1999.

[Gamma 95]

Erich Gamma, Richard Helm, Ralph Johnson, and John Vlissides. *Design Patterns: Elements of Reusable Object-Oriented Software*. Addison-Wesley, 1995.

[Geary 98]

David M. Geary. *Graphic Java 2, Mastering the JFC: AWT, Volume 1,* Third Edition. Prentice Hall, 1998.

[Geary 99]

David M. Geary. *Graphic Java 2, Volume 2, Swing, Third Edition.* Prentice Hall, 1999.

[Grand 1998]
Mark Grand. *Patterns in Java, Volume 1*. John Wiley & Sons, 1998.

[Horstmann 98]
Cay S. Horstmann and Gary Cornell. *Core Java 2, Volume 1: Fundamentals*. Prentice Hall, 1998.

[Horstmann 99]
Cay S. Horstmann and Gary Cornell. *Core Java 2, Volume 2: Advanced Features*. Prentice Hall, 1999.

[Joy 00]
Bill Joy, Guy Steele, Jar Gosling, and Gilad Bracha. *The Java Language Specification, Second Edition*. Addison-Wesley, 2000.

[Larman 97]
Craig Larman. *Applying UML and Patterns: An Introduction to Object-Oriented Analysis and Design*. Prentice Hall, 1997.

[Meyer 88]
Bertrand Meyer. *Object-Oriented Software Construction*. Prentice Hall, 1988.

[Meyer 97]
Bertrand Meyer. *Object-Oriented Software Construction,* Second Edition. Prentice Hall, 1997.

[Richter 99]
Charles A. Richter. *Designing Flexible Object-Oriented Systems with UML*. Macmillan Technical Publishing, 1999.

[Stevens 99]
Perdita Stevens and Rob Pooley. *Using UML: Software Engineering with Objects and Components,* Revised Edition. Addison-Wesley, 1999.

[Warren 99]
Nigel Warren and Philip Bishop. *Java in Practice: Design Styles and Idioms for Effective Java.* Addison-Wesley, 1999.

[Weiss 92]
Mark Allen Weiss. *Data Structures and Algorithm Analysis*. Benjamin/Cummings, 1992.

[Wirth 75]
Niklaus Wirth. *Algorithms + Data Structures = Programs*. Prentice-Hall, 1975.

INDEX